## Advanced Praise for
## *On Leadership: An Interdisciplinary Approach*

If you are looking for a cutting-edge resource regarding interdisciplinary leadership, I highly recommend *On Leadership*! Each chapter has a rich perspective, which contributes to the interplay between one's context, value system, level of authenticity, perspectives, and unique experiences. I highly recommend *On Leadership* and look forward to using this in the leadership courses I teach.

—**David De Jong**, Dakota State University

As both a scholar in school leadership and a former school leader, I thought I knew just about everything about leadership, but after reading this book, I was delightfully enlightened about the practical application of leadership in varying contexts around the world. Organized in three sections, this book clearly presents the practical application of leadership through an interdisciplinary approach. Fowler and Raehll provide a rich text with contributions of authors in both PK–12 schools and higher education, and this text would be a welcome addition to any educational leadership program.

—**Sonya D. Hayes**, The University of Tennessee, Knoxville

The concept of gender allyship in the organized workplace gains striking attention toward inclusive practices for women leaders. De-stigmatizing the biological experiences will allow for improved corporate culture. This book shares ways that men can support women leaders in the organized workplace by simply re-distributing the "virtual office housework" to include male leaders.

—**Dr. Shay Pursel**, CEO, So Very, LLC

Effective leadership development and corresponding leadership skills are not unique to any one profession, or leadership position. Effective leadership transcends all professions and effective leadership is evident in all effective leaders and leadership positions. Therefore, *On Leadership: An Interdisciplinary Approach,* is a timely must read for current and aspiring leaders. Siloed leadership development must be a thing of the past.

—**Dr. Michael Schwanenberger**, Department Chair & Associate Professor
Northern Arizona University

In our multifaceted, globalized, technologically complex world, leadership's context and content are transitioning from the traditional individual paradigm to a 21st-century one, which recognizes the critical need for interdisciplinary leadership. Fowler and Raehll have produced an essential resource for understanding highly effective contemporary leadership. Contributing authors (scholars and practitioners) provide new perspectives on the necessity of leadership being an interdisciplinary function.

—**Dr. Valerie A. Storey**, Professor Emerita
University of Central Florida

Undoubtedly forward-thinking content that will serve as key fundamentals in the future training of leaders in and out of the educational landscape. Centered on ethics and authenticity, this text truly represents a wholesome approach to modeling effective leadership practices in the 21st century.

—**Dr. Alexandrea Horton**
Former PreK–12 educator

A groundbreaking book on leadership, and a stark reminder that excellent leadership looks similar regardless of the setting. It is my hope that school leaders in the PreK–12 educational setting will utilize this text as Section III (focused on PreK–12 Education) of the book offers many insights on how to effectively lead in the educational setting, and as always, do what is best for students.

—**Mr. James C. Wrede**
Practicing high school principal, Southern California

The editors of *On Leadership* have assembled an international set of timely, relevant, thoughtful, and actionable information for leaders. This readable encyclopedia of interdisciplinary leadership is an essential reference for modern leaders!"

—**Dr. Michael Lubelfeld**
Practicing public school district superintendent, Midwest United States

# On Leadership

# On Leadership

## An Interdisciplinary Approach


***edited by***

**Denver J. Fowler**

***California State University, Bakersfield***

**Meghan B. Raehll**

***Franklin University***



IAP

INFORMATION AGE PUBLISHING, INC.

Charlotte, NC • www.infoagepub.com

**Library of Congress Cataloging-in-Publication Data**

A CIP record for this book is available from the Library of Congress
http://www.loc.gov

ISBN: 979-8-88730-092-4 (Paperback)
979-8-88730-093-1 (Hardcover)
979-8-88730-094-8 (E-Book)



Printed in the United States of America

# CONTENTS

## SECTION II

### HIGHER EDUCATION AND BEYOND

# SECTION III

## PRE-K–12 EDUCATION



# SECTION IV

## EXEMPLARS IN INTERDISCIPLINARY LEADERSHIP

# INTRODUCTION

Leadership is about influence. It is not bound to a siloed discipline or tied to a particular type of person, or place, or time. At its finest, leadership builds bridges and empowers people to work in order to collectively solve the complex problems of the day. At its worst, it can work to the determinant of individuals and groups on both small and global scales. It is precisely that potentiality in leadership that gives way to this book and the exploration of its inherently interdisciplinary nature. It is important to acknowledge from the outset, this work is intended as a response against the notion that leadership is a qualification for one industry or career over another. Instead, as you will find in this work, the authors showcase the transferability of leadership in a variety of industries to underscore how complex lived experiences can result in effective leadership.

As the reader will note, one challenge discussed throughout, and is unique to this work, is the how leaders were able to rely on interdisciplinary, multidisciplinary, and transdisciplinary approaches within the context of the COVID-19 pandemic, which began at the start of our preparation for this work. The COVID-19 pandemic exacerbated the digital divide in education and work, altered the field of healthcare, required a critical shift in approaches to physical and mental health, but also provided important insights into the interdisciplinary nature of crisis leadership and why it is necessary on an immediate and practical global scale. As such, several chapters focus directly or indirectly on interrelated COVID-19 pandemic issues.

*On Leadership*, pages ix–xvi

## Key Definitions

In addition, the reader will find varying definitions throughout this work to help shape and further explicate the intertwined nature of leadership. As a result, it is pertinent to define the difference between interdisciplinary, multidisciplinary, and transdisciplinary leadership. As the reader will discover, this book does include all three variations. It is interdisciplinary in the sense that higher education, PreK–12 education, business, public and nonprofit organizations, government, military, law enforcement, and the healthcare industry are all branches reflected within the varying sections and chapters of the book. However, it also very much multidisciplinary in the sense authors writing about these various branches (many of which are currently in the respective settings as practitioners or are former practitioners within these settings) are collaborating (in one book) in an effort to discuss best practices, aim to solve problems, review the extant literature, and share their own stories and journeys as it applies to leadership in an array of settings including the higher education setting, PreK–12 educational setting, business sector, within public and nonprofit organizations, government, military, law enforcement, and the healthcare industry. Finally, this book contains a variety of stories and situations that are transdisciplinary in nature, particularly in situations where leaders are drawing from multiple disciplines and backgrounds to create a holistic and novel approach to leading through change and complex problems.

## BOOK SECTIONS AND CHAPTERS

This work is divided into four sections with 23 chapters written by authors, scholars, practitioners, and researchers from across the nation and around the globe. The editors of this work took great care in curating relevant stories from experienced authors who not only reflect research expertise but lead by example in taking risks and transferring knowledge and engaging in the authentic manifestation of the influencing and complex work of leadership. The four sections include: (a) "Cultivating Interdisciplinary Leadership"; (b) "Higher Education and Beyond"; (c) "PreK–12 Education"; and (d) "Exemplars in Interdisciplinary Leadership." Within each section, readers will find between three and seven chapters focused on the accompanying section titles. Below, the reader will find each section and the supplementary chapters (with author name[s]) within the respective sections (in order) with a very brief description of the content one (the reader) might expect to find within said chapters.

## Section I: Cultivating Interdisciplinary Leadership

***Chapter 1: "Developing the Interdisciplinary Leader: A Wholistic Leadership Approach" by Valerie A. Storey***

In this chapter, the author argues that combinations of leadership styles, traits, attributes, integrated with conceptually meaningful ways, are more likely to develop and shape aspiring 21st-century interdisciplinary leaders than additive or independent contributions of several single factors. Furthermore, a defining core of this approach is the ability to flexibly lead in different ways across disparate organizational domains thereby creating new ways of thinking and new knowledge. Finally, the author proposes a wholistic leadership development framework (WLDF) that specifies influences on developing leadership processes and performance.

***Chapter 2 "Developing Capacity for Leading in a Digitally Transformed World" by Joe Lasley and Elizabeth Goryunova***

This chapter discusses the best practices, considerations, challenges, and strategies for the design and facilitation of impactful leadership instruction that results in developing skills important for leadership effectiveness in a digital environment across multiple contexts utilizing interdisciplinary approaches.

***Chapter 3: "The Interdisciplinary Acts of Leadership: Facilitating the Relationship Among the Head, Heart, Hands, and Holy" by Stan Amaladas***

In this chapter, the author offers a conceptual fourfold head-heart-hands-holy interdisciplinary leadership framework to address the problem of racism within a Canadian policing agency. The author argues that an interdisciplinary approach to leadership studies is governed by the interconnectedness of all four Hs (head, heart, hands, & holy) and its corresponding metaphors.

***Chapter 4: "Thoughtful Leadership: Developing Ethical and Authentic Leaders" by Elizabeth Ostler***

This chapter highlights a leadership program that draws from both authentic and servant leadership theories, and sheds light on how the program aims to develop thoughtful leaders who lead ethically and authentically.

***Chapter 5: "She Takes the Lead: Insights on the Shifting Landscape for Women in Leadership Roles" by Kathryn Woods***

This chapter explores historical and contemporary perspectives on women in organizational leadership roles. Supported by a plethora of published scientific research, this chapter addresses the importance of past influences on the challenges faced by women in the workforce, current issues that affect and perpetuate these challenges, and actions needed to overcome them in the future.

*Chapter 6: "Best Practices for Using Play in Business" by Joe Lasley and Akshay Sateesh*

In this chapter, the authors discuss playful leadership, including recommended practices for play in business through a much-needed analysis of how play is necessary for leading successfully in the 21st century and beyond. Theories of play and leadership are integrated to inform current best practices for using play in business settings and stories from field work/consulting professionals that help companies use play to transform the world of work to be more productive, creative, strategic, and motivated.

## Section II: Higher Education and Beyond

*Chapter 7: "Distinctive Characteristics in Interdisciplinary Academic Leadership Programs: A Multi-Program Case Study Analysis" by Kathy L. Guthrie and Pei Hu*

This chapter explores, through numerous case studies, distinctive characteristics in interdisciplinary higher education leadership programs, while supporting learning opportunities in higher education from an interdisciplinary framework.

*Chapter 8: "Higher Education in Crisis: Enabling Complexity Thinking and Adaptive Space for Ethical Decision-Making During the Time of COVID" by Benjamin Brooks*

Using COVID-19 crisis at its foundation, this chapter explores the value of engaging vanguard leadership constructs, complexity thinking, and adaptive space for improved ethical crisis leadership by higher education practitioners. The chapter gives an overview of crisis, stakeholders, interdisciplinarity and interdisciplinary leadership, ethics, and ethical crisis leadership before explaining complexity thinking and adaptive space, and how these constructs can be engaged for ethical, interdisciplinary leadership during a crisis. The chapter concludes by interrogating current issues in higher education governance and examines how complexity thinking and adaptive space could be applied to the COVID crisis in higher education for the re-opening college campuses.

***Chapter 9: "Educational Reprogramming: Leadership Perceptions and Practice of Academic Program Directors in a College of Education During COVID-19" by Joshua C. Tipton, Ashlee Hover, and Kyle Butler***

This chapter highlights the potential changes of collegiate leaders' perceptions and responsibilities to the students, faculty, and staff they serve as an impending result of the COVID-19 pandemic—especially leaders such as academic program directors who frequently engage both students and faculty in learning yet are often overlooked as potential change agents.

***Chapter 10: "Leadership in Education for Black Americans in Community Colleges" by Aishwarya Joshi and Seneka R. Gainer***

This chapter aims to (a) highlight the role of community colleges in fostering leadership among Black Americans, (b) explore the capacity of mentorship in supporting Black students in community colleges, (c) encourage policy and faculty development to increase student retention rates, and (d) offer interdisciplinary strategies and resources to systemically bridge the accessibility gaps toward an equitable educational experience.

***Chapter 11: "An Interdisciplinary STEM NIH Grant" by Anne Katz and Karla-Sue C. Marriott***

This chapter reflects on and summarizes both the participants and findings of a 5-year grant supported student-centered research education program. Through ADISRE (Achieving Diversity Through Integrative Scientific Research Experience), focused on "Creating a Desire" for learning and the ethical application of scientific information, the authors hope to expand, leverage and improve upon a previously successful research education model (NIBIB-EDEPS) conducted at an HBCU.

***Chapter 12: "Adaptive Informal Education Leadership During COVID-19" by Marlee J. Tavlin***

This chapter seeks to add an important component to literature by highlighting data collected during a phenomenological study which sought to explore urban high school students' experience transitioning to an online out of school time STEM learning environment during the COVID-19 pandemic.

***Chapter 13: "Narrow-Minded Military Education and Opportunity Lost: On the Possibility of Developing Future Army Officer Expertise in Mission Command at a Military Boarding School" by Richard Megahan***

This chapter sought to portray the problems and possibilities of future officers becoming proficient in mission command with a focus on improving opportunities for commissioning cadets in the Army, ROTC programs, and military boarding schools.

## Section III: PreK–12 Education

***Chapter 14: Leading From the Ranks: Teacher Leader Sensemaking of a District-Supported Mentorship Initiative" by Brianne Morettini and Lisa Vernon-Dotson***

This chapter shares the experiences and outcomes from a study of teacher leaders who participated in a grant-funded project focused on building teacher leadership capacity to support beginning teachers. Using sensemaking literature as a guide, the study sought to identify factors that enabled or hindered the work of teacher leaders in one school district as they embarked on facilitating a district-supported mentorship initiative. Ambiguity, empowerment, structural conflict, and tenacity were four predominant interdisciplinary themes that became relevant for the sensemaking of these teacher leaders.

***Chapter 15: "Developing Effective Professional Learning Communities for Senior Leaders" by Marie Stephenson, Carla Solvason, Tracey France, and Paul Sheehan***

This chapter builds upon the outcomes of longitudinal research into a leader development intervention, which took place 3 years ago involving primary (elementary) leaders across a range of educational settings and contexts. The authors argue that professional learning communities (PLCs) provide leaders with the optimum conditions to reflect, facilitating openness and transparency through trust-building, but simultaneously attend to the emotional dimensions of leadership.

***Chapter 16: "School Board Leadership to Improve Student Outcomes" by A. J. Crabill***

Focused on school board leadership, this chapter aims to shed light on how school boards can create the conditions for improvements in student outcomes, while sharing how this possibility is often not realized due to ineffective leadership practices. Key leadership practices are highlighted, namely as it applies to creating those conditions for the improvement of all students' outcomes.

***Chapter 17: "Charter Schools and Crisis Leadership" by David T. Marshall and Natilie M. Neugebauer***

The COVID-19 pandemic disrupted society in March 2020, including the operation of schools. When schools closed for in-person instruction, school leaders had a range of decisions to make as part of an effort to maintain the educational mission of their institutions. This chapter focuses on qualitative research that was conducted with charter school leaders during this pivotal time.

***Chapter 18: "Primary Resources and Public Pedagogy: A Case Study for Teacher Professional Development" by Minkie O. English***

This chapter focuses on an exploratory and descriptive case study demonstrating how a piloted Art as Activism workshop requested by education leaders at a higher education institution and a museum, in New York City, was customized for teachers' professional development. Using an interdisciplinary conceptual framework rooted in learning within and from community, for knowledge expansion and technical skills acquisition, this chapter shares how this workshop provided teachers with practical experiences to contextualize and re-contextualize historical and contemporary social issues and constructs best supported by public pedagogy critical theory.

***Chapter 19: "Serving Multiple Masters: Rural Ugandan Head Teachers Role in Attracting and Retaining Teachers" by Gilbert Arinaitwe and John Williamson***

This chapter reports how specific head teachers' practices work around the expectations and tensions among school boards, community leaders, and government agencies (i.e., multiple masters) as they attempt to attract and retain teachers. The role of the head teacher as policy and practical gatekeeper and how the head teachers balance individual school autonomy and the need to fit Ministry of Education policy, the expectations of teachers, parents and local community is presented. Finally, the chapter highlights how school head teachers adapt policies to fit their circumstances and to address the expectations of multiple masters to foster teacher attraction and retention.

***Chapter 20: "Distributed leadership in Tanzanian secondary schools: A Systematic Literature Review" by Revocatus C. Kuluchumila***

This chapter focuses on exploring distributed leadership in Tanzanian secondary schools. Utilizing a systematic literature review, the authors present numerous findings as it applies to school climate, fulfillment of school instructional objectives, school board members, teacher support, and mentorship, among many others. The authors generally concluded that Tanzanian secondary schools might benefit greatly in continuing moving from top–down leadership style and focus more on distributed leadership.

## Section IV: Exemplars in Interdisciplinary Leadership

*Chapter 21: "The Mutual Engagement Leadership Model Implementation and Outcomes at Conway Regional Health System" by Kateryna V. (Ligon) Pitchford*

This chapter focuses on interdisciplinary leadership within the healthcare industry. The author shares an instrumental case study to examine the implementation and outcomes of the mutual engagement leadership model in the healthcare setting. In doing so, multiple source databases are analyzed using deductive thematic analysis.

*Chapter 22: "Becoming an Integrated Leader" by Alyncia M. Bowen*

This chapter is an autoethnographic approach of this author's journey of becoming an integrated leader during disruption, both internally and externally, by capitalizing on the experience gleaned while leading in two nonprofit organizations, one a service organization and the other an institution of higher education.

*Chapter 23: Crossover Leadership: An Autoethnography on Interdisciplinary Leadership and Transformation" by John Nestor*

This chapter is an autoethnographic approach and examines the author's multi-industry leadership practices that have transformed underperforming organizations into best practices in manufacturing, law enforcement, K–12, and higher education. Key leadership principles, themes, and lessons learned shared within this unique chapter are grounded in 30 years of successful crossover leadership in both the public and private sectors that can support the development of today's leaders.

## FINAL THOUGHTS

In closing, the editors of this work have currently served in numerous leadership roles and extensively researched the field of leadership. As such, it is important to note that whether it be leadership in education, business, public and nonprofit organizations, government, military, law enforcement, or healthcare, the editors have yet to find an organization in any setting thriving under ineffective leadership. Thus, one might easily argue that leadership is perhaps the most important factor in determining the success or failure of a given organization, and therefore deserves considerable focus by practitioners, scholars, and researchers alike, perhaps especially as it relates to continued contributions to the extant literature on leadership—much like this book.

**—Denver J. Fowler**
**Meghan B. Raehll**

# FOREWORD

It would be easy to assume that there is nothing new for scholars or practitioners working in the field of leadership to study. A quick google search on the topic of leadership yields thousands of articles and books on the topic. Visit any bookstore or airport kiosk and you will be subjected to a multitude of tomes on the subject of leadership. The study of leaders and leadership theory is one of those rare crossover fields that attracts us all, scholars, practitioners, and lay people. One could reasonably argue that the field of leadership research has become saturated, for both the practitioner and the scholar. Yet, as Northouse (2021) so clearly articulates in *Leadership: Theory and Practice,* despite all of the research, all of the studies, just reaching a scholarly consensus on an overarching single definition of leadership has proven to be elusive.

If attempts by scholars to reach an agreement that simply defines leadership remains elusive, the study of leadership behaviors and the identification of an overarching theory of leadership remains even more debatable. From meta-analysis research conducted on leadership trait theory, leadership group theory, situational leadership, transformational leadership, mission driven leadership, and charismatic leadership, just to name a few leadership areas of focus, there is overwhelming evidence and agreement among scholars that if nothing else, modern leadership consists of a complex and interrelated set of skills, behaviors, and attributes.

As a practicing leader in both the K–12 sector and in higher education, I have personally learned a great deal from the research on leadership, despite the overwhelming and often contradictory nature of the research

*On Leadership,* pages xvii–xx

itself. As a researcher in the field of 21st century leadership, I have also come to recognize and appreciate the many complex and interrelated aspects of leadership that, in fact, cross all sectors and do not fit neatly into any one all-encompassing theory of practice.

In particular, I appreciate leadership research and analysis that combines the theoretical with the practical, that provides the reader with case studies from the field, along with exemplars of leadership theory in action, all embedded with scholarly rigor. With *On Leadership: An Interdisciplinary Approach,* Fowler and Raell have accomplished that elusive combination of scholar rigor and practical application.

*On Leadership* is a collection of scholarly work tied to practical applications organized to inform and support modern leaders. It is important to understand how successful leaders practice their craft; how they grow and evolve. Examining and understanding leadership from the context of interdisciplinarity provides leaders, and those who study leadership, one more context in which to navigate the complex and interrelated field that is leadership in the 21st century.

Fowler and Raehll, with the publication of *On Leadership: An Interdisciplinary Approach,* have accomplished what on the surface might appear to be an impossible task, they have clearly and concisely contributed in an impactful way to the field of leadership research in the 21st century. *On Leadership* examines leadership across major sectors of modern society. From PK–20 education and healthcare sectors to nonprofits, the military and government, Fowler and Raehll have assembled outstanding voices from these various organizational sectors.

The authors in *On Leadership* address a diverse and important set of leadership topics from a review of ethical leadership in the time of COVID-19 to examinations of leading in a digitally transformed world, and the interrelated nature of leadership as a function of the head, the heart, the hand, and the holy. Fowler and Raell have assembled an impressive array of researchers and practitioners who recognize the value of an interdisciplinary approach to leadership.

The views and insights of the authors presented in *On Leadership* provide a road map for understanding the interdisciplinary nature of leadership, as well as the advantages and challenges faced by today's leaders. Today's leaders' function in volatile, uncertain, complex, and ambiguous (VUCA) environments. These VUCA environments place stress on all systems within any organization, including the organization's leadership system. In these environments, there is little chance for success from the leader who is seen or who leads, as an isolated, independent figure, the leader as the lone hero coming to the rescue. As a result, in VUCA environments, understanding leadership as an interdisciplinary function is critical for leadership success.

It is through interdisciplinary leadership strategies that today's complex interrelated problems are best solved.

With a focus on providing lessons learned and specific exemplars in this field, as well as multiple examples of successful strategies to cultivate interdisciplinary leadership, *On Leadership* adds to the research in ways that are accessible and meaningful to both scholars and practitioners.

*On Leadership: An Interdisciplinary Approach*, is a welcome addition to the field of leadership research. With this collection of chapters from distinguished researchers and practitioners, the editors have produced a comprehensive analysis on the nature of leadership as an interdisciplinary venture. I know that you will enjoy, and benefit from, this welcome addition to the literature on leadership in the 21st century as I have.

**—Christopher Colwell**
Stetson University
Chair of the Department of Education
and Director of the Hollis Leadership Center

## REFERENCES

Northouse, P. G. (2021). *Leadership: Theory and practice.* SAGE Publications.

# SECTION I

## CULTIVATING INTERDISCIPLINARY LEADERSHIP

CHAPTER 1

# DEVELOPING THE INTERDISCIPLINARY LEADER

## A Wholistic Leadership Approach

**Valerie A. Storey**

### ABSTRACT

In this chapter, the author argues that combinations of leadership styles, traits, attributes, integrated with conceptually meaningful ways, are more likely to develop and shape aspiring 21st century interdisciplinary leaders than additive or independent contributions of several single factors. Furthermore, a defining core of this approach is the ability to flexibly lead in different ways across disparate organizational domains thereby creating new ways of thinking and new knowledge. Finally, the author proposes a wholistic leadership development framework (WLDF) that specifies influences on developing leadership processes and performance. The framework recognizes that the economic, ethical, and cognitive/emotional crises in contemporary society call for a deeper quest for meaning and individual wholeness and provides an inclusive pathway for aspiring leaders to follow. Without this completeness, the interdisciplinary leader may enjoy some success, but not the transformational success that leads to lasting results.

*On Leadership*, pages 3–18

In the 1930s a team of U.K. meteorologists led by Robert Watson-Watt developed a radar system for the detection of enemy planes. But one challenge was proving insurmountable, the ability to design small valves required for a miniature radar system. The problem was solved not by the team's knowledge and skill but by utilizing the expertise of others, that is, engineers who had built the first all glass valve for Philips's television sets. This sharing of discipline knowledge was fortuitous rather than deliberate. The discovery ultimately led to not only the development of the country's radar system (a system that, in 1940, was critical in winning the Battle of Britain) but also to the development of air traffic control, and the microwave. Undoubtedly, Watson-Watt's team of brilliant meteorologists would have eventually solved the valve problem, but how much time and money could have been saved if the development team consisted of experts from several fields, rather than one discipline all with the common capacity to lead? There are many examples when time and money have been saved by applying knowledge and expertise from a different discipline. Sometimes this may be systematic or as in the case of radar development in the United Kingdom, accidental. After World War II, leadership research developed in three major waves of conceptual, empirical, and methodological advances: (a) behavioral and attitude research; (b) behavioral, social-cognitive, and contingency research; and (c) transformational, social exchange, team, and gender-related research (Lord et al., 2017). Specifically, research progressed from a focus on personnel issues to contemporary multilevel models and meta-analyses on teams, shared leadership, leader-member exchange, gender, ethical, abusive, charismatic, and transformational leadership (Lord et al., 2017, p. 434).

Yet, many of the themes that characterize contemporary leadership research were also present in much earlier research (Kockelmans, 1979). For example, policy on interdisciplinarity constantly reiterate the fact that a diverse and inclusive team should effectively integrate multiple forms of knowledge and expertise across disciplines and not just incorporate disciplinary contributions additively, and that this integrative approach for addressing significant societal problems can lead to insights that enable new techniques or methodologies to be implemented. Imagine a multi-talented team that also shares a common body of leadership skills and competencies grounded on empirical research from a host of disciplines.

In developing interdisciplinary leaders, one approach is to deliver leadership training to all students on a higher education institution campus through leadership education (LE). LE employs an intentional approach to developing leaders with the capacity to practice effective leadership due to their deep, integrated, and applied knowledge. LE can also provide the skill base in leadership to reduce the learning cycle (Lindsay & Friesen, 2020) by providing opportunities for ongoing experiences and reflection as opposed to knowledge acquisition and absorption. Ultimately, this will lead to greater success in addressing complex, interdisciplinary issues and drive society forward.

A complementary approach is the development and application of a systemic, integrated leadership development framework which is useful in the process of setting leadership development strategies with both short-term and long-term trajectories. The objective of such a framework is to define elements of leadership that are generalizable and accurate; and enable aspiring leaders, consultants, or coaches to orient themselves and then to nurture the development of the capacities and skills required of a 21st century leader in any context. Furthermore, a framework is not only a learning and development tool, but also includes lifelong learning as an element of leadership capacities and skills. Building an interdisciplinary leader's capabilities is a process requiring social, emotional, physical, and cognitive development.

## Leadership in the 21st Century

In our multifaceted, globalized, technologically sophisticated world the context and content of leadership are transitioning from the traditional individual paradigm to a 21st century paradigm, which recognizes the critical need for interdisciplinary team leadership (Frantzeskaki & Rok, 2018; Irwin et al., 2018). This transition requires taking the best empirical knowledge on leadership from disciplines like philosophy, literature, the arts, psychology, sociology, political science, anthropology, and history; fields of study such as business, education, and agriculture; and even professions such as healthcare and social work (Boone et al., 2020; Frantzeskaki & Rok, 2018; Irwin et al., 2018; Lindsay & Friesen, 2020). If this cross-fertilization fails to occur then leadership will continue to be a fragmented field (Boone et al., 2020).

## Breaking Down Leadership Silos

The diverse field of leadership is unlike most other disciplines as it is informed, influenced, and enlightened by different bases of knowledge, approaches, and developmental strategies that transcend any single discipline (Riggio, 2011). In 1974, Stogdill noted that "four decades of research have produced a bewildering mass of findings . . . [but the] endless accumulation of empirical data has not produced an integrated understanding" (p. vii). An insight that still holds true today.

In 1985, Bennis and Nanus observed that despite the thousands of empirical leadership studies no undisputable understanding exists as to what distinguishes leaders from non-leaders, and effective leaders from ineffective leaders (p. 5). Further, in 2006, Yukl highlighted that the state of the field of leadership was one of ferment and confusion; that the field rushed from one fad to the next, but that theory development was slow.

Firstly, this chapter discusses interdisciplinary leadership, and the challenges of traversing across diverse knowledge forms and worldviews with prior knowledge and experience generally limited to a specific discipline with its language, goals, and strategies. Secondly, recognizing that leading interdisciplinary teams requires specific training and skills, a theoretically grounded aspiring leader development framework is described. Finally, contributions of the WLDF to the development of interdisciplinary leaders are discussed.

## Collaborative Approaches Contributing to the Understanding of Leadership Education

There are three different approaches to the understanding of LE: interdisciplinary, transdisciplinary, and multidisciplinary (see Table 1.1). First, interdisciplinarity requires the integration of many perspectives, highlighting the topic, issue, or problem to be addressed rather than individual

**TABLE 1.1 Three Approaches to the Understanding of Leadership Development (LE)**

| Approach | Definition | Source |
|---|---|---|
| Interdisciplinary | The integration of many perspectives, highlighting the topic, issue, or problem to be addressed rather than individual perspectives. | Klein, 1990 |
| | Involving two or more academic, scientific, or artistic disciplines. | Merriam-Webster Dictionary |
| Transdisciplinary | The study of underlying structures or relationships among disciplines, applying a theory or method to solve problems in individual disciplines. | Lattuca, 2001 |
| | A research strategy that crosses many disciplinary boundaries to create a holistic approach. This includes initiatives that support the capacity building required for the successful transdisciplinary formulation and implementation of research actions. | Merriam-Webster Dictionary |
| Multidisciplinary | The additive or cumulative approach to understanding and asking questions about leadership, foregrounding individual disciplinary contributions to a deeper understanding of leadership and leadership education | Klein, 1990 |
| | Combining or involving more than one discipline or field of study. | Merriam-Webster Dictionary |

perspectives (Klein, 1990). Second, transdisciplinarity involves the study of underlying structures or relationships among disciplines, applying a theory or method to solve problems in individual disciplines (Lattuca, 2001). Finally, multidisciplinarity is defined as the additive or cumulative approach to understanding and asking questions about leadership, foregrounding individual disciplinary contributions to a deeper understanding of leadership and leadership education (Klein, 1990). The benefit of these three approaches is that they cumulatively contribute to the evolution of leadership informed by varying disciplines, fields, and knowledge bases, all of which are needed to elevate the understanding of the development of effective leaders to solve complex problems in dynamic environments. In short, disciplinary, and field-specific methodologies can be brought to bear to solve complex 21st-century problems (Lindsay & Friesen, 2020).

These three approaches contribute to improved scholarship on leadership by ensuring that its development and practice are systematic, empirically grounded, and domain integrated. Such an approach sanctions a greater ethical practice of leadership, in all sectors of society, driving the change needed to address the complex issues being faced today (Kellerman, 2012).

***Challenges***

In higher education settings, LE and training can be found in numerous departments and programs which have the potential to create territorial silos. There is an urgent need to enhance interdisciplinary collaborative efforts to advance the field. Such collaboration has the potential to shift LE from interdisciplinary to transdisciplinary, or a synthesis of interdisciplinary efforts (Nicolescu, 1999). This synthesis can create a holistic perspective by promoting the emergence of new knowledge. To fully understand and develop leaders, access is required to disparate knowledge bases that are often separated by pedagogical and philosophical domains. Currently, there is a disjointed approach that lacks a unifying identity despite many calls by leadership educators to develop some guidelines and practices around the field of leadership (Kellerman & Douglas, 2019).

## LEADERSHIP EDUCATION AS A DISCIPLINE

In recent decades there has been an increasing number of studies that span more than one leadership approach, and the different lines of research are gradually meeting and converging. Overall, the findings from the varied lines of research are consistent, mutually supportive, and interrelated in a meaningful way (Yukl, 2006).

## The National Leadership Education Research Agenda

In the Fall of 2011, the National Leadership Education Research Agenda (NLERA) was developed by the Association of Leadership Educators to supplement the scholarship informing LE specifically within the United States higher education system (Andenoro et al., 2013). Described as a living document the intent is to provide direction for LE scholarship and practice for 5 years (2013–2018, 2020–2025), and that a new agenda will be presented every 5 years to inform the scholarship of LE concerning the evolution of the field and society (Andenoro et al., 2013).

The charge facing the Leadership Team (Andenoro et al., 2013, p. 42) responsible for the development of the inaugural NLER agenda was two-fold: (a) provide research priorities that can guide applied scholarship contributing to the development of future leaders and managers through higher education and (b) provide key elements that further define LE as a discipline (p. 2). The seven priorities identified by the NLERA guide the scholarship of LE, define it as a discipline and provide the foundation for increasing the applied nature of the scholarship guiding the development of leadership through higher education.

The second iteration of the NLER agenda (2020–2025) increases (a) legitimacy for the diverse fields of LE and (b) impact for our world by first promoting a collaborative multidisciplinary approach and second by validating Kellerman's (2018) calling for standards. The agenda emphasizes the need to advance the understanding of leadership through the development of guiding documents that frame best practices for interdisciplinary leadership programs. The authors of NLERA (2020–2025) again highlight the chaotic nature of leadership and the challenges and opportunities inherent to a call to action for LE.

## Collaboration and Consolidation

LE is described as the pedagogical practice of facilitating leadership learning to build human capacity, informed by an interdisciplinary knowledge base consisting of leadership theory and research. It specifically focuses on the activities and environments to develop leadership ability (Brungardt, 1997). The first agenda's priority is focused on teaching, learning, and curriculum development. Disciplines such as instructional and curricular design, program assessment, information processing, student development, competency-based learning, training and development, and educational psychology are identified as having the potential to inform how leadership educators view teaching and learning associated with LE (Andenoro et al., 2013, p. 5). Andenoro et al. (2013) argue that higher education has an opportunity to design and develop best practice leadership programs and cutting-edge teaching, learning, and assessment. They highlight the need to embrace and develop the interdisciplinarity nature of leadership education (p. 6) by learning valuable lessons from biology, anthropology, sociology, psychology, philosophy, the humanities, and several other areas of inquiry (NLERA, 2013–2018).

The third agenda priority highlights the fact that the intricacies of personality and self-awareness, along with other variables, require continued development and additional research that will provide perspective for leadership educators tasked with preparing the next generation of educational leaders. The following areas are recommended for exploration concerning the psychological development of leaders, followers, and learners:

- emotional intelligence
- emotional intelligent leadership
- critical leadership
- aversion and propensity for change
- motivation and initiatives in leadership contexts
- self esteem for leadership practice
- personality
- personal hardiness
- trust
- creativity
- self-agreement
- self-control
- self-sacrifice
- empowerment. (NLERA, 2013–2018, p. 14)

The purpose of the NLERA is not to guide practice but to initiate collaborative dialogue, break down independent silos, and create trajectory leadership educators as they plan their work (Andenoro et al., 2013). According to Andenoro (2013), the NLERA is a call to action grounded in credibility and linked to a process that can transform how leadership educators practice and how LE learners learn.

## Interdisciplinary Leadership and Problem-Solving

As can be seen from Table 1.1: Three Approaches to the Understanding of Leadership Development (LE) the leadership of interdisciplinary research is a process in which researchers, various stakeholders, and policymakers work together using a shared vision and language that draws together scientific, experiential, and contextual knowledge to innovatively address a common complex problem (Allen-Scott et al., 2015).

## INTEGRATING SCHOLARSHIP AND PRACTICE

In the last decade, there has been increasing advocacy for inter-and-trans-disciplinary (ITD) research teams (Olsen et al., 2013) due to the growing evidence that ITD research helps solve complex societal problems and achieve societal aspirations. This has been accompanied by theoretical reflection about the philosophy underpinning this shift. Conceptualized as a joint endeavor between academia and society and an encounter of different disciplinary, methodological, and epistemological perspectives, the success of an interdisciplinary approach requires leaders equipped with the skills to build, maintain, and sustain interdisciplinary teams (Nicolescu, 2012). For example, the European Commission's Science in Society Program, Horizon 2020 strategy articulates the need for interdisciplinary leadership to facilitate collaboration between social, natural, and physical sciences (Owen et al., 2012). Integral to the strategy is the inclusion of social science and humanities researchers early in the research design processes (Pedersen, 2016) to ensure that no social, political, or decision-making process required for moving policy recommendations into action is overlooked (Clark & Wallace, 2012).

The growth in ITD research has resulted in an increasing number of ITD teams and a growing demand for leadership training. The goal is to create a truly collaborative environment in which multiple people with specific expertise communicate and collaborate as one unit. This requires team members to recognize that a successful interdisciplinary team should be non-hierarchical and adopt a shared leadership model that encompasses a multiplicity of leadership attributes. Not surprisingly the road to becoming a team player can be rocky for talented individuals who excel in a specific knowledge domain. Transitioning from an expert individual to membership of a transformative team necessitates leadership training and support.

## AN INCLUSIVE FRAMEWORK

### Applied Scholarship

ITD leaders need to be multidimensional with skills and attributes that are specific to ITD interactions and that have the capacity to be transformative with real-world impacts (Boon et al., 2020). Required competencies and skills such as the ability to (a) create and foster a vision beyond status

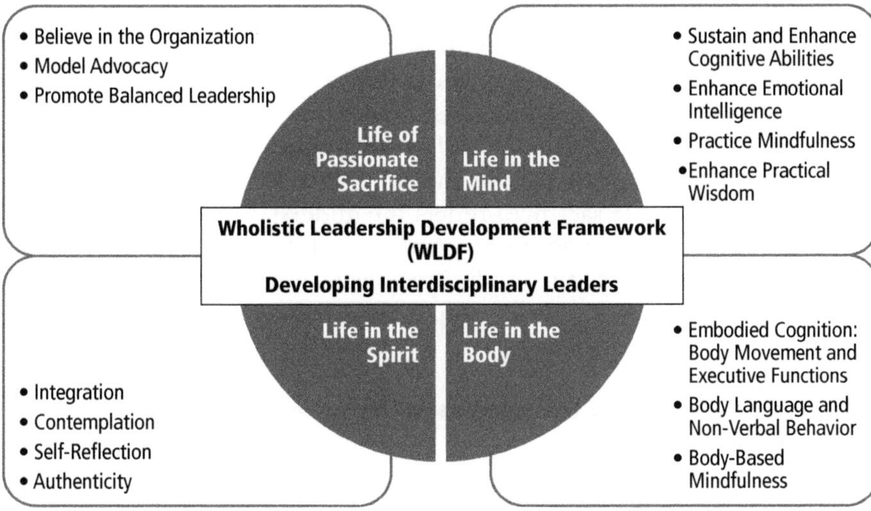


**Figure 1.1** Wholistic leadership development framework (WLDF).

quo, (b) develop a shared culture, (c) communicate to multiple audiences, and (d) evidence of adaptive behaviors such as humility and open-mindedness (Boone et al., 2020) contribute to the team's effectiveness. ITD leaders must also be adept at the three P's; namely, persuasion, perseverance, and patience. Whilst these leadership qualities, skills, and attributes are seldom characterized by one individual they should cumulatively characterize a successful team.

The WLDF (see Figure 1.1) is grounded on both an interdisciplinary and transdisciplinary approach, theoretically based, drawing on several different fields, such as philosophy, psychology, sociology, and ethics. Whilst the WLDF integrates disparate knowledge often separated by pedagogical and philosophical domains it remains grounded on social, emotional, physical, cognitive, and in some cases spiritual, approaches. This is essential in the 21st century if leaders are to solve today's complex interdisciplinary problems in a volatile environment. Otherwise, we will not only be doing a disservice to developing leaders, but leadership will also continue to be a disjointed field that does not fully utilize and leverage the expertise present.

## Why "Wholistic"?

To be whole means to understand the interconnectedness of individuals, organizations, society, and nature designed for common well-being, progress, and maximum happiness (Palmer, 2004); and requires awareness of weaknesses and strengths. To learn more about "wholeness" of the self as opposed to the society we turn to holistic medicine which is premised on the assumption that we are comprised of three components; physical, mental, and socio-emotional and that these components interact to encourage wholeness in self- and other relationships (Schuster, 1997).

The WLDF's quadrants (life in the mind, life in the body, life in the spirit, life of passionate sacrifice) reflect the understanding that leadership is not static but dynamic and transformative, and that each quadrant is mutually interdependent. As the model is wholistic, interrelated, and synchronous the implication is that leadership development is not a linear journey.

## Wholistic Leadership Development Framework Quadrants

### *Quadrant 1: Life in the Mind*

This quadrant of the WLDF adopts a neuroscience lens for an interdisciplinary leader to learn about the sustenance required to maintain general well-being, and to ensure that both body and mind are in the best of health. First, the importance of brain health is highlighted. This challenges an individual to identify important brain activities which when practiced daily impact brain health holistically, sustain cognitive ability, and enhance cognitive capacity.

Second, an awareness of the need to further develop emotional intelligence to lead a diverse group of people is essential. Whilst the first three components of emotional intelligence (self-awareness, self-regulation, and motivation/passion) focus on the management of emotions and behavior, the last two components (empathy and social skills) focus on relationship management. An interdisciplinary leader needs both empathy and the ability to self-regulate. In a diverse team, it is critical that team members can manage their emotions and impulses to control inappropriate reactions and channel energy in a positive manner. It matters as our level of self-control can impact decision-making. Anger, disrespect, impatience, irritability, failure to listen, and put-downs are all symptoms of poor self-regulation and self-awareness. These examples of negative behavior impact colleagues, team culture, and can ultimately result in moral failure.

Third, an interdisciplinary leader must lead a life of scholarship and mindfulness practices to address new and important intellectual challenges in a rapidly changing environment. Finally, embracing mindfulness practices will also enhance practical wisdom by promoting the capacity to think creatively, generate new ideas, and balance the interests of all team members:

1. *Sustain and enhance cognitive abilities*—Maintain lifelong learning to sustain and develop brain-based skills that are required to complete any task irrespective of complexity.
2. *Enhance emotional intelligence*—Learn the fundamentals of self-mastery.
3. *Mindfulness*—Practice mindfulness daily to enhance the ability to be fully present and self-aware.
4. *Enhance practical wisdom*—Balance reason, emotions, and behavior to create harmony.

***Quadrant 2: Life in the Body***

An interdisciplinary leader requires both mental and physical stamina to live a balanced life in an unbalanced world. The body's primary systems depend on each other. Energy connects the mind and body, a steady flow of electrical signals that activate cells and muscles in the body and neurons in the brain. Maximizing the body's full health by not only embracing a healthy lifestyle but by comprehending the relationship between specific physical activity, cognition, and executive functions is a relatively new but vibrant area of research.

A more traditional aspect of research that falls into this quadrant's domain is a focus on body language and non-verbal behavior as it is through body language that the strength of emotional intelligence becomes evident. Finally, as with Quadrant #1 Life in the Mind, Quadrant #2 Life in the Body endeavors to encourage the developing leader to embrace body-based mindfulness practices to support the development of practical wisdom.

1. *Embodied cognition: Body movement and executive functions*—Control and develop interactions between physical fitness, personality traits, and life skills.
2. *Body language and non-verbal behavior*—Increase awareness of body language and non-verbal behavior as this strengthens an individual's emotional intelligence.
3. *Body-based mindfulness*—Practices support the development of practical wisdom.

***Quadrant 3: Life in the Spirit***

An individual's understanding of spirituality can be polarizing (Marques, 2005). On the one hand, religion can be viewed as an expression of spirituality in search of the sacred, whilst on the other hand a humanistic view of spirituality has little or no religious connotations (Fisher, 2011). Nevertheless, irrespective of the perspective taken, living a life cognizant of spirituality is important to our general well-being (Mental Health Foundation, 2008). Spirituality represents whatever gives an individual's life meaning, purpose, and fulfilment; it is what makes life worth living or meaningful to live (Giacoline

& Jurkiewicz, 2014). An individual may consider themselves to be non-spiritual and yet still be guided by an internal set of goals, values, and beliefs, which are considered to be key components of spirituality (Samah et al., 2012).

A leader committed to living a "life in the spirit" motivates and stimulates colleagues and employees by instilling a vision and organizational culture based on altruistic values (Kolodinsky et al., 2008). Observed ethical behavior that aligns with a team mission or organizational values indicate integrity between the leader and the team/organization served. When colleagues see that integrity, it engenders relational respect and trust (Giacoline & Jurkiewicz, 2014). This quadrant is focused on the following:

1. *Integration*—See the relevance, interdependence, and interaction of individual actions to the order of things.
2. *Contemplation*—Engage with nature, the arts, and creative activities or practices such as yoga, Tai Chi, and team sports which all contribute to an individual's actions.
3. *Self-Reflection*—Integrate activities into daily life which prompt critical analysis, impact self-development, strengthen self-awareness, and contribute to better choices.
4. *Authenticity*—Live in the moment, be true to self, develop an open mind, and align actions with core beliefs and values.

***Quadrant 4: Life of Passionate Sacrifice***

Quadrant #4 is characterized by a leader who can sacrifice personal goals for the whole team, the collective benefit of everyone. Giving up a pay raise to keep people employed or devoting time to build up a team are examples. Sacrificial leadership does not necessarily mean the leader is totally altruistic, but instead, sees a bigger picture where delayed gratification can ensure even greater success. Sacrificial leadership is symbiotic in that it requires a commitment to the team and that commitment is reciprocated. It requires the authentic leader to show by words and actions that they believe in the value of their team/organization's mission, and the people served:

1. Believe in the organization
   a. Goodness of its mission
   b. Virtue of employees
   c. Defender of social justice
2. Model advocacy
   a. Of the present-day enterprise and the greater good of the organization
3. Promote balanced leadership
   a. Ensure positive developmental growth of individuals and organization

### Contributions of the Wholistic Leadership Development Framework

The WLDF (a) adds a leadership development theory reflective of interdisciplinary knowledge and practice, (b) enhances the relevancy of a unitary leadership development model, and (c) creates a framework for developing leaders aspiring to lead interdisciplinary teams reflective of 21st-century society.

#### *Contribution 1: Add to Existing Ring-Fenced Domain Leadership Theories*

20th-century leadership development theories were generally: (a) conceptualized and formulated through "a White male lens" and was subsequently applied to both males and females, (b) based largely upon theories from a corporate or military setting and experiences of White male administrators in the K–12 setting, and (c) define morality through a Christian lens that skewed morality and ethics. The WLDF purposefully includes both the male and female voice, and hard and soft skills thereby adding to the leadership development discourse.

#### *Contribution 2: Enhance Relevancy of Theory in Leadership Education Programs*

The urgent need to develop inclusive, non-discriminatory gender theory and practice, transdisciplinary leaders is not evident in current leadership education. The WLDF provides an interdisciplinary, inclusive framework to ground contemporary leadership development theory and practice.

#### *Contribution 3: Create a Framework for Leadership Development and Leadership Education*

Within the context of LE, the WLDF calls attention to interdependent quadrants that impact the development of an interdisciplinary leader's competencies, knowledge, and practice. Such a framework enables interdisciplinary leaders to critically self-analyze strengths and weaknesses thereby enabling supports via interventions or leader change to ensure that leadership effectiveness remains undiminished.

## CONCLUSION

Interdisciplinary leadership is a leadership paradigm focused on leadership practice that engages leaders to consider the dynamic wholistic nature of the varied systems within which they are engaging. Such leadership requires training and development in order to lead interdisciplinary teams committed to building the knowledge and consensus required to address complex problems.

To further confirm and/or refine the WLDF more interdisciplinary, and multi-paradigmatic research methodologies are required which align with the seven priorities found in the National Leadership Education Research Agenda. The primary means by which useful further investigations of WLDF can be conducted include (a) first-hand practice and phenomenological accounts of WLDF, (b) direct observation within the actual work context, (c) qualitative individual and group interviews, and (d) longitudinal case study methods.

The WLDF pushes beyond a specific area of study to (a) collectively drive the field forward with a deeper understanding of interdisciplinary leadership development and (b) create a synergy of learning and development in an integrated, intentional, and inspiring way.

## CLOSING REMARKS

In the 21st century, a high-functioning interdisciplinary team is an organizational necessity. Experience has shown that positing highly motivated individuals from multiple disciplines together with diverse but complementary skills does not necessarily create a high-functioning team. Whilst a specific leadership style is not a requirement for a high-performing interdisciplinary team what is critical is that each team member evidences adaptive leadership behaviors that are sensitive to the context and team members. Currently, interdisciplinary team members develop skills through personal experience with inconsistent degrees of success due to a lack of leadership education or training. Leadership training programs grounded on the WLDFs requirement of team members/leaders to critically self-analyze strengths and weaknesses in each of the four quadrants (life in the mind, life in the body, life in the spirit, life of passionate sacrifice) will contribute to the team's work efficiency and effectiveness.

## REFERENCES

Allen-Scott L., Buntain B., Hatfield J., Meisser A., & Thomas C. (2015). Academic institutions and one health: Building capacity for transdisciplinary research approaches to address complex health issues at the animal-human-ecosystem interface. *Academic Medicine: Journal of the Association of American Medical Colleges, 90*(7), 866–871.

Andenoro, A. C. (2013). The National Leadership Education Research Agenda: Strategic priorities and deepened perspectives. *Journal of Leadership Education, 12*(3), 1–9.

Andenoro, A. C., Allen, S. J., Haber-Curran, P., Jenkins, D. M., Sowcik, M., Dugan, J. P., & Osteen, L. (2013). *National Leadership Education Research Agenda 2013–2018: Providing strategic direction for the field of leadership education.* https://www.stu.edu/wp-content/uploads/sites/13/2020/09/NLEResearchAgenda.3.pdf

Bennis, W., & Nanus, B. (1985). *Leaders: Their strategies for taking charge.* Harper & Row.

Boone, C. G., Pickett, S. T. A., Bammer, G., Bawa, K., Dunne, J.A., Gordon, I. J., Hart, D., Hellman, J., Miller, A., New, M., Ometto, J. P., Tylor, K., Wendorf, G., Agrawal, A., Bertsch, P., Campbell, C., Dodd, P., Janetos, A., & Malleee, H. (2020). Preparing interdisciplinary leadership for a sustainable future. *Sustain Science, 15,* 1723–1733. https://doi.org/10.1007/s11625-020-00823-9

Brungardt, C. L. (1998). The new fact of leadership: Implications for training educational leaders. *On the Horizon, 6*(1), 7–8.

Clark S., & Wallace R. (2012). Interdisciplinary environmental leadership: Learning and teaching integrated problem solving. In D. R. Gallagher (Ed.), *Environmental leadership: A reference handbook* (pp. 420–429). SAGE.

Fisher, J. (2011). The four domains model: connecting spirituality, health and well-being. *Religious Journal, 2*(1), 17–28.

Frantzeskaki, N., & Rok, A. (2018). Co-producing urban sustainability transitions knowledge with community, policy and science. *Environmental Innovation and Societal Transitions, 29,* 47–51.

Giacalone, R. A., & Jurkiewicz, C. L. (2014). Toward a science of workplace spirituality. In R. A. Giacalone & C. L. Jurkiewicz (Eds.), *The handbook of workplace spirituality and organizational performance* (3rd ed., pp. 3–30). Routledge.

Irwin, E. G., Culligan P. J., & Fischer-Kowalski, M. (2018). Bridging barriers to advance global sustainability. *Nature Sustainability, 1,* 324–326. https://doi.org/10.1038/s41893-018-0085-1

Kellerman, B. (2012). *The end of leadership.* Harper Collins.

Kellerman, B. (2018, October 29). *Standards* [Bog post]. https://barbarakellerman.com/standards

Kellerman, B., & Douglas, D. (2019). The leadership system. *The Journal of Character & Leadership Development 6,* 52–60.

Klein, J. T. (1990). *Interdisciplinarity: History, theory, and practice.* Wayne State University Press.

Kolodinsky, R., Giacalone, R. A., & Jurkiewicz C. L. (2008). Workplace values and outcomes: Exploring personal, organizational and interactive workplace spirituality. *Journal of Business Ethics, 81*(2), 465–480.

Kockelmans, J. J. (1979). Why interdisciplinarity? In J. J. Kockelmans (Ed.), *Interdisciplinarity and higher education* (pp. 123–160). Pennsylvania State University Press.

Lattuca, L. R. (2001). *Creating interdisciplinarity: Interdisciplinary research and teaching among college and University Faculty.* Vanderbilt University Press.

Lindsay, D. R., & Friesen, D. L. (2020). Interdisciplinary leadership: Collectively driving the field forward: Priority 7 of the national leadership education research agenda. *Journal of Leadership Studies, 14*(3), 78–81.

Lord, R. G., Zaccaro, S. J., Day D. V., Avolio, B. J., & Eagly, A. H. (2017). Leadership in applied psychology: Three waves of theory and research. *Journal of Applied Psychology, 102*(3), 434–451.

Marques, J. F. (2005). The spiritual worker. *Journal of Management Development, 25*(9), 884–895.

Mental Health Foundation. (2008). *Need 2 know executive briefing: Spirituality and mental health.* https://www.bl.uk/britishlibrary/~/media/bl/global/social-welfare/pdfs/non-secure/s/p/i/spirituality-and-mental-health.pdf

Merriam-Webster's Collegiate Dictionary. (n.d.). New Edition. Merriam-Webster Inc.

Nicolescu, B. (1999). Manifest sur la transdisciplinarite. *Bulletin interactive du CIRET* (Centre de Recherche et Etudes Transdisciplinaires), *15*, 170–176.

Nicolescu, B. (2012). Transdisciplinarity: the hidden third, between the subject and the object. Human & Social Studies. *Research and Practice, 1*(1), 13–28.

Olsen, D. S., Borlaug, S. B., Klitkou, A., Lyall, C., & Yearley. S. (2013). *A better understanding of interdisciplinary research in climate change.* NIFU Nordic Institute for Studies in Innovation, Research and Education.

Owen R., Macnaghten P., & Stilgoe, J. (2012). Responsible research and innovation: From science in society to science for society, with society. *Science and Public Policy, 39*(6), 751–760.

Palmer, P. J. (2004). *A hidden wholeness: The journey toward an undivided life, welcoming the soul and weaving community in a wounded world.* Jossey-Bass.

Pedersen, D. B. (2016). Integrating social sciences and humanities in interdisciplinary research. *Palgrave Communications 2*, Article 16036. https://doi.org/10.1057/palcomms.2016.36

Riggio, R. E. (2011). Is leadership studies a discipline? In M. Harvey & R. E. Riggio (Eds.), *The dialogue of disciplines: Research companion to leadership studies* (pp. 9–19). Edward Elgar.

Samah, S. A. A., Silong, A. D., Jusoff, K., & Ismail, I. A. (2012). Relationship between spirituality and academic leader effectiveness. *Journal of Educational and Social Research, 2*(5), 33–40.

Schuster, J. (1997). Wholistic care: Healing a sick system. *Nursing Management, 28*(6), 56–59.

Stogdill, R. M. (1974). *Handbook of leadership: A survey of the literature.* Free Press

Yukl, G. A. (2006). *Leadership in organizations.* Prentice Hall.

CHAPTER 2

# DEVELOPING CAPACITY FOR LEADING IN A DIGITALLY TRANSFORMED WORLD

**Joe Lasley**
**Elizabeth Goryunova**

## ABSTRACT

The benefits of digital transformation for organizations such as increased innovation and efficiency are also accompanied by unique challenges and costs (technology, training, security). To effectively carry out essential leadership functions in a digital environment, leaders need to develop "digital savvy": a combination of technical savvy and the capacity to sense social interactions and organizational dynamics in digital environments. This chapter discusses the best practices, considerations, challenges, and strategies for the design and facilitation of impactful leadership instruction that results in developing skills important for leadership effectiveness in a digital environment across multiple contexts utilizing interdisciplinary approaches.

Digital transformation of global society, accelerated by the pandemic disruption of 2020, brought the attention of scholars and practitioners to the

*On Leadership*, pages 19–33

challenges of leading in a digital environment and revealed the importance of digital fluency for effective and responsible societal and organizational leadership of the future (Barnes, 2020; Pan & Zhang, 2020; Snyder & Barnakova, 2020). As the latitude of leadership functions widens, the tasks before leadership educators become more complex, as digital savvy is added to the responsible, effective, and other critical skills that leaders of the future need to actively contribute to building a better world (Cortellazzo et al., 2019). Digital savvy leadership means not only technology savvy, but also a capacity to work with social interactions and organizational dynamics in digital environments. Schrage et al. (2021) report that 88% of organizations believe in the importance of a critical mass of digital savvy leaders, but only 22% have achieved this objective thus far.

Accordingly, to be able to develop effective future leaders, leadership educators themselves have to master digital technology, integrate its benefits into their instructional practices, and further explore its potential in organizations and leadership contexts. Digital technology is commonly recognized for its benefits for organizational innovation and increased efficiency. Yet it also has enormous utility for successful leadership in the 21st century and beyond as the medium for communicating, leading, learning, and community-building that employs virtual tools to integrate online and in-person interactions (Fitzgerald et al., 2013). The same is true for leadership education that is currently adapting to the online learning environment and mastering new ways to evolve, design, teach, learn, and facilitate leadership development experiences in virtual and hybrid environments. Along the way, leadership educators discover the limits and affordances that virtual tools have for creating learning environments that facilitate leadership, and for engaging in the development and design of learning experiences and interventions.

In this chapter, we introduce the concept of digital leadership as the capacity for utilizing the advantages of digital technology to carry out essential leadership functions. We discuss the importance of digital leadership for future leaders' effectiveness and share the best practices as well as considerations, assumptions, challenges, and strategies for the design and facilitation of impactful leadership instruction. We conclude by envisioning the benefits of being digitally savvy in interdisciplinary leadership.

## LEADING IN THE DIGITAL ENVIRONMENT

The 2021 Global Leadership Forecast issued by Development Dimensions International (DDI) and showcased an analysis of the responses from 1,742 organizations and 15,787 leaders around the world. The results indicate that digital savvy leaders are 1.5 times as likely to lead innovation efforts, and to foster an inclusive culture, which results in an almost two-fold increase in an organization's agility and capacity for success (Neal et al., 2021). At the same time, respondents further acknowledged that developing the next generation of leaders is the biggest organizational challenge, with only 47% of companies currently capable of filling leadership roles. Of those currently filling leadership roles, only 23% report confidence in their digital acumen and ability to lead virtually.

Leadership scholars and practitioners are yet to come to a consensus on what the future of leadership is but there is a growing interest in identifying skills required to lead in a digital world and in conceptualizing digital leadership. Thus, Kane et al. (2019) point out that as compared to traditional leadership, digital leadership is uniquely characterized by a fast pace, digital literacy, adaptability, a culture of innovation, and perpetual connectivity. At the same time, they suggest that the traditional leadership competencies, such as effective communication, clear vision, business acumen, employees' support, and empowerment, as well as stakeholders' engagement, should not be ignored. Martins (2019) suggests that in contrast to hierarchies of business as usual, leading in a digitally transformed environment requires the ability to lead networks of people and teams. This transition highlights interdisciplinary networks and complex problem solving as becoming ever more salient within the emerging future of leadership. Buvat et al. (2018) state that to embrace the dizzying pace of technology innovation, organizations require a combination of digital capabilities (use of technology for organizational internal and external processes, such as operations or interactions with customers) and leadership capabilities (driving digital transformation).

The importance of balancing digital savvy with core leadership competencies is acknowledged in several models and frameworks developed for the leadership of the future. For instance, Van Laar et al. (2017) conceptualize the 21st-century digital skills framework as a combination of core skills (technical and information management competencies, problem-solving, collaboration) and contextual skills (ethical and cultural awareness, lifelong learning). Those skills increase employees' capacity to thrive in a rapidly changing environment, and to drive organizational innovation and competitiveness.

Barnakova et al. (2020) define "digital dexterity" (p. 1) as a combination of adaptive, strategic, innovative, and executional skills that enable leaders to support digital transformation of their organization. The digital dexterity competency model proposed by the authors is based on the three critical skills of digital leaders: digital strategist, digital innovator, and digital driver where strategist envisions the future, innovator disrupts the status quo while harnessing legacy assets, and driver builds trust and collaboration across diverse stakeholders to enable rapid action (Barnakova et al., 2020). Agility is at the core of the digital dexterity model, as it ensures adaptability, learning orientation, and growth mindset, similar to the performance of triathletes who have certain strengths in a specific athletic activity, but maintain potency in all three by preserving their agility.

Yet another model conceived by Green, Elson, and Linge (2012) characterizes leadership of the future by transformative authenticity and capacity to traverse the *third space*—a symbolic location that exists beyond individual differences and dualities, the evolving dynamic system of interactions and networked relationships that bring humanity back to unity. Humans naturally create dichotomies and binary explanations of issues, especially complex ones, to make them easier to analyze in chunks. Conceptualizing what is me and what is not me is a basic psychological function that gets expanded to groups as in-group vs out-group identification and various forms of othering, becoming a driver of dynamics contextualizing leadership (Haslam et al., 2011). The Third Space is creative potential that exists between and outside of these binaries in more complex interconnected networked forms. Neither side has an answer but integrating networked positions together into the proverbial third space can create new solutions that would not have been possible otherwise. Such opportunities for networking are proliferating at exponential rates thanks to communication technology.

Thus far, scholars concur that leading in a digitally transformed environment requires an expanded repertoire of competencies where traditional leadership skills are complemented by digital mastery. In this chapter, we define the capacity for utilizing the advantages of digital technology to carry out essential leadership functions (emphasizing underlying organizational dynamics) as digital leadership. Digital leadership is an example of an adaptive response to the increasingly complex and rapidly changing organizational ecosystems with newly emerging rules of economic and social engagement that permeate global society at every level. To prepare leaders of the future for digital leadership, educators must themselves demonstrate the adaptive response to the recent transformations in the educational landscape, particularly to the abrupt transition to fully online instruction brought about by the COVID-19 pandemic.

## LEADERSHIP EDUCATION IN A DIGITALLY TRANSFORMED ENVIRONMENT: PRINCIPLES

The core objective of leadership education is to build human capacity to shape the desired future, individually and collectively. This process is informed by leadership theory and research and engages diverse curricular and co-curricular activities and interactions (Adenoro, 2013; Senge et al.,

2008). Guthrie and Jenkins (2018) bring up the importance of engaging leadership learners as active participants of the educational process, that is ensuring experiential, relational, interactional, and interpersonal aspects of leadership learning. The authors further note that modeling the leadership process by inviting students to actively engage and build on existing knowledge through shared learning experiences is one of the effective leadership education practices (Guthrie & Jenkins, 2018).

While typical leadership education programs are conceived for physical spaces, leadership instruction increasingly takes place in blended and online modalities, both synchronously and asynchronously. As leadership education continues to expand to online platforms, modeling digital leadership that prepares leaders of the future for virtual interactions and distributed global organizations becomes critical to leadership instruction and the learning process (Siewiorek et al., 2012). Another tool that is increasingly employed to improve learning effectiveness (particularly for asynchronous learning) is the community of inquiry (COI). COI is the educational framework that can be defined as the confluence of social, cognitive, and teaching presence with an educational experience at their intersection (Garrison et al., 2000). Social presence implies established in-group trust and productive interaction, as well as the ability to express oneself through available means of communication, and it is enabled by open communication and group cohesion. Cognitive presence refers to learners' ability to construct meaning through reflection and collaborative critical discourse. And teaching presence focuses on mutually reinforcing processes of design, facilitation, and direct interaction that supports social and cognitive presence that builds understanding to achieve educational outcomes (Garrison et al., 2000).

Similar to Garrison et al. (2000), Law et al. (2019) acknowledge the importance of teaching presence, cognitive presence, and social presence, and demonstrate that in blended learning (with integrated online instruction) teaching presence becomes even more critical for students' learning behavior: It serves as a vital factor in ensuring learners' cognitive and social engagement, thus improving their performance. At the same time, online learning modalities, and utilizing technology platforms and information systems in general, introduce a particular form of stress and therefore adds a layer of uncertainty for embodying digital leadership (Tarafdar et al., 2019). In adaptive responses to these challenges, leadership educators discover innovative ways to design, teach, and facilitate leadership development experiences in online and hybrid environments. Thus, among the most creative learners' engagement tools are online educational games, simulations, and learning communities of varied quality and effectiveness (Superbetter.com, Habitica.com), some fully commercialized (Fligby.com, Ed Leadership SIMs, RealGame.com). Scholars recognize that meaningful online experience requires learners' behavioral, emotional, and cognitive engagement (Fredricks et al., 2004, Henrie et al., 2015). Pekrun (2011) argues that emotions can influence a "broad variety of cognitive processes that contribute to learning, such as perception, attention, memory, decision-making, and cognitive problem-solving" (p. 26). Therefore, it is important to create a learning environment that supports emotional experiences that foster learning.

In leadership education, regardless of modality, it is essential to create a psychological environment that is conducive to leading change, responding to disruption, and empowering learning. This aspect of leadership learning is called the "holding environment" or "container" (Bion, 1959; Winnicott, 1960). Holding refers to the way an authority figure, or group, contains and interprets what's happening in times of uncertainty to buffer distress and help others make sense of confusion. Holding is both interpersonal and institutional and applies in unique ways when interacting virtually (Petriglieri, 2020). Without holding, anxiety, anger, and fragmentation ensue, and therefore it is essential to create mutual support and continued engagement to allow for a truly shared vision to emerge.

These challenges are often addressed in leadership programs within adaptive leadership and group relations traditions. Adaptive leadership (Heifetz et al., 2009) distinguished between technical problems, which can be solved with expertise, and adaptive challenges in which expertise alone cannot accomplish required change. In situations with high degrees of uncertainty, authority functions (or dysfunctions) to regulate disequilibrium at a level that motivates deep learning without overwhelming a group's capacity to work through resistance and mobilize toward adaptive change.

Authority is also a core concept in group relations events, along with boundaries, roles, and tasks, referred to as BART (Green & Molenkamp, 2005; Turner et al., 2018). This framework is used to make sense of unconscious dynamics in groups and organizations operating within the "group-as-a-whole" (Schermer, 2012). The idea of a group-as-a-whole suggests that groups can be thought of "as if" they had an unconscious mind of their own (a metaphor to help us think about how unconscious group dynamics influence people in groups both intra-personally and in behavior). This approach enables learners to see patterns of emotions and behavior representing larger dynamics in the group that become expressed in individual behaviors. Sometimes this serves a working purpose and sometimes it serves survival tasks of the group, such as an irrational fear of uncertainty that detracts from group functioning. These dynamics are lying beneath the surface in organizations and effective leaders explore how they may be operating in any given system (Stapley, 2006). Understanding underlying group and organizational dynamics can have huge consequences. They are hard to observe even when interacting in face-to-face situations, which becomes more obscured but still workable and just as essential for leading adaptive change in digital environments.

Adaptive leadership and group relations traditions are well established, however, the heightened focus on using them online is a recent development. The incorporation of group relations methods in leadership education and more recently in online leadership education formats has highlighted characteristics of effective leadership including emotional intelligence, communicating across differences, growth mindset, community-building, and developing capacity to work with social interactions and organizational dynamics in digital environments. The process of developing the online manifestations of such programs has revealed important insights to inform best practices for digital leadership that are described next.

## LEADERSHIP EDUCATION IN A DIGITALLY TRANSFORMED ENVIRONMENT: ASSUMPTIONS

When facilitating online leadership education and development, we must be aware of implicit assumptions and how our mental models affect our strategies. Assumptions about online leadership education became apparent during the transition to online modalities. Some implications for practice also emerged while redesigning and implementing group relations and adaptive leadership programs in digital environments (see Table 2.1). The "savvy" in digital savvy leadership requires a continued attention to and awareness about our assumptions in online contexts.

Leadership educators should review these assumptions and adaptations, reflect on their own mental models, and then consider some strategies to incorporate in virtual leadership instruction. For example, one faulty assumption may be that the instructor is solely responsible for accommodating students' comfort zones, while in reality, students and teachers share responsibility for co-creating a learning environment that regulates a level of challenge at the edge of our comfort zones (French, 1997). After elucidating that assumption, instructors can address the challenge by designing activities that position the students as experts on their own learning edges. This and other assumptions are listed in Table 2.1 with corresponding adaptations to our mindset as leadership educators. The following section will further describe each assumption and adaptation.

### Getting Lost

There are two types of uncertainty that one can experience in the design and delivery of online instruction: productive (intrinsic to learning and

**TABLE 2.1 Assumptions and Adaptations in Facilitating Online Leadership Education and Development**

| Assumption | Adaptation |
|---|---|
| We should avoid getting lost in the material. Design to prevent confusion. | Get lost on purpose, be curious to explore the unknown, but don't panic. |
| Structure and scaffolding do not equal emerging experience. | Utilize both social structures and processes in tandem which are enabled by "virtual space" and form parallel social structure. |
| Intellectual cognitive engagement is a barrier to authentic developmental experiences. | Use intellectual approaches to get started and relieve some anxiety. Technical solutions reduce disequilibrium when it gets overwhelming. |
| Meetings or individual activities have a single purpose at a given time. | Name the purpose(s) in the design of each meeting, interaction, or activity. Group purposes can be at least two-fold: task, process, and/or social. Add intention to clarify purpose. |
| Education system: Grades are zero sums demanding finished products, prescribe learning, accommodate rather than buffer disequilibrium, the teacher is the responsible party, downloading knowledge is the focus, content = outcome. | Co-create learning, buffer and hold group disequilibrium, everyone is a source of learning, learning takes place at cognitive, emotional, and social levels. |
| Case-in-point is an ideal experiential pedagogy. | Experiment with how there are new affordances online that aren't reconstructions of physical spaces. Many methods are tremendous, and all have pros/cons. |

development process) and unproductive (anxiety about technical aspects and logistics of the course). While a valid best practice in online education is to have clear instructions, an explicitly designed curriculum, and thoroughly explained activities linked to learning outcomes, panic about course logistics can be detrimental to a developmental mindset. Extensive design helps reduce unnecessary uncertainty about the task, provides direction, and helps students with an orientation to the format and expectations of the course. However, this can be taken too far, on an assumption that there should always be a detailed map and prescribed sequence that predicts everything that will happen and prevents us from ever feeling lost. If we avoid exploration entirely, we lose out on valuable experiential and developmental learning opportunities that afford us valuable opportunities to question our understanding and be curious about the unknown (Winnicott, 1989). Therefore, an important strategy is to maintain a sense of purpose that will allow us to wander outside our comfort zone without knowing the path and still not be totally lost (Vygotsky, 1978). These approaches should involve deliberate practice of leadership behaviors and can be paired with contextually based debriefing (Rosch & Jenkins, 2020). The key here is to struggle with content and cognitive dissonance about self and others, not to be lost in logistics that would prevent participation entirely.

## Structuring Emergence

There are many elements of design and facilitation that impact learning and leadership experiences online by providing structure for the learning process. For example, course activities offer intentional directions for how to engage in learning, while learning outcomes provide scaffolding that aligns learning to the course and program objectives. Likewise, the learning process is impacted by the set-up of the physical and virtual spaces that often dictate what prompts are given, how many people are effective in small group discussions, a facilitator's ability to attend to learning that is happening in the moment, and so on. Additionally, leadership learning requires structures that allow for interaction and social learning thus its effectiveness depends on the way that social processes are arranged (Soria & Johnson, 2020). Leadership learning also requires adaptability and engaging with the discovery of learning potential as it unfolds during an experience. As we can see, social structures, physical layout, virtual space, and interaction processes all contribute to leadership learning environments and form intertwined elements of leadership learning. Yet while we intentionally design and structure online learning experiences, we need to allow flexibility to account for the emergence of unpredictable learning opportunities. The structure and group dynamic alone do not guarantee emergent learning, even the best of design has limitations thus underscoring the importance of masterful facilitation.

## The Cognitive Path to Affective Learning

A common challenge in leadership development is balancing the head and the heart: the thinking and feeling, or cognitive and affective aspects of learning and leadership. Many educators attend to the head, heart, and hand (cognitive, affective, and kinesthetic learning) and we know that leadership development requires experience, but intentional change is discontinuous, complex, and emotional (Boyatzis, 2006). Oftentimes in experiential leadership classrooms, we begin with cognitive development: knowing leadership and ourselves. The ability to reflect, observe, and analyze can enhance our self-awareness, equip us with new strategies, skills, behaviors, and increase our capacity to understand complex ways of being in the world. Affective development is also a crucial part of leadership learning: emotions impact the way we internalize information and the way we lead (Boyatzis et al., 2015).

Yet in digital leadership, there are unique barriers to emotional engagement. For instance, nonverbal communication and emotional cues are still very present in video conferencing or written communication on discussion boards, but they are less clear. This dynamic draws a lot of our energy for the emotional aspects of the experience (Bailenson, 2021). As a result, we might end up resisting the cognitive aspects of leadership learning, perceiving them as barriers to authentic emotional engagement. In fact, the opposite can be true: While the emotional demands of digital leadership (dealing with the lack of social cues) generate high amounts of stress, cognitive engagement can help soothe feeling overwhelmed by emotional confusion.

### Multi-Purpose

Learning activities need to be designed with an intended purpose in mind. This is necessary to guide individual learning activities and for group social learning experiences. Bion (1959) explains that groups often have both an intentional work purpose (to complete a specific task) and an unconscious purpose that can influence the emotional experience of the group. Commonly, there are tasks to achieve, learning to accomplish, along with social processes that contribute to an overarching shared experience that develops in parallel task and relational sequences (Tuckman, 1965). The social-emotional processes that happen in groups become useful for leadership learning when groups are intentional about how to engage together (Wheelan et al., 2020). If we design and facilitate leadership learning activities with these different kinds of purposes in mind, while recognizing that each activity may serve several purposes, we can enhance leadership learning and development while providing nuanced interdisciplinary guidance for engagement.

### The Education System

Education systems are massive, complex, and enmeshed in the culture of society. This means that values, beliefs, and assumptions about education run deep and have a tremendous impact on our mental models and approach to leadership instruction, including digital learning. The cultural assumptions inherent in our education system could constitute an entire book, at least. For now, we will briefly introduce some aspects that have become apparent in designing digital leadership instruction.

Frequently, grades are perceived as "the end game" rather than a step in continuous improvement with a growth mindset. Learning is prescribed and delivered from authority to ignorant masses. Freire (2003) calls this prescriptive and transactional approach the "banking model of education" (p. 72). In a class, whether traditional or online, the responsibilities of administrators and teachers are to accommodate students' comfort rather than buffer disequilibrium, and the focus is on downloading knowledge rather than on generating understanding. Content is the outcome that matters, so we test, test, test. These cultural assumptions are hard to overcome even if we are fully aware of them. External pressures, program expectations, and individual anxieties will all influence our experiences. Therefore, during the design and implementation of leadership instruction, it is essential to regularly reflect on how the underlying assumptions about education in society are impacting the learning process (Dugan et al., 2020; Jacobson & Mustafa, 2019).

Leadership education of all kinds should endeavor to transform learning mindsets. This is especially evident with digital savvy leadership, in which new ways of operating, understanding, and being are currently still unfolding in society. Adaptive leadership and group relations are becoming even more central in digital leadership due to the new demands of a global, networked society that is emerging. We should strive to co-create learning together and move beyond traditional student/teacher roles. It is paramount that leadership educators, leaders, and learners, together, buffer and hold group disequilibrium to allow for meaningful engagement that integrates cognitive/emotional/social learning and development. In closing, there are a number of practical steps digital savvy leaders can implement in an example of an online leadership education and development program. They include:

- The instructor(s) should be competent with the technology platforms being used and aware of how video/sound/text communication presents to learners. These platforms should be limited to a few and made clear in advance for participants. It is helpful to have an administrator role that assists in managing technology during larger events.
- *Resist* the temptation to control interactions provided by the technology platforms, while still ensuring secure online interactions. Test functions in advance.
- *Make* expectations explicit. Assume students are the experts on where their comfort zone transitions into discomfort that helps learning or when it is too much. Ask learners what they need. Create multiple ways to engage.
- *Be clear*, consistent, and explain activities in advance, including how the activity is linked to the learning objectives or purpose of the program.

- *Be clear* about the role of intellectualizing and sharing emotional experiences, model these forms of engagement.
- *Openly discuss* the challenges and range of experiences using technology. Discuss trustworthiness and how this group will interact online.
- *Make regular time* and space for learners to check in and communicate about their energy level and emotional experiences, even just to name them. Pause for mindfulness. "Are you existing, exhausted, or excited right now?"
- *Create* opportunities for casual online interaction. Online transitions can be stark. Formerly natural casual interaction needs to be intentional online. Utilize "hallway time" by not cutting the meeting off for everyone abruptly to promote social engagement.
- *Utilize small group* (~4 people) breakout rooms for discussions to help learners connect with each other differently than in larger video conference meetings.
- *Be aware* of how certain cues are not transmitted the same online and that there is much going on within individuals that may be affecting them.
- *Focus* on supporting social presence to balance the added challenges of interacting online. Provide opportunities for peer support and affirmation at higher rates or before critique.

## FUTURE RESEARCH AND PRACTICAL APPLICATIONS

The benefits of digital transformation are yet to be fully understood, embraced, and utilized. Its challenges are yet to be conquered, and potential yet to be unleashed. As scholars are focused on exploring the phenomenon, leadership educators and practitioners must respond to the need for groups and organizations to become capable of effectively functioning in a digital environment by identifying impactful pedagogies and practices. Bringing adaptive leadership and group relations traditions into online leadership instruction increases its effectiveness and emerges alongside digital leadership. Developing digital savvy leadership will enhance our abilities to sense emerging social dynamics and meet the demands of an evolving society. As leadership becomes increasingly global and interdisciplinary, capacity for developing digital leadership will become ever more salient and crucial.

## REFERENCES

Andenoro, A.C. (2013). The national leadership education research agenda: Strategic priorities and deepened perspectives. *Journal of Leadership Education, 12*(3), 1–9.

Barnakova, Y., Krupp, S., & Snyder, S. (2020). *Building digital dexterity in your leadership team.* https://www.heidrick.com/-/media/heidrickcom/publications-and-reports/building_digital_dexterity_in_your_leadership_team.pdf

Barnes, S. (2020). Information management research and practice in the post-COVID-19 world. *International Journal of Information Management, 55,* Article 102175. https://doi.org/10.1016/j.ijinfomgt.2020.102175

Bailenson, J. N. (2021). Nonverbal overload: A theoretical argument for the causes of Zoom fatigue. *Technology, Mind, and Behavior, 2*(1). https://doi.org/10.1037/tmb0000030

Bion W. R. (1959). Attacks on linking. *International Journal of Psychoanalysis, 40,* 308–315.

Boyatzis, R. E. (2006). An overview of intentional change from a complexity perspective. *Journal of Management Development, 25*(7), 607–623. https://doi.org/10.1108/02621710610678445

Boyatzis, R. E., Rochford, K., & Taylor, S. (2015). The role of the positive emotional attractor in vision and shared vision: Toward effective leadership, relationships, and engagement. *Frontiers in Psychology, 6,* Article 670. https://doi.org/10.3389/fpsyg.2015.00670

Buvat, J., Slatter, M., Puttur, R., Westerman, G., Bonnet, D., & Crummenerl, C. (2018). *Understanding digital mastery today.* Capgemini Research Institute. https://www.capgemini.com/wp-content/uploads/2018/07/Digital-Mastery-Report_Digital.pdf

Cortellazzo, L., Bruni, E., & Zampieri, R. (2019). The role of leadership in a digitalized world: A Review. *Frontiers in Psychology, 10,* Article 1938. http://doi.org/10.3389/fpsyg.2019.01938

Dugan, J. P., Randolph, P., Hightower, C., & Rossetti, A. M. (2020). The critical imperative: Evidence-based practices to strengthen leadership development. *New Directions for Student Leadership, 2020*(168), 19–30. https://doi.org/10.1002/yd.20405

Fitzgerald, M., Kruschwitz, N., Bonnet, D., & Welch, M. (2013). *Embracing digital technology: a new strategic imperative.* MIT Sloan Management Review. https://sloanreview.mit.edu/projects/embracing-digital-technology

Fredricks, J. A., Blumenfeld, P. C., & Paris, A. H. (2004). School engagement: Potential of the concept, state of the evidence. *Review of Educational Research, 74*(1), 59–109.

French, R. (1997). The teacher as container of anxiety: Psychoanalysis and the role of teacher. *Journal of Management Education, 21*(4), 483–495. https://doi.org/10.1177/105256299702100404

Freire, P. (2003). From pedagogy of the oppressed. In A. Darder, M. Baltodano, & R. D. Torres (Eds.), *The critical pedagogy reader* (pp. 57–96). Routledge Falmer.

Garrison, D. R., Anderson, T., & Archer, W. (2000). Critical inquiry in a text-based environment: Computer conferencing in higher education. *The Internet and Higher Education, 2*(2), 87–105.

Green, Z., Elson, O., & Van Linge, A. (2012). Unleashing possibilities: Leadership and the Third Space. In C. Pearson (Ed.), *The transforming leader: New approaches to the leadership for the 21st century* (pp. 211–219). Berrett-Koehler.

Green, Z. G., & Molenkamp, R. J. (2005). *The BART system of group and organizational analysis.* https://citeseerx.ist.psu.edu/viewdoc/download?doi=10.1.1.1075.504&rep=rep1&type=pdf

Guthrie, K., & Jenkins, D. (2018). *The role of leadership educators: Transforming learning.* Information Age Publishing.

Haslam, S. A., Reicher, S. D., & Platow, M. J. (2011). *The new psychology of leadership: Identity, influence and power.* Psychology Press

Heifetz, R. A., Linsky, M., & Grashow, A. (2009). *The practice of adaptive leadership: Tools and tactics for changing your organization and the world.* Harvard Business Press.

Jacobson, D., & Mustafa, N. (2019). Social identity map: A reflexivity tool for practicing explicit positionality in critical qualitative research. *International Journal of Qualitative Methods, 18,* 1–12. https://doi.org/10.1177/1609406919870075

Kane, G., Phillips, A., Copulsky, J., & Andrus, G. (2019, March 12). How digital leadership is(n't) different. *MIT Sloan Management Review, 60*(3), 34–39.

Law, K., Geng, S., & Li, T. (2019). Student enrollment, motivation and learning performance in a blended learning environment: The mediating effects of social, teaching, and cognitive presence. *Computers & Education, 136*(1), 1–12.

Martins, H. (2019). Digital transformation and digital leadership. *Healthcare Informatics Research, 25*(4), 350–351.

Neal, S., Boatman, J., Watt, B., & Bersi, J. (2021). *Global leadership forecast.* Development Dimensions International. https://media.ddiworld.com/research/GLF2021-final.pdf.

Pan, S., & Zhang, S. (2020). From fighting COVID-19 pandemic to tackling sustainable development goals: An opportunity for responsible information systems research. *Journal of Information Management, 55,* Article 102196. https://reader.elsevier.com/reader/sd/pii/S0268401220311154?token=0C396F5CFC86B89FB28C3439744C3E231E81085C672F95482C41FC653A8F40B8931CC8BC4C65E7B5DBC68960C86234BF

Pekrun, R. (2011). Emotions as drivers of learning and cognitive development. In R. Calvo and S. D'Mello (Eds.), *New perspectives on affect and learning technologies* (pp. 23–39). Springer. https://doi.org/10.1007/978-1-4419-9625-1_3

Petriglieri, G. (2020). *The psychology behind effective crisis leadership.* Harvard Business Review. https://hbr.org/2020/04/the-psychology-behind-effective-crisis-leadership

Rosch, D. M., & Jenkins, D. M. (2020). What do we know about formal leadership courses and their effects? *New Directions for Student Leadership, 2020*(168), 31–41. https://doi.org/10.1002/yd.20406

Schermer, V. L. (2012). Group-as-a-whole and complexity theories: Areas of convergence. *Group Analysis, 45*(3), 275–288.

Senge, P. M., Smith, B., Kruschwitz, N., Laur, J., & Schley, S. (2008). *The necessary revolution: How individuals and organizations are working together to create a sustainable world.* Broadway Books.

Siewiorek, A., Saarinen, E., Lainema, T., & Lehtinen, E. (2012). Learning leadership skills in a simulated business environment. *Computers & Education, 58*(1), 121–135.

Snyder, S., & Barnakova, Y. (2020). *Being a digital leader has never been more urgent.* Knowledge at Wharton. https://knowledge.wharton.upenn.edu

Soria, K. M., & Johnson, M. R. (2020). A Conceptual framework for evidence-based leadership development practices. *New Directions for Student Leadership, 2020*(168), 9–17. https://doi.org/10.1002/yd.20404

Stapley, L. (2006). *Individuals, groups, and organizations: Beneath the surface.* Karnac.

Tarafdar, M., Cooper, C. L., & Stich, J. (2019). The technostress trifecta–techno eustress, techno distress, and design: An agenda for research. *Information Systems Journal, 29*(1), 6–42. https://doi.org/10.1111/isj.12169

Tuckman, B. (1965). Developmental sequence in small groups. *Psychological Bulletin, 63*(6), 384–399.

Turner, J., Baker, R., & Morris, M. (2018). Complex adaptive systems: Adapting and managing teams and team conflict in organizational conflict. In A. A. Vilas Boas (Ed.), *Organizational conflict* (pp. 65–93). http://dx.doi.org/10.5772/intechopen.72344

Van Laar, E., Van Deursen, A. J. A. M., Van Dijk, J. A. G. M., & De Haan, J. (2017). The relation between 21st-century skills and digital skills: A systematic literature review. *Computers in Human Behavior, 72*, 577–588.

Vygotsky, L. S. (1978). *Mind in society: The development of higher psychological processes* (M. Cole, Ed.). Harvard University Press.

Wheelan, S. A., Åkerlund, M., & Jacobsson, C. (2020). *Creating effective teams: A guide for members and leaders.* SAGE Publications.

Winnicott, D. W. (1960). The theory of the parent-infant relationship. *The International Journal of Psychoanalysis, 41*, 585–595.

Winnicott, D. W. (1989). *Playing and reality.* Routledge.

CHAPTER 3

# THE INTERDISCIPLINARY ACTS OF LEADERSHIP

## Facilitating the Relationship Among the Head, Heart, Hands, and Holy

**Stan Amaladas**

### ABSTRACT

The author offers a conceptual fourfold head–heart–hands–holy interdisciplinary leadership framework to address the problem of racism within a Canadian policing agency. The question raised is: "How can enforcement officers commit themselves to the cause of treating all with respect and dignity rather than simply complying with an organizational command to do so?" Focusing on the unconscious and implicit biases in both a policing agency and in early leadership studies, the author argues that it is only by raising our consciousness of biases that exist (head), genuinely feeling the need for change (heart), and engaging in purposeful action (hands) for no other reason than to treat persons as persons, with dignity and grace (holy), can we begin to bring dwelling in this common place called Canada to the fullness of all that it can be. Emerging out of the reciprocity and oneness of the four Hs, the author concludes by offering four corresponding metaphors of leader-

*On Leadership*, pages 35–54

ship, namely, leadership as educating, as caring, as purposeful action, and as a moral undertaking. The author argues that an interdisciplinary approach to leadership studies is governed by the interconnectedness of all four Hs and its corresponding metaphors.

## A PERSONAL STORY

As a person of color, I worked with the Royal Canadian Mounted Police (RCMP) in my role as a civilian regional learning and change consultant within the Canadian Federal Public Service. My experience leads me to believe that police officers are decent and caring women and men who try to do what is right. While traveling with my family and one RCMP officer to visit my mother and siblings in Malaysia, I was encouraged to see that he defined his occupation when filling out the visitor's form at the point of entry, as peace officer. While I have witnessed a genuine interest in pursuing peace, today, I am perplexed and disturbed by the dissonance between what I know through my personal relationships and the allegations of racism against members of the RCMP.

## PURPOSE

The purpose of this chapter is three-fold. Expanding on Burns's (1978) formulation of the "essence" and "fundamental act" of leadership (p. 43), in Section 1 I introduce a conceptual fourfold head–heart–hands–holy framework for an interdisciplinary approach to leadership studies. In Section 2 I address the problem and implications of the unconscious and implicit bias that exists not only within the RCMP but more broadly in the field of leadership studies. To facilitate the brokenness of trust between citizens, especially those who have been harmed, and law enforcement officers, in Section 3 I propose *improvising* a "trust-building-learning-space" by combining familiar and unfamiliar acts of leadership to new and old situations.

## CONTEXT

The writing of this chapter is triggered by RCMP Commissioner, Brenda Lucki's response to the question of whether systemic racism permeated her policing agency. Shortly after Chief Allan Adam of the Athabasca Chipewyan First Nation in Alberta, alleged that "he was beaten by RCMP officers and that his wife was manhandled" (Haig, 2020, para. 2) after police stopped him for an expired license plate in March of 2020, she replied:

> That is an interesting question because in the last couple of days I have honestly heard about 15 or 20 definitions of systemic racism... If it refers to an unconscious bias that exists... we definitely have that in the RCMP and we are not immune to it at all. There are times when our members don't act in accordance with our core values, which includes racism, and it's those times that we have to make sure that that doesn't happen. (as cited in Haig, 2020, paras. 9–10)

If active members of the RCMP are not immune to an unconscious bias that feeds racism, and if there is an intent "to make sure that (racism) doesn't happen," how then can they commit themselves to the cause of safeguarding others from harm and treating all with respect for its own sake, rather than simply complying with an organizational command to do so? To answer this question, allow me to first re-construct Burns's (1978) understanding of the essence and fundamental act of leadership.

## SECTION 1: A FOURFOLD FRAMEWORK FOR AN INTERDISCIPLINARY APPROACH TO LEADERSHIP STUDIES

Burns (1978), who is considered by some as being the founder of leadership studies (Barbour, 2006), suggests that "the essence of leadership is consciousness raising" (p. 43). He further states that for the sake of "purposeful action" (p. 44), leadership's "fundamental act is to induce people to be aware or conscious of what they feel," because, and here he quotes an American educator, Susanne Langer, "where nothing is felt, nothing matters" (p. 44). A similar sentiment was expressed passionately by Marx (1856/1978), in reflecting on the glory and pain of industrialization in the 19th century: "But although the atmosphere in which we live weighs upon everyone like a 20,000 lb. force, do you feel it?" (p. 577). It is as if Marx also understood that if nothing is *felt,* nothing matters.

Thus far we see that for Burns (1978) leadership is a relationship among three Hs: the *head* (consciousness raising), *heart* (being aware of what they feel), and *hands* (used here as a metaphor for purposeful action). Several leadership scholars are familiar with connecting the work of leadership with these three Hs (Kouzes & Posner, 2017; Nicholls, 1994). Others, like Staub ll (1997), have written exclusively on the heart of leadership. However, Burns (1978) offers more "practical advice" (p. 462) on why we need to engage with the three Hs at all. For him, it is for no other reason than to "treat... all persons like *persons*" (p. 462, emphasis in original), and not like pawns or things to be manipulated, controlled, or exterminated. *Treating persons as persons,* as a "Thou" and not as an "It" (Buber, 1970), is a sacred and non-negotiable human gift that persons owe one other. Consequently, I place Burns's practical advice in the realm of a 4th H—the holy.

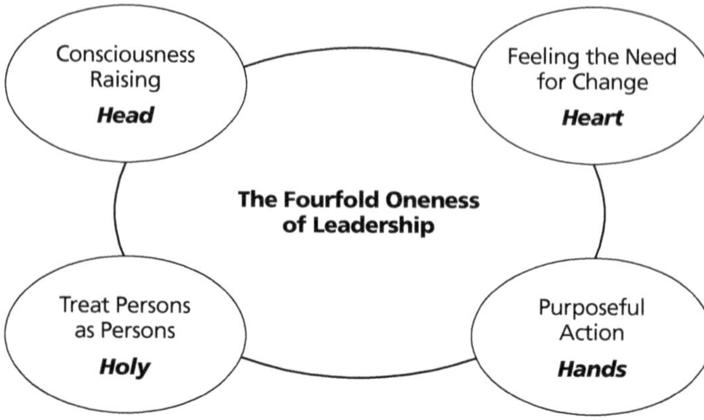


**Figure 3.1** The fourfold oneness of leadership.

The concept of "holy" is not used within a religious context. It is instead deeply humanistic. It is akin to Marx's (1848/1978) lament in the age of industrialization that "all that is holy is profaned" (p. 476) because human beings neglect their interpersonal responsibility to each other by reducing some to simply being an "appendage of a machine" (p. 479). As reflected in Figure 3.1, I will orient to the interdisciplinary relationship among the four Hs as the fourfold oneness of leadership.

## RELATIONSHIP AS RECIPROCITY

The philosopher Buber (1970) advises that in orienting to the relationship among the fourfold *as a relationship,* we "should not try to dilute the meaning of the relation: relation is reciprocity" (p. 58). The implications of this formulation of relationship as reciprocity are three-fold. First, the idea and practice of "lineal" cause–effect relationships where "a series of causes or arguments (are) such that the sequence does not come back to the starting point" (Bateson, 1979, p. 228), dilutes the meaning of relationships. Second, within the context of the fourfold it doesn't make sense to talk about crossing boundaries. There are no "boundaries" except in one's own mental construction of boundaries. In the fourfold, we have instead a "mix" or a "combination" of the dynamic interdisciplinary oneness that is both distinct and connected. Third, the interconnectedness of the fourfold, means that each H thinks of and orients to the other three Hs along with itself. They are not and cannot be separated from each other. Therein lies the dynamic and reciprocal nature of the fourfold oneness of leadership.

One anthropologist and cybernetics thinker, Bateson (1979), raises a particular problem with epistemology; namely, "How we can know anything?"

(p. 4). Bateson notes that in the Western world we have come to know by chopping up the oneness of the fourfold and treating them as independent and separate from each other. To be clear, Bateson was not talking about leadership but rather human relationships with nature. He was guided instead by an underpinning Oriental epistemology (Flemons, 1991); namely, an epistemology of connectedness. For me, what is particularly inviting is Bateson's call to situate our consciousness of leadership within an ecological connectedness of the fourfold. For far too long, our Western epistemology has been dominated by a dualistic either–or thinking. We are accustomed to think in terms of either black or white, either us or them, and so forth. This heady either–or thinking has led some in the field of leadership studies to claim that "leadership is not an affair of the head. Leadership is an affair of the heart" (Kouzes & Posner, 2017, p. 313). This bifurcation has also opened problematic either–or debates around head vs heart approaches to leadership and also calls to balance head and heart (Bartimote, 2020; Love, 2005).

To complicate matters, as Mary Catherine Bateson notes in the Preface to a later edition of her father's *Steps to an Ecology of Mind,* Western epistemology drives men and women to (a) "search for short term solutions that worsen the problem over time (often by mirroring it, such as violence used to oppose violence)" [parenthesis original] and (b) "focus on individual persons or organisms or even species . . . in isolation" (Bateson, 2000, p. xiv) from each other and from context. She further goes on to say that "even with current progress in chaos and complexity theory, we remain less skilled at thinking about interactions than we are at thinking about entities, things" (Bateson, 2000, p. vii).

Social scientists have become very proficient at thinking about entities and things since the founding days of positivistic sociology. As "demanded" by a co-founder of sociology, Emile Durkheim (1938/1966), the "proposition" that lies at the very heart of his *Rules of the Sociological Method* is "that social facts are to be treated as things" (p. xliii). This heady "It" proposition has moved empiricists to think about relationships in rationalistic and lineal terms of cause–effect. In contrast, I suggest that only when leadership scholars and practitioners gather with a view to raising their consciousness to the dynamic and reciprocal relationship among the fourfold, can they begin to gather with a mutually shared purpose (Amaladas, 2019).

## SECTION 2: CONSCIOUSNESS RAISING—A SHARED PROBLEM

The need to make conscious the unconscious and implicit biases that exist is passionately expressed by scholars from both the field of peace and conflict studies (PACS) and from leadership studies. Galtung (2001), the founder of PACS, speaks to how individual and collective trauma left behind by large-scale violence is passed on from one generation to the next. He further argues that violent conflict over the "root" conflict, can generate a "meta conflict"; namely, a "conflict that comes out of, or after, the root conflict, the over layer" (Galtung, 2001, p. 3). For Lumsden (1997), this meta-conflict can become an "*unconscious organizing principle*" (p. 377, emphasis in original) that determines how people see the world a generation later and how they choose to act. This unconscious organizing principle can perpetrate killing others or legitimize other violent forms of dealing with others.

To break the cycle of violence, Lumsden (1997) suggests that the "construction of a peaceful world society requires that individuals, groups, and nations negotiate shared meanings, including coherent but compatible identities and patterns of social relationship" (p. 378). Within the context of the fourfold, the purposeful effort to treat persons as persons is *not a matter of negotiation.* It needs to be a shared-non-negotiable-option and all must begin from a place of the holy. Furthermore, I argue that the unconscious bias that exists makes it necessary instead, the need to negotiate how we choose to live together in ways that *are governed* by the "holiness" of treating persons as persons.

Within the field of leadership studies, Ospina and Foldy (2009)—in their review of race and ethnicity in the leadership literature—sound the alarm that there is an "implicit bias in the mainstream literature to construct models that use western views and 'whiteness' as the referent from which to study and theorize leadership as a universal phenomenon" (p. 892). They conclude their review by saying that "unless leadership scholars raise their awareness" of the place and construct of race, "they may contribute to perpetuate stereotypes and use material as evidence that reproduces racist discourses and representations" (p. 889). To ignore this work of raising our own awareness is to be silently complicit in a process of cultural and intellectual colonization.

One "implicit bias" emerges from the trait approach, which Northouse (2022) identifies as being "one of the first systematic attempts to study leadership" (p. 27). In addressing the trait-based perspectives of leadership, Zaccaro (2007), for example, notes that the "quantitative analysis of leadership dates back to Galton's (1869) *Hereditary Genius*" (p. 6). Known for his pioneering studies in human intelligence, Galton's two basic premises have, as Zaccaro (2007) notes, "come to inform and misinform popular notions of leadership" (p. 6). The first is that leadership is a unique property of extraordinary individuals. The second is that these unique traits are either inherited or are a part of a leader's genetic makeup. For Galton, while "ability includes the effects of education . . . genius does not" (pp. viii–ix). However, Galton does not stop there. He further goes on to state:

> There is nothing either in the history of domestic animals or in that of evolution to make us doubt that a race of sane men may be formed who shall be as much superior mentally and morally to the modern European, as the modern European is to the lowest of the Negro races. (Galton, 1869, p. x)

In response to Galton's pseudo-biological claim, the first systematic attempts by scholars studying leadership was silence. From its early days, quantitative and empirical gatherers in the house of leadership proceeded instead to criticize "the practical implications" of Galton's view that "leadership quality is immutable and, therefore not amenable to developmental interventions" (Zaccaro, 2007, p. 6).

Today, it is encouraging to see leadership scholars moving away from such an ethnocentric thinking by centering race and racism within the dialogue and framework for leadership (Carney, 2016; Gooden, 2012; Gooden & Dantley, 2012). It is because race and ethnicity play a critical role in structuring and representing the social world, and because "communities and individuals are all informed by race" (Omi & Winant, 1994, p. 876), that Ospina and Foldy (2009) recommend that leadership studies must also include the construct and the place of race and racism. The "ism" of racism, I would suggest, is a short-handed way to avoid thinking about one's own attitudes or behavior while at the same time affirming one's membership in a primary group. If we accept that no behavior or "attitude" can maintain itself without a complementary behavior or "attitude," then it stands to reason that one can only go about affirming superiority by staying silent to the social construction of some others as being mentally and morally inferior.

## SUMMARY OF SECTION 2

I attended to the need to make conscious the unconscious and implicit biases that exist not only within a policing organization like the RCMP but also within the field of leadership studies. Biases need to be addressed on an ongoing basis because they can stand in the way of deliberately attending to the question of what it means to live together with dignity and respect. Insofar as *implicit and unconscious biases is a common problem,* it is an opportunity for *all* to address this problem. For leadership studies, the integrity of its field depends on the willingness of leadership scholars and practitioners to not remain silent to implicit biases informing the study of leadership. For those who serve as members of the RCMP, the "holiness" of their organization depends on their courage to confront their own unconscious biases for the sake of their core values: honesty, integrity, professionalism, compassion, accountability, and respect.

## SECTION 3: IMPROVISING A TRUST BUILDING LEARNING SPACE

I now move to Section 3 of this chapter by addressing the following questions:

- How can we go about the process of making conscious the unconscious biases that exist in a law enforcement agency like the RCMP, and in those who have been harmed, for the sake of treating persons like persons? (head/holy)
- How can we enable conditions where both police officers and persons harmed *feel* the need for *real* change? (heart)
- What can the persons harmed and those who put on a uniform do to live with each other without destroying each other? (hands/holy)

Intended for leadership learning facilitators, what follows does not offer a step-by-step technical guide to a learning curriculum. It does offer a reasoning that underlies each of the three recommended phases. In response to the first question, I propose the *improvisation* of a trust-building-learning-space (TBLS). The art of improvisation, rather than technical design, offers the flexibility of "recombining partly familiar materials" in ways that are "sensitive to *context, interaction, and response*" (Bateson, 1989, p. 2, emphasis added). But why a TBLS? Consider the story of von Foerster (1990):

> I have a dear friend who grew up in Marrakech. The house of his family stood on the street that divided the Jewish and the Arabic quarter. As a boy he played with all the others, listened to what they thought and said, and learned of their fundamentally different views. When I asked him once, "Who was right?" He said, "They are both right." "But this cannot be," I argued from an Aristotelian platform, "Only one of them can have the truth!" "The problem is not truth," he answered, "The problem is trust."

The singular quest for knowing "Who is right?" and "Who is wrong?" and that "only one . . . can have the truth," forecloses choices. Within the context of von Foerster's story, the singular quest for *the* truth closes off a quest for understanding that what is really at stake is trust. To accept this is to accept that *all* in this TBLS have *a* truth that not only needs *to be* heard, but also that *all need to feel* heard and understood. The presencing of trust would require all to suspend their claims of "right" and "wrong" and open themselves to listening to what the other has to say. It is fundamentally to stay open to the possible truths of others. For a hermeneutic philosopher, like Gadamer (1985), "without this kind of openness" there will be "no genuine human relationship" (p. 324). Consequently, for him, "belonging to one another always . . . means being able to listen to one another" and acknowledging that "I must accept" hearing "some things that are against myself" (Gadamer, 1985, p. 324).

As we venture into the realm of this proposed TBLS where all will be invited to speak and act together for the sake of all four Hs, Arendt (1958, 2013) reminds us of the unpredictable consequences of this proposed initiative. For her, we can never know the consequences of actions proposed in this TBLS because "one *cannot know*" (Arendt, 2013, p. 37, emphasis in original). Hence the venture and the nature of what it means to act. Second, and here lies a critical challenge, she also adds that "this venture is only possible when there is trust in people. A trust—which is difficult to formulate but fundamental—in what is human in all people. Otherwise, such a venture could not be made" (Arendt, 2013, pp. 37–38). What is particularly challenging for all in this TBLS is that they find themselves in the presence of the brokenness of trust. It is precisely because of this brokenness that I propose the *improvisation* of a trust-building-learning-space.

## FACILITATING DEUTERO LEARNING

For the sake of treating persons as *persons* (holy), how then can we begin to raise the consciousness (head) of the unconscious biases that exist without creating defensiveness and accusations? I recommend a three-phased deutero-learning process which Bateson and Bateson (1987), collect under categories like "learning to learn" and "character change due to experience" (p. 13). From the perspective of relationship as reciprocity, deutero-learning facilitates conversational spaces where gatherers learn to think "recursively," namely, where effects come back to their starting point (Bateson, 1979, p. 228). Thinking recursively means that we learn to see how we are a part of the system in which we are participating, and how what we do or not do while in our system continues to perpetuate and maintain our system, realities, identity, and character. For an organizational learning theorist, Senge (2006), this is indeed what it means to be truly proactive; namely, "*seeing how we contribute to our own problems*" (p. 21, emphasis in original). In the three phases that follow, I will offer a "how" and an interpretation as to "why" each of these phases are necessary and desirable.

## PHASE 1: A TURN TO POETRY (HEART/HANDS/HOLY)

In response to the second question, "How can leadership facilitators enable conditions where both police officers and persons harmed can *feel* the need for *real* change?" I recommend the use of poetry with a view to the non-negotiable treatment of each other as a "*Thou.*" It is critical to understand

Buber's (1970) distinction between "I–It" and "I–Thou." For him, the attitude of "I" towards "It" is one that treats the other not only as an object ("It") but also one that is separate from the "I." The attitude of "I" towards "Thou" is one in which I–Thou are not separated by discrete bounds. I–Thou is, instead, a living relationship among persons.

But why turn to what might be seen as an unlikely resource like poetry? The poet Robert Frost, for example, as President J. F. Kennedy (1963) noted in his speech at Amherst College,

> coupled poetry and power, for he saw poetry as the means of saving power from itself. When power leads men towards arrogance, poetry reminds him of his limitations. When power narrows the areas of man's concern, poetry reminds him of the richness and diversity of his existence. When power corrupts, poetry cleanses. For art establishes the basic human truth which must serve as the touchstone of our judgment. (para. 1)

Within the context of the brokenness of trust, I propose the use of James Patrick Kinney's (2012) poem "The Cold Within." Written within the socio-political context of the American civil rights movement—when people of color were fighting for their basic rights as citizens, and for the right to be treated with human dignity, Kinney's poem continues to be relevant today. Kinney speaks to the experiences of "six men" who not only find themselves "trapped in happen-stance, in bleak and bitter cold" but also amid a "dying fire in need of logs." Confronted with the crisis of a dying fire, each man, as Kinney tells his story, refused to feed the fire with their sticks of birch for different reasons. The first "held his back," because he noticed "one was black." The second "could not bring himself to give the fire his stick of birch" because he saw one "not of his church." A poor man in this group resentfully withheld his log: "Why should his log be put to use to warm the idle rich?" The rich man judges the poor as "lazy" and "shiftless." Hence *not* contributing his log would mean keeping what "he had earned" to himself and away "from the lazy shiftless poor." The "black man's face" was filled with the spirit of "revenge." All this man saw in his stick of wood was "a chance to spite the white." And the last of these men in this "forlorn group" played the transactional game of "giving only to those who gave." And since nobody gave, neither did he. Kinney completes his poem by defining a tragic consequence of this act of withholding:

> Their logs held tight in human hands was proof of human sin—
> They did not die from the cold without,
> They died from the cold within. (as cited in Hawkins, 2012, para. 8)

Kinney's (2012) poem taps into a particular aspect of humanity. The act of withholding our "logs" continues to reinscribe and polarize persons on the basis of racial and religious prejudices (Augoustinos & Haidt, 2012; Hoffer, 1951/2002). It continues to put humanity in crisis (our dying fire in need of logs). Holding tightly to one's own prejudices, righteousness, resentment, revenge, spite, and transactional giving, continue to perpetuate and sustain one tragic human reality: *We die from the cold within.* In this "un-holy" modern-day tragedy, there will be no winners. We will all lose.

When I share this poem with those whom I facilitate for *real* change, it is generally met with a few moments of silence. It is a silence that is then followed with a shaking of heads. It is as if they are thinking: "How can this be? Is there not a better way of being with each other?" The power and beauty of this poem is such that it captures the hearts and the imagination of all in the TBLS and opens their hearts to want to take a second look at their own unconscious biases.

Indeed, perhaps it is time to take a greater interest in an applied liberal arts education (ALAE) because it promises the possibility of an interdisciplinary approach to leadership studies. In a similar way that poetry taps into humanity, ALAE could offer us the possibility of addressing racism and making meaning of our lived experiences by mutually tapping into the dynamic and reciprocal interrelationship among the 4 Hs. For the sake of humanity, ALAE could offer us a way out of that which imprisons our thinking and acting.

## PHASE 2: A CASE STUDY (HEAD/HEART/HOLY: MUTUAL UNDERSTANDING, ACCOUNTING, INQUIRING)

Gatherers will be offered an opportunity to reflect and converse about their particular lived experiences, stories, and relationships through the story of Rosa Parks. In the 1950s Rosa Parks triggered the Montgomery bus boycott and moved the chains of democracy further along the road to social justice, by refusing to give up her seat. However, as Rosa Parks would constantly remind interviewers: "Over the years, I have been rebelling against second-class citizenship. It didn't begin when I was arrested" (as cited in Theoharis, 2013, p. 68). What is not talked about in greater detail is that Rosa Parks had been an activist for 2 decades before the bus stand. She worked alongside Raymond Parks in 1931, whom she married the following year, to organize in defense of the Scottsboro Boys—nine Black teenagers who were falsely accused of raping two White women. Indeed, as Professor Jeanne Theoharis notes, "One of the issues that animated her 6 decades of activism was the injustice of the (American) criminal justice system—wrongful accusations against Black men, disregard for Black women who had been sexually assaulted, and police brutality" (Theoharis, 2021, para. 4).

In this context, the question and the response she received from two White policemen who came to arrest her on that Montgomery bus will inform the conversation in this case study. But first, why turn to stories? As noted earlier, while "communities and individuals are all informed by race" (Omi & Winant, 1994, p. 876), stories not only inform culture and race but as psychologist Mair (1988) notes, we are also "lived by our culture and race" (p. 127). Furthermore, as a critical theorist Habermas (1984), remarks in his *Theory of Communicative Action*,

> When we tell stories, we cannot avoid also saying indirectly how the subjects involved in them are faring and what fate the collectivity they belong is experiencing. Nevertheless, we can make harm to personal identity or threats to social integration visible only indirectly in narratives. (p. 137)

It is because stories are one way of making "harm to personal identity or threats to social integration visible" that Mair (1988) cautions that we need to pay attention to the power and paradox of our stories in that they "hold us together and keep us apart" (p. 127). Stories can be like glue that holds a person or community together, and they can at the same time be like a sharp-edged sword, rip and tear persons or communities apart.

Let us reflect on Rosa Parks' story.

> One evening in early December 1955 I was sitting in the front seat of the colored section of a bus in Montgomery, Alabama. The white people were sitting in the white section. More white people got on, and they filled up all the seats in the white section. When that happened, we black people were supposed to give up our seats to the whites. But I didn't move. The white driver said, "Let me have those front seats." I didn't get up. I was tired of giving in to white people. "I'm going to have you arrested," the driver said. "You may do that," I answered. Two white policemen came. I asked one of them, "Why do you all push us around?" He answered, "I don't know, but the law is the law and you're under arrest. (Parks, 1999, p. 1)

Gadamer (1989), and the French philosopher, Levinas (1985) offer us a better understanding of what is really at stake. For Gadamer (1989), "Whoever opens his mouth wants to be understood; otherwise, one would neither speak out or write" (p. 55). Insofar as opening their mouths means that both Rosa Parks and the white policeman want to be understood, then understanding each other can only emerge through the messy process of *mutual understanding, accounting,* and *inquiring* rather than advocating for one's own point of view (Senge, 2006). Choosing not to listen and understand the other is in effect to perpetuate conditions of voicelessness. Choosing not to account for one's own actions, especially when those actions violate the dignity of human beings, is to perpetuate conditions of arrogance.

Choosing not to inquire is to choose to preserve conditions of ignorance ("I don't know but...").

In an effort to understand and offer an account to the other, Levinas (1985) surfaces Rosa Parks's invitation to the White police officer to talk to her through his distinction between "the saying" and "the said."

> The saying should include the said as a necessity of the same order as that imposed by a society with its laws, institutions, and social relationships. But the saying in a face-to-face encounter means that I'm not just there to contemplate, I reply... It is difficult to keep silent when in the presence of someone else; this difficulty is ultimately founded in the proper meaning of the saying, whatever has been said. You have to talk about something, the rain or good weather, who cares, but talk, respond to the other person and be accountable to him or her. (Levinas, 1985, p. 88)

In raising her question, I interpret Rosa Parks as asking this White uniformed officer to provide an account for the "order" of "the said" of his actions. It was her way of inviting him to attend to his assumptions in ways that allowed, as Senge (2006) notes, to "make one's view open to influence" (p. 231). I interpret Rosa Parks as inviting the White policeman to account for the "ingrained assumptions (and) generalizations" (Senge, 2006, p. 8), that influences his unconscious bias and informs his act of excluding Black Americans from fully participating in American democracy and citizenship.

For Senge (2006), talking as accounting, means shifting away from advocating one's opinion to inquiring into what one holds to be true. More than simply settling a conflict, it was Rosa Parks' way of asking the White policeman to address the very foundations that allowed him to do what he did because a life without questions is simply a life of dogmatic opinions. The "said" of the White policeman in Rosa Parks' story, is the "White privilege" that affords him the power to execute the coercive power of law without question or accounting. The "reply" (providing an account) that Rosa Parks was asking for, cannot, according to Levinas (1985), simply be a matter of contemplation or meditation. Talking in any face-to-face encounter is a social act. As a social act, talking is purposeful in that talkers take responsibility for providing an account for what they have come to accept—"*their* said," "*their* order"—as being "*the* said" or "*the* order of things."

## PHASE 3: WHAT NEXT? BEGINNING ANEW (HANDS/HEAD/HEART/HOLY)

What can all in this TBLS, both persons harmed and RCMP officers do to *live well* with each other without destroying each other? In this phase, for the sake of re-building the brokenness of trust and beginning anew, the focus will be on four familiar and unexpected actions, taking responsibility, forgiving, living in solidarity, and promising.

## Taking Responsibility

As we saw in the beginning of this chapter, if, as the RCMP commissioner, Brenda Lucki admits that an "unconscious bias" does exist in their organization, and that they "are not immune" to racism, then, would it not be necessary to attend to their unconscious biases for the sake of their organization's core values? Practically, they would be offered an opportunity to distance themselves from their unnoticed operating prejudices. This distancing is necessary because as Gadamer (1985) notes, "It is impossible to make ourselves aware" of our own prejudices, "while it is constantly operating unnoticed" (p. 266). For Gadamer, such a noticing can occur "when it is . . . stimulated" (p. 266). Their presence with those who have been harmed can serve as the stimulus to raise and address a question like: What are our unconscious biases or prejudices?

This question affirms that we cannot *not* have prejudices because we are all part of a group in which we have been socialized. In the case of the RCMP, their socialization in their group sanctions their roles as police officers. Rather than treating prejudices as a dirty word, or denying that one has prejudices, or rejecting the notion that prejudices can interfere with how they relate to some others, they will be invited to first raise their consciousness of their unnoticed operating prejudices. Second, they would be invited to raise another question: What can we do to transcend our prejudices for the sake of seeing and serving the humanity in all persons?

While this may be a risky enterprise, the courage to raise prejudices or biases *as a question* is, I suggest, a condition for healing the brokenness of trust and the possibility of beginning anew. If "the essence of the question is the opening up, and keeping open, of possibilities" (Gadamer, 1985, p. 266), then without having a meta-awareness of our own prejudices we will not be able to open up and keep ourselves open to new possibilities because we will forever be operating out of our unnoticed-socialized-prejudices.

## Forgiving

Second, the harmed in this gathering would be invited to think about what it means to live with the irreversibility of the consequences of past actions and of being unable to undo what has been done for the sake of a new beginning. Within this context, Arendt (1958) introduces us to the unexpected act of forgiving. Unlike the "Black man's face" in Kinney's (2012) poem, where vengeance and revenge are natural and automatic reactions to transgression and prejudices, Arendt argues that forgiving "is the only reaction which does not merely re-act but acts anew and unexpectedly, unconditioned by the act which provoked it" (p. 241). What are the consequences of an unforgiving and forgiving world?

Without forgiveness, "our capacity to act would... be confined to one single deed from which we could never recover" (Arendt, 1958 p. 58). A reality with forgiving (or not) is that it is both a burden and power that belongs to those who have been harmed. To choose not to forgive others is to never allow for the possibility of recovering from the irreversible consequences of what was done. Therein lies its power, in the sense that it is, as Arendt (1977) notes, "the only human attribute which applies solely to the worldly in-between space by which men are mutually related" (p. 175). Like *The Sorcerer's Apprentice* in Goethe's poem, where the apprentice bemoans, "Master's word I have forgotten" (Goethe, 1797/1995, para. 6), an unforgiving world forgets how to break the spell of action-reaction (revenge). In this respect, for Arendt (1958), "forgiveness is the exact opposite of vengeance, which acts in the form of re-acting against an original trespassing whereby... everybody (permits) the chain reaction in every action to take its unhindered course" (pp. 240–241).

Forgiving, on the other hand, frees "from its consequences both the one who forgives and the one who is forgiven" (Arendt, 1958, p. 241). For Arendt, the freedom of forgiveness "is the freedom from vengeance, which incloses both doer and sufferer in the relentless automatism of the action process, which by itself need never come to an end" (Arendt, 1958, p. 241). Consequently, without taking responsibility for one's own prejudices and without forgiving, we will continue to trap ourselves in our bitter coldness and die not from the cold without but from the cold within.

## Living in Solidarity

Third, in this process of beginning anew *all* will be invited to begin with a shared interest in orienting to the humanity in all persons (Thou) *and* living in solidarity by protecting each other from harm and danger. As dwellers in this common land called Canada, this shared interest *is not and cannot be open to negotiation.* Subsequently, the question for all in this TBLS would be: "How can we live together in ways that *live up* to this non-negotiable option and principle of solidarity (harmony, peace, fellowship)?"

Through this improvisatory art, I recommend turning our attention to an unfamiliar understanding of Canada's values of peace, order, and good government. But some might object. How can all in this TBLS willingly embrace what is essentially a legislative product of the British North American

Act of 1867; namely, of colonizers, and especially when "for Indigenous peoples, the story of Canada is one of myth, magic, deceit, occupation, and genocide" (Ladner, 2009, p. 279)? I suggest that we need to orient to all three Canadian values from other than a legislative/political platform because such a platform divides.

#### *Peace*

Galtung (1964), for example, distinguishes between negative peace and positive peace. Unlike negative peace, which intends a mere "absence of war" or conflict, positive peace refers to the quest for "social justice, harmony" and the "integration of society" (Galtung, 1964, p. 2). It is the quest for positive peace and not a government legislation that motivates Phase 3. The quest for positive peace shares in the interest of dwelling by caring for each other. Practically, caring can be addressed through this question: "What must we do to protect/safeguard each other from harm and danger?"

#### *Order*

The value of "order," I suggest, is not one of imposing "law and order" as it is conventionally understood and practiced, but rather one of being reasonably engaged in the act of dwelling by promoting the need for a new solidarity. For Gadamer (1981) solidarity "is the quest decisive condition and basis of all social reason" (p. 87; head). However, within the context of the oneness of the fourfold of leadership, insofar as the head simultaneously thinks of and orients to the other three Hs along with itself, I would propose that solidarity is the decisive condition and basis of all 4 Hs. While we are still a far cry from a common awareness that the quest for solidarity (harmony, positive peace, fellowship) is a matter of the destiny for everyone on this earth, I would also submit that for the sake of humanity it is never too late.

#### *Good Government*

By "good government," all within TBLS will be invited to engage in the question of what it would mean to *live up* to the values of social justice and solidarity. Good government is offered as a choice of governing well by *being governed* rather than ruling. It is a choice to be governed by the imagination of the best of what could be for *all* and not only for some at the exclusion of others.

## Promising

Finally, as a way of beginning anew, all present in this TBLS will be asked to make a promise (or promises) to follow through on what all say they will do. But why make promises especially when our Canadian story includes a string of broken promises? It is because, as Arendt (1958), notes, the act of making promises, emerges simultaneously out of (a) the "darkness of the human heart"; namely, "the basic unreliability of men who never can guarantee today who they will be tomorrow" and (b) "the impossibility of foretelling the consequences of an act within a community of equals where everybody has the same capacity to act" (p. 244).

For Arendt (1958), this human condition of unpredictability and unreliability which "the act of making promises partially dispels," is the "price" human beings must "pay for plurality and reality, for the joy of inhabiting together with others in a world whose reality is guaranteed for each by the presence of all" (p. 244). It is because of our human condition of unreliability and unpredictability, that we make promises and hold ourselves accountable to our promises. What other choice do we have, if we choose to relate to each other with grace and dignity and not neglect our interpersonal responsibility with each other? And so, we proceed as Frost (1923/1969) soulfully notes in his poem *Stopping by Woods on a Snowy Evening:* "The woods are lovely, dark, and deep, but I have promises to keep. And miles to go before I sleep, And miles to go before I sleep" (p. 224).

## CLOSING REMARKS

Expanding on Burns (1978) and appealing to writers from multiple disciplines, I attempted to situate an interdisciplinary approach to leadership as being grounded in a dynamic, reciprocal, and ecological oneness of four Hs. Conceptually, the four Hs can be collected under four corresponding leadership metaphors. The act of *consciousness raising* (head) is, I suggest, a metaphor of *leadership as educating.* Through deutero-learning, and from the perspective of the Latin *e-ducare,* leadership can be viewed as a process of leading (*ducare*) self and others out of (*e*) conditions that violate the holy. Second, inducing people to be conscious of what they feel, including feelings that emerge from one's unconscious biases is, I propose, grounded in the metaphor of *leadership as caring* (heart). But why feel the need to care at all? Because where nothing is felt, nothing matters. Third, in saying that the "fundamental act (of leadership) is to induce people to be aware or conscious of what they feel" so "that they can be moved to purposeful action" (Burns, 1978, p. 44), I interpret Burns as formulating the act of leadership not from the perspective of instrumental-means-end action, but rather as formulating *leadership as purposeful action* or *acting with purpose.* This is akin to the sociologist Weber's (1978) notion of "value-rational" action; namely, an act that is "determined by a conscious belief in the value for its own sake . . . independently of its prospects of success" (p. 25; hands). Finally, I submit that Burns's "practical advice" (p. 462) of treating persons

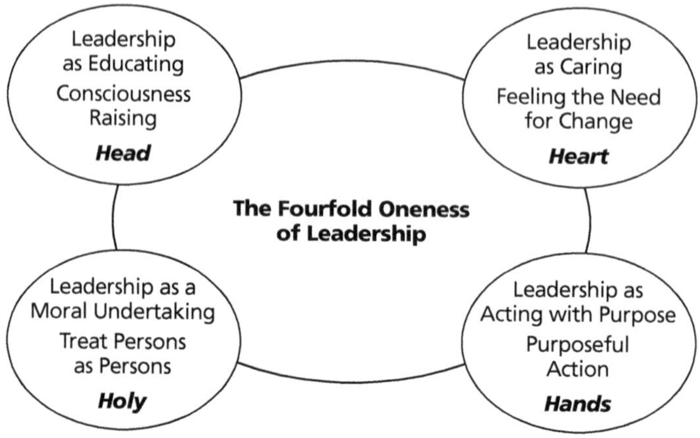


**Figure 3.2** Interrelatedness and oneness of the four Hs & corresponding metaphors of leadership.

as persons, is a metaphor of *leadership as a moral undertaking* (holy). Accordingly, I suggest that an interdisciplinary approach to leadership studies needs to be governed by the interrelationship and oneness of all four Hs and its corresponding leadership metaphors. Allow me to reconstruct Figure 3.1 which I presented earlier in this chapter (see Figure 3.2).

Practically, and within the context of racism, I proposed an *improvisatory* TBLS framework that is also *governed by* the ecology of the fourfold oneness of leadership. The promise of improvisation is that each speaker can "learn to say something new within a particular context and evoke a particular response, sometimes something of very great beauty or significance, but always improvisational and always adaptive" (Bateson, 1989, p. 3). How else can we answer this call to orient to the oneness of the four Hs, than by trying on our part, on our own, and in conversation with I–Thou, to bring dwelling in this common place called Canada to the fullness of trust, respect, and human dignity?

## REFERENCES

Amaladas, S. (2019). *Leadership studies and the desire for shared agreement.* Cambridge University Press.

Arendt, H. (1958). *The human condition.* The University of Chicago Press.

Arendt, H. (1977). *On revolution* (2nd ed.). Penguin Books.

Arendt, H. (2013). *The last interview and other conversations.* Melville Publishing House.

Augoustinos, M., & Reynolds, K. J. (2001). *Understanding prejudice, racism, and social conflict.* SAGE Publications.

Barbour, J. D. (2006). Burns, J. M. In F. W. English (Ed.), *Encyclopedia of educational leadership and administration* (pp. 93–94). SAGE.

Bartimote, H. (2020). *Leaders: How well do you balance your head and heart?* https://blog.container-solutions.com/leaders-how-well-do-you-balance-your-head-and-heart

Bateson, G. (1979). *Mind and nature: A necessary unity.* E. P. Dutton.

Bateson, G. (2000). *Steps to an ecology of mind.* The University of Chicago Press.

Bateson, G., & Bateson, M. C. (1987). *Angels fear.* Macmillan Publishing Company.

Bateson, M. C. (1989). *Composing a life.* Grove Press.

Buber, M. (1970). *I and thou.* Scribner & Sons.

Burns, J. M. (1978). *Leadership.* Harper Perennial.

Carney, N. (2016). All lives matter, but so does race: Black lives matter and the evolving role of social media. *Humanity & Society, 40*(2), 180–199.

Durkheim, E. (1966). *The rules of the sociological method* (G. Caitlin, Ed.). The Free Press. (Original work published 1938)

Flemons, D. (1991). *Completing distinctions.* Shambhala Publications, Inc.

Frost, R. (1969). Stopping by Woods on a Snowy Evening. In E. C. Lathem (Ed.), *The Poetry of Robert Frost.* Henry Holt & Company, Inc. (Original work published 1923)

Gadamer, H.-G. (Ed.). (1981). What is practice? The conditions of social reason. In *Reason in the age of science* (pp. 69–87). The MIT Press.

Gadamer, H.-G. (1985). *Truth and method.* The Crossroad Publishing Company.

Gadamer, H.-G. (1989). Reply to Jacques Derrida. In D. P. Michelfelder & R. E. Palmer (Eds), *Dialogue and deconstruction: The Gadamer-Derrida debate* (pp. 55–57). State University of New York Press.

Galton, F. (1869). *Hereditary genius.* Appleton.

Galtung, J. (1964). An editorial. *Journal of Peace Research, 1*(1), 1–4.

Galtung, J. (2001). After violence, reconstruction, reconciliation, and resolution: Coping with visible and invisible effects of war and violence. In M. Abu-Nimer (Ed.), *Reconciliation, justice, and coexistence: Theory & practice* (pp. 3–23). Lexington Books.

Goethe, J. (1995) *The sorcerer's apprentice.* (Original work published 1797) https://www.scottish-country-dancing-dictionary.com/sorcerers-apprentice.html

Gooden, M. (2012). What does racism have to do with leadership? *Educational Foundations, Winter-Spring,* 67–84.

Gooden, M., & Dantley, M. (2012). Centering race in a framework for leadership preparation. *Journal of Research on Leadership Education, 7*(2), 237–253.

Habermas, J. (1984). *The theory of communicative action* (Vol. 2). The Beacon Press.

Haidt, J. (2012). *The righteous mind: Why good people are divided by politics and religion.* Random House.

Haig, T. (2020). *Commissioner says RCMP must do more to confront 'unconscious bias.'* https://www.rcinet.ca/en/2020/06/11/commissioner-says-rcmp-must-do-more-to-confront-unconscious-bias

Hawkins, S. (2012). The Cold Within by James Patrick Kinney: *Poem, Purpose, Progress.* Retrieved from http://www.allthingsif.org/archives/1405

Kinney, J. P. (2012). *"The Cold Within" by James Patrick Kinney: Poem, purpose, progress.* http://www.allthingsif.org/archives/1405

Hoffer, E. (2002). *The true believer: Thoughts on the nature of mass movements.* Harper-Collins Publishers Inc. (Original work published 1951)

Kennedy, J. F. (1963). *President John F Kennedy: Remarks at Amherst College, October 26, 1963.* https://www.arts.gov/about/kennedy-transcript

Kouzes, J., & Posner, B. (2017). *The leadership challenge.* John Wiley & Sons.

Ladner, K. (2009). *Take 35: Reconciling constitutional orders.* https://cpsa-acsp.ca/papers-2006/Ladner.pdf

Levinas, E. (1985). *The face.* In E. Levinas (Ed.), *Ethics and infinity: Conversations with Phillipe Nemo* (R. A. Cohen, Trans; pp. 85–92). Duquesne University Press.

Love, C. (2005). Using both head and heart for effective leadership. *Journal of Family & Consumer Sciences, 9*(2), 17–19.

Lumsden, M. (1997). Breaking the cycle of violence. *Journal of Peace Research, 34*(4), 377–383.

Mair, M. (1988). Psychology as storytelling. *International Journal of Personal Construct Psychology, 1*(2), 125–138.

Marx, K. (1978) Manifesto of the communist party. In R. C. Tucker (Ed.), *The Marx-Engels reader* (pp. 469–500). Norton W. W., & Company. (Original work published 1848)

Marx, K. (1978). Speech at the Anniversary of the *People's Paper.* In R. C. Tucker (Ed.), *The Marx-Engels reader* (pp. 577–578). Norton W. W., & Company. (Original work published 1856)

Nicholls, J. (1994). The "heart, head, and hands" of transforming leadership. *Leadership & Organization Development Journal, 15*(6), 8–15.

Northouse, P. (2022). *Leadership: Theory and practice* (9th ed.). SAGE.

Ospina, S., & Foldy, E. (2009). A critical review of race and ethnicity in the leadership literature: Surfacing context, power, and the collective dimensions of leadership. *The Leadership Quarterly, 20*(6), 876–896.

Omi, M., & Winant, H. (1994). *Racial formation in the United States: From the 1960s to the 1990s.* Routledge.

Parks, R. (1999). *My story.* Penguin Group.

Senge, P. (2006). *The fifth discipline: The art and practice of the learning organization.* Doubleday.

Staub, R. E., II. (1997). *The heart of leadership.* Executive Excellence Publishing.

Theoharis, J. (2013). *The rebellious life of Mrs. Rosa Parks.* Beacon Press.

Theoharis, J. (2021, February 1). Rosa Parks's real story is better than a fairytale. *The New York Times.* https://www.nytimes.com/2021/02/01/opinion/rosa-parks.html?auth=link-dismiss-google1tap

Von Foerster, H. (1990). Ethics and second-order cybernetics. *Scandinavian Economic History Review, 4*(2). https://stream.syscoi.com/2018/10/21/ethics-and-second-order-cybernetics-heinz-von-foerster/

Weber, M. (1978). *Economy and society* (G. Roth & C. Wittich, Eds.). University of California Press.

Zaccaro, S. (2007). Trait-based perspectives of leadership. *American Psychologist, 62*(1), 6–16.

CHAPTER 4

# THOUGHTFUL LEADERSHIP

## Developing Ethical and Authentic Leaders

**Elizabeth Ostler**

### ABSTRACT

Leadership programs that adopt interdisciplinary practices and are mission-driven equipped leaders for complex challenges. The Thoughtful Leadership CertificationTM (TLC) program at the Gabelli School of Business at Fordham University is committed to forming such leaders. TLC is a year-long training program that provides theory, coaching, and experiential learning in thoughtful leadership to early and mid-career students. The program empowers students to recognize their leadership potential and develop leadership efficacy and capabilities. Grounded in Jesuit educational traditions and drawing from authentic and servant leadership theories, TLC seeks to develop thoughtful leaders who lead ethically and authentically.

On February 28, 2020, just weeks before the COVID-19 pandemic altered life on a global scale, Donna Rapaccioli, Dean of the Gabelli School of Business at Fordham University, spoke at the Fordham Women in Business

*On Leadership*, pages 55–66

annual conference. Addressing students, faculty, administration, and guests, she stated:

> In our rapidly changing world, one thing is clear: Smart and savvy leaders are needed now more than ever. At the Gabelli School, we not only teach you the skills you need to succeed in the business world, we teach you how to lead and act with thoughtfulness and empathy. (Rapaccioli, 2020)

The world changed rapidly as the pandemic disrupted the most basic ways of life, and a spotlight on racial injustices resulted in demands for equity and justice. The problems facing humanity are complex, interdependent, contradictory, and messy (Bloomquist et al., 2018). Such problems cannot be solved by one or a handful of leaders. "Solutions to global problems require leaders who are skilled in multiple disciplines, experienced integrative thinking, and willing to unite efforts in a quest for solutions" (Brock et al., 2015, p. 16). Approaching problems from interdisciplinary perspectives can challenge monolithic thinking and siloed development (Bloomquist et al., 2018) fostering creative and innovative solutions.

If an interdisciplinary approach is an ideal tool for addressing complex problems, then it is advantageous to consider what may be gained when coupled with a specific leadership style, such as thoughtful leadership. At the Gabelli School of Business, Thoughtful Leadership CertificationTM (TLC) teaches behaviors that form thoughtful leaders. A thoughtful leader acts "responsibly and ethically to develop people and systems with the intent of making positive changes within their spheres of influence (Gabelli School of Business, 2020a, p. 1). Though the TLC program does not explicitly teach interdisciplinary skills, students learn and practice leadership with peers from various business disciplines, such as finance, marketing, technology, and management.

## THOUGHTFUL LEADERSHIP CERTIFICATION

Within the United States higher education institutions are increasingly offering leadership programs to their students (Brock et al., 2015) as leadership skills are becoming more in demand in the workplace. A 2012 survey of over 500 executives reported that many executives prioritized leadership in their organization's development of human capital (McKinsey & Company and The Conference Board, 2012). More recently, a LinkedIn (2018) study reported that talent development managers, executives, and people managers ranked leadership as the most important soft skill to develop, over communications, collaboration, and role-specific skills. Leadership is a skill set that can be learned and taught (Komives et al., 2006). The correlation between leadership effectiveness and self-efficacy is well documented and shows if individuals believe they are capable of being an effective leader, they are more inclined to engage in behaviors that demonstrate effective leadership (Paglis, 2010; Seibert et al., 2017). Formal training in preparation for leadership opportunities can increase leadership self-efficacy and capacity (Seibert et al., 2017).

The TLC program brings together the disciplines of academia, business, and theology to form leaders who act "responsibly and ethically to develop people and systems with the intent of making positive changes within their spheres of influence" (Gabelli School of Business, 2020a, p. 1). Part of the Gabelli School of Business' (GSB) mission is to educate students to embody the Jesuit educational characteristics and make positive change in their personal and professional lives (Fordham University, n.d-a). Inspired by GSB mission, the TLC program is a year-long training program that provides theory, coaching, and experiential learning in thoughtful leadership to early and mid-career students that enables them to recognize their leadership potential and develop leadership efficacy and capabilities. The TLC guiding beliefs are (a) Individuals can and do make a lasting and meaningful impact within their spheres of influence; (b) Moral character is determined by aligning values and ethics with behaviors; (c) Everyone is a leader; (d) Leadership is how one chooses to be and to behave; and (e) The world needs more thoughtful leaders (Gabelli School of Business, 2020b).

GSB began offering a leadership certification program in the Fall of 2018 under the direction of the then associate dean of graduate studies, Travis Russ. Russ worked with an interdisciplinary team comprised of leadership experts in business, theater, humanities, education, and coaching to create an experiential learning (Kolb & Kolb, 2017) leadership program. The program utilizes small groups, high-engagement workshops to invite students to practice leadership skills through the interplay of communication, self-awareness, ethics, and interconnectedness. Throughout the certification process, students develop leadership efficacy by learning leadership theory and putting that knowledge into practice to cultivate a thoughtful leadership identity (Komives et al., 2006; Sorenson et al., 2016) and skill set.

## Theories and Frameworks

Servant leadership theory, authentic leadership theory, and Jesuit traditions provide the framework for the TLC program. They inform the program's focus on ethics, self-awareness, and common good. Thoughtful leaders are grounded in their values while attuning and adapting to an ever-changing world. This enables them to see individuals and communities as they are, that they may effectively enact positive change.

## Servant Leadership

Servant leadership differentiates from other leadership styles in that it positions leaders as servants to the organization and the people within that organization. Service can manifest as meeting the needs of direct reports, advocating for their participation in the organization, and mentoring them to become servant leaders (Wu et al., 2020). Servant leadership benefits an organization "by awaking, engaging, and developing employees as well as emphasizing the importance of listening to, appreciating, valuing and empowering people" (van Dierendonck & Patterson, 2015, p. 201). A seminal example of servant leadership within the United States was developed by Robert Greenleaf during his 40-year career at AT&T. Upon retiring, he founded the Greenleaf Center for Servant Leadership (Parris & Peachey, 2013; van Dierendonck & Patterson, 2015). Greenleaf believed effective leadership required introspection, moral character, purpose, and a deep commitment to serving others (Parris & Peachey, 2013; van Dierendonck & Patterson, 2015). Instead of a how-to-manual, Greenleaf provided an ethical framework for leaders to use to reflect on how their leadership impacted the individual growth and fulfillment of their direct reports. By being open, accountable, reflective, and willing to learn, servant leaders can develop trusting relationships within their organizations (Parris & Peachey, 2013).

## Authentic Leadership

Authentic leadership "draws upon and promotes both positive psychological capacities and a positive ethical climate, to foster greater self-awareness, an internalized moral perspective, balanced processing of information, and relational transparency on the part of leaders working with followers" (Walumbwa et al., 2008, p. 94). Authentic leadership is a pattern of behavior that is not ethically neutral. Research shows that individuals with high levels of self-awareness and self-acceptance tend to have higher levels of moral development (Walumbwa et al., 2008). Authentic leadership theory posits that effective leadership is the result of self-awareness and self-regulatory behavior. Authentic leaders internalize their moral perspectives by examining their beliefs and values and externalize their morals by behaving ethically. This includes being transparent in interactions, genuine in thoughts and feelings, and considering multiple perspectives when processing information (Walumbwa et al., 2008).

## Jesuit Education Characteristics

Jesuit ethos are foundational to the TLC program. A Jesuit education is a holistic integration of the intellect, faith, and civic lives of individuals (Geger,

2014). A dedication to excellence, understanding and engaging the whole person, learning through experience, and deep reflection are hallmarks of a Jesuit education (Fordham, n.d.-b). The TLC program draws on four Jesuit educational characteristics as part of its framework: *cura personalis, magis,* people for others, and forming and educating agents of change.

### *cura personalis*

*cura personalis* is often interpreted as care for the whole person by Jesuit institutions, including Fordham University (DeFeo & Keegan, 2020; Fordham University, n.d.-b; McCallum & Horian, 2013). "St. Ignatius wanted those involved in his schools to care for each student personally, always attentive to the particular needs and talents of each person" (Fordham University, n.d.-b, p. 12). This perspective directs educators to expand their views of students beyond intellect and to instruct and engage students holistically (DeFeo & Keegan, 2020; Geger, 2014).

### *People for Others*

People for others is more commonly known as men and women for others. TLC practices inclusivity and recognizes non-binary individuals; therefore, we adopt the modified phrasing of people for others. People for others are "persons who not only use their talents for the greater good, but who are also committed to standing in solidarity with the poor, the oppressed, the marginalized and with all whose human dignity is ignored, imperiled, or diminished" (Fordham University, n.d.-b, p. 15). There is a great need today for leaders who are people for others. Leaders who dedicate their lives to the erasure of margins and "seek to create a connection of hearts, to show others that they are seen, acknowledged, and embraced in the mutuality of value" (Boyle, 2017, p. 182).

### *Magis*

*Magis* can be understood as "the more universal good" (Geger, 2014, p. 6). This definition is derived from the teachings of Saint Ignatius of Loyola who taught the importance of behaving in ways that serve God and help others to thrive. It is an extension of the Society of Jesus's motto *Ad Majorem Dei Gloriam,* which means, "For the Greater Glory of God" (Mescher, 2018, p. 38). Saint Irenaeus of Lyons described glory to God as a person living their fullest life (Mescher, 2018). At Fordham University, *magis* is interpreted to mean striving for excellence. Excellence not limited by academic pursuits or quantifiable outcomes, but "always reaching for creative new horizons in the service of God and the service of others" (Fordham, n.d.-b, p. 14). In the context of serving others, Mescher (2018) expands the meaning of *magis* as "pursuing what will promote greater dignity, freedom, and responsibility for ourselves and others (or, what will alleviate the suffering of others)" (p. 39). *Magis* is not about personal gain or achievement; it's a call to be purposeful and work for the betterment of humanity.

***Formation and Education of Agents of Change***

A majority of emerging adults doubt their ability to make a difference in the world (Mescher, 2018). According to Komives et al. (2006), recognition that change is possible and that the individual can be an agent in that change is an important part of leadership development. The incorporation of the Jesuit traditions helps to bridge this gap. An explicit aspiration of Jesuit institutions is to form and educate agents of change (DeFeo & Keegan, 2020). "Now more than ever... our world can use more leaders who are guided by Ignatian wisdom" (Kelly & Moss Breen, 2020, p. 27).

## Praxis

Leadership development requires the changing of thoughts and behaviors (Komives et al., 2006). Guided by the leadership theories and Jesuit traditions outlined above, the TLC program draws from multiple disciplines (e.g., social sciences, education, business, theater, and theology) to create programming that challenges students to think and behave as thoughtful leaders. The first objective of the TLC program is to bring students attention to leadership and their awareness to how they are currently leading intentionally or unintentionally. This is done via a behavioral self-assessment, coaching, and experiential learning workshops. "For many students, identifying aspects of their own leadership identity is not realized until it is brought to their attention" (Sorenson et al., 2016, p. 32). Then students practice thoughtful leadership behaviors (see Table 4.1) and reflect on how this impacts themselves and others. Students have opportunities to practice in workshops throughout the academic year and during a case study simulation. As students practice introspection, engage in experiential learning, and receive positive encouragement they increase in their leadership efficacy (Paglis, 2010).

Leadership is demonstrated through behaviors (Komives et al., 2006; Lowney, 2003). The Thoughtful Leadership Certification LEAD Model™ (see Table 4.1) lists the behaviors that comprise thoughtful leadership. There are four core behaviors: listens, ethical, adapts, and develops along with the corresponding advancing behaviors. The advancing behaviors provide pointed ways to cultivate the core behavior. The Jesuit traditions give these behaviors a greater context and purpose than solely self-development and gain.

The core behaviors of listens, ethical, adapts, and develops are the praxis of TLC. A thoughtful leader is the embodiment of these behaviors, "acting responsibly and ethically to develop people and systems with the intent of

**TABLE 4.1 Thoughtful Leadership Certification LEAD Model**

| Core Behavior *Jesuit Tradition* | LISTENS *cura personalis* | ETHICAL *people for others* | ADAPTS *Magis* | DEVELOPS *forming & educating agents of change* |
|---|---|---|---|---|
| • Advancing<br>• Behaviors | • Shows empathy<br>• Builds trust<br>• Practices humility<br>• Seeks feedback | • Aligns with values<br>• Embodies integrity<br>• Models the way<br>• Treats people with dignity | • Increases self-awareness<br>• Learns from failures<br>• Strives for excellence<br>• Considers multiple perspectives | • Empowers others<br>• Builds community<br>• Critically examines systems<br>• Creates positive change |

*Source:* From Gabelli School of Business (2020a). *LEAD Model*, p. 1.

making positive changes within their spheres of influence" (Gabelli School of Business, 2020a, p. 1).

***Listens***

Thoughtful leaders listen from a place of curiosity and desire to understand. They listen while practicing *cura personalis.* Caring and connection are crucial to healthy and productive relationships between leaders and team members (Brown, 2018). They also become thoughtful listeners by showing empathy, building trust, practicing humility, and seeking feedback. Brown (2018) teaches that empathy is essential to building strong and trusting relationships. Her research shows that empathy is a choice and skill that can be developed through emotional literacy. Emotional literacy is demonstrated when one understands their own emotions, recognizes how others are feeling, and then communicates those feelings back to them. As a result, team members may feel listened to. And when people feel heard, they are more inclined to trust. Trust is further fostered when team members experience leaders as predictable, reliable, and compassionate (Tippett, 2020).

***Ethical***

"Ethics lie at the very heart of leadership" (Walumbwa et al, 2008, p. 94). Thoughtful leaders demonstrate their ethics by aligning their values, embodying integrity, modeling the way, and treating people with dignity. They have identified their values and strive to behave in ways that are congruent with those values (Brown, 2018; Walumbwa et al., 2008) through their thoughts, rhetoric, and actions (Brown, 2018). Thoughtful leaders model thoughtful behaviors. They are willing to do the hard things first and guide others through challenges with support, compassion, and encouragement.

***Adapts***

Thoughtful leaders develop adaptability by increasing self-awareness, learning from failures, striving for excellence, and considering multiple perspectives. Organizations and individuals are continually faced with change and the unexpected. Leaders who perceive organizational structures and systems as rigid tend to doubt their capabilities as a leader, whereas leaders who believe in the adaptability of organizations have hirer leadership efficacy (Paglis, 2010). Leaders who seek multiple perspectives, particularly those from other disciplines "obtain a broader sense of the world and the multiple views therein, helping them to develop flexible thinking skills essential for today's complex global problems" (Brock et al., 2015 p. 22).

***Develops***

Leaders develop people and systems (Brown, 2018). Thoughtful leaders do this by empowering others, building community, critically examining systems, and creating positive change. Thoughtful leaders are knowledgeable about power dynamics and how it manifests in organizations. They resist using their power to dominate or subjugate others. Instead, they use their privilege and power to enable others to be empowered (Mescher, 2018). Thoughtful leaders build communities that are diverse and inclusive. They build authentic communities that value social exchange over economic exchange (Walumbwa et al., 2008).

## Student Experience

Throughout the TLC program, students are encouraged to self-reflect on leadership and how they are developing as a thoughtful leader. The interdisciplinary practice of self-reflection (Bloomquist et al., 2018) is crucial to leadership identity development (Komives et al., 2006; Sorenson et al., 2016) and a fundamental Jesuit tradition (Brock et al., 2015). Students are encouraged to write down their reflections as a record of their leadership journey. Sometimes, they are asked to share their reflections in a workshop or coaching session.

The TLC program provides four areas of training for students: assessment, coaching, LEAD workshops, and simulation. The learning objectives for each training are derived from the LEAD model and scaffold from one training to the next. The trainings utilize the experiential learning cycle of experiencing, reflecting, thinking, and acting (Kolb & Kolb, 2017) to increase students' leadership self-efficacy. The trainings are usually conducted in small groups (5 to 12) and bring students together from diverse backgrounds and business disciplines, such as finance, technology, marketing, and management. By being in interdisciplinary groups, students have opportunities to expand their perspectives, cultivate humility, strengthen empathy (Bloomquist et al., 2018), and practice the LEAD behaviors.

***Assessment***

Students start their thoughtful leadership training by taking the DiSC® behavioral self-assessment. For many students, this is the start of bringing their attention to leadership and awareness to how they are currently leading. In this workshop, they are placed in small groups with students from different business disciplines and various DiSC® styles. A TLC facilitator guides the students through a series of thinking, acting, experiencing, and reflecting exercises (Kolb & Kolb, 2017) that promote self-awareness about how their personality influences their leadership style and how they can lead thoughtfully.

***Coaching***

Students then receive one-on-one thoughtful leadership coaching. They are coached through reflecting critically on their personal leadership journey, including past successes and their biggest recurring obstacles. They are taught a growth mindset framework to understand how their thoughts impact their emotions which impacts their behavior (Bloomquist et al., 2018). Students leave their coaching session with tangible action steps they can put into practice immediately to enhance their reality and begin making a positive impact.

***LEAD Workshops***

Throughout their thoughtful leadership training, students are offered a variety of shorter workshops to further develop thoughtful leadership behaviors (e.g., workshops in ethics, trust, communication). These workshops also provide opportunities to network with other students in the TLC program, faculty, alumni, and industry professionals which can increase students' leadership self-efficacy (Seibert et al., 2017) and expose them to other disciplines. Students are encouraged to attend as many of these workshops as possible. However, they are only required to attend two as part of their certification.

***Simulation***

Where the other three areas of training are designed to provoke self-awareness and internalization of a leadership identity (Komives et al., 2006), simulation is an opportunity for students to practice thoughtful leadership behaviors and receive individualized feedback. Humans learn in the doing. Ideally, in real life/real time situations (Cohen, 2019; Seibert et al., 2017). Due to logistical limitations this is not possible, so experiential simulations that approximate an actual experience are used instead. Simulated case studies have been shown to be effective in developing leadership efficacy and capabilities (Seibert et al., 2017). In small groups, students from multiple business disciplines work through the case study to generate solutions. A thoughtful leadership facilitator observes the students for demonstrations of LEAD Model behaviors and provides each student with individualized written feedback.

For the 2021 TLC simulation, Elizabeth Ostler, manager of the TLC program, partnered with Patrick Struebi, CEO and founder of Fairtrasa and peace activist and educator, Jerry White, to create a case study that would invite students to practice the LEAD behaviors in small groups in a virtual modality. This interdisciplinary team's case study drew from a leadership challenge the Struebi was facing at Fairtrasa. Within a month's time, Struebi was stepping down as CEO of Fairtrasa. Instead of hiring a new CEO, the senior management team would run the company as co-CEOs. The details of the case were shared with the students in a masterclass led by White and Struebi. Working in interdisciplinary cohorts, students were instructed to assume the role of new co-CEOs and create a transition plan, a one-year vision, and a team empowerment plan.

In a scenario where leaders from three different departments are charting new organizational territory as they equally share the authority and power of running that company, here are some questions students in the program are asked to consider:

- How does a co-CEO structure benefit the company, the employees, and stakeholders?
- How does a co-CEO harm the company, the employees, and stakeholder?
- What protocols and systems would need to be established to support a team of CEOs?
- What interdisciplinary practices could the co-CEO's adopt that would help them be successful?

This case study effectively challenges students to practice TLC behaviors. It also provides an opportunity to observe interdisciplinary leadership.

## CONCLUSION

Leadership programs that adopt interdisciplinary practices and are mission-driven equipped leaders for complex and messy challenges (Brock et al., 2015). The TLC program at the Gabelli School of Business at Fordham University is committed to forming such leaders. The interlinking of Jesuit education characteristics, servant leadership, and authentic leadership within one leadership program reveals behaviors that leaders can take to address issues holistically. In this program, students benefit from learning and practicing these behaviors in interdisciplinary cohorts. The world has become even more complex with the consequences of a global pandemic, wars, and global warming. Thoughtful leaders are needed who can ethically address these issues with the explicit intent to better the lives of all peoples.

## REFERENCES

Bloomquist, C. D., Georges, L., Ford, D. J., & Moss Breen, J. (2018). Interdisciplinary leadership practices in graduate leadership education programs. *Journal of Leadership Studies, 12*(2), 60–31. https://doi.org/10.1002/jls.21579

Boyle, G., (2017). *Barking to the choir: The power of radical kinship.* Simon and Schuster.

Brock, B. L., Cherney, I., Martin, J. R., Moss Breen, J., & Oltman, G. (2015). How to launch a doctoral interdisciplinary leadership program. *Creighton Journal of Interdisciplinary Leadership, 1*(1), 14–23.

Brown, B. (2018). *Dare to lead.* Vermilion.

Cohen, H. (2019). An inconvenient truth about leadership development. *Organizational Dynamics, 48,* 8–15.

DeFeo, J., & Keegan, B. (2020). Ignatian-centered and appreciative advising: Supporting the holistic development of students in 15-minute intervals. *Jesuit Higher Education: A Journal, 9*(2), 57–71.

Fordham University. (n.d.-a.). *Gabelli School of Business mission.* https://www.fordham.edu/info/21550/mission

Fordham University. (n.d.-b). *The Jesuit way at Fordham.* https://www.fordham.edu/download/downloads/id/259/the_jesuit_way_at_fordham.pdf

Gabelli School of Business. (2020a). *Thoughtful leadership certification* [Brochure]. https://www.fordham.edu/download/downloads/id/13646/thoughtful_leadership_certification_brochure.pdf

Gabelli School of Business. (2020b). *Thoughtful leadership certification* [PowerPoint].

Geger, B. T. (2014). Cura personalis: Some Ignatian inspirations. *Jesuit Higher Education: A Journal, 3*(2), 6–20.

Kelly, T. M., & Moss Breen, J. (2020). Ignatian leadership and the contemporary leadership landscape an exercise in counter-cultural engagement. *Jesuit Higher Education: A Journal, 9*(2), 16–29.

Kolb, A. Y., & Kolb, D. A. (2017). Experiential learning theory as a guide for experiential educators in higher education. *ELTHE: A Journal for Engaged Educators, 1*(1), 7–44.

Komives, S. R., Longerbeam, S. D., Owen, J. E., Mainella, F. C., & Osteen, L. (2006). A leadership identity development model: Applications from a grounded theory. *Journal of College Student Development, 47*(4), 401–418. https://doi.org/10.1353/csd.2006.0048

LinkedIn. (2018). *2018 workplace learning report* [Report]. LinkedIn. https://learning.linkedin.com/content/dam/me/learning/en-us/pdfs/linkedin-learning-workplace-learning-report-2018.pdf

Lowney, C., (2003). *Heroic leadership*. Loyola Press.

McCallum, D. C., & Horian, L. (2013). A leadership education model for Jesuit business schools. *Journal of Jesuit Business Education, 4*(1), 37–52.

McKinsey & Company, and The Conference Board. (2012). *The State of Human Capital 2012—False Summit: Why the human capital function still has far to go* (Report No. R-1501-12-RR). The Conference Board. https://www.mckinsey.com/~/media/mckinsey/dotcom/client_service/organization/pdfs/state_of_human_capital_2012.ashx

Mescher, M. (2018). Teaching *Magis* at college: Meaning, mission, and moral responsibility. *Jesuit Higher Education: A Journal, 7*(2), 37–55.

Paglis, L. L. (2010). Leadership self-efficacy: Research findings and practical applications. *Journal of Management Development, 29*(9), 771–782.

Parris, D., & Peachey, J. (2013). A systematic literature review of servant leadership theory in organizational contexts. *Journal of Business Ethics, 113*(3), 377–393.

Rapaccioli, D. (2020, February 28). *Remarks by Dean Donna Rapaccioli* [Remarks]. Fordham Women in Business 21st Annual Conference, New York, NY, United States.

Seibert, S. E., Sargent, L. D., Kraimer, M. L., & Kiazad, K. (2017). Linking developmental experiences to leader effectiveness and promotability: The mediating role of leadership self-efficacy and mentor network. *Personnel Psychology, 70*(2), 357–397.

Sorenson, T., McKim, A., & Velez, J. (2016). Leadership identity development through an interdisciplinary leadership minor. *The Journal of Leadership Education, 15*(1), 31–43.

Tippett, K. (Host). (2020, November 25). *This species moment* [Audio podcast episode]. OnBeing. https://onbeing.org/programs/agustin-fuentes-this-species-moment/

van Dierendonck, D., & Patterson, K. (2015). Compassionate love as a cornerstone of servant leadership: An integration of previous theorizing and research. *Journal of Business Ethics, 128*(1), 119–131.

Walumbwa, F. O., Avolio, B. J., Gardner, W. L., Wernsing, T. S., & Peterson, S. J. (2008). Authentic leadership: Development and validation of a theory-based measure. *Journal of Management, 34*(1), 89–126. https://doi.org/10.1177/0149206307308913

Wu, J., Linden, R. C., Liao, C., & Wayne, S. J. (2020). Does manager servant leadership lead to follower serving behaviors? It depends on follower self-interest. *Journal of Applied Psychology, 106*(1), 152–167. http://dx.doi.org/10.1037/apl0000500

CHAPTER 5

# SHE TAKES THE LEAD

## Insights on the Shifting Landscape for Women in Leadership Roles

**Kathryn Woods**

### ABSTRACT

This chapter explores historical and contemporary perspectives on women in organizational leadership roles. Supported by a plethora of published scientific research, this chapter addresses the importance of past influences on the challenges faced by women in the workforce, current issues that affect and perpetuate these challenges, and actions needed to overcome them in the future.

The journey a woman takes toward an organizational leadership role is not the same as a journey a man takes toward the same role. Long-standing gender stereotypes are rooted in sociological norms that have determined different "appropriate" roles for men and women at work for decades, and many of those have not yet been overcome. A recently renewed movement to focus on the benefits of diversity, equity, and inclusion in the workplace has led to additional efforts (both in research and practice) in examining the origins and current state of some of these issues and determining what

*On Leadership*, pages 67–87

actions are needed. To overcome current challenges and develop a culture that supports women moving into leadership roles in the workplace, leaders must work first to understand, and then to remove, the barriers that still exist. Organizations have a timely opportunity to educate employees and lay a foundation for this important work by integrating interdisciplinary approaches to removing obstacles to women's advancement, providing more opportunities for women to pursue leadership roles, and further supporting them in those roles. Workplaces can use this information to facilitate acknowledgment of gender stereotypes and the systems that reinforce them, ongoing gender discrimination issues, and real and perceived gender differences in work and communication styles. Acknowledging these inequities helps to inform policy and behavioral changes to advance women in the workplace, achieve the goals of more equal representation in leadership roles, support better handling of women's biological and maternity issues, and cultivate male allies to provide support for women in leadership.

## LEARNING FROM THE PAST

Many important historical events, shifts in culture, genetic predispositions, and systems of power have affected women in leadership roles. In recent years, organizations have been under pressure to provide more resources to help female employees advance in their organizations. The focus on diversity, equity, and inclusion in the workplace is only necessary because, historically, workplace culture was often built on homogeneity, inequity, and exclusion. In the past, organizations and industries manifested homogeneity by perpetuating the gendered stereotypes of males as breadwinners and females as home and family caretakers (Eagly, 1987). Upon entering the workforce, female workers experienced prolonged inequitable practices such as being paid less than men for the same work and receiving opportunities for advancement less than men (Correll et al., 2007; Grandey et al., 2020; Ko et al., 2015). Inequitable educational and employment opportunities resulted in women's exclusion from leadership roles in entire industries and social systems (Cundiff & Vescio, 2016; Guterres, 2020; Riggs, 1997, Sax, 2017). In this section, topics covered include historical gender roles and stereotypes in society, the rise of gendered careers, implied power structures, and legislation to promote equal opportunities.

### Gender Roles and Stereotypes in Society

For centuries, people have discussed and perpetuated behavioral stereotypes of men and women. While some stereotypes are socially constructed in the early years of life, others are rooted in real biological differences that exist between most men and women. Regarding behaviors, males have a predisposition to risk-taking and aggression significantly more often than females, and there is some evidence that they may frequently be developmentally less ready than girls to enroll and succeed in kindergarten. Girls tend to be under-confident about their own abilities, while boys tend to be overconfident. Boys' mental health is disproportionately negatively affected by excessive video game play, while girls' mental health is disproportionately negatively affected by social media usage (Sax, 2017). Traditional gender roles for heterosexual couples in the United States are heavily influenced by history, biology, and social norms that put pressure on men to be the breadwinners of the family and for women to take on the supporting roles of mom, caregiver, and housekeeper (Eagly, 1987). These long-held stereotypes have directly informed systems that support the rise of men as natural leaders in the workplace, while casting women in the professional supporting roles of secretary, nurse, or assistant (Cundiff & Vescio, 2016; Riggs, 1997; Sax 2017).

Another consideration for gender-based stereotypes is that some qualities typically attributed to one gender could be strengths or weaknesses on a situational basis. For example, a woman being viewed as a helper at home (perhaps as the default caretaker of the home itself or of children) and at work (being asked to take notes during a meeting or serve cake at the office birthday party) can be a barrier to her advancement in the workplace. If a woman is constantly cast in these helper roles, a negative consequence will be less time to devote to work that will help her earn a promotion or less consideration for a leadership role (Correll et al., 2007; Grandey et al., 2020; Ko et al., 2015). However, as further explored below, when women serve in leadership positions, they often draw on those qualities in a positive way to drive organizational success. For example, women are consistently rated as scoring higher on empathy scales (Di Tella et al., 2020; Rueckert & Naybar, 2008), and a heightened sense of empathy is proven to help leaders succeed in times of crisis (Zenger & Folkman, 2020). Complex situational and individual differences make it difficult to assess whether women are generally more empathetic due to the qualities that are nurtured in them as effects of these stereotypes or whether these qualities are more ingrained in female hormones and bodies in a biological way.

## The Rise of Gendered Careers and Implied Power Structures

As society is built on these gender-based stereotypes, some careers have historically been viewed as belonging to one gender. Over time, teaching, nursing, and childcare were deemed acceptable jobs for females, while positions in military service, finance, engineering, construction, and professional healthcare (medical doctors, dentists, psychiatrists) were deemed appropriate for males. This rise of gendered careers was influenced and reinforced in part by social views on how child-rearing and education should differ for boys and girls, and what subjects they should be encouraged to explore as they prepared for a career (Sax, 2017). Boys became the gender perceived to be good at science and math, while girls were pushed toward developing secretarial, caregiving, and other helping skills. These divisions across academic areas were compounded as more male students were encouraged to study and work in STEM fields and therefore continued to dominate the workforce in those careers. Gender-based inequalities in parenting, education, encouraged fields of study, and socially gender-appropriate employment led to large-scale gender imbalances in all facets of the workforce. Secretary General of the United Nations Antonio Guterres (2020) asserted, "Centuries of discrimination and deep-rooted patriarchy have created a yawning gender power gap in our economies, our political systems, and our corporations" (para. 4).

Systems that encourage men to prepare for high-paying jobs in male-led and male-dominated environments have produced more men who support men preparing for high-paying jobs in male-led, male-dominated environments. Famed philanthropist and gender equality advocate Melinda Gates has been quite vocal regarding barriers to gender equality worldwide, and has supported the notion that equal opportunities for women in the workforce can significantly advance the economy, family systems, and society in general, but only if each woman has control of her own decision-making power (Gates, 2019). Gates pointed out that male scientists are responsible for originally labeling subjects such as chemistry, biology, physics, as "hard sciences" and the behavioral sciences (to include gender studies) as "soft sciences" (Brown, 2021). Assigning a traditionally masculine adjective (hard) to one group of sciences and a traditionally feminine adjective (soft) to another group of sciences only served to reinforce which students opted for which programs (Gates, 2019).

## Legislation to Promote Equal Opportunities

After facing much discrimination, women have benefitted in the past 60 years from several legal efforts designed to promote equal opportunities and prevent gender discrimination at school and in the workplace. For example, the Equal Pay Act of 1963 prohibits paying women a lower wage based on their gender. Following the Civil Rights Act of 1964, Title VII was passed to prohibit organizations with 15 or more employees to discriminate against employees based on sex, race, religion, or national origin. Title IX (also known as the Patsy Takemoto Mink Equal Opportunity in Education Act) was passed as part of the Federal Education Amendments in 1972. This anti-discrimination legislation is still largely credited with creating a lasting shift in culture that has allowed for strides in gender equality with regards to educational opportunities in the United States (Melnick, 2018). The Pregnancy Discrimination Act of 1978 was passed to specify that women were not to be discriminated against based on pregnancy or pregnancy-related conditions. In 1993, the Clinton administration passed the Family Medical Leave Act, which (typically) requires companies with more than 50 employees to allow parents unpaid time off for 12 weeks to take care of a newly born or adopted child (Spiggle, 2019). These anti-discrimination laws have helped to reduce barriers to women's access to education, participation in athletics, and career opportunities. Access to these opportunities provides valuable informal and formal leadership experiences for women.

## ADDRESSING ISSUES IN THE PRESENT

Issues persist in society and the workplace that present obstacles for women serving in leadership roles today. While it is important to recognize and celebrate the achievements and progress made so far, women still face many barriers to earning leadership roles. Some of these challenges stem from issues that remain from the past and some are born from issues that are unique to the current context. In this section, topics covered include gender differences in leadership and communication styles, female representation in leadership, maternity leave and parenting responsibilities, and the disproportionate negative impact of the COVID-19 pandemic on working mothers.

### Gender Differences in Leadership and Communication Styles

As Baby Boomers continue to retire in droves, millennials are currently the majority group of employees represented in the workforce in the United States. Known for being open-minded and valuing relationship-building and open communication in the office, researchers have purported that millennials may be poised to abolish gender-related stereotypes for leaders sooner than later (Porter et al., 2019). These researchers concluded that millennial women may hold increased levels of confidence in their abilities to lead, and display more of the more traditionally "masculine" traits that have been linked to leader success at work (being direct, succinct communication) than women in previous generations. Researchers attribute at least some of these positive shifts to their experience with receiving a Title IX-influenced education, which allows for increased participation in organized sports and STEM activities. Representation in sports has allowed girls to take part in team membership and leadership, which provides access to skill-development previously mostly available for boys.

Researchers have studied differences in leadership styles exhibited by men and women in an organizational context for decades. More recently, researchers have also explored differences in how men and women (in the role of a follower) perceive leaders and their actions. One study found that while both genders have similar ideas about what makes for a "bad" leader, there are significant differences in how men and women rate "good" leader traits as they described their best and worst bosses (Singh et al., 2012). "More specifically, women perceived their best bosses more positively, at statistically significant levels, on the following attributes: knowledgeable, inspiring, developmental, visionary, humane, credible, encouraging, open-mindedness, and self-assured" (p. 11). They reported that these findings are consistent with the notion of tokenism present today in many organizations that employ few female leaders, which can lead to female employees' heightened awareness of their organizational status and opportunities for development. They also reported that women in their study had a nearly equal chance of identifying a male or female leader as their "best boss" or "worst boss" during their career, while men reported that a male leader was their "best boss" and "worst boss" 80% of the time. These findings are consistent with the notion that men still typically hold most upper-level managerial roles, and therefore most employees in many industries are still led predominately by men.

A large-scale study from Zenger and Folkman (2020) concluded that women leaders often perform as well or better than men in leading an organization through a crisis. Employees surveyed reported that the skills women ranked higher on were most important during times of crisis—to include providing inspiration and motivation, communicating effectively, promoting collaboration and teamwork, and building relationships. Specifically, the researchers reported, "Female leaders expressed more awareness of fears that followers might be feeling, concern for wellbeing, and confidence in their plans" (para. 9). This reported appreciation for empathetic responses is an encouraging indicator that female leaders shine while leading their employees through emergencies.

Gendered expectations of managers can also manifest in other ways. In a related study conducted by Abel (2019), workers reported no significant differences in the feelings evoked when receiving positive feedback from a male boss and from a female boss during a performance review, but employees stated negative feedback from a female boss carried twice as much negative implication on employee attitudes as negative feedback from a male boss. Both male and female employees expressed this more harsh negative view of criticism from their female managers. Abel also posits that discrimination by subordinates can create a self-fulfilling prophecy of sorts, and that an employee's view that female managers are less effective will lead to female managers being less effective. This study reveals that the disparity in perception is not necessarily rooted in implicit bias but more likely stems from a violation of expectations attributed to the long-standing gendered expectations of leadership traits. People of both genders expect (and therefore desire) praise from females and criticism from males—so, receiving criticism from a female leader feels worse. Providing critical feedback is a necessary task for anyone in a leadership role, and these skewed perceptions create a real barrier for women to succeed in those roles.

Women are also consistently found to be more critical of themselves when self-evaluating at work. They are more likely to absorb the feedback received from their managers and respond to it, while men tend to continue to inflate their own evaluations, even after receiving negative feedback (Mayo, 2016). Mayo offers the viewpoint that while this may seem like a criticism of both men and women, both can be viewed as positive qualities. Men are able to overcome harsh opinions and press on with their work, often all the way to a leadership position. Women could leverage their heightened sensitivity to feedback as an advantage to develop leadership competencies, since they are open to applying the feedback intended for their improvement. Identifying these qualities as strengths tempers the often-negative connotation of the stereotype of women as the emotional gender, and reflects how women can leverage their skills as fuel for effective leadership.

## Female Representation in Leadership

Women now hold the majority of jobs in the workforce and earn the majority of post-secondary degrees for both bachelor and master level, yet gender inequality persists in the workplace. Despite any progress made in this area, only 8% of Fortune 500 companies are led by female CEOs (Ward, 2020), and just over 25% of Congress is female (Blazina & Desilver, 2021). On the small business side, women-owned businesses have a more difficult path to venture funding than male-owned businesses (Helgesen, 2020).

Gender biases of both teachers and parents and the emotional responses to social norms and influences that men and women experience as they move through adulthood still prevail in holding women back (Frear et al., 2016). Historically, both males and females tend to perceive women as less authoritative than men, creating a continuing bias that has led to most upper-managerial positions to be thought of as "men's work" (Doering & Thébaud, 2017). Researchers also report that often, women are not promoted due to gendered assumptions that women already have too much on their plate to be offered an opportunity for advancement (Smith & Johnson, 2020a). Other studies show females are less likely to be promoted because they show less confidence than men when applying and interviewing for leadership positions, even when they are more competent than the male candidates (Chamorro-Premuzic, 2019; Exley & Kessler, 2019; Helgesen, 2020). Even as women have been recognized as valuable and productive employees with excellent leadership potential in many industries in recent decades, employers continue to promote them into leadership roles less than their male peers (Krivkovich et al., 2020). Melinda Gates (2019) asserted that the most efficient path to improving equality in the workplace involves accelerating progress for women specifically in finance, technology, politics, and media. All of these are systems that are very important in the fabric of society, but all of them currently lack a significant female influence (Brown, 2021; Gates, 2019).

## Maternity and Parenting Responsibilities

Pregnant women and women with children face additional challenges in the workplace regarding advancement to leadership roles. "Unlike every other industrialized nation, the United States doesn't guarantee paid parental leave through a permanent and universal federal law, which makes it impossible for some women to care for family members who fall sick or for kids who are suddenly without childcare" (Vesoulis, 2020, para. 11). Frear et al. (2018) found that the number of children in a family correlated with career success differently based on gender. Men with more children make more and advance in their careers at a higher rate than men with less children or no children. Women with more children make less money and advance in their careers at a slower rate than women with less children or no children. Much research underpins the notions that these unequal effects are born of (and reinforce) systems built on gender inequality. Grandey et al. (2020) explored the female specific bodily experiences that women contend with as barriers to success at work: menstruation, maternity, and menopause. Menstruation can commonly cause distress for young, early-career women acclimating to first jobs. Maternity typically occurs during early to mid-career, when full commitment to the workplace is expected in order to prepare for leadership roles. Menopause typically occurs during mid to late career, when leader emergence is most likely. Grandey et al. concluded all three of these specific biological functions of the female body are highly stigmatized in workplace settings and act as barriers to women's advancement. In particular, the study concluded symptoms and discomfort brought on by pregnancy and breastfeeding particularly hinder a woman's chances for a promotion during the same career stages in which men find themselves advancing rapidly.

Beyond the physical aspect of carrying and birthing children, in the United States, women still maintain the role of primary caregiver to their children. Research shows that women with children are at a disadvantage when interviewing for a job, even while men with equal qualifications are sometimes able to use fatherhood as an advantage (Correll et al., 2007). The same study concluded that even when mothers get the job, they are offered significantly less than non-mothers for their starting salaries. In addition to being paid less for the same work, "childless women are 8.2 times more likely than mothers to be recommended for management" (p. 1320).

## Impact of the COVID-19 Pandemic on Working Mothers

In March 2020, as the global COVID-19 pandemic made gathering in crowds and attending daycare or school suddenly unsafe, many employees began working from home. Faced with the bulk of childcare responsibilities, women in leadership and support positions experienced new types of fear and stress as they attempted to navigate working from home while caring for children and often managing their children's newly-online education (Calarco et al., 2020; Grose, 2020). Workloads become increasingly impossible while keeping up with the demands of childcare, and as the nation realized the start of the 2020–2021 school year would not see as much improvement in the spread of the virus as everyone had hoped, a mass exodus from the workforce ensued. Between August 2020 and September 2020, more than 1.1 million people dropped out of the American workforce—and over 860,000 of them were women (Gershon, 2020). Since women in heterosexual partnerships typically earn less than their partners (ACLU, 2020; Hegewisch & Barsi, 2020; Weber, 2020), and childcare responsibilities are still primarily "mom's job" (Kramer, 2020; Krivkovich et al., 2020), women were typically the ones to have to give up their jobs when faced with the reality that working from home full-time while caring for their children full-time was not sustainable long-term (Gershon, 2020).

While predictions vary, many scholars believe long-term negative effects will persist for women who no longer feel they have an option to work and their organizations that benefit from their presence and diverse perspectives (Calarco et al., 2020; Vesoulis, 2020). This massive wave of women leaving the workforce is predicted to reduce the number of women who are qualified for leadership positions, ultimately reversing progress that has been made toward closing the gender gap (Krivkovich et al., 2020). Mothers in academia who have been fortunate enough to be able to teach their courses online from home (therefore experiencing a new wave of stress, but avoiding immediate job loss) report that while they are keeping up with their courses, many are unable to find time to keep up with their research and writing expectations. The subsequent deficit in publications could lead to an inability to meet the requirements laid out for tenure by the time their probationary period ends. Less women earning tenure now will lead to a deficit in women in administrative leadership in the future (Kramer, 2020).

Researchers Zenger and Folkman (2020) were intrigued by the concept of the glass cliff, a term that describes instances in which women are placed in senior leadership positions only when an organization is already in a state of crisis. They conducted a large survey and found that employees viewed women leaders in a significantly more positive light than male leaders as they led their organizations or teams through crisis-mode changes during the early months of the COVID-19 pandemic. In the same survey, employees who reported to female leaders also admitted to feeling more engaged with their work than those who report to male leaders. This work highlights the need for organizations to make a concerted effort to keep women leaders in place as framed by what qualities employees report they need in a leader during a crisis—to include flexibility, adaptability, support for employee development, honesty, integrity, and a sensitive response to reports of stress and anxiety. Though many male leaders have certainly led and continue to lead organizations through crises, these reported employee perceptions (that women exemplify these traits) support the need for female representation in leadership during times of organizational crisis.

## LOOKING TOWARD THE FUTURE

Actions must be taken to overcome these issues and prepare women to seek and thrive in leadership roles in their careers going forward. Solutions to these issues are multi-disciplinary and multi-faceted, and cannot be carried out by women alone. Topics covered in this section include recent advancements for women in leadership, strategies to educate employees on gender issues, and effective corporate efforts to support the advancement of women in the workplace.

### Highlighting Recent Advancements for Women in Leadership

Despite the challenges mentioned in the previous section, an appropriate first step in thinking about action items for the future could be to recognize and celebrate recent progress for women in leadership. Though the road ahead is long and arduous, there are specific realizations and accomplishments that should be leveraged to sustain positive momentum for women. A study by Sergent and Stajkovic (2020) reported that states with female governors had fewer deaths caused by the COVID-19 pandemic than states with male governors. The corresponding qualitative analysis revealed that the female governors also conveyed messages with more empathy and confidence in their briefings on the subject than male governors did, which affirms a widespread positive view of women's ability to thrive in a leadership role during a crisis (Zenger & Folkman, 2020). Other research attributes the global success of women leading countries through the fight against COVID-19 to "family systems thinking" and caring for the vulnerable groups in their periphery, rather than focusing energy on their publicized metrics of "success" that may have more heavily influenced the actions of male leaders (Brown, 2021; Cutruzzula, 2020). Whether a predisposition to empathy and a care-taking mindset is biological or socially conditioned for women, these qualities can clearly be leveraged as strengths for women in leadership roles, rather than seen as weaknesses for decision-making. When women hold leadership positions alongside their male counterparts, they can work together to provide a more balanced perspective when determining what is best for the individuals within the organization in addition to what is best for the organization's bottom line.

While women still only occupy 8% of the CEO positions in Fortune 500 companies, the rate of progress has grown more rapidly in recent years, as female representation in C-suite executive positions went from 17% to 21% between 2015 and 2020 (Ward, 2020). Similarly, while women make up only 25% of the 117th United States Congress, this reflects a 50% increase over the past 10 years (Blazina & Desilver, 2021). Building on this success comes with many challenges, but it is important to recognize the progress made thus far.

## Educating Employees on the Value of Women in Leadership Roles

Highlighting the benefits for supporting women at work and the advancement of female leadership is perhaps the first step toward changing attitudes—both individually and collectively. Taking organizations as groups of individuals working together for a common purpose, continuing to study the benefits of female leadership, publishing the findings of these studies, and disseminating those publications to individuals who influence the culture of their workplace will remain a critical practice for years to come. Academic faculty in the discipline of organizational leadership have a unique and timely opportunity to connect theory to practice as this work continues.

Beyond follower preferences, women leaders also have a proven ability to significantly increase profits for their organizations when placed in executive leadership roles (Krivkovich et al., 2020). One large study found that "the 25 Fortune 500 firms with the best record of promoting women to high positions are between 18 and 69 percent more profitable than the median Fortune 500 firms in their industries" (Christoffer, 2019, para. 1). This increase in profits for firms with more female representation in leadership could be attributed to the synergy cultivated by men and women making important decisions together—both offering unique perspectives and diverse ideas for setting and achieving goals as an organization.

Additional research portrays gender allyship—or male sponsorship of women in the workplace—as an interdisciplinary practice that has just as many advantages for men as it does for women. Smith and Johnson (2020b) highlight many benefits for men as women are empowered and supported through their actions, including: improved mental health, more rewarding relationships, increasing revenues and profits, becoming even more influential, and an increased ability to comfortably serve as an ally to other marginalized groups in the future. The authors implore of their readers:

> Imagine a global culture of male allyship in which women are equally represented in decision making at every level of government—less armed conflict and violence, longer-lasting peace agreements, lower levels of corruption, and higher trust in government. Imagine allyship-fueled gender parity in the workplace where women have an equal voice in the economic decisions, leading to elimination of the gender wage gap, reductions in poverty, and an estimated $28 trillion added to the global GDP. (p. 215)

Other research suggests workplaces that recognize and encourage males who actively support females through gender allyship benefit from improvements in workplace culture. This practice is commonplace in some European countries and has been slow to catch on in the United States. Advocating for men to take paternity leave and be encouraged to focus on family/child care/elder care creates benefits for men, women, their organizations, and their families (Brown, 2021). Both men and women can further the notion of equality in the workplace by realizing and speaking out against the idea that in order for women to thrive, men must be cast aside. This is not the case. Organizations can focus on ways to promote excellence generated when men and women work together with synergy, rather than pitted against each other in competition for the best jobs, promotions, or leadership opportunities (Dzubinski & Diehl, 2018).

## Educating Men on How To Be Allies for Women in the Workplace

Recognizing the need to operationalize this allyship, Smith and Johnson (2020a) have outlined many concrete suggestions for ways men can successfully serve as allies to women in the workplace in their book, *Good Guys: How Men Can be Better Allies for Women in the Workplace.* They recommend that male allies specifically seek out feedback from their female colleagues and engage in generous listening sessions to validate and normalize women's experiences. When involved in hiring decisions, male allies should advocate for equal pay and hold hiring/promotion committees accountable to non-discrimination standards. During meetings, allies should recognize and correct sexist language and call attention to female employee expertise.

Though organizations have made some progress in cultivating gender allyship in recent years, the rise of remote work has brought on new challenges for men who are actively committed to supporting women in the workplace. With changes to the future of work and remote opportunities, Smith and Johnson (2020b) provided some specific updated practical recommendations for how men can support their female colleagues remotely. They suggest that men actively include and "sponsor" women by reaching out, checking in, and reinforcing their value at work by mentioning their good work to colleagues and supervisors. They can also seek out opportunities to ensure women have a chance to provide input during virtual meetings, deliberately provide women with updates and transparency on any information or decisions that affect them, and intentionally distribute "virtual office housework" (tasks like taking notes, committee work, virtual event planning, etc.) equitably between male and female employees. While the authors promote these actions as helpful in a virtual workspace, these suggestions could be equally beneficial when implemented in the face-to-face work environment.

Organizations can also review workplace needs and make minor, low-cost changes to encourage male allyship. Porter et al. (2019) found that organizations may benefit from offering informal leadership roles on a rotational basis to help prepare women for formal leadership roles. They also encouraged offering reciprocal mentoring programs and noted that both of these efforts are particularly valued by millennials. Male supervisors are encouraged to create these informal leadership roles and reciprocal mentorship programs as low-cost ways to create opportunities for female advancement. Formal mentorship programs are proven effective for both men and women, as employees of both genders can benefit from gaining insight into the perspectives of the other, growing their sense of professional wisdom and empathy, and getting informal feedback about skills and talents (Green, 2015).

Additionally, male supervisors and employees can educate themselves on the needs of pregnant and nursing women in the workplace, and provide time and space for them to take care of biological tasks privately and without guilt or negative consequences. Grandey et al. (2020) reported that recognizing challenges for women that become present with pregnancy and/

or breastfeeding "as a natural bodily experience offers a lens by which organizations can be more inclusive by acknowledging and valuing women's needs, rather than stigmatizing their biological experiences" (p. 24). Taking time to ask women what they need and then providing it in a supportive way is not resource-intensive, but makes a statement to women that helps them feel supported at work.

Studies show that male allyship programs do leave room for error, as some men are more skilled at helping to decrease harassment in the workplace than others (Cheng et al., 2019). Smith and Johnson (2020a) recommend several formal guidelines to build trust and ensure minimal discomfort between males and females in the workplace, especially as the relationship is being formed. Male leaders interested in supporting females should support multiple female colleagues instead of focusing on just one. They should also carefully consider the time and place of meetings, noting that public space is typically better than private space. Additionally, Smith and Johnson explicitly rule out all words and actions that a male leader would not use with a male colleague (hugs, flirting, pet names).

## Corporate Interdepartmental Efforts to Support the Advancement of Women in the Workplace

Once the good work of celebrating achievements and cultivating an environment in which both men and women feel ready to help break down barriers to women's advancement is underway, organizations must focus on re-working human resources systems and providing formal training to ensure women obtain and succeed in leadership roles. Frankiewicz (2020) highlighted the importance of attracting women to apply to leadership roles and retaining them in those roles, both of which can require organizational changes that increase job flexibility. While increased flexibility can benefit all employees, removing the requirement of a rigid schedule and set office hours can allow women more opportunities to lead as they continue to balance the needs of work and family life. While organizations are revising processes and policies, many will find that succession planning and recruiting processes also need review. Especially for roles that are traditionally heavily male-dominated, organizations must seek out women and train them in the skills needed to succeed. Organizations can partner with universities and search firms to help meet these goals by custom-designing training and recruiting programs. If organizations do not make changes in job flexibility and recruiting, gender imbalances in the workforce will likely never improve.

Organizations must also break down barriers in hiring, which necessitates revising interviewing and hiring processes to reduce bias. This can be addressed by focusing on relevant skills and adaptability (which are attainable for both genders) during an interview, rather than years of service and previous promotions, which skews toward males (Frankiewicz, 2020). Managers tend to hire candidates who remind them of themselves via cultural similarities, which can lead to increased gender disparities in organizations where the hiring managers are most often male (Rivera, 2012).

Similarly, shifts in systems have been proposed to combat gender bias in performance reviews. Cecchi-Dimeglio (2017) emphasized the benefits of providing short, weekly feedback sessions in lieu of annual reviews. Ideally, this feedback provides multiple data points and perspectives, as it is collected from clients, peers, and managers. This practice allows reviewers to be more specific and constructive instead of generalizing qualities to a full year of work, which is often where bias comes into play. Employees benefit from weekly feedback that can be used to adjust behaviors to optimize outcomes as needed. Leaders can benefit from amassing these reviews to more easily look for patterns in skill proficiencies and deficiencies, identify emerging leadership styles, and help employees identify their strengths and weaknesses of real work tasks, instead of forming sweeping statements about their impressions of the employee. Organizations benefit from reducing several forms of bias and creating a culture of constructive feedback.

As organizations move forward in an age with a growing population of employees who are enlightened and empowered by the strides made for and by women in the workplace thus far, many employers are making formal training programs and curricula available for their employees to further advance their thinking and develop their skills in this area. This work can be informed and supported by nonprofit organizations, consultants, institutions of higher education, or "homegrown" corporate diversity initiatives.

Examples of diversity initiatives include the Integrating Women Leaders Foundation, a nonprofit organization that exists to "accelerate the advancement of women to drive individual and organizational growth and impact" (Integrating Women Leaders, n.d., para. 1). The organization offers workshops, conferences, and other events focused on identifying and overcoming gender bias and promoting male allyship in the workplace. On a grander scale, the United Nations hosts a Generation Equality Forum, a global public society-centered assembly to promote gender equality. This effort is intended to "fuel a powerful and enduring coalition for gender equality, bringing together governments, activists, corporations, feminist organizations, youth, and allies to achieve transformative change" (Generation Equality Forum, n.d. , para. 3). The organization has also developed and disseminated a global set of women's empowerment principles, intended for use as guidelines for corporations to adopt best practices to improve gender equality within their organization.

For-profit leadership consulting and talent management organizations have also found ways to tap into the gender issues market via specialized diversity research and training initiatives offered to employees. Caver and Livers (2021) offer a three-pronged approach to overcoming women's barrier to promotion. First, the authors suggest careful examination of deep-rooted systems and processes. Going above and beyond awareness efforts favored by many individuals and organizations, the call becomes "actively making some organizational constituents uncomfortable with changes that may affect their prior status or unspoken privilege" (p. 27). Second, the researchers recommend leadership-driven elimination of harmful processes, policies, icons, and so on, that often masquerade as "tradition" but only serve to remind some marginalized groups of a long history of sexism or other discriminatory practices. Third, Caver and Livers emphasize the importance of empowering employees with support to sustain the benefits of these changes. This can entail restructuring, redistribution of resources, and a full shift in workplace culture.

Smith and Johnson (2020a) recommend that organizations launch a formal internal program for male employees that will allow the organization to develop a culture of allyship. They specifically recommend launching a formal community for male allies who are voluntarily interested in participating and strategically growing that community within the organization, clarifying specific desired outcomes, and cultivating the connections and collaborative efforts that develop and evolve with the program's success. Internal diversity, equity, and inclusion programming is an effort that has largely been handled by human resources departments in recent years. However, formal departments dedicated solely to this effort are becoming more commonplace as organizational needs continue to evolve and be addressed more proactively, and as resources allow.

Academic researchers studying organizational dynamics and issues related to gender equality in the workplace also generate and disseminate a plethora of information that organizations can use to shape messages to (and training for) their employees, often at low or no cost. For example, the business school at the University of Toronto maintains an Institute for Gender and the Economy, which hosts a very informative website with free resources organizations can use to promote gender equality in the workplace (Gender and the Economy, n.d.). The University of Toronto also offers non-credit short courses that employees can take as self-directed professional development. A number of universities, such as Austin Peay State University, have begun offering for-credit courses in gender and leadership and academic credentials in diversity, equity, and inclusion (Austin Peay State University, 2021). The focus of feedback from advisory boards and employers who help guide the curriculum for organizational leadership programs at institutions of higher education has increasingly pointed toward developing students as professionals who have a skillset that allows them to recognize, appreciate, and capitalize on the talents of a diverse group of employees. This feedback has also prompted an increase in the availability of this type of academic content.

While progress is being made in training and programming for women in leadership, the need for more research to help inform this type of curriculum is more crucial than ever. Formal research supports the continued study of: the preferences of male and female followers with regards to leader traits (Ko et al., 2015; Mroz et al., 2018; Singh et al., 2012; Zenger & Folkman, 2020), potential advancements in social safety nets for women (Grose, 2020; Vesoulis, 2020), the need for more effective, updated implicit bias detection and training (Frear et al., 2018; Krivkovich et al., 2020; Lyness & Grotto, 2018; Stephenson, 2020), how leadership and organizational culture affects how women manage female-specific biological functions in organizational spaces (Grandey et al., 2020), and how data collection and interpretation can be improved to fight gender inequality (Perez, 2019).

## CONCLUSION

Academics, industry employees, managers, administrators, and organizations must invest more effort and resources into educating employees about gender equality issues. This work will enable employees to identify their own biases and promote the advancement of women at work. Leveraging the unique strengths of men and women leaders can create a more balanced impact to inform lasting and meaningful change in workplaces and communities. Creating a climate in which women are provided more opportunities to develop their leadership skills and gain equal representation as decision-makers in organizations is a colossal task. This goal can only be accomplished through thoughtful delivery of information on these issues followed by informed, intentional shifts in policy and practice to remove these barriers for women.

## REFERENCES

Abel, M. (2019). *Do workers discriminate against female bosses?* IZA Institute of Labor Economics. https://www.iza.org/en/publications/dp/12611/do-workers-discriminate-against-female-bosses

ACLU. (2020). *Women's rights in the workplace.* https://www.aclu.org/issues/womens-rights/womens-rights-workplace/paycheck-fairness-act-50th-anniversary-equal-pay-act#:~:text=On%20average%2C%20women%20today%20earn,as%20compared%20to%20white%20men

Austin Peay State University. (2021). *Diversity, equity, and inclusion in the workplace graduate certificate.* https://apsu.edu/leadership/graduate/deicertificate.php

Blazina, C., & Desilver, D. (2021). *A record number of women are serving in the 117th Congress.* Pew Research Center Fact Tank. https://www.pewresearch.org/fact-tank/2021/01/15/a-record-number-of-women-are-serving-in-the-117th-congress/

Brown, B. (Host). (2021, January 20). *Brené with Melinda Gates on the moment of lift* (No. 40) [Audio podcast episode]. Cadence 13 Productions. https://brenebrown.com/podcast/brene-with-melinda-gates-on-the-moment-of-lift/#close-popup

Calarco, J. M., Anderson, E. M., Meanwell, E. V., & Knopf, A. (2020). *Let's not pretend it's fun: How COVID-19-related school and childcare closures are damaging mothers' well-being.* https://osf.io/preprints/socarxiv/jyvk4/

Caver, K., & Livers, A. (2021). The paradox of the seed and soil: Cultivating inclusive leadership for a "new normal." *Leadership, 17*(1), 18–31. https://doi.org/10.1177/1742715020976201

Cecchi-Dimeglio, P. (2017, April 12). How gender bias corrupts performance reviews, and what to do about it. *Harvard Business Review.* https://hbr.org/2017/04/how-gender-bias-corrupts-performance-reviews-and-what-to-do-about-it

Chamorro-Premuzic, T. (2019). *Why do so many incompetent men become leaders? (And how to fix it).* Harvard Business School Publishing.

Cheng, S. K., Ng, L. C., Traylor, A. M., & King, E. B. (2019). Helping or hurting? Understanding women's perceptions of male allies. *Personnel Assessment and Decisions, 5*(2), Article 6. https://doi.org/10.25035/pad.2019.02.006

Christoffer, J. (2019). *Women in the executive suite correlate to high profits.* W2T ORO. https://www.w2t.se/adler-web/

Correll, S. J., Benard, S., & Paik, I. (2007). Getting a job: Is there a motherhood penalty? *American Journal of Sociology, 112*(5), 1297–1338. https://doi.org/10.1086/511799

Cundiff, J. L., & Vescio, T. K. (2016). Gender stereotypes influence how people explain gender disparities in the workplace. *Sex Roles, 75*(3/4), 126–138.

Cutruzzula, K. (2020). *6 things we can learn from how women leaders have handled the pandemic.* TED Ideas. https://ideas.ted.com/6-things-we-can-learn-from-how-women-leaders-have-handled-the-pandemic/

Di Tella, M., Miti, F., Ardito, R. B., & Adenzato, M. (2020). Social cognition and sex: Are men and women really different? *Personality and Individual Differences, 162*(1), Article 110045. https://doi.org/10.1016/j.paid.2020.110045

Doering, L., & Thébaud, S. (2017). *The effects of gendered occupational roles on men's and women's workplace authority: Evidence from microfinance.* Gender and the Economy. https://www.gendereconomy.org/how-occupations-become-gendered/#:~:text=There%20is%20a%20general%20consensus,%E2%80%9Cmale%2Dgendered%E2%80%9D%20occupations

Dzubinski, L. M., & Diehl, A. B. (2018). The problem of gender essentialism and its implications for women in leadership. *Journal of Leadership Studies, 12*(1), 56–61.

Eagly, A. H. (1987). *Sex differences in social behavior: A social-role interpretation.* Psychology Press. https://doi.org/10.4324/9780203781906

Exley, C., & Kessler, J. (2019, December 19). Why don't women self-promote as much as men? *Harvard Business Review.* https://hbr.org/2019/12/why-dont-women-self-promote-as-much-as-men

Frankiewicz, B. (2020). *5 ways we lack gender balance in the workplace.* World Economic Forum. https://www.weforum.org/agenda/2020/01/5-ways-companies-can-progress-more-women-into-leadership-roles/

Frear, K. A., Paustian-Underdahl, S. C., Heggestad, E. D., & Walker L. S. (2018). Gender and career success: A typology and analysis of dual paradigms. *Journal of Organizational Behavior, 40*(4), 1–17. https://doi.org/10.1002/job.2338

Gates, M. (2019). *The moment of lift: How empowering women changes the world.* Flatiron Books.

Gender and the Economy. (2021, October 9). *About.* https://www.gendereconomy.org/about

Generation Equality Forum. (2021, October 9). *Generation equality forum.* https://africa.unwomen.org/en/get-involved/generation-equality/generation-equality-forum

Gershon, L. (2020, October 19). Covid-19's impact on working women is an unprecedented disaster. *Smithsonian Magazine: Smart News.* https://www.smithsonianmag.com/smart-news/covid-19s-impact-working-women-unprecedented-disaster-180976084/

Grandey, A. A., Gabriel, A. S., & King, E. B. (2020). Tackling taboo topics: A review of the three Ms in working women's lives. *Journal of Management, 46*(1), 7–35.

Green, M. P. (2015). *Creative mentorship and career-building strategies: How to build your virtual personal board of directors.* Oxford University Press.

Grose, J. (2020, October 14). Mothers are the 'shock absorbers' of our society. *The New York Times.* https://www.nytimes.com/2020/10/14/parenting/working-moms-job-loss-coronavirus.html

Guterres, A. (2020). *The gender power gap.* United Nations Secretary-General. https://www.un.org/sg/en/content/sg/articles/2020-03-02/the-gender-power-gap

Hegewisch, A., & Barsi, Z. (2020). *The gender wage gap by occupation 2019.* Institute for Women's Policy Research. https://iwpr.org/iwpr-issues/employment-and-earnings/the-gender-wage-gap-by-occupation-2019/

Helgesen, S. (2020). *The evolution of women's leadership.* Strategy + Business. https://www.strategy-business.com/article/The-evolution-of-womens-leadership?gko=35543

Integrating Women Leaders Foundation. (n.d.). *Our why.* https://www.iwlfoundation.org

Ko, I., Kotrba, L., & Roebuck, A. (2015). Leaders as males? The role of industry gender composition. *Sex Roles, 72*(7/8), 294–307.

Kramer, J. (2020, October 6). Women in academia face a new burden. *New York Times.* https://www.nytimes.com/2020/10/06/science/covid-universities-women.html

Krivkovich, A., Starikova, I, Robinson, K., Valentino, R., & Yee, L. (2020). *Women in the workplace 2020.* McKinsey & Company. https://www.mckinsey.com/featured-insights/diversity-and-inclusion/women-in-the-workplace

Lyness, K. S., & Grotto, A. R. (2018). Women and leadership in the United States: Are we closing the gender gap? *The Annual Review of Organizational Psychology and Organizational Behavior, 5,* 227–265. https://doi.org/10.1146/annurev-orgpsych-032117-104739

Mayo, M. (2016, August 31). The gender gap in feedback and self-perception. *Harvard Business Review.* https://hbr.org/2016/08/the-gender-gap-in-feedback-and-self-perception

Melnick, R. S. (2018). The strange evolution of Title IX. *National Affairs, 52*(Summer). https://www.nationalaffairs.com/publications/detail/the-strange-evolution-of-title-ix

Mroz, J. E., Yoerger, M. E., & Allen, J. A. (2018). Leadership in workplace meetings: The intersection of leadership styles and follower gender. *Journal of Leadership & Organizational Studies, 25*(3), 309–322. https://doi.org/10.1177/1548051817750542

Perez, C. C. (2019). *Invisible women: Data bias in a world designed for men.* Abrams Press.

Porter, T. H., Gerhardt, M. W., Fields, D., & Bugenhagen, M. (2019). An exploratory study of gender and motivation to lead in millennials. *The Journal of Social Psychology, 159*(2), 138–152. https://doi.org/10.1080/00224545.2019.1570902

Riggs, J. M. (1997). Mandates for mothers and fathers: Perceptions of breadwinners and care givers. *Sex Roles, 37,* 565–580. https://doi.org/10.1023/A:1025611119822

Rivera, L. A. (2012). Hiring as cultural matching: The case of elite professional service firms, *American Sociological Review, 77*(6), 999–1022. https://doi.org/10.1177/0003122412463213

Rueckert, L., & Naybar, N. (2008). Gender differences in empathy: The role of the right hemisphere, *Brain and Cognition, 67*(2), 162–167. https://doi.org/10.1016/j.bandc.2008.01.002

Sax, L. (2017). *Why gender matters: What parents and teachers need to know about the emerging science of sex differences.* Harmony Books.

Sergent, K., & Stajkovic, A. D. (2020). Women's leadership is associated with fewer deaths during the COVID-19 crisis: Quantitative and qualitative analyses of United States governors. *Journal of Applied Psychology, 105*(8), 771–783. https://doi.org/10.1037/apl0000577

Singh, P., Nadim, A., & Ezzedeen, S. R. (2012). Leadership styles and gender: An extension. *Journal of Leadership Studies, 5*(4), 6–19. https://doi.org/10.1002/jls.20239

Smith, D. G., & Johnson, W. B. (2020a). *Good guys: How men can be better allies for women in the workplace.* Harvard Business School Publishing.

Smith, D. G., & Johnson, W. B. (2020b, October 27). 4 ways men can support their female colleagues—remotely. *Harvard Business Review.* https://hbr.org/2020/10/4-ways-men-can-support-their-female-colleagues-remotely

Spiggle, T. (2019, March 13). Eight laws that helped women make history in the workforce. *Forbes.* https://www.forbes.com/sites/tomspiggle/2019/03/13/8-laws-that-helped-women-make-history-in-the-workforce/?sh=1a7a3ef617b5

Stephenson, A. (2020). *New tool to measure gender bias in the workplace may help finally eliminate it.* The Conversation. https://theconversation.com/new-tool-to-measure-gender-bias-in-the-workplace-may-help-finally-eliminate-it-137153

Vesoulis, A. (2020, October 17). 'If we had a panic button, we'd be hitting it.' Women are exiting the labor force en masse–and that's bad for everyone. *Time.* https://time.com/5900583/women-workforce-economy-covid/

Ward, M. (2020, November 30). There are now more women CEOs of Fortune 500 companies than ever before—but the numbers are still distressingly low. *Business Insider.* https://www.businessinsider.com/women-fortune-500-ceos-reaches-new-high-2020-11#:~:text=Despite%20the%20recent%20progress%2C%20roughly,the%20CEO%20of%20Yum%20China

Weber, L. (2020, July 15). Women's careers could take long term hit from Coronavirus pandemic: Disruption caused by Covid-19 related shutdowns highlights how women's careers often take a back seat when duty calls at home. *Wall Street Journal.* https://www.wsj.com/articles/womens-careers-could-take-long-term-hit-from-coronavirus-pandemic-11594814403

Zenger, J., & Folkman, J. (2020, December 30). Research: Women are better leaders during a crisis. *Harvard Business Review.* https://hbr.org/2020/12/research-women-are-better-leaders-during-a-crisis

CHAPTER 6

# BEST PRACTICES FOR USING PLAY IN BUSINESS

**Joe Lasley**
**Akshay Sateesh**

## ABSTRACT

Managers, and others in positions of authority, can maximize their success, the quality of their teamwork, and the culture of their organizations by incorporating play in their leadership practice. In this chapter we discuss playful leadership, including recommended practices for play in business through a much-needed analysis of how play is necessary for leading successfully in the 21st century and beyond. Theories of play and leadership are integrated to inform current best practices for using play in business settings and stories from the field work of Ziksana Consulting, consulting professionals that help companies use play to transform the world of work to be more productive, creative, strategic, and motivated.

The demands of 21st century businesses are dynamic, uncertain, and complex. Creativity, problem-solving, adapting to change, and continuous learning are increasingly essential. The connections between play and learning form a strong foundation that supports integrating organizational learning

*On Leadership*, pages 89–99

with playful leadership. Playful learning embodies multiple approaches and purposes that include motivation, psychological safety, identity development, affective, and socio-cultural growth (Plass et al., 2014). Because play, learning, and leadership are universal and studied across many disciplines, they are exciting topics for integration with interdisciplinary approaches to leadership. Current models of leadership are lacking this essential element of play. Play is linked to learning and is also helpful for creativity because it allows us to temporarily step away from the world as we know it, unlearn old mental models, and create new ways of being, seeing, feeling, and doing (Vygotsky, 1978; Winnicott, 1989). Seeing reality through multiple lenses is also at the heart of interdisciplinary leadership.

Business cultures often face barriers that bifurcate notions of work and play, even when considering experiences that are simultaneously work and play (Küpers, 2017). Given the potential for learning, creativity, problem-solving, and psychological safety that is afforded by play, businesses stand to benefit greatly by embodying playful leadership. There are implications of playful leadership at three levels: leaders, teams, and organization. This chapter discusses the implications of play at each level to help illustrate effectiveness of the Playductivity™ framework.

## PLAY

There are many forms of play, ways of thinking about play, and characteristics of playfulness. When applying play to business, we can think about playfulness as a personality characteristic of managers, self-perceptions of playfulness, experiencing play while at work, play for learning, entertainment, and developmental play.

*Playfulness* is defined by Proyer (2017) as a personality trait related to but distinct from previously researched measures. One prominent example of this is the Big 5 personality dimensions which lack the full scope of playfulness, resulting in a need for further exploration. In Poryer's (2017) research, four aspects of playfulness were found to be *other-directed* (enjoying playing with others, loosen tension, and playful interactions), *lighthearted* (seeing life as a game, not worrying, improvising, finding comedy rather than tragedy), *intellectual* (play with ideas, solving problems, preferring complexity, and word play), and *whimsical* (amused by strange situations, odd activities, or even mundane interactions). Play, like learning, is simple to recognize and central to human experience (Pavlas et al., 2012). As part of our experience, play can involve intrinsic and extrinsic motivations, freedom, focus, and whether we think of an activity as play (Pavlas et al., 2012). In a developmental sense, play is a semi-relaxed state in which we can experiment with new ways of knowing, feeling, being, and doing

(Winnicott, 1989). Vygotsky (1978) describes play in which we imagine situations, modify roles and social rules, and can begin to move beyond our current abilities.

Like other experiences and personality characteristics, humans have varying preferences for play. Bartle (1996) and subsequent studies using the same player types, have described how players prefer different aspects of games such as achievement (getting points and levels), exploration (immersion and discovery), socializing (interaction and connection), and competition (challenge and winning). Stuart Brown (2009) in *Play: How It Shapes the Brain, Opens the Imagination, and Invigorates the Soul,* describes how people enjoy play in varying types: physical, object, social, imaginative, creative, rough and tumble, and attunement.

## PLAYDUCTIVITY

The Playductivity framework (see Figure 6.1) is the model developed by Ziksana Consulting and illustrates the cyclical relationship between play and productivity. More specifically, it outlines a continuous process between learning and performance, people and results, creativity and execution, and energy and efficiency. These derivatives aid leaders to apply the framework to challenges they face.

For leaders, the Playductivity framework focuses on the tensions between mindsets that are people focused and results focused, the skills for performance and learning, and the capacity for managing energy and efficiency. From each of these leadership tensions, specific competencies can be identified in order to practically apply the framework to everyday leadership challenges. Sometimes a manager needs to coach an employee to improve performance and deliver better business results. While other situations with the same employee are better served if the manager facilitates

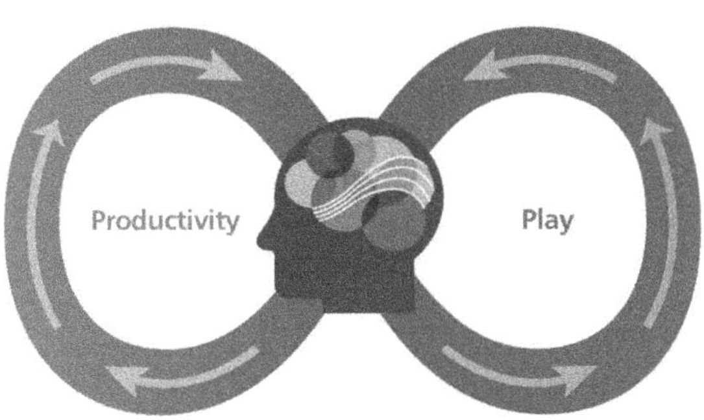


**Figure 6.1** Playductivity™ visual aid. *Note:* Trademark image provided with permission from Ziksana Consulting.

developmental coaching that focuses on the long-term learning and development of an employee based on the employee's aspirations. These approaches to coaching require different mindsets in which successful managers flow back and forth between performance and development loops in the Playductivity framework.

For teams, the Playductivity framework focuses on the tensions between creativity and execution, as well as team culture and strategy. And finally, for the organization, the Playductivity framework focuses on the tension between the values that define a motivated culture, and the priorities that define an efficient strategy to achieve the vision of the company. On the team and organizational levels, the Playductivity framework flows between challenging processes with accountability and supporting people to foster engagement and enjoyment in working together. Sometimes organizations (and leaders) need to focus on putting people in the right roles with resources to achieve team goals while at other times balancing a culture that motivates teams to enjoy going above and beyond together. Play on the development/culture side of the loop fuels curiosity, disruption, and innovation. Play on the performance/strategy end of the loop uses that innovation to fuel business results with iterative improvements. Organizations need to build cultures that support flowing between these loops and harnessing success when they intersect.

## PLAY FOR LEADERS

Consider the story of Malcolm. After rising through the ranks from an engineer, to become senior leader of a life science company, Malcolm was stuck. His technical experience and background were unmatched, and through the years he had learned how to manage individuals, and eventually manage teams. The company was struggling to produce unique and creative solutions for their customers, and their engineering design teams seemed to hit a wall each time they developed potential products. As it turns out, their leader Malcolm, had a hand in their troubles. He was often entering design meetings and asking questions that would stifle the team's creativity. He would say things like, "Why aren't you thinking about...?" and "We've tried that idea in the past."

Malcolm realized that his presence was being perceived as controlling and purely results oriented. He was coached to experiment with new behaviors that would shift how his team perceived him while still meeting the expectations to perform and produce results. In short, he needed to be more playful in order to improve his approachability and connect authentically with each team member and demonstrate that he cared about their success, not just the end outcome of the work.

Over the course of 4 months, Malcolm started to take on a more playful mindset when interacting with team members: He would ask questions about people's motivation and personal lives, he listened and accepted others' ideas, suggestions, and concerns, no matter what they shared, and he spent time in meetings finding enjoyable moments to share with others as much as he could. His shift to a more balanced approach to having both a productive mindset AND a playful mindset, empowered his teams and accelerated goal achievement. Employing his playful mindset also gave him the courage to try new behaviors and be open to new possibilities of types of outcomes.

Business leaders like Malcolm need to be productive and solve problems fast, often with a lack of space to be creative at the same time. Play, as evidenced in game-based learning, provides space for creative problem-solving and metacognition that is useful for leadership (Plass et al., 2015). Theories of leadership development and play can frame an approach to leader identity development (Kark, 2011). In addition, playfulness is viewed as a personal characteristic (Proyer, 2017) similar to characteristics of transformational leadership (Carless et al., 2000; Tucker et al., 2010). Transformational leaders are known for using creative and imaginative communication to express their visions with group members (DuBrin, 2013). Leaders that engage in playful experiences and playful moments with others are better able to balance a range of abilities such as a learning mindset and a performance skill set. Play encompasses a range of activities that can have varying degrees of spontaneity or goal orientation (Küpers, 2017). The ability for leaders to flow between a playful learning mindset and a playful performance skill set builds leadership capacities.

## PLAYFUL TIPS TO BALANCE A PRODUCTIVE AND PLAYFUL MINDSET AS A LEADER

1. Listen appreciatively to your employees and team members:
   a. Say "Yes, and" versus "Yes, but" in most conversations to enable acceptance of others' perspectives.
   b. Ask open-ended questions to get people to share more about their perspective or opinions.
   c. Establish clear boundaries for when judgment of ideas or suggestions are acceptable in the creative process.
2. Find ways to connect with others through various types of play:
   a. Identify what types of play team members enjoy (social, object, imaginative, creative, and physical) to help them manage their own energy to be more productive. Consider the following de-

scriptions to help team members identify their favorite types of play:

i. Social play refers to activities that are done for the mutual joy of connecting with others in fun ways. Examples of social play include team sports, foosball, and attending happy hours with friends.

ii. Object play refers to activities that are driven by curiosity and the joy found in manipulating tangible objects. People who enjoy object play are often adept problem solvers who like to "tinker" with objects to solve problems. Examples of object play include doing a puzzle, building Legos, and fixing a car for the fun of it.

iii. Imaginative play shows up in activities where players freely move back and forth between pretend and reality. Examples include storytelling, acting, and daydreaming.

iv. Creative play encompasses activities that enable us to think outside the confines of our ordinary lives and imagine new possibilities. It is largely tied to imagination, and is expressed in activities such as drawing, writing, and even redecorating a room.

v. Physical play encompasses activities that mobilize the body, and consequently, the brain. Examples of physical play include yoga, swimming, running, and dance.

b. Find ways to share common experiences with various play preferences so team members feel motivated and connected to one another.

c. Balance your time spent on strategy and decisions, with personal connection and fun team experiences.

## PLAY FOR TEAMS

The COVID-19 pandemic brought a new challenge to a medical diagnostic manufacturing team. Their company was producing tests for COVID-19 specifically, and their challenge was to produce 600% more capacity than they had ever achieved in the past. Each individual was being pushed to their limit of the sheer number of hours it took to produce results, and the team was suffering from unhealthy communication and shared mental models that stifled their productivity. These norms prevented the team from sharing knowledge to help one another perform. Team members were hiding information that would help others learn from their mistakes, they were not willing to handle conflict directly with one another, and they were unable to challenge one another in productive ways.

Over the course of 6 months, the team received team coaching support in order to overcome their challenges and achieve their shared goals. Due to the highly stressed environment, the team was unable to connect with one another beyond the functions they represented. Play-based coaching involves a combination of experiential activities with practical coaching that helps develop psychological safety. Through a series of play-based group coaching sessions, the team was able to speak more openly about successes and failures with each other. They felt safer to be seen as imperfect and vulnerable in times of ambiguity and stress, and realized that team members were available to help one another solve problems.

The team also spent time in redefining their roles during these challenging times. Using play as a learning tool provided insight that not everyone is great at everything when it comes to collaboration. Team members that matched their roles closer to responsibilities they truly enjoyed, found their intrinsic motivation and energy increased, thereby helping them to manage the workload and their ability to collaborate effectively.

Finally, the team was more open to new ideas and suggestions from one another to improve end outcomes and find creative solutions that enhanced their team performance. It was a playful approach to creating safety to learn from mistakes, and fueling connection to have difficult conversations, that enabled the team to achieve its massive goal during a global pandemic.

Play is innately human and linked to learning, creativity, and development in social relatedness (Vygotsky, 1978; Winnicott, 1989). In addition to shared experiences that promote team development, social play allows teams to experiment with roles and modify situations that are normally constricted by power dynamics and rigid mental models. Play experience (Pavlas et al., 2012) may simultaneously facilitate an individual's ability to communicate openly, establish a learning mindset, develop psychological safety, and promote team development. Lasley (2020) observed how a group that engaged in play generated a creative group environment and psychological safety by using gaming activities to facilitate group development processes. Group processes designed for play can be used to provide opportunities for focusing attention, experimentation, ongoing reflection, and learning at the team and cultural levels of an organization (Küpers, 2017).

## PLAYFUL TIPS TO ESTABLISH HIGH-PERFORMING TEAMS

1. Measure Psychological Safety of the team:
   a. Use a simple diagnostic measure with a balanced approach to "supportive" and "challenging" team behaviors. For example, ask team members to what degree
      i. it is easy to ask members of the team for help (supportive).

ii. members of the team raise concerns they have about team plans or decisions (challenging).

b. Use a collaborative approach to generate ideas to improve specific team norms and/or behaviors. Then identify fun ways to motivate team members to start doing them.
c. Hold the team accountable by using the diagnostic again in 3 months and celebrate successes.

2. Establish a process for Innovation:
   a. Ensure team members are consistently engaging in both creative and execution processes. Practice using various parts of the innovation process in meetings to adhere to boundaries and rules as needed for each step of the process.
   b. Establish expectations for improvement individually and collectively in coaching conversations with team members. Support each team member with "play projects" that are self-directed and have milestones that ensure progress.
   c. Hold meetings that acknowledge, accept, and even celebrate failures and mistakes in order to create a culture that makes it enjoyable to learn from each other.

## PLAY FOR CULTURE

A recent case of successfully implementing a playful business culture involved a marketing and technology firm that established a presence in the real estate industry and over the course of 5 short years, boasted year on year revenue growth rates of 40%. The executives were talented founders that quickly realized truly scaling their company required hiring more experienced leaders that could unlock the company's potential. The executives also had intuition that the culture of the small firm would need to pivot as well.

An effort to re-connect the executives with the vision, values, and strategy of the company was exactly what the team needed. Through a playful approach to envision the future of the company, the team was able to identify a common vision. Identifying their values was the tall order ahead. What they knew was that they wanted to create a place to work where people were motivated, innovative, and having fun. And they wanted to shoot past their goals for the company as quickly as possible. They wanted it all.

Using a balanced approach to focus the culture on both people as well as results, the team was able to co-create pairs of values that were in tension with each other. Since these executives have to make many decisions with little or incomplete information, they were used to debating multiple sides and risks of key decisions. In this case, they realized that by naming the values consistently underlying their debates, they could create a culture that held both the impact of any decision on people and the ultimate business result of that decision. In other words, they identified a culture that balanced both play and productivity in order to achieve their vision.

Their next steps were to inculcate the rest of the organization into the culture they had connected with and co-created. Department by department, the simple yet effective four values (two pairs straddling productivity and play), were shared and fine-tuned to ensure every single person understood how to live them out on a daily basis. The executives' openness to use a balanced approach to establishing a company culture was rewarded two years later when they sold the organization for five times the revenue-base.

Successful business cultures in the 21st century must master a form of leadership that generates learning, motivation, and innovation. Transformational leaders have used storytelling as a way to build company culture, as well as getting group members to embrace change (DuBrin, 2013). Leaders and followers engaging in transformational leadership increase levels of motivation for everyone (Wren, 1995). Organizational cultures that employ play are able to create learning cultures that sustain high levels of motivation, engagement and innovation. For instance, businesses can boost motivation and engagement on a day-to-day basis by normalizing the practice of coaching individuals to be responsible for work that is considered playful. Given the potential usefulness of play in organizations and for leaders, playful values warrant consideration in organizations along with understanding the relationships between play and productivity that inform everything we do.

## PLAYFUL TIPS TO ESTABLISH AN ORGANIZATIONAL CULTURE

1. Use a balanced approach to setting values, not a linear one:
   a. Establish a list of values that everyone on a team share. Then start to pair values together as opposing pairs. For example, pair "We learn from failure" with "We execute efficiently."
   b. Choose only 2–3 pairs of values (4–6 total values) to share with the organization. Ensure leaders understand how they will use the values in communication, collaboration, innovation, and decision-making.
2. Role model and demonstrate the company culture in various ways:
   a. Key leaders, especially those at high levels, need to consistently demonstrate the balanced approach of being productive while staying playful in their work. This is the only way to guide the rest of the organization through stories and connection. Host events and social gatherings that are connected to each of the values, and ensure senior leaders are engaged.

b. Use the company values in performance reviews. Rate each person on how they live out the values in order to reinforce and reward the balanced approach to productivity and play.

## CONCLUSION

As the demands of business continue to expand in a globally networked society, 21st century skills including creativity, problem-solving, adapting to change, and continuous learning are increasingly essential. The volatile, uncertain, complex and ambiguous business environment requires managers, those in positions of authority, teams, and entire organizations to adapt dynamic interdisciplinary approaches in order to succeed. Play, learning, and leadership are universal and can be practiced across disciplines to help in creating new understandings of our evolving society. Play helps managers, teams, and organizations not only balance, but integrate productive and developmental mindsets, styles, practices, strategies, and cultures that will propel our success into an emerging future. At all levels, leadership that adopts interdisciplinary and multifaceted approaches will enable businesses to meet complex challenges.

## REFERENCES

Bartle, R. (1996). *Hearts, clubs, diamonds, spades: Players who suit MUDs.* http://www.arise.mae.usp.br/wp-content/uploads/2018/03/Bartle-player-types.pdf

Brown, S. L., & Vaughan, C. C. (2009). *Play: How it shapes the brain, opens the imagination, and invigorates the soul.* Avery.

Carless, S. A., Wearing, A. J., & Mann, L. (2000). A short measure of transformational leadership. *Journal of Business & Psychology, 14*(3), 389–406. https://doi.org/10.1023/A:1022991115523

DuBrin, A. J (2013). *Leadership: Research findings, practice, and skills.* South-Western Cengage Learning.

Kark, R. (2011). Games managers play: Play as a form of leadership development. *Academy of Management Learning & Education, 10*(3), 507–527. https://doi.org/10.5465/amle.2010.0048

Küpers, W. (2017). Inter-play(ing)—Embodied and relational possibilities of "serious play" at work. *Journal of Organizational Change Management, 30*(7), 993–1014. https://doi.org/10.1108/JOCM-12-2016-0267

Lasley, J. (2020). *An examination of gaming environments in Dungeons & Dragons groups* [Unpublished doctoral dissertation]. University of San Diego.

Pavlas, D., Jentsch, F., Salas, E., Fiore, S. M., & Sims, V. (2012). Play Experience Scale (PES) [Database record]. APA PsycTests. https://doi.org/10.1037/t21710-000

Plass, J. L., Homer, B. D., & Kinzer, C. K. (2014). *Playful learning: An integrated design framework* [White paper].

Plass, J. L., Homer, B. D., & Kinzer, C. K. (2015). Foundations of game-based learning. *Educational Psychologist, 50*(4), 258–283. https://doi.org/10.1080/00461520.2015.1122533

Proyer, R. T. (2017). A new structural model for the study of adult playfulness: Assessment and exploration of an understudied individual differences variable. *Personality & Individual Differences, 108*, 113–122. https://doi.org/10.1016/j.paid.2016.12.011

Tucker, S., Turner, N., Barling, J., & McEvoy, M. (2010). Global transformational leadership scale—Adapted version. *PsycTESTS.* https://doi.org/10.1037/t11628-000

Vygotsky, L. S. (1978). *Mind in society: The development of higher psychological processes* [M. Cole, Ed.]. Harvard University Press.

Winnicott, D. W. (1989). *Playing and reality*. Routledge.

Wren, J. T. (1995). *The leader's companion: Insights on leadership through the ages.* The Free Press.

# SECTION II

## HIGHER EDUCATION AND BEYOND

CHAPTER 7

# DISTINCTIVE CHARACTERISTICS IN INTERDISCIPLINARY ACADEMIC LEADERSHIP PROGRAMS

## A Multi-Program Case Study Analysis

**Kathy L. Guthrie**
**Pei Hu**

## ABSTRACT

An interdisciplinary approach has been widely employed in academic leadership programs to create leadership learning opportunities in higher education. This chapter highlights three academic leadership programs that include: North Central College's minor in ethical leadership in the leadership, ethics, and values program; Florida State University's undergraduate certificate in leadership studies; and Kansas State University's leadership studies minor, as case studies to explore distinctive characteristics in interdisciplin-

*On Leadership*, pages 103–117

ary leadership programs. Through reviewing these programs' website information and communicating with program contacts, this chapter highlights distinguishing program characteristics: intentionally designed programs, authentic leadership learning environments, application of knowledge, skills, and values, meaning making through reflection, and continuous program improvement. Together, these case study analyses offer an introductory understanding of distinctive characteristics in interdisciplinary academic leadership programs and will assist in supporting leadership learning opportunities in higher education from an interdisciplinary framework.

Leadership as an interdisciplinary, multidisciplinary, and transdisciplinary field of study continues to be a critical part of higher education. Guthrie and Osteen (2016) challenged higher education to reclaim their role in the leadership development of students. Further, Chunoo and Osteen (2016) argued higher education's purpose, mission, and context directly aligns with the environment and resources necessary to provide quality leadership education in both academic and co-curricular contexts. Due to the alignment with higher education's purpose, mission, and context, professionals in higher education are constantly asked to provide opportunities for students to learn leadership. Whether this is in the context of academic classrooms or occurring outside-of-the-class in co-curricular contexts, educators are working towards developing leaders: leaders in various industries, social change, and around the world.

One way of reclaiming this purpose of leadership development in higher education is to continually expand the discussion on how to intentionally provide leadership learning opportunities for all students using an interdisciplinary, multidisciplinary, and transdisciplinary approach. In this chapter, we provide a broad perspective of academic leadership programs in the United States. We first frame leadership learning in interdisciplinary, multidisciplinary, and transdisciplinary ways, then provide a general landscape of academic leadership programs, and highlight three distinctive academic leadership programs that intentionally frame their offerings through an interdisciplinary lens.

## DEFINING LEADERSHIP

Over the years, defining leadership has become more debated than agreed upon (Dugan & Komives, 2011). When discussing how leadership is defined, many scholars and practitioners cite Kellerman's (2012) meta analysis of leadership literature that emerged with over 1,500 definitions and 40 models of leadership. Others emphasize the importance of the language used when discussing leadership (Bertrand Jones et al., 2016; Dugan, 2017). This chapter focuses on the interdisciplinary nature of leadership, but first we want to discuss how interdisciplinary, multidisciplinary, transdisciplinary, and social construction informs leadership as a concept.

## Interdisciplinary and Multidisciplinary

For decades, learning and practicing leadership from diverse constructs, perspectives, and contexts has been viewed as advantageous (Riggio et al., 2003). Various perspectives such as historical, psychological, sociological, political, linguistic, and cultural are perspectives that enhance students' understandings of various leadership approaches (Harvey & Riggio, 2011). As leadership studies evolves as a discipline, so does the approach scholars and practitioners take to develop and provide leadership learning opportunities. *Multidisciplinary* includes one thematic topic, for example, leadership, where multiple disciplines work within their individual disciplinary approach to examine that thematic topic without consulting other disciplines. However, *interdisciplinary* approaches cross disciplinary boundaries, analyzes, and synthesizes the links between disciplines. If leadership learning is enhanced by various constructs, then leadership education should not only be drawn from multiple disciplines, but integrated across disciplines in the development of new knowledge. Leadership being both interdisciplinary and multidisciplinary is beneficial to both the scholarship and practice of this complex concept (Guthrie & Jenkins, 2018; Sowcik & Komives, 2020).

## Transdisciplinary Leadership

Although leadership has been identified widely as being interdisciplinary and multidisciplinary, the idea of leadership being transdisciplinary has not been as widely discussed in research. Introduced by Piaget (1972), *transdisciplinary* approaches suggest an integration of ideas (Nicolescu, 2008) between and across disciplines. As Bernstein (2015) offers, the goal of transdisciplinary is to create a holistic approach that can provide a better understanding of the present world. Transdisciplinary connects with leadership (Francovich, 2020) and provides a stronger framework because of the integration of ideas and brings it into the complexities of current times, which is where leadership and leadership learning is situated. Transdisciplinary leadership education brings this integration of ideas to construct new knowledge and elevates learning to more complex cognitive abilities (Guthrie et al., 2021).

## Social Construction

Leadership scholars have generally agreed that leadership is socially constructed when discussing how to define leadership (Dugan, 2017; Guthrie & Jenkins, 2018; Owen, 2020). Socially constructed means that over time, our understandings of a complex idea have been jointly created from shared assumptions within a particular cultural community. In leadership, it means how we understand leadership as a phenomenon has evolved as our cultural shared assumptions have as well. Shared assumptions have incredible influence because of the collective nature and overall cultural impacts they have. Social construction centers on the idea that meanings are developed with others rather than separately within everyone. Jones et al. (2013) point out constructivism and constructionism are often mistakenly interchanged. As Crotty (1998) differentiates, constructivism indicates developing individual meaning while social constructionism takes social cultural influence to generate and transmit meaning. This difference is important to note, especially when applying it to how individuals define leadership, which influences how they learn and practice it. Honoring the complexity and nuances of approaches is essential in creating intentional leadership learning opportunities in higher education spaces.

With approaching leadership learning from interdisciplinary, multidisciplinary, and transdisciplinary framework and acknowledging how leadership is socially constructed, this chapter builds off these assumptions to provide an overall landscape of academic leadership programs in higher education institutions in the United States. We note that although we are making a case of the importance of how leadership education should be moving towards transdisciplinary frameworks, we focus on interdisciplinary programs, as this term is what is widely used even though when digging deeper, some programs are framed more in transdisciplinary approaches. Understanding these differences are critical in developing an influential framework for leadership learning opportunities.

## DISTINCTIVE INTERDISCIPLINARY ACADEMIC LEADERSHIP PROGRAMS

Developing leadership learning opportunities for students can take several formats. Whether it is an academic program where students gain credit or a co-curricular training workshop, thoughtful leadership program planning is essential. Contextualizing program development and implementation is an important step in the development of leadership learning opportunities, as is understanding and implementing distinctive program characteristics, which is discussed in this section.

### Landscape of Interdisciplinary Academic Programs in the United States

The data for this chapter is based on the largest known dataset of current academic leadership programs in the United States, which is managed by the Leadership Learning Research Center (LLRC) at Florida State University. This data was originally based on self-reported academic leadership programs included in the 2016 International Leadership Association (ILA) directory (ILA, n.d.). The LLRC has continually updated the data since 2017. Through over 3,000 hours of vigorous cleaning, updating, and building on the original ILA directory, the LLRC research team developed an Academic Leadership Programs dataset (Guthrie et al., 2018; Guthrie et al., 2019). This dataset includes 1,526 academic leadership programs within 489 higher education institutions in 49 states across the United States (Guthrie et al., 2019). Among this sample of academic leadership programs in higher education within the United States, there are 289 interdisciplinary based leadership programs currently offered.

Within the 289 identified interdisciplinary academic leadership programs, there are 41 bachelor's degree programs, 80 master's programs, 45 doctoral programs, 43 certificate programs, and 80 minor programs. Through examining these interdisciplinary academic leadership programs, three programs will be highlighted in this chapter, including the minor in ethical leadership in the leadership, ethics, and values program at North Central College, the undergraduate certificate in leadership studies at Florida State University, and the leadership studies minor at Kansas State University. These three programs serve as a case study to highlight the program characteristics that make them distinctive and provide examples for leadership educators with a fundamental understanding of interdisciplinary leadership programs.

## Distinctive Leadership Program Characteristics

After an extensive literature review, Guthrie and Jenkins (2018) offered five major characteristics for distinctive leadership programs. They defined distinctive programs as those having a positive influence on student leadership learning. Distinctiveness is based on high-quality, well-developed programs which demonstrate the ability to meet their stated learning outcomes. Eich (2008) suggested high-quality leadership programs focus on opportunities for students to practice leadership in various ways. Some suggestions Eich (2008) provided to practice leadership are specifically applying skills and concepts learned in the program, engaging in out-of-classroom projects, and participating in positions related to the leadership program responsible for developing and teaching. Expanding on Eich (2008), Guthrie and Jenkins (2018) observed five characteristics of distinctive leadership programs, including:

1. Intentionally designed programs
2. Authentic leadership learning environments

3. Application of knowledge, skills, and values
4. Meaning making through reflection
5. Continuous program improvement

Intentional creation of a program is the first characteristic of a distinctive leadership program. As we know, developing a program with purpose is critical to overall program success and to the achievement of student learning. Wiggins and McTighe (2005) share how a scaffolding approach to planning and executing curriculum is a strategy for well-designed programs. Intentionally designed programs should include clear learning outcomes and instructional and assessment strategies that are connected to the learning outcomes.

Another characteristic of a distinctive program Guthrie and Jenkins (2018) outline is creating a positive learning environment. A few key considerations when developing learning environments should include the role and influence of instructors, creating supportive, yet challenging environments, developing integrative learning environments, and incorporating culturally relevant leadership learning (Bertrand Jones et al., 2016).

Another distinctive program characteristic involves providing opportunities for learners to apply leadership knowledge, skills, and values to real-life situations. Experiential learning, service-learning, and experiences in the process of leadership frames and encourages application of knowledge, skills, and values.

Volpe White et al. (2019) offered a "reflection in leadership" learning model, which supports another characteristic of a distinctive leadership program. Reflection is essential to making meaning of leadership learning and instructors can support meaningful reflection by creating environments that encourage and value reflection as a continuous process. "Distinctive leadership programs have reflective environments, created through intentional spaces and instructional strategies throughout the program" (Guthrie & Jenkins, 2018, p. 112).

The final distinctive characteristic is engaging in continuous assessment, feedback, and improvement. As Guthrie and Jenkins (2018) noted, assessment should be included with the goal of program improvement and not simply be an afterthought. Deliberately designing assessment and opportunities for feedback when developing a program's learning outcomes, instructional strategies, and overall program design should be part of the program design process.

These five distinctive program characteristics (Guthrie & Jenkins, 2018) will provide a framework in highlighting three interdisciplinary academic programs, which can illuminate what we can learn about creating intentional leadership learning opportunities in higher education contexts. As Guthrie and Jenkins (2018) state, "Developing, delivering, and assessing high-quality programs for students needs to role model purpose, inclusivity, empowerment, reflection, and the process-oriented framework of leadership to advocate for students to become the best leaders they can be" (p. 115).

## INTERDISCIPLINARY ACADEMIC LEADERSHIP PROGRAM HIGHLIGHTS

Interdisciplinary approach has been employed widely in academic leadership programs in higher education (Guthrie & Jenkins, 2018). Including various disciplines and approaches to creating leadership learning opportunities serve the broad goal of teaching leadership. We offer three interdisciplinary academic leadership programs as case studies. In each of these case studies, we provide how the program demonstrates distinctive characteristics as well as how institutional context influences the development of interdisciplinary leadership learning opportunities in an academic, for credit context. The highlighted programs include North Central College's minor in ethical leadership in the Leadership, Ethics, and Values program, Florida State University's undergraduate certificate in leadership studies, and Kansas State University's leadership studies minor.

### North Central College

According to the Carnegie Classification of Higher Education Institutions (n.d.), North Central College is a small, private, not-for-profit institution located in Naperville, Illinois. The minor in ethical leadership at North Central College is one of degree options within the leadership, ethics, and values (LEV) program, which focuses on a commitment to develop students into changemakers (North Central College, n.d., para. 1). The minor in ethical leadership requires a minimum of 20 credit hours consisting of four required courses and at least one elective. The curriculum of this minor is specifically designed to engage students with learning leadership theory to assist in development of their knowledge in ethics and values with the goal to develop ethical leaders in current political, social, and cultural climates.

The LEV program at North Central College was founded more than 30 years ago rooted in the college's mission statement to produce "curious, engaged, ethical, and purposeful citizens and leaders in local, national, and global contexts" (North Central College, n.d., para. 1). The minor in ethical leadership program is among several programs added to the LEV program over years with the initiative to enhance the broader LEV program and leadership education at North Central College (T. Cavenagh, personal communication, April 5, 2021). It is evident both the minor in ethical leadership and the entire LEV program at North Central College was intentionally designed with extensive consultation with both individuals, organizations, and overall industry both on and off campus (T. Cavenagh, personal communication, April 5, 2021). The interdisciplinary leadership program has been intentionally developed from individual faculty expertise and efforts in working with academic departments and colleagues across campus. Resultantly, the LEV program, including the minor in ethical leadership, contribute to the designation of the North Central College as an "Ashoka Changemaker Campus"—"We (North Central College) are one of just 48 in the world" (T. Cavenagh, personal communication, April 5, 2021). Such a designation recognizes institutions "with a proven track record of campus-wide excellence for social innovation and changemaking" (AshokaU, n.d., para. 1).

Creating authentic leadership learning environments are standard in the LEV program. In addition to intentional design, learning environments are created by including various methods in delivering learning opportunities to maximize engagement. The core values and guiding operational principles of the LEV program, such as "we will endeavor to touch every student with leadership, ethics, and values experiences" (T. Cavenagh, personal communication, April 5, 2021), have been underscored for the contribution to the leadership learning environments.

The application of knowledge, skills, and values is important in any program, which makes it a characteristic for distinctive programs. Three specific examples in which the minor in ethical leadership at North Central College provides opportunity for application are provided. One example is that several courses in the minor "have formal community engaged learning dimensions" within their curriculum design, which require their students to apply what they learned from classrooms to their work with community (T. Cavenagh, personal communication, April 5, 2021). Another example of the application of learning is the close relationship between the LEV program and student affairs at North Central College. This partnership provides opportunities for students in the interdisciplinary leadership program to put their knowledge into practice through a wide range of campus leadership positions. The final example is the *Changemaker Challenge,* which is a competition for students with ideas on how to make a positive social impact to "pitch" their ideas. This provides funding opportunities for students to initiate their own projects on campus or in the local community, which is valuable to students' leadership knowledge, skills, and values application.

In the minor, there are courses that focus on reflection as the cornerstone of the curriculum design. This aligns with the liberal arts tradition. For example, two courses, LEAD 250, *Designing Your Life* and LEAD 260, *Inner Transformation and Leadership,* are both designed based on a reflective and practical approach to help students find "purpose and meaning in life and career" and "inner character transformation," respectively (T. Cavenagh, personal communication, April 5, 2021). The fifth characteristic of distinctive programs is continuous program improvement is also represented in this interdisciplinary minor. Several approaches for improvement span gathering feedback from stakeholders to enhancing instructor professional development to assessing student growth in the program. The LEV program evaluates its impact through the Multi-Institutional Study of Leadership and has certified trainers in the Gallup StrengthsFinder and Entrepreneurial Mindset who contribute to the continuous assessment and improvement of the program by reviewing learning with outcomes for alignment and offering professional development of educators. As shared, not only is the program focused on continuous improvement regarding environment, instructional methods, and assessment strategies, but "students are given the information and tools to assess themselves in meaningful, structural ways" (T. Cavenagh, personal communication, April 5, 2021). As you can see, the LEV program at North Central College and the minor in ethical leadership is a program that is distinctive because of the aspects discussed here. Another interdisciplinary program we want to highlight is the undergraduate certificate in leadership studies at Florida State University.

## Florida State University

The undergraduate certificate in leadership studies is an 18-credit interdisciplinary program open to all undergraduates at Florida State University (Florida State University, n.d.). Different from North Central College, Florida State University is a large, four-year public university with very high research activity located in Tallahassee, Florida. To complete the undergraduate certificate requirements, students are required to take five core courses and one elective. The goal of the certificate is to prepare students for leadership learning through experiential and service-learning projects within the context of social change. An interdisciplinary curriculum design is critical to achieve this goal, as well as in offering various electives across academic departments.

The certificate was created in 2003, after the Southern Association of Colleges and Schools' (SACS) Accreditation Committee charged Florida State University with developing a Quality Enhancement Plan (QEP), which focused on institutional improvement in an area of student learning (Guthrie & Bovio, 2014). One of the main initiatives of the QEP is the undergraduate certificate in leadership studies. Distinctive program characteristics are seen in this program through intentional program design, creating a meaningful environment, application of learning, inclusion of reflection, and continuous program improvement.

The intentional program design and creating an authentic learning environment are interconnected in this program. As the lead advisor for the program stated, "Students are coming into the classes from a wide variety of majors, this creates a robust environment where students can learn from each other's understanding and perspectives of leadership" (J. LeBlanc, personal communication, April 5, 2021). The peer-to-peer learning opportunities are accomplished through peer facilitation, which "allows them (certificate students) to synthesize the course content from their own perspective to deliver content to their peers" (J. LeBlanc, personal communication, April 5, 2021).

Application of knowledge, skills, and values is another distinctive program characteristic and is a main priority for this program. By design, students select one supporting course, often from their own academic discipline, which not only highlights the interdisciplinary nature of the program, but focuses on application of knowledge, skills, and values; students "make connections between their discipline and leadership studies" (J. LeBlanc, personal communication, April 5, 2021). Another example is LDR 3263: Leadership Experience; this course takes an application-based approach for students to experience leadership in a specific site of their choosing for 120 hours during one semester (J. LeBlanc, personal communication, April 5, 2021). This experience not only allows students to see "leadership in action," but also provides opportunities for students to "apply their knowledge, skills, and values, and also critique and synthesize how leadership is enacted at their site" (J. LeBlanc, personal communication, April 5, 2021).

The last two characteristics for distinctive programs, meaning making through reflection and continuous program improvement, are each seen in the program in various ways. Although reflection is incorporated in each leadership course through class activities and course assignments, there are two core courses that is based on meaning making from experience, LDR 3263: Leadership Experience and LDR 2162: Groups and Communities, in which "all assignments are reflective in nature asking students to make meaning of their experiences (individually and in groups)" (J. LeBlanc, personal communication, April 5, 2021). The program faculty "believe in the power of individual and collective reflection" in enhancing students' learning throughout the leadership certificate program (J. LeBlanc, personal communication, April 5, 2021). Continuous program improvement occurs through yearly evaluation of curriculum at both individual course and program curriculum level and suggested revisions are planned and implemented in the appropriate manner. For example, recently a complete revision of an online course was done to better meet the needs of students in successfully achieving the established course learning outcomes and a program assessment was completed in how the leadership learning framework is used throughout all courses (Guthrie & Jenkins, 2018). These distinctive characteristics are essential from the program to continually create influential leadership learning opportunities for students.

## Kansas State University

As a large public institution, Kansas State University provides an interdisciplinary minor in leadership studies in the Staley School of Leadership Studies (Kansas State University, n.d.). This minor requires 16 credits of leadership studies, which includes 12 credits of core courses and four credits of elective courses. This differs from Florida State University in its designation as a minor and requirements. Students could select a minimum of four credits from a list of elective courses from campus-wide academic departments to adapt to their own academic majors or academic goals. This interdisciplinary minor in leadership studies at Kansa State challenges students to practice leadership in each of their career, community, and personal life and the program prepares their students with the confidence to innovate change for the common good.

Analysis on the qualitative data collected from the chair for leadership, Dr. Mary Toler (personal communication, March 23, 2021) at Kansas State University also revealed the leadership studies minor program is an intentionally well-designed interdisciplinary program which met all five distinctive program characteristics. Specifically, M. Toler (personal communication, March 23, 2021) shared the historical background of their leadership minor program: "The minor began with one course, co-designed and co-taught with students in a leadership honor society in the mid 1990s." With an increasing number of students interested in this course, it has been developed to an interdisciplinary leadership minor that was intentionally designed by instructional faculty members based on their knowledge on leadership studies and other academic fields. M. Toler (personal communication, March 23, 2021) also mentioned that feedback and suggestions from students, student affairs professionals, and senior faculty from different academic departments have been incorporated into this minor program's on-going development. Currently, they have an 80-person advancement council, including stakeholders from the industry, community, and university (students, alumni, legendary football coach, senior administrators) to help with the program enhancement who make general recommendations about the program including development of learning outcomes.

M. Toler (personal communication, March 23, 2021) introduced the inclusive leadership learning environments of the leadership studies minor. She noted that several important elements they consider while creating learning environments to maximize student learning outcomes within the program, which include "learning by doing... scaffolding concepts and theories throughout the four core courses, utilizing learning activities that engage in real world... and appreciating that all students come with lived experiences, knowledge, and expertise that contribute to their and others' learning" (M. Toler, personal communication, March 23, 2021). The inclusive leadership learning environment created by the minor leadership program aligns with their mission statement: "Developing knowledgeable, ethical, caring, inclusive leaders for a diverse and changing world" (M. Toler, personal communication, March 23, 2021). Creating inclusive leadership learning environments requires paying attention to the voices in leadership curriculum and in the classroom and to make physical, technical, and social-emotional resources available to all students.

Application and reflection are core to the learning activities of the leadership studies minor as the chair of leadership noted. In the course syllabus, application of knowledge, as well as development of skills and values are stated as expectations and learning outcomes for the students in the minor. M. Toler (personal communication, March 23, 2021) added, "We understand that leadership is learned by practicing... and we also assess application of knowledge, skills, and to some extent values in our academic program assessment activities of the university." Similarly, reflection activities have been incorporated throughout the leadership courses. For instance, in the capstone course of the minor, one of the major assignments "is built on individual self-reflection and goal setting as students transition from college to what follows" (M. Toler, personal communication, March 23, 2021).

As to the fifth distinctive program characteristic—continuous program improvement, M. Toler (personal communication, March 23, 2021) shared that they conduct course assessment within the minor program, which is coordinated by the university's office of assessment. Also, they have teaching teams for all courses of the minor program to "assess progress regularly—formally and informally" (M. Toler, personal communication, March 23, 2021). Additionally, faculty assesses the program regularly through faculty retreats, student evaluations, peer faculty observations, special faculty meetings, focus groups, and exit surveys for program improvement.

As seen from the interdisciplinary programs highlighted from North Central College, Florida State University, and Kansas State University, intentional design, authentic learning environments, application, reflection, and continuous program improvement are critical to distinctive programs. From exploring these case studies in more depth through an open coding method, a few themes emerged to what we can learn from such programs.

## ENHANCING LEADERSHIP LEARNING OPPORTUNITIES

As educators, we are always searching for new strategies to enhance student learning. From exploring the interdisciplinary programs at North Central College, Florida State University, and Kansas State, a few lessons emerged. One of the components of successful interdisciplinary academic leadership programs is that faculty's efforts are critical to program design, implementation, continuous program, and ultimately defining the achievement of successful measures for program outcomes. Course instructors can teach in their single course, but enhanced student learning occurs when faculty break out of artificial silos and work across courses to focus on the program unit. In interdisciplinary programs, reaching beyond one discipline to integrate all disciplines only enhances overall student learning and is often done through relationships built from program faculty across campus. Collaborating within the community is also essential to provide quality experiential and service-learning opportunities.

Program development and location within a higher education institution is often the outcome of historical policies and funding. The college, discipline, and department an academic leadership program is in influences the resources in which it is given. This is true with any academic program, but this becomes more complex when it is an interdisciplinary program. Different types of institutions and operations funding and support may influence how an interdisciplinary program can be situated and supported. This, in turn, influences how leadership learning opportunities are created and offers better understanding how institutional types, mission statements, and teaching tradition, such as liberal arts or research focused, can enhance development of leadership learning opportunities.

In considering interdisciplinary leadership programs, clear program mission, values, expectations, and goals should be developed and provided for not only program guidance, but for students who are interested in an interdisciplinary framework. This clarity can not only strengthen the intentionality of program design, but the creation of opportunities to apply leadership learning, and gain feedback for continuous improvement.

The interdisciplinary academic leadership programs at North Central College, Florida State University, and Kansas State University highlighted in this chapter provides a case study but there are more than 289 interdisciplinary leadership programs currently existing in U.S. higher education. Through employing Guthrie and Jenkins's (2018) distinctive leadership program characteristics framework, we aimed to provide both leadership educators and students who are interested in interdisciplinary programs with a solid understanding of critical factors in considering the distinctiveness of an interdisciplinary leadership program.

## REFERENCES

AshokaU. (n.d.). *AshokaU changemaker campus.* https://ashokau.org/changemaker campus/

Bernstein, J. H. (2015). Transdisciplinary: A review of its origins, development, and current issues. *Journal of Research Practice, 11*(1), Article R1. https://www.researchgate.net/publication/282285072_Transdisciplinarity_A_Review_of_Its_Origins_Development_and_Current_Issues

Bertrand Jones, T., Guthrie, K. L., & Osteen, L. (2016). Critical domains of culturally relevant leadership learning: A call to transform leadership programs. In K. L. Guthrie, T. Bertrand Jones, & L. Osteen (Eds.), *New directions for student leadership: No. 152: Developing culturally relevant leadership learning* (pp. 9–21). Jossey-Bass.

Chunoo, V. S., & Osteen, L. (2016). Purpose, mission, and context: The call for educating future leaders. In K. L. Guthrie, & L. Osteen (Eds.), *New directions for higher education: No. 174: Reclaiming Higher Education's Purpose in Leadership Development* (pp. 9–20). Jossey-Bass.

Crotty, M. (1998). *The foundations of social research: Meaning and perspective in the research process.* SAGE.

Carnegie Classification of Higher Education Institutions. (n.d.). *Institutional lookup.* https://carnegieclassifications.acenet.edu/lookup/lookup.php

Dugan, J. P. (2017). *Leadership theory: Cultivating critical perspectives.* Jossey-Bass.

Dugan, J. P., & Komives, S. R. (2011). Leadership theories. In S. R. Komives, J. P. Dugan, J. E. Owen, C. Slack, W. Wagner, & Associates (Eds.), *The handbook of student leadership development* (2nd ed.; pp. 35–58). Jossey-Bass.

Eich, D. (2008). A grounded theory of high-quality leadership programs: Perspectives from student leadership programs in higher education. *Journal of Leadership & Organizational Studies, 15*(2), 176–187. https://doi.org/10.1177/1548051808324099

Florida State University. (n.d.). *Leadership learning research center.* https://thecenter.fsu.edu/llrc

Francovich, C. (2020). Leadership studies at the crossroads. *Journal of Leadership Education, 19*(4), 163–174. https://doi.org/10.12806/v19/i4/t2

Guthrie, K. L., Batchelder, J. M., & Hu. P. (2019). *Examining degree types of academic leadership programs in the United States.* Leadership Learning Research Center, Florida State University.

Guthrie, K. L., Beatty, C. C., & Wiborg, E. (2021). *Engaging in the leadership process: Identity, capacity, and efficacy in college students.* Information Age Publishing.

Guthrie, K. L., & Bovio, R. (2014). Undergraduate certificate in leadership studies: An opportunity for seamless learning. *Journal of College and Character, 15*(1), 25–31. https://doi.org/10.1515/jcc-2014-0004

Guthrie, K. L., & Jenkins, D. M. (2018). *The role of leadership educators: Transforming learning.* Information Age Publishing.

Guthrie, K. L., & Osteen, L. (Eds.). (2016). *Reclaiming higher education's purpose in leadership development.* Jossey-Bass.

Guthrie, K. L., Teig, T. S., & Hu, P. (2018). *Academic leadership programs in the United States.* Leadership Learning Research Center, Florida State University.

Harvey, M., & Riggio, R. E. (Eds.). (2011). *Leadership studies: The dialogue of disciplines.* Edward Elgar.

International Leadership Association. (n.d.). *Leadership program directory.* http://www.ila-net.org/Resources/LPD/index.htm

Jones, S. R., Torres, V., & Arminio, J. (2013). *Negotiating the complexities of qualitative research in higher education: Fundamental elements and issues* (2nd ed.). Routledge.

Kansas State University. (n.d.). *Staley School of Leadership Studies.* https://www.k-state.edu/leadership/academics/undergradprograms/minor.html

Kellerman, B. (2012). *Cut off at the pass: The limits of leadership in the 21st century.* Governance Studies at Brookings Institution. https://www.brookings.edu/wp-content/uploads/2016/06/0810_leadership_deficit_kellerman.pdf

Nicolescu, B. (2008). *Transdisciplinarity: Theory and practice.* Hampton Press.

North Central College. (n.d.). *Leadership, ethics, and values.* https://www.northcentralcollege.edu/interdisciplinary-programs/leadership-ethics-and-values

Owen, J. E. (2020). *We are the leaders we've been waiting for: Women and leadership development in college.* Stylus.

Piaget, J. (1972). The epistemology of interdisciplinary relationships. In Centre for Educational Research and Innovation (Ed.), *Interdisciplinarity: Problems of teaching and research in universities* (pp. 127–139). Organisation for Economic Co-operation and Development.

Riggio, R. E., Ciulla, J. B., & Sorenson, G. J. (2003). Leadership education at the undergraduate level: A liberal arts approach to leadership development. In S. E. Murphy & R. E. Riggio (Eds.), *The future of leadership development* (pp. 223–236). Lawrence Erlbaun.

Sowcik, M., & Komives, S. R. (Eds.). (2020). *How academic disciplines approach leadership development.* Wiley & Sons.

Volpe White, J. M., Guthrie, K. L., & Torres, M. (2019). *Thinking to transform: Reflection in leadership learning.* Information Age Publishing.

Wiggins, G., & McTighe, J. (2005). *Understanding by design* (2nd ed.). Association for Supervision and Curriculum Development.

CHAPTER 8

# HIGHER EDUCATION IN CRISIS

## Enabling Complexity Thinking and Adaptive Space for Ethical Decision-Making During the Time of COVID-19

**Benjamin Brooks**

### ABSTRACT

Using the COVID-19 crisis as its foundation, this chapter will explore the value of engaging vanguard leadership constructs, complexity thinking, and adaptive space for improved ethical crisis leadership by higher education practitioners. The chapter gives an overview of crisis, stakeholders, interdisciplinarity and interdisciplinary leadership, ethics, and ethical crisis leadership before explaining complexity thinking and adaptive space, and how these constructs can be engaged for ethical, interdisciplinary leadership during a crisis. The chapter concludes by interrogating current issues in higher education governance and examines how complexity thinking and adaptive space could be applied to the COVID-19 crisis in higher education for the reopening of college campuses. Higher education is facing a very real-world problem that has long been in the making and is not going away any time soon. New leadership approaches are needed to confront this crisis and to be better prepared to act ethically concerning the future of higher education.

*On Leadership*, pages 119–144

We are in an unprecedented time in world history. We face a global pandemic that has upended the fabric of day-to-day life. At the time of this writing in 2021, 204 million people worldwide have been infected with COVID-19 and over 4.3 million people have died. In the United States alone, over 35 million people have been infected and 615,000 people have lost their lives (Centers for Disease Control [CDC], 2021). The virus, and measures to stop the spread of the virus, have caused extreme and long-lasting economic hardship around the world (see Center on Budget and Policy Priorities [CBPP], 2021). Furthermore, the isolation individuals are experiencing from a lack of interaction with family, friends, and traditional workplace environments has caused a mental health crisis alongside the public health challenges (Panchal et al., 2021; Wang et al., 2020). Specific to the United States, the detrimental effects of COVID-19 have been felt most egregiously by historically marginalized populations (see Kantamneni, 2020; Panchal et al., 2021). While vaccines are available, the infection rate is still high and the implications of this crisis on our lives is far from over.

We are also in an unprecedented time in the history of higher education in the United States. Higher education is a bedrock institution in American society, but that bedrock is cracking under the stress of this moment. College and university enrollment is down, and along with it, revenue (Ellis, 2021; Gardner, 2021; Hoover, 2021). In 2020, students enrolling immediately after high school declined by a rate of 6.8% over the prior year (Hoover, 2021). The economic loss tied to the pandemic and pandemic-related state legislative decision-making has been estimated at over $180 billion (Natow, 2021). This economic decline has been linked to, or used to explain, several colleges and universities ceasing operations (Gardner, 2021; Natow, 2021) and countless others eliminating faculty and staff positions, sports programs, and entire academic departments (Brown, 2021; Stripling, 2021b). Laying off workers, including tenured faculty, and shuttering programs in many cases has contributed to a culture of distrust and animosity among employees and college and university administrators (Brown, 2021; Fischer & Ellis, 2021; Stripling, 2021b; Gardner, 2021). In addition, across the country there are examples of employees who, to keep their jobs, were exposed to what they deemed unsafe work environments (Brown, 2021; Gardner, 2021; Stripling, 2021b).

The lack of trust is not limited to the relationship between employees and administration in higher education. Students are also concerned with how institutions are handling this crisis and are suffering deeply. One recent study found that 50% of students believe universities only care about the money students give to them (Eisenberg et al., 2020). There are also many examples of students being upset with COVID-19 protocols on campus and with some of the same cuts that have upset faculty and staff (Brown, 2021).

The pressures of pandemic life related to schooling, work, and socialization have contributed to an unprecedented rise in mental health issues. Approximately 4 in 10 college-age adults have reported feeling anxious or depressed, while rates of eating disorders and substance abuse have also increased dramatically (Eisenberg et al., 2020). The direct impact of COVID-19 and its economic and mental health fallout has disproportionately impacted students of color (Bauman, 2021; Eisenberg et al., 2020; Laidler, 2020; Panchal, 2021; Wang et al., 2020).

The communities that depend on colleges and universities, which often have trying relationships with their institutions in the best of times, have seen those relationships strained even further. These communities have seen revenues drop by not having students living on or near campus and where there are students living in the community there have been examples of viral spread contributed to by students (Stripling, 2021a). Communities have regularly put the blame for this at the feet of the institutions for not testing enough, not enforcing safety protocols, and deciding to reopen campuses in the first place (Stripling, 2021a). To further complicate matters, there are colleges and university administrators, like those who are part of the state systems in Idaho, Pennsylvania, Kansas, and South Carolina, to name only a few, who are not fully in control of COVID-19-related decision-making and are, instead, following the directives of state governing boards that can appear to be more aligned with political agendas than pandemic considerations (Fischer & Ellis, 2021; Gardner, 2021; Pettit, 2021). There are examples of universities and colleges supporting the communities they live in; supporting their students intellectually, emotionally, economically, and medically; and supporting faculty and staff through the pandemic (for examples, see Carroll, 2021; Huber, 2020). These positive examples of college and university leadership, however, appear to be more the exception than the rule.

Compounding the complexity of the issues higher education and its institutions are facing during this crisis is that none of these issues are new. The pandemic is a novel event, but the underlying issues it is exposing—student and employee health and well-being; financial solvency; inequitable treatment toward traditionally marginalized communities; and mistrust, lack of communication, and poor collaboration between stakeholders—are ethical issues that have been festering in higher education for decades (Al-Sharafi & Al-Rubaíey, 2020; Lapworth, 2004; Maguad, 2018; Nordberg & Andreassen, 2020). Where higher education has suffered during this COVID-19 time, it did so not only because of the pandemic, but because it was not prepared for the crisis the pandemic brought. Crises are complex and interdisciplinary by their very nature (Repko, 2012; Seeger et al., 2003) and it is incumbent that leaders act ethically in confronting them if they are to have a chance at having a positive long-term impact on their organizations and stakeholders (Johnson, 2018; McNulty & Marcus, 2020). Higher education leaders who failed to act ethically during this crisis did so because they failed to account for the complexity of their institutions under normal operations and were thus ill-prepared to organize, mobilize, and lead the wide array of stakeholders needed to analyze the complex nature of this crisis and propose and enact ethical solutions to confront it.

So, how *should* higher education have responded to this crisis? What roles should this institution and its leaders have played in confronting and potentially alleviating some of the horrors of this moment and serve its vital role in society into an uncertain future? Perhaps most importantly, what can be learned from this past year to better prepare colleges and universities for not just the next crisis, but for better governance and a more sustainable institution in general?

Higher education's leaders need to embrace the interdisciplinary nature of the contexts in which they lead, generally, and the interdisciplinary nature of this crisis, specifically, and apply appropriate interdisciplinary leadership strategies to ethically lead through these difficult times. No two institutions are the same and no two institutions are impacted the same by a crisis. There can be no single answer, then, as to how higher education *should* confront a crisis. What there can be is an ethical leadership approach to engage during a crisis that is interdisciplinary, equitable, and transparent. Further, higher education would be wise to implement just such an interdisciplinary leadership approach when not in crisis. Not only will this prepare stakeholders for when crises do occur, it may decrease the amount of unethical decision-making that occurs at the onset of crisis events, mitigate the damage caused by a crisis, and aid in creating a just and value-based environment for ethical leadership on the complex issues facing institutions daily.

Using the COVID-19 crisis as its foundation, this chapter will explore the value of engaging the vanguard leadership constructs of complexity thinking and adaptive space for improved ethical crisis leadership by higher education practitioners. The chapter will begin by giving an overview of crisis, ethics, interdisciplinarity, and ethical crisis leadership before explaining complexity thinking and adaptive space, and how these constructs can be engaged for ethical, interdisciplinary leadership during a crisis. The chapter will then conclude by interrogating current issues in higher education governance and examine how complexity thinking and adaptive space could be applied to the COVID-19 crisis in higher education for reopening college campuses. Higher education is facing a very real-world problem that has long been in the making and is not going away any time soon. New leadership approaches are needed to confront this crisis and to be better prepared to act ethically concerning the future of higher education.

## ETHICAL CRISIS LEADERSHIP: CRISIS, STAKEHOLDERS, INTERDISCIPLINARY LEADERSHIP, AND ETHICS

A crisis is any major event that is unanticipated and poses a substantial threat to those experiencing the crisis (Johnson, 2018). Pearson and Clair (1998) offer this definition of crisis in an organizational context, "An organizational crisis is a low-probability, high-impact event that threatens the viability of the organization and is characterized by ambiguity of cause, effect, and means of resolution, as well as by a belief that decisions must be made swiftly" (p. 60). Crises are "wicked problems," which is defined as complex and large impact issues that affect multiple stakeholders in a multitude of ways (Bloomquist et al., 2018). The concept of "stakeholders," as popularized by Edward Freeman, posits that "to be an effective . . . strategist, you must deal with those groups that can affect you, while to be responsive (and effective in the long run) you must deal with those groups that you can affect" (Freeman, 1984, p. 46). The assumption underlying a stakeholder-based leadership approach then is that an individual, group, or organization should make decisions with all constituents' interests in mind (Laplume et al., 2008) and that "values are necessarily and explicitly a part of doing business" (Freeman et al., 2004, p. 364).

Confronting a crisis in a manner that embraces the varied concerns of stakeholders is an interdisciplinary undertaking. Interdisciplinarity, generally, is predicated on integrating knowledge bases together to better understand and hopefully, solve real world problems (Repko, 2012). Interdisciplinary leadership, specifically, embraces the complexity of these real-world problems and accepts the need for a shared sense of accountability and responsibility by all stakeholders engaged in the leadership process. Bloomquist, Georges, Ford, and Moss Breen (2018), put it this way,

> Interdisciplinary leadership is not just a collection of individuals with different perspectives mobilizing others to action. Instead, interdisciplinary leadership is a distinct approach that incorporates the complex interplay between context, culture, accountability, power, values, beliefs, ethics, and decision-making in which all members share responsibilities for processes and outcomes. (p. 60)

Ethical considerations are central to engaging in interdisciplinary leadership and to engaging stakeholders in the leadership process. Given the nature of crises, it is not surprising that most crisis experts argue that on a core values level, leaders have an ethical responsibility to prepare for crises (Pauchant & Mitroff, 1992) and act ethically during crises (Johnson, 2018). Ethics, not unlike leadership itself, is a term whose definition is not universally agreed upon. For the purposes of this chapter, though, ethics will be defined as "well-founded standards of right and wrong that prescribe what humans ought to do, usually in terms of rights, obligations, benefits to society, fairness, or specific virtues" (Velasquez et al., 1987/2010, para. 10). An organization's core values should reflect its ethical standards regulating right and wrong conduct. If an organization does not have an expressed set of core values or the stakeholders engaged in crisis leadership question whether the organization stands behind its expressed set of core values, the stakeholders will lack a solid foundation upon which to build their ethical crisis response.

## The Types and Stages of a Crisis

There are many different types of crises, ranging from public perception crises and natural disasters to terrorist attacks and economic calamity (for a complete discussion of crisis types, see Seeger et al., 2003). A crisis on the magnitude of the COVID-19 pandemic has such an expansive scope that it can engage multiple, intertwined crisis types. Regardless of type, though, all crises share a trajectory, passing through three stages: pre-crisis, crisis event, and post-crisis (Seeger et al., 2003). The pre-crisis stage is the period of regular operation for an organization. During this stage, nothing appears wrong, and the organization maintains its regular operating procedures. It generally believes it is not at risk or that it is prepared, due to some previous post-crisis analysis and examination of underlying conditions that could impact response, should issues arise (Marcus et al., 2019). The crisis begins with some triggering "crisis event."

For the United States and its higher education institutions that event was COVID-19 being detected in the country, combined with the realization of just how easily spreadable and deadly the virus is. It is during this time that an organization's crisis management team, if it has one, will implement its crisis management plan, if it developed one (Johnson, 2018). It is generally during this period that the public becomes aware of the crisis and the leadership, or lack thereof, of an organization is on display. The crisis event is a time of uncertainty and is commonly marked by fear, stress, anger, and confusion by all those impacted by the crisis (Johnson, 2018). This stage and its associated feelings will continue until the crisis is resolved. At this point, the post-crisis stage will commence and it is during this period after the crisis when investigation, analysis, and recovery of and from the crisis will occur with the hopes that the organization will return to normal and be better prepared for the next crisis (Johnson, 2018).

## Ethical Leadership Behaviors During Crisis

The set of crisis stages is illustrative of what happens in a crisis and allows for crisis experts to analyze a crisis in a narrative structure with a beginning, middle, and end. The crisis event, situated as the middle stage, becomes the focal point of analysis, and is the concern of much academic and popular crisis writing, with a particular focus on what leadership should look like during crisis events. In a review of the literature, Johnson (2018) identifies six actions or behaviors individuals engaging in ethical leadership should carry out during a crisis namely, assuming broad responsibility, practice transparency, demonstrate care and concern, use their heads as well as their hearts, improvise from a strong moral foundation, and build resilience:

- *Assuming broad responsibility* is the foundation of ethical crisis leadership (Johnson, 2018; Seeger et al., 2003). Leaders and followers have an ethical responsibility to prepare for, act upon, and critically reflect on crisis situations. In addition, leaders should be held accountable for their choices and actions before, during, and after a crisis.
- *Practicing transparency* means leaders and their organizations are open and forthright about all decisions and actions taken throughout the crisis, including making public any errors that were made along the way.
- *Demonstrating care and concern* means not only accepting responsibility for decisions and actions throughout a crisis but showing genuine empathy for those negatively impacted by a crisis. This concept is based in care theory and requires leaders to address the needs of the "whole person" throughout the crisis (Johnson, 2018; see Noddings, 2002 for a complete discussion of care theory).
- *Using their heads as well as their hearts* asks leaders to engage both rationality and emotion when choosing courses of action throughout a crisis and encouraging followers to do the same.
- *Improvising from a strong moral center* is an acknowledgement that leaders must keep their moral and ethical code at the front of their mind while confronting the ambiguity of crises and the quick actions that are often required during them. By extension, followers, too, must improvise in this manner and be empowered by leaders to do so (Argenti, 2002; Johnson, 2018).
- *Build resilience* encapsulates the idea that leaders must foster an environment of support that allows an organization and all external stakeholders to come back from the hardships faced during the crisis in a manner stronger or wiser than they were before. That environment is fostered through trust, building social capital, and the

diffusion of power (Marcus et al., 2019; McNulty & Marcus, 2020; Petriglieri, 2020).

## Crisis Leadership Without Ethics and Interdisciplinarity

The previous few sections demonstrate key elements of ethical crisis leadership. Through a focused engagement with stakeholders, an embrace of the interdisciplinarity nature of the crisis, and an understanding and modeling of its ethics and core values, an organization can carry out ethical crisis leadership. The problem that too often arises during crises, however, is that leaders do not engage in these actions and, correspondingly, do not make ethical decisions (Marcus et al., 2019; McNulty & Marcus, 2020; Nichols et al., 2020; Petriglieri, 2020). The stress of the crisis causes many leaders to fall back into a management role that feels familiar to them, instead of maintaining their leadership role, and allows them the illusion that they are "in control" of the situation (McNulty & Marcus, 2020). Leadership and management, however, are not the same thing and that demarcation is particularly evident during a crisis (see Bennis & Nanus, 2012). McNulty and Marcus (2020) describe the dynamic thusly, "Crises, replete with both complexity and change, require executives to both lead and manage effectively. Addressing the urgent needs of the present is the work of management...Leading, by contrast, involves guiding people to the best possible eventual outcome over this arc of time" (para. 3). Essentially, leaders lose vision and fail to see the bigger picture. Decision-making becomes rote and immediate. A leadership void is created and long-term hope of ethically handling a crisis diminishes.

There is a significant body of literature that shows that leaders engaging in ineffective crisis management compound this mistake by leading more autocratically or top–down than the situation requires (Kezar, 2012). Autocratic leading usually lacks the adherence to core values, collaboration, communication, and transparency that are hallmarks of ethical crisis leadership. It can foster significant distrust amongst the organization (Johnson, 2018). Bazerman and Tenbrunsel (2011) note that all people have what they call "ethical blind spots." These are essentially biases, often unconscious, that can negatively impact our ethical decision-making practices. These biases include overestimating our own ethicality (the belief that we will act more ethically than we actually will), forgiving our own unethical behavior (being more forgiving of ourselves than we might be toward others when we fall short of our ethical standards), in-group favoritism (giving benefits to individuals with whom we share some social identity grouping), and implicit bias (unconscious preferences for groups of people that may lead to discriminatory behavior toward people not in those groups; Banaji & Greenwald, 2013; Bazerman & Tenbrunsel, 2011; Johnson, 2018).

Autocratic leaders engage these ethical blind spots when they try to take control of a crisis instead of embracing the tension of the ambiguous situation and remove agency from the stakeholders directly engaging the crisis (McNulty & Marcus, 2020). By not relying on the expertise of individuals and groups within an organization, not only will the quality and speed of the "task-oriented" elements of the crisis response suffer, but it will hurt the personal, emotional relationship leadership has with employees and stakeholders (McNulty & Marcus, 2020). The ethical foundation will have cracked and building resilience may not be possible. It takes significant mental energy and a desire to guard against these blind spots to develop stronger ethical judgment. This work becomes more manageable and has greater ethical safeguards on it when the crisis leadership process is carried out by well-formed, interdisciplinary groups (Johnson, 2018; Repko, 2012) and within an organization that knows what its values are.

The benefits of ethical leadership are robust. Ethical leadership has been linked to numerous workplace and personal well-being benefits for followers (Bedi et al., 2016). Research has linked follower perceptions of ethical leadership to positive job satisfaction, job performance, job engagement, work effort, organizational identification, and personal well-being as well as a negative relationship to job stress. Research also supports that follower perception of ethical leadership is positively associated with trust in the leader, leader honesty, interactional fairness, leader effectiveness, and satisfaction with the leader (for a complete discussion of these findings, see Bedi et al., 2016). Additionally, there appears to be a trickle-down effect. Followers are more likely to act ethically if their leaders act ethically (Wang et al., 2018).

If the negative impact of "leading" in a manner that fails to engage the bigger picture impact of the crisis is so well-documented and the benefits of ethical leadership so great, why do we continue to see so many instances of unethical leadership? Research indicates one primary reason is biological. As McNulty and Marcus (2020) state, "The human brain is programmed to narrow its focus in the face of a threat. It's an evolutionary survival mechanism designed for self-protection" (para. 5). The human brain, however, is also capable of learning and adapting new strategies of behavior based on exposure to novel experiences (Kahneman, 2011). A situation becomes less threatening and our focus less narrow, the more prepared we are to adapt to unique circumstances. The same thinking can apply to organizations. As Pauchant and Mitroff (1992) point out, for organizations some amount of crisis is inevitable, but many instances of crisis can be mitigated or prevented. These mitigation and prevention efforts cannot be developed once the crisis event has occurred, only before. Leaders and their organizations will suffer during the crisis event and in its aftermath if they are not already leading in a manner during "normal times" that can be successful during crisis times (McNulty & Marcus, 2020). Put simply, if leaders are not leading ethically when not in crisis, they have almost no chance of doing so when in crisis. To achieve ethical crisis leadership, then, organizations must create an environment that mitigates the likelihood of leaders becoming autocratic and being ruled by their ethical blind spots. Complexity thinking and adaptive space are two constructs that can help leaders and organizations do just that.

## Complexity Thinking

Complexity thinking is a mode of analysis that embraces the "emergent, interactive dynamic" of situations and behaviors within a system (Uhl-Bien et al., 2007). Complexity thinking is a central component of complexity science, which "is the study of dynamic behaviors of complexly interacting, interdependent, and adaptive agents under conditions of internal and external pressure" (Marion, 2008, p. 3). Uhl-Bien and Arena (2017) describe complexity by its "rich interconnectivity," arguing that a system is complex when "things interact, they change one another in unexpected and irreversible ways" (p. 9). They further differentiate *complexity* from *complicated* by stating, "Complicated systems may have many parts but when the parts interact they do not change each other" whereas the components of complex systems are "fundamentally changed" by their interactions in that the "system is not decomposable back to its original parts" (Uhl-Bien & Arena, 2017, pp. 9–10). Most, if not all, organizations and institutions fit the definition of complex systems, which is why complexity science's appeal and usefulness has expanded beyond the natural sciences and is used by fields as diverse as philosophy, computer science, human resources, and now, leadership studies (Arena, 2018; Dugan, 2017).

There are several leadership theories that embrace elements of complexity science, all of which fit under the umbrella term of "complex system leadership theory" (for discussions of the major theories and models, see Dugan, 2017). Each of these theories and models emphasize different points, but they are united by the fundamental idea that our world and its organizations and institutions are becoming increasingly complex and that previous approaches to understanding leadership were ill-equipped to understand and embrace the full-scope of that complexity (Uhl-Bien & Arena, 2017). In short, according to complex system leadership theory, complex leadership problems should be met with complex thinking. This complexity even extends to how the field considers the concept of *leadership*. In complex system leadership theory, leadership is not synonymous with leader, nor is it a top–down understanding of behaviors in connection with situations. Rather, leadership is an "emergent, interactive dynamic that is productive of adaptive outcomes" (Uhl-Bien et al., 2007, p. 299), while leaders are "individuals who act in ways that influence this dynamic and the outcomes" (Uhl-Bien et al., 2007, p. 299). This move toward complexity in defining leadership was a rejection of popular "Industrial Era" managerial leadership theories as they seemed incongruous with "Knowledge Era" leadership which values knowledge and ideas as our greatest commodity (Manville & Ober, 2003; Uhl-Bien et al., 2007).

Leadership, in this consideration, is a shared process by everyone involved in understanding and acting upon the challenges a constantly changing context requires, making it a perfect approach for acting ethically during a crisis. Interestingly, and perhaps surprisingly, not all complex system leadership theories directly address ethics and values, and, frankly, they are weaker for it. Nonetheless, these theories have a sense of ethics built into their design, whether explicitly articulated or not. Complex leadership theories engage with and understand the needs and ideas of appropriate stakeholders. For that engagement to work, a structure, however informal it may be, must have a care and concern for those engaging in the work. In seeking the solutions to complex problems these theories require a structure that engages interdisciplinarity thought and diversity of ideas and gives voice to those without power. Power and decision-making are not condensed at the top but diffused across stakeholders to the extent its hierarchy affords.

A move towards complexity thinking must include an organization's ethical values at its core. This move acknowledges that staying true to those values (or allowing them to evolve as new pressures dictate) is incredibly difficult in our increasingly complex world, thus requiring leadership approaches that can rise to that level of complexity. For organizations and institutions, there is no pressure more complex and in need of ethical leadership than a crisis.

## Adaptive Space

A central requirement for complexity thinking to occur within an organization is what complexity theorists call a "complex adaptive system." Uhl-Bien and Arena (2017) define a complex adaptive system (CAS) as "a dynamic system that is able to adapt in and evolve with a changing environment... [I]t is a collection of dynamic networks of interactions with each network comprised of a collection of many agents acting in parallel" (p. 11). Uhl-Bien and Arena (2017) note that in the natural sciences, "complex adaptive systems are described as having no centralized control and no fixed order. They are self-organizing, continually adapting and changing in relation to environmental conditions" (p. 11). This is not true of how most organizations, including higher education institutions, are formed and structured. Organizations and the systems in which they exist were designed to have a hierarchy. Hierarchies require a "chain of command" and hierarchical leaders (Uhl-Bien & Arena, 2017) and it is extremely difficult to remove a hierarchy once it is in place. With hierarchy comes bureaucracy, and bureaucracies do not deal well with change, innovation, and adaptability. These constructs lead an organization toward disorder or, at least, uncertainty, and bureaucracies want order (Uhl-Bien & Arena, 2017). Our institutions and organizations are not going to get rid of their hierarchies, so instead, complex leadership theories call for an embrace of the tension between bureaucracy (order) and uncertainty (disorder), or as Uhl-Bien and Arena (2017, 2018) put it, not privileging either the operational system (order) or the entrepreneurial system (disorder).

Some complex leadership theories acknowledge that change, uncertainty, and the need for adaptation is not only hard for bureaucratic systems, but for individuals within those systems (Heifetz, 1994; Heifetz & Linksy, 2002; Ospina & Foldy, 2010). Individuals within, not just between, layers of organizational structure can resist adaptive change because it makes those individuals confront potentially problematic elements of their values or in areas where their actions do not match their espoused values (Heifetz, 1994; Heifetz & Linksy, 2002). Embracing the need for change and engaging in this kind of "adaptive work," necessary as it may be, is not always easy or enjoyable (Dugan, 2017). It is, however, in confronting and carefully balancing these tensions that exist within individuals and across organizations that complexity thinking can be fostered and, eventually, implemented (Heifetz, 1994; Heifetz & Linsky, 2002), thus establishing a new sense of order. For "productive tension" to be realized, leaders let go of some of the authority (and power) typically associated with their positions and create the structures that diffuse some of that authority to the collective group and *enable* (Arena, 2018; Heifetz, 1994; Uhl-Bien & Arena, 2017; Uhl-Bien et al., 2007) complexity thinking to occur and stakeholders must be willing to engage in this taxing work. This process may happen organically in nature, but in organizations it must be intentionally designed in the form of adaptive space.

Adaptive space is an environment that allows for the free flow of ideas through "discovery, development, diffusion, and disruption" (Arena, 2018, p. 18). Adaptive space constitutes "the relational, emotional, and sometimes physical space necessary" (Arena, 2018, p. 9) for those ideas to be formed and shared across an organization. The relationships and connections that are formed in this space transcend the silos that often exist within organizations and foster the interdisciplinary spread of knowledge and ideas (Heifetz, 1994; Uhl-Bien & Arena, 2018). In short, it is the space that makes complexity thinking possible. For that complexity thinking to take place, leaders have to embrace the fact that it is not their job to have all of the answers and then instruct their subordinates on how to carry out their orders. Their job is to enable adaptive space (Arena & Uhl-Bien, 2018). The remainder of this section will discuss the conditions necessary for enabling adaptive space and explain some of the organizational, ethical, stakeholder, and individual components of adaptive space that make it so challenging and rewarding to perform.

***Group Cohesion***

To fully realize complexity thinking in adaptive space, group cohesion is required. Group cohesion is "how connected an agent is with others in a group" (Uhl-Bien & Arena, 2017, p. 12). There is a wealth of research that effective groups or teams lead to favorable outcomes for organizations, including, but not limited to greater productivity, better decision-making and problem-solving, and greater innovation and creativity (see Kozlowski & Ilgen, 2006; Parker, 1990). If a group is cohesive, both in terms of task cohesion (understanding and agreeing upon what the group is being asked to accomplish) and interpersonal cohesion (trust, openness in communication, effective perspective-taking, and group pride), they will be more likely to share information, engage in meaning-making, form mutual understandings of issues, iterate and test their ideas, be open to giving and receiving constructive feedback, and avoid the pitfalls of groupthink (Dugan, 2017; Johnson, 2018; Kozlowski & Ilgen, 2006; Ospina & Foldy, 2010; Uhl-Bien & Arena, 2017). Additionally, groups are more effective the more diverse they are, both in terms of diverse individual expertise and social identity diversity (Phillips et al., 2014), making the engagement of an array of interdisciplinary stakeholders a crucial component of group formation. The closer a group can get to achieving this type of cohesion and this level of diversity, the more likely the group is to produce creative solutions (Phillips et al., 2014; Uhl-Bien & Arena, 2017) and weather increased levels of stress (Dugan, 2017; Heifetz & Linsky, 2002). The challenge, though, is in maintaining this cohesion within groups under times of pressure, like during a crisis. Heifetz and Linsky (2002) call for designing "a space . . . within which people can tackle tough, sometimes divisive questions without flying apart" (p. 102). A major way to create that space and foster the diversity needed for effective complexity thinking comes in the linkages created through brokerage.

***Brokerage***

Brokerage refers to the connections formed between groups and creates the "conditions to facilitate discovery and introduction of novel ideas and help amplify them for scale across a system" (Uhl-Bien & Arena, 2017, p. 12).

Brokerage must be fostered by leaders. They have to enable individuals, perhaps even by targeting specific individuals best suited for the role in a certain situation, to build these connections by giving them early access to information, cross-pollinating membership in established groups, or just simply creating the mechanism for those without positional authority to *safely* share ideas with those that do (Arena & Uhl-Bien, 2018; Heifetz, 1994, Uhl-Bien & Arena, 2017). Protection of those without power or authority is crucial to enabling the formation and expression of creative ideas. Individuals must believe they will not face negative repercussions for stepping outside of the normal, operational structure, otherwise, there is little value and great risk in their doing so (Heifetz et al., 2009). Through brokerage, individuals can realize they have overlapping ideas, interests, values, and identities, and form new groups to consider pressures associated with what they share. They can create the rich interconnectivity needed for complexity thinking, and the more of these interrelated, informal groups that have been created up and down an organization, the more prepared an organization will be when adaptive pressures, particularly in the form of a crisis, arise.

### *Adaptive Pressures*

Adaptive pressures are what force a system or organization out of equilibrium and promote the productive tension needed to enable complexity thinking and adaptive space. These pressures are caused by events, either internal or external to the organization, but that have the potential to have a significant impact on the organization (Arena & Uhl-Bien, 2018). To realize an organization is facing an adaptive pressure, leaders must be able to step outside of situations, gain greater perspective on them, and then articulate the challenges of that situation in such a manner that work of adaptive space can begin (Arena & Uhl-Bien, 2018; Heifetz & Linsky, 2002). This type of monitoring practice is an ethical action. Comprehensive ethical crisis leadership cannot occur if leaders are unaware that an adaptive pressure is building that may lead to a crisis. While challenges will come and go and specific adaptive spaces will open and close, adaptive pressures are almost always present. Ethical crisis leadership requires leaders and stakeholders to be vigilant in monitoring for adaptive pressures and ready to engage them when the moment calls.

A pandemic, like COVID-19, was, unfortunately, a perfect example of an adaptive pressure and the "moment calling." The next section will explore how complexity thinking and adaptive space could have been engaged by higher education institutions to lead ethically on the question of whether campuses should have reopened during the COVID-19 crisis.

## HIGHER EDUCATION IN CRISIS: SHOULD CAMPUSES HAVE REOPENED?

By the middle of March 2020, most campuses around the country closed alongside most other institutions and businesses that were "non-essential" and did not require working in person. The decision to initially close campuses was, in the scope of this pandemic, an easy one to make in that it was the only choice. Collectively, we knew next to nothing about COVID-19 other than it could be transmitted between people and that it was deadly. The decision to close campuses was, of course, fraught, but unavoidable. It was the decision of if, when, and how to reopen campuses that truly called for ethical crisis leadership and provided the real adaptive pressure of this crisis, that sent colleges and universities into disequilibrium, and in need of engaging complexity thinking and adaptive space.

### Applying Complexity Thinking and Adaptive Space to Campus Reopening

Institutions of higher education are ethically obligated to prepare for the next crisis. A major element of that preparation is the crafting of a crisis plan. All crises are unexpected, but some can be specifically planned for. In the case of an active shooter on campus, for example, the crisis plan can tell everyone exactly what to do and how to carry out their role. Most crises, however, are both unexpected and ambiguous, and so the crisis plan is less about what to do and more about how to figure out what to do. Complexity thinking and adaptive space get at the "how." For them to be successfully engaged during a crisis, though, they must be cultivated throughout the institution and across time so that stakeholders have trust in each other and their administration. This means they must be part of the everyday running of the institution—even when it is not in crisis. This can only be undertaken, however, if an institution's leadership and governance structure create and foster the environment in which it can happen.

#### *Non-Autocratic Governance: A Necessary Antecedent*

If your university president or your governing board never posed the question of "Should campus reopen?" but instead told the campus community, "Campus is reopening. Classes will happen in-person. Figure it out." Then, complexity thinking will not be occurring, adaptive space will not be created, ethical decision-making has been compromised, and ethical crisis leadership has already failed even though the crisis is far from over.

In the 1960s, shared governance became the prevailing governing principle for U.S. colleges and universities and was "intended to foster constructive joint thought and action, both within the institutional structure and in protection of its integrity against improper intrusions" (American Association of University Professors [AAUP], 2021, para. 1). In general, then, "shared governance is... complex; it is a delicate balance between faculty and staff participation in planning and decision-making processes, on the one hand, and administrative accountability on the other" (Olson, 2009, para. 6).

Since the 1960s, however, the principle of shared governance has been understood quite differently by different institutions and at different times (Eckel & Trowers, 2018). Crucially, shared governance does not mean that all stakeholders share in the decision-making of institutions. As Olson (2009) puts it:

> The truth is that all legal authority in any university originates from one place and one place only: Its governing board... Typically, the board then formally delegates authority over the day-to-day operation of the institution... to the president, who, in turn, may delegate authority over certain parts of university management to other university officials. (para. 7)

Hierarchical governance structures are embedded in higher education institutions and are not going away, but they do not need to be an impediment to enabling complexity thinking and adaptive space. These structures cause problems for institutional stakeholders when the individuals in the positions of authority in that structure minimize the role of shared governance (Ekler & Trowers, 2018; Kezar & Eckel, 2004) from one of interdisciplinary collaboration in decision-making to one of information gathering for decision-making (Kezar et al., 2008; Kezar & Fries-Britt, 2020), or, in its most autocratic, top–down, form, no role in decision-making at all. This lack of, or minimizing of, collaboration in decision-making effectively rules out leaders enabling stakeholders to form networks and broker relationships. Instead of fostering ideation, it stifles the possibility of change (Siemens et al., 2018). There are definite concerns that this type of autocratic governance has become deeply rooted in some higher education institutions (Brown, 2021; Kezar, 2012; Kezar & Fries-Britt, 2020; Siemens et al., 2018). While there is and will continue to be much debate concerning the validity of this perceived trend, in institutions where this type of leadership occurred throughout the pandemic crisis, complexity thinking and the creation of adaptive space did not, and the road ahead is likely to be fraught and filled with an unhealthy level of tension.

#### *Know Your Institution's Core Values*

Every college and university has values. Those values will be articulated through vision and mission statements and realized through the enactment of strategic plans. While each set of values will be unique from school to school, these institutions generally have values centered on supporting growth, development, and opportunity for students, and likely, for the faculty, staff, administrators, and the community, as well (Blumenstyk, 2015; Siemens et al., 2018; Thompson, 2014). Everyone in an organization engaging in complexity thinking, from the leaders on down, must know what it values. For universities and colleges, those values must guide the ethical crisis leadership and decision-making concerning campus reopening.

#### *Identifying Stakeholders, Enabling Agents, and Fostering Group Cohesion*

To enable complexity thinking and adaptive space, college and university leadership would have needed to first identify the stakeholders impacted by the COVID-19 crisis and who might be useful in undertaking the work of best dealing with it. They needed to enable stakeholders to form interdisciplinary cohorts. It was clear early in the pandemic that the crisis consisted of several overlapping crisis types. COVID-19 represented a public health crisis, a mental health crisis, and a financial crisis, and it was likely to impact marginalized communities (which has, sadly, clearly come to fruition). The stakeholders for the public health portion of this crisis would at least include outside experts on disease control and epidemiology, internal experts on disease control and epidemiology-colleges and universities must never forget that they are filled with experts and that those experts can be brought to task to solve real world problems—student affairs professionals, facilities management, ethicists, and pedagogy specialists. The mental health crisis portion would require stakeholders from student affairs, counseling and advising services, residence life, and internal and external experts on mental health. The financial crisis portion would require the university's finance office, the financial aid office, budget officers from units across campus, governing boards, alumni boards or foundations, and internal and external experts on higher education finance. Additionally, each of these crisis portions should contain experts on diversity, inclusion, and social justice, community representatives, the legal department, the communication department, IT, staff, faculty, and, yes, students (often the forgotten stakeholder). Finally, while each of these groups is clearly multidisciplinary, it is imperative to include experts in interdisciplinarity and interdisciplinary leadership who can speak across boundaries (Repko, 2012). These burgeoning networks need individuals who can understand and interpret the languages spoken by different stakeholder groups, so that meaning-making and ideation can occur (Ospina & Foldy, 2010; Repko, 2012). These individuals may also eventually serve as the brokers as networks within and between each of these crisis portions begin to form ideas that should be shared more broadly.

It is important to note that public health, mental health, finance, and the inequitable treatment of marginalized groups were all pressurized issues, if not full-blown crises, on college campuses before the pandemic hit. This may sound like 20/20 hindsight, but leaders needed to be enabling these stakeholder groups and their agents to create adaptive space and networks around these issues long before this crisis. Enabling complexity thinking and adaptive space must be practiced and cultivated; it has to be part of the culture of an organization (Marcus et al., 2019; McNulty & Marcus, 2020; Siemens et al., 2018). If it was not, it is far more likely that colleges and universities fell back on more autocratic and less ethical decision-making approaches when the pandemic crisis began.

It is important to reiterate that the agents representing these stakeholder groups are not being placed into networks by leaders. These are not formal structures. In complexity leadership, leaders enable stakeholders or their agents to form these networks when they detect pressures. In describing how not to handle race-based crises on campus Kezar and Fries-Britt (2020, p. 10) describe a common practice to confronting these issues where administrative leaders set up a task force, collect data, and write a report with recommendations. This is not what enabling complexity thinking and adaptive space looks like. In many ways, it is the opposite. In the approach Kezar and Fries-Britt (2020) describe, the leaders have created a formal group (the task force) with specific charges and a clear delineation of their place within the hierarchy. Instead of embracing the pressure, the leaders turned to administrative leadership and bureaucracy (Uhl-Bien et al., 2007). Additionally, however considered the administration was in determining the membership for the task force, it will ultimately be limited by who is on it. Colleges and universities are filled with excellent, diverse minds well-equipped to generate novel ideas (Siemens et al., 2018). Leaders determining who is best to serve on a task force, again, however well-meaning those leaders may be, is an exercise in control and does not allow for bottom-up innovation (Kezar, 2012; Siemens et al., 2018).

Compounding that issue is that groups that are not self-organized do not have an established sense of group cohesion. Any group has the potential to go through the stages of group development (Tuckman, 1965) and develop that cohesion, but it will not be present immediately. Pressures, in general, and crises specifically, require speed in creative ideation and ethical decision-making (Seeger et al., 2003) and group cohesion is needed for the meaning-making that leads to that ideation and decision-making.

Leaders who take this task force approach in response to the crisis will not end up creating a new sense of order and equilibrium but will more likely maintain the existing order through an exercise in control and muted ideation. What may have seemed like the safe course of action, will instead cause the tension to grow, foster a greater lack of trust between the administration and other stakeholders and could exacerbate and extend the crisis (Kezar & Fries-Britt, 2020). Colleges and universities that chose this approach with the COVID-19 pandemic, will likely be headed back to campus with some very disaffected stakeholders.

***Constructing Knowledge and Brokering Ideas***

If higher education leaders are open to the formation of these networks, they have to also be open to enabling transparency. Transparency is a mark of good ethical leadership (Johnson, 2018), but transparency in this context really means opening the books, sharing information, and providing constructive feedback (Siemens et al., 2018). Knowledge construction and the brokering of ideas cannot happen without it. For example, if the pandemic crisis is broken down into the crisis networks described in the previous section, but those networks are not privy to the same information and are not interconnected, they will very likely arrive at different answers to the question of reopening campus. Consider these simplified network solution examples:

- *Problem:* The public health networks determine that the best course of action is for everyone to shelter in place off campus.

  *Solution:* Classes can be moved online. Faculty can switch their classes to online and be quickly trained on how to use those systems. Most non-faculty employees can also work from home as there will be no need to have face-to-face interactions with faculty, students, and administrators. It will cost some money to get everyone the technology needed to do this, but it is worth the cost. They will be safe. The communities around the school will be safer, too, as there will be no interaction between students and residents. It is true that not everyone has a stable "home" life to return to, but it is clearly the safest option given the density of people and extensive interactions typical of the campus.
- *Problem:* The COVID-19 pandemic will exacerbate mental health crises.

  *Solution:* The mental health networks determine that the extent of the mental health crisis is so severe that it would be best to keep some portions of the campus open to aid students in need of mental health services or related services, like food, shelter, and personal interaction. This will be particularly valuable to traditionally marginalized students who are at greatest risk for mental health issues during this time. For many students and faculty, it is probably best to minimize the risk of exposure to the virus and spending extended periods of time in enclosed rooms. Greater care should be taken to reach out and connect with students and coworkers. Expenditures will need to be made to physically safeguard the parts of campus that are going to open and for hiring and technology that will enable a more robust online counseling presence in students' lives. This level of interaction may lead to more infection than keeping campus closed, but it will lower the mental health strain for those most susceptible.

- *Problem:* The pandemic resulted in a significant financial loss.

  *Solution:* The finance networks determine that the campus has to open at as full a capacity as possible. This not only includes in-person classes, but dorms, food halls, the gym, library, and sports venues. The operating budget minus any tuition and fees we gave back for finishing the Spring 2020 semester online and the projected loss in enrollment for the fall due to students not wanting to pay full tuition to be online and not paying room and board will put us in a deficit that forces administration to "let go" of a significant portion of the workforce. If the campus was to remain closed for three semesters, the loss in revenue would likely cause the institution to close for good. There will be costs to make the physical plant as safe as possible, so some employees will still lose their jobs, and this will lead to increased infection rates among students, faculty, staff, their families, and the community, but this is the way to ensure the long-term sustainability of the institution.

Each network's decision is imperfect but is the best decision each can make based on data, ideas, and perceptions available to them. Each decision becomes more imperfect and appears less ethical considering the data, ideas and perceptions of the other networks. Because these networks, and the information made available to each, was siloed, they are not capable of making the most ethical decision. The lack of transparency in sharing information and having constructive feedback loops has led to insufficient knowledge construction and complexity thinking has not been fully enabled. There is an ethical obligation that these networks be allowed and encouraged to work interdisciplinarily and across networks to gather the most data to make the best decisions moving forward. If brokers from each of these networks created linkages between the networks there would be the adaptive space to fully enable complexity thinking. Every campus has individuals positioned to take on these roles. There are interdisciplinary scholars who focus on race and public health. There are students who are also staff. There are administrators who are also counselors. There are board members with a background in epidemiology. Engaging these intersectional identities serve agents well in enabling brokerage. These questions may still have a public health, mental health, or financial focus, but the rich interconnectedness created through enabling these networks now tries to answer the reopening campus question by asking (and eventually) answering more nuanced questions in a collaborative, interdisciplinary, and ethical manner. These questions might include:

- *Public Health and Safety:* How do we safely have students on campus? What is the science telling us about interpersonal interactions? Should there be a mask mandate? Should we have smaller class sizes? In bigger rooms? Should we have more hybrid classes? Should (and would) faculty, temporarily, change their workload plans to accommodate teaching more smaller classes? Should classes be held outside or in open-air environments? Should we change the length of classes? Should we change the length of courses? Of the semester? Should facilities be updated for better ventilation? Would technology and teacher training improve the online learning experience? Should students serve as ambassadors of safety protocol? Should we put significant limits on community interaction to safeguard communities from the influx of people a campus reopening would create? Should there be significant penalties for not adhering public health protocols?
- *Mental Health:* How do we support our stakeholders' mental health during this crisis, whether the campus is open or not? Should we eliminate the limit on counseling sessions? Should we have a 24-hour video counseling hotline? Should we have free, pre-prepared meals for anyone who needs one? Should we create a free "store" of necessary items (food, toilet paper, diapers, etc.) for anyone in the community who needs them, built on community donations? Should we create peer-support groups for students? Staff? Faculty? Administrators? Should we form mentoring relationships between faculty/staff and students, particularly targeted toward first generation students and students of color?
- *Financial:* How much are we willing to spend on COVID-19-related public health improvements and where is that money coming from? What are the alternatives to "letting go" of people? How do we raise revenue and/or cut costs without impacting employment? Should we change the way our endowment is spent? Do we have donors we can access for operating funds? What grants can we apply for? What non-profit or corporate partnerships can we form? Should we take temporary furloughs or pay cuts? Should we postpone infrastructure spending and redistribute those funds? Should we be transparent with students about why costs may need to go up even while they are taking classes online? What non-employee, operational cuts can be made?

Most of these questions, and many more, were probably asked at campuses around the country, but who was enabled to answer them? If the answer to that question was not "everyone," then complexity thinking and adaptive space were not truly engaged. Ethical crisis leadership does not always result in the best outcomes or even good outcomes. There was no choice a college or university could make that would have benefitted all its stakeholders fully or equally. All that we should ask, then, of higher education's leaders is to enable an environment that continuously allows us the opportunity to discover the most ethical choice based on the data and information and then grieve, heal, and learn together.

## CONCLUSION

For all the horrors the COVID-19 pandemic has brought, most colleges and universities are going to survive this crisis. That's a good thing. But, will the leaders of these institutions have learned anything from it? Survival is a necessary but not sufficient condition for thriving, complex organizations. Most colleges and universities will not have thrived during the pandemic and their leaders will have disaffected stakeholders on their hands who do not feel valued. The postcrisis phase is when leaders reflect on how the crisis was handled and determine what they need to improve about their organization before the next crisis hits. It is never too late, then, to reengage values, build back trust, embrace interdisciplinarity, and start enabling complexity thinking and adaptive space for ethical crisis leadership. After all, the next crisis is only a matter of time.

## REFERENCES

Al-Sharafi, A. G., & Al-Rubaíey, F. (2020). Managing stakeholder conflicting expectations in higher education: A hybrid approach. *Journal of Educational and Psychological Studies, 14*(4), 627–641.

American Association of University Professors. (2021). *Statement on government of colleges and universities.* https://www.aaup.org/report/statement-government-colleges-and-universities

Arena, M. J. (2018). *Adaptive space: How GM and other companies are positively disrupting themselves and transforming into agile organizations.* McGraw-Hill Education.

Arena, M. J., & Uhl-Bien, M. (2016). Complexity leadership theory: Shifting from human capital to social capital. *People + Strategy, 39*(2), 22–27.

Argenti, P. (2002). *Crisis communication: Lessons from 9/11.* Harvard Business Review.

Banaji, M. R., & Greenwald, A. G. (2013). *Blindspot: Hidden biases of good people.* Delacorte.

Bauman, D. (2021, April 19). Here's who was hit hardest by higher ed's pandemic-driven job losses. *Chronicle of Higher Education.* https://www.chronicle.com/article/heres-who-was-hit-hardest-by-higher-eds-pandemic-driven-job-losses

Bazerman, M. H., & Tenbrunsel, A. E. (2011). *Blindspots: Why we fail to do what's right and what to do about it.* Princeton University Press.

Bedi, A., Alpaslan, C. M., & Green, S. (2016). A meta-analytic review of ethical leadership outcomes and moderators. *Journal of Business Ethics, 139,* 517–536. https://doi.org/10.1007/s10551-015-2625-1

Bennis, W. G., & Nanus, B. (2012). *Leaders: The strategies for taking charge.* Harper Business.

Bloomquist, C. D., Georges, L., Ford, D. J., & Moss Breen, J. (2018). Interdisciplinary leadership practices in graduate leadership education programs. *Journal of Leadership Studies, 12*(2), 60–63.

Blumenstyk, G. (2015). *American higher education in crisis? What everyone needs to know.* Oxford University Press.

Brown, S. (2021, March 11). The impossible conversation. *The Chronicle of Higher Education.* https://www.chronicle.com/article/the-impossible-conversation

Carroll, A. E. (2021, January 31). The colleges that took the pandemic seriously. *The Atlantic.* https://www.theatlantic.com/ideas/archive/2021/01/colleges-took-pandemic-seriously/617879/

Center on Budget and Policy Priorities. (2021, April 22). *Tracking the COVID-19 recession's effects on food, housing, and employment hardship.* https://www.cbpp.org/research/poverty-and-inequality/tracking-the-covid-19-economys-effects-on-food-housing-and

Centers for Disease Control. (2021, August 10). COVID Data Tracker. Retrieved August 10, 2021, from https://covid.cdc.gov/covid-data-tracker/#datatracker-home

Dugan, J. (2017). *Leadership theory: Cultivating critical perspectives.* John Wiley & Sons.

Eckel, P. D., & Trower, C. A. (2019). *Practical wisdom: Thinking differently about college and university governance.* Stylus Publishing.

Eisenberg, D., Ketchen Lipson, S., Heinze, J., & Zhou, S. (2020). *The healthy minds study: Fall 2020 data report.* The Healthy Minds Network. https://healthymindsnetwork.org/wp-content/uploads/2021/02/HMS-Fall-2020-National-Data-Report.pdf

Ellis, L. (2021, February 17). New diversity. Striving for prestige. Limited money. Meet the 'broke' research universities. *Chronicle of Higher Education.* https://www.chronicle.com/article/new-diversity-striving-for-prestige-limited-money-meet-the-broke-research-universities

Fischer, K., & Ellis, L. (2021, January 27). The heavy cost of an empty campus. *The Chronicle of Higher Education.* https://www.chronicle.com/article/the-specter-of-semesters-past

Freeman, R. E. (1984). *Strategic management: A stakeholder approach.* Cambridge University Press.

Freeman, R. E., Wicks, A. C., & Parmar, B. (2004). Stakeholder theory and "the corporate objective revisited." *Organization Science 15*(3), 364–369.

Gardner, L. (2021, February 15). The great contraction. *The Chronicle of Higher Education.* https://www.chronicle.com/article/the-great-contraction

Heifetz, R. A. (1994). *Leadership without easy answers.* Harvard University Press.

Heifetz, R. A., & Linsky, M. (2002). *Leadership on the line: Staying alive through the dangers of leading*. Harvard Business School Press.

Heifetz, R., Grashow, A., & Linsky, M. (2009). Leadership in a (permanent) crisis. *Harvard Business Review, 87*(8), 62–70.

Hoover, E. (2021, March 25). Decline in students' going straight to college in 2020 was sharp—but not catastrophic. *The Chronicle of Higher Education*. https://www.chronicle.com/blogs/live-coronavirus-updates/decline-in-students-going-straight-to-college-in-2020-was-sharp-but-not-catastrophic

Huber, S. (2020, September 10). As colleges move classes online, families rebel against the cost. *New York Times*. https://www.nytimes.com/2020/08/15/us/covid-college-tuition.html

Johnson, C. E. (2018). *Meeting the ethical challenges of leadership: Casting light or shadow* (6th edition). SAGE Publications.

Kahneman, D. (2011). *Thinking, fast and slow*. Penguin.

Kantamneni, N. (2020). The impact of the COVID-19 pandemic on marginalized populations in the United States: A research agenda. *Journal of Vocational Behavior, 119*, 1–5.

Kezar, A. (2012). Bottom-up/top-down leadership: Contradiction or hidden phenomenon. *The Journal of Higher Education, 83*(5), 725–760.

Kezar, A., & Eckel, P. D. (2004). Meeting today's governance challenges: A synthesis of the literature and examination of a future agenda for scholarship. *The Journal of Higher Education, 75*(4), 371–399.

Kezar, A., Eckel, P. D., Contreras-McGavin, M., & Quaye, S. J. (2008). Creating a web of support: An important leadership strategy for advancing campus diversity. *Higher Education, 55*(1), 69–92.

Kezar, A., & Fries-Britt, S. (2020). Navigating a campus racial crisis: Building capacity, leading through trauma and the recovery process. *Change: The Magazine of Higher Learning, 52*(2), 89–93.

Kozlowski, S. W. J., & Ilgen, D. R. (2006). Enhancing the effectiveness of work groups and teams. *Psychological Sciences in the Public Interest, 7*(3), 77–124.

Laidler, J. (2020, October 28). COVID's triple whammy for black students. *The Harvard Gazette*. https://news.harvard.edu/gazette/story/2020/10/covid-carries-triple-risks-for-college-students-of-color/

Laplume, A. O., Sonpar, K., & Litz, R. A. (2008). Stakeholder theory: Reviewing a theory that moves us. *Journal of Management, 34*(6), 1152–1189.

Lapworth, S. (2004). Arresting decline in shared governance: Towards a flexible model for academic participation. *Higher Education Quarterly, 58*(4), 299–314.

Maguad, B. A. (2018). Managing the system of higher education: Competition or collaboration? *Education, 138*(3), 229–238.

Manville, B., & Ober, J. (2003). *Beyond empowerment: Building a company of citizens*. Harvard Business Review.

Marcus, L. J., McNulty, E. J., Henderson, J. M., & Dorn, B. G. (2019). *You're it: Crisis, change, and how to lead when it matters most*. Public Affairs.

Marion, R. (2008). Complexity theory for organizations and organizational leadership. In M. Uhl-Bien & R. Marion (Eds.), *Complexity leadership part 1: Conceptual foundations* (pp. 1–15). Information Age Publishing.

McNulty, E. J., & Marcus, L. J. (2020). *Are you leading through the crisis . . . or managing the response?* Harvard Business Review. https://hbr.org/2020/03/are-you-leading-through-the-crisis-or-managing-the-response

Natow, R. S. (2021, March 1). Why haven't more colleges closed? *The Chronicle of Higher Education.* https://www.chronicle.com/article/why-havent-more-colleges-closed

Nichols, C., Chatterjee Hayden, S., & Trendler, C. (2020). *4 behaviors that help leaders manage a crisis.* Harvard Business Review. https://hbr.org/2020/04/4-behaviors-that-help-leaders-manage-a-crisis

Noddings, N. (2002). *Educating moral people.* Teachers College Press.

Nordberg, T. H., & Andreassen, T. A. (2020). Challenging professional control? Reforming higher education through stakeholder involvement. *Journal of Education and Work, 33*(2), 169–183.

Olson, G. A. (2009, July 23). Exactly what is 'shared governance'? *The Chronicle of Higher Education.* https://www.chronicle.com/article/exactly-what-is-shared-governance/

Ospina, S., & Foldy, E. (2010). Building bridges from the margins: The work of leadership in social change organizations. *The Leadership Quarterly, 21*(2), 292–307.

Panchal, N., Kamal, R., Cox, C., & Garfield, R. (2021). *The implications of COVID-19 for mental health and substance abuse.* KFF. https://www.kff.org/coronavirus-covid-19/issue-brief/the-implications-of-covid-19-for-mental-health-and-substance-use/

Parker, G. M. (1990). *Team player and teamwork: The new competitive business strategy.* Wiley.

Pauchant, T. C., & Mitroff, I. (1992). *Transforming the crisis-prone organization: Preventing individual, organizational, and environmental tragedies.* Jossey-Bass.

Pearson, C. M., & Clair, J. A. (1998). Reframing crisis management. *The Academy of Management Review, 23*(1), 59–76.

Petriglieri, G. (2020, April 22). The psychology behind effective crisis leadership. *Harvard Business Review.* https://hbr.org/2020/04/the-psychology-behind-effective-crisis-leadership

Pettit, E. (2021, April 5). 'Anti-American', pushing 'Marxism', and more: Do you recognize your college here? *The Chronicle of Higher Education.* https://www.chronicle.com/article/anti-american-pushing-marxism-and-more-do-you-recognize-your-college-here

Phillips, K. W., Medin, D., Lee, C. D., Bang, M., Bishop, S., & Lee, D. N. (2014). How diversity works. *Scientific American, 311*(4), 42–47.

Repko, A. F. (2012). *Interdisciplinary research: Process and theory.* SAGE Publications.

Seeger, M. W., Sellnow, T. L., & Ulmer, R. R. (2003). *Communication and organizational crisis.* Praeger.

Siemens, G., Dawson, S., & Eshleman, K. (2018). Complexity: A leader's framework for understanding and managing change in higher education. *EDUCAUSE Review, 53*(6), 27–42.

Stripling, J. (2021a, February 15). For town and gown, a pandemic pressure test. *The Chronicle of Higher Education.* https://www.chronicle.com/article/for-town-gown-a-pandemic-pressure-test

Stripling, J. (2021b, February 24). Lower pay. Less job security. More COVID-19 risk? *Chronicle of Higher Education.* https://www.chronicle.com/article/lower-pay-less-job-security-more-covid-19-risk

Thompson, R. J. (2014). *Beyond reason and tolerance: The purpose and practice of higher education.* Oxford University Press.

Tuckman, B. W. (1965). Developmental sequence in small groups. *Psychological Bulletin, 63*(6), 384–399.

Uhl-Bien, M., & Arena, M. (2017). Complexity Leadership: Enabling people and organizations for adaptability. *Organizational Dynamics, 46*(1), 9–20.

Uhl-Bien, M., & Arena, M. (2018). Leadership for organizational adaptability: A theoretical synthesis and integrative framework. *The Leadership Quarterly, 29*(1), 89–104.

Uhl-Bien, M., Marion, R., & McKelvey, B. (2007). Complexity leadership theory: Shifting leadership from the industrial age to the knowledge era. *The Leadership Quarterly, 18*(4), 298–318.

Velasquez, M., Andre, C., Shanks, T., & Meyer, M. J. (2010). *What is ethics?* Markkula Foundation. (Original work published 1987) https://www.scu.edu/ethics/ethics-resources/ethical-decision-making/what-is-ethics/

Wang, X., Hegde, S., Son, C., Keller, B., Smith, A., & Sasangohar, F. (2020). Investigating mental health of US college students during the COVID-19 pandemic: Cross-sectional survey study. *Journal of Medical Internet Research, 22*(9), e22817. https://www.jmir.org/2020/9/e22817/

Wang, Z., Xu, H., & Liu, Y. (2018). How does ethical leadership trickle down? Test of an integrative dual-process model. *Journal of Business Ethics, 153*(3), 691–705.

CHAPTER 9

# EDUCATIONAL REPROGRAMMING

## Leadership Perceptions and Practice of Academic Program Directors in a College of Education During COVID-19

**Joshua C. Tipton**
**Ashlee Hover**
**Kyle Butler**

### ABSTRACT

Educational leadership is commonly envisioned from the perspectives of organizational structure, scheduling, instructional supervision, and assessment. Additionally, the extant research regarding leadership in higher education, unlike literature focused upon K–12 education, is scarce and has rarely included analyses of leader effectiveness. While research on organizational leadership has more recently emphasized the importance of adaptability, vulnerability, and emotional awareness for leaders in an ever-changing, global economy, leadership in higher education institutions has remained slow to change compared to leadership development efforts in other settings. In con-

*On Leadership*, pages 145–157

trast, interdisciplinary leadership encompasses notions of identity and transformative approaches to organizational and systemic challenges and promotes competencies such as self-awareness, strategic planning, innovation, and decisiveness. This chapter highlights the potential changes of collegiate leaders' perceptions and responsibilities to the students, faculty, and staff they serve as an impending result of the COVID-19 pandemic—especially leaders such as academic program directors who frequently engage both students and faculty in learning yet are often overlooked as potential change agents. Furthermore, case examples are highlighted throughout the chapter to display how the infusion of transformational leadership helped academic program directors in the educational leadership department of a college of education fulfill the administrative demands of their role while also reflectively serving as a colleague, confidant, counselor, and coach to effectively guide their programs and support the faculty and students they lead.

Educational leadership is commonly envisioned from the perspectives of organizational structure, scheduling, instructional supervision, and assessment (Bass, 1990; DiPaola & Hoy, 2014; Hoy & Miskel, 2013; Palestini, 2012; Spillane, 2004; Yukl, 2008). Tosas (2016) suggested that much of what has been presented as educational leadership within research literature would be more appropriately identified as educational management. More specifically, literature related to leadership in higher education has often failed to establish a clear distinction between leadership—most broadly defined as an individual's ability to impact organizational effectiveness by influencing others toward a shared purpose and achievement of common goals—and managerial or administrative activities such as allocation of resources, organizational operations, competitive strategy, and fiscal accountability (Astin & Astin, 2000; Basham, 2012; Bass, 1985; Bryman, 2007; Burns, 1978; Coyle, 2018; Esen et al., 2018; Kotter, 1990; Northouse, 2013; Spillane, 2004; Tosas, 2016). Additionally, the extant research regarding leadership in higher education, unlike literature focused upon K–12 education, is scarce (Bryman, 2007; Bryman & Lilley, 2009; Esen et al., 2018; Gmelch, 2013; Gumus et al., 2018) and has rarely included analyses of leader effectiveness (Bryman, 2007; Esen et al., 2018; Gomes & Knowles, 1999; Harris et al., 2004; Kok & McDonald, 2017).

While research on organizational leadership has more recently emphasized the importance of adaptability, vulnerability, and emotional awareness for leaders in an ever-changing, global economy (Burkus, 2016; Coyle, 2018; Gostick & Elton, 2018; Heath & Heath, 2010), leadership in higher education institutions has remained slow to change compared to leadership development efforts in other settings (Gigliotti & Ruben, 2017; Gmelch, 2013; Ruben et al., 2017). Certainly, academic programs, course offerings, and methods of instructional delivery have been modified to accommodate both the demands of the market and the needs of diverse learners, but the perception of leadership in higher education has remained fixed upon effective and efficient management and traditional approaches to leadership (Anthony & Antony, 2017; Bolden et al., 2012; Burnette, 2015; Gigliotti & Ruben, 2017; Gonaim, 2019). Simply put, leadership in higher education has predominately been defined by the fulfillment of roles and managerial responsibilities rather than reflective practice or relationships with students and colleagues. Due to the many operational and educational challenges present during the COVID-19 pandemic; however, leaders in higher education, particularly academic program leaders, have had to exhibit flexibility and fluidity while serving as colleagues, confidants, counselors, and coaches to guide programs and support the faculty and students they lead. Such leaders have had to remain vigilant during COVID-19 and, as in the case of the educational leadership department example, were often required to employ interdisciplinary and transformational leadership practices to mitigate personal, professional, and academic challenges to lead their programs effectively.

## Academic Program Leadership in Higher Education

Academic program directors, the focus group of this paper, frequently engage both students and faculty in learning while simultaneously serving in faculty and program supervision roles but are often overlooked as potential change agents. Like department chairs, academic program directors serve in the dual role of administrator and colleague (Gonaim, 2019; McArthur, 2002; Riley & Russell, 2013). However, other than representing the program within the context of the department, college, and graduate school, they do not hold a formal administrative position in the leadership hierarchy of the university. Instead, they serve in a faculty role and are usually provided with release time or additional compensation for their administrative work. At many post-secondary institutions, academic program directors—though not always recognized as a formal leadership position throughout higher education—serve in some of the same leadership roles under the supervision of department chairs (Bryman, 2007; Smith, 2005). Still tasked with teaching duties and pursuit of scholarly activity, academic program directors are also responsible for administrative oversight of their academic programs, development of course schedules and planning, staffing, academic advising, course revisions, and engaging with stakeholders such as university administration, faculty, students, and accreditation officers.

To highlight the changing dynamics of leadership, the educational leadership department at a southeastern state university serves as the context for the case examples presented within this chapter. This department offers approximately 20 graduate programs for students seeking initial teacher licensure, additional endorsements, and/or advanced degrees. The graduate faculty who work in these post-baccalaureate programs serve as instructors, advisors, and mentors for graduate students from multiple school districts and counties in the region. Depending on the number of programs in a respective department, the number of academic program directors varies. The title of each academic program director is related to the unique nature and niche of the program within the institution (e.g., MEd in curriculum and instruction (ESL) program coordinator), and the professional challenges and complexity of such a role aligns to existing research focused upon higher education leaders at the departmental level, which has consistently emphasized the ambiguous and demanding nature of their work (Delener, 2013; Hecht, 2006; McArthur, 2002).

At the department and college levels, academic program directors are in a unique position regarding demands for both program efficiency and effectiveness, which can make this role a potential paradigm for the development of interdisciplinary leadership competencies such as self-awareness, shared vision, and collaboration. In his analysis of research regarding leadership in higher education Bryman (2007) argued, the organizational units at the departmental level are "crucial units of analysis in universities, as it is often, if not invariably, a key administrative unit for the allocation of resources, and the chief springboard for the organization's main teaching and research activities" (p. 694). To be effective in such work requires a high level of collegiality, credibility, trust, and consideration (Ambrose et al., 2005; Bryman, 2007; Burnette, 2015; Kennie, 2016; Kok & McDonald, 2017; McCaffery, 2018; Spendlove, 2007; Trocchia & Andrus, 2003). Therefore, academic program directors must on one hand dutifully meet the administrative and managerial requirements of the institution, while on the other serve as academic leaders who, like effective department heads, wield their influence to support and advocate for change on behalf of students and faculty (Benoit & Graham, 2005; Creswell & Brown, 1992; Riley & Russell, 2013). Yet, little research has been conducted regarding the perceptions of leaders within departmental programs or units, such as academic program directors (Bryman, 2007; Esen et al., 2018; Smith, 2005), or how such leaders perceive their own leadership of university faculty and students.

Boone et al. (2020) proposed that interdisciplinary leadership requires leaders to evolve, foster long-term vision, communicate and collaborate with multiple stakeholders, consistently evaluate programs, exhibit perseverance, and continually reflect upon their own identity as a leader. In dealing with the challenges of the COVID-19 pandemic, the reflexivity and leadership influence of academic program directors has undoubtedly been tested as they worked to meet the individual needs of faculty and students. Though the program director role might be commonly viewed as representative of middle management between faculty and university administration, academic program directors have the potential to spearhead change efforts that benefit both the human and organizational elements of the institution.

The leadership of the academic program directors in the college of education discussed in this chapter exemplified tenets of interdisciplinary leadership through their transformative approach to meeting the unique instructional and scheduling needs of the graduate students they serve, increased and intentional support for the faculty members they supervise, and their responsive and reflective programmatic adaptations to address both state and local school district demands. Northouse (2013) described transformation leadership as "concerned with emotions, values, ethics, standards, and long-term goals. It includes assessing followers' motives, satisfying their needs, and treating them as full human beings" (p. 185). The transformational leadership model proposes that effective leadership not only produces organizational success but also emphasizes individual needs and potential to achieve sustained individual success for followers and subordinates. Similarly, interdisciplinary leadership emphasizes lifelong learning, collaborative decision-making, inclusivity, reflective practice, and attentiveness to societal problems. Interdisciplinary leaders must at times be willing to prioritize the needs and concerns of others and facilitate change via adaptability and advocacy (Alonso-Yanez et al., 2019).

The response to COVID-19 has necessitated adaptations to traditional operating procedures that have provoked reflective approaches to academic quality, academic equity and accessibility, and guided academic program directors toward greater emphasis upon active leadership, advocacy, and social-emotional supports for faculty and students. Effectively preparing and supporting teacher candidates has demanded a more personalized, adaptive, and empathetic approach than ever before. For example, university students, whose lives and academic plans were impacted by the pandemic, wanted reassurance that their individual needs would be accommodated, and faculty wanted to effectively support teacher candidates in developing the skills necessary to succeed. The core characteristics of transformational leaders—idealized influence, individualized consideration, intellectual stimulation, and inspiration have more intentionally been exhibited during the pandemic. Examples of this type of leadership can be found in the processes of programmatic decisions, course delivery decisions, practicum experience decisions, student success/advising decisions, and academic philosophical decisions.

## Program Reprogramming and Delivery

Serving adult students has previously influenced leadership approaches in higher education and prompted the development of specific programs and services to meet the needs of students (Burnette, 2015; Burns, 2011).

The case example of academic programs in a college of education designed for graduate students seeking licensure to become teachers is especially unique; many candidates enrolled in this program are nontraditional students with both professional and family obligations. COVID-19 spurred a broad range of programmatic modifications, from admissions and scheduling to faculty accessibility and instructional delivery. The rate and expanse of revisions and changes to programs and services were hastened out of necessity to recruit and retain students. As a result, many faculty members expressed being unprepared for and overwhelmed by the vast changes that have been required of their courses. Indeed, university and college faculty nationwide have reported higher rates of dissatisfaction, emotional stress, and burnout, which could result in high numbers of collegiate faculty leaving higher education (McMurtrie, 2020; Nietzel, 2020; Turk & Ramos, 2020). Therefore, to effectively lead their programs, academic program directors had to engage in organizational change while also increasing levels of professional and personal support for faculty and students. Faculty ability to adapt effectively has required ongoing, specific, and timely training and support for implementation to sustain effective programs and stabilize enrollment. Academic program directors needed to exercise forward-thinking and empathy. For example, COVID-19 protocols required program directors to move entire programs to an online/remote format, which demanded intense faculty and student collaboration, instructional technology training, and iterative professional development to continue offering these programs with fidelity. In addition, although cohort models of course offerings and the prerequisite nature of the courses were still in place, COVID-19 protocols created a situation that required a high level of individual consideration and case-by-case analysis of student needs. Management and compliance-oriented roles and responsibilities could no longer be prioritized over transformational actions such as individualized consideration, idealized influence, intellectual stimulation, and inspiration. Therefore, the success of graduate students in the respective programs required academic program directors to model greater flexibility, adaptability, and accessibility while balancing course requirements with current school contexts and adequate attention to the unique individual needs of teacher candidates academically and personally.

To fully meet both the demand for and academic needs of candidates, academic program directors also revised programs of study so that courses were offered more frequently to support the adaptability of scheduling. The result was a transition to a loose cohort format that allowed students to enter the program at any time, reduced the number of courses, forced the redesign of many of the courses to an online asynchronous experience, and changed the instructional delivery of all licensure courses to either weekly face-to-face meetings during the school week (Monday–Friday), a three-weekend seminar (Friday–Saturday), or in-person meetings during the summer session (see Figure 9.1). In addition, academic program directors adapted coursework to incorporate a flipped learning model. In this model of instruction:

> Class time is used for students to engage in hands-on learning, collaborate with their peers and evaluate their progress rather than traditional direct instruction delivery. Instructors can provide one-on-one aid, guidance, and inspiration. This facilitates a shift...from an instructor-centered classroom to a student-centered learning environment. (Aronson et al., n.d., para. 1)

The program directors' adaptation of these courses from traditional models to co-taught, flipped model designs provided students with more opportunities to collaborate with classmates who were seeking certification in the same content areas (e.g., business, English, history, math, music, performing arts, physical education, science, visual arts, world languages). The change in course formats supported both the academic and social-emotional well-being of course instructors and candidates alike. Therefore, idealized influence, individualized consideration, and intellectual stimulation, all elements of the transformational approach to leadership, have become embedded into course instruction and design via heightened collaboration, specific attention to individual areas of expertise and candidate development, and routine emphasis upon individual interest and motivation.

## Practicum Reprogramming

COVID-19 brought many challenges to the graduate coursework that required K–12 field placements as well. Such challenges included the lack of

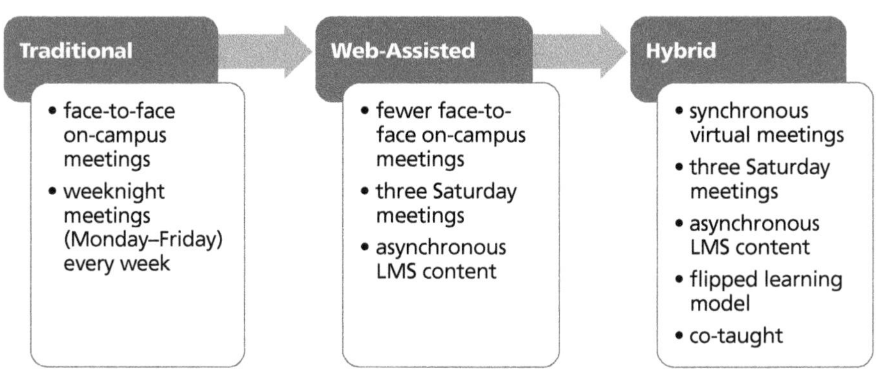


**Figure 9.1** Course format progression.

time in the local schools due to periodic school closures and limitations or restrictions regarding the number of people allowed in the buildings. Additionally, the reopening strategies varied—some K–12 schools gradually allowed specific groups of children to return to school in-person (e.g., students with disabilities, specific grade levels) while others implemented a hybrid model that mixed in-person and virtual learning with alternating groups of children on different days of the week (Russo, 2020). Due to these variations, the regular practice of pairing initial licensure candidates with teacher mentors in the field to observe and practice teaching was disrupted and academic program directors were required to assign school placements based on the candidates' preferences between on-site and virtual learning experiences in K–12 classrooms. However, it was often difficult for the candidates to practice working with the students in either of these instructional environments due to social distancing guidelines or the nature of the virtual learning environment. Furthermore, because teachers, even veteran educators, were overwhelmed with the new workload requirements brought on by the pandemic, facilitators often hesitated to ask them to take on the additional responsibilities of mentoring candidates. In this case, academic program directors exercised another example of individualized consideration to balance the academic expectations for the program with an empathetic, flexible approach toward school leaders and classroom mentors who could not always provide the depth of mentorship normally available for students in their field placement settings.

Likewise, the job-embedded candidates' (candidates who are already teaching in the field while still earning a teaching license) work environment was like a revolving door; based on quarantine procedures and the parents' selected learning preference, teachers rotated teaching students (a) face-to-face in the school building; (b) virtually from home; and (c) face-to-face in the school building while others learned virtually at home. Thus, school-based mitigation of COVID-19 further elevated the stress levels of candidates who were new to the teaching profession and had little to no pedagogical training. During these challenging times, academic program directors modeled transformational leader behaviors of idealized influence by remaining accessible and responsive to student needs and developing trust with candidates through personal support; individualized consideration by working with candidates to develop individualized academic plans and more personalized scheduling options for field-based and class assignments; intellectual stimulation by innovatively structuring field experiences and mentor assignments in multiple school districts and classroom environments; and inspiration by emphasizing collaboration amongst faculty, students, and school leaders and building belonging amongst teacher candidates via virtual meetings and debriefing sessions.

## Rethinking Advising

The implementation of advising sessions following class meetings was yet another change made based upon the academic program directors' intentional emphasis on supporting teacher candidates in managing academic and professional demands during the pandemic. Before the pandemic, candidates were required to meet with each director one on one to complete advising sessions and fill out necessary paperwork. However, once the pandemic occurred, the academic program directors created group advising sessions after virtual classes concluded to address common themes of inquiry for large group discussions and individualized discussions related to course assignments, licensure requirements, evaluations, classroom management, instructing diverse learners, and navigating university and school district policy. Additionally, academic directors arranged advising sessions that included time for candidate reflection, recognition of personal challenges, and reasons for celebration. These sessions further constructed a sense of belonging and collegiality amongst students and faculty who retained a shared objective of seeking to serve as exceptional educators in an exceptionally challenging time.

## Managing Philosophical Decisions

As was the case for institutions of higher education across the nation, COVID-19 required academic program directors to adapt and redesign course schedules and instructional delivery to ensure that the personal well-being and academic needs of faculty and students were considered. For example, graduate teacher licensure courses that had traditionally been scheduled as evening and weekend in-person classes were redesigned to remote, hybrid, and online formats. Despite the directors' attempt to provide diverse course delivery types, it remained difficult for some students to maintain consistent attendance. In addition to normal responsibilities at their respective schools, many students were planning for and assessing three different student profiles for each class they taught (in-person, virtually at home, or hybrid with some students in-person and others at home) within the K–12 environment. Because of this, the program directors allowed candidates to connect to class meetings via Zoom while driving home from work, at school functions they had been tasked with supervising, and/or missed class altogether, which resulted in the need to watch class recordings and complete alternative assignments. Therefore, not only did the academic program directors need to make sure faculty teaching in their respective programs had the prerequisite knowledge and skills to teach future teachers (including how to teach them virtually), but they also needed to mitigate diverse faculty philosophies and dispositions regarding the proper balance between student equipping (e.g., listening, teaching, coaching, mentoring) and student accountability.

## CONCLUSION

Bush (2007) suggested that authentic educational leadership influences and initiates change. Tosas (2016) proposed that "educational leadership should instead aim at helping students fulfill their unique, singular potential, a potential that is impossible to anticipate beforehand" (p. 355). Academic program directors in the educational leadership department of a college of education who serve graduate students in an educator preparation licensure program have had to become more engaged with, and aware of, the multitude of challenges that faculty and students have encountered during the COVID-19 pandemic. Defining characteristics of transformational leadership such as individualized consideration, innovation, intellectual stimulation, and inspiration have been critical to programmatic sustainability and student success. Program leadership has required an extraordinary level of adaptability and flexibility regarding course scheduling and instructional delivery that has included both faculty and student input. The abrupt transition from the traditional classroom setting to remote, hybrid, or online formats, even for experienced faculty members and practicing teachers, was challenging and demanded individual attention to professional development needs and support for faculty and academic engagement and connection for students. Program directors' need to navigate the mandatory expectations of field experience service and supervision necessitated more creativity and frequent communication between program directors, students, and school district personnel to ensure that all parties felt supported and safe with consideration of COVID-19 protocols and transmission. Finally, and most importantly, academic program directors emphasized and exercised empathy in serving their students and faculty during the pandemic. Course content and instruction, though important, became secondary to care and concern for others. Effective leadership, and teaching, are ultimately about our knowledge and attentiveness to the individual motivation and needs of others. For academic program directors in a college of education, COVID-19 resulted in a re-programming that realigned their focus from efficiently managing the program itself to effectively serving the people they lead.

## REFERENCES


Alonso-Yanez, G., House-Peters, L., Garcia-Cartagena, M., Bonelli, S., Lorenzo-Arana, I., & Ohiro, M. (2019). Mobilizing transdisciplinary collaborations: Collective reflections on decentering academia in knowledge production. *Global Sustainability, 2*, E5. https://doi.org/10.1017/sus.2019.2

Ambrose, S., Huston, T., & Normal, M. (2005). A qualitative method for assessing faculty satisfaction. *Research in Higher Education, 46*(7), 803–830.

Anthony, S. G., & Antony, J. (2017). Academic leadership—special or simple. *International Journal of Productivity and Performance Management, 66*(5), 630–637.

Aronson, N., Arfstrom, K. M., & Tam, K. (n.d.). *Flipped learning in higher education.* Pearson. https://flippedlearning.org/wp-content/uploads/2016/07/HigherEdWhitePaper-FINAL.pdf

Astin, A. W., & Astin, H. S. (2000). *Leadership reconsidered: Engaging higher education in social change.* W. K. Kellogg Foundation.

Basham, L. M. (2012). Transformational leadership characteristics necessary for today's leaders in higher education. *Journal of International Education Research, 8*(4), 343–347.

Bass, B. M. (1985). *Leadership and performance beyond expectations.* Free Press.

Bass, B. M. (1990). *Handbook of leadership: A survey of theory and research.* Free Press.

Benoit, P., & Graham, S. (2005). Leadership excellence: Constructing the role of department chair. *Academic Leadership: The Online Journal, 3*(1). http://www.academicleadership.org/volume3/issue1/index.html

Bolden, R., Gosling, J., O'Brien, A., Peters, K., Ryan, M., & Haslam, A. (2012). *Academic leadership: Changing conceptions, identities and experiences in UK higher education.* Leadership Foundation for Higher Education.

Boone, C. G., Pickett, S., Bammer, G., Bawa, K., Dunne, J. A., Gordon, I. J., Hart, D., Hellmann, J., Miller, A., New, M., Ometto, J. P., Taylor, K., Wendorf, G., Agrawal, A., Bertsch, P., Campbell, C., Dodd, P., Janetos, A., & Mallee, H. (2020). Preparing interdisciplinary leadership for a sustainable future. *Sustainability Science, 15*, 1723–1733. https://doi.org/10.1007/s11625-020-00823-9

Bryman, A. (2007). Effective leadership in higher education: A literature review. *Studies in Higher Education, 32*(6), 693–710.

Bryman, A., & Lilley, S. (2009). Leadership researchers on leadership in higher education. *Leadership, 5*(3), 331–346.

Burkus, D. (2016). *Under new management: How leading organizations are upending business as usual.* Houghton Mifflin Harcourt.

Burnette, D. (2015). Negotiating the mine field: Strategies for effective online education administrative leadership in higher education institutions. *The Quarterly Review of Distance Education, 16*(3), 13–25.

Burns, J. (1978). *Leadership.* Harper and Row.

Burns, E. C. (2011). The adult learner: A change agent in postsecondary education. *Online Journal of Distance Learning Administration, 14*(2), 29–45.

Bush, T. (2007). Educational leadership and management: Theory, policy, and practice. *South African Journal of Education, 27*(3), 391–406.

Coyle, D. (2018). *The culture code: The secrets of highly successful* groups. Bantam Books.

Creswell, J., & Brown, M. L. (1992). How chairpersons enhance faculty research: A grounded theory study. *Review of Higher Education, 16*, 41–62.

Delener, N. (2013). Leadership excellence in higher education: Present and future. *Journal of Contemporary Issues in Business and Government, 19*(1), 19–33.

DiPaola, M. F., & Hoy, W. K. (2014). *Improving instructional supervision, evaluation, and professional development.* Information Age Publishing.

Esen, M., Bellibas, M. S., & Gumus, S. (2018). The evolution of leadership research in higher education for two decades (1995–2014): A bibliometric and content analysis. *International Journal of Leadership in Education, 23*(3), 259–273. https://doi.org/10.1080/13603124.2018.1508753

Gigliotti, R. A., & Ruben, B. D. (2017). Preparing higher education leaders: A conceptual, strategic, and operational approach. *Journal of Leadership Education, 16*(1), 96–114.

Gmelch, W. H. (2013). The development of campus academic leaders. *International Journal of Leadership and Change, 1*(1), 26–35.

Gomes, R., & Knowles, P. A. (1999). Marketing department leadership: An analysis of a team transformation. *Journal of Marketing Education, 21*(3), 164–174.

Gonaim, F. A. (2019). Leadership in higher education in Saudi Arabia: Benefits, constraints and challenges of adopting servant leadership model by department chairs. *International Journal of Education and Practice, 7*(2), 101–111.

Gostick, A., & Elton, C. (2018). *The best team wins: The new science of high performance.* Simon & Schuster.

Gumus, S., Bellibas, M. S., Esen, M., & Gumus, E. (2018). A systemic review of studies on leadership models in educational research from 1980 to 2014. *Educational Management Administration & Leadership, 46*(1), 25–48.

Harris, J., Martin, B. N., & Agnew, W. (2004, November 11–14). The characteristics, behaviors, and training of effective educational/leadership chairs. In D. C. Thompson & F. E. Crampton (Eds.), *The changing face(s) of educational leadership: UCEA at the crossroads.* Conference of the University Council for Educational Administration, Kansas City, MO, United States.

Heath, C., & Heath, D. (2010). *Switch: How to change things when change is hard.* Broadway Books.

Hecht, I. W. (2006). Becoming a department chair: To be or not to be. *Effective Practices for Academic Leaders, 1*(3), 1–16.

Hoy, W. K., & Miskel, C. G. (2013). *Educational administration: Theory, research, and practice* (9th ed.). McGraw-Hill.

Kennie, T. (2016). Academic leadership: Dimensions, dysfunctions and dynamics. *International Scientific Journal of Universities and Leadership, 2*, 1–16.

Kok, S. K., & McDonald, C. (2017). Underpinning excellence in higher education—An investigation into the leadership, governance, and management behaviours of high-performing academic departments. *Studies in Higher Education, 42*(2), 210–231.

Kotter, J. P. (1990). *A force for change: How leadership differs from management.* Free Press.

McArthur, R. C. (2002). Democratic leadership and faculty empowerment at the community college: A theoretical model for the department chair. *Community College Review, 30*(3), 1–10. https://doi.org/10.1177/009155210203000301

McCaffery, P. (2018). *The higher education manager's handbook: Effective leadership and management in universities and colleges.* Routledge.

McMurtrie, B. (2020, November 5). The pandemic is dragging on. Professors are burning out. Overwhelmed and undersupported, instructors see no end in site. *The Chronicle of Higher Education.* https://www.chronicle.com/article/the-pandemic-is-dragging-on-professors-are-burning-out?utm_source=Iterable&utm_medium=email&utm_campaign=campaign_2042358_nl_Academe-Today_date_20210226&cid=at&source=&sourceId=

Nietzel, M. T. (2021, February 26). Pandemic toll: More than half of college faculty have considered a career change or early retirement. *Forbes.* https://www.forbes.com/sites/michaeltnietzel/2021/02/26/pandemic-toll-more-than-half-of-college-faculty-have-considered-a-career-change-or-early-retirement/?sh=1bbac24e12da

Northouse, P. G. (2013). *Leadership: Theory and practice.* SAGE Publications.

Palestini, R. (2012). *A commonsense approach to educational leadership: Lessons from the founders.* Rowman & Littlefield.

Riley, T. A., & Russell, C. (2013). Leadership in higher education examining professional development needs for department chairs. *Review of Higher Education & Self-Learning, 6*(21), 38–57.

Ruben, B. D., De Lisi, R., & Gigliotti, R. A. (2017). *A guide for leaders in higher education: Core concepts, competencies, and tools.* Stylus.

Russo, A. (2020, November 12). School reopening 2020: The surge that never happened. *Forbes.* https://www.forbes.com/sites/alexanderrusso/2020/11/12/school-reopening-2020-the-surge-that-never-happened/?sh=6b0984085484

Smith, R. (2005). Departmental leadership and management in chartered and statutory universities. *Educational Management, Administration and Leadership, 33*(4), 449–464.

Spendlove, M. (2007). Competencies for effective leadership in higher education. *International Journal of Educational Management, 21*(5), 407–417.

Spillane, J. (2004). Educational leadership. *Educational Evaluation and Policy Analysis, 26*(2), 169–172.

Tosas, M. R. (2016). Educational leadership reconsidered: Arendt, Agamben, and Bauman. *Studies in Philosophy & Education, 35*(4), 353–369.

Trocchia, P. J., & Andrus, D. M. (2003). Perceived characteristics and abilities of an effective marketing department head. *Journal of Marketing Education, 25*(1), 5–15.

Turk, J., & Ramos, A. M. (2020). *College and university presidents respond to COVID-19: 2020 fall term survey.* American Council on Education Research Report. https://www.acenet.edu/Research-Insights/Pages/Senior-Leaders/College-and-University-Presidents-Respond-to-COVID-19-2020-Fall-Term.aspx

Yukl, G. (2008). How leaders influence organizational effectiveness. *The Leadership Quarterly, 19*(6), 708–722.

CHAPTER 10

# LEADERSHIP IN EDUCATION FOR BLACK AMERICANS IN COMMUNITY COLLEGES

**Aishwarya Joshi**
**Seneka R. Gainer**

## ABSTRACT

Higher education aims to support next-generation leaders' development and competencies that possess the essential characteristics to lead and foster sustainable changes (Nohria & Khurana, 2010). However, there remains a disparity in access to higher education and leadership opportunities for Black American students, despite continued demonstration of excellent leadership and successful contributions to American society. Black students are confronted with experiences that test the self-identity instilled by parents and role models and yet are provided less training and leadership development opportunities. As it relates to access to higher education, community colleges can play a crucial role in closing the leadership opportunities gap. And yet, the retention rates of Black Americans in community colleges are the lowest (see Harper, 2013, Pérez Huber, 2015, Saenz et al., 2016, etc.). Hence this chapter aims to (a) highlight the role of community colleges in fostering leadership among Black Americans, (b) explore the capacity of mentorship

*On Leadership*, pages 159–174

in supporting Black students in community colleges, (c) encourage policy and faculty development to increase student retention rates, and (d) offer interdisciplinary strategies and resources to systemically bridge the accessibility gaps toward an equitable educational experience.

*A genuine leader is not a searcher for consensus, but a molder of consensus*

—Martin Luther King Jr.

The disparity between Black and White students' completion rates of 2-year community colleges is 24%, with attrition rates of Black men the highest at 41.1% (Shapiro et al., 2017). Due to the disparity, there is a lack of focus on developing Black leadership in community college settings. Despite community colleges' successful contributions to develop and support future leaders, a gap continues to persist in the long-term retention and sustainability of Black student populations in community colleges. The focal point of the chapter is to inquire how leadership traits can be identified and developed in Black students to foster success in the future.

A "leader" or "leadership" concept is complex, nuanced, highly contextual (Guba & Lincoln, 1989), and ever-evolving. Therefore, it is imperative to understand that no one definition sufficiently encapsulates all the tenants of an effective leader or an effective leadership style (Shead, 2016). Leadership is further understood within the context of culture and/or environment in which leadership traits are fostered. For the purpose of this book chapter, a working definition of an effective leader is "a person or a group of people who provides direction, establishes interpersonal and intrapersonal trustworthiness and holds the ability to lead and represent an institution or organization all while adhering to the values and cultures of the institution and people" (Bryman, 2008; Winston & Patterson, 2006). Through this chapter the author aims to highlight the integration of interdisciplinary approaches to serve as the vehicle to address the barriers and offer long-term solutions to promote Black leadership identity within higher education.

## Fostering Leadership Among Black Americans in Community Colleges

The contributions of Black leaders in developing and enhancing American society have been countless, and they continue to demonstrate excellent leadership in this movement towards an equitable and progressive society. The significance of Black leadership is not only due to the achievement of leadership roles. It is also attributed to navigating oppressive interpersonal and professional spaces. Black leaders obtain advanced positions while dismantling systemic, academic, and institutional barriers meant to hinder their positionality and identity development as successful leaders.

Community colleges are often the first step towards success as future leaders within higher education. For example, community colleges' prioritization and success rates in developing leaders were featured when, during his presidency, Barack Obama shared the ambitious goal of producing 5 million new community college graduates (Berhane, 2018). In addition, community colleges are also deemed the primary economically feasible options for post-secondary education (Evans et al., 2017). Being an initial step and with economic feasibility in view, greater focus should be placed on the investment in developing and creating means to foster leadership among Black students in community colleges. Mentoring, teaching pedagogies, and student-led organizations are examples of initiatives that support the development of Black leaders in community college settings. Along with these are two specific leadership styles that have been deemed a success, especially with Black students. These initiatives and leadership styles require representation and training and offer an approach that supports student identity development.

***Mentoring***

A nationally representative survey of over 30,000 college graduates found that the ability to establish a mentor for each college student predicts greater work engagement and subjective well-being in the years preceding graduation (Raposa et al., 2020). The knowledge, relationships, and experiences students attain during the college years are pivotal and fundamentally define their lifetime personal and career outcomes (Wood & Palmer, 2013). A mentor's role in higher education provides a more significant opportunity for choice and exploration and aids in developing leadership skills.

Mentors in community college settings likely influence students in a variety of ways. As young adults achieve new levels of independence and engage in decision-making processes related to their social lives and careers, adjusting to college and transitioning to adulthood are often met with elevated anxiety and risk rates (Raposa et al., 2020). Specifically, Black American students, whose culture or worldview is viewed through a collective lens, may experience immense pressure to mature and produce. Mentors can help offset this risk by supporting students as they navigate identity issues inherent in the transition to adulthood and offer and provide encouragement and guidance while facilitating students' academic and career opportunities (Eby et al., 2008).

Efficient and competent mentorship is defined by career and psychosocial support, trust, and responsiveness (Crisp et al., 2017). The American Association of Community Colleges (AACC, 2017) further emphasizes the significance of mentorship to support the retention and successes of Black students in community college settings. Moreover, Cornwall (2020) asserts that to understand the factors that affect the quality of mentorship for underrepresented students, one must examine those experiences and cultural differences. He further identifies five crucial factors that can help underrepresented students gain access and help mentors recognize student competence and achievements without minimizing social identities or causing harm. These practices can be incorporated in community college settings providing mentors with an outline to engage with Black American students:

- *Mindfully broach crucial conversations about barriers.* Mentors are encouraged to recognize the role culture plays in students' development and broach the topic in mentorship relationships. Being vulnerable in this way highlights positionality and identity, awareness of privilege, and how one navigates it. It is imperative to create opportunities for open conversation and complex topics. Mentorship transcends discussion on academic and career pursuits. Inclusive mentorship includes intentional work toward social justice and is approached individually, collaboratively, holistically, and systematically (Cornwall, 2020).
- *Develop a balance between practical help, emotional support, and encouragement.* Mentors have an opportunity to demonstrate how they can "show up" for their mentees. Mentors must be cautious not to exercise performative allyship and operationalize their support through collaborations, continuing education, and engagement in action-oriented initiatives. Mentors are uniquely positioned to assist in their areas of expertise and capacity and show up fully and organically for students.
- *Ask for feedback candidly and consistently.* Cornwall (2020) promotes listening and incorporating the ideas of the mentees. Being willing to listen to Black American students, for example, and their specific needs are imperative for mentors. Offering a confidential survey for students to provide anonymous feedback is also pertinent to the mentor's development and highlights minoritized voices.
- *Do not try to provide all needed mentoring support by yourself.* Dismantling systems that lack diversity and equity are individual, collective, and systemic efforts. Growth and development do not occur in isolation, and a sense of community is essential in any given field. Having the opportunity to develop interdepartmental/ interdisciplinary mentoring and collaborative relationships is vital to support a well-rounded and holistic professional and interpersonal development. Several researchers have recognized and attested to the strengths and benefits of having multiple mentoring relationships.

For instance, participants in Mazerolle et al.'s (2018) study reported having multiple mentors provided them with flexibility and mobility to develop a sense of community and belonging and have their individual needs met adequately and appropriately. Mentors are encouraged to build a network with peer mentors and leaders and facilitate the students' connections. Mentors may encourage students to attend conferences and workshops to put them in the proper position to network effectively and open the door for opportunities. Mentors can further call upon this extended network to provide specific expertise that the primary mentor may not possess.

- *Seek to learn more about best practices in mentoring.* The Center of Mentoring Excellence (2015) highlights best practices for mentors that includes: engaging in meaningful and authentic conversation; balancing talking and listening; examining personal implicit and explicit biases. It is imperative for mentors to continually engage in self-exploratory practices that foster continued growth and development.

Although mentoring is a proven way to promote student growth and development (Center for Mentoring Excellence, n.d.), it is only one aspect of the Black student leader identity development. To develop successful Black leader identities, a holistic and multifaceted approach is required. The following section speaks to another tenant supporting Black leader identity development and the Black community college experience.

***Culturally Responsive Teaching Pedagogies***

Educators agree that competent teaching requires mastery of content knowledge and pedagogical skills (Gay, 2002). This applies to awareness and recognition of student populations, students' needs, and subject matter. Thus, it is imperative that teachers develop a culturally diverse foundation and knowledge base. Culturally responsive teaching uses cultural experiences, attributes, and perspectives as conduits for teaching minoritized students. Researchers suggest that mentorship, coupled with self-reflection, are pertinent tenants associated with effective culturally responsive pedagogy. The development of culturally responsive teachers who acknowledge and respect their students for their personal stories and backgrounds represents a crucial pursuit in education (Lucey & White, 2017).

However, new educators report feeling inexperienced when broaching culture in the classroom and find that coursework addressing these issues provides little help in classroom practice (Castro, 2010; Dwyer, 2008). Mills and Ballantyne (2010) developed a systemic classification of three hierarchical stages (self-awareness/self-reflectiveness, openness, and commitment to social justice) representing educators' transition to diversity-responsive dispositions (Lucey & White, 2017). This uniquely positions educators to create safe and trusting environments, encourage vulnerability, foster attentive listening, and connect teaching and learning with students' community-based culture (Darling-Hammond et al., 2019; Lucey & White, 2017; Sleeter, 2011).

Research emphasizes the strength of caring relationships in education and the impact of students' attitudes and beliefs on their ability to learn (Noddings, 1984, 1992, 2005, 2010; Owusu-Ansah & Kyei-Blankson, 2016). According to Beland (2014), students who regard their teachers as caring individuals have a better sense of belonging in school and exhibit more learning progress. The exercise of care is exemplified by the representation of the faculty. The student-faculty relationship is bi-directional and can further bolster the recruitment and retention of Black faculties in community colleges.

The constructs of care and connectedness are essential at all levels of education (Owusu-Ansah & Kyei-Blankson, 2016). Such care and connection are particularly important for Black students in the community college setting who simultaneously withstand systemic and institutional obstacles during the transitions to college life and adulthood. Nodding's (2008) model for a caring classroom includes four valuable elements that can inform culturally responsive pedagogical practices—(a) modeling, (b) dialogue, (c) practice, and (d) confirmation. Table 10.1 elaborates on each component of Nodding's (2008) model.

These elements serve as a collaborative tool for developing academic settings by demonstrating empathy, reflexivity, compassion for student's views, and building trust with each individual in the class community (Lucey & White, 2017). In this framework, Black students are likely to encounter an intentional

**TABLE 10.1 Nodding's Approach to Fostering Care in Academic Settings**

| Nodding's Model (2008) | Explanation |
|---|---|
| Modeling | Caring behavior is not innate and requires learning through reflexive modeling. This includes veracity and accountability on the educator to operationalize caring relationships into an action-oriented, tangible approach. |
| Dialogue | Academic discourse is essential to understanding what students are thinking. Educators can employ instructional strategies to keep students engaged. |
| Practice | Increased visibility and access to resources allows students to experiment and implement the learned behaviors in a safe manner. |
| Confirmation | Faculty representation confirms identity. Black faculties represent relatedness to the student experience and fosters community within the classroom setting. |

*Note:* This table demonstrates the elements of Noddings (2008) model, with explanations modified and defined specifically to cater to the Black student population.

sense of safety. Students may express personal vulnerability about their social views. As a result, they may develop exposure to care that models responsibility to (a) support one another and (b) integrate a collectivist culture into the learning space (Lucey & White, 2017). Utilizing culturally responsive pedagogy within community college settings can create spaces that foster solidarity through collaboration and mutual respect. Consider the following question: What factors play a role in the effective teaching of Black students?

### *Student-Led Organizations and Leadership*

Student-led organizations have been and continue to be an excellent platform to cultivate leadership skills among students in higher education institutes. Rios-Aguilar et al. (2015) report that 1 in 4 undergraduate students are involved in student-led organizations in their first year of college. Student-led organizations are perceived as spaces where learning occurs through peer interactions and modeling new behaviors and skills. Additionally, they also provide a pipeline for professional networking and future career advancements.

Moreover, as evidenced in decades of literature (see Kezar & Maxey, 2014; Kuh, 1995; McFarland & Thomas, 2006; Mayhew et al., 2016), is the impact of student-led organizations on the cultivation of leadership skills such as effective communication, developing bureaucratic strategies, collective engagement with stakeholders in various communities. They further transcend student skill development and nurture their psychosocial and emotional advancement (Keating et al., 2014). For Black students, this is crucial as they move through the minority status stressors and biases. Assertions can be made that student-led organizational involvement is a stepping stone for Black student populations to engage in systemic leadership positions and create a pathway for their social and career advancements.

For Black students in community colleges, student-led organizations play a pivotal role in creating a space for them to engage in leadership positions and navigate the institutional biases and barriers that hinder their professional and personal development. Furthermore, these organizations go beyond interpersonal peer learning and interactions and are also grounds for advocacy and activism involvement. An excellent example is a student-led organization, The Congress of Racial Equity (CORE), that gained national attention as a significant civil rights organization that emerged from the leadership of Black undergraduate students at the Chicago Theological Seminary (Altbach, 1997).

### *Integrating Leadership Styles*

To develop Black leaders in community college settings, a culturally responsive leadership framework is vital. Culturally responsive leadership involves interpreting one's leadership style using the lens of intersectionality and displaying leadership that is culturally responsive (Lopez, 2015, 2016; Peters et al., 2020). This not only includes the racial identity but is a culmination of individual social identities and positions on the spectrum of power, privilege, and oppression. For example, Lopez (2016) built upon such a framework in developing her culturally responsive leadership model, which consisted of four components: critical self-reflection, construction and deconstruction, agency and action, and support and sustenance. These four elements focus on learning and unlearning all forms of discrimination, inequity, and oppression. Blanken (2019) suggests eight common leadership styles, two of which—coaching style leadership and transformational style leadership—demonstrate cultural responsiveness and an integrated approach to leadership for cultivating success in the development of influential Black student leaders.

Leadership is understood and modeled differently based on a leader's professional specialty, identities, culture, discipline, system, or contextual factors. The coaching leadership style was first defined by Paul Hersey and Kenneth Blanchard in the late 1960s. They described this as a leadership style that a leader can adapt based on a specific situation and current attitude. In coaching-style leadership, group members engage in a personalized plan to achieve individual goals. Leaders who integrate this style facilitate the engagement of others, empathize with specific and unique motivations, and support and challenge group members collaboratively to achieve set personal goals (Hogan, 2020). Rathmell et al. (2019) assert this leadership style to be effective with Black students in academia due to this approach's collectivistic and nurturing underpinnings.

Similarly, group members in the transformational leadership process are inspired to work towards a goal collectively. This approach embraces a relational style of motivating action (Jacob et al., 2017). Leaders incorporating this leadership style are often energetic, passionate, and enthusiastic, as this approach focuses on motivating, inspiring, and attending to the needs of others. Based on Piccolo and Colquitt's 2006 study on leadership, Jacob et al. (2017) purport that the tenets of transformational leadership include idealized influence (encompassing confidence, power, and trust), inspirational motivation, intellectual stimulation (demonstrating new ways of viewing problems), and individual consideration. Researchers have further noted transformational leadership to yield higher levels of performance as well as group satisfaction (Jacob et al., 2017). Exemplars of this leadership approach are Oprah Winfrey, Reeds Hastings, and Hubert Joly.

Furthermore, the leadership styles mentioned above evolve and vary in representation as determined by the context in which it is demonstrated. In this chapter, the emergence of an effective leader/leadership style is discussed within the context of Black Americans' historical and continued marginalization in community college settings.

## CHALLENGES TO LEADERSHIP IDENTITY DEVELOPMENT

According to the National Center for Education Statistics (NCES, 2020), Black American undergraduate students represent 37% of the minoritized student population in community colleges. Community colleges are an affordable and accessible means to higher education. They are estimated to be essential by 2050 for Black Americans' personal and professional success (Wood & Palmer, 2013). Also, community colleges are grounds for fostering diversity and equity. For example, around 61% of undergraduate students in community colleges identify themselves as a part of the minoritized subgroups (e.g., Black Americans, Hispanic/Latinx Americans, and/or Asian Americans; NCES, 2017). At the same time, the retention rates of Black Americans in community colleges appear to be at their lowest (Harper, 2013). Several factors contribute to the early departure of Black Americans from academia and deter them from continuing higher education. Racism and the experiences of microaggressions are the most researched factors that hinder the professional and personal development of Black Americans in higher education systems (Alinia, 2014; Preston-Cunningham et al., 2015; Mushonga & Hennenberger, 2020; Perez & Carney, 2018). These experiences impact them individually and contribute to the intergenerational barriers of race-based trauma and poverty resulting from everyday oppression and discrimination.

On the other hand, the identity of a Black American individual in the United States is layered and complex and simply not based on their race alone. Research scholars such as Crenshaw (2018), Collins (1991), and hooks (2014) have pushed back and negated the stereotype that the Black American identity is a monolith. Instead, these scholars highlight the intersecting identities within the Black culture, often of varying values, ideas, and beliefs. However, these intersecting factors are often overlooked when Black Americans pursue advancement opportunities or leadership roles, resulting in implicit and explicit biases and stereotype threats. Moreover, these stereotypes and stereotype threats are primary contributors to Black students in academia experiencing the impostor phenomenon (Cokley et al., 2013; Chao et al., 2014; Gibson-Beverly & Schwartz, 2008), which impacts student retention, early departure, and sense of belongingness.

Imposter phenomena tend to attribute success to external factors and expose a subjective sense of intellectual fraudulence (Stone et al., 2018). A new University of Texas at Austin study suggests that this phenomenon, in some cases, can exacerbate the mental health of minority students who already experience prejudices against them (Bauer-Wolf, 2017). Black Americans that experience imposter feelings have difficulty grasping or believing in their own successes. A 2018 study developed a culturally informed model of the imposter phenomenon construct. The model highlights additional culturally relevant factors that hinder individual progression for Black students (Stone et al., 2018). These factors include awareness of low racial representation, expectations, psychosocial costs, and explaining success externally (Stone et al., 2018). The phenomenon is well researched and occurs on an individual basis, an important point to consider when discussing and addressing Black students' barriers in continued education and retention of Black leaders in community colleges.

## Retention of Black Students Leaders in Community Colleges

Historically, college faculties and administrators, particularly advisors and counselors, have been tasked with developing the "whole" student (American College Personnel Association, 1994; Hamrick et al., 2002). The primary focus includes a holistic approach, considering personal development and actualizing personal goals (Kitzrow, 2009; Stebleton & Schmidt, 2010). Thus, a multifaceted and interdisciplinary approach is necessary to increase the retention of Black student leaders in community colleges. These approaches can be broadly categorized into (a) interpersonal development and (b) systemic/institutional development.

### *Interpersonal Development*

Given the array of challenges (e.g., tokenism, isolation, microaggression, racism, etc.) that Black student leaders experience in community colleges, their social, emotional, and mental well-being must be prioritized by both student and faculty alike as they develop and hone their leadership skills. These can be addressed in two ways—one through the intentional engagement of Black students in peer-to-peer group settings in classrooms and creating space to bring their "funds of knowledge" (Daddow, 2016, p. 744) into their own vocabularies. As discussed previously, the bi-directional approach to increase the representation of both Black faculty and students is imperative for the interpersonal development of Black leaders.

Another aspect of the Black student leader's interpersonal development is their mental and emotional well-being. Accessibility to counseling resources and integration of wellness models can be monumental in addressing the complexities of the Black student experience in community colleges. Simultaneously, access to mental health services is not a singular problem, as Black students have historically been hesitant in seeking mental health services due to poor experiences with White counselors and the lack of representation of Black mental health professionals in the field (Hudson et al., 2016). However, Easterwood (2016) recommends reducing the stigma around mental health by allowing frequent and open conversations about the importance of mental wellness and normalizing it in academic settings. Particularly, seeking mental health services and incorporating emotional wellness in their daily lives have demonstrated reduced life stressors and better coping abilities among Black students in higher education (Snyder et al., 2016).

## Systemic/Institutional Development

Student leaders and faculty taking ownership and accountability for leadership identity development is only one aspect of the developmental trajectory. Without the support of the institutions and the systems (e.g., administration), any steps towards equity will be harder to achieve and, most importantly, sustain. At the administrative level, people in leadership positions are crucial to aid the longevity of measures taken to make academia more culturally responsive. An example of a systemic strategy would be developing policies that ensure diversity and equity training is administered continually. Still, it is infused on a continuum at varying levels (e.g., administration staff, educators, students, etc.) in the institution.

Another strategic example is to develop specific diversity and equity leadership programs for administrative leaders, such as chancellors, presidents, CEOs, and superintendents. One such program is the Wheelhouse Leadership training program designed by the University of California, Davis campus that ensures systematic measures are put in place to continually combat anti-Blackness and racist attitudes in academia. Finally, incorporating an intersectionality framework in classroom and administrative settings can significantly create emotionally and psychologically safe spaces for critical conversations and operational change. Black student leadership identity development is layered and cannot be fully developed without considering the intersections of their social identities and positionality on the systems of power, privilege, and oppression. An example would be integrating students and faculty's intersecting identities into academic discourse, reflexive activities, and cultural immersion experiences. Thus, systemic and institutional development supports Black students' efforts in cultivating their leadership traits on a macro level, ensuring sustainability and successful retention in community colleges.

## SUMMARY

Black student leaders stand on the shoulders of many past leaders that share their heritage. However, Black students are more adversely impacted by institutional inconsistency in leadership education and opportunities in their post-secondary studies (Anderson, 2021). Community colleges are uniquely positioned to develop and adopt culturally conscious practices that foster awareness, inclusion, and relationship, explicitly adapting to the collectivistic nature that is culturally responsive. A collaborative approach between students, faculty, and administration is necessary to create a sustainable space for Black students to develop their leadership identities. Interdepartmental and interdisciplinary approaches within the community college setting address the complex challenges impacting leadership identity development. It further supports Black students venturing into a highly competitive and fast-paced society as prominent and successful leaders. Moreover, the call to address the challenges faced by Black students in community colleges as they develop their leadership identities is necessary and can no longer be ignored or negated. Integrating interdisciplinary approaches is the answer to address the barriers and offer long-term solutions to promote Black leadership identity development success.

## REFERENCES

Altbach, P. G. (1997). *Student politics in America: A historical analysis.* Transaction Publishers.

Alinia, M. (2015). On black feminist thought: Thinking oppression and resistance through intersectional paradigm. *Ethnic and Racial Studies, 38*(13), 2334–2340. https://doi.org/10.1080/01419870.2015.1058492

American Association of Community Colleges. (2017). *Competencies for community college leaders.*

American College Personnel Association. (1994). *The student learning imperative: Implications for student affairs.*

Anderson, G. (2021, February 26). A racial trust deficit in higher ed. *Inside Higher Ed.* https://www.insidehighered.com/news/2021/02/26/black-students-trust-college-leadership-less-white-peers

Bauer-Wolf, J. (2017, April 6). Feeling like imposters. *Inside Higher Ed.* https://www.insidehighered.com/news/2017/04/06/study-shows-impostor-syndromes-effect-minority-students-mental-health#.YFzmARCin_o.link

Berhane, B. T. (2018, April 29–May 2). *On becoming a "transfer institution": Research on a community college that supports diverse black students in their transfer aspirations* [Paper presentation]. The Collaborative Network for Engineering and Computing Diversity Conference, Crystal City, VA.

Beland, K. (2014). Easing the transition to middle adolescence. *Journal of Research in Character Education, 10*(1), 61–67.

Blanken, R. (2016). *8 Common leadership styles.* https://www.asaecenter.org/resources/articles/an_plus/2019/december/eight-leadership-styles-and-when-to-use-them

Bryman, A. (2008). *Social research methods* (3rd ed). Oxford University Press.

Castro, A. J. (2010). Themes in research on preservice teachers' views of cultural diversity: Implications for researching millennial preservice teachers. *Educational Researcher, 39*(3), 198–210. https://doi.org/10.3102/0013189X10363819

Center for Mentoring Excellence. (n.d.). *Mentoring strategies for success.* https://www.centerformentoring.com/services/mentoring-strategies-for-success

Center for Mentoring Excellence. (2015). *Top 10 best practices for mentors.* https://www.centerformentoring.com/top-10-best-practices-for-mentors

Chao, R. C., Longo, J., Wang, C., Dasgupta, D., & Fear, J. (2014). Perceived racism as moderator between self-esteem/shyness and psychological distress among African Americans. *Journal of Counseling & Development, 92*(3), 259–269. https://doi.org/10.1002/j.1556-6676.2014.00154.x

Cokley, K., McClain, S., Enciso, A., & Martinez, M. (2013). An examination of the impact of minority status stress and impostor feelings on the mental health of diverse ethnic minority college students. *Journal of Multicultural Counseling and Development, 41*(2), 82–95. https://doi.org/10.1002/j.2161-1912.2013.00029.x

Collins, P. H. (1995). Black women and motherhood [1991]. In V. Held (Ed.), *Justice and care* (pp. 117–136). Routledge. https://doi.org/10.4324/9780429499463-11

Crenshaw, K. (2018). Demarginalizing the intersection of race and sex: A Black feminist critique of antidiscrimination doctrine, feminist theory, and antiracist politics [1989]. In K. T. Bartlett & R. Kennedy (Eds.), *Feminist legal theory* (pp. 57–80). Routledge. https://doi.org/10.4324/9780429500480-5

Cornwall, A. (2020, January 13). Mentoring underrepresented minority students. *Inside Higher Ed.* https://www.insidehighered.com/advice/2020/01/13/advice-mentoring-underrepresented-minority-students-when-you-are-white-opinion

Crisp, G., Baker, V. L., Griffin, K. A., Lunsford, L. G., & Pifer, M. J. (2017). Mentoring undergraduate students. *ASHE Higher Education Report, 43*( 1), 7–103. https://doi.org/10.1002/aehe.20117

Daddow, A. (2016). Curricula and pedagogic potentials when educating diverse students in higher education: Students' *Funds of Knowledge* as a bridge to disciplinary learning. *Teaching in Higher Education, 21*(7), 741–758. https://doi.org/10.1080/13562517.2016.1183619

Darling-Hammond, L., Flook, L., Cook-Harvey, C., Barron, B., & Osher, D. (2020). Implications for educational practice of the science of learning and development. *Applied Developmental Science, 24*(2), 97–140. https://doi.org/10.1080/10888691.2018.1537791

Dwyer, C. A. (2008). *America's challenge: Effective teachers for at-risk schools and students.* Public Agenda and National Comprehensive Center for Teacher Quality. https://files.eric.ed.gov/fulltext/ED543777.pdf

Easterwood, A. (2016). *Racial stressors and the black college experience at predominately white institutions* [Unpublished master's thesis]. University of Kansas. https://kuscholarworks.ku.edu/bitstream/handle/1808/22359/Easterwood_ku_0099M_14812_DATA_1.pdf?sequence=1

Eby, L. T., Allen, T. D., Evans, S. C., Ng, T., & Dubois, D. (2008). Does mentoring matter? A multidisciplinary meta-analysis comparing mentored and non-mentored individuals. *Journal of Vocational Behavior, 72*(2), 254–267. https://doi.org/10.1016/j.jvb.2007.04.005

Evans, W., Kearney, M., Perry, B., & Sullivan, J. (2017). *Increasing community college completion rates among low-income students: Evidence from a randomized controlled trial evaluation of a case management intervention* [Working paper]. https://doi.org/10.3386/w24150

Gay, G. (2002). Preparing for culturally responsive teaching. *Journal of Teacher Education, 53*(2), 106–116. https://doi.org/10.1177/0022487102053002003

Gibson-Beverly, G., & Schwartz, J. P. (2008). Attachment, entitlement, and the impostor phenomenon in female graduate students. *Journal of College Counseling, 11*(2), 119–132. https://doi.org/10.1002/j.2161-1882.2008.tb00029.x

Guba, E. G., & Lincoln, Y. S. (1989). *Fourth generation evaluation.* Sage.

Hamrick, N., Cohen, S., & Rodriguez, M. S. (2002). Being popular can be healthy or unhealthy: Stress, social network diversity, and incidence of upper respiratory infection. *Health Psychology, 21*(3), 294–298. https://doi.org/10.1037/0278-6133.21.3.294

Harper, A. (2013). *Leadership styles of California African American community college chancellors and self-perceptions of the effectiveness of their recommendations* [Unpublished doctoral dissertation]. Argosy University

Hogan, M. J. (2020) Collaborative positive psychology: Solidarity, meaning, resilience, wellbeing, and virtue in a time of crisis. *International Review of Psychiatry, 32*(7/8) 698–712. https://doi.org/10.1080/09540261.2020.1778647

hooks, b. (2014). *Teaching to transgress.* Routledge.

Hudson, D. L., Eaton, J., Banks, A., Sewell, W., & Neighbors, H. (2016). "Down in the sewers": Perceptions of depression and depression care among African American men. *American Journal of Men's Health, 12*(1), 126–137. https://doi.org/10.1177/1557988316654864

Jacob, C. J., Stoler, J., & Roth, G. (2016). A pilot study of transformational leadership and college counseling outcomes. *Journal of Creativity in Mental Health, 12*(2), 180–191. https://doi.org/10.1080/15401383.2016.1201033

Keating, K., Rosch, D. M., & Burgoon, L. (2014). Developmental readiness for leadership: The differential effects of leadership courses on creating "ready, willing, and able" leaders. *Journal of Leadership Education, 13*(3), 1–16.

Kezar, A., & Maxey, D. (2014). Collective action on campus toward student development and democratic engagement. In C. J. Broadhurst & G. L. Martin (Eds.), *New directions for higher education: No. 167: "Radical academia"? Understanding the climates for campus activists* (pp. 31–41). Jossey-Bass.

Kitzrow, M. A. (2009). The mental health needs of today's college students: Challenges and recommendations. *Journal of Student Affairs Research and Practice, 46*(4), 646–660. https://doi.org/10.2202/1949-6605.5037

Kuh, G. D. (1995). The other curriculum: Out-of-class experiences associated with student learning and personal development. *Journal of Higher Education, 66*(2), 123–155.

Lopez, A. E. (2015). Navigating cultural borders in diverse contexts: Building capacity through culturally responsive leadership and critical praxis.

*Multicultural Education Review, 7*(3), 171–184. https://doi.org/10.1080/2005615X.2015.1072080

Lopez, A. E. (2016). *Culturally responsive and socially just leadership in diverse contexts: From theory to action.* Palgrave MacMillan.

Lucey, T. A., & White, E. S. (2017). Mentorship in higher education: Compassionate approaches supporting culturally responsive pedagogy. *Multicultural Education, 24*(2), 11–17. https://eric.ed.gov/?id=EJ1150567

Mayhew, M. J., Rockenbach, A. N., Bowman, N. A., Seifert, T. A., Wolniak, G. C., Pascarella, E. T., & Terenzini, P. T. (2016). *How college affects students: Vol. 3: 21st-century evidence that higher education works.* Jossey-Bass.

Mazerolle, S. M., Nottingham, S. L., & Coleman, K. A. (2018). Faculty mentorship in higher education: The value of institutional and professional mentors. *Athletic Training Education Journal, 13*(3), 259–267. https://doi.org/10.4085/1303259

McFarland, D. A., & Thomas, R. J. (2006). Bowling young: How youth voluntary associations influence adult political participation. *American Sociological Review, 71*(3), 401–425.

Mills, C., & Ballantyne, J. (2010). Preservice teachers' dispositions towards diversity: Arguing for a developmental hierarchy of change. *Teaching and Teacher Education, 26*(3), 447–454. https://doi.org/10.1016/j.tate.2009.05.012

Mushonga, D. R., & Henneberger, A. K. (2020). Protective factors associated with positive mental health in traditional and nontraditional Black students. *American Journal of Orthopsychiatry, 90*(1), 147–160. https://doi.org/10.1037/ort0000409

NCES. (2020). *The condition of education 2019.* Claitor's Pub Division.

Noddings, N. (1984). *Caring: A feminine approach to ethics and moral education.* University of California Press.

Noddings, N. (1992). *The challenge of care in schools: Care in schools.* Teachers College.

Noddings, N. (2005). *An alternative approach to education* (2nd ed.). Teachers College Press.

Noddings, N. (2008). Caring and moral education. In L. P. Nucci & D. Narvaez (Eds.), *Handbook of moral and character education* (pp. 161–174). Routledge

Noddings, N. (2010). *The maternal factor: Two paths.* University of California Press.

Nohria, N., & Khurana, R. (2010). *Handbook of leadership theory and practice.* Harvard Business Press.

Owusu-Ansah, A., & Kyei-Blankson, L. (2016). Going back to the basics: Demonstrating care, connectedness, and a pedagogy of relationship in education. *World Journal of Education, 6*(3). http://dx.doi.org/10.5430/wje.v6n3p1

Pérez Huber, L., & Solorzano, D. G. (2015). Racial microaggressions as a tool for critical race research. *Race Ethnicity and Education, 18*(3), 297–320.

Pérez, J. F., & Carney, J. V. (2018). Telling of institutional oppression: Voices of Minoritized counselor educators. *Counselor Education and Supervision, 57*(3), 162–177. https://doi.org/10.1002/ceas.12108

Peters, H. C., Luke, M., Bernard, J., & Trepal, H. (2020). Socially just and culturally responsive leadership within counseling and counseling psychology: A grounded theory investigation. *The Counseling Psychologist, 48*(7), 953–985. https://doi.org/10.1177/0011000020937431

Piccolo, R. F., & Colquitt, J. A. (2006). Transformational leadership and job behaviors: The mediating role of core job characteristics. *Academy of Management Journal, 49*(2), 327–340. https://doi.org/10.5465/AMJ.2006.20786079

Preston-Cunningham, T., Boyd, B., Elbert, C., Dooley, K., & Peck-Parrott, K. (2016). What's up with this leadership thing? Voices of African American male college undergraduates. *Journal of Leadership Education, 15*(3), 53–74. https://doi.org/10.12806/v15/i3/r1

Raposa, E. B., Hagler, M., Liu, D., & Rhodes, J. E. (2020). Predictors of close faculty–student relationships and mentorship in higher education: Findings from the Gallup–Purdue Index. *Annals of the New York Academy of Sciences, 1483*(1), 36–49. https://doi.org/10.1111/nyas.14342

Rathmell, W. K., Brown, N. J., & Kilburg, R. R. (2019). Transformation to academic leadership: The role of mentorship and executive coaching. *Consulting Psychology Journal: Practice and Research, 71*(3), 141–160. http://dx.doi.org/10.1037/cpb0000124

Rios-Aguilar, C., Eagan, K., & Stolzenberg, E. B. (2015). *Findings from the 2015 administration of the your first college year (YFCY) survey.* Higher Education Research Institute.

Shapiro, D., Dundar, A., Huie, F., Wakhungu, P., Yuan, X., Nathan, A., & Hwang, Y., A. (2017). *A national view of student attainment rates by race and ethnicity—Fall 2010 cohort* (Signature Report No. 12b). National Student Clearinghouse Research Center.

Shead, M. (2016). *Leadership trait theory.* http://www.leadership501.com/leadership-trait-theory/22/

Sleeter, C. E. (2011). An agenda to strengthen culturally responsive pedagogy. *English Teaching: Practice and Critique, 10*(2), 7–23. https://eric.ed.gov/?id=EJ944889

Stebleton, M. J., & Schmidt, L. (2010). Building bridges: Community college practitioners as retention leaders. *Journal of Student Affairs Research and Practice, 47*(1), 78–98. https://doi.org/10.2202/1949-6605.6018

Stone, S., Saucer, C., Bailey, M., Garba, R., Hurst, A., Jackson, S. M., Krueger, N., & Cokley, K. (2018). Learning while Black: A culturally informed model of the impostor phenomenon for Black graduate students. *Journal of Black Psychology, 44*(6), 491–531. https://doi.org/10.1177/0095798418786648

Winston, B. E. (2006). An integrative definition of leadership. *International Journal of Leadership Studies, 1*(2), 6–66. https://www.regent.edu/wp-content/uploads/2020/12/winston_patterson.pdf

Wood, J. L., & Palmer, R. T. (2013). Understanding the personal goals of Black male community college students: Facilitating academic and psychosocial development. *Journal of African American Studies, 17*(2), 222–241.

CHAPTER 11

# AN INTERDISCIPLINARY STEM NIH GRANT

**Anne Katz**
**Karla-Sue C. Marriott**

## ABSTRACT

Achieving Diversity Through Integrative Scientific Research Experience (ADISRE) is about "creating a desire" for learning and the ethical application of scientific information. This is a 5 year (2018–2023) National Institutes of Health NIBIB-ESTEEMED student-centered research education program. The purpose of ADISRE is to expand, leverage, and improve upon a previously successful research education model (NIBIB-EDEPS) conducted at an HBCU by accomplishing the following objectives: (a) expanding the number of high-achieving student participants; (b) increasing the emphasis on doctoral careers in the biomedical sciences through the nature of our training activities, including a holistic summer bridge program; (c) enhancing the ability of ADISRE scholars to gain entrance into competitive doctoral programs through rigorous and interactive training, negating the need for them to garner post baccalaureate experience; and (d) creating a broad, long-term institutional impact of integrative teaching and learning through laboratory courses for freshmen and sophomores.

*On Leadership*, pages 175–197

Over the past 10 years, an HBCU with over 90% of its students drawn from groups underrepresented in the sciences has built its research training capacity. This accomplishment can be attributed to an institutional commitment and external support from a number of STEM (science, technology, engineering, and mathematics) training programs, including a NIBIB (National Institute of Biomedical Imaging and Bioengineering) funded research training program titled: Expanding Diversity in Engineering and the Physical Sciences (EDEPS). A successful outcome of the EDEPS program included its 92% graduation rate in 4.5 years. This figure is in stark contrast to the 9% institutional rate and 33% rate for matched students admitted with GPA >3.0 over the same period. We anticipate a 100% 5-year graduation rate for the EDEPS cohort, in contrast to the institution's 27% 6-year graduation rate typical of similar institutions. Over 46% of the EDEPS cohort transitioned directly into biomedical related post graduate studies; an additional 39% conducted post baccalaureate work to enhance competitiveness for admission into competitive doctoral programs.

This successful model for student training was facilitated by a one-time NIBIB contractual funding of modest student stipends. In addition, ancillary instruction as well as mentored academic year and summer research experiences facilitated high achievement. This was combined with an intensive mentoring model, unlike any other training programs on the campus. As a result of our evaluation, we believe that a combination of these unique components, including the attention to the quality of mentorship, resulted in the exceptional outcomes.

We now expand, leverage, and improve upon this model in the Achieving Diversity Through Integrative Scientific Research Experience (ADISRE) program. In 2018, the HBCU was one of only two institutions in the nation to successfully obtain funding of $1.3 million from the National Institute of Health, for a NIH-NIBIB-ESTEEMED: ADISRE undergraduate research training program. This 5-year program provides earned scholarships for seven incoming freshmen majoring in biology, chemistry, forensic science, and mathematics each year. These students receive $12,000 per year during the academic year for two years and are involved in biomedical research during the summer.

The goal of this program—funded by NIBIB as a component of the enhancing science, technology, engineering, and math educational diversity (ESTEEMED) initiative—is to expand, leverage, and implement the program through achieving the following objectives:

- Expand the number of student participants from 13 to 28. Each year seven new ADISRE scholars are selected, with scholars from the previous cohort serving as big brother/sister to the newly selected scholars.

- Increase the emphasis on doctoral careers in the biomedical sciences through the nature of our training activities, including a holistic summer bridge program.
- Enhance the ability of ADISRE scholars to gain entrance into competitive doctoral programs through rigorous and interactive training, negating the need for them to garner post baccalaureate experience.
- Create a broad, long-term institutional impact of integrative teaching and learning.

The principal investigator for this program, Dr. Marriott, is a colleague that Dr. Katz met through a Governor's Teaching Fellows Program through the Institute of Higher Education at the University of Georgia. Dr. Marriott served as the founding coordinator for the Forensic Science degree program since its approval by the University System of Georgia Board of Regents in 2011; she previously served as interim chair of the Chemistry and Forensic Science Department at the HBCU. Dr. Katz is an associate professor of literacy education at another local university in the college of education and was invited to collaborate on this NIH project. Dr. Katz is presenting workshops on close reading and critical thinking skills at several points throughout the year; she obtained IRB approval to monitor students' literacy self-concept and close reading strategy implementation in both their academic and personal reading repertoires.

The ADISRE program conducts an intentional and selective recruitment of seven high-achieving incoming freshmen per year with GPA of 3.0 or higher and declared majors in NIBIB-ESTEEMED relevant STEM disciplines until the junior year. Training includes a high impact summer bridge program, summer research, and academic year professional development. This consists of multiple interactive interdisciplinary workshops covering basic science, computation, scientific communication and their application in the real world.

## GRANT PROJECT OVERVIEW

ADISRE is about "creating a desire" for learning and the ethical and useful application of scientific thought and method. The forensic science (FSCI) program at the HBCU has been successfully implementing integrative, immersive STEM learning projects through an interdisciplinary leadership model. The FSCI framework serves as inspiration for the development of this ADISRE program. The overarching goal is to produce STEM graduates with an internal drive to serve their community by pursuing a career in biomedical sciences. ADISRE creates a space for our students and faculty to grow, enjoy learning, and engage in research, while simultaneously fostering environmental awareness, personal discovery, and STEM interdisciplinary leadership development.

## STRENGTHS OF AN INTERDISCIPLINARY FRAMEWORK

The NIH-NIBIB-ESTEEMED ADISRE program is currently in its third year of implementation. To date, the program has accomplished the following outcomes:

1. Selected and supported 21 STEM freshmen scholars majoring in biology, chemistry, forensic science, and mathematics.
2. All ADISRE scholars have been trained in RCR starting during the summer bridge program, as well as during each academic year.
3. All ADISRE scholars have explored multiple research laboratories during the freshmen year and shadowed multiple research professors.
4. All ADISRE scholars have conducted on-campus research including literature review with a designated research advisor during their rising sophomore and rising junior AY year.
5. All ADISRE scholars have attended at least 1–3 scientific research conferences.
6. All ADISRE scholars are members of the honors program.
7. 95% (20/21) of ADISRE scholars have been retained at the HBCU in their STEM major. One scholar transferred to a nursing program at another institution. The HBCU does not have a nursing program.

By providing university students who are in the early stages of their degree programs with this interdisciplinary curricular experience, these workshops are accomplishing the strategic goals of providing transformative student learning experiences and increasing retention. Our goal is to provide students with the experience of professionally presenting their ideas, both orally and in written form, while they receive constructive feedback and guidance from the professor and colleagues. As students collaborate to provide comments, ask questions, and/or offer suggestions to their peer(s), they are displaying growth as problem-solvers and leaders.

Interdisciplinary leadership models such as the partnership described in this chapter can serve as a framework for constructing space for students and faculty to grow and enjoy learning. ADISRE connects STEM with content-area literacy skill development, inspiring creativity, and promoting interdisciplinary collaboration. Zenkov et al. (2016) coined the idea of "partnership literacies" (p. 87). The concept revolves around the collaborative efforts of university and community partners. When literacy programming is approached in this manner, it provides students with access to a wider range of resources.

## COLLABORATIVE METAVERSE RESEARCH FACILITY: VIRTUAL REALITY AND HALOSCREEN

A virtual reality (VR) facility, established at the HBCU within the forensic science program, is used to conduct STEM teaching and research sessions in a collaborative virtual reality. This can also be projected onto a Haloscreen, allowing maximum interaction and collaboration within an immersive environment, locally or remote (see Figure 11.1).

In Fall 2021, these facilities will be used at the HBCU for early impact gateway biology, chemistry, and forensic science STEM laboratory courses. The Haloscreen allows the institution to expand the impact of VR into chemistry and biology. It is exciting to expand interdisciplinary leadership development and collaborative learning in the Metaverse (see Figure 11.2).

Exposure of science students to interdisciplinary leadership is essential for students to become more resourceful in terms of experimentation, removing unnecessary boundaries that limit thought processes, and generating connections between multiple disciplines. ADISRE is designed to improve student depth of understanding, communication across disciplines,

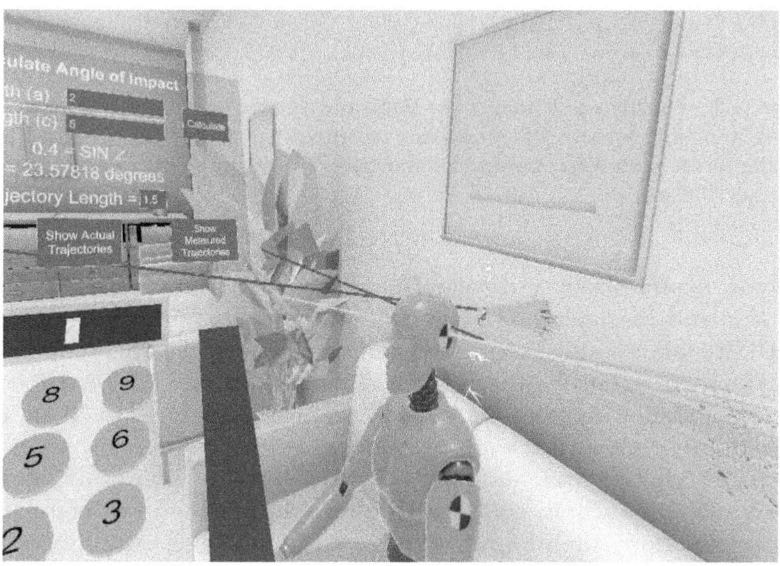


**Figure 11.1** Forensic science blood spatter analysis in VR. *Source:* Marriott, 2020.

**Figure 11.2** Faculty and students can build and analyze small and complex molecules using Nanome. VR rooms can accommodate professor and students together in the same VR room for collaborative VR learning experiences. *Source:* Marriott, 2020.

ability to troubleshoot and solve complex problems, as well as enhance creativity and risk-taking. We believe that the successful implementation of ADISRE will provide learning experiences for our STEM students that will assist them in developing the critical tools, skills, and knowledge necessary to graduate with confidence. This will enable students to create their own unique space in this world with benefits to society. Thus, we expect the successful implementation of this program will result in the following achievements: increased student retention, the transition of competitive undergraduates in their rising junior year into our new institutional honors program, and finally acceptance into a graduate degree program and a career in biomedical sciences.

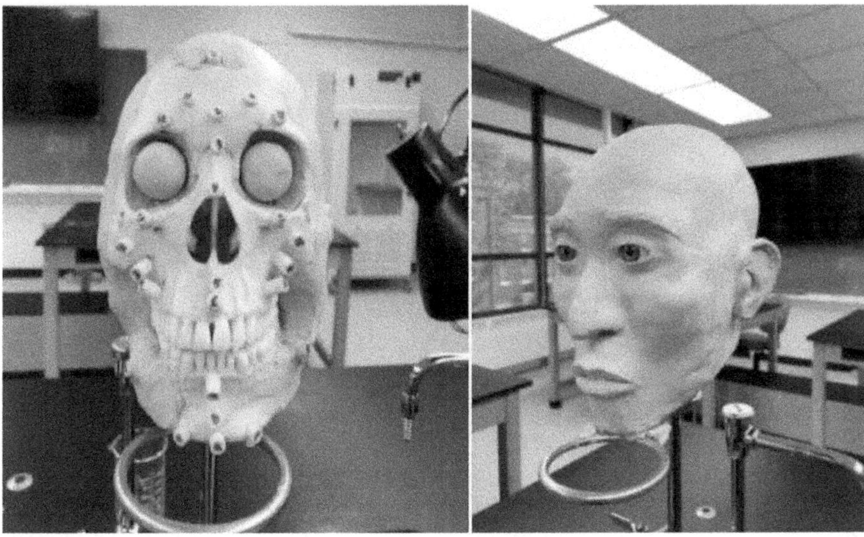

(a) (b)

**Figure 11.3** Facial reconstruction project images: "before" with depth markers on skull (left image) and "after" when the oil-based clay has been applied to give a finished product (right image).

ADISRE incorporates an interdisciplinary leadership curriculum, integrating design-related strategies in conjunction with content-area literacy skills development as an outgrowth of traditional STEM curriculum. For example, a successful forensic science and art collaboration—Facial Reconstruction—serves to reinforce the value of interdisciplinary leadership, immersive learning, and teamwork facilitated by professors that allow students to explore, make connections, and take risks (see Figure 11.3). The project was conducted in student groups over two semesters (through Crime Scene 1 and Crime Scene 2 courses). The collaboration serves as a model for conducting and strengthening mutually beneficial team-based scientific research that is engaging, relevant, immersive, and interdisciplinary. The process required studying anthropology, anatomy, mathematics, 3D digital imagery, and artistry (Marriott, & Clark, 2019).

## SUMMER BRIDGE

First generation college attendees experience numerous challenges, generally being less academically prepared for college than their non-first-generation counterparts. Fifty-nine percent of our students at the HBCU are first generation college attendees. The ADISRE program focuses on conducting a highly integrative, high-impact, and immersive summer bridge program to appropriately prepare and acclimatize incoming STEM freshmen to college life and academic expectations. ADISRE scholars are positioned to be propelled by curiosity, and possess a need for depth of understanding throughout their studies. The ADISRE summer bridge program ensures that our scholars develop a connection with the campus and Savannah community. This goal is accomplished by implementing a holistic approach involving faculty and professional academic advisors.

ADISRE scholars develop critical college knowledge during the summer bridge program which assists in ensuring their retention and success. Summer bridge workshops include the following: Metacognition and Learning, Appreciative Advisement, Close Reading, Critical Thinking, Integrative Learning: Creative Design and Productive Teamwork, Applied Mathematics, Applied Chemistry, Creating Good Study Habits, Applied Science: Real Life CSI Anthropologist, Biostatistics, Blood Spatter Analysis and "Population Genetics, Get the Most Out of Your Institutional Resources, The Graduate School Experience, Professional Etiquette, and Music Appreciation. Scholars who participate in the summer bridge program emerge empowered, having developed critical knowledge, ensuring their academic retention and success.

## CLOSE READING AND CRITICAL THINKING SKILLS

The ADISRE program places special emphasis on Close Reading and Critical Thinking workshops, which are conducted by Dr. Katz. Cervetti and Hiebert (2019) explain that research has demonstrated that different kinds of knowledge have a positive impact on comprehension, from "knowledge of the topic of the text . . . to knowledge of the broader domain . . . to cultural knowledge and general world knowledge" (p. 499). Close reading of science-based articles from a range of sources (such as PBS NewsHour, NPR, CBS News, and poetry) enables students to set a purpose for each reading task and read in a more thorough manner. In addition, articles from these sources that cultivate a sense of personal and cultural heritage were included in these close reading exercises. The process helps students concentrate on what is being read, encourages sustained effort to fully understand the text, encourages personal discovery and individual development, and enables learners to become strategic and independent readers. Kundu (2020) describes how "having agency helps a person to initially visualize and care about certain goals, which is the first step to attaining them. Individuals must be able to see goals as both personally significant and within the realm of possibility. Then they can develop strategies for attaining them" (p. 27).

Close reading encourages the development of skills and strategies through an interdisciplinary leadership framework, such as the ability to interpret words and phrases, analyze structural—visual and textual elements, understand the author's reasoning and use of evidence, ask text-based questions, promote connections, and integrate ideas and knowledge from the text (Lehman & Roberts, 2013). ADISRE scholars greatly benefit from these workshops, as reading is crucial to understanding and extends to writing clearly for meaningful communication. Vaughn et al. (2020) explain that student agency—"the ability of individual students to influence and to create opportunities in the learning context through intentions, decisions, and actions"—merits consideration as students develop as future scientific leaders through an interdisciplinary lens (Vaughn, 2018, p. 62).

Close reading requires prompting students to "unpack" the text to promote deeper comprehension. Regular practice with complex texts and a range of text types (including narrative, informational, and poetry) facilitates students' ability to succeed with college-level text as well as text that they encounter in their everyday lives. Close reading enables students to become critical readers as they build their knowledge through evidence gathered from narrative, informational, and other text types. Sample texts unpacked throughout the workshops included the following (see Table 11.1).

## CLOSE READING METHODS AND TECHNIQUES

Students were invited to participate in multiple close reading demonstrations and writing applications throughout the course of each workshop. An initial close reading activity was structured as follows, using Avery colored dots as a tool to document student insights as they read. For the first reading, students focused on an overview of the text. They were asked to figure out what the text *says* after establishing a purpose for the reading task. For the second reading, the aim was to discern how the text *works*. As workshop facilitator, Dr. Katz modeled the process for students with a sample text. The process for the second reading was as follows:

1. Record a text-to-self connection you made with the text with the orange dot. Jot down connection in margin.
2. Record a memorable word choice or sentence with the green dot.
3. Record the author's perspective as you read with the yellow dot. Jot down why you selected this language as contributing to the author's point of view.

**TABLE 11.1 Sample Texts**

| Article | Link | Close Reading Activity |
|---|---|---|
| "Students Serve up Stories of Beloved Family Recipes in a Global Cookbook" (Harlan, 2017) | https://www.npr.org/sections/thesalt/2017/03/25/519041220/students-serve-up-stories-of-beloved-family-recipes-in-a-global-cookbook | Avery colored dots (text-to-self connection with orange dot, memorable word choice with green dot, author's perspective with yellow dot) |
| "Samin Nosrat Is Making Space at the Table" (Bates, 2019) | https://www.houstonpublicmedia.org/npr/2019/05/30/726375712/samin-nosrat-is-making-space-at-the-table/ | Creating student-generated discussion questions to accompany a text |
| "Love of Words Brings Child, Poet Together" (Robbins, 2010) | https://www.npr.org/templates/story/story.php?storyId=131192480#:~:text=Love%20Of%20Words%20Brings%20Child%2C%20Poet%20Together%20Three%2Dyear%2D,of%20poetry%20with%20one%20another | "What Do You Notice?" chart<br>Rewriting the text as a series of tweets or text messages |
| "A Young Mississippi Woman's Journey Through a Pioneering Gene-Editing Experiment" (Stein, 2019) | https://www.npr.org/sections/health-shots/2019/12/25/784395525/a-young-mississippi-womans-journey-through-a-pioneering-gene-editing-experiment | "Knew-New-Q" (K-N-Q) activity<br>Visual outlines |
| "Why Octopuses Might Be the Next Lab Rats" (Boyce, 2019) | https://www.npr.org/sections/health-shots/2019/06/03/727653152/why-octopuses-might-be-the-next-lab-rats | Creating student-generated discussion questions to accompany a text<br>Text codes |
| "How to Make the Most of Online College This Fall" (Nadworny & Nguyen, 2020) | https://www.npr.org/2020/09/11/911933161/how-to-make-the-most-of-online-college-this-fall | Avery colored dots (text-to-self and text-to-text connection with orange dot, memorable word choice with green dot, author's perspective with yellow dot) |

*(continued)*

**TABLE 11.1 Sample Texts (continued)**

| Article | Link | Close Reading Activity |
|---|---|---|
| "The Age-Old Practice of 'Gleaning' Is Feeding People Through the Pandemic" (Weber, 2020) | https://www.pbs.org/newshour/show/the-age-old-practice-of-gleaning-is-feeding-people-during-the-pandemic | Text codes<br>Thinking hats |
| "A COVID-19 Vaccine May Be Only 50% Effective. Is That Good Enough?" (Aubrey, 2020) | https://www.npr.org/sections/health-shots/2020/09/12/911987987/a-covid-19-vaccine-may-be-only-50-effective-is-that-good-enough | "Knew-New-Q" (K-N-Q) activity<br>Discussion circles<br>Visual outline |
| "An Electrical Line Worker's Brief but Spectacular Take on Empowering Her Community" (Taylor, 2020) | https://www.pbs.org/newshour/show/an-electrical-line-workers-brief-but-spectacular-take-on-empowering-her-community | Thinking hats<br>Rewriting the text as a series of tweets or text messages |
| "Jonah Larson, a 12-Year-Old Crochet Prodigy, Will Bring You Pure Joy" (Copeland, 2020) | https://www.oprahmag.com/life/a33262498/jonah-larson-crochet/ | Avery colored dots (text-to-self connection with orange dot, memorable word choice with green dot, author's perspective with yellow dot) |
| "The US Isn't Even Close to Getting COVID-19 Down to Where It Needs to be by Fall, Medical Experts Say" (Yan & Holcombe, 2020) | https://www.cnn.com/2020/09/14/health/us-coronavirus-monday/index.html | "Knew-New-Q" (K-N-Q) activity<br>Discussion circles |

An additional close reading activity was the "Knew-New-Q" (K-N-Q) activity (Gambrell, 2014). This activity provided a means for students to annotate the text, as follows:

- K—Put a "K" in the margin if the information is something that you already knew.
- N—Put an "N" in the margin if the information is new to you.
- Q—Put a "Q" in the margin if you have a question about the information.

After annotating the text independently, students verbally shared their reflections with a peer:

- I already knew that...
- I learned something new. I learned that...
- I have a question about...
- I wonder about...
- I'd like to know more about...
- The author's purpose in writing the text is...

Finally, each student wrote a rationale for their annotation to solidify their "Knew-New-Q" insights, guided by the following sentence starters:

- Write a sentence about something you already knew. (I already knew...)
- Write a sentence about something new that you learned. (I learned...)
- Write a sentence about something you would like to know more about. (I would like to know more about...)

Additional close reading strategies were introduced and reinforced throughout the workshops. This included a "What do you notice?" chart to record ideas and spark discussion while reading. After recording items that were noticed, students were invited to discuss their rationale for selecting the concept, strengthening their presentation skills. Strategies with a focus on digital literacy connections, such as rewriting the text as a series of tweets or text messages, were included. It is important to integrate literacy strategies that align with students' daily repertoire, as leaders need to be equipped with creative strategies for communication success.

Discussion circles were modeled as a sample format, with four roles. Person A is designated as the summarizer. Pre-discussion, this individual writes a short summary of the reading. During the discussion, the individual's role is to summarize the discussion as it proceeds (in writing) and to maintain the group's momentum. The individual needs to be knowledgeable about the reading so that he/she has the ability to direct peers to a specific point or fact. Person B is designated as the inquirer. This individual develops three open-ended questions for the group to discuss, using their questions to spark conversation. Person C is designated as the clarifier. Pre-discussion, this individual chooses three sections that are particularly salient, interesting, unusual, or difficult to understand. Page numbers for each item as well as a rationale for each selection will be provided to the group. During the discussion, this individual will share their choices one at a time to spark discussion. Person D is the connector. Pre-discussion, this individual will write about connections they see between the reading and their own experiences, as well as connections between previous material studied or read, academically or personally. During the discussion, this individual will ask colleagues to share connections they noticed as they read. This individual will bring connections up one at a time to ensure that all voices are heard as the discussion evolves.

Analyzing a text from different viewpoints (deBono, 1999) was introduced to students to cultivate interdisciplinary leadership skills. The six thinking hats concept was originally designed for a group to analyze a problem, but can also be used as a strategy to analyze a piece from different viewpoints. Each "thinking hat" represents a different approach to a topic. Sample "thinking hats" are as follows:

1. Focus on the piece itself and the facts it contains. Look at the information you have, and see what you can learn from it. Look for gaps in your knowledge, and either try to fill them in or recognize that they exist.
2. Look at the piece using intuition and emotion. Also, consider how other individuals might react to it emotionally. Try to understand the responses of others who may not fully know your reasoning.
3. Look critically at the piece. What in the piece is problematic? Where does the piece not supply as much information as you need?
4. This is the lens that allows you to think positively about the piece. It is the optimistic viewpoint that allows you to see its strengths and contributions.
5. This is the creative lens. This is where you can consider how you could apply this piece to your own life.
6. This lens stands for process control. This is the hat that you assume when you encounter difficulties, as it allows you to stop and generate a plan. This is an important thinking hat for when you need to reflect and consider other positions.

Creating student-generated discussion questions to accompany a text were introduced and practiced with various articles. Students were encouraged to generate questions which would inspire critical thinking on the topic. Additional strategies included creating visual outlines and self-generated annotation strategies. A discussion regarding selecting and applying strategies that work better for facilitating one's own comprehension and critical thinking skills followed, with a focus on both academic and personal reading.

Due to COVID-19 pandemic in 2020, the face-to-face close reading and critical thinking workshops were adapted to virtual sessions through Zoom during Summer and Fall 2020. Students were invited to join via Zoom, with preparation materials and attachments sent in advance to build background knowledge. Sample introductory activities for the virtual format were as follows in order to build a sense of community in this alternate format:

Please read the article—take notes as a series of tweets for a few lines and post here! https://www.pbs.org/newshour/show/how-schools-are-coping-with-constantly-changing-landscape-of-covid-19. Responses included the following tweets: #student-keep track of learning-on my own; #school harder-remote learning; #school-keeps-changing; #learn-read-write

After introducing Jason Reynolds, the National Ambassador for Young People's Literature appointed by the Library of Congress, I invited students to watch this brief video: https://www.loc.gov/item/webcast-9175/. I then posed the question—"What item would you frame? Why was it significant? Where would you hang it and why?" Responses included, "I would frame my adoption papers because family pushes me to succeed. With them being framed, it would remind me that I have family at home and it would motivate me to do better every day."; "I would frame my first workplace. This is because it was a very memorable experience for me." The chat box provided a forum for student response and facilitated our virtual learning, as students read and were able to think aloud through the text with peers before our discussion, enabling literacy leadership development to thrive in an alternate format.

## DATA SOURCES AND RESULTS

Pre-and post-surveys on reading memories and self-concept as a reader today as well as a "self-portrait as a writer" were distributed at the beginning of each session with each cohort. (Please see Tables 11.A1, 11.A2, and 11.A3 in Appendix).

### Self-Concept as a Reader

1. What kinds of books do you like to read—both in school and at home? Please tell me about them (topics/genre/information/narrative).

2. Please explain the kind of reading that you do in these formats. Please be specific. eBooks (Kindle, Nook, iPad); computer/laptop/iPad; communication—email, IM, blog, Twitter, Facebook, post, chat
3. How do you find out about books/reading materials/online resources you might like to read?
4. What are some of your immediate reading goals? School and Home
5. What could professors do to make reading for school more enjoyable? Please be specific.

## Self-Portrait as a Writer

As a writer, please share your feelings about writing and your writing history including:

- a experience that you remember as a young writer;
- writing courses taken in school and for leisure;
- which writing tasks you find to be enjoyable, easy, and/or challenging;
- aspects of writing with which you have the most/least experience; and
- please make a list of your writing activities, no matter how small, over the past two days.

## Post-Workshop Survey

1. Have you applied any of the specific "close reading" strategies from the workshop in your own reading? If so, which ones?

   Colored dots; text-to-text/text-to-self connections; memorable word choice; author's perspective; K-N-Q strategy; annotation coding strategy; thinking hats; discussion circles in a study group.
2. What kind of reading material have you used to apply the strategy/strategies?
3. Have you applied any of the note-taking strategies presented from the workshop in your own reading? If so, which ones?

   Taking notes as tweets; Post-it note diagram; sketches of key points with captions; 3-2-1 discussion strategy; outline with your own connections; create own discussion questions.
4. What kind of reading material have you used to apply the strategy/strategies? Please be specific and explain.
5. Did the close reading strategies workshop make you a more effective and strategic reader/increase your comprehension? Please be specific and explain.

In addition to results from the surveys, an audit trail was kept to document student learning. This included tracking workshop activities and student applications of the strategies in notebooks. Finally, a postworkshop survey was sent to students at 2-month intervals between workshops to document their progress as close readers with feedback sent to encourage continued growth.

## WRITERS AS LEADERS

"I am From" poems (Lyon, 1999) were introduced as a tool to reflect on what is important to us and what shapes our identities. Students were provided with a general template, and I shared a sample poem. An excerpt of a student's poem is as follows:

> I am from my parents and grandparents—
> The future that they thought would come.
> I am from the shabby home made from bare hands and built with lots of love,
> It's a generational home with books,
> Full of memories.
> I am from my mother, a passionate gardener with her azaleas, tulips, and roses—
> It is always important to remember.
> I am from an independent woman, loud and demanding high expectations.
> I am from the mischievous adventures of me and my sister.
> I am from kindness and goodness.

Writing as a tool for self-identity was explored through activities such as the six-word memoir (National Public Radio, 2010). Reading the article and listening to the audio clip led to a discussion of distilling our central story to a short phrase. I modeled by sharing my current six word memoir with students—"authentic teaching and learning and creating." Sample student six-word memoirs included "from a nobody to a somebody"; "little kid to young adult here"; "finishing what my parents started first"; and "infinite to finite back to infinite."

This writing activity positioned students as future leaders, as they were invited to consider how they could present the material to colleagues in an engaging manner that represented their personal leadership style. As a writing extension, students were asked to select an article at the end of each workshop and consider how they could represent their discussion and application of the material in a different format—"How else can I write/create this?" Students were provided with a menu of choices: meme, personal narrative, social narrative, comic strip, op-ed for the newspaper, tweet,

Facebook post, 2-minute video, poem, letter, blog post, series of text messages, song, spoken word, play vignette, or photo essay. Sample student responses to this activity were as follows:

- "You could write a blog post with the PBS article. It would be used as a way to voice your opinion."
- "You could make a 2 minute video with the CNN article, showing images and captions with the main highlights telling the audience what they need to know about this important information."
- "You could use the Jason Reynolds article for a photo essay, taking pictures of his framed items and explaining their significance to him."

## PLAN FOR INSTRUCTION IN THE RESPONSIBLE CONDUCT OF RESEARCH (RCR)

The NIBIB-ESTEEMED ADISRE program is designed with responsible conduct of research (RCR) at its core. As stated at the beginning of this chapter, ADISRE is about creating a desire for learning and the ethical and useful application of scientific thought and method. As such, instructions on RCR are conducted starting during the summer bridge program as well as during each academic year covering the following subject matter: (a) laboratory safety: all freshmen scholars, beginning of the first year in the laboratory (laboratory safety awareness will be conducted in Years 1, 2, 3, and 4); (b) research misconduct; (c) research ethics; (d) conflict of interest; (e) authorship; (f) data management; and (g) human subjects and animal use.

In addition, a general 2-hour discussion session with case studies covering multiple RCR topics is conducted during the summer bridge program to introduce new scholars to the importance and relevance of RCR. We emphasize to our scholars that RCR is a part of a scientist's daily life and should always be at the forefront of our scientific thinking, applications, presentations, and documentations. ADISRE scholars are held accountable to the highest standards of responsible conduct within their scientific disciplines, in keeping with the established RCR training plan, which conforms with NIH NOT-OD-10-019.

## RESEARCH PREPARATION AND RESEARCH EXPERIENCES

Scholars are trained and prepared for internships in both internal and external research programs beginning in the rising sophomore summer, and continuing through to the rising junior summer. After summer experience as rising juniors, scholars will be well prepared for entrance into the institution's honors program and others such as the NIH-MARC.

### Presentation at Regional and National Conferences

Beginning in their sophomore year, the scholars are supported to attend and present at scientific conferences such as PSLSAMP, ABRCMS, ACS, HBCU-UP. Conference attendance presents the scholars with important opportunities to meet with scientists and form professional connections.

## CONCLUSION

Participants in the study emerge as interdisciplinary leaders with a unique skill set, prepared to solve complex problems with a well-grounded scientific framework. Interdisciplinary leadership skills are cultivated as ADISRE freshman prepare and acclimatize to college life, professional etiquette, and academic expectations. Leadership skills are further strengthened as sophomores prepare for honors programs, graduate school, and a meaningful career in biomedical sciences. Through ADISRE, we hope to spark a desire and capacity in students to become self-directed learners, as well as open-minded, caring, and ethical leaders in biomedical sciences. Interdisciplinary workshops are designed to nurture integrative learning, effective study skills, depth of understanding through close reading strategies, creativity, and innovation through teamwork and service to the community through scientific contributions. The collaborators approach this work from a leadership framework that suggests all learning is social. "We learn literacies via many types of text, including, but not limited to, all forms of print/digital media and interactions with other human beings and our environments. However, our concept relies on a physical, community, contextual form of collaboration, with real people being involved in real contexts, across settings and communities" (Zenkov et al., 2016, p. 89). The interdisciplinary STEM NIH grant thrives on this very notion.

## ACKNOWLEDGMENT

This work is supported by the National Institutes of Health NIH-NIBIB-ESTEEMED (5R25EB025768-02) grant award.

## APPENDIX

Sample of Reading Workshop Results

**TABLE 11.A1 Reading Memories**

| Student | Earliest Reading Memory | Kinds of Reading Materials | Feelings Associated With Experience | Key People- Influenced Reading Opinions | How Did You Acquire Reading Materials? |
|---|---|---|---|---|---|
| A—freshman/male | Nursery rhymes and songs. | Fiction books with a focus on reading comprehension. | A content feeling that I was safe and learning. | My kindergarten teacher encouraged me to read and provided me with books to read on my own. | School library, teachers, bookstore. |
| B—freshman/female | Mom reading stories to me and my sister. | Bedtime stories about animals (caterpillar changing into a butterfly, a duck at the park). | Joy and happiness. I am lucky to still have most of my childhood books. | My elementary teacher. We would read for AR (accelerated reader) points. We would earn prizes depending on how much we read. | The local library. |
| C—freshman/female | Joke books and simple nursery rhyme books. Soon, I began to read non-fiction books about animals and plants. | Nursery rhymes, non-fiction, science articles, mythology. | The experience of finding out something new, but also the feeling of familiarity. | My uncles, who would encourage me to read about science. | Family, friends, the library in my neighborhood. |
| D—freshman/male | Cereal boxes- my mom reading them to me. Menus from restaurants. Educational books. | "When you give a mouse a cookie . . ." series. | Love | My mom and kindergarten teacher drove me to read more because they loved hearing me read. | School or mom always bought books for me if I wanted to read them. |

**TABLE 11.A2 Self-Concept as a Reader**

| Student | Kinds of Books I Like to Read Today (Home & School) | Kind of Reading You Do in Different Formats | How Do You Find Out About Books/Reading Materials/Online Resources You Like to Read? | What Are Some of Your Immediate Reading Goals? | What Could Professors Do to Make Reading for School More Enjoyable? |
|---|---|---|---|---|---|
| A—freshman/male | Fantasy, mystery, and biographies (successful people and how they achieved success). | Social media posts, school email, textbooks, reading for school on laptop, and Kindle (read fiction book). | Google search, social media, recommendations from other people | I want to dedicate myself to more structured reading and study time. I would like to set a reading goal for a specific number of books to read and achieve that. | Choose textbooks that don't have a monotonous style and that are more engaging. Associate everyday analogies with the material. |
| B—freshman/female | Drama, action, graphic novels. | Checking updates on Facebook, schoolwork on laptop, read eBooks during downtime. | I read the summaries, and decide if it interests me. | I want to be more interested in reading textbooks for school. I want to read more books for personal enjoyment. | Use eBooks and include reading with more images. |
| C—freshman/female | Books about plants and business structures (school). At home, I read books about medicine and chemical affinity. | I honestly prefer hardcopy books rather than electronic, unless it is an article about recent findings. | I look at the back of books as references to see if I would find some of the resources interesting. | At school, I want to read as much information as I can that is valuable. At home, I like to read for confirmation. | Have interesting reading material available, and recommend other resources. |
| D—freshman/male | Classical novels, poetry, science fiction, fantasy, mystery. | My friends and I will sometimes share poetry we write online or with each other. | Through friends or past books or authors that I like who are publishing a new series. | Read to learn and develop in school. Learn to see others' lives through the eyes of the characters while reading for fun. | Find ways to connect readings into everyday lives, when possible. |

**TABLE 11.A3 Post-Workshop Survey**

| Student | Application of Close Reading Strategies in Own Reading | Applied to ____ Kind of Reading Material | Application of Note-Taking Strategies | Applied to ___ Kind of Reading Material | Did the Close Reading Workshop Make You a More Strategic Reader? |
|---|---|---|---|---|---|
| A—freshman/male | annotation coding strategy<br>discussion circles in a study group | Science text<br>Research articles | create own discussion questions | Science text | It has made reading and studying more effective. It helps me problem solve as I read. |
| B—freshman/female | K-N-Q strategy<br>colored dots<br>text-to-text / text-to-self connections | English literature<br>History class | taking notes as tweets<br>3-2-1 discussion strategy<br>post-it note diagram | English literature<br>History class | I learned new ways to read and annotate text. I like using the visual comprehension strategies. |
| C—freshman/female | colored dots<br>memorable word choice<br>thinking hats | Science text<br>News articles for current events | create own discussion questions<br>outline with your own connections | Science text<br>News articles for current events | It gave me ways to engage in the readings and look at them from different perspectives. |
| D—freshman/male | author's perspective<br>K-N-Q strategy | Science text<br>Science lab | post-it note diagram<br>sketches of key points with captions<br>3-2-1 discussion strategy | Science text<br>Science lab | I have used many of these methods since I took the workshop. It made studying so much easier by letting me focus on key notes rather than everything I read. I have also increased my presentation and writing skills. |

## REFERENCES


Aubrey, A. (2020, September 12). *A COVID-19 vaccine may be only 50% effective: Is that good enough?* NPR. https://www.npr.org/sections/health-shots/2020/09/12/911987987/a-covid-19-vaccine-may-be-only-50-effective-is-that-good-enough

Bates, K. G. (2019, May 30). *Samin Nosrat is making space at the table.* Houston Public Media. https://www.houstonpublicmedia.org/npr/2019/05/30/726375712/samin-nosrat-is-making-space-at-the-table/

Boyce, N.G. (2019, June 3). *Why octopuses might be the next lab rats.* NPR. https://www.npr.org//sections/health-shots/2019/06/03/727653152/why-octopuses-might-be-the-next-lab-rats

Cervetti, G. N., & Hiebert, E. H. (2019). Knowledge at the center of English language arts instruction. *The Reading Teacher, 72*(4), 499–507.

Copeland, S. (2020). *Jonah Larson, a 12 year old crochet prodigy, will bring you pure joy.* Oprah Daily. https://www.oprahmag.com/life/a33262498/jonah-larson-crochet

deBono, E. (1999). *Six thinking hats.* Little, Brown, and Company.

Gambrell, L. (2014, October 14). *Reading informational text with pleasure, proficiency, and passion* [Keynote presentation]. Georgia Reading Association Conference, Macon, Georgia.

Harlan, B. (2017, March 25). *Students serve up stories of beloved family recipes in a global cookbook.* NPR. https://www.npr.org/sections/thesalt/2017/03/25/519041220/students-serve-up-stories-of-beloved-family-recipes-in-a-global-cookbook

Kundu, A. (2020). *The power of student agency: Looking beyond grit to close the opportunity gap.* Teachers College Press.

Lehman, C., & Roberts, K. (2013). *Falling in love with close reading: Lessons for analyzing texts—and life.* Heinemann.

Lyon, G. E. (1999). *Where I'm from.* Absey and Co. http://www.georgeellalyon.com/where.html

Marriott, K-S. C. (2020). [Forensic science blood splatter analysis in VR].

Marriott, K-S. C., & Clark, E. B. (2019, June 26). Forensic facial reconstruction: Integration of science and art. In D. P. Domizi (Ed.), *Engaged student learning: Essays on best practices in the University System of Georgia* (Vol. 1; pp. 38–44). University System of Georgia. https://www.usg.edu/teaching-and-learning-excellence/assets/facultydevelopment/documents/ebook/MarriottClark.pdf

Nadworny, E., & Nguyen, A. (2020, September 14). *How to make the most of online college this fall.* NPR. https://www.npr.org/2020/09/11/911933161/how-to-make-the-most-of-online-college-this-fall

National Public Radio. (2010, February 3). *Can you tell your life story in exactly 6 words?* https://www.npr.org/2010/02/03/123289019/can-you-tell-your-life-story-in-exactly-six-words

Robbins, T. (2010, November 9). *Love of words brings child and poet together.* NPR. https://www.npr.org/templates/story/story.php?storyId=131192480#:~:text=Love%20Of%20Words%20Brings%20Child%2C%20Poet%20Together%20Three%2Dyear%2D,of%20poetry%20with%20one%20another

Stein, R. (2019, December 25). *A young Mississippi woman's journey through a pioneering gene-editing experiment.* NPR. https://www.npr.org/sections/health-shots/2019/12/25/784395525/a-young-mississippi-womans-journey-through-a-pioneering-gene-editing-experiment

Taylor, S. (2020, July 2). *An electrical line workers 'Brief but Spectacular' take on empowering her community.* PBS. https://www.pbs.org/newshour/show/an-electrical-line-workers-brief-but-spectacular-take-on-empowering-her-community

Vaughn, M. (2018). Making sense of student agency in the early grades. *Phi Delta Kappan, 99*(7), 62–66.

Vaughn, M., Premo, J., Sotirovska, V., & Erickson, D. (2020). Evaluating agency in literacy using the Student Agency Profile. *The Reading Teacher, 73*(4), 427–441.

Weber, S. (2020, September 6). *The age-old practice of 'gleaning' is feeding people during the pandemic.* PBS. https://www.pbs.org/newshour/show/the-age-old-practice-of-gleaning-is-feeding-people-during-the-pandemic

Yan, H., & Holcombe, M. (2020, September 14). *The US isn't even close to getting Covid-19 down to where it needs to be by fall, medical experts say.* CNN. https://www.cnn.com/2020/09/ 14/health/us-coronavirus-monday/index.html

Zenkov, K., Bertrand, S., Clark, E., Taylor, L., Newman, K., Sciarrino, S., von Topel, K., Angle, D., & Pellegrino, A. (2016). Partnership in/as/for literacies. *Journal of Adolescent & Adult Literacy, 60*(1), 87–90. https://doi.org/10.1002/jaal.563

CHAPTER 12

# ADAPTIVE INFORMAL EDUCATION LEADERSHIP DURING COVID-19

**Marlee J. Tavlin**


## ABSTRACT

Despite declining interest in STEM, there is extensive research which demonstrates that out of school time (OST) learning helps motivate students and that it has an especially positive influence on typically underrepresented students. Although the COVID-19 pandemic forced many OST institutions to shut down in March 2020, there were a few OST STEM leaders who decided to continue with programming virtually. This chapter seeks to add an important component to literature by highlighting data collected during a phenomenological study which sought to explore urban high school students' experience transitioning to an online OST STEM learning environment during the COVID-19 pandemic. Semi-structured interviews, observations and archival material analysis were conducted. Data was coded and analyzed thematically. Reliability and validity were accomplished through verbatim transcription of audio-recorded interviews and triangulation. Findings suggest that to face the struggles of COVID-19, informal education leaders should embrace an interdisciplinary leadership approach in being mindful of personal needs, em-


*On Leadership*, pages 199–211

> bracing other experts, being flexible, leaning into the community, mentoring others including fellow leaders and looking at what positive changes may come out of this crisis. Although it may remain difficult to engage in hands-on learning while staying physically distant, this chapter serves as a preliminary glimpse into what a particular institution did when the pandemic began, as well as cite literature that may be helpful to other leaders facing this crisis.

According to UNESCO, the COVID-19 pandemic has as of 2020 put 1.6 billion young people out of school and "turned educators' (and students') worlds upside down" (Verma et al., 2020, p. 487) with no end in sight. UNESCO's (2020) report states that to enact an appropriate and strong educational response to COVID-19, leaders should develop partnerships with institutions of informal learning. Although information remains scarce on how educational leaders can best respond and support those they serve, a new report produced by the UNESCO Institute for Lifelong Learning (UIL) asserts that this "pandemic has allowed us to recognize and demonstrate the value of non-formal and informal learning" (p. 2). UNESCO's report aims to explain lessons learned from examining how various cities across the world have utilized informal learning and suggests concrete measures for action. It urges educational leaders to utilize informal learning as they respond to the COVID-19 crisis, highlighting the particular importance of libraries, museums and other institutions of informal learning during this time because they "support learning, promote well-being and foster solidarity" (p. 5). This echoes research which states that to address complex issues, leaders must enact an interdisciplinary approach through integrating knowledge from multiple disciplines and stakeholders (Bammer et al., 2020).

Several large research, education, and science organizations, such as the National Science Teachers Association and the National Science Board, emphasize the importance of informal or out of school time (OST) science learning. They help students to connect science to their everyday lives and bridge the gap between informal and formal science learning by helping to strengthen concepts that students are already learning in school (National Research Council, 2009). Research indicates that out of school time science programming has an especially positive influence on low-income students who often come from schools that have inadequate science educational resources (Rahm, 2008).

At the time of this writing, according to data collected by the American Alliance of Museums this past summer, a third of museums are expecting to close their doors before the end of 2021. Another 41% had to reduce staff and 33% are expecting to lose almost half of their annual operating income before 2021. This reflects the larger informal education's financial landscape; non-profits have already lost about one million jobs and 22,000 more are expected to close permanently. Because many museums and other institutions of informal learning will have to survive on smaller budgets, their leaders have to make the hard decisions of what programming and staff must be reduced until they are able to recover financially (Merritt, 2020). This is why it is of the utmost importance to examine existing educational programs and to explore what methods their leaders have utilized to adapt to be successful or even merely survive through this crisis (Verma et al., 2020).

## PURPOSE

Many informal education institutions were forced to shut their doors in March 2020, forcing leaders to decide which programming to suspend, including any type of outreach programming planned for the summer. However, there were a few OST STEM leaders who decided to continue with programming virtually. Genspace is a nonprofit community laboratory in Brooklyn, New York whose main purpose is making science more accessible to those both with and without a formal background in science by enabling them to pursue laboratory projects. Biorocket is Genspace's paid 6-month Biotech internship program for New York City high school students whose immediate purpose is to increase its interns' science knowledge and lab skills by exposing them to work in a real lab. The program's ultimate goal is to motivate students from traditionally underrepresented groups in STEM to pursue science after high school (Center for an Urban Future, 2020).

Genspace's director of education and executive director, Beth Tuck, believes that the important difference between this community lab internship program and other informal STEM programs is its autonomous nature. Interns are afforded the freedom to "craft their own experience" by enabling them to have a greater voice and a choice in their experience. She believes that being in control of their own experience may help them with their science identities and motivate them to continue on in science (B. Tuck, personal communication, February 7, 2020).

This chapter seeks to add an important component to literature by highlighting data collected during a phenomenological study which explored Biorocket's experience transitioning to a completely virtual out of school time learning environment during the COVID-19 pandemic. Although all interns were assigned pseudonyms, Beth and the program itself were not assigned pseudonyms to highlight this particular program. Biorocket should be considered an example of a successful OST STEM program during COVID-19 in that it was able to transition from an in-person lab-based program to completely online while keeping all twelve interns involved, with some even planning to return to the program's teen council in the fall.

## The Importance of Hands-On Learning

Hidi and Renninger (2006) created a four-phase model which describes the development and deepening of learning interests. They believe that how learning occurs is also important because interest development is partly context dependent. Therefore, the resources that informal institutions of science can offer (e.g., special exhibits, lab equipment, hands on experiences) can greatly affect the interest development and learning that takes place.

Price and Hein (1991) found that the most effective museum encounters included opportunities for children to actively engage with and handle objects and scientific materials. Emdin (2010) firmly believes that student interest in science is directly linked to their ability to engage in hands-on activities. He found that when students are not able to explore scientific concepts using hands-on activities and tools, it is "invariably linked to the limited agency of students in the classroom to be fully connected to science" (p. 15). Unfortunately, COVID-19 requires that students be removed from any type of hands-on experience.

Hamilton et al. (2020) utilized findings from the 2020 COVID-19 AEP surveys which aimed to provide a nationally representative summary and "wide-ranging picture of teaching, leading, and learning during an unprecedented time" (p. 13). One of the major findings was that educational leaders at all levels expressed a noted loss of engagement from their students at all educational levels which they attributed to the loss of hands-on learning opportunities.

However, interdisciplinary leadership "presents itself wherever there are complex, real-world problems" (Bloomquist et al., 2018, p. 60). Arguably there may be no more fitting issue facing our generation than the COVID-19 pandemic and the impact it has and will continue to have on all aspects of our society, especially our youth and learners. This type of leadership focuses on addressing complex issues through the creation of an environment which embraces uncertainty, focuses on the whole rather than the individual and does not shy away from how complex issues may influence multiple aspects of the lives of those they lead. Interdisciplinary leaders are willing to learn from those they lead by creating an open dialogue, coproducing solutions, changing course when necessary and having a growth mindset (Block, 2013; Dweck, 2016; Hornett & Lee, 2017). This chapter demonstrates the importance of a leader such as Beth who embodies the qualities of interdisciplinary leadership through a crisis and the positive effect it had on her informal learning community.

## CASE STUDY: HOW DO WE HAVE A COMMUNITY LAB WITH NO LAB?

On July 6, 2020, Beth wakes up early again. It is 5 months into the COVID-19 pandemic and she has recently made the difficult decision not to continue working on a grant. Although this grant would bring funds that the nonprofit so desperately needs to survive, it would be a long shot for their small organization. The time spent working on it would most likely be more lucratively spent on figuring out how to transition their hands-on lab to a remote one, if that is even possible. As she logs in for their first Zoom session of the summer, she worries about securing funding for the next year within this economic depression. Even if she receives the funds, how will she run a community lab space with no lab? As she takes another sip of her coffee, she puts all that aside and smiles as her 12 interns start to enter the Zoom session, all but two of whom keep their cameras off.

> Welcome back, everyone! I know it's been a long time since we've met together so let's start off today by doing a "brain dump" in our shared Google document about anything you remember from our few sessions we were able to meet in the lab. Before that though let's speak a bit about how the summer is going to go now that we are no longer in the lab. Although we expect you to attend every session and if we do not hear from you, we will be forced to adjust your stipends . . . we understand that especially now that may not be possible so please just communicate with us as much as possible! This summer we are going to start with some "sciency stuff" but then later go on to do more change making thinking. We've seen hardship in our lives and we're going to see more and we are going to try and come up with science based solutions on how we can work to make the world a better place for the next generation. (observation notes, July 6, 2020)

As the students start filling out the document under various headings such as "Mutations → variation" or "Gene Regulation" with their microphones and cameras off, she asks, "Does anyone remember where genetic code comes in?" No one answers. "That's okay . . . no one person has to know everything, together we can know all the things!" In the past it has been hard enough speaking in a physical class and getting no response, but not being able to even see them adds another layer. She tries again, "I'll add my favorite gene which is the sonic hedgehog gene partly because of its funny name." That finally receives some chuckles. "The knotch gene is my favorite," one intern unmutes his microphone and says, which opens the floodgates to other interns speaking and debating both on the Zoom and chat functions. As a student named Fatima fills out a part of the google document, Beth cheers her on: "Yesss Fatima, keep going!" (observation notes, July 6, 2020).

In this vignette, Beth displays multiple aspects of an interdisciplinary leader such as: being open to change, embracing uncertainty, being aware of how those she leads may be affected and being open to co-producing solutions to problems such as them not being able to attend every session (Block, 2013; Dweck, 2016; Hornett & Lee, 2017).

## EDUCATIONAL LEADERSHIP AND THE COVID-19 CRISIS

Leithwood and Riehl (2005) illustrate how successful educational leadership cannot be separated from its context, "the goals being perused, the individuals involved, resources and timeframes and many other factors" (p. 20). Leadership during a crisis is a unique field of leadership because each "crisis" is different from the last and may have various lasting effects that may change its field. Although one type of leadership may have been effective before the crisis, a leader may need to change to accommodate this particular crisis.

### Findings From Unfolding Literature: Themes of Note

From the limited literature regarding the COVID-19 crisis, several themes have emerged that informal learning leaders should keep in mind while making decisions which may impact their institutions. For example, an important characteristic of an effective leader during the COVID-19 crisis is flexibility, which includes understanding the personal situations of those they lead as well as the ability to "change course" and enact/adapt to a new way of doing things (Kaul et al., 2020; Mutch, 2015).

Gabrielle, a rising high school junior and member of the 2020 Biorocket cohort, was asked if she believed that OST STEM programming could survive if it had to remain remote. Although initially worried about the transition online, she felt that "Biorocket made a way... everything just shifted but they made it seem like it was the plan the whole time" (G. Smith, personal communication, September 2, 2020). However, Beth and the other leaders of Biorocket had no blueprint of how to turn an internship that relied on making scientific equipment accessible and using a community lab to a virtual setting "without losing the integrity of what makes the program and the community itself really special and unique" (B. Tuck, personal communication, January 7, 2021). She described how she embraced uncertainty and through having the flexibility to be open to change, an element crucial to successful interdisciplinary leadership, was able to maintain the integrity of her program.

> So, certainly some of it was trial by fire in terms of how we adapted... It was a lot of patching together, but it was purposeful in its intention of trying to make sure that the students were building knowledge, skills, getting more prepared for what college and careers in STEM could look like.... all of those elements, we were able to still maintain, even though we were doing it in a remote or virtual format. (B. Tuck, personal communication, January 7, 2021)

Various examples of flexibility were evident throughout observations of Biorocket. In addition to Biorocket staff and various guest mentors, only two interns would keep their cameras on regularly and everyone would keep themselves "muted." Although this made observing interns' reactions and engagement difficult, it was also possible that the interns could possibly be in a different room altogether. Beth described that the decision to give the students this autonomy was purposeful for a few reasons. They wanted to be cognizant of the wi-fi and broadband issues that many students were facing as well as wanting to respect their privacy and not force them to show their homes. However, the main reason Beth gave was closely tied to her leadership style which is adaptive in nature:

> I am a firm believer that people need to be comfortable in their learning environment. There are plenty of fidgety people and if you ask them to sit still in front of a computer for 12 hours a day you're begging for trouble. So if they need to walk around or if they need to go on errands for their families or whatever else was going on, it's not my responsibility to police that. Really they know themselves and they know their families so they can be responsible for making those calls. We still maintained the expectation that they were going to participate. So we would split them out into breakout rooms, we would make sure that they were participating in the chat, we would have poles, you know whatever other structure we could create was to make sure that they were in it. But if that serves them as a moment to like reset and re-engage we didn't want to serve as a place of judgment, we wanted to make sure that they felt like they could take advantage and participate to the degree that they wanted to. And they did... they were in it. So, you know I wasn't feeling like we were missing out on them because they didn't have their cameras on. I think what we saw in the final products especially was a pretty strong indicator that they were engaged in their learning and that they were taking it seriously so I like giving them their own autonomy. (B. Tuck, personal communication, January 7, 2021)

This echoes the American Psychological Association's (2020) findings that during crises such as the COVID-19 pandemic, people often feel helpless and an extreme loss of control. It is crucial for leaders to do whatever they can to recognize the differences in the way people may react and allow them to have a sense of control, even if that is just over the way they are communicating. Interdisciplinary leadership is flexible to "changing course" when necessary (Bloomquist et al., 2018). Hannah, one of the college leaders, described how Biorocket had the flexibility to move to 3 days a week to minimize the amount of time that students would have to sit in front of a computer as well as incorporating "dry labs." Additionally, Beth led her students through a lab which included elements that she had sent to them through the mail and they all did together online.

***The Importance of Mentorship: Positive Adults Who Genuinely Care***

Researchers highlight the importance of leaders during crises who humanize themselves and put the needs of those they lead at the forefront. They also emphasize the importance of staying calm while simultaneously acknowledging the immense stress those they lead are going through (American Psychological Association, 2020; Kaul et al., 2020; Mutch, 2015). Observing Beth, demonstrated how she used Biorocket to consistently encourage both her students and teachers to make her OST STEM program work during the summer.

The 2020 cohort participants who were interviewed praised her encouragement and mentorship this past summer. Beth described the amount of stress and uncertainty she knew many of her interns were facing between transitioning online, their parents being out of work and even getting sick. She also acknowledged the stress that she and her co-leaders felt trying to imagine the future of Genspace. However, she said that in spite of all this uncertainty, her priority was making Biorocket as successful an experience for the students as possible. The way she was able to accomplish this was by "stripping away the noise" and focusing on what was most important to her as a leader:

> Making sure that we could stay as anchors for the students and provide a space for them to come every week or every couple of days where it was very low pressure but they knew that we were going to be there no matter what. So there was just kind of that feeling of like, how can we just be an anchor while the sea is roiling around us? (B. Tuck, personal communication, January 7, 2021)

Boone et al. (2020) highlights how successful interdisciplinary leaders recognize the importance of bringing in outside expertise reasoning that: "Such engagement elicits new ideas, perspectives, and initiatives, contributing to the dynamism" (p. 5). For Beth, a crucial element to Biorocket is including a myriad of mentors and guest scientists with various areas of expertise who would "log on." For example, a July 23, 2020 observation showed the students attempting to learn how to use a coding language called "R." Although typically difficult to teach even in person, these interns were being taught virtually with the help of a special guest scientist through the use of screen sharing and by working slowly with a lot of patience.

Research highlights the importance of "horizontal" lateral leadership; during a crisis "strong leaders who enable others to lead are catalysts for widespread change" (Kaul et al., 2020, p. 809). Beth displayed this important characteristic through including young mentors in the Biorocket program and empowering them to lead their own sessions. For example, Brad, a college mentor and extremely involved member of Biorocket, emphasized the importance of the mentorship he received from other Biorocket leaders which got him through this unprecedented time. As he observed:

> The amount of mentorship and support that I got from my mentors was just like amazing! I had mentioned coming into this remote learning and a rough semester my motivation wasn't completely there. Even though this summer was mainly about the high school students, my mentors made me feel really special as well. I think that's one of the things that really stood out to me and kind of pushed me to be a better version of myself. 'Cause I came into it not wanting to fully be there, but because of the people that I was surrounded by it kind of pushed and elevated me to step up. I'm surrounded by people who love what they do and I love what they do and I also want to be a part of this so it kind of made me more motivated and on top of my stuff and just challenging myself. So definitely my mentors 1000% need all the praises that they deserve for finishing off this program. It is such a success and without them it wouldn't have been as amazing. (B. Smith, personal communication, August 8, 2020)

Biorocket cohort member Amy said in her interview that Beth learned of her love of reading and recommended books to enhance her STEM learning while in quarantine. She also motivated her to stay in science by getting her and another cohort member involved in a virtual class that Genspace would be holding that upcoming fall. This was in stark contrast to the STEM leadership that Amy experienced in school where she did not feel a personal connection to her chemistry teacher and likely would not have continued in STEM. As of Fall/Winter 2020, Amy is still involved in Genspace and is both taking their "Bad Science" virtual course as well as being actively involved in their newly developed teen council.

#### *The Importance of Community*

Mutch (2015) found that "building strong relationships, developing a sense of community, engendering loyalty, and fostering collaboration are typical relational characteristics of successful crisis leaders" (p. 192). Leaders are responsible for creating and maintaining the kind of culture necessary and multiple Biorocket participants, including Hannah, a college aged leader/mentor, reported that they felt a sense of community during the 2020

Biorocket session even after they abruptly switched online. She described this during an interview conducted via phone about how they triumphed through the transition online: "You have to adjust to it...we had small groups where we went over how we were going to collaborate and help each other. We still felt an overall sense of community; it just was online" (H. Smith, personal communication, September 2, 2020). She said that even after the day was over she would check in on her mentees to see how they were doing.

Successful interdisciplinary leaders recognize the specific and important knowledge that community members hold and the importance of looking to and incorporating that knowledge (Bammer et al., 2020). Communities are a key resource for a successful educational leader during a crisis, as they host a wealth of knowledge, are experts in their own needs and creating strong links within them is a "necessity to deal with the many issues that COVID-19 has generated particularly for vulnerable, marginalized, or isolated young people" (Harris & Jones, 2020, p. 245). Beth echoed this sentiment and emphasized the importance of Biorocket leaning into their community as a key to their success.

> I mean that in the broadest sense...so leaning into our teens as drivers in their own experience to help us define what learning is going to look like and feel like. Leaning into partners who are willing to volunteer their time, their energy, their expertise to share that knowledge with our young people, leaning into funders that want to see your programs succeed. So, checking in with them, asking them for advice, leaning on them as partners as best as you can, or as much as you feel trusting of that relationship, leaning on your colleagues and your workplace, getting their feedback. If you're having a rough day just asking them to step in, you know, it's really about you're not in it alone and as much as you can lean on your community as well as support your community will make your experience more successful. (B. Tuck, personal communication, January 7, 2021)

***Learning From This Crisis: Becoming a Better Leader***

Although leaders may have an instinct to rush to "returning to normal" as soon as possible, research highlights how a crisis such as COVID-19 may present an important opportunity for an institution to improve itself. It is important for an organization's core mission and values to remain at the forefront and "effective leaders take this opportunity to reemphasize these values to motivate and galvanize those around them" (Kaul et al., 2020, p. 810). Verma et al. (2020) exemplifies how one science education leader in particular reported that COVID-19 has allowed her institution to reach more people, especially those in rural areas, by increasing engagement with webinars.

As UNESCO (2020)'s report illustrates: "Cities can thrive on what they achieve during the crisis and benefit from the momentum that follows by continuing to place importance on non-formal and informal learning and promoting lifelong learning for all" (p. 7). During an interview conducted via Zoom, 2020 Biorocket cohort member Gabrielle discussed how Biorocket remained committed to their core values of "accessibility and communication. I think they're really crucial for people who come from underrepresented backgrounds like myself because it kind of gives us hope and gives us resources we wouldn't otherwise have" (G. Smith, personal communication, August 12, 2020).

Although the financial situation may seem bleak for many informal educational institutions, Merrit (2020) describes how senior museum leaders had to determine how they could move forward and continue to serve their communities. President and CEO of the Science Museum of Minnesota, Alison Rempel Brown and her leadership team looked at their museum's mission statement and found that they could still serve the needs of the community in some capacity by immediately creating online experiences for families with children who had to be at home.

## CONCLUSION AND LOOKING FORWARD WITH INTERDISCIPLINARY LEADERSHIP

As Harris and Jones (2020) describe in their editorial about school leadership during COVID-19, educational leaders are "walking a tightrope without a safety net" (p. 244). Biorocket is an example of a successful informal learning environment during the COVID-19 pandemic where students were able to use and create real data that was led by their interests and utilized their collaboration. When asked if she believed that her leadership style changed, Beth remarked:

> I would say it got more clear... when you're faced with a crisis like this you really have to strip away all of the extra and focus back on what really matters and that clarity of what really matters in this experience was the driver for how we chose all the different things that we did. (B. Tuck, personal communication, January 7, 2021)

Although it may remain difficult to engage in hands-on learning while staying physically distant, this chapter serves as a preliminary glimpse into what a particular institution did when the pandemic began, as well as cite literature that may be of help to other leaders facing this crisis. Findings suggest that to face the struggles of COVID-19, informal education leaders should embrace an interdisciplinary leadership approach in being mindful of personal needs, embracing other experts, being flexible, leaning into the community, mentoring others including fellow leaders and looking at what positive changes may come out of this crisis.

## REFERENCES

American Psychological Association. (2020). *How leaders can maximize trust and minimize stress during the COVID-19 pandemic psychologists' research shows how to boost leaders' communication in times of crisis.* https://www.apa.org/news/apa/2020/03/covid-19-leadership

Bammer, G., O'Rourke, M., O'Connell, D., Neuhauser, L., Midgley, G., Thompson Klein, J., Grigg, N. J., Gadlin, H., Elsum, I. R., Bursztyn, M., Fulton, E. A., Pohl, C., Smithson, M., Vilsmaier, U., Bergmann, M., Jaeger, J., Merkx, F., Vienni Baptista, B., Burgman, M. A., . . . Richardson, G. P. (2020). Expertise in research integration and implementation for tackling complex problems: when is it needed, where can it be found and how can it be strengthened? *Palgrave Communications, 6*(5), 1–12 https://doi.org/10.1057/s41599-019-0380-0

Block, P. (2013). *Stewardship: Choosing service over self-interest.* Berrett-Koehler Publishers.

Boone, C. G., Pickett, S., Bammer, G., Bawa, K., Dunne, J. A., Gordon, I. J., Hart, D., Hellmann, J., Miller, A., New, M., Ometto, J. P., Taylor, K., Wendorf, G., Agrawal, A., Bertsch, P., Campbell, C., Dodd, P., Janetos, A., & Mallee, H. (2020). Preparing interdisciplinary leadership for a sustainable future. *Sustainability science, 15,* 1723–1733.

Bloomquist, C. D., Georges, L., Ford, D. J., & Breen, J. M. (2018). Interdisciplinary leadership practices in graduate leadership education programs. *Journal of Leadership Studies, 12*(2), 60–63. https://doi.org/10.1002/jls.21579

Center for an Urban Future. (2020). *Plugging in: Building nyc's tech education & training ecosystem.* https://nycfuture.org/pdf/CUF_TechNYC_Plugging_In_final.pdf

Dweck, C. (2016). *Mindset: Changing the way you think to fulfill your potential.* Penguin Random House.

Emdin, C. (2010). *Urban science education for the hip-hop generation.* Sense Publishers.

Hamilton, L. S., Kaufman, J. H., & Diliberti, M. (2020). *Teaching and leading through a pandemic: Key findings from the American educator panels spring 2020 COVID-19 surveys.* Rand. https://www.rand.org/pubs/research_reports/RRA168-2.html

Harris, A., & Jones, M. (2020). COVID 19—School leadership in disruptive times. *School Leadership & Management, 40*(4), 243–247. https://doi.org/10.1080/13632434.2020.1811479

Hidi, S., & Renninger, K. A. (2006). The four-phase model of interest development. *Educational Psychologist, 41*(2), 111–127. https://doi.org/10.1207/s15326985ep4102_4

Hornett, A., & Lee, P. D. (2017). Developing strategic leaders: Three studies of wicked problem-solving. *Global Business and Organizational Excellence, 37*(1), 28–38. https://doi.org/10.1002/JOE.21826

Kaul, V., Shah, V.H., & El-Serag, H. (2020). Leadership during crisis: Lessons and applications from the COVID-19 pandemic. *Gastroenterology, 159*(3), 809–813.

Leithwood, K., & Riehl, C. (2005). What we know about successful school leadership. In W. Firestone & C. Riehl (Eds.), *A new agenda: Directions for research on educational leadership* (pp. 22-47). Teachers College Press. https://www

.researchgate.net/publication/44836425_A_New_agenda_for_research_in_educational_leadership

Merritt, E. (2020). *Downsizing our museum in the face of a pandemic.* American Alliance of Museums. https://www.aam-us.org/2020/10/20/downsizing-our-museum-in-the-face-of-a-pandemic/

Mutch, C. (2015). Leadership in times of crisis: Dispositional, relational and contextual factors influencing school principles' actions. *International Journal of Disaster Risk Reduction, 14*(1), 186–194. https://doi.org/10.1016/J.IJDRR.2015.06.005

National Research Council. (2009). *Learning science in informal environments: People, places, and pursuits.* The National Academies Press. https://www.nap.edu/catalog/12190/learning-science-in-informal-environments-people-places-and-pursuits

Price, S., & Hein, G. E. (1991). More than a field trip: Science programmes for elementary school groups at museums. *International Journal of Science Education, 13*(5), 505–519. https://doi.org/10.1080/0950069910130502

Rahm, J. (2008). Urban youths' hybrid positioning in science practices at the margin: A look inside a school-museum-scientist partnership project and an afterschool science program. *Cultural Studies of Science Education, 3*(1), 97–121. https://doi.org/10.1007/s11422-007-9081-x

UNESCO. (2020). *How cities are utilizing the power of non-formal and informal learning to respond to the COVID-19 crisis.* https://unesdoc.unesco.org/ark:/48223/pf0000374148

Verma, G., Campbell, T., Melville, W., & Park, B. Y. (2020). Science teacher education in the times of the covid-19 pandemic. *Journal of Science Teacher Education, 31*(5), 483–490, https://doi.org/10.1080/1046560X.2020.1771514_

CHAPTER 13

# NARROW-MINDED MILITARY EDUCATION AND OPPORTUNITY LOST

## On the Possibility of Developing Future Army Officer Expertise in Mission Command at a Military Boarding School

**Richard Megahan**

### ABSTRACT

This chapter aims to highlight the problems and possibilities of future officers becoming proficient in "Mission command" with a focus on improving opportunities for commissioning cadets in the Army, ROTC programs, and military boarding schools. Interestingly, the literally hundreds of American observers who were regularly sent to the old continent during the course of the 19th century to study the constantly warring European armies completely missed out on the decade long discussion about the revolutionary command philosophy of Auftragstaktik. Instead they focused on saddle straps, belt buck-

*On Leadership*, pages 213–233

> les, and drill manuals. This is one reason why the most democratic command concept never found a home in the greatest democracy. The U.S. officers simply missed the origins because of their own narrow-minded military education. (Muth, 2013, p. 44)

## STARTING WITH WHY

The stark reality of constant decentralized operations in Operation Iraqi Freedom (OIF) and Operation Enduring Freedom (OEF) demonstrated flaws and weaknesses in the Army's conventional command methods (Horton, 2014; McCauley, 2012). At the onset of the 21st century, the Army found itself questioning its long-standing "detailed command" approach to leadership in units. The traditional "American Way of War," emphasizing overwhelming firepower, material and technological advantages, caused leaders to stumble in the face of combat with low-tech forces (Orsini, 2019). The culture of top–down, process-driven planning and detailed guidance proved too plodding and methodical for leaders against an agile, nimble, free-wheeling foe (Vandergriff & Webber, 2018).

In response to the needed change, the mission command doctrine provided the Army with a means to examine operational complexity through an open-mindedness that seeks opportunities for leader education and training in interdisciplinary leadership practices (Vangjel, 2018). The result was Army Doctrinal Publication 6-0 (ADP 6-0), *Mission Command: Command and Control of Army Forces,* published in July 2019. Mission command is the current U.S. Army doctrinal approach to operations, training, and leadership development. The manual has come closer to identifying and incorporating the characteristics of interdisciplinary leadership than any previous paradigm (Orsini, 2019). Mission command and interdisciplinary leadership concepts mirror one another. For example, both incorporate the criticality of context, recognition of culture, dealing with complexity and "wicked" problems, practicing open-mindedness, being adaptable, embracing a growth mindset, employing shared leadership and decision-making, and focusing on outcomes and not processes (Bloomquist et al., 2018; ADP 6-0, 2019).

Nevertheless, where and how does the U.S. Army begin to inculcate interdisciplinary leadership practices in leadership development for mission command? The answer is that the Army does so by focusing on the education and training of its officer corps—the men and women, the trusted professionals, who will lead units in complex environments—in pre-commissioning training (Mele, 2020). Army Reserve Officer Training Corps (ROTC) is the largest source of new 2d lieutenants every year, and is located at 274 colleges, universities, and junior and senior military colleges where aspiring officers receive their first installment of mission command (Department of the Army, U.S. Army Cadet Command, 2019).

While the U.S. Army Training and Doctrine Command (TRADOC) oversees all institutional training and education occurring at Army professional development schools and courses, its subordinate arm, the U.S. Army Cadet Command (USACC), is responsible for the nuts-and-bolts delivery of mission command/interdisciplinary leadership education and training in ROTC programs. The most historic and unique ROTC programs are at the military boarding schools: four military junior colleges (MJC) and six senior military colleges (SMC). These schools offer a tremendous opportunity to teach mission command doctrine and ensure there is the transfer of experiential learning into daily operations, procedures, and the leadership development culture of their resident corps of cadets. To analyze this open-minded approach to leadership and command, and the opportunities to take advantage of the phenomenal experiential learning potential at military boarding schools, the first step is to understand why junior officers' interdisciplinary leadership development and professional expertise in mission command is important.

## What is Mission Command?

Mission command is the Army's doctrinal guidance for command, leadership, and management in operations, training, and garrison duties. Mission command doctrine encapsulates an approach to command and control, a pedagogy for leader training and education, and a leadership philosophy (ADP 6-0, 2019). As an approach to command and control, mission command focuses on outcomes, not details of accomplishing the task or mission. Commanders capitalize on subordinate ingenuity, innovation, and decision-making to achieve the commander's intent when conditions change or current orders are no longer relevant. Subordinates must seek opportunities, and commanders accept risk for subordinates trying to meet their intent. Subordinate decision-making and decentralized execution appropriate to the situation help manage uncertainty and enable the necessary tempo at each echelon during operations. Employing the mission command approach during all garrison activities and training events is essential to creating the culture for its employment in high-risk environments (ADP 6-0, 2019, pp. 1–4).

As a pedagogy, mission command is a learner-centric practicum oriented on adaptive leadership challenges addressed with deep learning, coaching and mentoring by instructors, and growth in expertise (Green & McBride, 2015). Peer-to-peer learning, choices, learner autonomy, and experimentation are instructional approaches that demonstrate the critical link between pedagogy and mission command (Barlett, 2019; Kvernbekk et al., 2008; Vandergriff, 2019; Vandergriff & Webber, 2017; West, 2020; Williams, 2020). Leaders must be educated and trained to be agile and open-minded in their approach to wicked problems. Using an interdisciplinary schema to apply critical thinking skills to search for opportunities, to examine multiple perspectives. Training and education foundations provide occasions to transfer learning to "what you see is what you get" experienced-based intuition and decision-making skills (Vangel, 2018).

As a leadership philosophy, commanders empower subordinates to use their initiative to accomplish their assigned tasks. Commanders provide direction to subordinates who can execute without the need for continuous guidance. Commanders realize that the complexity of operation means they alone cannot make every important decision in every critical situation and must lead, coach, and train subordinates to apply initiative and sound judgment in the time-constrained, simultaneous decision required during combat (Department of Army, 2019). Young leaders are empowered—and expected—to make crucial decisions based on their training and education, connecting observations and determinations of what is taking place on the ground (Heyward, 2013). The common thread is a trust—trust relationship that binds all unit echelons, from commanders to soldiers (Vangjel, 2019). Mission command is a *culture* of commanders providing direction but not tight control. Mission command is a culture of trust; it is a culture of "thinking like a commander" (Shadrick & Lussier, 2004), that emphasizes a mindset of growth in professional expertise (Muth, 2013).

The Army's mission command doctrine includes guiding principles that describe the mindset and highlight the focus for the development of professional expertise: competence, mutual trust, shared understanding, commander's intent, mission orders, disciplined initiative, and risk acceptance (ADP 6-0, 2019). Operating within the philosophy of mission command, in combat, training, or garrison, requires Army officers to understand how to apply the principles of mission command as leaders and staff officers. While the Army issued an unambiguous articulation of its expectations of all members of the force to apply, learn, and train in mission command, there has been narrow-mindedness in training and opportunities lost in education (Muth, 2013; Orsini, 2019; Orsi & Mundell, 2019; Vandergriff, 2019). This dysfunction has had the most harmful effect on ROTC precommissioning training and education (R. Megahan, personal communication, July 20, 2020).

Therefore, if military schools are preparing future leaders for the mission command environment of the Army, learning *and* applying *m*ission command *in school* is a crucial first step.

## Research Questions

1. Mission command is the Army's philosophy of operating, educating, and training. Are ROTC programs at military schools and colleges "narrow-minded" in instructional approach? What factors cause programs to fail to apply the current Army focus and conduct training on the seven principles of mission command philosophy?
2. The development of professional expertise in mission command is imperative of USACC for the training and education of future officers. What factors cause ROTC programs at military schools and colleges to experience opportunities lost by failing to take advantage of training transfer and curricular alignment-enhanced experiential learning within the school corps of cadets?

## Methodology

The methodology employed for this research project is qualitative content analysis (QCA; Schreier, 2012). QCA systematically explicates texts, images, and expressions within the contexts of everyday life to make sense of the communications intended between people in organizations (Krippendorf, 2013, p. xxi). QCA is a sound methodology for this study. It is interpretative, naturalistic, and situational, reflexive, emergent, flexible, inductive, case-oriented, and emphasizes validity. These elements are crucial attributes resident in mission command and the development of leadership expertise (Elvira et al., 2017; Schreier, 2012, pp. 21–36; see ADP 6-0, 2019; Department of the Army, 2019).

For this study, relevant/purposeful sampling (Krippendorf, 2013, p. 120) occurs by analyzing only those texts related to answering the research questions. QCA examined 8 SMC and 4 MJC Academic Year 2019–2020 ROTC program course syllabi and 30 SMC and 30 MJC Corps of Cadets Training Schedules before the effects of COVID-19 on college campuses. In addition, this study assessed ROTC syllabi and regimental training schedules for the frequency of manifest (Schreier, 2012, pp.176–179; Krippendorf, 2013, p. 1) evidence of training and education activities in mission command (ADP 6-0, 2018; Department of the Army, USACC, 2019).

The study examined Army ROTC syllabi for scheduled course lesson periods with mission command instruction, and assessed corps of cadets weekly training schedules for dedicated training periods demonstrating evidence of ROTC mission command training transfer. QCA of course syllabi and weekly training schedules sought to highlight interpretations and inferences about the organization's cultural approach to learning in mission command. Also, QCA was applied to identify what the documents promote, discount, enable, inhibit, expand, or limit within the educational and organizational contexts to be used (Krippendorf, 2013, p. 24; Schreier, 2012, p. 2).

The study's methodology used "formal segmentation" to divide the material into the most relevant categories to answer the research questions (Schreier, 2012, p. 134). The design of coding for data collection ensured a "fit" between categories and codes. This study adapted the classification methodology of content analysis research of undergraduate syllabi conducted by Welch (2005, p. 3). The approach for this study facilitated a focus on manifest evidence of mention for mission command (no mention; key words only; short statement of one or two sentences; paragraphs of three or more sentences; extensive comment of two or more sections).

The study methodology achieved reliability in analysis through a consistent coding frame devised to assess stable AY 2019–2020 syllabi and training documents (Schreier, 2012, p. 167). "What-You-See-Is-What-You-Get" Face and Content Validity (Neuendorf, 2002, p. 115) of the coding was achieved through a break-down of categories that support the research questions, using subject matter expert evaluation (Schreier, 2012, p. 189).

## Mission Command in the Military Boarding School

The U.S. Army expects all officers to become experts in the philosophy and principles of mission command (ADP 6-0, 2019). The first step on this pathway to expertise occurs in the demonstration of proficiency in mission command in pre-commissioning programs at the U.S. Military Academy (USMA), Officer Candidate School (OCS), and ROTC. Within the genre of 274 Army ROTC programs, though, there is a subset of schools that are as historic as they are unique in providing an extraordinary organizational context for mission command: the Senior Military College and Military Junior College boarding schools.

The SMC in the study has an on-campus student body of approximately 2,600 students, including 1,800 cadets and around 800 civilian students. The school offers Army, Navy/U.S. Marine Corps, and Air Force ROTC programs, with Army ROTC the largest with around 700 cadets. The Military Junior College in the study is a cadet-only 2-year junior college and high school (about 550 cadets in Grades 9–12), with approximately 450 junior college cadets enrolled in the Early Commissioning Program (ECP) of Army ROTC. Both schools follow Army doctrine in the ROTC programs and in nearly every aspect of cadet life in the corps of cadets.

These two schools are not just known for rigorous academics, emphasis on fitness, and focus on developing leaders; they are the closest representation to a "unit" organizational culture a prospective junior officer will find in pre-commissioning training and education. The Army's unit culture, its organizational culture (Schein, 2017, pp. 3–5), is evident every day in military boarding schools (Coulter, 2017, p. 4). Nevertheless, it is essential to recognize that academic policy and other institutional programs affect this formative representation of Army unit culture. This makes Army organizational structure and the number and type of leadership opportunities in ROTC and the cadet regiment crucial components for enacting the development of professional expertise of aspiring future officers in mission command. How closely interconnected the ROTC battalion *unit* is with the corps of cadets *unit*—and vice versa—is a clear indicator of the degree of authenticity and realism of the Army culture at each school, and signals the propensity to facilitate the deliberate practice of mission command (Borce, 2012; Finney & Klug, 2016).

The ROTC battalion constitutes the first of two unit venues where leadership practice occurs within an Army organizational context. Both SMC and MJC Army ROTC programs conduct USACC syllabi-directed lessons and labs through their student ROTC battalions, which must be organized to replicate the structure and function of an actual Army Infantry battalion or cavalry squadron organizational context and culture (Department of the Army, USACC, 2019).

Beginning with the SMC in the study, the Army ROTC battalion consists of approximately 700 cadets, organized in 4 companies and a battalion staff, providing cadets with opportunities to practice in 72 leadership positions (from team leader to battalion commander). The MJC ROTC unit differs slightly in that instead of a standard infantry battalion, it consists of a USACC-approved cavalry squadron of three troops (companies) and squadron (battalion) staff, with 24 leadership positions in the squadron (squad leader to squadron commander).

The second unit venue is the cadet experience in each school's corps of cadets. This is the largest, more realistic Army-based unit venue in both schools for daily deliberate practice in Army organizational leadership. While the SMC Army ROTC battalion clearly resembles the standard Army Infantry battalion, the SMC Corps of Cadets unit structure is radically different from its ROTC unit organization.

At first glance, the 1,800-cadet strong corps of cadets mirrors a standard Army regimental structure, with two line battalions of four companies and one "special troops" battalion of five companies. There are 245 leadership roles from team leader to regimental commander. However, it is in the subordinate battalion level of the organization of the SMC Corps of Cadets where there is a significant departure from both the standard Army regimental structure, and no resemblance to the ROTC battalion. The two line battalions are unique: Each battalion has two new cadet (freshmen) companies and two old cadet, upper class (sophomore-to-senior) companies. This structure is designed to be more conducive to a plebe system (Muth,

2013) than an adaptive leader organization. On top of this non-standard organization, cadet leaders in these units (and across the regiment) are participants in four different service ROTC programs, who naturally tend to defer to their respective service doctrinal concepts of leadership in the execution of their duties.

Comparatively, the MJC ROTC and cadet regiment unit venues are much more straight-forward. The Army ROTC squadron and the cadet regiment follow a U.S. cavalry organizational model. Unlike the SMC, however, the MJC Army ROTC student squadron aligns coherently with the corps of cadets unit structure, organized into one U.S. Cavalry-style regiment of four squadrons, five troops (companies) per squadron (battalion). The MJC Corps of Cadets numbers approximately 1,000 cadets. Usually, there are 175 leadership roles (squad leader to regimental commander) but this is complicated by what positions are available to high school cadets and those held only by junior college cadets. However, compared to the SMC, the congruence of the MJC ROTC squadron and the cadet regiment suggests a much greater possibility of essential training transfer between the MJC Army ROTC instruction and duties in the corps of cadets.

Thus, the organization of the ROTC battalion, the organization of the corps of cadets (cadet regiments), and the number of leadership positions and opportunities to practice leadership in these unit entities are crucial components to examine. For both schools, the problem is not positions, but practice. In the ROTC battalions and cadet regiments at both schools, there is woefully inadequate preparation and practice opportunities before cadets assume leadership duties, professional development while performing in assigned positions, or training for future positions of greater responsibility. These are serious shortfalls which directly affect the deliberate practice required for proficiency in mission command.

These issues occur because the SMC and MJC ROTC battalion leadership position preparation is assumed to occur at ROTC Summer Camp. Consequently, there are no ROTC battalion professional development activities before the start of the academic year, only possibilities for some on-the-job training during ROTC labs twice a week. Similarly, for both schools, all corps of cadets training and preparation for leadership roles in the academic year take place in an intense 5-day period before the arrival of the new cadets. Known as "cadre" training, it is very heavily oriented on receiving new cadets and reinforcing the plebe system. Neither school has a planned official cadet professional development sequence of positions (like the Army) that provide echelon-by-echelon progressive experience for higher ranking billets over the course of cadet time at their schools (a cadet could be a platoon sergeant one year, and a company commander the next).

The fundamental contributing factor at both schools is that dedicated corps of cadets training time is severely constrained by academic scheduling

(SMC training is 6 hours per week; MJC is 3 hours). Since there is minimal professional development conducted throughout a SMC/MJC cadet leaders' year-long tenure in any position, there is significant "tribal knowledge" influencing suboptimal "on-the-job" performance. Ultimately, due to a lack of dedicated training, the cadet leaders at both schools naturally gravitate toward behaviors that reflect how they survived the plebe system.

There is one more major contributor to the representation of Army organizational culture and the pathway to professional expertise in mission command: academic leadership courses. There are academic leadership courses offered at both schools that are outside ROTC programs or corps of cadets duties. The SMC conducts over two dozen academic leadership courses and offers a leadership minor program. These courses are interdisciplinary and draw from most of the academic departments. Course objectives and outcomes do not specifically connect with SROTC courses, but military sciences course credit applies to the minor. The MJC conducts five academic leadership courses (not including Junior ROTC). The business and athletic departments and the school leadership center instruct these courses. Course objectives and outcomes do not connect or intersect with either SROTC or JROTC curricula. For both the SMC and MJC, it is the ROTC curriculum and the academic leadership courses that are credit bearing courses. The largest experiential leadership learning opportunities at the schools—the corps of cadets—are deemed extra-curricular by accrediting agencies, with no academic credits awarded.

Between just these two schools, over 3,000 cadets are members of a corps of cadets (student body), organized, trained, and educated using Army doctrine, occupying over 400 direct corps of cadets organizational leadership positions each year, participating in 370 hours of scheduled training. Both schools conduct over 320 SROTC lessons, have over 100 ROTC battalion leadership positions, and ultimately provide over 125 new officers to the Army every year. Each graduate/commissioned second lieutenant must demonstrate proficiency in mission command (ADP 6-0, 2019; Department of the Army, U.S. Army Training and Doctrine Command, 2017; Department of the Army, USACC, 2019). The research question is, given their respective environments, how well are military boarding school ROTC cadets trained and educated to achieve this *proficiency* in mission command?

## Findings: Senior Military College (SMC) and Military Junior College (MJC)

The QCA revealed near-identical findings regarding manifest mention of mission command in ROTC syllabi and corps of cadets training schedules. For the SMC, 8 AY 2019–2020 AROTC syllabi (MS I, II, III, IV), in 216 class periods/activities across eight full semesters, only two of eight syllabi (25%) contained manifest mention of mission command as a specifically designed learning task, exercise, or event. Of the 216 total scheduled class period topics listed in those eight syllabi, instruction in mission command occurred in only two 60-minute class periods (0.93%). A closer reading of all eight syllabi reveals the Army's four learning outcomes for mission command are present in syllabi introduction portions (demonstrate proficiency in mission command philosophy; demonstrate proficiency in mission command leader and commander tasks; demonstrate proficiency in mission command staff tasks and demonstrate proficiency in mission command systems). However, there is no further elaboration of how cadets achieve proficiency in these learning outcomes.

The study examined 4 MJC AY 2019–2020 AROTC syllabi (MS III, IV). Syllabi listed 108 class periods/activities across four full semesters. The findings of the analysis for manifest mission command content mirrored those of the SMC. Only two syllabi (25%) contained manifest mention of mission command as a discrete learning task, activity, or event. Of the 108 scheduled class period topics listed in the four syllabi, instruction in mission command occurred in only two class periods (1.85%). Like the SMC, the Army learning outcomes for mission command appeared in the syllabi introductions of all four syllabi.

Thirty SMC AY 2019–2020 Corps of Cadets Training Schedules, accounting for 90 training periods, were analyzed for mission command content. 0 (0%) contained manifest mention of mission command as a discreet training or leader development task, activity, or event. While nearly training events referred to Army doctrine as a basis for execution, *ADP 6-0,* mission command, was not among the list. 30 MJC AY 2019–2020 Corps of Cadets Training Schedules, accounting for 90 training periods, were analyzed for manifest mission command content. 0 (0%) contained manifest mention of mission command as a discreet training or leader development task, activity, or event. Again, similar to the SMC, training schedules consistently referred to Army doctrine, except ADP 6-0 (R. Megahan, personal communication, 2020).

Across both schools, within 12 entire semesters and 324 total syllabi-driven class periods of Army ROTC course work, the manifest evidence of mission command instruction occurred in 4 class periods—just 1.23% of classes—where mission command was the specifically assigned instructional topic. Additionally, there was no manifest mention of mission command in 60 weeks of both schools' corps of cadets training schedules.

These findings suggest that mission command is missing-in-action in ROTC and military school programs. The first step of the pathway to expertise from cadet to colonel is absent. Despite the fact that the Army's official declarations about developing professional expertise in mission command, it has not yet caught on in the training and education of future leaders. Furthermore, this is especially true in the military boarding school environments that are most conducive to its practice.

The study of syllabi and training schedules suggest a primary conclusion that there is narrow-mindedness and opportunity lost in the instruction for the development of professional expertise in mission command, and it occurs due to culture and mindset, curriculum and pedagogy, praxis and training transfer, and instructor effectiveness.

The absence of focus on mission command suggests the Army culture remains unconvinced of the imperative nature of the concept. It signals the Army's return to an emphasis on discipline-oriented rather than interdisciplinary leadership development. Instead of synthesizing multiple disciplines, the ROTC curriculum isolates them in favor of technical military skills orientation. Instead of connecting an interdisciplinary array of perspectives and viewpoints to contextual decision-making, the curriculum disassociates other approaches in favor of process-driven status quo thinking. Instead of hinging leadership education on experiential learning to develop professional expertise in mission command, it appears the Army is taking the most convenient route with classroom-laden instruction. As highlighted by Vaill (1996, in Owen, 2015), this does not seem to help emerging Army leaders prepare to "navigate the permanent whitewater" (p. 50) turbulence of the 21st-century world.

Where, then, can the interdisciplinary approach to mission command instruction be found? This next section will amplify the research question findings and offer a solution.

## Professional Expertise for Mission Command

The absence of manifest evidence of attention devoted to mission command instruction in ROTC programs and any hint of its application within the military boarding schools underscores the USACC failure to truly make mission command the priority.

The study points to narrow-mindedness and opportunities lost in establishing an organizational culture and mindset for mission command, creating a comprehensive interdisciplinary curriculum and deliberate praxis pedagogy for mission command, and ensuring instructor effectiveness in mission command education. Sadly, the most consequential narrow-mindedness and opportunity lost is the absence of mandated policy, focused supervision, and staff and schedule resourcing for deliberate praxis and training transfer for professional development in mission command in the everyday "potent" (Komives et al., 2011) experiential learning of a military school environment.

Considering the military boarding schools rely exclusively on Army doctrine for everything from uniforms and regulations to drill and ceremonies and leadership and training, the cadet system's culture is just as large an obstacle as the Army culture. To overcome a culture of pedagogical narrow-mindedness and lost opportunities for deliberate practice, according to Muth (2013, p. 165; Van Benken, 2017), means recognizing mission command instruction and deliberate practice support... the real notion that there are no perfect solutions in war. Things would constantly go wrong or break down, intelligence would be faulty, a company would get lost, and so on. Therefore flexibility of mind is the most important thing to teach an officer—that he would be able to make do, no matter the situation, that he would be able to command unruffled amid the turmoil and chaos of war, which would in itself calm the situation. He would "command into the uncertain," but command he would.

## "Unit" Context and Culture

Preparation for command into the uncertain begins with learning about leadership in a unit context. Without a unit, the entire organizational and military context is negated. The deliberate practice of mission command leadership simply cannot be conducted outside the unit environment, and the corps of cadets at military boarding schools provide a tantalizing opportunity for the ROTC department to see military science students learn and grow in the most realistic example they will find of a unit until they report to their first one in the Army. A cadet unit presents most of the conditions a leader will confront on active duty, from diverse populations with multitudinous motivations and goals to training and resourcing issues, senior-subordinate relationships, and planning, preparing, executing, and assessing missions and tasks. And this organizational and military context is right on campus.

Both ROTC programs and commandant's staff struggle with enough leader "repetitions" in situations in which to assess and evaluate cadets. Officially connecting the two gives each a complete school year of everyday, practical mission command leadership situations, compared to minimal ROTC lab syllabi unit leadership episodes and virtually none by design in the corps of cadets. This creates a powerful synergy of departments, which in turn fuels unparalleled potent experiential learning opportunities.

## Instructor Identity: Alignment With Mission Command

The enhancement of leadership educator professional identities—identifying and aligning with mission command—directly influence instructor leadership effectiveness in teaching, coaching, and mentoring (Hastings & Kane, 2018; Seemiller & Crosby, 2019) within the organizational and military unit contexts. However, this identification and alignment cannot end there. In the military schools of study, not only are there the ROTC pre-commissioning training requirements of USACC and the training and leader development programs of the cadet regiment, but the third line of effort exists with academic leadership courses. If there is any wonder why cadets are confused about how to perform as leaders, this triad of competing approaches is evidence.

One of the military boarding schools in our study prides itself in being a "leadership laboratory." Following this analogy, the most effective ROTC instructors and the commandant's staff trainers/leadership advisors would be the "chemistry teachers" who enable cadets to "experiment" with mission command leadership. The instructor/trainer's leadership effectiveness creates an indelible impact on cadet leader development (Luria et al., 2019), and directly affects the organization and military contexts that undergird cadet unit development. A crucial part of that military "unit" context is the leadership trainer's identity as a role-modeling of effective leadership behaviors, which promotes "accelerated" skills, knowledge, and "actual effectiveness" of cadets (Luria et al., 2019, p. 575) in the real-life units of the cadet regiment. Coaching offers distinct benefits at the individual leadership task learning level. Mentoring is effective for promoting organizational effectiveness. Advising occurs as a routine intervention (Roupnel et al., 2019).

## Interdisciplinary "Core" Leadership Curriculum "for the Corps"

A comprehensive interdisciplinary curricula for leadership development should formally align mission command with other leadership courses and programs. It involves a conspicuous and legitimate campus-wide curricular mapping that establishes a "core" (Watt, 2003, p. 14) interdisciplinary leadership curriculum for "learning that sticks" (Department of the Army, U.S. Army Training and Doctrine Command, n.d., p. 4). It aligns teaching and learning processes (Hart et al., 2014; Webb, 2007; Williams, 2020), and accreditation and evaluation (Komives et al., 2011; Owen, 2012). It insists upon ongoing professional learning of faculty and staff as educators in the instructional principles for the development of professional expertise (Elvira, et al., 2017; West, 2012). Alignment enables effective instructor/trainers to be able to "stitch together" (Owen, 2012; Perruci & Hall, 2018, p. 262) leadership education, leadership training, and leadership development with practice venues in mission command.

Instructional principles for the pathway of the development of professional expertise are central to the aligned curriculum and its progression (Boshuizen et al., 2004; Elvira et al., 2017; Ericsson, 2009; Ericsson & Pool, 2016; Ericsson & Smith, 1991; Ericsson et al., 2018; Tynjala et al., 1997). This requires revisiting Army definitions of proficiency, mastery, and expertise (Dreyfus & Dreyfus, 1980; FM 7-0, 2019), the application of the Army Experiential Learning Model (AELM; Department of the Army, USACC, 2019; Department of the Army, U.S. Army Training and Doctrine Command, n.d) and aligning them with learning outcomes of an interdisciplinary core leadership curriculum (Reyes et al., 2019; Steeves, 2018).

### Deliberate Practice and Training Transfer Within the Unit Context

Deliberate praxis and training transfer should constitute the center of gravity of a comprehensive, interdisciplinary, mission command-grounded leadership development program at military boarding schools, but do not. Growing leadership takes extensive deliberate practice (Ericsson & Pool, 2016) tightly networked with an aligned curricula, actionable, overtly measurable outcomes and practice-oriented evaluation, and a campus-wide commitment.

There is no substitute for deliberate practice in mission command leadership in the cadet regiment any more than there is for practice of any collegiate sports team. And just as coaches continuously teach, coach, train, and evaluate players and team elements in every practice, and expect growth (proficiency, mastery, expertise) in individual and team skill performance, in preparation for the uncertainties of a game. This should be the pedagogy for mission command instruction in the corps of cadets. Sports team skill development and game situation practice is the ideal methodology to emulate to achieve mission command experiential learning, and it deserves the resources of time and priority and faculty and staff commitment comparable to the athletic department.

## RECOMMENDATIONS

Leadership development occurs in the context of the organization. As an Army leadership philosophy, mission command must become the preeminent approach of leader and unit training. While there are many obstacles to inculcating mission command in Army ROTC programs and achieving training transfer into the military boarding school cadet regiments, not all opportunities are lost.

Arguably, one of the most impactful and prescient research studies conducted by the Army Research Institute at the onset of the era of persistent conflict was *Think Like a Commander* (Lussier et al., 2003; Ross & Lussier, 1999; Shadrick & Lussier, 2002). Based on the extensive review of the development of professional expertise in mission command, it is time to resurrect and refresh this training program and apply it to the ROTC programs at military boarding schools and make it the training and education vehicle for the corps of cadets.

*Think Like a Commander* (TLAC) was tested by the developers at the Armor Captain's Career Course (then at Ft. Knox, KY) in 2004. This training program emphasizes deliberate practice to develop expertise in critical thinking, decision making, problem-solving, provided focused feedback and active coaching. It reinforced the immediacy of performance, emphasized challenging aspects, and of seeing "the Big picture"—all necessary to mission command proficiency. TLAC accounts for all elements revealed in this chapter: it establishes a defined culture and mindset; supplies a curriculum and pedagogy; promotes movement along the pathway of the development of professional expertise; emphasizes deliberate practice, reflection, and training transfer; and it requires instructors to coach and mentor as subject matter experts, not lecturers, and sets conditions for an evaluation scheme for proficiency in mission command.

TLAC is, in a more updated phrasing, an adaptive course model pedagogy. TLAC can educate and train cadets through adaptive leader soldier training and education (ASLTE). These methods dovetail with what the Army expects to see of mission command-proficient junior officers. These approaches teach, coach, and train to the intangibles of adaptive leaders: training to grow problem-solving teaches soldiers to "teach themselves" the skills necessary to the success of their mission; training to increase intangibles develops the intangible attributes of confidence, accountability, and initiative; training to increase understanding and awareness teaches through the contextual understanding of the task and its mission application; training to increase deliberate thought conditions soldiers to always exercise a deliberate thought process while under stress; and training to improve combat performance conditions soldiers to overcome the psychological and physiological effects of combat. ASLTE intangibles are perfect for Army ROTC instruction and are just as viable when applied to the cadet regiments at the military boarding schools of our study. Accepting TLAC/ASLTE as the engine for leader development, the following components in our study must be adjusted to support and reinforce the mission command leader training and education.

The most significant issue is with an Army culture and mindset that still has not embraced mission command. This issue is pervasive in the ROTC pre-commissioning programs of USACC. Status quo approaches to leadership development in ROTC amplify problematic university and college approaches to leadership education. Diagnosing and changing organizational culture is an enormous task, but we have learned from the analysis of mission command in military boarding schools that remarkable opportunities exist to make adaptations.

The change in culture and mindset must begin with viewing the corps of cadets as a "unit." The *corps as unit* solidifies the organizational context within which mission command can take place every day. Mission command then becomes the leadership philosophy of the corps of cadets, a platform for ROTC cadets to conduct definitive training transfer, deliberately practicing in mission command. Like the approach to combat advising, mission command is taught and trained "by, with, and through" the corps of cadets (R. Megahan, personal communication, 2019). ROTC instructors and commandant's staff leadership advisor can combine to establish a more robust, decisive, and in-depth mission command proficiency assessment amid daily practice.

Mission command, after all, requires a mission. Neither of the military boarding schools in our study has determined what their respective cadet regiments must be, know, or do as an organizational entity of their school. The cadet experience is vastly more than being a student at a military boarding school. While not the purview of this chapter to explore the absence of mission analysis of cadet regiments, it remains a glaring deficiency in addressing the *reason* for the corps of cadets—the *why* of being part of the unit, and striving for becoming an accomplished unit. No unit in the Army is without a mission, and this should be no different for the "cadet units," where so many Army-related activities occur. For mission command to be embraced and performed in the corps of cadets, it has to have a clearly articulated mission, be trained to that mission, develop leaders for that mission, and evaluate its mission. Now a cultural platform for mission command is present, legitimate, and *all cadets, instructors, and staff benefit.*

The platform of the cultural narrative of the cadet regimental mission must also be officially and unambiguously aligned and intertwined with USACC's ROTC organizational culture narrative. This narrative codifies the cadet regiment's cultural DNA: It incorporates observed behavioral regularities when cadets interact; describes an organizational climate; outlines formal rituals and celebrations; declares espoused values; establishes a formal philosophy; identifies group norms; establishes rules of the game; determines identity and self-image; lists embedded skills; reinforces habits of thinking, mental models, or linguistic paradigms; designs shared meaning; and develops "root metaphors" (Schein, 2017, pp. 3–10). Append the phrase "of mission command" into any one of these elements, and immediately, the power of a culture of mission command in ROTC and the corps of cadets organization is evident.

One of the schools in our study describes its cadet regiment with the slogan, "One Corps, One Standard." Unfortunately, this actually refers to disciplinary actions, not leader development. The center of gravity of the school is the corps of cadets, not ROTC programs, not academic departments. Therefore, the cultural narrative of the corps should not be any more separate from that of ROTC than it should be of other academic programs. Central to this point is the necessity to establish and reward a culture of shared understanding, decision space, and empowered execution of mission command. There is simply no substitute for practice, and cadets in ROTC courses and in their respective regiments must get more time to do so. As the training schedules analysis revealed, the cadet week is full of required events. Why couldn't an athletic department approach to practice be conveyed to the corps of cadets? Imagine an innovative and creative schedule with many opportunities for practice in mission command as the school football, basketball, or baseball teams.

The mission command cultural platform emphasizes a growth mindset for deliberate practice. Here, the school culture must underwrite and enable "psychological safety" for growth as a leader. Psychological safety is a crucial component of moving down the pathway of mission command expertise development. The leadership education and training approach must also account for new definitions of success and the role of failure in rich and full learning experiences. A culture of psychological safety ensures the ROTC mission command training transfers into organization leadership behaviors. *The entire corps benefits.*

Too many different organizational contexts only serve to detract from the power of the synergies of a comprehensive and synchronized leadership development program. Instead of "One Corps, One Standard," how about "One Corps, *Mission Command*"? "One Corps, Mission Command" would simplify the pedagogical approach to leadership education and training. It would enable an interdisciplinary leadership curriculum, build multi-departmental, university-wide learning outcomes that drive mission command education, training, and praxis. The entire school develops a new mental model supporting and reinforcing mission command novice and advanced beginner certification. The novice level of proficiency learning outcome includes clear, overtly measurable performance measures and applies them to other disciplines. Gone are those esoteric goals of unreasonably unachievable expertise 10 years into the future. Fully understanding what is achievable with undergraduate neophyte leaders removes the mystery of instructional technique, provides for in-stride benchmarks, and sets a valid evaluation program for proficiency in mission command.

## CONCLUSION

Mission command is all about interdisciplinary leadership. Learning about mission command, and conducting the deliberate practice in it, is what the U.S. Army expects of the new generation of army officers. The military boarding schools are unique institutions in our country and offer a tantalizing environment for a much more robust daily practice and evaluation of mission command.

This chapter sought to portray the problems and possibilities of future officers becoming proficient in mission command. There is much more to be studied, many more options to analyze. Not all options will succeed; some are just enough to get things moving. Nevertheless, every academic year the Army, the ROTC programs, and the military boarding schools that house them fail to take a concerted step forward is a colossal opportunity lost for those commissioning cadets. We must continue to seek options to make things better.

Our future officers deserve nothing less.

## REFERENCES

Bloomquist, C. D, Georges, L., Ford, D., & Breen, J. M. (2018, September 26). Interdisciplinary leadership practices in graduate leadership education programs. *Journal of Leadership Studies, 12*(2), 60–63, https://doi.org/10.1002/jls.21579

Borce, L. (2012). *Outcomes based training and education: In the Department of Military Instruction, United States Military Academy* [Unpublished paper]. Center for Teaching Excellence, United States Military Academy. http://pinnacle-leaders.com/wp-content/uploads/2018/02/Outcomes-Based-Training-and-Education_-in-the-Department-of-Military-Instruction-United-States-Military-Academy.pdf

Boshuizen H. P. A., Bromme R., & Gruber H. (Eds.). (2004). *Professional learning: Gaps and transitions on the way from novice to expert.* Kluwer Academic Publishers.

Coulter, J. A., II. (2017). *Cadets on campus: History of military schools of the United States.* Texas A&M University Press.

Department of the Army. (2019, November 25). *ADP 6-22: Army leadership and the profession.* https://armypubs.army.mil/epubs/DR_pubs/DR_a/ARN20039-ADP_6-22-001-WEB-0.pdf

Department of the Army. (2021, June 14). FM 7-0, Training

Department of the Army, U.S. Army Cadet Command. (2019, June 18). *USACC regulation 145-3 army senior reserve officers training corps on-campus training and leadership development.*

Department of the Army, U.S. Army Training and Doctrine Command. (n.d). *Adult teaching and learning user's guide.* The Army University Center for Teaching and Learning Excellence Faculty and Staff Development Division.

Department of the Army, U.S. Army Training and Doctrine Command. (2017, April 13). *TRADOC pam 525-8-2: The U.S. army learning concept for training and education, 2020–2040.* U.S. Army Training and Doctrine Command.

Dreyfus, S. E., & Dreyfus, H. (1980). *A five-stage model of the mental activities involved in directed skill acquisition.* Operations Research Center. https://apps.dtic.mil/dtic/tr/fulltext/u2/a084551.pdf

Elvira, Q., Imants, J., Dankbaar, B., & Segers, M. (2017). Designing education for professional expertise development. *Scandinavian Journal of Educational Research, 61*S(2), 187–204. https://doi.org/10.1080/00313831.2015.1119729

Ericsson, K. A. (Ed.). (2009). *Development of professional expertise: Toward measurement of expert performance and design of optimal learning environments.* Cambridge University Press.

Ericsson, K. A., & Pool, R. (2016). *Peak: Secrets from the new science of expertise.* Eamon Dolan.

Ericsson, K. A., & Smith, J. (Eds.). (1991). *Toward a general theory of expertise: Prospects and limits.* Cambridge University Press.

Ericsson, K. A., Hoffman, R., Kozbelt, A., & Williams, A. M. (2018). *The Cambridge handbook of expertise and expert performance* (2nd ed.). Cambridge University Press.

Finney, N., & Klug, J. (Eds.). (2016). *Mission command in the 21st century: Empowering to win in a complex world.* The Army Press.

Green, C., & McBride, J. F. (2015). *Teaching leadership.* Kansas Leadership Center.

Hart, P. L., Brannan, J. D., Long, J. M., Maguire, M. B. R., Brooks, B. K., & Robley, L. R. (2014). Effectiveness of a structured curriculum focused on recognition and response to acute patient deterioration in an undergraduate BSN program. *Nurse Education in Practice, 14*(1), 30–36. doi:http://dx.doi.org/10.1016/j.nepr.2013.06.010

Hastings, L., & Kane, C. (2018). Distinguishing mentoring, coaching, and advising for leadership development. *New Directions for Student Leadership, 158*(Summer 2018), 9–22. https://doi.org/10.1002/yd.20284

Heyward, R. (2013). *Embedding mission command in army culture* [Unpublished master's thesis]. U.S. Army War College.

Horton, A. (2014). *Mission command: Challenges to implementation and institutionalization in the Army* [Strategy research paper]. U.S. Army War College.

Komives, S., Dugan, J., Owen, J., Slack, C., & Wagner, W. (2011). *The handbook for student leadership development* (2nd ed). Jossey-Bass.

Krippendorf, K. (2013). *Content analysis: An introduction to the methodology* (3rd ed.). SAGE Publications.

Kvernbekk, T., Simpson, H., & Peters, M. (Eds.). (2008). *Military pedagogies: And why they matter.* Sense Publishers.

Luria, G., Kahana, A., Goldenberg, J., & Noam, Y. (2019). Leadership development: Leadership emergence to leadership effectiveness. *Small Group Research, 50*(7), 571–592.

Lussier, J. W., Shadrick, S. B., & Prevou, M. (2003). *Think like a commander prototype: Instructor's guide to adaptive thinking.* U.S. Army Research Institute for the Behavioral and Social Sciences, Fort Knox, KY.

McCauley, D. (2012, June 21). The facets of mission command. *Small Wars Journal.* https://smallwarsjournal.com/jrnl/art/the-facets-of-mission-command

McPhail, P. (2020). The search for deep learning: a curriculum coherence model. *Journal of Curriculum Studies, 53*(4), 420–434. https://doi.org/10.1080/00220272.2020.1748231

Mele, P. (2020). Army ROTC and military science: Developing trusted army professionals. *New Directions for Student Leadership, 2020*(165), 137–148.

Muth, J. (2013). *Command culture.* University of North Texas Press.

Neuendorf, K. A. (2002). *The content analysis guidebook.* Sage.

Orsi, D., & Mundell, B. (2019). *Will new doctrine fix mission command?* https://warroom.armywarcollege.edu/articles/new-doctrine-mission-command/

Orsini, R. (2019). *U.S. army mission command at a crossroads.* The Strategy Bridge. https://thestrategybridge.org/the-bridge/2019/10/29/us-army-mission-command-at-a-crossroads

Owen, J. E. (2012). *Findings from the Multi-Institutional Study of Leadership institutional survey: A national report.* National Clearinghouse for Leadership Programs.

Owen, J. (2015). Integrative and interdisciplinary approaches to leadership development. *New Directions for Student Leadership, 145*(Spring 2015), 49–58.

Perruci, G., & Hall, S. W. (2018). *Teaching leadership: Bridging theory and practice.* Elgar.

Reyes, D., Dinh, J., Lacerenza, C., Marlow, S., Joseph, D., & Salas, E. (2019). The state of higher education leadership development program evaluation: A meta-analysis, critical review, and recommendations. *The Leadership Quarterly, 30*(5), 365–382. https://doi.org/10.1016/j.leaqua.2019.101311

Ross, K. G., & Lussier, J. W. (1999). *A training solution for adaptive battlefield performance.* Proceedings of the 1999 Interservice/Industry Training, Simulation, and Education Conference, Orlando, FL.

Roupnel, S., Rinfret, N., & Grenier, J. (2019). Leadership development: Three programs that maximize learning over time. *Journal of Leadership Education, 18*(2), 126–137. https://doi.org/10.12806/V18/I2/T1

Schein, E. (2017). *Organizational culture and leadership* (5th ed.). Wiley.

Schreier, M. (2012). *Qualitative content analysis in practice.* SAGE Publications.

Seemiller, C., & Crosby, B. (2019). Exploring and enhancing leader, educator, and leadership educator professional identities. *New Directions for Student Leadership, 2019*(164), 71–86.

Shadrick, S., & Lussier, J. (2004). *Assessment of the Think Like a Commander training program.* U.S. Army Research Institute for the Behavioral and Social Science. https://apps.dtic.mil/dtic/tr/fulltext/u2/a425737.pdf

Steeves, W. (2018). Scholarship in practice: Leadership in action. *Marine Corps Gazette, 102*(9), 1–5.

Vandergriff, D. (2019). *Adopting mission command: Developing leaders for a superior command culture.* Naval Institute Press.

Vandergriff, D., & Webber, S. (Eds). (2017). *Mission command: The who, what, where, and why an anthology* (Vol. 1). CreateSpace Independent Publishing Platform.

Vandergriff, D., & Webber, S. (Eds). (2018). *Mission command: The who, what, where, and why an anthology* (Vol. II). CreateSpace Independent Publishing Platform.

Vangjel, P. (2018). Mission command: A clarification. In D. Vandergriff & S. Webber (Eds.), *Mission command: An anthology, Vol. II.* CreateSpace Independent Publishing Platform.

Von Benken, D. (2017). *Averse to initiative: Risk management's effect on mission command* [Monograph]. School of Advanced Military Studies, U.S. Army Command and General Staff College.

Watt, W. (2003). Effective leadership education: Developing a core curriculum for leadership studies. *Journal of Leadership Education, 2*(1). https://doi.org/10.12806/V2/I1/RF1

Webb, N. (2007). Issues related to judging alignment of curriculum standards and assessments. *Applied Measurement in Education, 20*(1), 7–25. https://www.cehd.umn.edu/edpsych/c-bas-r/docs/webb2007.pdf

Welch, L. (2005). A content analysis of traditional undergraduate course syllabi: Reinforcing the message of academic honesty? *Journal of College and Character, 6*(6), https://doi.org/10.2202/1940-1639.1470

West, C. (2012). Teaching leadership to undergraduates: Lessons from U.S. military colleges. *Journal of College Teaching & Learning, 9*(2), 135–146.

Williams, T. (2020). An evidence-based approach to unit-level teaching and learning. *Journal of Military Learning, 4*(1), 57–67. https://www.armyupress.army.mil/Portals/7/journal-of-military-learning/Archives/April-2020/JML-April-20-BOOK.pdf

# SECTION III

## PRE-K–12 EDUCATION

CHAPTER 14

# LEADING FROM THE RANKS

## Teacher Leader Sensemaking of a District-Supported Mentorship Initiative

**Brianne Morettini**
**Lisa Vernon-Dotson**

### ABSTRACT

This study examines the experiences of teacher leaders who participated in a grant-funded project focused on building teacher leadership capacity to support beginning teachers. Using sensemaking literature as a guide, the study sought to identify factors that enabled or hindered the work of teacher leaders in one school district as they embarked on facilitating a district-supported mentorship initiative. Data for this qualitative study was collected from teacher leader participant interviews, observations of school improvement committees, field notes, transcripts from professional learning series meetings, a teacher leader blog, and relevant documents. Ambiguity, empowerment, structural conflict, and tenacity were four predominant interdisciplinary themes that became relevant for the sensemaking of these teacher leaders.

Over the past 2 decades, educational policies have attempted to frame problems, adopt solutions, and guide classroom practices in an effort to

*On Leadership*, pages 237–256

improve P–12 student outcomes by addressing teaching conditions and teacher quality (e.g., merit-based pay, class size, teacher evaluation). In recent years, teacher leadership has surfaced in practice, research, and educational policy. While there is no consensus on the definition of teacher leadership (Neumerski, 2013), the key idea of teacher leadership is grounded in teachers influencing others to contribute to school improvement or educational practice (Katzenmeyer & Moller, 2009; York-Barr & Duke, 2004) with the goal of promoting effective leadership, quality teaching, and improved student learning.

In 2004, in what is widely considered the seminal review of literature on teacher leadership, York-Barr and Duke indicated the need for more scholarly studies documenting how teacher leadership develops and its impact on teaching practices and student outcomes. Still, most of the teacher leadership literature focuses on the roles of teacher leaders (e.g., Fairman, & Mackenzie, 2014) or how principals distributed power to teacher leaders (e.g., Thoonen et al., 2012). Yet, little emphasis is paid to teacher leadership development in the changing school context (Cheng & Szeto, 2016; Lear et al., 2015b) or on how it enhances professional practice leading to improved instruction and increased student learning (Lear et al., 2015a; Wenner & Campbell, 2016). In addition, we continue to build the knowledge base on interdisciplinary and pragmatic approaches to solving complex challenges related to teaching and teacher leadership.

This study tells a story about how to get from the concept of teacher leadership to the implementation of teacher leadership within one large school district. The researchers aimed to explore this initiative using sensemaking as a theoretical perspective. Using a distributed leadership framework, the researchers set out to document teacher leaders' sensemaking (Rom & Eyal, 2019) of their district's mentorship program, which was designed to support and ultimately retain beginning teachers. Specifically, this research seeks to better understand teacher leaders' sensemaking (Rom & Eyal, 2019) of their roles as teacher leaders during their participation in a professional development program aimed at building their capacity to mentor beginning teachers in the hard-to-staff school district of Smithville.

This research is part of a larger study entitled, *The Beginning Teacher Project,* that focused on building teacher leader capacity in order to support beginning teachers in one school district in the southern region of a state. Supported by state level No Child Left Behind funding, the project was a partnership between a P–12 school district and a university's college of education and college of arts. In this study, the researchers aspired to document and analyze the ways that teacher leaders and school improvement teams made sense of the ambiguity and uncertainty in their roles as mentors of beginning teachers. To situate this work within the literature, we connect our work to literature on the distributed leadership framework.

## THEORETICAL FRAMEWORK AND LITERATURE REVIEW

The history of research on teacher leadership tends to lack full theoretical grounding. As documented by Wenner and Campbell (2016), it is "only partially theoretical as just over a majority of the literature was framed by theory" (p. 161). The theoretical basis of teacher leadership points to distributed leadership. According to Gronn (2000), distributed leadership is "fluid and emergent, rather than a fixed phenomenon" (p. 324), and is characterized as "a group activity that works through and within relationships, rather than individual action" (Bennett et al., 2003, p. 3).

### Distributed Leadership

Klein and colleagues (2018) maintain "distributed leadership is most valuable as a framework when it considers teacher leadership activities as situated and examines the social processes at the intersection of leaders, followers, and the situation or context" (p. 94). Spillane and Diamond (2007) described distributed leadership as a practice distributed over leaders, followers, and their situation. To that end, distributed leadership is based on the willingness of school leaders to share their authority and power with others. In an organization that follows a distributed leadership model, teachers and other school personnel collaborate as they engage in discussions and use decision-making models that allow for problem-solving. In order to support and facilitate interactions, school leaders use a democratic participation process (Hord, 2009).

To that end, distributed leadership is indeed considered a perspective—as opposed to a management technique—whereby all members of the organizational community contribute sources of knowledge, skills, and insights (Vernon-Dotson, 2008). According to Klein et al. (2018), teacher leaders move from isolation in the classroom setting to a new role that focuses on supporting colleagues; thus, "teacher leadership is intrinsically tied to opportunities to form relationships and the supports that are necessary for these relationships to be sustained" (p. 92). Hence, by virtue of their role, teacher leaders are integral to a distributed leadership perspective.

The effects of distributed leadership on teachers, however, are not well documented in empirical research (Harris et al., 2007) although it has emerged as the most frequently used theoretical lens for examining teacher leadership (Wenner & Campbell, 2017). Of the literature that does exist, most is overwhelmingly positive; however, it should not be assumed that all distributed leadership models are always a good thing (Harris, 2008). Hargreaves and Fink (2006) cautioned that distributed leadership has the potential to "enhance the sustainability of deep and broad learning, or disintegrate into the kind of turmoil that sucks the energy and enthusiasm out of students and staff" (p. 136). Further, they described distributed leadership as having the impending power to "emerge as a dynamic community practice... [or] sabotage a school's efforts at improvement" (p. 137).

Communication is the key to supporting and sustaining a collaborative distributed leadership model. While having the potential to be extremely successful, distributed leadership is very sensitive to disruption and lack of support. Hargreaves and Fink (2006) cautioned those debating the use of a distributed leadership model to be wary of its tenuous nature, but in the end still champion its use. The warnings fail to outweigh the benefits of positive daily collaborative interactions between school leaders and members of the organization, which allow problem-solving and decision-making to be managed by those vested in the education process (Hargreaves & Fink, 2006; Harris, 2008; Harris et al., 2007; Sergiovanni, 2007; Spillane & Diamond, 2007; Vernon-Dotson, 2008). As such, "distributing leadership across schools and other organizations isn't just common sense; it is the morally responsible thing to do" (Hargreaves & Fink, 2006, p. 97). According to Mayrowetz (2008), the field of educational leadership has endorsed the usage of distributed leadership; however, researchers have not yet agreed on a common definition or even the practice of the term. Further, he publicized, "these significant discrepancies allow researchers to talk past each other" (p. 425).

To assist in alleviating some of these discrepancies, the researchers aimed their work toward "the idea of distributed leadership as a human capacity development strategy... [which] has promise as a link to school improvement" (Mayrowetz, 2008, p. 432) and sets the stage for teacher leadership. Supporting Cheng and Szeto (2016), the researchers of this study, argue that "as the principal and teachers work collaboratively..., the mutual influence of the two parties on teacher leadership development is possible" (p. 141). Whether teacher leaders have formal or informal roles, the distributed leadership theory allows teacher leaders to surface organically as they share their practice with one goal in mind—improving teaching for all students.

## Sensemaking

To understand the factors that influence teacher leaders' sensemaking of a district-supported, grant-funded initiative, the researchers pulled on the theory of sensemaking. Sensemaking is "the process through which individuals work to understand novel, unexpected, or confusing events" (Maitlis & Christianson, 2014, p. 57). Sensemaking allows for the construction of understanding or frameworks for understanding, beyond interpretation, that involve identifying, acting on, remembering, and applying patterns to lived experiences (Weick et al., 2005). Sensemaking often relies on different texts and meanings from tradition, ideology, and professional paradigms (Allen & Penuel, 2015), thus suggesting the interdisciplinary nature of sensemaking. The literature describes sensemaking as narratives and/or mental maps that people develop to fill cognitive gaps and turn untenable situations into circumstances brimming with meaning (Powell & Colyvas, 2008; Weick, 1995).

Sensemaking validates and acknowledges the ways that individuals "notice, select, and interpret ideas in their environment, but also how they enact them so as to be rendered meaningful" (Rom & Eyal, 2019, p. 63). The researchers focused on the actions of teacher leaders who participated in the grant project on the reorganization of their district's mentorship program. With that in mind, the purpose of this research was to document and analyze the ways that teacher leaders made sense of the ambiguity and uncertainty in their new roles as mentors of beginning teachers (Rom & Eyal, 2019; Weick et al., 2005).

According to Tsoukas and Chia (2002), "Organization is an attempt to order the intrinsic flux of human action, to channel it toward certain ends, to give it a particular shape, through generalizing and institutionalizing particular meanings and rules" (p. 570). Because the work of teacher leaders is largely informal and undefined in schools and "meanings and rules" during a district level school reform initiatives tend to be ambiguous and uncertain, we sought to document how teacher leaders make sense of what occurred during the 3 year partnership grant focused on building the capacity of teacher leaders in order to support beginning teachers.

## METHODOLOGICAL FRAMEWORK

As described by Milner (2012) in his evolving typology of urban education, the P–12 partner district of Smithville could be considered an urban characteristic school (Milner, 2012). Urban characteristic schools are those that have many of the indicators of urban schools but are not located in cities. For example, Smithville has a population that is 44% Hispanic or Latina/x/o, 35% African American, and 19% White. Nearly 45% of the residents are foreign born, as it is host to many migrant and seasonal farmworkers; one-third of the population are non-native English speakers. And, over 33% of the entire documented population live in poverty (U.S. Census Bureau, 2010). The district's seven schools serve more than 5,800 students, and more than half of those students receive free or reduced-rate meals.

## Study/Project Design

Criteria-based sampling (Creswell, 2007) was used to select the teacher leader participants for this qualitative study. The criteria for participating in the project included: (a) at least 5 years teaching experience, (b) a teacher performance rating of effective or better for the most recent 2 years, (c) good attendance record (defined as missing 6 days or fewer each year of the previous 3 years), (d) record of significant contributions to the district with willingness to commit to working beyond their contractual agreements, and (e) a completed letter of application addressing their aspirations for teacher leadership. Thirty-six participants were selected for the initiative—24 in the first year of the project and an additional 12 in the second year of the 3 year project. Participants represented all seven schools in the district and were monetarily compensated for their participation in activities outside of normal business hours. By design, teacher leader selection in the third year was not part of the grant initiative. The project utilized a gradual release model that moved from mostly outside professional learning facilitated by the university partners in the first year, to a train-the-trainers or mentor-the-mentors approach in the second year. In the third year, the teacher leaders worked with the district administration to select and lead the mentorship process.

After participants were selected as teacher leaders, they participated in a variety of professional learning opportunities which included a professional learning series (monthly meetings), a teacher leader blog, summer institutes, and a regional teacher leadership symposium where the teacher leaders shared their work (e.g., learning modules, mentor–mentee guide, formal presentations). To capture the thoughts of the participants and the work of these teacher leaders, the researchers conducted and semi-structured interviews with teacher leaders. The interviews were audio recorded and then transcribed verbatim. The researchers also attended multiple school improvement committee meetings at each of the individual schools with the purpose of observing and soliciting feedback. Documents related to The Beginning Teacher Project (e.g., agendas, minutes, field notes, external evaluation feedback, surveys, emails) were also collected.

Transcripts, blogs, observation data, and documents were repeatedly read and reread to identify possible themes (Miles & Huberman, 1994; Patton, 1990). The analysis was aligned to two preset themes (e.g., ambiguity/uncertainty, empowerment) from sensemaking literature and allowed for the others to be added as they became apparent through the identification of categories and subcategories. After two additional rounds of systematic coding consistent with the themes, the researchers met again to compare the thoughts, categories, and themes until all discrepancies were resolved. To allow for member checking, the findings were shared with a small group of teacher leaders who agreed with the findings.

## Context

The Beginning Teacher Project was designed to leverage the power of a partnership between two colleges at one university (education and arts) and a public school district to improve the support provided for beginning teachers in the school district. To that end, the project had specific goals with measurable outcomes that align with implementation activities for the purposes of increasing beginning teacher persistence; improving student outcomes; and building community between teachers, district and school leaders, and community stakeholders. (See Figure 14.1 for the Theoretical context guiding The Beginning Teacher Project.)

The project was deliberately framed by research related to signature pedagogies, a collaborative professional learning model, Critical Friends Group®, and community engagement. Using this research as a framework, the project unfolded as a sustainable, tiered model of support for beginning teachers that drew on the expertise of teacher leaders. The researchers, who served as the grant co-principal investigators, used a

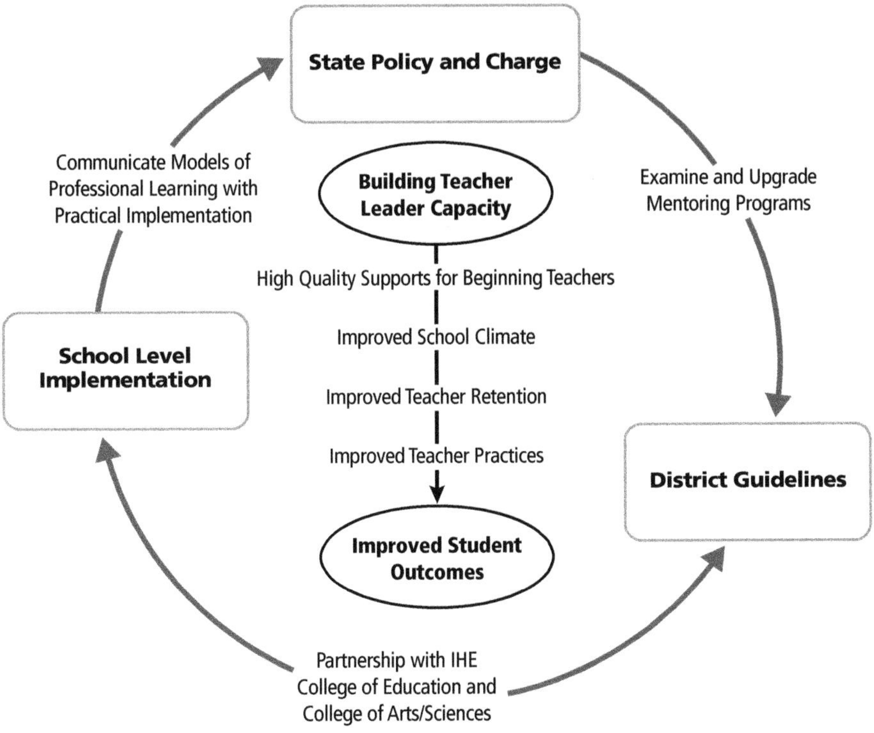


**Figure 14.1** Theoretical context guiding The Beginning Teacher Project.

cognitive-developmental approach to mentoring that assisted teacher leaders in building trust with beginning teachers and engaging in courageous conversations around context-based student engagement and growth.[1]

The project rolled out in four phases: (a) Creating a Foundation, (b) Community Building and Critical Reflection, (c) Constructing Knowledge and Skills for Mentoring, and (d) Crafting Future Plans. During each phase, there were planned learning opportunities for teacher leaders as well as district and school leaders. Additionally, eight after school sessions in a professional learning series approach were held monthly as professional learning opportunities for teacher leaders that enabled them to systematically support beginning teachers. During certain sessions in the professional learning series, district and school leaders as well as members of the grant project's newly established community advisory board were invited. Separate learning opportunities for school leaders also occurred through quarterly meetings.

Finally, in order to effectively meet the needs of the beginning teachers and teacher leaders in the school district, the researchers systematically collected data at several points during the four phases of the project. In addition to meeting the grant requirements, the purpose of the data collection was to ensure that the professional learning series addressed the needs of teacher leaders in an effort to support those who were targeted for the grant—beginning teachers. As such, this model was an organic and sustainable approach to building teacher leadership capacity to support beginning teachers.

## FINDINGS

According to Killion et al. (2016), a systematic approach to teacher leadership is necessary if teachers are to lead and take responsibility for what matters most to them. With proper professional learning opportunities, teacher leaders have the looming power "to promote effective, collaborative teaching practices in schools that lead to increased student achievement, improved decision-making at the school and district level, and create a dynamic teaching profession for the 21st century" (Teacher Leadership Exploratory Commission, 2011, p. 3).

Findings from the qualitative data analysis reflect the significance of interdisciplinary approaches to leadership; the findings revealed four primary themes related to how teacher leaders make sense of their roles as mentors. These themes were ambiguity/uncertainty, empowerment, goal conflict, and tenacity. In addition to two preset themes (ambiguity/uncertainty, empowerment), two themes (structural conflict, tenacity) emerged. The following provides an overview of each theme. How the teacher leaders made sense of the district initiative and operationalized it within their schools is addressed in the following section.

## Ambiguity or Uncertainty

Drawing on sensemaking (Rom & Eyal, 2019) as a guide, the researchers were particularly interested in sources of ambiguity and uncertainty that emerged from teacher leaders and school improvement teams throughout the mentorship initiative. Specifically, we analyzed the data with an eye toward how teacher leaders made sense of the ambiguity and uncertainty they encountered as a result of working as teacher leaders. Support for the project originated from the central office. The district's grant manager contacted the college of education's dean to solicit partnership for the grant project. The team consisted of four district administrators, three representatives from the college of education, and one representative from the college of arts (required by the grant). During the first professional learning series meeting, a teacher leader commented on the variety of people available in the room:

> It is helpful to be able to talk to the union representative, as well as people from the central office rather than speculating about official policies, you can go right to the source.

While side conversations began along with the previous comment, another teacher leader asked about where this project would go after the grant project was finished. She indicated that she'd been there long enough to see initiatives appear and then disappear when the projects leave.

> Like several of us here, we see these things come and we do them because we want to do better and then next thing you know, they are gone. How do we know this is going to stay? We are here because we want to be district mentors and were told that we had to do this to be a mentor next year. Is everyone going to do this to be a mentor?

The assistant superintendent, who was an active participant in the project during the first year and was revered by the teachers in the district, stood and addressed the teacher leaders.

> At an administrative level, the structure that we build is in your hands. You've been identified and vetted. We have the capacity within the district to meet our internal needs. We want a mentoring program that's not restricted to building[s]. We want best fits.... The district is committed [to] and invested [in] building the program pipeline... The district wants to create a system of

> sustainability. We invest a lot of resources [and] money in human capital, and we need to sustain them.

The teachers often noted inconsistencies in policies within their school district and a lack of understanding of practices that occurred, particularly around mentorship. A teacher noted in her blog post:

> Throughout my tenure in this district, and in our school, our new teachers have been randomly assigned a mentor. I have always observed how mismatched some of the pairs were. I think with this training, the matches will be better and the pool of teachers who are trained to be mentors will be an asset.

During the second year, the assistant superintendent retired and, although the central administrators participated in other grant activities, active participation from the district administration waned at the professional learning series. The teacher leaders noted this during the meetings, "Are [they] coming today?" and "Where is our support?"

When it was time for the new assignments for district leaders during the third year of the grant, the teachers became concerned and angry when the list of new district mentors was shared. Only three of the 36 teachers who participated in the teacher leader grant project were selected as paid mentors. The email was sent the day of one of the professional learning series meetings and the buzz was heard. Participants were looking over each other's shoulders reading the email and scrutinizing the names on the list: "Do you know [this person]?"; "How did [she] get picked?"; and "I thought they said everyone who wanted to be a mentor HAD to be trained in this program!" The teachers wanted answers, but the administrator who was slated to attend this afterschool meeting had a conflict and could not attend.

## Empowerment

Another theme that emerged from this data surrounded empowerment. Teacher leaders participating in the project became noticeably more confident and indicated feeling empowered at the district level. As stated by one of the teacher leaders who participated in all 3 years of the project, "I absolutely love the opportunity this grant has given us. We get to build the new mentor program and serve as mentors next year." With 14 years of experience, she was never selected to serve as a formal mentor. Another teacher leader, expressed apprehension:

> My concern is to have gone through the project and not being allotted the opportunity to implement the training for the success of other educators because of the difference in grade/subject levels.

The school improvement committees provided feedback on the mentor–mentee supplemental guide, created by the first cohort of teacher leaders. A teacher leader who also served on her building's school improvement committee indicated, "This Guide could be adapted to assist cooperating teachers and teacher candidates as well." Another team member who was not a grant participant shared, "We like the section about conversation starters, because we usually spend most of our time on areas of concern the new teacher brings up. If they don't have any concerns, it's a short conversation." One school improvement committee member provided the following written feedback:

> The [district] *Public Schools Mentor & Mentee Guide* is a phenomenal resource! It is evident that it was thoughtfully prepared and well-organized...We are looking forward to sharing it with our staff.

The teacher leaders took ideas and information back to their schools and shared it with their colleagues. They were proud of the relationships they had with the other teacher leaders across the district, the community, and the university partners and believed that they had control of the future of mentorship in their district. One teacher leader shared on the blog post:

> The support from community members, parents, [the] university, and the [district] leadership team will no doubt be a huge asset and help us to be better mentors and teachers. They are our mentors!

Another responded to her colleague:

> I am also looking forward to strengthening relationships with my colleagues who are at other schools in the district, learning new information, and having a larger network of resources.

The teacher leaders felt that they had the power to make change and they had the confidence to facilitate and promote the new mentorship initiative at their schools with their colleagues—the hallmarks of empowerment.

## Structural Conflict

Structural conflict refers to miscommunication between entities that affect school operations. For example, in Year 1 of the grant, the district administrators determined that only teachers who participated in the professional learning series (grant participants) could serve as formal mentors. During an observation of a school improvement committee meeting when members were talking about the mentor-mentee handbook, the vice principal indicated, "One teacher is upset because she has been a mentor for 20 years and didn't know she had to do this [professional development with the grant] to be a mentor. [My principal] didn't even know." Structural conflict not only occurred between the district and school levels, but also between teachers and district administrators. Many teachers—both participants and non-grant participants—indicated that information was not shared with all schools/teachers. When visiting school improvement teams, teachers reacted more to the lack of information about the project than to the information being shared: "We didn't know"; "Why are there no [school] representatives on the [grant project]"; and "They had to apply?" Two schools refused to allow the researchers to attend their school improvement team meeting, even though it was arranged in advance by the district administrators.

Formal mentor assignments were designated at the district level and mentors and their mentees (beginning teachers) were physically located at different schools. This created disparity in the quality and quantity of mentorship available as formal mentors are paid by the mentees for their support per teacher union agreement and state regulation. The teacher leaders selected to participate in the project were all eligible to become or have served previously as formal district mentors. They had varying degrees of training. One teacher leader recalled:

> I was new to the school and new to that [teaching] position, and I did [the mentoring of a new teacher]. I really didn't have any training and when I did have questions... it was like pretty much, "We'll get back to you" or "We'll train you down the road," but it's like I needed answers to questions now. So I think, as a mentor, to know that you have someone who you can communicate and learn from, and they can answer your questions immediately... some type of formal training would be great.

Principal and school improvement committee involvement in the mentoring process ranged from no involvement at all to the creation of a school-based mentorship network. Evidence from the data confirmed that across the seven individual schools, implementation of the district's state approved mentorship plan was not consistent and the role of the principal in the mentorship process was not defined. When participating in a school improvement committee meeting in order to share progress and gain feedback on documents created through the project, a principal who had the project listed on his agenda explained to his team:

> [The researcher] is here to talk about the teacher leadership initiative. This is the good work that [our two team school improvement members]have been participating in and sharing with us... I reviewed the [mentor/mentee

> guide] and I think it will be useful... I agreed to allow this committee to review it and share it with our faculty for feedback.

Great disparities were noted from school to school, most surrounding the consistency of practice and communication. The teacher leaders were from across the district which allowed for ongoing comparison conversations and discussions about the mentorship initiative and project. When inconsistencies arose, it was noticed and became the headliners for the professional learning series.

## Tenacity

Tenacity encompasses spirit, courage, and determination. Both teacher leaders in the project and those serving on the school improvement committees demonstrated tenacity. Observations that were conducted during the school improvement committee meetings and the formal feedback that was obtained clearly revealed the tenacity of teachers on these committees. They demonstrated spirit by remaining positive about their schools, their students, and their colleagues. When talking about how she was planning to support beginning teachers, one teacher leader stated that "encouraging beginning teachers to maintain a positive attitude... helping them increase their productivity and dedication to the workplace" was going to be her primary focus.

Another example of tenacity was demonstrated when the state minimum qualifications for teachers to serve as formal mentors was discussed. Two different school improvement teams indicated that the minimum qualifications were not stringent enough. They wanted to create their own mentor qualifications. Their mentor qualifications went beyond demonstrated performance and experience to include characteristics related to knowledge, skills, and professional dispositions. Responses included, "collaborator, friendly, organized" (school improvement committee member); "strong presence, willing to work and take a vested interest in the mentee's success" (teacher leader on school improvement committee); and "strong school leadership skills, current on latest and most beneficial teacher practices, ability to effectively differentiate instruction to meet the various challenges in the classroom, and strong class management skills" (written feedback from school improvement committee).

Teacher leaders were determined to make a difference for beginning teachers, regardless if they were assigned to them as formal or district mentors. One teacher boasted,

> Not to toot my own horn, but I'm very knowledgeable about the subject matter. I don't have a master's degree in secondary education or anything, but I know I'm doing a good job. I've seen a lot of people, when we do those

> rare articulation meetings who struggle to make a topic interesting. I think I can help somebody do that. I've made a lot of mistakes when I was a young teacher... I would like to make a younger teacher aware of the mistakes I've made and let them know that if they make the same mistakes, it's not the end of the world.

Mrs. Branch only participated in the project for 2 years. She enjoyed learning from her peers who facilitated the second year's professional learning series. She was cognizant of the need for continuous learning:

> I'm very strong in my content and I love teaching. The [previous] district mentor training was three hours... and I went to [a local university] for a one-day training. I'm at a hard school, so I came to this [project]. They ask me to do a lot at [the school], but I really want to help the other teachers. The kids need good teachers and I can help with that.

Throughout the course of the project, the teacher leaders were overwhelmingly positive and maintained a focus on improvement of their own practice to improve their work with the students. While some cited struggles with taking the information back to their colleagues, they were determined to make a difference through creating a network of supports at their individual schools.

## TEACHER LEADERS' SENSEMAKING OF THE MENTORSHIP INITIATIVE

Pulling from the implementation study literature, the researchers looked at The Beginning Teacher Project and the mentorship initiative as a means of "gaining targeted employees' appropriate and committed use of an innovation" (Klein & Sorra, 1996, p. 1055). Further, the researchers expected and planned for an implementation burst where the teacher leaders would experience excitement and anticipation for the innovation and then experience the struggles of practical implication and use of the innovation (Klein & Sorra, 1996). Despite the research-based program design, pre-planning, and district buy-in, teacher leaders still experienced ambiguity, uncertainty, and structural conflict over the course of the mentorship initiative.

The teacher leaders understood the context of their district and their respective schools. It was clear that they were realistic about how they would be involved in the mentorship initiative and how they would then facilitate what they learned with their colleagues. In general, they were excited about planning for and writing the new mentorship plan. When the district's mentorship plan was shared with them at a professional learning series meeting in the first year, the teacher leaders noted that it was already approved by the state for the following year. A teacher leader hesitantly asked an administrator in attendance, "If this is already approved, what are we doing?" The administrator explained that the plans were required to be submitted a full year in advance and that they would "take the recommendations from the teachers and consider them for the next year's plan." The participants' dispositions notably changed. Although they were hopeful that their work would be appreciated and applied, an underlying and voiced concern was that their input would be discarded. Fast-forward another year, to the teacher leaders' dismay, they found that the previous administratively developed mentorship plan was submitted to the state and again approved. The fact that their input was not incorporated serves as additional evidence of tenacity.

Fortunately, the teacher leaders did not see the mentorship plan as an obstacle. They focused on what they could do to support all teachers. For example, two teacher leaders who were at the same school also served as members of the school improvement committees. They were well respected by their principal and other teachers. One of The Beginning Teacher Project signature practices was Critical Friends Groups (Bambino, 2002). After the professional learning series that focused on the process for implementing Critical Friends Groups, these teachers took the signature practice back to their schools and with support of their principal demonstrated how to use it. They created a support group for any teacher with a problem of practice to explore options for addressing the problem and returning to his/her class with actionable steps to implement. It is important to note that this was a completely voluntary group that could not be mandated due to union restrictions; however, it became a sought after exercise for more than just beginning teachers. The teacher leaders saw immediate use of a process shared from the project and translated it into practice to support all teachers in their buildings.

This was not an isolated example. Teacher leaders continuously took the knowledge and skills they acquired from working on The Beginning Teacher Project and mentorship initiative back to their schools and implemented it. The scale of this implementation varied greatly from school to school. The project helped the teachers build their identities as teacher leaders and added legitimacy to the work they were doing. They saw themselves as leaders who were determined to make a difference—and it mattered. These teacher leaders were dedicated to helping other teachers and were making a difference (empowerment). They had difficult conversations with other teachers and administrators in which feedback was given, and they kept a positive outlook while demanding change (tenacity). These participants were teacher leaders who were committed to improving their practice to benefit the students in their schools.

## DISCUSSIONS AND CONCLUSIONS

The work of the teacher leaders in this study clearly aligned to the Teacher Leader Exploratory Consortium (2011). Over the course of the 3-year Beginning Teacher Project that focused on developing a mentorship model, the teachers continuously focused on

- fostering a collaborative culture to support teacher development and student learning (Domain I),
- accessing and using research to improve teacher practice and student outcomes (Domains II),
- promoting professional learning and facilitating improvements in instruction for continuous improvement within their schools (Domain III and Domain IV),
- promoting the use of assessment and data for school and district improvement (Domain V), and
- improving outreach and collaboration with families through advocating for student learning and the profession (Domain VI and Domain VII).

Although ambiguity, uncertainty, and structural conflict contribute to the outcomes of this project, so did empowerment and tenacity. Teachers returned to their schools to negotiate ways to employ teacher leadership and find time to support the beginning teachers within their buildings. The teacher leaders in this study engaged in sensemaking processes as they sought to lead from the ranks. When not selected as formal mentors, they met with beginning teachers and developed informal mentorship programs at the building level. They educated the school leaders and other teachers on teacher leadership and recruited teachers to serve in professional learning communities and in Critical Friends Groups. This supports the notion that teachers who are empowered believe that they can make a difference; they have vision and purpose, are vested in the effort, and make change happen. The findings also signal the rich interdisciplinary approaches that teacher leaders take up in the enactment of their roles. To that end, the findings demonstrated teacher leaders' responsiveness to the varied needs of their own particular school contexts as they made sense of what was required from them as teacher leaders.

It was clear that the members of school improvement committees were seeking ways to improve their schools. Further, the teacher leaders who were participating in the grant sought the same goal. The disconnect was in structural conflict. Either the principals were unaware of the work associated with the grant or it was not a priority for them. As accountability on the part of schools continues to remain on the forefront of our educational system, we need ways for teacher leaders and school improvement committees to scrutinize their school's organizational climate so that all educators can continue to seek ways of improving their schools. Teachers need more experience in engaging in sensemaking activities around school reform, in general.

Unfortunately, empirical evidence exploring the greater impact of teacher leadership on student learning remains meager (Leithwood et al., 2004; Neumerski, 2013; Wenner & Szeto, 2016; York-Barr & Duke, 2004). What principals and school leaders need to do to support teacher leaders is clearly indicated across several decades of the research on teacher leadership (e.g., Angelle & Teague, 2014; Crowther et al., 2002; Kahrs, 1996; Lambert, 2003; Lieberman, 1988; Muijs & Harris, 2007; York-Barr & Duke, 2004). According to York-Barr and Duke (2003), evidence suggests "that principal support of teacher leadership is more readily espoused than enacted" (p. 274) which is unfortunately supported by this study. The real significance of this work may be implications surrounding the need to revisit principal and school leader preparation and professional development and to ensure that it is aligned to policy guiding the work of teachers and teacher leaders. As asserted by York-Barr and Duke, "While generally supportive of the concept of teacher leadership, principals may lack the knowledge and experience required to effectively support high levels of such leadership" (p. 274).

Finally, the data suggest the need to hold principals accountable for supporting and drawing upon interdisciplinary approaches to teacher leadership. As the [state] Department of Education is using data from this grant (and six others across the state focused on building teacher leader capacity to support beginning teachers) to guide the legislatively mandated teacher leadership endorsement, this study may provide evidence for the need to include teacher leader support in "principal evaluations." Further, this study may spark the importance of building a tool for the evaluation of the work of teacher leaders focusing specifically on improved student outcomes.

## NOTE

1. For more detailed information on the *Beginning Teacher Project,* please see Morettini, B., Luet, K., Vernon-Dotson, L., Nagib, N., & Krishnamurthy. (2018). Developing teacher leaders using a distributed leadership model: Five signature features of a school-university partnership (pp. 217–233). In J. Hunzicker (Ed.), *Teacher Leadership in Professional Development Schools.* Emerald Publishing.

## REFERENCES

Allen, C. D., & Penuel, W. R. (2015). Studying teachers' sensemaking to investigate teachers' responses to professional development focused on new standards. *Journal of Teacher Education, 66*(2), 136–149. https://doi.org/10.1177/0022487114560646

Angelle, P., & Teague, G. M. (2014). Teacher leadership and collective efficacy: Teacher perceptions in three US school districts. *Journal of Educational Administration, 52*(6), 738–753. https://doi.org/10.1108/jea-02-2013-0020

Bambino, D. (2002). Redesigning professional development: Critical friends. *Educational Leadership, 59*(6), 25–27.

Bennett, N., Wise, C., Woods, P. A., & Harvey, J. A. (2003). *Distributed leadership.* National College of School Leadership.

Cheng, A. Y. N., & Szeto, E. (2016). Teacher leadership development and principal facilitation: Novice teachers' perspectives. *Teaching and Teacher Education, 58,* 140–148. https://doi.org/10.1016/j.tate.2016.05.003

Creswell, J. W. (2007). *Qualitative inquiry and research design: Choosing among five approaches* (2nd ed.). Sage.

Crowther, F., Kaagen, S. S., Ferguson, M., & Hann, L. (2002). *Developing teacher leaders: How teacher leadership enhances school success.* Corwin Press.

Fairman, J., & Mackenzie, S. (2014). How teacher leaders influence others and understand their leadership. *International Journal of Leadership in Education, 18*(1), 61–87.

Gronn, P. (2000). Distributed properties: A new architecture for leadership. *Educational Management Administration & Leadership, 28*(3), 317–338.

Hargreaves, A., & Fink, D. (2006). *Sustainable leadership.* Jossey-Bass.

Harris, A. (2008). Distributing leadership according to the evidence. *Journal of Educational Administration, 46*(2), 172–188.

Harris, A., Leithwood, K., Day, C., & Hopkins, D. (2007). Distributed leadership and organizational change: Reviewing the evidence. *Journal of Educational Change, 8*(4), 337–347.

Hord, S. M. (2009). Professional learning communities: Educators work together towards a shared purpose. *Journal of Staff Development, 30,* 40–43.

Kahrs, J. R. (1996). Principals who support teacher leadership. *New Directions for School Leadership, 1,* 19–40.

Katzenmeyer, M., & Moller, G. (2009). *Awakening the sleeping giant: Helping teachers develop as leaders* (3rd ed.). Corwin Press.

Killion, J., Harrison, C., Colton, A., Bryan, C., Delehant, A., & Cooke, D. (2016). *A Systemic approach to elevating teacher leadership.* Learning Forward.

Klein, E. J., Taylor, M., Munakata, M., Trabona, K., Rahman, Z., & McManus, J. (2018). Navigating teacher leaders' complex relationships using a distributed leadership framework. *Teacher Education Quarterly, 45*(2), 89–112.

Klein, K., & Sorra, J. (1996). The challenge of innovation implementation. *The Academy of Management Review, 21*(4), 1055–1080.

Lambert, L. (2003). Leadership redefined: An evocative context for teacher leadership. *School Leadership and Management, 23*(4), 421–430. https://doi.org/10.1080/1363243032000150953

Lear, J., Godin, S., Werner, S., & Flamisch, M. (2015a, June). *Distributed leadership: Behaviorally anchored development of the instructional teacher leadership rating scale for building school capacity (ITLRSBSC).* Canada International Conference on Education: CICE-2015: Infonomics Society, Mississauga, ON, Canada.

Lear, J., Godin, S., Werner, S., & Flamisch, M. (2015b). Two-phase development of the instructional teacher leadership rating scale for building school capacity (ITLRSBSC): Model emergence through pervasive empirical grounding and mixed method evaluation. *International Journal for Cross-Disciplinary Subjects in Education, 5*(2), 2523–2532. https://doi.org/10.20533/ijcdse.2042.6364.2015.0343

Leithwood, K., Louis, K. S., Anderson, S., & Wahlstrom, K. (2004). *Review of research: How leadership influences student learning.* Wallace Foundation.

Lieberman, A. (1988). Teachers and principals: Turf, tension, and new tasks. *Phi Delta Kappan, 69*(9), 648–653.

Maitlis, S., & Christianson, M. (2014). Sensemaking in organizations: Taking stock and moving forward. *The Academy of Management Annals, 8*(1), 57–125. https://doi.org/10.1080/19416520.2014.873177

Mayrowetz, D. (2008). Making sense of distributed leadership: Exploring the multiple usages of the concept in the field. *Educational Administration Quarterly, 44*(3), 424–435.

Miles, M. B., & Huberman, A. M. (1994). Qualitative data analysis: An expanded sourcebook (2nd ed.). SAGE Publications.

Milner, R. (2012). But what is urban education? *Urban Education,* 47(3), 556–561.

Morettini, B., Luet, K., Vernon-Dotson, L., Nagib, N., & Krishnamurthy, S. (2018). Developing teacher leadership using a distributed leadership model: Five signature features of a school-university partnership. In J. Hunzicker (Ed.), *Teacher leadership in professional development schools* (pp. 217–233). Emerald Publishing.

Muijs, D., & Harris, A. (2007). Teacher leadership in (in)action: Three case studies of contrasting schools. *Educational Management Administration and Leadership, 35*(1), 111–134. https://doi.org/10.1177/1741143207071387

Neumerski, C. M. (2013). Rethinking instructional leadership, a review: What do we know about principal, teacher, and coach instructional leadership, and where should we go from here? *Educational Administration Quarterly, 49*(2), 310–347. https://doi.org/10.1177/0013161x12456700

Patton, M. Q. 1990. *Qualitative evaluation and research methods* (2nd ed.). SAGE Publications.

Powell, W. W., & Colyvas, J. A. (2008). Microfoundations of institutional theory. In R. Greenwood, C. Oliver, K. Sahlin, & R. Suddaby (Eds.), *The Sage handbook of organizational institutionalism* (pp. 276–298). Sage.

Rom, N., & Eyal, O. (2019). Sensemaking, sense-breaking, sense-giving, and sense-taking: How educators construct meaning in complex policy environments. *Teaching and Teacher Education, 78,* 62–74.

Sergiovanni, T. (2007). *Rethinking leadership.* Corwin Press.

Spillane, J. P., & Diamond, J. B. (2007). *Distributed leadership in practice.* Teachers College Press.

Teacher Leadership Exploratory Consortium. (2011). *Teacher leader model standards.* http://teacherleaderstandards.org/downloads/TLS_Brochure.pdf
Thoonen, E., Sleegers, P., Oort, F., & Peetsma, T. (2012). Building school-wide capacity for improvement: The role of leadership, school organizational conditions, and teacher factors. *School Effectiveness and School Improvement, 23*(4), 1–20.
Tsoukas, H., & Chia, R. (2002). Organizational becoming: Rethinking organizational change. *Organization Science, 13*(5), 567–582.
U.S. Census Bureau. (2010). *QuickFacts.* Retrieved from http://www.census.gov/quickfacts/table/PST045215/3407600
Vernon-Dotson, L. J. (2008). Promoting inclusive education through teacher leadership teams: A school reform initiative. *Journal of School Leadership, 18*(3), 543–554.
Weick, K. E. (1995). *Sensemaking in organizations.* Sage.
Weick, K. E., Sutcliff, K. M., & Obstfeld, D. (2005). Organizing and the process of sensemaking. *Organizational Science, 16*(4), 409–421. https://doi.org/10.1287/orsc.1050.0133
Wenner, J. A., & Campbell, T. (2016). The theoretical and empirical basis of teacher leadership: A review of the literature. *Review of Education Research, Online Version.* https://doi.org/10.3102/0034654316653478
Wenner, J. A., & Campbell, T. (2017). The theoretical and empirical basis of teacher leadership: A review of the literature. *Review of Educational Research, 87*(1), 134–171. https://doi.org/10.3102/0034654316653478
York-Barr, J., & Duke, K. (2004). What do we know about teacher leadership? Findings from two decades of scholarship. *Review of Educational Research, 74*(3), 255–316. https://doi.org/10.3102/00346543074003255

CHAPTER 15

# DEVELOPING EFFECTIVE PROFESSIONAL LEARNING COMMUNITIES FOR SENIOR LEADERS

**Marie Stephenson**
**Carla Solvason**
**Tracey France**
**Paul Sheehan**

## ABSTRACT

This chapter builds upon the outcomes of longitudinal research into a leader development intervention, which took place 3 years ago involving primary (elementary) leaders across a range of educational settings and contexts. Evidence showed that the leadership learning and wider impacts from these collaborative cluster groups was significant for a range of stakeholders. In this chapter we return to the data, examining it from an interdisciplinary lens to reveal the key role that professional learning communities (PLCs) play for leaders in sharing tacit knowledge based upon insight, intuition, and experience. We argue that this initiative is the perfect leader development tool—constructive and interdisciplinary. PLCs provide leaders with the op-

*On Leadership*, pages 257–277

> timum conditions to reflect, facilitating openness and transparency through trust-building, but simultaneously attend to the emotional dimensions of leadership. In essence, highly quality collaborative leader development programs such as this can help leaders address pressing leadership challenges and increase leader effectiveness by accommodating the complex and interdisciplinary nature of organizations, people, and societies.

In 2019 one of the authors of this chapter published an article which discussed the impact of the formation of collaborative clusters across schools in an English region to support the development of head teachers (Solvason & Kington, 2019). The data made clear that the considerable impact of the program was not achieved through productivity targets, but through trusting and respectful relationships. These relationships were nurtured through carefully planned collaborative sessions involving between two and seven head teachers, guided by skilled facilitators. The facilitators were not academics, but experienced and successful head teachers themselves from a range of primary (elementary) schools scattered across England in both rural and urban settings serving a range of socio-economic communities. They were seconded to the role by the university tasked with implementing the development program and welcomed the chance to work with a diverse group of colleagues as an invaluable opportunity to continue to widen their own professional skills and knowledge. They arranged and chaired the cluster groups of head teachers, decided on key development goals for the sessions and introduced key theoretical literature. For clarification, the role of the head teacher in the United Kingdom equates to that of school principal; the person who takes ultimate responsibility for the general, day-to-day running of the school and its administration.

In the aforementioned article by Solvason and Kington (2019), the *what* was discussed; the significant impact that the program had upon the head teachers. In this chapter, we shift the focus to the method behind the results, or the *how.* As one of the reviewers of the previous article pointed out, it is all well and good presenting the impressive results of these collaborative nurture groups, but what was the secret, how were such positive cultures created and what leadership lessons can we learn from this type of intervention? Here, we present a fusion of perspectives to further unpack these original concepts and draw upon a range of viewpoints and disciplines; these include the researcher who led on the original project, a specialist in ethical leadership, and two of the facilitators who were involved in, and who continue to implement collaborative working groups. Through fresh lenses we explore effective approaches to leadership collaborations, revealing what works and *why.* We present a wealth of practical information for those interested in developing professional learning communities (PLCs) and argue that, when set up correctly and carried out skilfully, these collaborative partnerships are not only a highly effective holistic leadership development tool for head teachers but have much to offer leaders in other settings and contexts.

Firstly, it is important to position this research broadly in the educational leadership literature, to understand the important role that professional relationships play in enhancing leadership practice and as corollary, school effectiveness.

## SITUATING EDUCATIONAL LEADERSHIP

Educational leadership is traditionally conceptualized through the lens of the wider leadership literature (Stephenson, 2017), where constructs are adopted, applied, and replaced depending on their popularity. However, over time, scholars have agreed that there are commonalities regarding what is required for good and effective leadership, such as the notion of influence, facilitating goals and shared objectives (Kort, 2008; Yukl, 2013). But a deeper analysis shows that educational leadership may be different. Schools are values expressive according to Jeavons (2005, p. 205), they are "sustained by the bonds of trust... their very existence and practices convey a public statement of what their members see as a better, or more caring or just world" (Rothschild & Milofsky, 2006, p. 137). School leadership is emotional (Hargreaves, 2008), sophisticated, and nuanced (Hodges & Howieson, 2017); in short, it is relational work (Duignan, 2006; Helstad & Møller, 2013). School leadership operates in a "field of relationships" (Ospina & Uhl-Bien, 2012, p. 6), in the dynamic spaces between people, their interdependencies and intersubjectivities (Cox & Hassard, 2018, p. 535). Schools are a network of interactions, structures, and cultures, where principals play a critical role in ensuring that trusting relationships and collaboration can flourish (Helstad & Møller, 2013, pp. 259–260). As such, schools appear interdisciplinary in nature, their leaders are competing and engaging in complex problem-solving to sustain, cultivate, and facilitate the needs and interests of others.

Although relationships are at the heart of leadership constructs such as leader member exchange, distributed leadership, shared leadership and complexity leadership theory, relational aspects tend to focus on reciprocal behavior, mutual dependence, loyalty, and support (Yukl, 2013, p. 222). In schools, leadership relationships extend past dyadic and vertical structures; they are networked and concern a range of wider stakeholders (Duignan, 2006; Helstad & Møller, 2013). Educational leaders must be experts in demonstrating relational intelligence and relational skills (Maak & Pless, 2006, p. 104). If so, then it would be feasible that they use these same relational approaches to facilitate their own professional development. It is clear from the original research undertaken by Solvason and Kington (2019) and a further deeper analysis of the data presented here, that professional collaborative groups provide the necessary space for self-observation, self-appraisal, and self-assessment (Caldwell & Hayes, 2016, p. 116) which results in a high quality, critical, reflective, and engaging learning opportunity (Kochan et al., 2002), which in turn, enhances leader effectiveness.

## PROFESSIONAL LEARNING COMMUNITIES

According to Stoll and Louis (2007) a PLC is an *enterprise*, which is "ongoing, reflective, collaborative, inclusive, learning-oriented" and "growth promoting" (p. 2). They normally involve teacher groups within a school but can also encompass professional educational networks across localities (Mitchell & Sackney, 2007), or even countries (Stoll & Louis, 2007). PLCs are deliberate, based on voluntarist freedom and collective responsibility, as such, "an architecture or design" (Hargreaves, 2014, p. 139) is required to create and build a sense of stability (Stoll & Louis, 2007), ensure sustainable improvement, and allow for contextual flexibility.

Successful PLCs are dependent upon positive relationships and collegiality, "sincere and candid collaborations... relationships founded in faith in self and others and belief in the potential of the whole" (Beatty, 2007, p. 322). They draw upon deeper understandings and new knowledge (Bolam et al., 2005, p. 21), offering a forum for peers to "help make critical decisions, share in the creation of new knowledge, the collective ownership of the ideas of the day and the responsibility for outcomes" (Beatty, 2007, p. 328, Solvason & Kington, 2020). This unique platform enables school leaders to safely explore context specific personal and professional challenges, affirm identities and attend to the human side of change (Stoll & Bolam, 2005). On review, PLCs are an interdisciplinary leader development tool, allowing leaders to explore deeper, more sustained leadership learning to transform the organization, its partners, and others. In a school we see a positive impact on pupils, morale, educational practice (Bolam et al., 2005), the hallmarks of effective leadership (Huguet, 2017).

### Honesty, Vulnerability, and Trust

In order to facilitate sharing, reflection, and change (as is evidenced in the collaborative groups described in this chapter), Hallam et al. (2014, p. 146) note that group members must make themselves vulnerable to one another. Vulnerability is a key antecedent to trust. In demonstrating vulnerability, leaders show willingness to accept personal risk and undertake a mutual agreement not to violate trust (Tschannen-Moran, 2007, pp. 47–48).

Over time, and as parties interact, trust deepens and becomes more authentic, strong enough to withstand the occasional disappointment or disagreement. Bolam et al. (2005) lists mutual trust, respect, and openness as key, whereas Lasater (2016) settles for trust, rapport, and communication. But the consensus is that trust is the common denominator, without it "there can be no cooperation, no community, no commerce, no conversation" (Solomon, 1998, p. 99). It embodies "cultural meanings, emotional responses, and social relations... one not only thinks trust, but feels trust" (Kramer, 2011, p. 137).

Trust is regarded as a reciprocal transformational dimension of leadership, a core fiber running through the effective leader (Stephenson, 2017), it is also a fundamental element of relational leadership. Nicholas and West-Burnham (2016) explain that relational trust is about "building social capital, creating learning communities which are exemplified in the strength of social networks, interdependency, engagement, shared purpose, parity of esteem and genuine reciprocity" (p. 171). It involves respect, competence, personal regard, and integrity (Bryk & Schneider, 2003), it also engenders candor, openness, and honesty (Tschannen-Moran, 2014). The latter is key according to Hallam et al. (2014) and Lasater (2016), honesty is essential to show vulnerability because without it, Brooks (2015) argues, there is no trust. These concepts are tightly tied, but collectively, they create the optimum conditions for action and collaboration (Helstad & Møller, 2013, p. 258), disclosure, problem-sharing, and professional dialogue. In short, the most effective communities of practice are predicated on heightened levels of trust played out in the relational interactions between peer group members.

## REFLECTION AND EMOTIONAL DIMENSIONS

The practice of reflection has long been considered fundamental for teachers' professional development (Postholm, 2018). Its origins can be traced to scholars such as Dewey (1916) and Schön (1987) who envisaged reflection as an *in situ* or *post-situ* performative act most often performed in isolation. However, individuals need the support and counsel of others to facilitate genuine reflection and critical thinking, or, as Ersozlu (2016) contends, they need opportunities to "witness the continuity of their development" (p. 803). Daniëls et al. (2020) suggest that group reflective learning through sharing experiences involves a focus on thoughts and feelings. According to Zembylas (2014), this is a departure from the traditional thinking of both Dewey (1916) and Schön (1987) who acknowledge the emotional dimensions of reflection, but neglect to put emotions at the center of the reflective process.

Similarly, as Solvason and Kington (2019) assert, the emotional aspects of leadership have not received due attention in the leadership literature; but this is beginning to change. Scholars such as Salvador and Folger (2009) have renewed efforts to understand the role of emotions, breaking what Beatty (2007) described as a "professional silence." Emotions can be positive, influential for moral motivation (Johnson, 2012), moral awareness, and moral judgment, they are crucial in shaping decision-making (Salvador & Folger, 2009). Feelings lubricate social transactions and reflect the structure and culture of organizations (Fineman, 1993, p. 9) and are key to understanding human dynamics (Fineman, 1993, Uhl-Bien, 2006). Those engaging in the practice of critical emotional reflexivity (Zembylas, 2014) open themselves to deeper dimensions of the reflective experience, a process which helps individuals rationalize their roles and behavior and strengthen character.

To summarize, head teachers are emotional beings, and schools are emotional contexts for decision-making (Crawford, 2007). This means that educational leaders need new types of opportunities to not only explore the professional and rational, but to understand the nature and meaning of extreme feelings such as shame, anxiety, and grief, and work on ways to deal with the emotions of others.

## THE ORIGINAL RESEARCH

This research arose as a means of evaluating the impact of an ongoing leadership development program delivered by a U.K. university. It was based upon the development of PLCs for head teachers across primary schools (ages 4–11) in the Midlands, a central region of England, and took place across an academic year. Because the intervention was based upon open, trusting relationships it was vital that this was mirrored in the research approach. As such, a collaborative, co-constructed approach was taken in order to research *with* the teachers and facilitators, in partnership rather than them being researched *on* (Cohen et al., 2018). The full details of the research approach can be found in Solvason and Kington (2019), but a brief overview of how data were collected is provided below. The research design bore the hallmarks of constructivist, participative research, allowing for the perceptions, views, and voices of all to be heard from inception to conclusion (Rossman & Rallis, 2017). Ethical boundaries were transparently established with all involved, and the British Educational Research Association ([BERA]; 2011) *Ethical Guidelines* followed closely. All participants were fully informed of the intentions of the research and advised of the ways in which the data could be used (including for chapters such as this) before consenting to be involved.

From initial discussions between the researcher and seven of the head teachers (representing seven PLCs) it was agreed that a mixed method approach (Bryman, 2015) would be suitable for the head teachers; comprising three sources of data collection. First, the head teachers completed a school audit of impact. This audit, based upon the findings of Baker's (2015) research into school collaborations, was completed throughout the year and aggregated the views of all 29 head teachers involved in the seven PLCs and concerned the ways this interdisciplinary collaboration had impacted upon their own schools. The main foci were based on Baker's (2015) research, and included the following:

- pedagogy
- increased motivation
- openness/sharing of good practice
- shift towards an enquiry-based culture
- CPD and career enhancement
- innovation
- curriculum development

For each of these areas head teachers were asked to provide evidence of the impact of their collaboration with other head teachers on their own setting, but they were also encouraged to share any barriers that they may have experienced.

There were also three focus group discussions spaced through the year (the numbers involved in these varied from five to nine head teachers) and lastly, there were individual interviews with the 15 head teachers who volunteered. The areas outlined by Baker (2015) also steered the semi-structured group and individual interviews, but the head teachers were also given the space to explore those key points that they believed were most significant in demonstrating the impact of their collaborative development sessions. Additionally, some points raised in focus group interviews were then explored in more depth in the discussions that followed. In this way, the data collection was organic and responsive to the direction chosen by the head teachers. Mid-way through the study 12 facilitators also participated in a one-off focus group discussion, to reflect upon their perception of their own role, as well the more general impacts of the cluster groups.

A staged approach was taken to analysis of the data collected through audit and interview. This involved becoming familiar with the data as a whole, through listening and transcription, and then categorizing into broader themes and relationships (Denscombe, 2010). When clear themes began to emerge very early on in the data collection they were further explored in the focus group discussions. The latter were particularly effective in generating "thick descriptions" (Geertz, 1973) as the leaders and facilitators reflected and expanded upon one another's ideas. The audit data, collected towards the end of the year, was instrumental for generating more directive questions (Cohen et al., 2018, p. 260) to shape the interviews with leaders. At the conclusion of the data collection period all data were triangulated using a data reduction grid, enabling the various data sources to be compared across the prevalent themes. A non-partisan expert in data analysis was asked to confirm the topics which had been identified as most prevalent within the data.

As indicated earlier, the general areas of impact were addressed in Solvason and Kington (2019), whereas in this chapter we take a fresh look at the data in terms of the dynamics of a PLC based upon relational interdependencies. Two lead facilitators involved with the original leadership development intervention have added their reflections and perceptions as new data for this chapter and a specialist in leadership literature has offered her expertise in terms of how the data intersects with emerging leadership theory and current thinking regarding professional learning in communities of peers. As such, the analysis of the data and the discussion which follows demonstrates a multi-faceted richness for anyone involved or who wishes to be involved in designing, facilitating and sustaining similar communities of practice which acknowledge and celebrate the emotional aspects of collaborative working and the dynamics of relational skills and intelligence.

Below we present what emerged from a re-examination of the original data collected from head teachers and facilitators. It serves to, not only evidence the significant role that PLCs play in head teachers' own, and school development, but, more significantly for this chapter, *how* that happened. We share the voices of head teachers and facilitators (given pseudonyms to protect their identity) with just a short commentary on the key issues we identified. These themes are then explored in relation to the literature in the discussion section which seeks to understand the comments in terms of the leadership lessons learned, and their importance for effective leader development.

## LAYING THE GROUNDWORK FOR EFFECTIVE PLCS

Firstly, it was important that facilitators established themselves as peers within the groups, to demonstrate that they had the capacity to understand and to empathize, they did this by explaining shared and similar experiences with the head teachers in the clusters. Each facilitator remained with a designated group over time and this consistency helped to secure the group dynamic and impetus. Amongst other tasks, facilitators co-created the aims of each session with their respective groups using research articles and think pieces as motivation for members to identify what was important to them. From this process, they agreed on a common language and shared understanding regarding the purposes and intentions of the sessions. When discussing their role in directing the groups, facilitators were keen to establish that their work was about people and relationships, and that they understood their role as catalyst:

> The competence, knowledge, and neutrality of the facilitation team were cornerstones to the clusters' success. Time, skill, careful communication and planning were crucial to creating the conditions necessary to reduce the inevitable mixed-motive situations that are common in highly accountable and increasingly market driven systems.
>
> **Jane, Facilitator**
>
> We make them think by the articles... this might take you in a direction, but we are not determining the direction.
>
> **Ian, Facilitator**
>
> Not being the rescuer. Not stepping in and rescuing them... that then allows them to bond, because they become each other's rescuers.
>
> One of the other things that has been important is to listen, to listen carefully to who they are, get to know them as people... So that not only do they build trust with each other, but they build trust with you and they do trust us with the things that they are going to say.
>
> **Beth, Facilitator**

## THE DEVELOPMENT OF TRUST

The data above clearly shows that facilitators created the conditions for trust to develop. Over the length of the program, they strengthened and nurtured mutual trust by encouraging members to revisit their values and beliefs, take risks without fear, and engage in the free exchange of information. This enabled the development of the cohort's collective capacity through the creation of high levels of confidence, coupled with a climate of safety and honesty. Members worked towards developing greater empathy, insight, and an openness to change as relationships developed and matured:

> What's been really fascinating to see is how these groups of people have grown together. So, some of them starting from quite disparate beginnings,

> when we began this, they've grown together in a professional, but also a personal way and you can see those relationships growing.
>
> **Simon, Facilitator**

> That trust for me is key...we formed a very trusting band of head teachers.
>
> **Michelle, Head Teacher**

> And therefore, by the end of the day their trust was even higher because they had experienced having to put themselves in a vulnerable position and it was safe.
>
> **Ian, Facilitator**

The head teachers also stressed the importance of visiting one another's schools for "opening up" regarding their strengths and weaknesses with one another; this was a key step toward sustaining mutual trust in the PLC. Head teachers simultaneously exposed vulnerabilities to one another, in the knowledge that they would also be "held safe" by the unconditional positive regard of their peers as demonstrated in the data below:

> It was that, the breaking down of the barriers and having the tour of each other's school... warts and all.
>
> **Niki, Head Teacher**

> When we walk round each of the schools again, you are on show, you are vulnerable.
>
> **Angela, Head Teacher**

> You are letting someone come into a fairly dusty dirty corner of your school... and I think making yourself vulnerable is important to development.
>
> **Stuart, Head Teacher**

> We are building people's confidence within a safe environment. They are more powerful individually, but also as a group.
>
> **Ian, Facilitator**

> I'd already got that network of people there, that I could ask those questions to that, you know, might sound a bit stupid...
>
> **Sue, Head Teacher**

### Openness and Transparency

The facilitators explained how the cohort meetings typically began with a review of the last gathering and centered on activities or key questions, such as sharing things that had recently gone well, with a partner. This dedicated time to re-establish relationships with peers allowed members to share and explore the challenges they faced in their complex roles since they had last met and proved to be a powerful tool in drawing the cohort together. By articulating their values as they reflected upon actions in their own settings, they were able to better understand that they all faced similar issues, which created a feeling of safety, solidarity, and unity.

Developing non-judgemental conditions and behaviors was an essential feature of the group delivery. The facilitators understood the need to be passionately curious and to demonstrate the right behaviors for listening. They understood that sometimes it was important to acknowledge and respect any personal issues that the leaders brought to the meetings which were particularly pressing at the outset. Without these being addressed they would linger as a barrier to engagement—but sharing emotions also enabled further bonding. A space was provided for those who needed to "vent" and to have their feelings validated by peers who had shared similar experiences. By knowing when and how to change the direction of the conversation, the facilitators were then able to move the conversation forward in a gentle and considered way.

I was just bowled over by how honest they were. Not navel gazing, but really honest... and one person had only joined the group two months before but had really opened up.

**Ian, Facilitator**

The brutal honesty in our meetings.

**Angela, Head Teacher**

It is one of the first things we did, and it was about being honest, open, and transparent really. So about challenging one another.

**Sharon, Head Teacher**

The whole purpose of [the university collaboration] was to create an open atmosphere of professional discussion and school improvement... And I think that's what's been done.

**Stuart, Head Teacher**

That transparency I think, which obviously leads on, goes hand-in-hand I think with the trust... transparency has been instrumental really in moving all of our schools forward... everything is out in the open in every school... there is no hiding place.

**Marie, Head Teacher**

## Building Respect

The facilitators explained how there were always opportunities built into the collaborative sessions for members to undertake further exploration of their strengths, to reaffirm positive values, and to use their personal assets to appreciate and engage with others in the cohort. Time was given for members to build reciprocity, to pay attention to one other's assets and to appreciate self and others. Through encouraging the leaders to ask experienced peers for help, relationships were co-created, strengthened, and deepened. The head teachers were able to use the other cohort members as a support system, knowing they had someone "rooting for them." This provided a sense of community connection and a safe outlet for anxiety and stress.

To have that time to listen, again, to those experienced people.

**Liz, Head Teacher**

We soon developed a professional respect for one another as heads.

**Nikki, Head Teacher**

We were all just saying, "Look, what do you think?" And some people would be better than you, some people would be as good as you... We were all very open about that.

**Lindsay, Head Teacher**

We do have strengths, so to look at each other's strengths and learn from it. Not to be afraid to share or to say, "This is rubbish here."

**Michelle, Head Teacher**

And as leaders we put hands up and say, well actually, we are not very good at that. It's not a strength and can we learn from you?

**Angela, Head Teacher**

Facilitators used case studies as artefacts to enable cohorts to focus on assertion and facilitate structured discussion. From these exemplars, members were encouraged to identify specific aspects of their own practice that they would like to develop further. Subsequent sessions would then include a focus on progress against identified targets, which gave group members the opportunity to explore and revisit aspects that they had found personally useful.

Other activities centered on self-reflection, looking at personal strengths, or analyzing team dynamics within their school. This established greater understanding of personal style and orientation, whereby members gained greater understandings about what was working well and what needed to be changed. By setting up coaching triads to explore complex issues, and structuring these opportunities using coaching models, such as OSCAR (Rogers et al., 2012) or GROW (Whitmore, 2017), time and space were created for critical evaluation and the identification of new (rather than the re-processing of existing) priorities.

## Supporting One Another's Progress

In order to "push and nudge," facilitators created the conditions for effective, purposeful dialogue where leaders were able to share their knowledge. This was achieved by asking, "So what?" or "What else?" and brought an element of challenge and tension to discussions. Probing in this way encouraged deeper thinking and reframing. The collaborative group could identify clear actions that might ultimately lead to a positive impact on children's learning and the wider educational experience.

The leaders worked on whole school action plans together and challenged each other constructively, as exemplified by Simone (see below) when questioning targets, or evidence which appeared insufficiently convincing. Such challenges were not approached in a discouraging or disparaging way, but in a friendly and supportive way which said, "You can do better than that, let me show you what I mean." These exchanges were about honesty, role modeling, and sharing expertise. In recognizing the sense of forward motion which had emerged from their time spent together, the head teachers duplicated this approach to peer development for their subject leads across the cluster of schools. They visited one another's schools, shared their pupils' work, and shared their planning, "They did things differently," and this had a significant impact upon pupil attainment.

> We are looking at one another's results and you want to do as well as everybody else. So, it's almost like a healthy competition. We want all of us to do well.
>
> **Sharon, Head Teacher**

I can remember [other head in cluster] saying, "Yes that's lovely—but so what?" He didn't mean it like that, but it did make me think, yes, well actually, yeah, so what?

**Simone, Head Teacher**

Don't the Zulus call it Ubuntu? Where we are all lessened by a failure of our own.

**Stuart, Head Teacher**

I think not only are you in control of what's being looked at, but if you are doing it right (and I think we are) then you pick an area that you know you've not got right... do some reflection on it and come up with some ideas.

**Pete, Head Teacher**

So actually, having the comfort of your buddies and people you love and have kind of chosen to actually help you solve those problems has been a real saving grace.

**Angela, Head Teacher**

I just think that kind of level of knowing that other people are really gunning for you is really important.

**Mandy, Head Teacher**

## Maintaining Perspective

The role that the collaborative group played in acting as a "sounding board" when individuals were faced with seemingly insurmountable problems was valued by the members. The concept of being re-grounded, or maintaining perspective, as mentioned below, arose during several interviews. The facilitators perceived competence, knowledge and neutrality as being the cornerstones to successfully dealing with these situations. They explained that skillful communication was crucial to creating the conditions necessary to reduce the inevitable mixed-motive, challenging situations that are common in highly accountable and increasingly market driven systems. Because of these pressures it was essential that the facilitators' guidance focused upon both task support and social and emotional support by building time into the sessions for systematic reflection on the complexity and multifaceted nature of their head teacher roles. From these explorations they gained a more nuanced perspective and understanding, which led to improvements in their own performance and in the sustained collaborative leadership of the group.

I think it's nice because you can go, and somebody will say, "Does anybody else feel like this?" or "Has anyone else found this?" and it's nice to feel that other people are feeling that way.

**Mandy, Head Teacher**

Yeah, that your own school issues are not isolated just to your school, that can be reassuring, can't it?

**Angela, Head Teacher**

You've got someone to say, "I've got this person saying this and I've got this person saying that" and they'll ground you and say, "Well, you need to think about what your school needs."

**Janet, Head Teacher**

It was almost like group therapy.

**Simone, Head Teacher**

Partly because it's cathartic, they can have some time to share things and to maintain a perspective. Because I think each of us goes off in our lives and we are thinking, "This is a really big issue." And then you talk to colleagues and think, "No, it isn't actually, it's part of the real world, it's manageable, and we can do this, this and this." So, it helps to maintain a perspective, I think, or to get shared input to help somebody to maintain a perspective or address an issue.

**Simon, Facilitator**

I think that in the modern educational world, [that model of accountability] sometimes tends to forget that schools are about people... and that's what's exciting about this work.

**Elliott, Facilitator**

## DISCUSSION

This chapter set out to reflect on *how* the positive leadership cultures discussed in Solvason and Kington (2019) were created, managed, and sustained. What we have shown is that a confluence of specific conditions proved fundamental for successful PLCs of educational leaders. As reported by Stoll and Louis (2007), PLCs are not easy to set up and that membership must be carefully managed. The right environment is crucial and optimum conditions are necessary for the "magic" to happen. As Cooper et al. (2009) suggest, boundaries must be agreed whereby members respect each other's views and uphold shared democratic principles. Halverson (2007) recommends that processes are creatively co-constructed with the purpose of challenging members both intellectually and professionally. Resources, or "artifacts" were used by our facilitators as crucial tools to build trust, these were the lenses with which to see how leaders would think and act (Halverson, 2007, pp. 94–95). This enabled PLC members to grow and develop with each other, but also move at their own pace, albeit supported and nudged by facilitators and peers (Hargreaves, 2014, p. 132).

We have described a real and constructive and interdisciplinary approach, which engendered feelings of affiliation and cohesiveness. Markedly, it provided psychological safety, empowered members and gave them the freedom to take risks and show vulnerability. Similar to the findings of Wahlstrom and Louis (2008), needs were recognized and understood, which set the optimum conditions for honest exchange. This was a safe place to speak the truth, where members felt free to develop a collective awareness of the challenges to their roles. Although we have detailed the kinds of conditions necessary for the successful PLC, the real magic was not immediately visible. On close examination it became clear that there was a golden thread connecting and underpinning the network of relationships.

Trust is a "particular quality of a social system" according to Van Maele et al. (2014, p. 1). It is woven through a school, evident in every relationship, and is a key element of successful and effective educational leadership. Kramer (2011) describes trust as fundamental for "coordination, cooperation and other positive forms of collective behavior" (p. 139). It could be argued that head teachers are familiar with building organizational trust in their schools, but working in a PLC, with a group of your peers offers a new context with which to understand the notion of trust. Kramer (2011, p. 142) describes this type of trust as "thickening" or "thinning," dependent upon interactional histories, which calibrate and update in line with member expectations. These were not the normal leader-centric decision-making events experienced in a school; this was a high-capacity community, which shared perceived social similarity. As such, the leaders were able to open their minds to novel insights, perspectives, and imagine alternatives they had not previously realized. They were able to transform their organizations through using their relational skills and relational intelligence in collaboration with each other.

Although Bolam et al. (2005) claim that PLCs provide benefits beyond the individual and impact on a wide range of educational stakeholders, it is the relational aspects that take center stage in our chapter. Being part of a PLC gives value to professional development by providing the means for reflection and growth. Like Kochan et al. (2002) we found the process of reflection to be at the root of effective leadership development, self-observation, self-appraisal, and self-assessment (Caldwell & Hayes, 2016). Our research suggests that the PLC provided the much-needed "mind space" for testing ideas and collaborative thinking. This stands in contrast to the traditional notions of reflection as lonely (Dewey, 1916), post hoc (Schön, 1987), and episodic events carried out in the margins of a school day. This intervention can be typified as quality retro—and introspection from shared professional and experiential narratives (Postholm, 2018). With the PLC as conduit, head teachers were able to retain perspective, experience belonging, unity, and solidarity as they normalized the problems of practice (Little & Horn, 2007, p. 79). In summary, we assert that when set up skillfully, PLCs are one of the most complete and effective professional development tools currently available to educational leaders.

## CONCLUSION

As can be seen, the success of this initiative was based upon several key factors, such as setting up the cohorts, creating the optimum environment, and sustaining success. But, as Stoll and Bolam (2005) argue, real progress and professional development within a PLC are only possible if we also attend to the human side of things. In this chapter we universally acknowledged the importance of strong, mutually respectful personal, and professional relationships amongst all members. This requires careful management, hard work, and high levels of emotional maturity. Like Zembylas (2014), we agree that emotions are linked with cognition and perception, but our data goes further and demonstrates how a skilfully facilitated PLC enables emotions to be exposed, but crucially holds them safe. Our members showed their vulnerabilities, were open, honest, and transparent. Emotions were carefully moderated and mediated through a solutions-focused and a forward-facing culture of listening, valuing, and understanding. The PLC was the figurative safety net, where members simultaneously challenged and encouraged each other in constructive ways.

Finally, there are important lessons to be drawn from this research in terms of leadership and its interdisciplinary nature. According to Owen (2015) leaders must possess the ability to work in integrative and intentional ways, as learning communities in a networked world. The time has come to repair the fragmentation of knowledge; other disciplines have much to learn from subspecialities, alternative experiences, and innovative research in educational leadership. Whilst there are challenges to overcome, the research presented here demonstrates the real benefits of constructing new knowledge and approaches and epistemologies using an evidenced based approach to address pressing leadership challenges. We contend that PLCs offer all leaders the opportunity to engage in highly effective leadership development whilst also acknowledging the complex and interdisciplinary nature of organizations, people, and the societies in which they exist.

## REFERENCES

Baker, A.C. (2015). *Catalytic conversations: Organizational communication and innovation.* Routledge.

Beatty, B. (2007). Going through the emotions: Leadership that gets to the heart of school renewal. *Australian Journal of Education, 51*(3), 328–340.

Bolam, R., McMahon, A., Stoll, L., Thomas, S., Wallace, M., Greenwood, A., Hawkey, K., Ingram, M., Atkinson, A., & Smith, M. (2005). *Creating and sustaining effective professional learning communities* (Research Report No. 637). DfES Publications, University of Bristol.

British Educational Research Association. (2011). *Ethical guidelines for educational research.* https://www.bera.ac.uk/wp-content/uploads/2014/02/BERA-Ethical-Guidelines-2011.pdf?noredirect=1

Brooks, M. C. (2015). School principals in Southern Thailand: Exploring trust with community leaders during conflict. *Educational Management Administration & Leadership, 43*(2), 232–252.

Bryman, A. (2015). *Social research methods* (4th ed.). Oxford University Press.

Bryk, A. S., & Schneider, B. (2003). Trust in schools: A core resource for school reform. *Educational leadership, 60*(6), 40–45.

Caldwell, C., & Hayes, L. (2016). Self-efficacy and self-awareness: Moral insights to increased leader effectiveness. *Journal of Management Development, 35*(9), 1163–1173.

Cohen, L., Manion, L., & Morrison, K. (2018). *Research methods in education* (8th ed.). Routledge.

Cooper, C. W., Allen, R. A., & Bettez, S. C. (2009). Forming culturally responsive learning communities in demographically changing schools. In C. A. Mullin (Ed.), *The handbook of leadership and professional learning communities* (pp. 103–114). Palgrave Macmillan.

Crawford, M. (2007). Rationality and emotion in primary school leadership: an exploration of key themes. *Educational Review, 59*(1), 87–98.

Cox, J. W., & Hassard, J. (2018). From relational to relationist leadership in critical management education: Recasting leadership work after the practice turn. *Academy of Management Learning & Education, 17*(4), 532–556.

Daniëls, E., Hondeghem, A., & Heystek, J. (2020). Exploring outcomes of group reflective learning for school leaders. *Reflective Practice, 21*(5), 604–618.

Denscombe, M. (2010). *The good research guide for small-scale research projects* (4th ed.). Open University Press

Dewey, J. (1916). *Democracy and education.* Macmillan.

Duignan, P. (2006). *Educational leadership: Key challenges and ethical tensions.* Cambridge University Press.

Ersozlu, A. (2016). School principals' reflective leadership skills through the eyes of science and mathematics teachers. *International Journal of Environmental & Science Education, 11*(5), 801–808.

Fineman, S. (1993). *Emotion in organizations.* SAGE Publications.

Geertz, C. (1973). Thick description: Toward an interpretive theory of culture. In C. Geertz (Ed.), *The interpretation of cultures: Selected essays* (pp. 3–30). Basic Books.

Hallam, P. R., Dulaney, S. K., Hite, J. M., & Smith, H. R. (2014). Trust at ground zero: Trust and collaboration within the professional learning community. In D. Van Maele, P. B. Forsyth, & M. Van Houtte (Eds.), *Trust and school life: The role of trust for learning, teaching, leading, and bridging* (pp. 145–170). Springer.

Halverson, R. (2007). How leaders use artefacts to structure professional community in schools. In L. Stoll & K. S. Louis (Eds.), *Professional learning communities divergence, depth and dilemmas* (pp. 93–105). McGraw-Hill Education, Open University Press.

Hargreaves, A. (2008). The emotional geographies of educational leadership. In B. Davies & T. Brighouse (Eds.), *Passionate leadership in education* (pp. 129–152). SAGE Publications.

Hargreaves, A. (2014). Push, pull and nudge: The future of teaching and educational change. *LEARNing Landscapes, 9*(1), 119–142.

Helstad, K., & Møller, J. (2013). Leadership as relational work: Risks and opportunities. *International Journal Leadership in Education, 6*(3), 245–262.

Hodges, J., & Howieson, B. (2017). The challenges of leadership in the third sector. *European Management Journal, 35*(1), 69–77.

Huguet, B. C. S. (2017). Effective leadership can positively impact school performance. *On the Horizon, 25*(2), 96–102.

Jeavons, T. H. (2005). Ethical non-profit management. In R. D. Herman & Associates (Eds.), *The jossey-bass handbook of non-profit leadership and management* (2nd ed.). John Wiley & Sons.

Johnson, C. E. (2012). *Meeting the ethical challenges of leadership: Casting light or shadow.* SAGE Publications.

Kochan, F. K., Bredeson, P., & Riehl. C. (2002). Rethinking the professional development of school leaders. *Yearbook of the National Society for the Study of Education, 101*(1), 289–306.

Kort, E. D. (2008). What, after all, is leadership? 'Leadership' and plural action. *The Leadership Quarterly, 19*(4), 409–425.

Kramer, R. K. (2011). Trust and distrust in the leadership process: A review and assessment of theory and evidence. In A. Bryman, D. Collinson, K. Grint, B. Jackson, & M. Uhl-Bien. (2016). *The SAGE handbook of leadership* (pp. 136–150). SAGE Publications.

Lasater, K. (2016). School leader relationships: The need for explicit training on rapport, trust, and communication. *Journal of School Administration Research and Development, 1*(2), 19–26.

Little, J. W., & Horn, I. S. (2007). 'Normalizing' problems of practice: Converting routine conversation into a resource for learning in professional communities. In L. Stoll & K. S. Louis (Eds.), *Professional learning communities divergence, depth and dilemmas* (pp. 70–92). McGraw-Hill Education, Open University Press.

Maak, T., & Pless, N. M. (2006). Responsible leadership in a stakeholder society—A relational perspective. *Journal of Business Ethics, 66,* 99–115.

Mitchell, C., & Sackney, L. (2007), Extending the learning community: A broader perspective embedded in policy. In L. Stoll & K. S. Louis (Eds.), *Professional learning communities divergence, depth and dilemmas* (pp. 30–44). McGraw-Hill Education, Open University Press.

Nicholas, L., & West-Burnham, J. (2016). *Understanding leadership: Challenges and reflections.* Crown House Publishing.

Ospina, S. M., & Uhl-Bien, M. (2012), Exploring the competing bases for legitimacy in contemporary leadership studies. In M. Uhl-Bien & S. M. Ospina (Eds.), *Advancing relational leadership research: A dialogue among perspectives* (pp. 1–42). Information Age Publishing.

Owen, J. E. (2015). Integrative and interdisciplinary approaches to leadership development. *New Directions for Student Leadership, 2015*(145), 49–58.

Postholm, M. B. (2018). Reflective thinking in educational settings: An approach to theory and research on reflection. *Educational Research, 60*(4), 427–444.

Rogers, J., Gilbert, A., & Whittleworth, K. (2012). *Manager as coach: The new way to get results.* McGraw-Hill Education.

Rothschild, J., & Milofsky, C. (2006). The centrality of values, passions, and ethics in the non-profit sector. *Non-profit Management and Leadership, 17*(2), 137–143.

Rossman, G. B., & Rallis, S. F. (2017). *An introduction to qualitative research: Learning in the field.* SAGE Publications.

Salvador, R., & Folger, R. G. (2009). Business ethics and the brain. *Business Ethics Quarterly, 19*(1), 1–31.

Schön, D. A. (1987). *The reflective practitioner: How professionals think in action.* Ingram Publishers.

Solomon, R. C. (1998). Ethical leadership, emotions and trust: Beyond charisma. In J. B. Ciulla (Ed.), *Ethics, the heart of leadership* (pp. 87–107). Praeger Publishers.

Solvason, C., & Kington, A. (2020). How subject leader collaborations across schools can act as a source of personal and curriculum development. *Curriculum and Teaching Dialogue, 22*(1/2). https://www.infoagepub.com/products/Curriculum-and-Teaching-Dialogue-Vol-22

Solvason, C., & Kington, A. (2019). Collaborations: Providing emotional support to senior leaders. *Journal of Professional Capital and Community, 5*(1), 1–14. https://doi.org/10.1108/JPCC-05-2019-0010

Stephenson, M. E. (2017). *Ethical decision-making: Learning from prominent leaders in not-for-profit organisations* [Unpublished doctoral dissertation]. University of Worcester. https://eprints.worc.ac.uk/8294/1/Ethical%20decision-making-%20Learning%20from%20prominent%20leaders%20in%20not-for-profit%20organisations.pdf

Stoll, L., & Bolam, R. (2005). Developing leadership for learning communities. In M. J. Coles & G. Southworth (Eds.), *Developing leadership: Creating the schools of tomorrow* (pp. 50–64). Open University Press.

Stoll, L., & Louis, K. S. (2007). *Professional learning communities divergence, depth and dilemmas.* McGraw-Hill Education, Open University Press.

Tschannen-Moran, M. (2007). Becoming a trustworthy leader. In *The Jossey-Bass reader on educational leadership* (2nd ed.; pp. 99–114). Jossey-Bass.

Tschannen-Moran, M. (2014). The interconnectivity of trust in schools. In D. Van Maele, P. B. Forsyth, & M. Van Houtte (Eds.), *Trust and school life: The role of trust for learning, teaching, leading, and bridging* (pp. 57–82). Springer.

Uhl-Bien, M. (2006). Relational leadership theory: Exploring the social processes of leadership and organizing. *The Leadership Quarterly, 17*(6), 654–676.

Van Maele, D., Forsyth, M., & Van Houtte, M. (2014). *Trust and school life: The role of trust for learning, teaching, leading, and bridging*. Springer.
Wahlstrom, K. L., & Louis, K. S. (2008). How teachers experience principal leadership: The roles of professional community, trust, efficacy, and shared responsibility. *Educational Administration Quarterly, 44*(4), 458–495.
Whitmore, J. (2017). *Coaching for performance: The principles and practice of coaching and leadership* (5th ed.). Nicholas Brealey Publishing.
Yukl, G. A. (2013). *Leadership in organizations*. Prentice Hall.
Zembylas, M. (2014). The place of emotion in teacher reflection: Elias, Foucault and 'critical emotional reflexivity'. *Power and Education, 6*(2), 210–222.

CHAPTER 16

# SCHOOL BOARD LEADERSHIP TO IMPROVE STUDENT OUTCOMES

**A. J. Crabill**


## ABSTRACT

School boards can create the conditions for improvements in student outcomes, but this possibility is often not realized due to ineffective leadership practices. Key leadership practices that support the effectiveness of school boards include an aligned focus on student outcomes, setting student outcomes focused goals, routinely monitoring progress toward those student outcomes focused goals, aligning adult behaviors with the student outcomes focused goals, and receiving student outcomes focused coaching. Student outcomes don't change until adult behaviors change—and that change begins with the school board.


When school boards lead effectively, their work can create the context for improvements in what students know or are able to do—not by teaching, but by their leadership (Delagardelle, 2006; Ford, 2013; Lorentzen, 2013; Plough, 2014; Waters & Marzano, 2006). Unfortunately, many school

*On Leadership*, pages 279–309

boards fail to have this impact because their actions are not focused on students' outcomes (CGCS, 2021; Holman, 2016). They fail to set appropriate goals and do not monitor progress toward their goals, even when they authentically believe that they are doing both. Bridging the gap between biased self-perceptions and effective school board governance practice requires training and coaching. But analysis shows that more than 95% of school board annual conference training sessions and mandatory school board member training in all but a few states fail to address these key areas of deficiency. When school boards receive training to distinguish effective leadership behaviors and coaching to support implementation, their work can create the necessary conditions for school systems to improve student outcomes (CGCS, 2021; Howard, 2019; TEA, 2019). This chapter explores five aspects of these challenges and highlights promising practices that can serve as paths forward for school board leaders seeking to intensely focus on improving student outcomes.

## Align Focus on Student Outcomes

Political and practical realities can entice education leaders into focusing on adult inputs rather than student outcomes, which leads to declaring victory when adult needs have been satisfied even if student needs have been neglected. A practical understanding of the distinction between adult inputs and student outcomes, when applied to observations of two school board meetings, reveals both the problem and a potential solution.

## Set Student Outcomes Focused Goals

Much has been written about education leadership, but it is largely written from the perspective of management rather than governance. When leadership lessons written for management are applied in the governance context without translation, the resulting behavior disrupts organizational alignment rather than improves it. Evaluating the "before" goals and "after" goals for a large school district reveals which lessons translate from managerial goal setting to governance goal setting and which lessons do not.

## Monitor Progress Toward Goals

The practice of setting goals or creating grand plans only to leave both on the metaphorical shelf completely undermines the value of having engaged in either process. A national review of recent school board conference sessions reveals a dearth of training focused on progress monitoring and wide variation based on who is leading the session—despite evidence suggesting that consistency in monitoring progress towards goals can create the context for improved student outcomes.

### Leadership That Aligns Adult Behaviors

When school board leaders receive training that helps illuminate which governance behaviors are most and least aligned with improvements in student outcomes, they have a framework that allows them to meaningfully influence the school system's ability to improve student outcomes. Unfortunately, a review of school boards' required training across all 50 states reveals only four states where training on student outcomes focus, goal setting, and/or goal progress monitoring is even suggested, and only one where it is required. But that one example has a lot to teach the rest of the nation.

### Coaching That Creates a Space for Changing Adult Behaviors

Training is important but results come from ideation *plus* implementation. A recent statewide analysis suggests that school board leaders sitting through a workshop alone does not appear to make a difference for students. The gap, however, between common school board practice and the habits of school board leadership that create the context for improved student outcomes is significant. Further, a recent analysis suggests that school boards that attempt to bridge the gap with coaching are likely to experience much higher positive results than those who do not receive coaching.

## ALIGNING FOCUS ON STUDENT OUTCOMES

We lie all the time—to children, to others, and to ourselves. And while some of those lies may have only mild consequences, some of them deprive children and ourselves of a healthy grasp on reality. Such is the case with the story of the emperor's new clothes. In this deceptive account, children are led to believe that if they are the one who points out that the leaders are completely lacking in the very things they most pride themselves in having, that things will go well for them. This is often not at all the case.

In the same way that the emperor truly thought himself to be wearing fine garments, school board members truly believe themselves to be focused on student outcomes. When I ask a room of 1,000 school board members whether or not their school board is focused on student outcomes, invariably there will be at least 950 heads nodding in affirmation. These leaders are not attempting to deceive, but as this chapter will explore, their actions do not always align with the intention of improving student outcomes. Thus, it is unsurprising that suggesting to the school board that they are in fact very often not focusing on the outcomes of their students, rather than applause, garners a response that can be quite angry.

The challenge is that school board leaders are saying the words, "student outcomes" but meaning very different things without realizing it. In these moments, the potency that school boards could truly bring to bear goes unexpressed. What school boards need is a more accurate conception of behavior that is truly focused on student outcomes.

## Inputs, Outputs, and Outcomes

I love to cook. The most predictable and controllable part of the process is the selection of ingredients. Once you start combining ingredients, it takes skill to create something that actually tastes great. But even the most delicious dishes will not satisfy someone if they have a specific food allergy and can not eat what you have made. This is an example of inputs, outputs, and outcomes.

The inputs are the ingredients. *Inputs* are generally known at the start of a process or cycle and they are the resources and effort applied. Inputs are the most predictable because they are the most easily controlled. Either you buy basil or you do not. Either you have some habaneros or you do not. Inputs certainly come in a variety of qualities as well; not every tomato tastes like a locally grown, vine fresh, perfectly ripe tomato. In a professional kitchen, knowing exactly which ingredients/inputs to select requires a chef of exceptional training. Sure, the investors in the restaurant may provide the funding to purchase the produce, but you certainly don't want them at the farmer's market telling the chef which peppers to buy. Selection of inputs is clearly a job for professionals, not amateurs.

The completed dish is the output. *Outputs* are generally known in the middle of a process or cycle and they are a measure of the implementation. Having the perfect inputs is no guarantee that you will get the outputs you intended. Just as inputs require expertise, it takes special care and attention to translate a recipe into a culinary masterpiece. Output measures provide feedback, letting you know if you are on track or not so you can take corrective action early. So, if it becomes apparent that the chef cannot create basic dishes, the restaurant investors have clear information that their restaurant is not going to succeed. Seeing that the desired outputs are not being delivered, they know changes need to be made immediately.

But restaurants do not make food for the sake of having made food. The output—their dishes—are important but having made the dish is not why restaurants exist. They make it for the purpose of satisfying their guests. This is the outcome chefs intend. The *outcome* describes whether or not the intended result was accomplished and is generally not known until the end of the process or cycle. Just because the chef created a great dish does not mean it satisfied the guests and that they will become loyal fans who will return again and again. You need the ingredients/inputs and dishes/outputs, but the measure of a restaurant's success is in whether or not the guests were satisfied. If the inputs and outputs were perfect but no guests were satisfied, the restaurant failed; it did not meet its objectives/desired outcomes.

## School-Based Inputs, Outputs, and Outcomes

These same ideas hold true for schools. Take a moment and consider: What are the inputs in a school system? Common examples include books, buses, teachers, technology, and so forth. Like ingredients in a recipe, these are the things that are generally known at the beginning of a school year. These are the resources or activities the school system has planned for prior to the students arriving. And like ingredients in a restaurant, great results rely on the professional chef (superintendent) selecting the appropriate ingredients—selecting between properly ripened and unripened tomatoes, choosing between appropriate and inappropriate learning materials—not the restaurant's investor representatives (school board members). Sure, the school board has approval authority for expenditures (inputs) but that is not the same as the board making the selections; selection requires someone with professional expertise.

What are examples of outputs in a school system? Think grade cards, benchmark tests, semester grades, quarterly financials, and the like. These are outputs in that, like dishes in a restaurant, they reflect the implementation and use of the inputs. Work has been done, and the outputs are the demonstration of that work. Outputs are the evidence we can look at in the middle of the school year to get a sense of whether or not things are headed in the intended direction; like grade cards at midterm, they help us know if we are likely to get the desired end of year outcomes. Outputs provide critically important feedback, allowing school systems to course correct without waiting until the end of the year when it is clearly too late. If there is evidence that students have not learned what school leaders expected by midyear, school boards should expect the superintendent to adjust at midyear.

And finally, think of outcomes in a school system. A common example is the graduation rate. But it could also be end of year assessments, balanced budget, retention of effective teachers, construction completion, and many more. Outcomes are the measurable results that schools are aiming for by the end of the year and are a culmination of all the inputs and outputs. Just because people like which inputs were chosen (the "right" pencil, textbook, teacher) does not mean the outcomes will be what was intended. It is essential to recognize that effectiveness and "rightness" cannot be determined by inputs but, rather, only by outcomes. This distinction clarifies why school boards must be invested in outcomes, not just in inputs: school leaders can know everything there is to know about inputs but it will never reveal if the leaders made the "right" choices because only the outcomes can do that. School boards can spend every meeting entirely focused on inputs and that will never reveal whether the intended results were achieved; only the outcomes can do that. Boards don't drive improvements in student outcomes by hyper focusing on or evaluating their superintendent based on inputs. They must focus on and evaluate the superintendent based on outcomes. The school board that focuses on inputs to the exclusion of focusing on the outcomes is a school board that is setting children up to fail.

## Student Outcomes Versus Adult Outcomes

Being able to differentiate between inputs, outputs, and outcomes is only the first step. The next step is distinguishing between the two kinds of outcomes that school systems create: student outcomes and adult outcomes. Student outcomes are the results that school systems create which measure what students know or are able to do. Adult outcomes are results that the school system creates that are not a measure of what students know or are able to do. Still valuable and necessary, but not the same as a student outcome. Is retention of effective teachers an important outcome? Yes! Very important, actually. But it is not a student outcome. Knowing the percentage of effective teachers retained does not reveal whether or not students are more literate or numerate this year. While retention of effective teachers may lead to higher literacy and numeracy, teacher retention is an adult outcome, not a student outcome. In this example, the student outcome that retention of effective teachers might contribute to could be improved literacy and numeracy. But the only way to know that for certain is to measure what students know or are able to do. School boards should never use results about adults in their goal-setting as a proxy for results about students.

Improving adult outcomes is only valuable insomuch as they contribute to improvements in student outcomes. If the school board is discussing the fidelity of implementation of the literacy curriculum, it is not discussing a student outcome. Literacy curriculum fidelity is also an important outcome and may increase literacy, but it does not tell a school board leader whether or not *the students* are more literate; only measures of how well students can actually read can do that. When the outcome is implementation fidelity, staff can implement an ineffective program for this particular group of students, and implement it extremely well. That does not mean that what students know or are able to do has improved.

School systems don't exist for adult outcomes; they exist to improve student outcomes. Effective school boards focus on student outcomes (CGCS, 2021). It is important for the adult outcomes to improve as well. But improving adult outcomes is not why a school system exists.

## Case Study: DeSoto Independent School District

By May 2020, DeSoto Independent School District (DISD) was in trouble and not merely because of the pandemic. The school board correctly surmised that their district was struggling academically and in need of significant improvement. Observing their May 11th meeting through an inputs/outputs/outcomes lens, it is clear that the school board's chosen strategy for addressing the situation is to manage the inputs. Pushback on the school board's lack of focus on student outcomes was not well received.

Just as the emperor proceeded to parade, confident in his believed non-nudity, school board members became increasingly engaged in ever more granular detail—all of it divorced from an examination of actual data describing what students know or are able to do. Table 16.1 shows the result of utilizing the inputs/outputs/outcomes logic model to evaluate the discussion taking place during each section of the meeting. Completing the analysis provides objective data on how school boards are spending their time and where their attention is focused.

There is much to notice here. First, this one meeting lasted 8 hours with 5 of those hours being in front of the public. Meaningful work can be difficult to sustain after only a few hours; it is hard to imagine that a leader's best thinking will be done at 2:00 a.m. at the tail end of an 8-hour gathering. Second, the exclusive focus was on adult inputs. Third, during the public meeting the item with the largest use of time was a discussion of laptops for students (Item 5e). It may be that school boards are often inclined to spend more time on items that are tangible *because* they are tangible. Student outcomes are not something that can be held in one's hand; district-wide literacy rates are not as tangible a product as textbooks (Items 4a & 5b) and technology.

Perhaps it is unsurprising that this group of leaders could not avoid the nearly inevitable frustration given voice throughout the meeting. From the prosaic (Item 5i, the shortest non-consent item, which was about an obscure financial matter) to the passionate (Item 5f, one of the more contentious items considered during the public meeting), the one consistency is

**TABLE 16.1 DeSoto ISD May 11, 2020 Meeting—Time Use Analysis (DeSoto ISD, 2020)**

| Agenda Item | Agenda Description | Minutes Spent | Time Use Analysis |
|---|---|---|---|
| *Meeting Convenes at 6:31 p.m.* | | | |
| Item 1 | Call workshop to order; pledges and establish quorum | 4:30 | NA |
| Item 2 | Citizen comments | 6:01 | Adult Inputs |
| Item 3 | Consent items | 1:08 | Adult Inputs |
| Item 4a | Action Items 9–12 ELAR textbook Adoption approval | 13:16 | Adult Inputs |
| Item 4b | Consider and act on an order authorizing the issuance of unlimited tax refunding bonds; appointing a pricing officer and delegating to the pricing officer the authority to approve the sale of the bonds; establishing certain parameters for the approval of such matters; approving an escrow agreement, and paying agent/registrar agreement; levying an annual ad valorem tax for the payment of the bonds; and enacting other provisions relating to the subject | 12:06 | Adult Inputs |
| Item 4c | HB 3 reading academies memorandum of understanding | 6:36 | Adult Inputs |
| Item 5a | Possible action items HB3 reading academies purchase | 28:28 | Adult Inputs |
| Item 5b | Collaborative classroom libraries purchase | 32:49 | Adult Inputs |
| Item 5c | 2020 educator appraisal waiver | 36:14 | Adult Inputs |
| Item 5d | Board resolution to address waiving local policies regarding ranking/GPA and employee evaluations | 12:04 | Adult Inputs |
| Item 5e | Technology 1:1 purchase | 38:26 | Adult Inputs |
| Item 5f | Redesign: Competency-based discovery and capacity building | 27:15 | Adult Inputs |
| Item 5g | (Part 1 of 2)—Princeton Review summer programming | 4:53 | Adult Inputs |
| Item 5h | Recommendation regarding DeSoto ISD auditor services | 6:07 | Adult Inputs |
| Item 5i | Consider approval of resolution amending authorized representatives for TexPool investment funds | 1:30 | Adult Inputs |
| Item 5j | Board crisis priorities | 21:04 | Adult Inputs |
| Item 5g | (Part 2 of 2)—Princeton Review summer programming | 1:47 | Adult Inputs |
| *Went into Executive Session at 10:55 p.m.* | | | |
| Items 8 | Executive Session | 3:13:00 | Unknown |
| *Returned From Executive Session at 2:08 a.m.* | | | |
| Items 9 & 11 | Open Session Action Item, Adjourn | 26:48 | Adult Inputs |

*Meeting Adjourned at 2:25 a.m.*
Percentage of the 5 hours of public meeting focused on student outcomes: 0%

the lack of a student outcomes focus. In this example, it is not merely a confusion between student outcomes vs adult outcomes that is consuming the school board, because they are not discussing adult outcomes either. No school system created results of any kind are the focus of this meeting. In fact, in this instance, paying attention to adult outcomes might actually be an improvement in practice by lending an opportunity to pivot in focus from a discussion of adult-created results to one of student-created results. Instead, the culprit in this meeting is the narrow focus on adult inputs ungrounded by a shared agreement on student outcomes.

Purpose lends meaning to practice. The first thing the DeSoto ISD school board needed to do was acknowledge that it was entirely nude—that none of its current practices were yet focused on student outcomes. In the absence of a clarifying leadership purpose, little is left to leaders but to squabble over differences in opinion over practice. This DeSoto ISD meeting was unlikely to ever elevate to the level of the leader's intentions not because they are not well intended but because there is not the grounding influence of a clearly defined and honored set of student outcomes against which the various strategies can be evaluated. Without this, instead of having some objective means of determining the merits of the superintendent's proposals, the school board members are left to opine on whatever narrow set of observations they have made from their relevant but disjointed perspectives. Add that unintentional but very real leadership failure to an exhaustingly long meeting and this is a recipe for inspiring the worst in a group of leaders rather than the best.

What is remarkable about the DeSoto ISD story is not where the school board started, however, but where it went next. A few months after this meeting, the school board began the work of reimagining its governance practices. While they had already heard about the difference between adult inputs and student outcomes, evidence reveals that they never internalized the message to the point of allowing it to drive changes in adult behavior.

In the Fall of 2020, 4 months later, the school board began an aggressive redesign of their operating procedures, school board calendar, and school board meetings all in pursuit of a singular aspiration: to become intensely focused on improving student outcomes. The lens for every policy revision and every practice change became: How does this allow us to be more focused on improving student outcomes. If it met that threshold, it stayed. If it did not—no matter how sacred and beloved—it was eligible to be scrapped. After several months of labor toward this intention, there was a noticeable shift towards a student outcomes focus (see Table 16.2).

To the untrained eye based on the agenda descriptions, these meetings may seem nearly identical. The differences, however, couldn't be more neon. For starters, the more recent public meeting in Table 16.2 only lasted 2 hours. Second and perhaps the single most important change to facilitate, the school board shifted to a commitment of investing at least

**TABLE 16.2 DeSoto ISD March 22, 2021 MeetingTime Use Analysis (DeSoto ISD, 2021b)**

| Agenda Item | Agenda Description | Minutes Spent | Time Use Analysis |
|---|---|---|---|
| *Meeting Convenes at 6:30 p.m.* | | | |
| Item 1 | Call meeting to order | 0:44 | NA |
| *Went Into Executive Session at 6:31 p.m.* | | | |
| Item 2 | Closed session items | 59:00 | Unknown |
| *Went Into Executive Session at 7:30 p.m.* | | | |
| Item 3 | Public session, welcome, invocation by pastor, pledges, student recognition | 14:51 | NA/Student Outputs |
| Item 4 | Public comments | 0:00 | Adult Inputs |
| Item 5 | Board monitoring: Goal #4 individual growth (4.1, 4.2, 4.3) | 1:05:59 | Student Outcomes |
| Item 6a & 6b | January tax collections, January financials | 10:09 | Adult Outputs |
| Item 6c | Administrative corrective action plans | 7:09 | Adult Outputs |
| Item 6d | Board corrective action plans | 6:02 | Adult Outputs |
| Item 7 | Consent items (all items shall be acted upon at the same time) | 0:38 | Adult Inputs |
| Item 8 | Action/discussion items (action requested) | 0:03 | Adult Inputs |
| Item 9 | public comments on non-agenda items | 0:03 | Adult Inputs |
| Item 10 | Adjourn | 1:13 | Adult Inputs |

*Meeting Adjourned at 9:20 p.m.*

Percentage of the 2 hours of Public Meeting Focused on Student Outcomes: 60%

50% of each school board meeting to monitor progress regarding its adopted student outcome goals (Item 5). While this meeting did not provide a highly effective example of goal monitoring (CGCS, 2021), it was a massive shift in that direction. Unlike the previous year's meeting which was painful to watch both for its length and its tone, this meeting was brief and measured. Another noteworthy aspect is the school board's choice to front-load the monitoring of their goals rather than placing it after other business. Doing so allows the school board to monitor student progress early in the meeting to enhance focus.

Hidden in plain sight is another artifact of the school board's student outcomes focus. During this particular month, all of the action items were handled via the consent agenda (Item 7). Consent agendas are a common practice used by governing bodies to address multiple routine business items all at once without the need for individual debate or multiple votes. It is a time saving device used when a board wants to preserve time during the meeting to invest in other matters it deems more needing of the body's attention. Notice that both meetings make use of a consent agenda, but that many items from the first meeting are also handled by an action agenda (Item 5). This two-step practice—some items on consent agenda and then some on the action agenda—is actually a highly appropriate and normative practice among school boards. That makes its absence at the March 2021 meeting (Item 8) all the more curious. An investigation of the school board's revised policies solves the mystery.

In order to facilitate an increased focus on student outcomes, the school board began requiring the superintendent to provide all of the board's materials 14 days prior to the meeting. During the intervening 14-day period, board members could submit questions and 5 days prior to the meeting the superintendent provided a written copy of responses to all of the submitted questions. At that point, board members are then invited to remove items from the consent agenda if they still have questions—otherwise the item remains on the consent agenda. Either way, a copy of all questions asked and responded to is made available to the public so that inquiry that took place prior to the public meeting is still transparent and available for public consumption. This process revision has allowed the DeSoto ISD board to have the best of both worlds: They still transparently enact a high degree of oversight and review of expenditures, but only the most vital matters to be discussed by the full board make it onto the action agenda to be verbally discussed. This leaves more time and attention for what these education leaders most want to focus their energies on: To what extent are our students learning and what adjustments are being made to accelerate it?

## Summary

The distinction between adult inputs and student outcomes can be transformative in the hands of a determined group of education leaders. The implications for all leaders are clear as well. Organizations exist to improve the outcomes of their constituencies. Hospitals exist to improve patient outcomes. Banks exist to improve depositor outcomes. Schools exist to improve student outcomes. Inside the clarity that this taxonomy enforces, organizational leaders are able to discern between the ingredients and the satiation of customers. Only when empowered by this level of clarity can observations about the emperor's nudity be met with invitation—and improvement—rather than derision.

## SETTING STUDENT OUTCOMES FOCUSED GOALS

The function of the school board is to represent the vision and the values of the community; the ends that the school system must accomplish. The function of the superintendent is to implement the vision and values of the community, as communicated to them by the school board; the means by which the ends are accomplished. Governance in this context requires practitioners whose expertise is in community representation—people who have a deep understanding of the community's will and the reasons for it. Management in this context requires practitioners whose expertise is in operating large education institutions—people who have a deep understanding of classroom instruction and the operational systems that support it. This understanding establishes the boundary between governance which is responsible for selecting the ends and management which is responsible for selecting the means. Only when these separate but interwoven functions collaborate effectively can each be its most effective.

When the boundary is imprecise or permeated, managers make policy decisions about community values that they cannot possibly have the context or community understanding for, and governors make day-to-day operational decisions that they cannot possibly have the context or organizational understanding for. In both cases, the organization experiences dysfunction—not in the colloquial sense, but in the sense that the functions that need to be accomplished to improve student outcomes are conducted inadequately.

Adding to the challenge is that most texts on effective leadership are penned from a managerial perspective. Boards may read about goal setting but not realize that the advising often focuses on the tactical means, rather than the strategic ends.

For school boards to be effective, they must have goals. But those goals can best create the context for improving student outcomes when they adhere to governance-appropriate criteria.

### Effective School Board Governance Goals

The most critical distinction between goals for governing and goals for managing is that governing goals should always describe what it will look like once the organization has taken the next step in the trajectory of why the organization exists. They won't describe how the organization will get there—that is the domain of managerial goals. Because school systems only exist to improve student outcomes, school board goals should only ever be about what the next tranche of student outcomes will be. Not adult inputs. Not even student outputs. Effective school board goals are only ever about student outcomes—what students know and are able to do. This is what it means for the school board to represent the vision of the community.

Once the school board provides the superintendent with the goals, the superintendent will need to create management-level objectives for how the goals about student outcomes will be accomplished by the organization. Managerial objectives—and this is often where confusion starts, because these are often also referred to as goals—are how the school board's goals cascade throughout the organization from the boardroom to the classroom. Where governance-level goals focus on what the community's vision for children is, managerial objectives focus on how the organization will implement the vision of the community.

An example of the intrusion of managerial practice into governance goal setting can be found in Philadelphia School District's 2018 goals. Of the four goals in Table 16.3, only the first one makes an effort at describing why the school system exists. School systems don't exist to be transparent, have quality schools, or be financially stable. These are all important because they are all means to the end: improving student outcomes. But none of them actually describes the end state, they describe critical strategies to be implemented with the intention of achieving the end state. Contrast this behavior with the district's revised 2020 goals shown in Table 16.4.

Each of the five goals clearly articulates where the district is starting relative to the community's vision for what students should know and be able to do. The revised goals lack any description of *how* this will be achieved, but that's the point. Effective strategic governance makes the vision of where the organization must get to completely clear, then leaves it to management to determine the most effective means of reaching the destination.

| **TABLE 16.3 Philadelphia School District Board Goals, Announced January 2018** |
|---|
| *Goal 1: Student Achievement.* Our students' potential is limitless. The achievement and safety of our students will drive all of our decisions and we will invest in programs and initiatives that are proven to support all students in reaching their potential |
| *Goal 2: Transparency and Accessibility.* Effective school governance requires the intentional inclusion of diverse populations and viewpoints in order to support and strengthen decision-making. All voices matter. |
| *Goal 3: One System of Quality Schools.* All of our students deserve access to quality schools. While the school board oversees district schools and charter schools differently, both types of schools exist to provide quality educational opportunities to all Philadelphia students. We will work to make sure that all children attending public schools—regardless of life circumstances, zip code, behavioral challenges, or disability—have access to great schools. |
| *Goal 4: Financial Stability.* In the end, none of our goals will be possible without balancing the ability to make additional investments while maintaining our financial stability. We will manage our financial resources prudently and seek to secure additional sustainable funding. |

**TABLE 16.4 Philadelphia School District Board Goals, Adopted December 2020**

| |
|---|
| **Reading: Every student reads on or above grade level.** |
| *Goal 1:* The percentage of students in Grades 3–8 who are proficient on the state ELA assessment will grow from 35.7% in August 2019 to 65.0% by August 2026. |
| *Goal 2:* The percentage of 3rd grade students who are proficient on the state ELA assessment will grow from 32.5% in August 2019 to 62.% by August 2026. |
| **Math: Every student performs on or above grade level in math.** |
| *Goal 3:* The percentage of students in Grades 3–8 who are proficient on the state math assessment will grow from 21.5% in August 2019 to 52.0% by August 2026. |
| **College & Career: Every student graduates ready for college and careers.** |
| *Goal 4:* The percentage of students who are proficient on all three state high school assessments (algebra, literature, and biology) by the end of their 11th grade year will grow from 22.2% in August 2019 to 52% by August 2026. |
| *Goal 5:* The percentage of career and technical education (CTE) students who pass an industry standards-based competency assessment by the end of their 12th grade year will grow from 49.9% in August 2019 to 80% in August 2026. |

It's also worth noting that the revised goals create more clarity by employing goals that are specific, measurable, attainable, results-focused, and time-bound (SMART). The more exacting the governing body chooses to be, the clearer the delegation of expectation from the school board to the management team. The vague operational objectives from the 2018 "goals" do not accomplish this; the SMART goals from 2020 do.

Effective governance practice doesn't end with goals, however. That's only the beginning. Once a governing team has established goals, the school board's next step is to ensure clarity regarding how progress toward the goals will be measured (CGCS, 2021). Without a progress measuring system in place, goals will soon be placed on a shelf to be forgotten while the inevitable vicissitudes of daily serving tens of thousands of children conspire to distract leadership attention.

Unfortunately, school boards that adopt management-oriented goals are doomed to adopt management-oriented progress monitoring. This is evident in the Philadelphia school board's work (see Table 16.5).

While each of these activities are likely wise actions to pursue, with the exception of 1a, none of them will ever describe for the school board whether or not the organization's reason for existing—to improve student outcomes—is being achieved. The school board that is not routinely evaluating whether or not the vision of the organization is being accomplished is a governing team that is, as previously defined, not representing the vision of the community. The mistake, however, was not in identifying progress measures that aligned to the goals. That represents exceptional attention to

**TABLE 16.5 Philadelphia School District 2018 Board Goals, Monitoring Progress**

**Goal 1: Student Achievement**

a. Adopt a set of key indicators of student performance and create a schedule for monitoring these indicators.
b. Promote student achievement by investing in strategies that create safe, welcoming, and trauma-informed learning environments in every school.
c. Adopt an effective facilities maintenance program that ensures timely capital investments in order to promote the health and safety of students and staff and to support academic programming.
d. Attract and retain highly qualified, talented, and passionate staff by implementing policies that build both strong leadership pipelines and capacity within the district.

**Goal 2: Transparency and Accessibility**

a. Establish a committee structure to promote transparency in board decision-making and create opportunities for public engagement on district matters.
b. Develop a communication strategy that is transparent about board actions and welcomes all stakeholders to participate in the board's decision-making process.
c. Establish a greater board presence outside of district headquarters and in school communities.
d. Explain the processes by which decisions are made, when they are made, who made them, how public input was used, who is responsible for executing the decisions and how success is measured and evaluated.

**Goal 3: One System of Quality Schools**

a. Set and communicate clear standards for a quality education and hold both district schools and charter schools responsible for meeting these standards.
b. Invest in strategies and policies that grow the ability of all Philadelphia students to access quality schools. Hold schools accountable for practices that impede access.
c. Advocate for funding and a funding formula that invests in Philadelphia public schools and alleviates inequities between district and charter schools.

**Goal 4: Financial Stability**

a. Adopt a long-term strategy that will allow us to continue to stabilize our finances and make investments in support of teaching and learning.
b. Educate the public on our financial realities and build a broad base of support for public education that will create a sense of pride in the district and lead to investments in our schools.
c. Adopt an effective facilities maintenance program that ensures timely capital investments in order to promote the health and safety of students and staff and to support academic programming.
d. Ensure that all decision-making and investments reflect our beliefs and are in the best interest of Philadelphia's students. Collaborate with stakeholders across the city and commonwealth around school funding needs.

duty on the part of the school board. Instead, the mistake was the management-focused goals to which the progress measures were aligned.

Part of the challenge for school boards is that they are frequently assigned non-governance responsibilities by state legislatures and over time have come to identify them—and adjacent behaviors—as governance behaviors. But because they were always managerial behaviors, the adjacent activities that they step into also tend to be managerial activities. The classic example of this is the school board's approval of the annual budget. Annual budgets are not governance tools, they're managerial tools. The nature of governance is to be more focused on the ends than the means. Having a great budget is a means, it is not an end. But because legislatures nationwide have obligated school boards to adopt annual budgets through state laws, this is commonly considered to be a governance practice. Absent statutory obligation, school boards would care less about what the superintendent's budget is and more about improving student outcomes. But the current reality is that school boards are generally required to adopt the budget, and without training they will come to associate that—and adjacent activities like approving expenditures, selecting vendors, negotiating with vendors—as being governance work. But all of these are adult inputs, not student outcomes. As school boards grow increasingly focused on adjusting adult inputs, it's easy for them to lose track of focusing on student outcomes. Such was the behavior exhibited by the Philadelphia school board in 2018.

The revision of the goals in 2020 gave rise to a corresponding revision of progress measures (see Table 16.6). Notice how, inspired by the goals' focus on student outcomes, the progress measures all focus on student outputs. In this manner, the school board secures for itself the possibility of conducting monthly monitoring into the extent to which student learning is propelling them toward the community's vision.

Not all lessons from a managerial approach to goal setting are inadvisable. It's worth noting several of the management-oriented lessons that Philadelphia was wise to adhere to in both sets of goals. In both cases they selected no fewer than one and no more than five goals. This may sound trivial but it is not unusual to come across school boards that have no goals or to come across school boards with more than thirty goals. Both are suboptimal practices that most goal-setting resources—whether governance-oriented or management-oriented—will advocate avoiding.

In addition, both sets of goals have between two and four progress measures. While it is recommended to have either two or three, four is not an unreasonable number (CGCS, 2021). And like with goal-setting, having four is a better plan than not having them at all.

## Summary

The managerial books on leadership are absolutely right: Having goals matters and having progress measures matters. The school board with only one or with neither has abdicated its accountability to the community's vision. But for goals to work at the governance level:

**TABLE 16.6 Philadelphia School District 2020 Goals and Guardrails, Monitoring Progress**

**Goal 1: Reading**

- *Leading Indicator 1.1:* The percentage of students in Grades 3–8 who score at or above grade-level on the district's within-year reading assessment in Fall, Winter, and Spring each year.
- *Leading Indicator 1.2:* Closing the gap—The percentage of students, by subgroup, in Grades 3–8 who score at or above grade-level on the district's within-year reading assessment in Fall, Winter, and Spring each year.

**Goal 2: Reading**

- *Leading Indicator 2.1:* The percentage of students in Grades K–3 who score at or above grade-level on the district's within-year reading assessment in Fall, Winter, and Spring each year.
- *Leading Indicator 2.2:* Closing the gap—The percentage of students, by subgroup, in Grades K–3 who score at or above grade-level on the district's within-year reading assessment in Fall, Winter, and Spring each year.

**Goal 3: Math**

- *Leading Indicator 3.1:* The percentage of students in Grades 3–8 who score at or above grade-level on the district's within-year math assessment in Fall, Winter, and Spring each year.
- *Leading Indicator 3.2:* Closing the gap—The percentage of students, by subgroup, in Grades 3–8 who score at or above grade-level on the district's within-year math assessment in Fall, Winter, and Spring each year.

**Goal 4: College and Career**

- *Leading Indicator 4.1:* The percentage of students in Grades 9–11 who score at or above grade level on the district's within-year math and reading assessments in Fall, Winter, and Spring each year.
- *Leading Indicator 4.2:* The percentage of students who are proficient on all three state high school assessments (algebra, literature, and biology) by the end of their 10th grade year.
- *Leading Indicator 4.3:* Closing the gap—The percentage of students, by subgroup, who are proficient on all three state high school assessments (algebra, literature, and biology) by the end of their 10th grade year.

**Goal 5: College and Career**

- *Leading Indicator 5.1:* The percentage of 11th grade CTE students who pass their CTE Level 2 coursework (with a grade of A or B).
- *Leading Indicator 5.2:* The percentage of 10th grade CTE students who pass their CTE Level 1 coursework (with a grade of A or B).

- They must be about student outcomes, not adult input or adult outputs or even student outputs.
- There should be between one and five of them.
- Each goal should be SMART.
- Each goal should be accompanied by two or three progress measures.
- Progress measures are only about student outputs, not adult outputs.
- Each progress measure should be SMART.

## MONITORING PROGRESS TOWARD GOALS

Student outcomes don't change until adult behaviors change. Or said differently, when placed in the context of school board leadership, patterns of behavior that are exhibited in the boardroom can reasonably be expected to be found paralleled in the classroom. This concept, which offers a summation of the current literature on school board leadership behaviors and their relationship to improving student outcomes, is as simple as it can be confounding because changing adult behaviors can be challenging.

When school board members are selected, they often come to the role having no practical knowledge about effective leadership in the context of school board governance. Having been an educator doesn't prepare someone to lead in a governance context; at best it just helps understand what the data means. Having served on non-profit boards doesn't prepare someone; few non-profit board members are selected by the general public and few such organizations deal with such vast budgets. Having served on a corporate board doesn't prepare someone; few corporate board meetings are held in public or have labor units intimately involved in board member selection. Instead most school board members arrive with an authentic desire to serve children and little applicable knowledge about how best to do so in this capacity.

One attempt to bridge that gap comes in the form of annual school board conferences which draw in many thousands of school board members each year. The challenge doesn't live in the intention; bringing school board members together to learn can be a powerful opportunity for changing adult behaviors. The challenge, rather, lies in the execution—what is being taught and by whom.

### What Should Be Taught

The school board behaviors that most create the context for improvements in student outcomes are setting goals, monitoring progress toward goals, and aligning resources with the goals (CGCS, 2021; Howard, 2019; Waters & Marzano, 2006). The practice of setting goals should be collaborative, should focus on desired student outcomes, the resulting goals should be SMART, and there should be between one and five of them. The practice of monitoring progress toward goals should result in two or three progress measures that are student outputs, that are SMART, and that are predictive of the goals they are intended to monitor. The practice of aligning resources with the goals should involve identifying the most effective educators and the largest available sources of funding, and disproportionately applying both in ways that increase the likelihood of achieving the progress measures and, through them, the goals. But aligning to progress measures cannot happen without first having progress measures. And conducting goal monitoring using the progress measures cannot happen without first having goals. Because of the pivotal role that goal setting and goal monitoring play in effective school board leadership, these are skills that should be at the forefront of school board member training.

## What Is Being Taught

Unfortunately, conference sessions that teach school board members about goal setting and about monitoring progress relative to those goals are rare. After coding more than 800 annual school board conference session offerings from 2015–2017, a stark picture emerges. (*Note*: The names of the conference host organizations included in this analysis are excluded for privacy.) Of the many hundreds of sessions offered, the percentage of sessions available that were focused on setting goals, monitoring goals, or even more tangentially on the vague topic of the school board's role in strategic planning is low (see Table 16.7).

Those results are not a typo. At annual conferences designed explicitly for school board members to attend and receive training relevant to their effectiveness in their leadership role, the percentage of sessions devoted to the school board leader behavior with the strongest correlation to improvements in student outcomes—setting and monitoring goals about what their students should know or be able to do—is less than 4%.

The logical question that follows is: "What are the sessions about, if not setting and monitoring goals about student outcomes?" The good news is that there really are a great number of topics that would be incredibly helpful to school board members. Beyond goal setting and monitoring, there are many other issues where the work is appropriately initiated by governing teams rather than the management team. Board-initiated topics covered during the coded sessions include:

- superintendent selection based on prior history of accomplishment regarding board goals,

**TABLE 16.7 Annual School Board Conference Sessions 2015–2017, Topic Focus**

| Sessions Focused on Goal Setting/ Goal Monitoring | Sessions Not Focused on Goal Setting/ Goal Monitoring |
|---|---|
| 3.78% | 96.22% |

- superintendent evaluation based on progress toward and/or accomplishment of board goals,
- budget alignment with board goals,
- bond election design based on board goals, and
- how to train future school board candidates regarding goal setting and monitoring.

The list goes on. And each of these topics was present to some degree. The bad news is that the majority of session topics were focused on a very different audience—the management team.

Just as there are some issues that are appropriately initiated by the governing team, there are other issues that are most appropriately initiated by the management team. Examples of management-initiated topics include:

- construction and maintenance of athletic facilities
- selection of technology
- selection of textbooks
- selection of energy systems
- selection of vendors
- selection of disciplinary strategies
- evaluation of teachers
- evaluation of programs

This list too goes on—and for quite a lot longer than the board-initiated list of issues. Some issues vary—they could be appropriately initiated by the board or by the superintendent. These issues include:

- updates on federal law
- updates on state law
- advocacy at the national capital
- advocacy at the state capital
- stakeholder engagement
- board/superintendent relationship
- general topics about leadership

The distinction between board-initiated vs management-initiated is important because even though one group may begin a task, much of the work that is initiated by one group is eventually worked on by another. For example the budget is initiated by the superintendent but later voted on by the school board. And the superintendent evaluation is initiated by the board but at some point includes the superintendent. Few items that are board initiated go untouched by the superintendent at some point in their process and the same is true for much of the superintendent's work. So

**TABLE 16.8 Annual School Board Conference Sessions 2015–2017, Audience Focus**

| A Topic That Is Board-Initiated | A Topic That Is Management-Initiated | A Topic That Varies in Initiation Between Board and Management | Other |
|---|---|---|---|
| 19.61% | 56.42% | 16.63% | 7.34% |

while there is often not a bright line between which group works on which item, there is often a bright line delineating which group has responsibility for initiating most items.

In the 3-year analysis, Table 16.8 shows the breakdown of session prevalence by audience type.

One concern inspired by this analysis is that the sessions in the conference program were not labeled as being board-focused or management-focused. Unless a board member knew exactly what they were looking for, it would not be immediately apparent to them whether they were attending a session about board-initiated topics or management-initiated topics. Based on these percentages, school board members have a significant chance of attending annual school board conferences and never once being exposed to board-initiated content—as are the chances of them never even hearing the words goal setting or goal monitoring.

## Who Is Doing the Teaching

The coded sessions revealed another pattern when coding both the session and the lead presenter. This shed light on a potential misalignment of interests between the lead presenters and the school board members attending the conference (see Table 16.9).

One explanation for the strong prevalence of vendor-led sessions could be profit motive. Annual conferences for many school board-serving organizations are fundraisers that help sustain the organization's annual budget. Another potential explanation could be avoiding the risk of alienating members; it is not necessarily beneficial to point out if the emperor is entirely nude.

Additional coding was completed to identify which presenters *were* presenting on goal setting and goal monitoring. Nearly half of all such sessions were provided by staff from regional organizations whose focus is school boards. Superintendents and their staff provided just under a quarter of the remaining sessions and school board members themselves just over a quarter (see Table 16.10).

**TABLE 16.9 Annual School Board Conference Sessions 2015–2017, Lead Presenter**

| Lead Presenter | Percentage of Presentations |
|---|---|
| School Board Member | 9.29% |
| Central Office-Based Staff | 20.87% |
| School-Based Staff | 3.21% |
| Students | 0.46% |
| State Association Staff | 12.16% |
| National Association Staff | 6.65% |
| Keynote Speakers | 3.33% |
| College/University Affiliated | 3.10% |
| State/Federal Agency Staff | 0.34% |
| Vendors | 40.60% |

**TABLE 16.10 Annual School Board Conference Sessions 2015–2017, Which Presenters Offered Goal-Focused Sessions**

| State Association Staff | Central Office-Based Staff | School Board Members | National Association Staff |
|---|---|---|---|
| 45.45% | 24.24% | 27.27% | 3.03% |

This also begged the question about the prevalence of this focus within these presenters' larger portfolio of sessions: Out of all of their sessions, what percentage of those were the goal setting and monitoring-focused sessions? (see Table 16.11).

These results suggest that it's not safe to assume that any presenter will offer a goals-focused session. But regional staffers and school board members themselves offer the highest probability of success. Indeed, every other group—teachers, students, university professors, government representatives, and especially vendors—was at 0%.

## Summary

Unfortunately, the most direct conclusion is that if school board members want to grow in the area that will allow them to have the strongest

**TABLE 16.11 Annual School Board Conference Sessions 2015–2017, Presenter Likelihood of Goal-Focused Session**

| State Association Staff | Central Office-Based Staff | School Board Members | National Association Staff |
|---|---|---|---|
| 14.15% | 4.40% | 11.11% | 1.72% |

impact on improving student outcomes, don't attend school board conferences that are dominated by vendors. Or cause the organizations to change and start providing school board members with a more significant dose of student outcomes focused training. If those changes are not made but leaders still choose to attend these conferences, actively seek out goal-focused sessions that are most likely led by staff from region-specific organizations or school board members themselves. Of particular note, if the intention is to learn about adult behavior changes in the boardroom that most correlate with improvements in student outcomes, avoid all sessions by vendors—which will be quite difficult.

## LEADERSHIP THAT ALIGNS ADULT BEHAVIORS

Training that is focused on student outcomes is vital, but annual school board conferences are unlikely to provide this type of training. Another place to look for possible training is the state's required courses for school board members. Unfortunately, a review of the professional development requirements that states place uniquely on public school board members reveals that this is also unlikely.

The first issue is that many states have no required or even recommended training for school board leaders. Table 16.12 shows the breakdown of what was found on the legislative websites for all 50 states.

But even among the states with school board-specific requirements, not all requirements are created equally. A topical analysis of the requirements shows that among states with training requirements for school board members, the majority of those requirements focus purely on legal and financial matters. To be clear, these are important areas of focus; in many parts of the country the local public school district is the largest employer and/or one of the largest governmental bodies. Ensuring that these outsized institutions are conducting business in a manner that honors the resources and values of the communities they serve is an important part of their job.

**TABLE 16.12 States That Do and Do Not Have Training Requirements as of May 2021**

| States With Training Requirements | States Without Training Requirements |
|---|---|
| Alabama, Arkansas, Delaware, Florida, Georgia, Illinois, Kentucky, Louisiana, Massachusetts, Minnesota, Mississippi, Missouri, Nevada, New Jersey, New Mexico, New York, North Carolina, Oklahoma, Pennsylvania, Rhode Island, Tennessee, Texas, Virginia, West Virginia | Alaska, Arizona, California, Colorado, Connecticut, Hawaii, Idaho, Indiana, Iowa, Kansas, Maine, Maryland, Michigan, Montana, Nebraska, New Hampshire, North Dakota, Ohio, Oregon, South Carolina, South Dakota, Utah, Vermont, Washington, Wisconsin, Wyoming |
| Total: 24 | Total: 26 |

**TABLE 16.13 States With Training Requirements Concerning Student Outcomes as of May 2021**

| States With Training Requirements That Include a Student Outcomes Focus | States With Training Requirements but That Do Not Include a Student Outcomes Focus |
|---|---|
| Arkansas, Rhode Island, Texas, West Virginia | Alabama, Delaware, Florida, Georgia, Illinois, Kentucky, Louisiana, Massachusetts, Minnesota, Mississippi, Missouri, Nevada, New Jersey, New Mexico, New York, North Carolina, Oklahoma, Pennsylvania, Tennessee, Virginia |
| Total: 4 | Total: 20 |

But even though legal and financial matters are important, they are not the reason school systems exist. School systems exist to improve student outcomes. If the school system spends 50% less money this year but educates zero children, the taxpayers still did not get a good deal.

The measure of whether a school system is being efficient with taxpayer resources lives in how much student outcomes have improved for each dollar spent. Merely spending less money is not automatically a measure of efficiency. It could, in fact, be a measure of inefficiency because there may be more bang for the buck to spend $110 and see a doubling in student performance than to spend $90 and see a halving of student performance. Table 16.13 shows which states have begun to move in this direction. Unfortunately, of the 50 states surveyed, only four contain an expectation that school board members be trained in student outcomes focused topics—setting goals about student outcomes, monitoring those goals monthly, or aligning district operations with those goals.

## One Exemplar

Standing apart from nearly all other states in this conversation is Texas. In 2017, the Texas legislature passed Senate Bill 1566, the first law of its kind in Texas declaring

1. that school boards are responsible for improving student outcomes,
2. that school board members should have 3 hours of training every other year regarding evaluation and improvement of student outcomes, and
3. that the state's department of education would be responsible for certifying individuals who were eligible to lead the 3 hour course.

The first statutory provision sounds like a no-brainer, but reading state statutes regarding school board duties tells a different story. Often, if such an assertion even exists, it is in amongst a long list of statutory obligations that range from the normal (the school board shall be responsible for hiring and evaluating the superintendent) to the absurd (the school board shall install the accounting software). The second provision creates one of the only statutory expectations in the nation that points toward the school board implementing a focus on student outcomes. And the third provision is exceptional in that while many states require school board trainers to be registered with the state, few conduct significant screening of that registry, and fewer still actively create certification programs for potential school board trainers.

In response to this law, the state department of education created a certification training and a certification test. During the first year of implementation, roughly 60% of those taking the test to become certified school board trainers under the new law failed the test their first time taking it. This degree of expectation regarding the content combined with quality control in the trainer led to Texas' roughly 7,000 school board members receiving a standardized introduction to student outcomes focused principles.

## State Roles

Mandatory or suggested school board professional development is typically adopted by either a state legislature, a state board of education, or both in collaboration. This analysis does not suggest that state leaders do not care about effective school board governance, but it does suggest that they do not actually know what it looks like (see section above, "Aligning Focus on Student Outcomes"). Creating the expectation that school board members should be focused on improving student outcomes matters because in the absence of clear direction, ambient leadership behavior is likely to have an outsized impact on individual leadership behavior. Said differently, a new school board member is unlikely to know what effectiveness in school board leadership looks like, and will often default to imitating the behaviors of other school board members.

Even if state leaders do not mandate professional development that teaches a student outcomes focus, they can create a student outcomes focused framework and invite school board leaders to opt in. Or they can create a legislative framework that aligns the interests of the adults in the boardroom with improvements for students in the classroom. Examples might include:

- automatic recall elections for school boards whenever student outcomes decline in growth beyond a certain threshold,

- regional grade cards for school boards that are largely composed of student outcomes data, and
- current student outcomes data being mandated to appear on school board ballots next to the incumbent's name.

Even if regional governments do not take reasonable steps to improve the effectiveness of school board members, school board members can take it upon themselves to lead the conversation. First by seeking out training that is student outcomes focused. And then by advocating for their regions to follow their lead.

### Summary

Regional governments are almost entirely non-entities in the conversation about how school boards create the context for improved student outcomes, but they can be. And even in the absence of guidance from regional leaders, local school board leaders can seek out external opportunities for student outcomes focused training, and they can advocate for their regional leaders to learn about options available to them that could truly make a difference.

## COACHING THAT CREATES A SPACE FOR CHANGING ADULT BEHAVIORS

Recapping, this chapter has (a) identified that school boards often are not focused on student outcomes—even when they think they are—and that (b) having a student outcomes focus is a prerequisite to crafting effective school board goals. But complicating these observations is the reality that (c) most school board conferences don't help with either of the topics, and (d) neither do most state mandated school board trainings.

The challenge requires even further unraveling, however. Even when quality training is available, it will only take a school board so far. In a report released by the Texas Education Agency based on state accountability data and implementation of the agency's student-outcomes focused Lone Star Governance (LSG) framework for school board training and coaching, the agency found that there was only minor variation in average school system performance between school boards that participated in the framework training (without coaching) and school boards that did not. Training that was student outcomes focused appears to positively correlate with average increases in academic performance, but the magnitude of improvement was slight.

The same report also found that on average, school boards that went through the training and received ongoing guidance from an agency-certified student outcomes focused coach experienced 2× improvement in the state accountability system over a 2 year period. As shown in Figure 16.1, while these are extremely preliminary findings (the entire initiative was only begun in 2016 so reliable data remains limited) and suggest a corollary—though by no means a causal—relationship, it is fair to speculate that effective coaching that leads to measurably increased student-outcomes focused adult behavior in the boardroom *may* be positively correlated with improvements in system-wide student performance in the classroom.

The key term, however, is "effective"; not just any coaching will do. The measure of effectiveness in coaching is whether the adult behaviors in the boardroom actually change over time in response to the coaching. But to measure adult behavior change, a governance-specific rubric is needed. The agency, recognizing this, designed a quarterly self-evaluation for the LSG coaches to conduct with school boards using a rubric made available in the LSG manual. The excerpt in Figure 16.2 shows one page of the LSG rubric, this one showing the various conditions that must be met and the corresponding score for increased student outcomes focus. On this page of the rubric, school boards can behave in ways that confer between 0 and 15 points out of a 100 point scale.

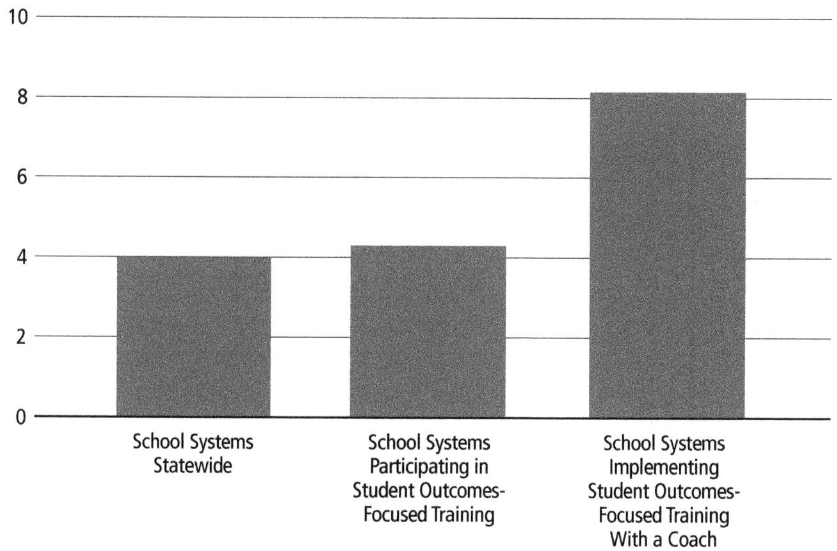


**Figure 16.1** TEA 2019 statewide average accountability system score increase, coaching use (TEA, 2019).

| TEXAS FRAMEWORK: VISION & GOALS | | | | |
|---|---|---|---|---|
| **Vision & Goals 1: The Board has adopted student outcome goals** | | | | |
| **Does Not Meet Focus** 0 | **Preparing to Focus** 1 | **Approaches Focus** 4 | **Meets Focus** 12 | **Masters Focus** 15 |
| *The Board does not meet focus if any of the following statements are true:* | *The Board is preparing to focus if all the following conditions are true:* | *The Board approaches focus if all prior conditions and the following conditions are true:* | *The Board meets focus if all prior conditions and the following conditions are true:* | *The Board masters focus if all prior conditions and the following conditions are true:* |
| The Board does not have a **vision**.<br><br>The Board does not have **goals**.<br><br>The Board does not consistently distinguish between **inputs**, **outputs**, and **outcomes**. | The Board has:<br>☐ adopted a vision statement;<br>☐ owned the vision development process while working collaboratively with the Superintendent;<br>☐ adopted 3 to 5 goals; and<br>☐ owned the goal development process while working collaboratively with the Superintendent. | All goals are specific, quantifiable, **student outcome goals** that include:<br>☐ a **population**;<br>☐ a 5-year **deadline** of a month and year;<br>☐ a **baseline**; and<br>☐ **annual student group targets**. | All Board Members and the Superintendent agree that the student outcome goals:<br>☐ will challenge the organization;<br>☐ require adult behavior change;<br>☐ are **influenceable** by the Superintendent; and<br>☐ are the Superintendent's first priority for resource allocation.<br><br>☐ The Board relied on a root cause analysis, comprehensive student needs assessment, and/or similar research-based tool to inform the identification of and prioritization of all student outcome goals. | All Board Members and the Superintendent:<br>☐ have committed the vision and student outcome goals to memory;<br>☐ know the current status of each student outcome goal; and<br>☐ agree there is broad community ownership of the Board's vision and student outcome goals through involvement and communication with students, staff, and community members. |

**Figure 16.2** TEA 2020 *Lone Star Governance Manual* (TEA, 2021).

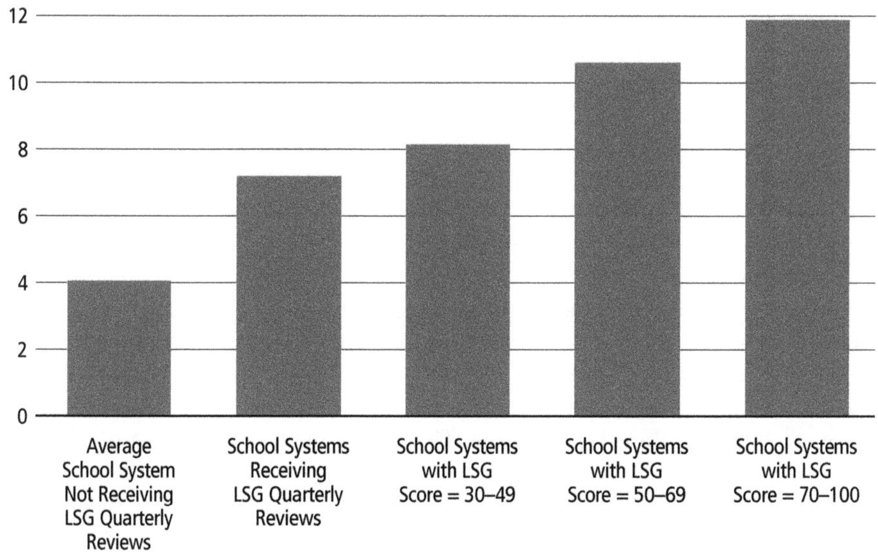


**Figure 16.3** TEA 2019 statewide average accountability system score increase, self-evaluation rating (TEA, 2019). *Source:* Texas Education Agency, 2019.

As LSG coaches led school boards through the 2-year long coaching cycle, they would support the school boards in conducting quarterly self-evaluations. Figure 16.3 documents the average school system improvement based on the school board's LSG self-evaluation scores.

While preliminary, early indications suggest that, even though the magnitude cannot yet be ascertained longitudinally, training in student outcomes focused methodologies followed by intensive coaching over time seems to aid a school systems' efforts to improve student outcomes.

## Summary

School boards can create the conditions for improving student outcomes and there are examples across the nation of where this is occurring. But it requires changes in knowledge, skill, and mindset on the part of individual board members. And those shifts appear to be most likely when there is student outcomes focused training followed by student outcomes focused coaching.

## CONCLUSION

It is hard to consider the five practices—(a) aligning focus on student outcomes, (b) setting goals focused on student outcomes, (c) monitoring progress toward those goals, (d) aligning adult behaviors with the goals, and (e) receiving coaching to support all of the above—and avoid the conclusion that there is not a sufficiently systematic approach nationwide to ensuring that school board leaders are set up to succeed. Instead, it appears the exact opposite: The support that school board leaders most need is not coming from the sources that they most rely on. And the behaviors that are common practice, absent a student outcomes focused framework and deep coaching, are generally misaligned with creating the context for improving student outcomes.

However, there is still cause for optimism that changing the behavior of adults that serve on school boards can lead to improved outcomes for students. School board leaders are in a meaningful position to create the context for improved student outcomes, but there are specific factors that can increase their likelihood of doing so. Drawing on the wisdom garnered from a variety of disciplines beyond public education—such as corporate management, non-profit leadership, performance coaching, and public administration—school board leaders who want to maximize their effectiveness can

- identify gaps between belief and action—as exemplified by the gap between the perception of a student outcomes focus and the reality of an adult inputs focus—and then act to diminish those gaps;
- set goals about student outcomes and then monitor progress with interim goals about student outputs;
- avoid trainings that are adult inputs focused, even if they claim to be student outcomes focused;
- encourage state and regional entities to adopt board professional development expectations, and related legislation, that reflect a student outcomes focus; and
- hire a coach to support the school board and board members on their path to being more fully student outcomes focused.

## REFERENCES

Council of the Great City Schools. (2021). *Student outcomes focused governance manual.* https://www.cgcs.org/cms/lib/DC00001581/Centricity/Domain/4/StudentOutcomesFocusedGovernanceManual.pdf

DeSoto Independent School District. (2020, May 11). *Special board of trustees meeting.* http://desotoisdtx.swagit.com/play/05112020-1138

DeSoto Independent School District. (2021b, March 22). *Special board of trustees meeting.* http://desotoisdtx.swagit.com/play/03232021-518

Delagardelle, M. (2006). *Roles and responsibilities of local school board members in relation to student achievement* [Unpublished doctoral dissertation]. Iowa State University. https://lib.dr.iastate.edu/cgi/viewcontent.cgi?article=2504&context=rtd

Ford, M. (2013). *The impact of school board governance on academic achievement in diverse states* [Unpublished doctoral Dissertation]. University of Wisconsin-Milwaukee. http://dc.uwm.edu/cgi/viewcontent.cgi?article=1334&context=etd

Holman, J. (2016). *School boards and student achievement: The relationship between previously identified school board characteristics and improved student learning* [Unpublished doctoral dissertation]. Seattle Pacific University. https://digitalcommons.spu.edu/cgi/viewcontent.cgi?&article=1013&context=soe_etd

Howard, D. (2019). School governance matters: Best practices for school boards to improve student outcomes. *Journal of the Effective Schools Project, 26*, 6–9. https://www.tarleton.edu/esp/_view-journal/ESP-JOURNAL-2019—Final.pdf

Lorentzen, I. (2013). *The relationship between school board governance behaviors and student achievement* [Unpublished doctoral dissertation]. University of Montana. http://scholarworks.umt.edu/cgi/viewcontent.cgi?article=2406&context=etd

Plough, B. (2014). School board governance and student achievement: School board members' perceptions of their behaviors and beliefs. *Educational Leadership and Administration, 25*, 41–53. https://files.eric.ed.gov/fulltext/EJ1028871.pdf

The School District of Philadelphia. (n.d.). *Evaluation, research, and accountability: Goals and guardrails.* https://www.philasd.org/era/goals-and-guardrails/#1614014403026-52974bfb-4e25

Texas Education Agency. (2018, April 27). *Trustee training requirement and senate bill 1566.* https://tea.texas.gov/about-tea/news-and-multimedia/correspondence/taa-letters/trustee-training-requirement-and-senate-bill-1566

Texas Education Agency. (2019, July 30). *Lone star governance efficacy report.* https://drive.google.com/file/d/1kV4mx5-dzSwiO0SAfnxc00Cuc8Vn9oO0/view.

Texas Education Agency. (2021). *Lone star governance participant manual.* https://tea.texas.gov/sites/default/files/LSGParticipantManual.pdf

Waters, J., & Marzano, R.J. (2006). School district leadership that works: The effect of superintendent leadership on student achievement (Mid-Continent Research for Education and Learning Working Paper). https://files.eric.ed.gov/fulltext/ED494270.pdf

CHAPTER 17

# CHARTER SCHOOLS AND CRISIS LEADERSHIP DURING COVID-19

**David T. Marshall**
**Natalie M. Neugebauer**

## ABSTRACT

The COVID-19 pandemic disrupted society in March 2020, including the operation of schools. When schools closed for in-person instruction, school leaders had a range of decisions to make as part of an effort to maintain the educational mission of their institutions. This chapter focuses on qualitative research that was conducted with charter school leaders during this pivotal time. We interviewed 33 charter school leaders in the summer and early fall of 2020 to understand the extent to which they effectively engaged in crisis leadership during the pandemic. Findings focus on initial responses to the pandemic, including assessing student needs, making decisions about remote instruction, and finding a balance between rigor and the humanity of the moment. Four overarching themes emerged in terms of how our participants engaged in crisis leadership and include: (a) the extent to which charter school leaders anticipated the crisis, (b) how well charter school leaders delegated tasks, (c) what charter school leaders communicated with stakeholders, and

*On Leadership*, pages 311–328

(d) what charter school leaders learned from mistakes during the crisis. We conclude by locating our findings within the broader context of interdisciplinary crisis leadership.

In March 2020, the COVID-19 viral pandemic disrupted virtually all aspects of life, and schooling was no exception. By March 23, all but two states had closed their schools (Marshall & Bradley-Dorsey, 2022). During this time, schools had to pivot and provide instruction to students without the benefit of being in-person. Many hoped this interruption would only span a couple of weeks; however, schools across the United States completed the school year with remote instruction. Schools and school districts varied in their approaches to deliver remote instruction in terms of how instruction was delivered, the extent to which assignments were graded, and the nature of the interactions that students and parents had with teachers and building leaders (Love & Marshall, 2022; Marshall et al., 2020). The Fall 2020–2021 school year began with many schools remaining online to start the school year, although decisions about learning modalities varied across schools, districts, and states (Marshall & Bradley-Dorsey, 2020).

## Crisis Leadership and Crisis Management

For many years, crisis management has been explored in the context of educational leadership (Gouwens & Lander, 2008; McLaughlin, 2015; Mutch, 2015; Smith & Riley, 2012; Sutherland, 2017; Tarrant, 2011). Since the emergence of the COVID-19 pandemic beginning in early 2020, educational leadership has been put to the test and many scholars have studied the attributes of effective leadership in schools during this unprecedented time (Brinkman et al., 2021; Harris, 2020; Hemmer & Elliff, 2020; Varela & Fedynich, 2020). Some of these attributes include clearly communicating with stakeholders, such as parents, students, and teachers, as well as delegating responsibilities to team members (Fernandez & Shaw, 2020; Harris & Jones, 2020; Vanourek, 2020). These attributes are reflected in educational leaders' responses to the pandemic. Schools across the country quickly transitioned to remote instruction after the initial closure of schools (Marshall & Bradley-Dorsey, 2020). This included planning for remote instruction while also addressing students' immediate needs outside of the classroom. Because many students did not have access to the internet and technological devices outside of school, school leaders prioritized acquiring, distributing, and introducing devices. Teachers and administrators alike worried about their students' well-being and academic success, especially students facing inequality. Some educational leaders felt prepared to engage with effective crisis management and leadership while others did not (Varela & Fedynich, 2020).

However, a clear distinction between crisis management and crisis leadership becomes salient particularly when looking at educational leaders' responses to the pandemic and how they planned for a future with many unknowns. McNulty and Marcus (2021) describe the relationship between crisis management and leadership, "as two circles in a Venn diagram. At the moment crisis strikes, the two circles largely overlap. As the event unfolds over the arc of time, the two activities move apart. The two circles never fully separate because the present and the future are interdependent" (p. 6). Crisis management assesses and solves immediate problems while crisis leadership seeks to solve immediate problems and anticipate future unforeseen problems. Crisis leadership distinguishes itself further from crisis management in that it aims to "increase organizational resilience before, during, and after a crisis" (McLeod & Dulksy, 2021, p. 2). Engaging with effective crisis leadership "involves planning, implementing, assessing and acting, and in each phase, there is time for reflection on how each phase is being processed, including how goals and targets are being met" (Brinkmann et al., 2021, p. 9). It is essential for educational leaders to reflect on current circumstances and errors that have been made, in order to learn from their mistakes and provide better solutions in the future. This can be achieved by establishing transparency and open communication with community stakeholders (Fernandez & Shaw, 2020). Overall, it is more difficult to engage with effective and proactive crisis leadership than crisis management.

## CONTEXT OF STUDY

Charter schools are independent public schools that have more flexibility to make decisions that are appropriate for their teachers, students, and communities than traditional public school building leaders (Bulkley & Wohlstetter, 2003). In exchange for additional flexibility, charter schools have greater accountability and can be shut down if they perform poorly. In a traditional public school system, decisions are often made by central office personnel and then handed down to school leaders. School leaders who want to do something that differs from what is directed often have to first appeal to an assistant superintendent, and if that person agrees with the decision, they might need to get approval from the school district superintendent, and the superintendent might still need to obtain approval from the school board at their next meeting (Osborne, 2017). The process varies but can often take an extended period of time. However, in a crisis such as the COVID-19 pandemic, decisions often need to be made quickly in order to be effective (Fernandez & Shaw, 2020; Humphrey, 2013). These layers of bureaucracy often do not exist for charter school leaders (Nathan, 1996; Oberfield & Henig, 2017; Pendergrass & Kern, 2017). In some cases, a charter school leader might need to consult with their board of directors prior to making a decision, but most often they are at the top of the organizational chart for their schools. It is worth noting that charter management organizations (CMOs) that oversee multiple charter schools also have some bureaucracy. However, many larger multi-region CMOs allow a large amount of flexibility region by region. For example, the Knowledge is Power Program (KIPP) CMO operates more than 250 schools in more than 30 regions in the United States (KIPP, n.d.). While a set of core values are evident in all of their schools, KIPP schools are operated regionally allowing those closest to the schools to make decisions that work best for their students (Okwara, 2015). In this study, charter school leaders' perspectives were solicited precisely because of their flexibility to make decisions that might deviate from those made by a larger bureaucracy. The authors' work was guided by the following question: To what extent did charter school leaders effectively engage in crisis leadership during the COVID-19 pandemic?

To answer this question, we interviewed 33 charter school leaders from 31 different charter school organizations across the United States. In two of our interviews, two charter school leaders participated. Fifteen of our participants were female (45.5%) and 18 of our participants were male (55.5%). In terms of race/ethnicity, 15 of our participants were African American/Black (45.5%), 16 were Caucasian/White (48.5%), and 2 were of Asian descent (6.0%). More than two-thirds of the charter school leaders we spoke to were school building leaders; the rest worked for a CMO. See Figure 17.1 for a map displaying where our participants' schools were located.

All of the interviews we conducted took place between July 13, 2020 and October 1, 2020 and lasted between 30 to 60 minutes in length. During the interviews, participants were asked about the decisions they made during the transition to remote instruction, what went well, and what challenges they faced during that time. We also asked them about how they approached decisions they had made for reopening schools for the 2020–2021 school year.

A constant-comparative approach (Corbin & Strauss, 1990) was used to analyze the interview transcripts and identify emerging patterns. We met and created an initial list of codes related to crisis management and crisis leadership; the list of codes was then expanded based on the transcripts (Maxwell, 2013). We initially coded one interview and then met as a team to review coding, discuss new codes that were created, discuss interpretations, and resolve coding discrepancies. We coded an additional three interviews and met again to do the same. Following that meeting, we coded

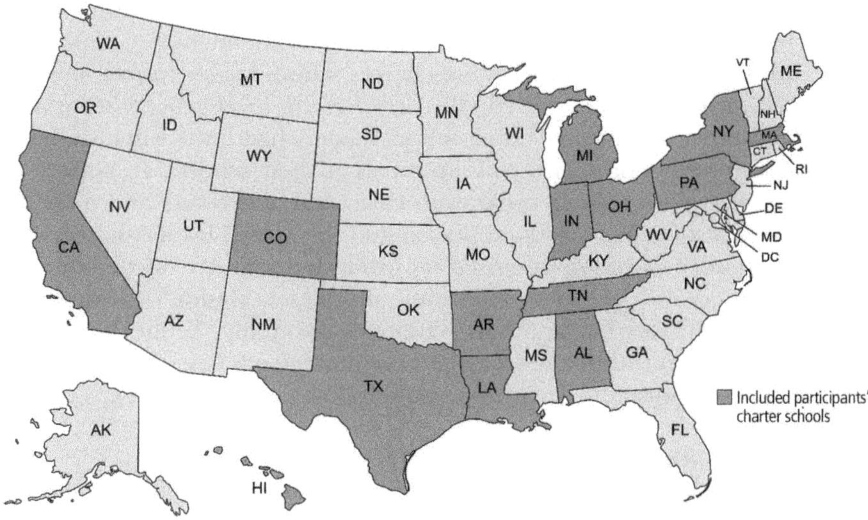


**Figure 17.1** Location of participants' charter schools.

the remaining transcripts and met a final time to identify emerging themes. Data analyses were conducted using Atlas.ti version 9.

## WHAT WE LEARNED

We organize what we learned from this work in two ways: (a) initial responses to the pandemic and (b) crisis leadership. The first section describes decisions that were made when schools were forced to close for in-person instruction in March 2020. The second section explores elements of crisis leadership described by our participants.

### Initial Responses to the Pandemic

The initial responses to the pandemic in the spring of 2020 reflected many facets of crisis management, including (a) addressing student needs, (b) making decisions about what remote instruction was going to look like at their school(s), and (c) finding a balance between rigor and recognizing the humanity of the moment.

#### *Addressing Student Needs*

School leaders almost universally shared that among their first tasks was making sure that they addressed the immediate needs of their students. These needs included providing food for those who relied on school for meals, as well as technology needs necessary for remote learning including digital devices and access to the internet. One charter school leader from Colorado shared that his school purchased gift cards for the local grocery store and distributed them to students. Other school leaders had times when students and families could come and pick up meals at their schools. In almost all cases, the school leaders we spoke with described addressing and meeting these needs before they discussed pedagogy. One school leader shared, "So those are some of the main things I'd say we started with. We needed the Wi-Fi and we needed to get them their basic supplies... Maslow's hierarchy of needs was much more important than Bloom's taxonomy." School leaders all acknowledged that without addressing these basic needs first, there was little chance that any substantive learning would follow.

***Learning Modalities***

When schools were forced to close for in-person instruction, they shifted to deliver instruction remotely. This took on a range of forms across school contexts. Some schools pivoted to provide instruction completely online (either synchronous, asynchronous, or a combination of the two), some schools began remote instruction by putting together hard-copy instructional packets and distributing them to students, and some schools offered families the choice of which they preferred. The single greatest determinant of what a school's initial remote learning looked like was the extent to which they were already using technology in their classrooms. Schools that were not using as much technology before COVID-19 were much more likely to deploy instructional packets. In hindsight, these packets likely did little to bring about any meaningful learning—a point our participants who used them readily conceded. One elementary principal shared, "We realized real quick that packets weren't working and that they're not a long-term solution." Another school leader shared, "We sent home work, I don't think it was the highest quality of work... I remember one of the eighth graders walking out and he was like, 'This isn't two weeks' worth of work. I was like, 'Come on, keep it moving.'"

Schools that were already housing their curriculum and assignments online and using learning management systems tended to have an easier transition to remote learning compared to schools that were not using as much technology before the pandemic. The head of an alternative high school shared:

> We've been fortunate for a couple of reasons. One is that we utilize Google Classroom and Chromebooks and technology for blended learning all through our core curriculum. Students were familiar with the general structures, but we did use them in the classroom as much more of a supplementary tool, not a primary tool. And so, when COVID hit and we had to switch to

> virtual instruction, then the supplementary nature of instruction moved to primary. That's one reason we were fortunate, we had some familiarity with tools for teachers and students as supplementary in-class instruction.

Another high school principal shared, "We already did e-learning days. And so, students understood the process and we worked out some of the kinks of attendance and tracking students and we didn't have to teach students how to log on in March." A CMO leader shared, "We had the advantage of having a lot of technological resources already in place. We were using Google Classroom pretty much across the board in our schools. So, it wasn't a total shock to teachers to have to deliver instruction remotely." The decision to invest in learning technologies provided these schools with a greater range of options during this pivotal time than would have existed absent those pre-pandemic investments.

***Finding Balance***

Some of the more difficult decisions that our school leaders faced involved knowing where to draw the line between maintaining high expectations for their students and recognizing the reality of a viral pandemic. One California leader shared, "I think that's been one of the toughest challenges and tensions we've had to keep is, we want to make sure that our students are still learning of course. But this is such a burden for our students and families." A K–8 school leader shared, "I think the spring was tough because we worked hard to balance the humanity of the moment with that urgency of our kids can't come out from this [even further] behind." Another leader was clear to describe what occurred as "an emergency response," noting that they "couldn't push too much." This is not the default setting for most of the school leaders we spoke with, given their insistence on setting high expectations for all students. Similarly, school leaders shared that they had to find where the appropriate balance was for their teachers. A Midwest secondary school leader shared:

> Teachers are trying to figure out how to do virtual learning and our teachers are killing it and they're rock stars and they're going above and beyond. I've actually said... We hate saying this because we really believe in high expectations, but you have to lower the bar for a bit. Not because you're killing it... Literally one teacher said that... she's not going to her friend's baby shower because she has too much work to do.

Especially at the start of the pandemic, teachers were being asked to teach online and very few were trained to do so (Marshall et al., 2020). This often resulted in teachers working far more hours than usual (Kaden, 2020), and our participants echoed this finding.

## Crisis Leadership

Four overarching themes emerged for crisis leadership: (a) anticipating the crisis, (b) all hands on deck, (c) communication with stakeholders, and (d) learning from mistakes.

### *Anticipating the Crisis*

An important component of effective crisis leadership is the ability to anticipate a crisis. Several of our participants candidly shared that they had not done enough to plan for the possibility of closing schools for in-person instruction. One charter school leader from New Orleans shared, "I think we had not done a lot of pre-planning and pre-work of, 'hey, schools might be dismissed.' It seemed to pick up momentum very fast, right?" Another shared, "Looking back on it, it probably shouldn't have caught us by surprise as much as it did." Another leader from the Midwest shared, "It was very abrupt and we knew that it was a possibility about a week before we shut down."

This was not the case for everyone. Several leaders in this study were much more proactive in their preparation for the crisis. One Midwest charter school leader explained that he had been following international news closely and went to his board in January 2020 explaining that there was a good chance that they would need to shut down their schools and that they needed to begin investing in the technology to deliver instruction online. Although highly skeptical of what seemed like a far-fetched idea at the time, they approved his project. By March 1, 2020, they had all of their classes up and running online. When schools closed for in-person instruction 2 weeks later, their transition was almost seamless. He shared, "So I think a lot of that was just good foresight and seeing what was coming in. You know, a good charter leader should always run a pretty high level of risk management, and I always plan for the worst and we did a good job of that through this." A New York City CMO leader described attending a small conference with other charter school leaders three weeks before schools shut down. He described a moment before the conference was set to begin where he and other charter school leaders were sitting around drinking coffee and making small talk, and a lot of their conversation was about the pandemic. Finally, one of the other school leaders in attendance suggested that it was not "if, but when" schools were going to shut down for in-person learning. He responded, "Well we got this whole agenda where we're talking about all this mundane stuff, and you're saying that? That's all we should be talking about. This is it." The group of leaders pivoted from their planned agenda and spent the entire time planning for different scenarios they anticipated potentially facing as a result of COVID-19.

***All Hands on Deck***

One component of crisis leadership that goes beyond crisis management is delegating tasks and responsibilities among team members. In order to quickly and effectively prepare and transition to remote instruction, charter leaders had to not only provide open communication, but also clear guidance and instruction to their teachers and administrators. With the addition of many new responsibilities and tasks at hand, the majority of our participants employed an "all hands on deck" approach. One middle school leader described the shifting roles in her school as follows:

> So yeah, we've had to restructure staff. I have two staff members right now that spend most of their day just helping the e-learning families while the other teachers are teaching in classrooms. It's definitely been "all hands on deck." Little things like, now when you take the kids to the bathroom, they can't congregate. They can't stand in lines. We have people on bathroom duties a lot of hours during the day, because you have to have a staff member standing there watching the kids and then the other staff member has to be back in the classroom waiting for the kids to come back. It's silly. It's little things, but those little things do require manpower, so that we can kind of run the building in a way that meets all the guidelines.

Similar to the "all hands on deck" sentiment, charter leaders and CMOs referenced utilizing a "divide and conquer" strategy to best serve their students during the initial transition to remote learning. Similar to what Fernandez and Shaw (2020) found, many spoke of forming working groups and designating teams to plan for and execute tasks ranging from instruction over technical support to tracking attendance. One CMO leader with campuses in different states and policy contexts shared, "One thing that [we] started to... build up [was] the number of working groups. So, within the regional structures, you'd have a working group that was focused on apps, and a working group that was focused on instruction, a working group that was focused on social emotional learning."

In addition to forming teams and assigning specific tasks, many charter leaders also incorporated co-teaching across grade levels to accommodate different modalities in the fall semester of 2020. One elementary leader described how his teachers manage virtual and in-person instruction, "So the one full-time teacher teaches [K–2] virtually... our fourth and fifth grade teachers who teach in person, they teach third and fourth grade virtually. Our sixth grade teachers teach fifth and sixth grade virtually and sixth grade in person." Overall, teachers and administrators alike had to show great flexibility in order to assume different roles and new responsibilities to best serve their students and school during this unprecedented time.

### *Communication With Stakeholders*

The school leaders we spoke with recognized the importance of strong communication with families. Many of our participants worked in charter schools that were located in areas with high concentrations of poverty. The schools were founded in these locations as part of an intentional effort to be accessible to this student population. School choice has always been available to families with means; these charter schools were founded to offer educational opportunities to families without the means to move or afford private school tuition (Marshall, 2017). Yet, many of their students come from homes that do not have the same resources as wealthier families.

Several of the school leaders we spoke with explained that before the pandemic they were "ambivalent" about their students' families. They further explained that it was not that they were uninterested in engaging with parents; rather, it was part of the ethos of their schools that a student's home situation was not going to dictate their educational outcomes. For these leaders, the pandemic changed that. One leader shared, "You need the family. You need that relationship. It really flips the script from having heavy duty academic rigor that we have within the building that has to be heavy duty relationship building when we're in the e-learning environment." A Northeastern urban CMO leader shared, "We began to coauthor school with families because we could not do it without them in ways that we could when you drop off your child in the building." Another principal in New Orleans shared, "I will say our family engagement and our family communication, they weren't as strong as they needed to be before March 13th (2020). We should be able to come out of this more connected with families than we've ever been." Where school leaders could ensure that learning took place within their buildings, they relied on parents to ensure that it continued with remote instruction.

School leaders shared with us that they were not able to involve teachers in the decision-making process as much as they would have liked when schools initially shut down, mostly because decisions had to be made with a sense of urgency. One middle school leader from Pennsylvania shared:

> Our teachers were a part of the fall implementation from day one, when we started planning, because, really to be honest with you, we kind of left them out. They were not involved as much as they would've been in the spring because we had to hurry up. We couldn't gather every group. We couldn't do every survey. We had to implement something fast in the spring. But now we had time to really get and pick their brains around what the schedule should look like.

Similarly, another CMO leader shared, "We've also included teachers in all of our planning, all of our committees that are doing planning. We've tried to get teacher input on that, and tried to keep that communication going."

Effectively communicating with teachers and seeking their input with decision-making was an important task for school leaders during the pandemic.

***Learning From Mistakes***

Another hallmark of effective leadership is the ability to learn from missteps and improve. The school leaders we spoke with shared a number of ways in which they learned from early mistakes, including (a) not adequately anticipating the pandemic early enough, (b) early choices in learning modality, and (c) the manner in which they managed their teachers. An elementary school principal shared, "We should have been more ready for that. And I think that's hard to know. Right? . . . But I still think that the writing was on the wall and we didn't pay close enough attention in terms of our baseline preparation for it." This was echoed by most of the school leaders who had not anticipated the crisis and only began preparing for it during the week that schools were closed.

One school leader who exclusively employed asynchronous online instruction shared that they recognized there were missed opportunities to engage students by not having any synchronous components in their spring schedule. She shared, "I would definitely add a couple of synchronous [sessions] weekly, so that there was face time with children. I know the benefit of it, but we didn't necessarily provide that." A New York City CMO leader shared that their schools went through several iterations before arriving at a learning modality that worked for them in the spring of 2020. He shared:

> I think the place where we've made significant pivots, in the beginning, we tried to model as much as possible with synchronous learning, just doing what we were doing on a daily basis and sending it home. That didn't work. Then what we tried to do was have as much asynchronous learning that we could possibly have, and teachers filming themselves and sending that home. That didn't work. So, what we've sort of honed in on is a model that is primarily synchronous, but specialized, but different.

They also experimented with what synchronous instruction looked like, eventually cutting their class sizes by one-third to one-half, offering students 1–2 synchronous lessons per week, with 1–2 small group sessions, an assessment, and feedback each week instead of having students meet synchronously 5 days per week. He shared, "That [it] is much better than trying to have four . . . or five mediocre classes over the week." School leaders made several adjustments to learning modalities early in the pandemic.

Finally, school leaders shared some areas where they believed they learned from mistakes in terms of managing teachers. A Midwest CMO leader shared that his failing was assigning everyone a specific role, which led some of his teachers to work an incredible amount and allowed some of his teachers to get by without doing as much. He shared:

> Half my staff, I think, worked 80 to 100 hours a week through spring break, through the summer. I mean, they just didn't stop. There was no break, and we had to really try to encourage the folks to take some time. You've been running hard since March 19th. But half my staff quietly disappeared and caught up on Netflix shows, and other things of the sort. So, that part of us just didn't have time to get everybody a specific role. Now, we know we have basically 15 distinct positions in our school. Everybody has a role, and everybody has accountability.

About one in five of the school leaders we spoke with shared that they recognized that there were opportunities to check in with their teachers more than they did—both in terms of the instruction they were providing remotely as well as in terms of their wellness and mental health. An elementary school leader in a southern state shared that they did not observe teachers as often during the early stages of the pandemic. She shared:

> We did not observe teachers as much during virtual learning. We looked at lesson plans, but we did not keep the professional development piece going. And so, I think that's something that would have done differently to continue to, in that spirit of continuous improvement, for our teachers.

In each of these instances, school leaders approached these as moments to learn and make adjustments ahead of the 2020–2021 school year—which for everyone was going to involve some amount of remote learning and engagement with students and teachers.

## Long-Term Impact of the Pandemic on Schools

David Tyack and Larry Cuban (1995) suggested in their book *Tinkering Toward Utopia* that creating change in public education is a slow process. They observe that "some innovations seem to die on contact with the institutional reality of school" (p. 60). Traditional public school systems have been historically resistant to change. By contrast, a common refrain among the leaders we spoke with was that "we can't go back" to pre-pandemic ways of doing school. As one middle school leader shared with us: "If you look at classrooms, they look very similar to what they did decades and decades and decades ago... So I think this is going to raise the bar for us. I know it has for me... to do better in regards to how we teach children." The COVID-19 crisis puts these two ideas on a collision course. Our participants viewed the pandemic as a moment of disruption and permanent change; however, history has demonstrated that our institutions can be quite resistant to that.

The vast majority of the school leaders we spoke with believe that online learning options are here to stay, and this might take several different forms.

One-third of our participants indicated that they intend to have an online-only option for students who want that after the pandemic, something almost none of these leaders would have entertained prior to the crisis. One Midwest school leader shared, "We want to add a virtual school... super controversial and super against everything I've ever said [about] virtual schools up to COVID." Like this leader, several of our participants were very skeptical of online learning, but now see this as an option that speaks to the needs of some students. One CMO leader in New York City shared that "a small group, I would say about 10% of our population actually does better in online learning interestingly." We heard this from several other participants as well. Participants also suggested that various hybrid learning options might be part of a post-pandemic K–12 landscape. One Midwest high school principal shared that they elected to employ a hybrid model for the 2020–2021 school year that included having asynchronous instruction every Wednesday. This allowed for the building to be cleaned and for faculty and staff to have time to hold office hours and plan. Other participants shared about the possibility of using video-conferencing software like Zoom to hold virtual meetings that have been historically held in person, including faculty meetings, IEP and 504 meetings for special education services, and parent–teacher conferences.

In-person instruction will likely see changes in a post-pandemic world as well. Several participants noted that they envision replacing paper-based assignments with digital assignments to be completed online. One elementary principal in Philadelphia shared:

> I keep saying... teaching is forever going to be changed because I think the days of printing and laminating things for centers are over. Now you can just pick up your iPad and do that. I think things like having virtual discussions about books, like the way teachers use technology in the classroom will forever be changed. I think class assignments of the writing-it-by-hand, little things like that are going to probably change forever, and I think that's a good thing, some things needed to be changed.

One of the greatest impediments to meaningful instruction in the classroom occurs when a teacher fails to maximize learning time (Vander Ark, 2018). Several of our participants told us that their state purchased a learning management system for them, and they will likely continue to use them for the foreseeable future. Using a learning management system to house documents that previously would have required paper and ink (and a functional printer, which anyone who's been an educator can appreciate). It also cuts down on taking time in class to pass out paper assignments, collect paper assignments, and affords the potential for tasks that once consumed a lot of class time at the expense of high-level learning to be eliminated. Learning management systems also create the potential for more immediate feedback on assignments (Lonn & Teasley, 2009), which in turn makes feedback more meaningful and actionable (Feden & Vogel, 2003).

## INTERDISCIPLINARY LEADERSHIP

Our findings are in line with how leaders in many other disciplines, including higher education, business, hospitality, government, and healthcare have shaped what effective crisis leadership looked like during this unprecedented time. Across disciplines, effective crisis leadership is defined by responding quickly and decisively, acknowledging mistakes and learning from them, as well as communicating openly and actively with stakeholders and community members (Haslam et al., 2021; Mather, 2020; Stoller, 2020). Another key component of effective crisis leadership, distinct from immediate crisis management, is being proactive and anticipating future crises and disruptions (Forster et al., 2020; Kaul et al., 2020). Some of the charter school leaders we spoke with anticipated the crisis and began planning, in some cases well in advance of schools closing in March 2020. Other leaders seemed caught off guard and were not as good at anticipating the crisis.

To successfully navigate their businesses, hotels, hospitals, and schools through the COVID-19 pandemic, leaders had to "reinvent their organizations [...] and both create and take new opportunities as they develop" (Mather, 2020, p. 580). During this time, hospitality leaders adapted to new challenges by introducing special offers and other marketing practices, reducing, and reallocating employees, and implementing preventative practices, such as access to PPE and additional cleaning (Lai & Wong, 2020). Similarly, educators took this opportunity to launch into a new era of remote and hybrid learning. In line with our findings, other examples across industries yielded similar results. For example, leadership in the healthcare industry shifted from a top-down approach to a dispersive model by involving stakeholders in the decision-making process and delegating tasks to other team members (Gerada, 2021; Kaul et al., 2020).

In light of the above changes, Mather (2020) speaks of the "next normal" and what might persist after the pandemic. In business, some of these lasting changes may include working from home, as well as increased demand for contactless and cashless commerce (Mather, 2020). In healthcare, telemedicine has become a permanent fixture and government-sponsored vaccinations have opened a dialogue about the possibility of accessible and affordable public healthcare (Kaul et al., 2020). As previously stated, the charter school leaders with whom we spoke believe that online learning and increased parent involvement will remain as some of the permanent fixtures in schools—features of the "next normal" in K–12 education.

## CONCLUDING THOUGHTS

Our overall findings vary but suggest that charter school leaders largely engaged in effective crisis management and crisis leadership. At the start of the pandemic when schools initially closed, the school leaders we spoke with prioritized addressing student needs and sought to find a balance between maintaining rigorous expectations for teachers and students and recognizing the "humanity of the moment," as one leader put it. In terms of crisis leadership, charter school leaders effectively communicated with stakeholders including parents, teachers, and other school leaders. Several school leaders shared instances where they learned from initial mistakes and used those moments as opportunities to improve.

Decisions made prior to the pandemic dictated the range of decisions school leaders could make regarding remote instruction modality. Schools that had invested more in technology prior to the pandemic were better situated for the moment. This finding reminds us that it is important to consider crisis leadership not as an isolated set of decisions made in response to an isolated event. The decisions that school leaders are making now will dictate the range of options at their disposal for the next crisis. Most of the school leaders we spoke with seemed to recognize this. Almost everyone recognized that some form of online learning and the use of digital tools would remain in place beyond the pandemic. Even leaders who were quite skeptical of online learning prior to the pandemic have developed a new appreciation for the possibilities that these technologies can bring to public education. Our world and educators need effective crisis leadership for students to continue to flourish and thrive. While Tyack and Cuban (1995) may have been right about the slow nature of change in public education historically, this time might be different.

## REFERENCES

Brinkmann, J. L., Cash, C., & Price, T. (2021). Crisis leadership and coaching: A tool for building school leaders' self-efficacy through self-awareness and reflection. *International Journal of Mentoring and Coaching in Education, 10*(2), 234–246. https://doi.org/10.1108/ijmce-01-2021-0009

Bulkley, K. E., & Wohlstetter, P. (2003). Introduction. In K. E. Bulkley & P. Wohlstetter (Eds.), *Taking account of charter schools: What's happened and what's next?* (pp. 1–8). Teachers College Press.

Corbin, J., & Strauss, A. (2014). *Basics of qualitative research: Techniques and procedures for developing grounded theory* (4th ed.). SAGE Publications.

Feden, P. D., & Vogel, R. M. (2003). *Methods of teaching: Applying cognitive science to promote student learning.* McGraw-Hill Humanities, Social Sciences & World Languages.

Fernandez, A. A., & Shaw, G. P. (2020). Academic leadership in a time of crisis: The coronavirus and COVID-19. *Journal of Leadership Studies, 14*(1), 39–45. https://doi.org/10.1002/jls.21684

Forster, B. B., Patlas, M. N., & Lexa, F. J. (2020). Crisis leadership during and following COVID-19. *Canadian Association of Radiologists Journal, 71*(4), 421–422. https://doi.org/10.1177/0846537120926752

Gerada, C. (2021). Reflections on leadership during the Covid pandemic. *Postgraduate Medicine, 133*(7), 717–720. https://doi.org/10.1080/00325481.2021.1903218

Gouwens, J., & Lander, D. (2008). School leadership in changing cultural contexts: How Mississippi superintendents are responding to hurricane Katrina. *Journal of Education for Students Placed at Risk, 13*(2/3), 273–296. https://doi.org/10.1080/10824660802350276

Harris, A. (2020). COVID-19—School leadership in crisis? *Journal of Professional Capital and Community, 5*(3/4), 321–326. https://doi.org/10.1108/jpcc-06-2020-0045

Harris, A., & Jones, M. (2020). COVID 19—School leadership in disruptive times. *School Leadership & Management, 40*(4), 243–247. https://doi.org/10.1080/13632434.2020.1811479

Haslam, S. A., Steffens, N. K., Reicher, S. D., & Bentley, S. V. (2021). Identity leadership in a crisis: A 5R framework for learning from responses to COVID-19. *Social Issues and Policy Review, 15*(1), 35–83. https://doi.org/10.1111/sipr.12075

Hemmer, L., & Elliff, D. S. (2019). Leaders in action: The experiences of seven Texas superintendents before, during, and after Hurricane Harvey. *Educational Management Administration & Leadership, 48*(6), 964–985. https://doi.org/10.1177/1741143219873073

Humphrey, R. H. (2013). *Effective leadership: Theory, cases, and applications* (1st ed.). SAGE Publications.

Kaden, U. (2020). COVID-19 School closure-related changes to the professional life of a K–12 teacher. *Education Sciences, 10*(6), 165. https://doi.org/10.3390/educsci10060165

Kaul, V., Shah, V. H., & El-Serag, H. (2020). Leadership during crisis: Lessons and applications from the COVID-19 pandemic. *Gastroenterology, 159*(3), 809–812. https://doi.org/10.1053/j.gastro.2020.04.076

KIPP Public Schools. (n.d.). *KIPP regions.* https://www.kipp.org/schools/kipp-regions

Lai, I. K. W., & Wong, J. W. C. (2020). Comparing crisis management practices in the hotel industry between initial and pandemic stages of COVID-19. *International Journal of Contemporary Hospitality Management, 32*(10), 3135–3156. https://doi.org/10.1108/ijchm-04-2020-0325

Lonn, S., & Teasley, S. D. (2009). Saving time or innovating practice: Investigating perceptions and uses of Learning Management Systems. *Computers & Education, 53*(3), 686–694. https://doi.org/10.1016/j.compedu.2009.04.008

Love, S. M., & Marshall, D T. (2022). Teacher experiences during COVID-19. In D. T. Marshall (Ed.), *COVID-19 and the classroom: How schools navigated the great disruption* (pp. 21–65). Lexington Books.

Marshall, D. T. (2017). Equity and access in charter schools: Identifying issues and solutions. *Educational Policy Analysis Archives, 25*(83), 1–18. https://doi.org/10.14507/epaa.25.2745

Marshall, D. T., & Bradley-Dorsey, M. (2020). Reopening America's schools: A descriptive look at how states and large school districts are navigating fall 2020. *Journal of School Choice, 14*(4), 534–566. https://doi.org/10.1080/15582159.2020.1822731

Marshall, D. T., & Bradley-Dorsey, M. (2022). Reopening schools in America. In D. T. Marshall (Ed.), *COVID-19 and the classroom: How schools navigated the great disruption* (pp. 147–164). Lexington Books.

Marshall, D. T., Shannon, D. M., & Love, S. M. (2020). How teachers experienced the COVID-19 transition to remote instruction. *Phi Delta Kappan, 102*(3), 46–50. https://doi.org/10.1177/0031721720970702

Mather, P. (2020). Leadership and governance in a crisis: Some reflections on COVID-19. *Journal of Accounting & Organizational Change, 16*(4), 579–585. https://doi.org/10.1108/jaoc-08-2020-0123

Maxwell, J. A. (2013). *Qualitative research design: An interactive approach* (3rd ed.). SAGE Publications.

McLaughlin, D. V. (2015). *Insights: How expert principals make difficult decisions* (1st ed.). Corwin.

McLeod, S., & Dulsky, S. (2021). Resilience, reorientation, and reinvention: School leadership during the early months of the COVID-19 pandemic. *Frontiers in Education, 6,* 1–13. https://doi.org/10.3389/feduc.2021.637075

McNulty, E. J., & Marcus, L. (2020, March 25). *Are you leading through the crisis . . . or managing the response?* Harvard Business Review. https://hbr.org/2020/03/are-you-leading-through-the-crisis-or-managing-the-response

Mutch, C. (2015). Leadership in times of crisis: Dispositional, relational and contextual factors influencing school principals' actions. *International Journal of Disaster Risk Reduction, 14*(2), 186–194. https://doi.org/10.1016/j.ijdrr.2015.06.005

Nathan, J. (1996). *Charter schools: Creating hope and opportunity for American education* (1st ed.). Jossey-Bass.

Oberfield, Z. W., & Henig, J. R. (2017). *Are charters different? Public education, teachers, and the charter school debate.* Harvard Education Press.

Okwara, O. (2015). *KIPP: Changing lives one student at a time.* Technology and Operations Management. https://digital.hbs.edu/platform-rctom/submission/kipp-changing-lives-one-student-at-a-time/

Osborne, D. (2017). *Reinventing America's schools: Creating a 21st century education system.* Bloomsbury USA.

Pendergrass, S. A., & Kern, N. (2017). The case for charters. In N. K. Buchanan & R. A. Fox (Eds.), *The Wiley handbook of school choice* (1st ed.; pp. 237–251). Wiley-Blackwell.

Smith, L., & Riley, D. (2012). School leadership in times of crisis. *School Leadership & Management, 32*(1), 57–71. https://doi.org/10.1080/13632434.2011.614941

Stoller, J. K. (2020). Reflections on leadership in the time of COVID-19. *BMJ Leader, 4*(2), 77–79. https://doi.org/10.1136/leader-2020-000244

Sutherland, I. E. (2017). Learning and growing: trust, leadership, and response to crisis. *Journal of Educational Administration, 55*(1), 2–17. https://doi.org/10.1108/jea-10-2015-0097

Tarrant, R. (2011). Leadership through a school tragedy: A case study (Part 1–The first week). *Australasian Journal of Disaster and Trauma Studies, 2011*(3), 65–76. http://trauma.massey.ac.nz/issues/2011-3/AJDTS_2011-3_01_Tarrant.pdf

Tyack, D. B., & Cuban, L. (1995). *Tinkering toward utopia: A century of public school reform.* Amsterdam University Press.

Vander Ark, T. (2017). The problem is wasted time, not screen time. *Education Next, 18*(1). https://www.educationnext.org/problem-is-wasted-time-not-screen-time-forum-scoggin-vander-ark

Vanourek, G. (2020). *Schooling Covid-19: Lessons from leading charter networks from their transition to remote learning.* The Thomas B. Fordham Institute. https://fordhaminstitute.org/national/research/schooling-covid-19-lessons-leading-charter-networks-their-transition-remote

Varela, D. G., & Fedynich, L. (2020). Leading schools from a social distance: Surveying South Texas school district leadership during the COVID-19 pandemic. *National Forum of Educational Administration and Supervision Journal, 38*(4), 1–10. http://www.nationalforum.com/Electronic%20Journal%20Volumes/Varela,%20daniella%20Surveying%20South%20Texas%20School%20District%20Leadership%20NFEASJ%20V38%20N4%202020.pdf

CHAPTER 18

# SERVING MULTIPLE MASTERS

## Rural Ugandan Headteachers' Role in Attracting and Retaining Teachers

**Gilbert Arinaitwe**
**John Williamson**

### ABSTRACT

Attracting and retaining teachers in rural schools is an issue that impacts communities around the world. Head teachers play a critical role in the recruitment, management, and development of teachers and they do so in the context of serving multiple stakeholders—the school community, parents, central and local education authorities—who often have conflicting expectations. The ability to address these tensions is key to the school's success in attracting and retaining teachers, yet the way Ugandan head teachers do so remains poorly understood. This chapter reports how specific head teachers' practices "work around" the expectations and tensions among school boards, community leaders, and government agencies, that is, "multiple masters" as they attempt to attract and retain teachers. The role of the head teacher as policy and practical "gate-keeper" and how the head teachers balance individual school autonomy and the need to fit Ministry of Education policy, the expectations of teachers, parents, and local community is presented. This study

*On Leadership*, pages 329–350

thus highlights how school head teachers adapt policies to fit their circumstances and to address the expectations of multiple masters to foster teacher attraction and retention.

Globally, effective leadership of the school head teacher has a significant role to play in promoting school improvement (Leithwood et al., 2020; Player et al., 2017). Research in the West has identified the major roles of head teachers, including, to articulate an explicit school vision and culture (MacBeath, 2008); generate high expectations and goals for all students and monitor schools' performance through regular use of data and frequent classroom observations (Goodwin et al., 2005; Preston et al., 2017); implement reforms from the central government (Chapman et al., 2010); hire high-quality teachers as well as to improve teacher motivation and working conditions (Engel et al., 2018; Huff et al., 2018); and to reach out to parents and community to strengthen the ties between local school professionals and the community they serve (Fullan, 2000).

Roles have been widely articulated by studies from the West, including the task to ensure ethical leadership of the schools in their care (Fowler, 2010; Fowler et al., 2018), and the task to provide better working conditions for teachers and other school staff (Burkhauser, 2017). This chapter will focus on the widely published role of head teachers in attracting and retaining other school teachers, a major issue in the West (Engel et al., 2018; Hughes et al., 2015; Player et al., 2017), through findings from Uganda, a non-Western context, and elucidate how Ugandan head teachers worked around and localized the central government policies in ensuring schools run and develop.

In their roles, Kafka (2009) argued that U.S. head teacher's position is "neither at the top of the educational hierarchy nor at the ground level, but is somewhere in the middle, answering to district officials, policy makers, parents, students, teachers, and community member" (p. 329). Like in most other countries whose education is modeled after the British education system (Mahoney et al., 1998; Mestry, 2018), Ugandan school head teachers are answerable to the Boards of Governors (BOG) and Parents–Teachers Association (PTA) which represent other constituencies (students, parents, teachers, the foundation bodies and government) and attenuate the powers of the head teacher in school leadership. Consistent with studies in the West (Hallinger, 2017; Kafka, 2009), the head teacher's role is to manage the implementation of stakeholders' expectations. Given these needs the head teacher's behavior is often conforming to external compliance criteria rather than the exercise of autonomous decision-making.

In the United Kingdom, for example, MacBeath (2009) argued that the devolution of decision-making to school level resulted in increased tensions and dilemmas as it sandwiched head teachers between students, parents, staff, local community, and government agencies each with their own conventions, protocols, and implicit value systems whom head teachers paradoxically is accountable to. This raises ethical leadership challenges, defined as how head teachers perceive what is and is not ethical conduct based on what is socially desirable or acceptable (Fowler et al., 2018). As a result, head teachers act differently in different situations and stakeholders' expectations may be treated as guidelines for action, not steps to be followed (Fullan, 2000).

Some Western scholars have noted the circumstances considered to be breaking rules with right reasons (Dahling, 2012) especially in the context of contradictory requirements from organizational stakeholders (Pérezts et al., 2011). Rule breaking is the way to get things done and, it has been asserted, shaping of activities to achieve a goal, that is, micro-politics (Altrichter, 2001) cannot be practiced without a flexible attitude to the rules (MacBeath, 1998). These behaviors have been treated in cognate literature, such as business, as adapting service experience by frontline workers in organizations who create alternatives to meet the needs of customers (Chung Beth & Schneider, 2002; Wilder et al., 2014).

As noted by Leithwood et al., (2020) head teachers demonstrate responsiveness to, rather than dictation to, the contexts in which they work. Leadership may involve the notion of loose coupling (Bush, 2017) defined as "coupled events are responsive, but that each event also preserves its own identity and some evidence of its physical or logical separateness" (p. 6). Leadership is then distributed to various organs and individuals. Distributed leadership foregrounds how actors engage in tasks that are "stretched" or distributed across the organization. It means seeing leadership activities as a situated and social process at the intersection of leaders, followers, and the situation (Gronn, 2000). Western literature argues that the role of head teachers is therefore not an individual act but a collective effort to cater for interests and expectations of various stakeholders. Whereas published literature is mostly studies from English-speaking countries of Australia, the United Kingdom, the United States, Canada, and New Zealand, there are many fewer reports on the leadership of school head teachers in Africa and other non-Western countries (Hallinger, 2017). The Western literature may help form a basis of understanding Ugandan head teachers' experiences. There are similarities and differences in the way that head teachers execute their roles in the West and in Uganda and therefore this chapter aims to delineate the head teacher's role in the context of attracting and retaining teachers in country-specific rural public schools.

## COUNTRY CONTEXT

As in many other British Commonwealth countries, school education in Uganda was initially established and controlled by religious bodies, local community, and private individuals (Higgins & Rwanyange, 2005). Later, the government established its own schools to provide access to education for those who do not "fit"—culturally, religiously, economically—within religious and privately founded schools (Ssekamwa, 1997). Some of the non-government established schools later started receiving government funding and staff (Ssekamwa, 1997). As a result, government took over the control and administration of the government-aided schools. Ugandan education policy is designed and implemented by the Ministry of Education, one of the major agencies of the government.

Since 2007, universal secondary education (USE) has been implemented in selected schools, usually one school per sub-county. As of 2018, USE schools comprise 89% of the Ugandan public school system and are mostly located in rural areas (geographic places outside gazetted urban areas). In a developing country such as Uganda the designation of a school as USE or non-USE is important, firstly, as the former are government supported and are prohibited from levying fees for education; however, they are permitted to collect ("request") voluntary school contributions from parents towards "emergencies" and, secondly, they are not permitted to exclude students whose parents do not make the voluntary contribution (Chapman et al., 2010; Huylebroeck & Titeca, 2008). These "voluntary" contributions are typically used for teacher remuneration and in their retention on the school's staff. Politicians in Uganda portray USE as a government scheme which provides completely free education to the entire population (Huylebroeck & Titeca, 2008). However, due to government's underfunding and delayed funding to schools, head teachers turn to parents and, what is known as, "the foundation body," to generate income for purposes including to pay teachers, and provide critical operational needs (Omoeva & Gale, 2016; Ssekamwa, 1997).

The board of governors (BOG) which oversees the school operations at the local government level on behalf of the Ministry of Education (MoE; 2 Act, 2008) is comprised of 50% of members, including a Chairperson, who are appointed by the relevant foundation body, and the remaining 50% are MoE appointees. The foundation body is (a) the owner of the land and buildings for these schools; (b) consulted by government on fundamental matters such as staffing decisions and remain with keen interest in schools which they founded; (c) have a specially posted staff (e.g., a chaplain in religious founded school) to oversee the adherence of the school ethos and values; and (d) schools exclusively offer a type of religious education that is professed by the foundation body. The parish priest where the school is located represents the religious foundation body and plays an oversight role for the schools founded by the religious body within such a community (Muwagga et al., 2013). As a result, the government ideology and national identity is difficult to inculcate in schools receiving government funding but religiously owned. The Ugandan Education Act (2008) mandates a head teacher of a school to (a) exercise such functions of the BOG as the BOG may delegate to him or her, (b) be personally responsible to the BOG, (c) advise the BOG when required to do so, and (d) furnish a report on his or her conduct of the affairs of the school to the Permanent Secretary of MoE. Therefore, the interplay of MoE and foundation body expectations influences the head teacher's decisions for individual schools. Tensions arise when head teachers act in disregard of, try to be independent of or are not keen to work closely with, the foundation body and BOG; and rather, work directly and closely with the central government on matters of school administration.

By policy, the recruitment of teachers in public schools is conducted by the Education Service Commission (ESC) and the Ministry of Public Service (MoPS) pays teachers as civil servants. Teachers recruited by MoE are appointed according to the public service pay structure and paid by MoPS directly into individual bank accounts. Salaries are fixed at annual rates and paid in twelve equal monthly installments. As in African countries, such as Gambia, Zambia, Namibia, South Africa, and other countries, such as Australia (Kelly & Fogarty, 2015; Pugatch & Schroeder, 2014; UNICEF, 2014), the Ugandan government provides a location allowance for government appointed teachers in hard to reach and hard to staff districts to increase their level of motivation and retention (Ellis & Bahiigwa, 2003). The location allowance is paid to teachers on the government payroll as a top-up of 30% to their basic salary. It is non-pensionable and non-gratuitable and is paid only during the period such a teacher is posted in designated hard-to-reach areas (MoPS, 2010).

However, certain circumstances encourage USE schools to supplement government payments for teachers. First, teachers are paid differently by the government according to the individual teacher's subject specialty, with science teachers earning more than non-science teachers to attract and retain science teachers (Ministry of Public Service, 2019). For example, non-science teachers at their top of salary scale earn less than the starting salary of science teachers within the same rank/position. This differential demotivates non-science teachers and means school relations are sometimes difficult for school head teachers to manage. Second, the government suspended teachers' incremental salary progression in 2012 and as a result, most teachers who upgrade their qualifications (e.g., from diploma to bachelor degree) remain earning the same salary on which they commenced. Besides, when salary increments are made for a select category of teachers, they are usually small in size. As an outcome, government payroll teachers receive payments from both government and locally generated school income, the latter acting as a supplementary pay depending on the school's available resources.

As a result of low government revenue and budget funding competition, the government has appointed and deployed less than the required number of teachers in rural schools. Based on the MoE teacher recruitment policy procedure described above, the government takes an inordinate amount of time to appoint and, when it does, still underemploys (Crawfurd, 2017). This is partly because the staff ceilings were established many years ago and the staff numbers agreed by the MoE do not increase to match the growth in student numbers (Namusoke et al., 2017). Consequently, schools often recruit their own teachers to fill immediate teaching needs while waiting for the government to announce positions. Schools pay the teachers they recruit independent of government financial support, and it is done through locally generated income, such as philanthropic support from affluent local parents, community members, and donations from the foundation body, as described above as voluntary contributions for MoE permitted school emergencies. Therefore, within the same public school, there are both school BOG and government recruited teachers and these two bodies remunerate teachers differently. This means each school has some teachers employed under its own terms and conditions of service and these vary between schools, and, on the other hand, all schools have teachers employed by the MoE, under a unified teaching service, and accorded the same status as civil servants with the same qualifications.

When government announces positions for filling staffing gaps, head teachers (a) recommend teachers who were temporarily recruited by the school to be officially confirmed in the position and (b) provide cover letters for teachers seeking transfer from one school to another. These behaviors disregard the merit recruitment and transfer policy procedure (Arinaitwe et al., 2020) where head teachers were to only submit information on staffing needs and the MoE, in turn, was to publicly advertise and interview eligible applicants (MoE, 2014).

In 2010, the Ugandan government identified schools and areas that were described as both hard to staff and hard to reach school districts. Several characteristics explain these hard to reach and hard to staff districts. First, the hard to reach and hard to staff districts within the southwestern part and the highland areas in eastern Uganda experience a range of weather temperatures that are difficult for year-round habitation.

Second, some hard-to-reach districts experience conflict and insecurity challenges. The hard-to-reach districts located along the international borders host refugees from Democratic Republic of Congo, South Sudan, and Rwanda. The rebel insurgencies by Lord's Resistance Army (LRA) in northern Uganda since 1987 and the Allied Democratic Forces (ADF) in western Uganda since 1996, have both contributed to the insecurity of most Ugandan border districts. These border areas, particularly those that are heavily forested, with low population densities and a mountainous terrain, project the government's inability to exercise authority over vast distances and therefore are more open to insurgency (Day, 2019).

Third, the absence of service utilities, such as electricity and running water delivered to the house, greatly affects non-Western countries but mostly rural communities. This deficit is widespread in Uganda: only 5% of Uganda is connected to the national electricity grid and approximately 2% of rural areas are connected to this grid (Gore, 2009). As a result, the lack of access to electricity to pump water, to allow work beyond dusk and sociable leisure time is severely restricted in areas without the connection to the electricity grid. Not surprisingly, teachers seek to reside in areas with an established electricity connection. This desire is similar in the access to clean, piped water.

Fourth, hard to reach districts are further characterised by hindered access to services from other districts, including teacher training institutions, banks, and referral hospitals. The National Teachers Colleges and Universities are mostly located in larger towns in districts adjacent to the hard-to-reach districts. The teacher's salary is available only through a bank and in the hard-to-reach district this institution might not be accessible. Similarly, in the case of serious illness the hard-to-reach districts are not likely to have a major hospital to treat the complaint. The lack of referral hospitals, banks, and teacher training institutions reinforces the teachers' desire for commuting to and from the hard-to-reach districts and increases the cost of living. This has implications for teachers accepting deployment in hard-to-reach districts.

Fifth, hard to reach districts in central and eastern part of Uganda are an amalgamation of tiny island areas within Lake Victoria and they experience travel difficulties as it is by canoe boat only and, in addition, the environment promotes a myriad of diseases less experienced in mainland Uganda (Kabatereine et al., 2011).

## RESEARCH APPROACH

This chapter reports findings from a larger qualitative study that explored why some teachers stay while others leave rural teaching positions in Uganda. An embedded single case study of two districts (Kanungu & Kisoro) selected from 24 districts that the MoPS (2010) described as both hard to reach and hard to staff was chosen with ethics approval obtained from the relevant authorities. The two districts—namely, Kanungu and Kisoro—are adjacent to each other in the extreme southwestern corner of Uganda's international borders with the Democratic Republic of Congo (DRC) in the west, and Rwanda to the south. It takes a long time traveling on bad roads from Kampala, the capital of Uganda and its largest city to other parts of the country. The main trunk roads and major inter-district roads are sealed all weather tarmac roads but the roads within districts are a "marram," that is, non-sealed road. Whereas access to public transport on the highway roads to and from the district is available any time, access within the district's rural communities is severely restricted. During the two rainy seasons, March to May and October to November, the roads are likely to be slippery and there are landslides which block roads. During the two dry seasons, June to September and December to February, the roads become very dusty resulting in reduced visibility when driving at the legal speed limit. This has major implications for teachers who need to commute to work if they do not own a car.

The study began with a reconnaissance and mapping exercise of all 22 rural public secondary schools in both districts; 12 in the Kanungu district and 10 in the Kisoro district. All the schools were implementing the USE program. The schools were typically not performing as highly as elite schools in urban areas in national assessments. The schools were mostly attended by students who come from the surrounding villages for the day, that is, "day schools"; in larger villages there are occasionally some minimum boarding facilities for students from distant communities and who could not travel safely to school and then home again each day. While the schools admitted most students from within immediate rural communities, it is likely that students from wealthier families who could afford boarding fees attended urban schools. The schools were established by different foundation bodies, including 11 Anglican Church of Uganda founded schools, four Roman Catholic Church founded schools, five local community founded schools, and two government founded schools. A total of eight schools had a complete cycle of secondary education (from S1–S6) and 14 schools had only lower secondary (S1–S4) which meant that some rural students who complete lower secondary may either drop out of school or be required to leave their home rural communities to attend school in other larger rural or urban areas.

Of the 22 schools, 21 were coeducational and one was a single sex school, for girls. Overall, 10% more boys were enrolled in the two districts. While the MoE does not mandate male students to be taught by males or female students to be taught by females the published employment data shows a significant predominance of male teachers in primary and secondary schools. This workforce is likely the result of cultural norms, the country's history, and socio-economic factors, such as valuing boy's education more than females. In the 22 schools studied, there were few female teachers which had implications for support for girls in both curriculum areas and pastoral care; in the curriculum provision this was particularly evident in science, technology, and mathematics subjects (Brotman, 2009; Skelton et al., 2009).

Finally, schools varied in the number of teachers and attending students. The largest school had almost two-and-a-half times as many teachers as the smallest school. Teachers of the senior classes within the same school taught fewer students than their counterparts deployed in junior classes. In addition, teachers for optional or elective subjects within the same school and class level taught fewer students than their counterparts teaching MoE mandated compulsory subjects. This combination of school size and MoE compulsory subjects has meant schools have varying student–teacher ratio (STR) within and across the schools, and influences school staffing decisions.

Following the reconnaissance and mapping exercise, a total of four schools, two from each district, were selected for an in-depth case study (Ridder, 2017; Yin, 2014) because they had relatively high teacher retention for their district. The head teachers of all four schools participated in the study. The head teachers were then requested to invite all teachers who were in school at the time of the researchers' visits for an information session. In these meetings, teachers could meet the researchers to build rapport and trust, review ethical considerations and complete consent forms. The researchers explicitly requested teachers' voluntary participation in the study during the information session in the staff room. The head teacher could not find out which teachers had volunteered. Head teachers were also asked for addresses of all members of the PTA executive committee, BOG members, and five key community leaders. This record provided the address for all members without disclosing to the head teacher the participants who eventually expressed interest to participate in the study. A total of 31 participants were selected including four head teachers, three PTA chairpersons, two BOG chairpersons, two community leaders, and 20 teachers. As described above, a combination of opportunistic and purposeful sampling techniques (Ritchie et al., 2003; Robinson, 2014) was used to select all participants. These techniques allowed for on-the-spot sampling decisions that emerged during fieldwork (Suri, 2011). Data were gathered through document analysis and semi-structured interviews (Creswell & Poth, 2017). To establish rapport, there was a prolonged and intense exposure with participants within their context. An average of 2 weeks per study site was spent and 8 months of the entire data collection process was spent engaging with participants. As a result, multiple perspectives were collected and understood and hence reduced potential for social desirability responses in interviews.

Following thematic analysis steps of Braun and Clarke (2006), data were analyzed deductively and inductively using an iterative process (Bazeley, 2013) to re-identify themes. First, a verbatim transcription was conducted for the audio recorded interviews and a member checking (Birt et al., 2016) was conducted with all participants. There was repeated reading of the transcripts, searching for meanings and patterns. While reading, notes were taken, and ideas marked for coding. All data set was read at least twice before coding began. The rereading continued throughout all steps of the analysis and writing up of the report. As an initial step, a deductive, theory driven analysis (Gibbs, 2007) was used, that is, a codebook was developed from literature reviewed, key summary points identified during data collection as well as personal hunches gained from the researchers' years of experience in living and working in rural areas. However, further rereading led to clearer insights about the interview data (DeCuir-Gunby et al., 2011) and a shift from theory-driven codes to data-driven codes that closely suit the nuances of participants and context. Subsequently, the initial theory-driven codes were aligned with data-driven codes as a blueprint to generate trustworthy codes. The codes were collated into broader themes by looking at the list of codes and their associated extracts to find matching patterns. A tree map or hierarchy of codes was drawn using NVivo and codes moved around to identify those that fit together to form themes. Consistent with Braun and Clarke (2019) and Guest et al. (2011), some themes were collapsed into each other (those that had little data to support them), some themes were dropped (those that were not coherent with the developing pattern), and other themes were broken down into separate themes (those that had a large, diverse data set). This chapter reports one of the themes. Some theme names were revised to fit the story under the theme. The first author conducted all of the interviews and in reporting the findings, schools' and participants' names are anonymized to protect confidentiality.

## FINDINGS

The following section describes the role of Ugandan head teachers in serving their school communities within central government policies including (a) circumventing statutory employment conditions, (b) interpreting voluntary contributions as compulsory contributions from parents, and (c) concealing from parents the teachers' pay inherent within permitted contributions. These examples will demonstrate how the focus of the typical Ugandan rural head teacher is on operating in the context of mandated policies to keep their school open and operating rather than some of the roles seen in the typical Western head teacher.

## CIRCUMVENTING STATUTORY EMPLOYMENT CONDITIONS

As head teachers faced simultaneous understaffing and underfunding by the government (Arinaitwe et al., 2020), they operated in a constrained policy space (Dagher, 2019) while serving in low-income rural school communities (Fowler & Jouganatos, 2020). Nonetheless, head teachers ensured that students had teachers and that these teachers were paid. Faced with these circumstances, the head teachers performed a "leadership dance"; that is, through a localization of action within the context of a national policy (Sausman et al., 2016) they developed on-the-ground strategies and tactics to attract and retain teachers. First, as described above, head teachers paid school board payroll teachers about one quarter of the wage that teachers on the government payroll received. This in-school differentiation was acknowledged by Participant A (personal interview, April 12, 2018):

> Teachers who entirely depend on school pay are not comfortable. You find somebody is a graduate, he is recruited locally, working in a government school, but government has not appointed him. He is only paid 200,000 UGX (56.75 USD) per month (by the school). They are not comfortable really. The reason is that we do not have money as a school.

Participant A clearly indicated that school board payroll teachers were paid much less than government appointed teachers because of the inability of the school to pay the higher salary. Head teachers, therefore, operated within a two-track salary scale system which affected teacher's psychological well-being and attitudes (Castaing, 2006; Conway & Briner, 2002; Lester et al., 2002) and which they had to manage.

Second, some head teachers worked around the national employment policy by (a) describing the school board payroll teachers as "temporary staff" even though they worked as permanent teaching staff, (b) not providing them with written contracts of service in accordance with the Employment Act 2006 but instead used the permitted oral contracts without explicit written agreement on remuneration, (c) avoiding deductions required by law from teachers' remuneration, and (d) not paying the full-time school board payroll teachers during school holidays. In adopting this strategy head teachers were able to save money by avoiding compulsory employment obligations. In addition, head teachers set different terms of payment for teachers, including the amount paid, duration of payment, and regularity of payment. Participant A (personal interview, April 12, 2018) succinctly said:

> When you compare with some of these schools around, in terms of facilitation, I think our school is doing fairly well. Because we pay (school board payroll teachers' salary) all the 12 months in a year and some of the schools around they do not pay teachers during the school holidays. And although it is little money, but when you compare with other government USE schools around; we are still leading.

Some schools paid a higher amount and for all months in the year than did counterpart rural schools that paid less and only during school session time. Participant B (personal interview, June 13, 2018) stated other terms of employment:

> We recruit them on temporary terms... They stay because they have no alternative. If they had, they would go away... We know we pay them little... We do not pay salary to them. We call it transport refund. We do not give them appointment letters.

Participant B reported how head teachers were able to recruit teachers who were waiting for a government offer of a permanent government position. In return, head teachers "worked around" the MoE merit recruitment procedure to ensure that these *in situ* teachers secured the government job by recommending these teachers for employment by the MoE. In this situation, despite the very unfavorable terms of employment faced by the school board payroll teachers, teachers perceived that working in rural locations provided a pathway for entry into government service. However, in this careful dance between the obligations of MoE policy and actual school staffing, the head teachers acknowledged the risk of legal disputes with teachers. This practice raises issues of accountability and transparency which schools recognised but, in practice, simply ignored and/or worked around.

Third, whereas the stated MoE employment policy required head teachers to ensure that they recruit teachers who are not holding another full-time teaching position in another school, the head teachers worked around this policy. Because of low and delayed pay for teachers, the head teachers worked around the full-time employment policy by reducing or compressing workload and ensuring that they had a flexible timetable for the teachers' class instruction responsibilities to allow teachers engage in part-time employment in other schools, that is, to work unofficially at one or more schools while holding a full-time position at their school. As a result, teachers had an approved leeway to engage in part-time employment in preferred areas with neighbouring schools. Participant A (personal interview, April 12, 2018) said:

> There is an issue of flexibility in administration. We give them gaps to do some things to help them. For example, we can say from Monday to Friday, you have a right to declare two days you are free. Teach 24 periods (16 hours) in three days. We try to sensitise them to use their two days profitably... So, we do not compel them to sit here from Monday to weekend. We try to be flexible to give them a chance to make more money.

As described above many teachers are school board employed and are paid much less than government payroll teachers, in all of these schools the head teachers supported the practice of part-time employment in other schools to retain and assist teachers to earn a living wage. For example, Participant C (personal interview, April 17, 2018) said, “In my [school’s] timetable, I accommodate that because I know they do part-time jobs in other schools and for us our timetable accommodates a teacher for three days. I encourage them to work [elsewhere] to bring some income.” The practice of holding more than one job was perceived by heads, chairs of BOG, and teachers as an appropriate coping mechanism on account of the low salaries. Participant D (personal interview, April 11, 2018) explained: “It is not appreciating it. I would talk of coping mechanisms. There is nobody who does part-timing and likes it. It is a coping mechanism so that maybe they can get a package to meet their needs.” In addition, the head teacher used the practice as a mechanism for buying talent to support the weaker full-time staff.

As previously noted (Arinaitwe et al., 2020), nearly half of the teachers did not meet the MoE requirements of a bachelor degree to teach upper secondary level (S5–S6) curricula. This was confirmed by Participant E (personal interview, April 18, 2018) who said, “At times we employ some people who are not competent and for that matter it affects the performance of our students.” Participant D (personal interview, April 11, 2018) explained:

> The competences of teachers are a big challenge. Not all can teach the upper section S3, S4 and others may lack competences to handle A Level. Because what happens is “star,” that is, very good teachers with high competences tend to remain in urban areas. Then those who lack certain competences go to rural areas. If you are in high demand, you go to urban. If you are not on high demand, you go to or remain in rural. We found that as a big challenge. So as a Board we have encouraged the head teacher to hire. If you know a teacher who has certain competences which are lacking, is it possible to hire this person for few hours to bridge in the gap? Those are kind of mechanisms that rural schools have tried to adapt to compete with other urban schools.

Participant D reported that rural schools were often staffed by low quality teachers who, in turn, were not able to improve the poor student performance. He observed that competent teachers qualified to teach a high demand subject area tended to be appointed to an urban school. On the other hand, through a process of informal sifting, teachers with little or no curriculum expertise and weaker teaching competencies were employed by the rural school. This, in turn, weakened and limited the options available for the rural students to learn effectively and maximise their potential (Arinaitwe et al., 2020).

As a coping strategy, the head teacher’s role was to supplement their existing less qualified or out-of-subject teachers with competent and high demand subject area teachers from urban schools on a part-time basis.

These better qualified urban government employed teachers would earn additional wages by teaching some classes in the rural schools. For the head teachers this was described as a "game of buying talent," to teach those curriculum areas and levels that existing staff could not. This action ignored the guidelines from the MoE discouraging full-time teachers from part-time employment in other schools.

The practice of part-time employment in other schools had implications for teacher attendance and punctuality (Chaudhury et al., 2006) and the quality of education in rural schools. The common school practice of compressing face-to-face teaching instructional time within a few days of a week rather than spreading lessons for a whole week had several flow-on consequences. First, it was likely to affect student learning as the teacher was not only focused on their teaching but also the next off-school job. Second, the absence of teachers from the school was likely to deny student consultations outside class instructional time. In practical terms, this action was working around the MoE policy that was predicated on spaced practice or distributed practice of student learning of 40–80 minutes per day per subject.

## BREAKING THE MOE POLICY: MAKING "VOLUNTARY" CONTRIBUTIONS "COMPULSORY"

The practical outcome of schools, through BOGs and head teachers, using the policy relating to voluntary contributions towards emergency funding requests meant they were in effect made compulsory contributions. Notwithstanding the policy the head teachers described their actions as for the betterment of their school and staff and this was acknowledged as a deliberate ignoring of MOE policy. The head teachers carefully calibrated their request for "the donations" on an understanding of what their BOG would advise and what their community could afford, and they considered a balance between cash and non-cash contributions. As seen in the rural schools the most common approach that head teachers took were barter exchange, that is, negotiating with parents to supply materials to the school and or parents/students to do work for the school to cover voluntary school contributions. Participant F (personal interview, April 18, 2018) reported:

> The head teacher normally arranges with those students who fail to pay school fees (voluntary school contributions), they remain here during holidays to clear the bush or to make some odd jobs around for the school as part of clearance of school fees (voluntary school contributions).

Similarly, Participant E (personal interview, April 18, 2018) said:

> Then others are working at school. Most of the people who work at school are parents. They work and after that they deduct that money to pay school fees (voluntary school contributions). And others provide firewood. They deduct money from them. When we are building classrooms most of the people who do work there are parents. So, they [parents] are assisted in that way. Most of them you see working are parents, for example, this gatekeeper you came with here is a parent.

The rural head teachers devised a "work study program" outside school hours and holidays which enabled students to help pay for their own education. While this enabled the students to stay in school, the national test data suggest that their levels of academic performance were negatively impacted when compared to their urban, more affluent peers who could concentrate on academic study (Namubiru, 2017). Participants E and F reported two options which head teachers orchestrated the ways parents paid for voluntary school contributions, namely, working for the school or supplying the school with materials. The strategies of parents offering school supplies and working for the school engendered a sense of school ownership by the parents. As seen by Participant C (personal interview, April 17, 2018), "This is their school; this is their property and the school itself belongs to this community." Participant C illustrated the head teacher's practical leadership in working with his local community to address the school's funding needs to attract and retain teachers. While the literature describes philanthropic support (Rohayati et al., 2016) and parent's contribution (Thompson et al., 2019) for schools internationally, the head teachers in this study reported similar funding practices in Uganda but typically these were now made compulsory rather than voluntarily.

## CONCEALING TEACHERS' PAY IN MOE POLICY PERMITTED SCHOOL CONTRIBUTIONS

The Ugandan Education Act states the government was responsible to pay for all teachers and therefore teachers' pay was not included in what were described as "the unforeseeable" school funding needs (Education Act, 2008). However, head teachers often classified the school-based teacher salaries and incentives as "emergencies," and the following tactics were employed. First, head teachers acted in concert with BOGs and PTA executive committees to conceal from both the MoE and parents the use of permitted "emergency" money, from allowable voluntary school contributions, to pay fully or supplement teachers' wages. This concealment of purpose was elaborated by Participant D (personal interview, April 11, 2018) who in conjunction with the head teacher subverted the MoE policy:

> I think PTA fees (voluntary school contributions) they label it something else because the government says since in USE you are not supposed to charge fees. But there is a way parents come and say this is for remedial teaching or something. They get a certain name that will not implicate them. You find all in all, a student is paying around 200,000 UGX (52 USD) which is not realistic. The school capitation grant is 40,000 per student. Is that enough? And it does not come on time.

Similarly, Participant A (personal interview, April 12, 2018) reported:

> There is a way government has limited us on charging fees (voluntary school contributions), even the little we are charging, we charge it in the disguise of food expenses. At first, they said USE schools should not levy any money from the parents. But you must create other excuses so that you save some little money to pay these other teachers. So, the fees (voluntary school contributions) we charge we call it a development fund. This being a rural school, students are paying only 100,000 UGX (26 USD).

As noted by Participants A and D, head teachers concealed the amount, either in-full or in-part, to teachers' pay from the policy permitted reasons for collecting contributions from parents. The head teachers ignored MoE policies regarding the use of voluntary contributions from parents and hid the fact it was used for teachers' remuneration.

## CONCLUSION

The Ugandan rural school head teachers—because of their context: political, policy, rurality, cultural, financial—are acting to keep their schools operating through balancing competing needs/directions and in doing so are performing a "skillful dance" between competing masters (e.g., MoE, foundation bodies, local community, and parents). The study demonstrated how head teachers face numerous dilemmas in deciding what to do in very challenging circumstances and how they need to act differently in different situations, for example, interpreting stakeholders' expectations as guidelines for actions rather than steps to be followed. The head teachers were skilled in forming alliances with different stakeholder representative constituencies, especially the BOG chairpersons, PTA committee chairpersons, and teachers, to work around other stakeholder expectations to reach their goals. While making the best of serving different masters, in these dynamic contexts, head teachers partnered with (a) BOG and PTA chairpersons to exploit school board payroll teachers who, in turn, accepted these lesser conditions while waiting to secure a recommendation to obtain a government payroll position in the future, (b) teachers in having direct personal communication with the community re the needs for them to make contributions allowable under the MoE policy of "unforeseen emergencies" to keep their local school operating, and (c) parents in negotiating a barter system so that there was a cash or service contribution to the school's operation notwithstanding the Govt rhetoric re "free education."

Head teachers in this study have all demonstrated skills, abilities, and dispositions in their interactions with multiple stakeholders that have allowed their schools to succeed in very challenging circumstances. In that sense they have shown a very varied and interdisciplinary leadership skill set. While exercising their roles, they have demonstrated a collective effort working with stakeholders to respond to the contexts in which they work, breaking rules with right reasons and localizing central government policies. The head teachers worked collaboratively with local stakeholders to develop and shape the on-the-ground actions, which in some instances were against MoE policy. However, as described by all stakeholders, the head teachers acted rationally (MacBeath, 2008) and for the larger good (Fowler et al., 2018) firstly, to attract, secondly to pay, and thirdly, to retain teachers by a range of strategies. They did this through subverting policy resulting in poorer remuneration of some teachers, the encouraging of teachers to engage in part-time employment in other schools and interpreting policy relating to voluntary school contributions in ways not intended by the MoE. However, these actions while defensible—and sensible—in context also need to be seen as having a negative impact on rural students and ultimately the country through not providing an educational system that extends the advantages of a full education to all learners. The movement from a local on-the-ground practical outcome to a truly national equitable education system for all learners will be the big challenge for rural head teachers.

## REFERENCES


Altrichter, H. (2001). Schools, micropolitics of. In N. J. Smelser & P. B. Baltes (Eds.), *International Encyclopedia of the Social & Behavioral Sciences* (pp. 13594–13598). Pergamon. https://doi.org/10.1016/B0-08-043076-7/02455-4

Arinaitwe, G., Williamson, J., & Kilpatrick, S. (2020). 'Birds of a feather flock together!': Rural teacher recruitment policy and retention in and for hard-to-staff Ugandan schools. In J. Fox, C. Alexander, & T. Aspland (Eds.), *Teacher education in globalised times: Local responses in action* (pp. 295–310). Springer Singapore. https://doi.org/10.1007/978-981-15-4124-7_16

Bazeley, P. (2013). *Qualitative data analysis: Practical strategies*. SAGE Publications.

Birt, L., Scott, S., Cavers, D., Campbell, C., & Walter, F. (2016). Member checking: A tool to enhance trustworthiness or merely a nod to validation? *Qualitative Health Research, 26*(13), 1802–1811. https://doi.org/10.1177/1049732316654870

Braun, V., & Clarke, V. (2006). Using thematic analysis in psychology. *Qualitative Research in Psychology, 3*(2), 77–101. https://doi.org/10.1191/1478088706qp063oa

Braun, V., & Clarke, V. (2019). Reflecting on reflexive thematic analysis. *Qualitative Research in Sport, Exercise and Health, 11*(4), 589–597. https://doi.org/10.1080/2159676X.2019.1628806

Brotman, J. S. (2009). Girls and science: A review of four themes in the science education literature. *Journal of Research in Science Teaching, 45*(9), 971–1002. https://doi.org/10.1002/tea.20241

Burkhauser, S. (2017). How much do school principals matter when it comes to teacher working conditions? *Educational Evaluation and Policy Analysis, 39*(1), 126–145. https://doi.org/10.3102/0162373716668028

Bush, T. (2017). School improvement through government agencies: Loose or tight coupling? *Improving Schools, 20*(1), 35–47. https://doi.org/10.1177/1365480216650949

Castaing, S. (2006). The effects of psychological contract fulfilment and public service motivation on organizational commitment in the French civil service. *Public Policy and Administration, 21*(1), 84–98. https://doi.org/10.1177/095207670602100106

Chapman, D. W., Burton, L., & Werner, J. (2010). Universal secondary education in Uganda: The headteachers' dilemma. *International Journal of Educational Development, 30*(1), 77–82. https://doi.org/10.1016/j.ijedudev.2009.08.002

Chaudhury, N., Hammer, J., Kremer, M., Muralidharan, K., & Rogers, F. H. (2006). Missing in action: Teacher and health worker absence in developing countries. *The Journal of Economic Perspectives, 20*(1), 91–116.

Chung Beth, G., & Schneider, B. (2002). Serving multiple masters: role conflict experienced by service employees. *Journal of Services Marketing, 16*(1), 70–87. https://doi.org/10.1108/08876040210419424

Conway, N., & Briner, R. B. (2002). Full-time versus part-time employees: Understanding the links between work status, the psychological contract, and attitudes. *Journal of Vocational Behavior, 61*(2), 279–301. https://doi.org/10.1006/jvbe.2001.1857

Crawfurd, L. (2017). School management and public–private partnerships in Uganda. *Journal of African Economies, 26*(5), 539–560. https://doi.org/10.1093/jae/ejx021

Creswell, J. W., & Poth, C. N. (2017). *Qualitative inquiry and research design: Choosing among five approaches* (2nd ed.). SAGE Publications.

Dagher, R. (2019). Policy space under a constraining combination—Open economies, austerity and small island states. *Third World Quarterly, 40*(6), 1040–1063. https://doi.org/10.1080/01436597.2019.1574563

Dahling, J. J. (2012). Breaking rules for the right reasons? An investigation of pro-social rule breaking. *Journal of Organizational Behavior, 33*(1), 21–42. https://doi.org/10.1002/job.730

Day, C. R. (2019). "Survival mode": Rebel resilience and the Lord's Resistance Army. *Terrorism and Political Violence, 31*(5), 966–986. https://doi.org/10.1080/09546553.2017.1300580

DeCuir-Gunby, J. T., Marshall, P. L., & McCulloch, A. W. (2011). Developing and using a codebook for the analysis of interview data: An example from a professional development research project. *Field methods, 23*(2), 136–155.

Ellis, F., & Bahiigwa, G. (2003). Livelihoods and rural poverty reduction in Uganda. *World Development, 31*(6), 997–1013. https://doi.org/10.1016/S0305-750X(03)00043-3

Engel, M., Cannata, M., & Curran, F. C. (2018). Principal influence in teacher hiring: Documenting decentralization over time. *Journal of Educational Administration, 56*(3), 277–296. https://doi.org/10.1108/JEA-05-2017-0061

Fowler, D. J. (2010). The ethics of educational leadership. *Academic Leadership: The Online Journal, 8*(3), Article 45. https://scholars.fhsu.edu/alj/vol8/iss3/45

Fowler, D. J., Edwards, R., & Hsu, H.-Y. (2018). An investigation of state superintendents in the United States: Ethical leadership perspectives, state leader demographics, and state education characteristics. *Athens Journal of Education, 5*(3), 209–246. https://doi.org/10.30958/aje.5-3-1

Fowler, D. J., & Jouganatos, S. M. (2020). Leadership practices for supporting equity in the PreK–12 educational setting. In R. Papa (Ed.), *Handbook on promoting social justice in education* (pp. 399–411). Springer International Publishing.

Fullan, M. (2000). The role of the principal in school reform. *Occasional Paper Series, 6*(2), 1–24.

Gibbs, G. R. (2007). *Analysing qualitative data* (U. Flick, Ed; 2nd ed.). SAGE Publications.

Goodwin, R. H., Cunningham, M. L., & Eagle, T. (2005). The changing role of the secondary principal in the United States: An historical perspective. *Journal of Educational Administration and History, 37*(1), 1–17. https://doi.org/10.1080/0022062042000336046

Gore, C. (2009). Electricity and privatisation in Uganda: The origins of the crisis and problems with the response. In D. MacDonald (Ed.), *Electric capitalism: Recolonising Africa on the power grid* (pp. 359–399). HSRC Press.

Gronn, P. (2000). Distributed properties: A new architecture for leadership. *Educational Management and Administration, 28*(3), 317–338. https://doi.org/10.1177/0263211X000283006

Guest, G., MacQueen, K. M., & Namey, E. E. (2011). *Applied thematic analysis.* SAGE Publications.

Hallinger, P. (2017). Surfacing a hidden literature: A systematic review of research on educational leadership and management in Africa. *Educational Management Administration & Leadership, 46*(3), 362–384. https://doi.org/10.1177/1741143217694895

Higgins, L., & Rwanyange, R. (2005). Ownership in the education reform process in Uganda. *Compare: A Journal of Comparative and International Education, 35*(1), 7–26. https://doi.org/10.1080/03057920500033464

Huff, J., Preston, C., Goldring, E., & Guthrie, J. E. (2018). Learning-centered leadership practices for effective high schools serving at-risk students. *Teachers College Record, 120*(9), 1–38.

Hughes, A. L., Matt, J. J., & O'Reilly, F. L. (2015). Principal support is imperative to the retention of teachers in hard-to-staff schools. *Journal of Education and Training Studies, 3*(1), 129–134. https://doi.org/10.11114/jets.v3i1.622

Huylebroeck, L., & Titeca, K. (2008). Universal secondary education (USE) in Uganda: Blessing or curse? The impact of USE on educational attainment and performance. *Journal of Educational Development, 28*, 161–175.

Kabatereine, N. B., Standley, C. J., Sousa-Figueiredo, J. C., Fleming, F. M., Stothard, J. R., Talisuna, A., & Fenwick, A. (2011). Integrated prevalence mapping of schistosomiasis, soil-transmitted helminthiasis and malaria in lakeside and island communities in Lake Victoria, Uganda. *Parasites & Vectors, 4*(1), Article 232. https://doi.org/10.1186/1756-3305-4-232

Kafka, J. (2009). The principalship in historical perspective. *Peabody Journal of Education, 84*(3), 318–330. https://doi.org/10.1080/01619560902973506

Kelly, N., & Fogarty, R. (2015). An integrated approach to attracting and retaining teachers in rural and remote parts of Australia. *Journal of Economic & Social Policy, 17*(2), 1–19.

Leithwood, K., Harris, A., & Hopkins, D. (2020). Seven strong claims about successful school leadership revisited. *School Leadership & Management, 40*(1), 5–22. https://doi.org/10.1080/13632434.2019.1596077

Lester, S. W., Turnley, W. H., Bloodgood, J. M., & Bolino, M. C. (2002). Not seeing eye to eye: Differences in supervisor and subordinate perceptions of and attributions for psychological contract breach. *Journal of Organizational Behavior, 23*(1), 39–56. https://doi.org/10.1002/job.126

MacBeath, J. (1998). Seven selected heresies of leadership. In J. MacBeath (Ed.), *Effective school leadership: Responding to change* (pp. 1–19). Paul Chapman Publishing Ltd.

MacBeath, J. (2008). Stories of compliance and subversion in a prescriptive policy environment. *Educational Management Administration & Leadership, 36*(1), 123–148. https://doi.org/10.1177/1741143207084064

MacBeath, J. (2009). Recruitment and retention of senior school leaders: Meeting the challenge. *European Educational Research Journal, 8*(3), 407–417. https://doi.org/10.2304/eerj.2009.8.3.407

Mahoney, P., MacBeath, J., & Moos, L. (1998). Who really runs the school? In J. MacBeath (Ed.), *Effective school leadership: Responding to change* (pp. 112–124). Paul Chapman Publishing Ltd.

Mestry, R. (2018). The role of governing bodies in the management of financial resources in South African no-fee public schools. *Educational Management Administration & Leadership, 46*(3), 385–400. https://doi.org/10.1177/1741143216665838

Ministry of Education. (2014). *Teacher issues in Uganda: A shared vision for an effective teachers policy.* UNESCO. https://unesdoc.unesco.org/ark:/48223/pf0000229777

Ministry of Public Service. (2010). *Payment of the hardship allowance in the public service.* Ministry of Public Service. https://www.publicservice.go.ug/policy?page=1

Ministry of Public Service. (2019). *Public service salary structure for 2019–2020. Kampala, Uganda.* https://publicservice.go.ug/download/public-service-salary-structure-for-fy-2019-2020-pages-1-9/

Muwagga, A. M., Genza, G. M., & Ssemulya, R. (2013). School leadership and denominational identity: The case of Roman Catholic-founded schools in

Uganda. *American Journal of Educational Research, 1*(8), 327–333. https://doi.org/10.12691/education-1-8-10

Namubiru, L. (2017). *UCE results by school 2011–2016.* http://catalog.data.ug/dataset/uce-school-results-2011-2016

Namusoke, K. S., Akulume, M., Tetui, M., Muhumuza, K. R., Bua, J., & Ekirapa, K., Elizabeth. (2017). Balancing the cost of leaving with the cost of living: Drivers of long-term retention of health workers: An explorative study in three rural districts in eastern Uganda. *Global Health Action, 10*(sup4), 60–70. https://doi.org/10.1080/16549716.2017.1345494

Omoeva, C., & Gale, C. (2016). Universal, but not free: Household schooling costs and equity effects of Uganda's universal secondary education policy. *International Journal of Educational Development, 50*(C), 41–50.

Pérezts, M., Bouilloud, J.-P., & Gaulejac, d. V. (2011). Serving two masters: The contradictory organization as an ethical challenge for managerial responsibility. *Journal of Business Ethics, 101*(1), 33–44. https://doi.org/10.1007/s10551-011-1176-3

Player, D., Youngs, P., Perrone, F., & Grogan, E. (2017). How principal leadership and person-job fit are associated with teacher mobility and attrition. *Teaching and Teacher Education, 67,* 330–339. https://doi.org/10.1016/j.tate.2017.06.017

Preston, C., Goldring, E., Guthrie, J. E., Ramsey, R., & Huff, J. (2017). Conceptualizing essential components of effective high schools. *Leadership and Policy in Schools, 16*(4), 525–562. https://doi.org/10.1080/15700763.2016.1205198

Pugatch, T., & Schroeder, E. (2014). Incentives for teacher relocation: Evidence from the Gambian hardship allowance. *Economics of Education Review, 41,* 120–136. https://doi.org/10.1016/j.econedurev.2014.04.003

Ridder, H.-G. (2017). The theory contribution of case study research designs. *Business Research, 10*(2), 281–305. https://doi.org/10.1007/s40685-017-0045-z

Ritchie, J., Lewis, J., & Elam, G. (2003). *Designing and selecting samples.* SAGE Publications.

Robinson, O. C. (2014). Sampling in interview-based qualitative research: A theoretical and practical guide. *Qualitative Research in Psychology, 11*(1), 25–41. https://doi.org/10.1080/14780887.2013.801543

Rohayati, M. I., Najdi, Y., & Williamson, J. C. (2016). Philanthropic fundraising of higher education institutions: A review of the Malaysian and Australian perspectives. *Sustainability, 8*(6), 541.

Sausman, C., Oborn, E., & Barrett, M. (2016). Policy translation through localisation: Implementing national policy in the UK. *Policy & Politics, 44*(4), 563–589. https://doi.org/10.1332/030557315X14298807527143

Skelton, C., Carrington, B., Francis, B., Hutchings, M., Read, B., & Hall, I. (2009). Gender 'matters' in the primary classroom: Pupils' and teachers' perspectives. *British Educational Research Journal, 35*(2), 187–204. https://doi.org/10.1080/01411920802041905

Ssekamwa, J. C. (1997). *History and development of education in Uganda.* Fountain Publishers Limited.

Suri, H. (2011). Purposeful sampling in qualitative research synthesis. *Qualitative Research Journal, 11*(2), 63–75. https://doi.org/10.3316/QRJ1102063

Thompson, G., Hogan, A., & Rahimi, M. (2019). Private funding in Australian public schools: a problem of equity. *The Australian Educational Researcher, 46*(2), 1–18.

Uganda Education Act. (2008). *The Education (pre-primary, primary and post-primary) Act, 2008.* Government of Uganda. http://www.unesco.org/education/edurights/media/docs/5d1b721a509097c2833561341ead3d788906cf4a.pdf

UNICEF. (2014). *The impact of incentives for the recruitment and retention of qualified teachers in Namibia's remote schools.* https://docplayer.net/23946952-The-impact-of-incentives-for-the-recruitment-and-retention-of-qualified-teachers-in-namibia-s-remote-schools.html

Wilder, K. M., Collier, J. E., & Barnes, D. C. (2014). Tailoring to customers' needs: Understanding how to promote an adaptive service experience with frontline employees. *Journal of Service Research, 17*(4), 446–459. https://doi.org/10.1177/1094670514530043

Yin, R. K. (2014). *Case study research: Design and methods* (5th ed.). SAGE Publications.

CHAPTER 19

# DISTRIBUTED LEADERSHIP IN TANZANIAN SECONDARY SCHOOLS

## A Systematic Literature Review

**Revocatus C. Kuluchumila**

### ABSTRACT

The book chapter aimed at exploring distributed leadership in Tanzanian secondary schools, it adopted the systematic literature review model. The search engines and other sources on distributed leadership came up with 100 articles. About fulfilment of school instructional objectives, findings revealed that distributed leadership was directly linked to attainment of instructional objectives. However, some researchers suggested that hierarchical leadership limited accomplishment of their schools' instructional objectives. About school climate, findings indicated the subsequent components linked to distributed leadership: teachers' appreciation by heads; teachers' empowerment; transparent and communicative school leadership. Nevertheless, several researchers showed inadequacy of school infrastructure, particularly classrooms, toilets, and utilities. The connection between distributed leadership

*On Leadership*, pages 351–376

and procurement and/or distribution of resources was also looked at. Findings revealed that school board members in various secondary schools lacked information to assist them participate in making sound decisions, for instance planning. The last but one aspect was on supporting teachers' growth and development and how it is linked to distributed leadership. Findings revealed teachers being happy with the facilitation led by their fellow teachers (the potentiality of informal leadership). Regarding ICT competence, both school heads and teachers needed support from higher education authorities. However, findings revealed that teachers were more satisfied with mentorship from their heads. Lastly, about school culture, findings revealed that both school heads and teachers had limited knowledge about schools' cultural symbols. It was generally concluded that, Tanzanian secondary schools might benefit greatly in continuing moving from top-down leadership style and give much attention to distributed leadership.

*Distributed leadership* is defined by Harris (2013) as "actively brokering, facilitating, and supporting the leadership of others" (p. 546). In this definition, Harris basically describes distributed leadership as the leadership style which involves others. That is, leadership practice is stretched to even those who are not in the leadership hierarchy. In the school organization context, distributed leadership simply refers to the process of mobilizing leadership knowledge, skills and competence at all levels in the school in order to generate more opportunities for change and to build the capacity for improvement. Therefore, distributed leadership is a leadership style where responsibilities and leadership actions are shared amongst various personnel. In schools as other organizations, Spillane and colleagues describe distributed leadership as the leadership style which has two aspects: "the leader-plus aspect and the practice aspect" (Spillane et al., 2009, p. 49). The leader-plus aspect is about leading and managing schools through engaging multiple individuals, in formal and informal hierarchies. Whereas the leadership practice aspect focuses on the action of leading and managing. For this reason, the leadership practice aspect does not focus on leaders or what is done by leaders, rather on leadership activity (Spillane et al., 2004, p. 10). Leadership activity is simply defined by the interactions of school leaders, followers, and the situation or context and all elements depend on each other. This basically means that leadership practice is constituted in the interaction of all three elements as shown in Figure 19.1.

Furthermore, Spillane and colleagues illustrate the concept of the situation as social-cultural context which includes: artifacts (e.g., forms, memos, curricular documents, tools for representing test scores, and meeting agenda), language, and organizational structure (Spillane et al., 2004, p. 11). In another article, Spillane (2006) emphasizes, "Distributed leadership encompasses both formal and informal forms of leadership practice within its framing, analysis, and interpretation" (p. 58). Leithwood et al. (2009, p. 13) also

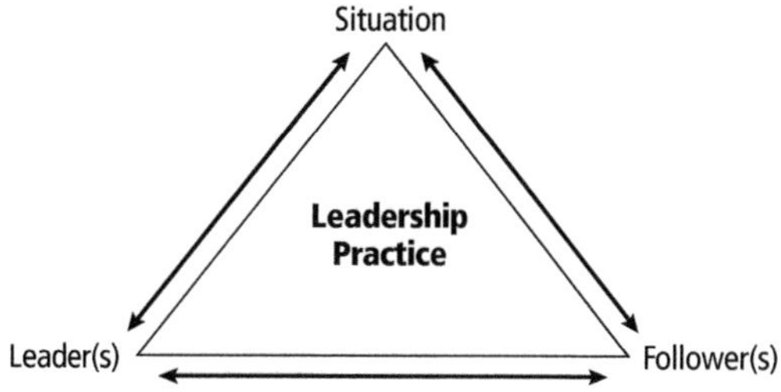


**Figure 19.1** Elements of leadership practice. *Source:* Adopted from Spillane, Halverson, & Diamond (2004, p. 11).

assert that formal and informal leadership in the organization do co-exist and are inter-related. Harris (2013) also asserts, "Formal and informal leadership are not incompatible or oppositional... but are rather different parts of leadership practice" (p. 546). MacBeath et al. (2003) as well acknowledge that distributed leadership gives a room for all members of staff in the given organization to participate in leadership responsibilities (p. 13).

The concept of distributed leadership in various earlier literatures to a certain extent is equated to shared, collaborative, democratic, collective, and participative leadership styles (see Delgado, 2014, p. 2; Kilicoglu, 2018, p. 7; Spillane & Sherer, 2004, p. 2). Furthermore, the recent literature by Kilicoglu, affirms a strong connection between democratic leadership and distribution of leadership functions (Kilicoglu, 2018, p. 7). However, Spillane (2005, p. 149) does not support that democratic leadership, team leadership, and shared leadership are synonymous for distributed leadership. The reason behind that is teams do not automatically possess authority or leadership and teamwork does not necessarily involve a distributed leadership perspective, since teams can function hierarchically and be run undemocratically (Heikka et al., 2013, p. 34). But, in another literature, Spillane (2006, p. 6) acknowledges distributed leadership as a diagnostic tool for studying leadership. According to Harris and Spillane (2008), "Within distributed leadership literature, the emphasis is on leadership practice rather than on leadership roles and it is the nature and quality of leadership practice that matters" (pp. 52–53).

Gkoros (2021, p. 96) describes five dimensions necessary for implementing distributed leadership in an organization as illustrated in Figure 19.2. The five dimensions include: distributed leadership emanates from the school leadership (leaders influence distributed leadership among members of staff); distributed leadership depends on flexibility, absence of conflict, and precision-planned practice; distributed leadership could be effective through building members of staff leadership skills, trust that allows collective decision-making; building trust between leadership and followers

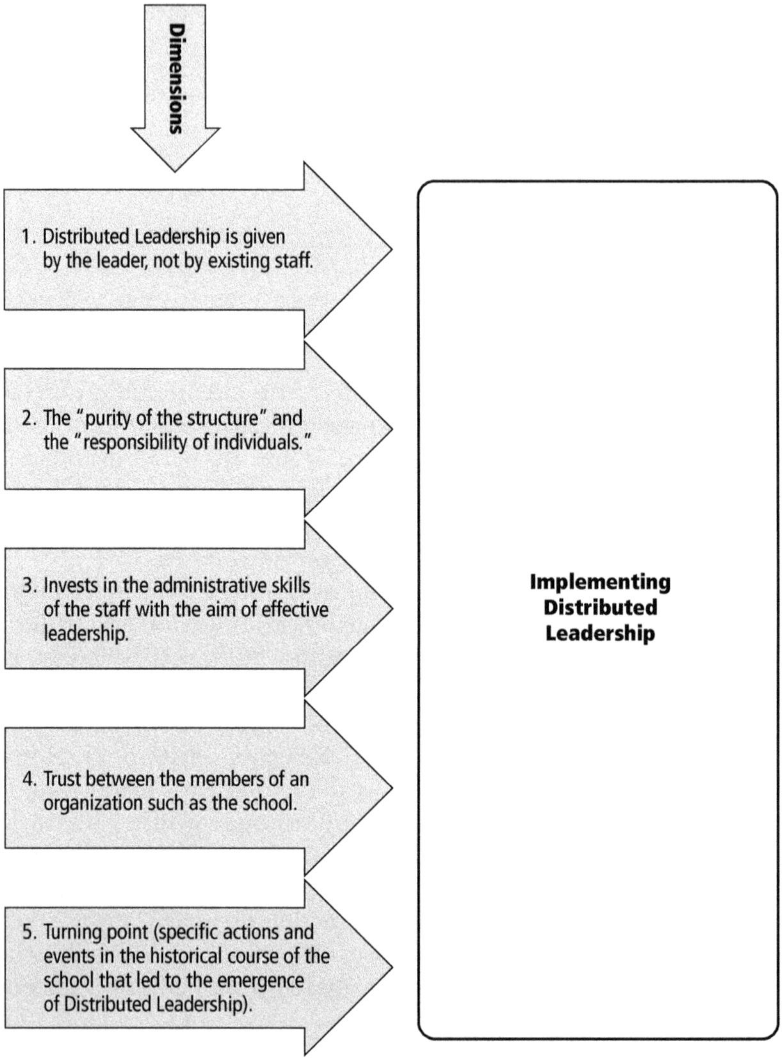


**Figure 19.2** Distributed leadership dimensions. Source: Adapted from Gkoros (2021, p. 96).

and trust among followers is inevitable for success of distributed leadership; and consideration of historical school's contextual factors which brought distributed leadership is as well inevitable.

Few research projects conducted in Tanzania show in some way that distributed leadership is practiced in Tanzanian schools. For instance, the recent research carried out by Boniface (2019, p. 176) revealed that teachers living in remote areas valued so much the act of being involved in building a friendly school working environment. In the different research, however, findings scarcely revealed a fair connection between distributed leadership and teachers' performance (Aunga & Masare, 2017, p. 49).

Earlier, several studies were done outside of Africa to establish the connection between distributed leadership and students' academic achievement. That is, the efficacy for adopting distributed leadership in relation to learners' achievement and school effectiveness. The research by Sheppard and Dibbon, for example, revealed a 55% positive trend on how teachers, school heads, assistant heads, and other education stakeholders, parents, and the community focused on student learning (Sheppard & Dibbon, 2010, as cited in Sheppard et al., 2010, p. 3).

The present systematic literature review (SLR) explores distributed leadership in Tanzanian schools basing on key leadership functions (the leadership practice aspect) namely: Fulfilment of school instructional objectives; managing and developing school culture; procuring and distributing resources; supporting teachers' growth and development; and establishing a school climate.

## THE RESEARCH QUESTION

The present desk research therefore, aimed to establish how and the extent to which school leadership in several secondary schools in Tanzania is distributed under following school functions: fulfilling school instructional objectives; establishing a school climate; procuring and distributing resources; supporting teachers' growth and development; and managing and developing school culture.

## METHODOLOGY

The present desk research adapted pragmatism as a research paradigm. The benefit attached to pragmatism is that it uses whatsoever combinations to work to help the researcher to attain his/her epistemological justification status (Dewey, 1938/1998, p. 161). Furthermore, the desk research used a SLR method. The benefits of SLR include: It is objective, systematic, and transparent, and likewise, it is replicable. Moreover, the SLR features transparency, clarity, equality, and accessibility, it is unified and focused (Thorpe et al., 2006, p. 258). The SLR as well assists the researcher to pinpoint major themes from different literature so as they can be viewed holistically (Pittaway & Coope, 2007, pp. 4–5). The steps taken in this SLR included:

1. Identifying academic bases: Academic bases identified include Google Scholar, SSRN, ERIC, and Opendoar.org/Directory of Open-Access Repositories website.
2. Journal articles related to distributed leadership and/or key terms attached to leadership functions were sought from given search engines.
3. Both published and unpublished articles and/or theses and dissertations from university repositories were sought.
4. Published and unpublished articles and/or theses and dissertations were reviewed and evaluated.
5. Relations, contradictions, gaps, and inconsistencies in the literature (e.g., by proposing a new conceptualisation or theory which accounts for the inconsistency) were explored and identified.
6. Formulation of general statements or an overarching conceptualisation was done.
7. Comments were done to substantiate the arguments raised in the researched sources.
8. Directions for future research were done.

In the present research, searching for resources used the subsequent review question: How and to what extent is school leadership in several secondary schools in Tanzania distributed? The subsequent phrases under school functions as aligned to distributed leadership were also used in the searching process: fulfilling school instructional objectives, managing and developing school culture, procuring and distributing resources, supporting teachers' growth and development, and establishing a school climate. Moreover, the subsequent terms were used in the search: leadership, distributed leadership, shared leadership, collaborative, democratic leadership, collective leadership, participative leadership, school culture, school climate, school environment, procurement and distribution process, teachers' development, teachers' growth, teachers' professional growth in Tanzanian secondary schools.

The searches from Google Scholar, SSRN, ERIC, and Opendoar.org (https://www.jisc.ac.uk/opendoar) resulted in 100 articles and other sources on distributed leadership and/or related terms. The number of published sources which met the inclusion criteria was 73. The unpublished dissertations and/or research and other sources found were 27; all were included in the review.

## RESULTS

The subsequent sub-headings guided the presentation of results in connection to distributed leadership functions: Distributed leadership and school instructional objectives; distributed leadership and school climate; distributed leadership and procuring and distributing resources; distributed leadership and supporting teachers' growth and development; and distributed leadership and developing school culture.

## Distributed Leadership and School Instructional Objectives

Meeting school instructional objectives is one of the prime aims of any educational institution simply because it describes that learning is taking place. An instructional objective is a statement that will describe what the learner will be able to do after completing the instruction. That is, instructional objectives are specific, measurable, short-term, and observable students' behaviors. Thus, instructional objectives indicate the desirable knowledge, skills, or attitudes to be gained by the learners. This means, planning for teaching needs to meet the needs of the three learning domains namely, cognitive domain for knowledge, affective domain for attitudes, and psychomotor domain for skills. Dooley et al. (2006) emphasize "an instructional objective is a statement describing a proposed 'change' of what the learner can do when (s)he has successfully completed a learning experience" (p. 1). Instructional objectives need to be specific, measurable, attainable, relevant, and timed bound (SMART).

Schools are meant to fulfil the teaching and learning process so as to come up with learned individuals and school leadership needs to ensure that all students learn and not just go to school. In fact, learning happens when a learner changes his/her behavior. That is, what the learner is able to do. For example, when a teacher teaches a swimming skill, the learner(s) should be able to swim; when a teacher teaches his/her students to write a poem, we can say that learning has taken place if the learners are able to construct a poem; and if learners are taught principles for writing an essay, they should be able to use taught principles to write an essay. Moreover, if learners are taught how to ride a bicycle, we can describe that learning has taken place if those learners are able to ride a bicycle.

Several studies have attempted to show the extent to which school leadership in Tanzanian secondary schools is working collaboratively (a component of distributed leadership) with teachers and non-teaching staff to ensure learning takes place, that is, teaching is changing learner's behaviors. For instance, a study carried in Arusha revealed how school leadership involved teachers in decision-making, and the act of involving teachers contributed to good academic performance of their students (Aunga & Masare, 2017, p. 50). Another research by Maige as well indicated teachers' job satisfaction and effective commitment resulted from being involved in school leadership (Maige, 2016, p. 33). Earlier, a different research by Urio (2012, para. 1) too acknowledged distributed leadership as one of the influencing factors for good academic performance.

One more study by Felician (2013, para. 1), the study was carried out in Kilombero district in Tanzania. The researcher investigated the influence of teacher's participation in decision-making on their job performance in public secondary schools. The research findings showed vividly that secondary school teachers enjoyed active participation in decision-making processes. Findings from Felician's research as well revealed the likelihood of fulfilment of instructional objectives through distributed leadership in connection to good learners' outcome (para. 1). Moreover, findings in Felician's research (2013, para. 1) showed that teachers' day-to-day participation in the leadership increased their experiences. The research results further revealed teachers' participation in the leadership activities reduced boredom, disappointments and enhanced their work commitment, job satisfaction, and efficiency.

On the contrary, the different researcher, who carried out a study in Mpwapwa district, Tanzania, found autocratic leadership causing a negative contribution towards schools' achievement (Camara, 2014, para. 1). It is more likely that autocratic leadership is to a great extent linked to solo leadership, and solo leadership contradicts distributed leadership. Solo leadership is also described by Mgani (2013, para. 1), and Chua and Mosha (2015, p. 6), whereby a large proportion of teachers were not aware of school vision, mission, and school goals. However, research findings in Komba (2015), the research which was carried out in Tanzania, indicated the existence of distributed leadership in the form of participatory leadership as follows: "Teachers were involved in decision-making and decentralization and delegation of duties was done by school leadership" (para. 1). Nevertheless, it should be known that decentralization and delegation of duties is not linked to distributed leadership, this is a stretch of top–down leadership style. The findings further indicated participatory style of leadership being a catalyst for teachers' performance in their day-to-day teaching and learning activities (Komba, 2015, para. 1).

One more researcher, Manaseh (2016, p. 5), investigated at length the various ways heads of school managed instructional programs in their respective schools in Tanzania. Findings showed that instructional programs were not well managed because head of departments were poorly involved in curriculum coordination. In addition, results showed that subjects' syllabi were not covered because of poor coordination. The research by Manaseh supports what was found in researches by Camara (2014, para. 1), Mgani (2013, para. 1), and Chua and Mosha (2015, p. 6) whereby dominance of solo leadership led to ineffective learning due to failure of meeting instructional objectives.

In the different research conducted in Tabora municipality by Kambambovu (2018), findings revealed that "democratic leadership style mostly influenced students' academic achievement" (p. 34). In Kambambovu's research, one of the components of distributed leadership, namely, consultation, triggered the school's achievement because the majority of teachers were happy to be consulted by their school heads before making decisions. Kambambovu's research is similar to that of Raphael (2011, para. 1), Justus (2013, para. 1), Hassan (2014, para. 1), and Aunga and Masare (2017, p. 50) who as well found that teachers were happy with style of school leadership, the leadership style which involves other members of staff. Kilicoglu emphasises, "In schools where democratic approaches are embraced, all school members engage to work as a team in the decision-making, implementation, or monitoring processes, and sense of ownership is developed with the participation of all school members" (Kilicoglu, 2018, p. 7). Moreover, Kilicoglu (2018, p. 7) quoting Delgado (2014), acknowledges that distributed leadership fits well within the democratic and collective approaches to leadership.

## Distributed Leadership and School Climate

The literature by Thapa et al. (2013) describes school climate as "based on patterns of people's experiences of school life and reflects norms, goals, values, interpersonal relationships, teaching, and learning practices, and organizational structures" (p. 2). Mkumbo (2013, para. 1) mentions various elements of school climate namely safety, relationships, teaching and learning, institutional environment, motivation of students to learn, and parents involvement in school activities. Cohen et al. (2009, p. 184) also enumerate a number of features of school climate which are similar to that of Thapa and colleagues and those of Mkumbo. The characteristics of school climate mentioned by Cohen and colleagues (2009, p. 184) include: students' and teachers' perceptions of their school environment; the school's personality factors, environmental factors (such as the physical buildings and classrooms, and materials used for instruction); academic performance; feelings of safeness and school size; and feelings of trust and respect for students and teachers as illustrated in Figure 19.3.

School climate is also termed as school environment; however school climate is not the same as school culture. According to Dernowska (2014a) and Tłuściak-Deliowska (2014), as quoted in Dernowska (2017, p. 65), school culture and climate have similar characteristics, however school climate is concerned with the process and style of a school's organizational life while school culture is concerned with content and substances of the school organization. According to Sergiovanni, "climate, more than culture, is

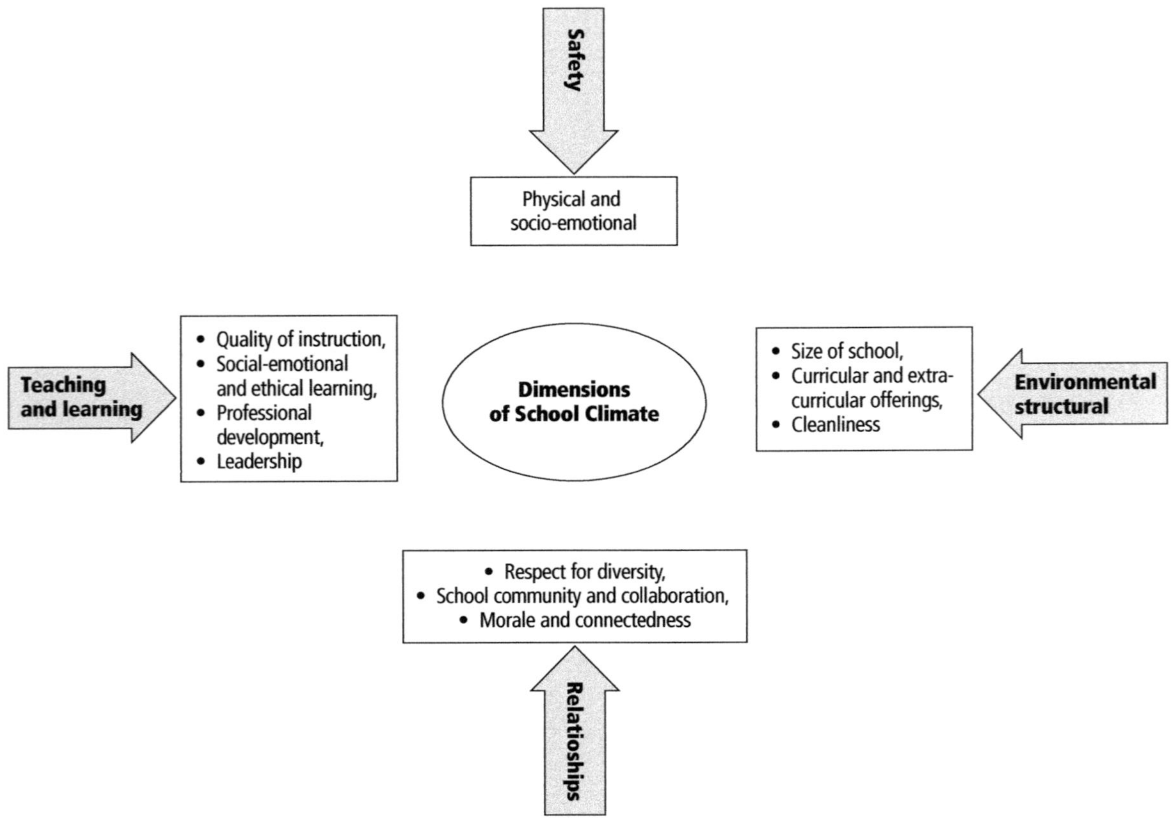


**Figure 19.3** School climate. *Source:* Adapted from Cohen, McCabe, Michelli, & Pickeral (2009, p. 184).

interpersonal in tone and is manifested in the attitudes and behaviours of teachers, students, supervisors and principals at work..."(Sergiovanni, 1991 cited in Dernowska, 2017, p. 56 ). Hoy and Feldman (1999) quoted by Dernowska (2017, p. 56) distinguish culture from climate as follows: "Culture (are shared norms) and climate (are shared perceptions)."

A number of researches have been carried out in Tanzanian schools attempting to describe and show the connection between distributed leadership and school climate. One of these researches was conducted by Mkumbo (2013, para. 1). Research findings revealed that the large percent (73.1%) of teachers agreed to be recognized by the school authority. This basically means that the school administration valued the teachers' contribution, that is, the school administration–teachers relationship was positive in nature. It can be argued that, the school heads valuing what teachers are doing (teachers' actions) is connected to distributed leadership, and this is the leadership practice aspect advocated by Spillane et al. (2004, p. 11).

Chachage et al. (2019) studied the issue of educational caring (an element of school climate) in primary schools in Tanzania. The study was done in a primary school environment, but findings could shed much light in secondary school settings because the environmental factors in the two settings in Tanzanian context are somehow similar. One of research objectives, in Chachage and colleagues' study was to establish the extent to which school leadership met various needs of teachers (p. 41) including: requirement for teachers to be empowered so as to solve various problems in schools, and the necessitate for educational caring so as to improve teachers' education, and policy planning for quality education in schools. Regarding educational caring, research findings revealed that the head teachers needed monitoring, instilling, and facilitating positive teacher–student relationships (p. 50). For instance, one respondent said, "As a head teacher... the way you handle students, should not be the way you handle the teachers" (p. 50). The research findings emphasize the importance of distributed leadership in view of accountability, expectations, and professionalism as they differ when you consider students as opposed to teachers. However, in Chachage and colleagues' research, the school leadership is viewed having the key role of effecting and enhancing the relationship, which brings in features of top–down approach of leadership.

School climate and its influence on learners' academic performance is as well looked at by other researchers in Tanzania. For example, Nkuba and Massomo (2019, para. 1) did the study in several secondary schools available in Morogoro, Tanzania. One of the elements looked at was the influence of school heads towards learners' achievement. Findings indicated the following: "The subtests of headmaster/mistress influence and academic emphasis both indicated a strong significant ($r = 0.848$ and $r = 0.860$) correlations with division I and II, respectively" (para. 1). The findings from

Nkuba and Massomo's research suggests that wherever school heads are transparent and communicative to members of staff about school plans, there is a strong possibility of getting much support consequently leads to fulfilment of school plans and obtaining good students' academic outcomes, that is, most of the learners can achieve Division I (first class) and Division II (second class) in their final examinations.

Another study that relates distributed leadership research and school climate was carried out by Katera and Msafiri (2020). The study was commissioned by Poverty Alleviation (REPOA), a not-for-profit organization together with the World Bank. It was a service delivery indicator (SDI) survey carried out between 2014 and 2017 in Tanzanian primary schools. Research findings showed that, in terms of school infrastructure (electricity, water, and sanitation), 44% of schools met the required minimum infrastructure. A half of the schools, that is, 54% owned toilets meeting the standard, but teachers shared toilets with pupils. Furthermore, in total, less than 61% of the schools visited for the research owned private toilets for teachers (Katera & Msafiri, 2020, pp. 3–4).

The research findings by Katera and Msafiri (2020, p. 3–4) indicate that many primary schools fail to meet the minimum standard of safety for teachers and students. These research findings could shed much light on what is available in Tanzanian secondary schools because the situation is not very different in secondary schools when compared to what is available in primary schools. The similar research recently carried out by Lyanga and Ming-kun in several secondary schools available in Bukoba Tanzania showed that an increase in number of students in secondary schools because of fee-free education led to a big shortage of classrooms (Lyanga & Ming-kun, 2020, p. 44). The pertinent question which could be raised is to what extent school leadership involved teachers and the community to solve the mentioned shortages. It is most likely that heads relied on government to respond to the mentioned limitations.

The study carried out by Lauwo and Mkulu (2021, p. 80) highlights poor leadership as one of the factors limiting involvement of the community so as to improve the educational quality of community secondary schools in Meru district in Tanzania. Inadequacy and/or failure to involve other members of staff in school leadership is not connected to distributed school leadership. Generally, in the reviewed studies, the subsequent components of school climate are inadequately present and do not directly indicate the linkage to distributed leadership: environmental factors such as the physical buildings and classrooms (few classrooms and toilets), and interpersonal relationships (little involvement of teachers and the community).

## Distributed Leadership and Procuring and/or Distributing Resources

Purchase, storage, and distribution of supplies and equipment are several of the key functions of the school heads in Tanzania. According to Babyegeya (2002, p. 182), the school administrator does the purchasing, storage, and distribution of instructional materials. Babyegeya further mentions that the school bursar, the store keeper, and the secretaries have a responsibility for ordering or purchasing storage and distribution of the instructional materials on behalf of the school heads. Thus, ordering, purchasing, storage responsibility is delegated to the support staff. Nevertheless, accountability for finance, purchased materials and equipment remains in the hands of the head of schools. It is well known that delegation of responsibilities is not linked to distributed leadership. Delegation of responsibilities is just extending leadership responsibilities, while the leader maintains authority. Now the pertinent question which can be raised is how the purchase and distribution function is shared among members of staff in secondary schools available in Tanzania?

Several studies have been carried out in Tanzania which attempted to make a connection between distributed leadership and procuring and distributing resources. One research was carried out by Masue and Askvik (2016) and the study focused on school committees. School committees may empower school leadership, teachers, and parents/guardians on finance and procurement matters. Findings revealed that school committees empowered school members in many areas including expenditure decisions, procurement of books and stationery (Masue & Askvik, 2016, p. 7). That is, school committees involved the school leadership and other members of staff in making decisions; this is one of the elements of distributed leadership. Despite the fact that the school committees' work in primary schools, still the findings might shed light to what is done in Tanzanian secondary schools, where school boards (top school authorities) are available. School boards are more similar to school committees in composition and their role. In fact, a school committee is a structure of authority in primary schools, while school board is a structure of authority in secondary schools. Furthermore, findings revealed that school committees involved parents and/or guardians in making decisions including making decisions on expenditure, choice, and procurement of books, and giving contracts (Masue & Askvik, 2016).

The different research was carried out in Moshi Rural District Council and Hai District Council by Maeda. The study aimed at establishing how the school boards' empowerment contributed to accomplishment of their role. Findings revealed that the school board members lacked key information to help them participate in making schools' decisions like planning

(Maeda, 2021, p. 166). Absence of information among members of school boards most likely limited their ability to perform their duties including making decisions on procurement. Moreover, lack of information most likely limited their ability to share responsibilities among themselves; they just worked as symbolic representatives.

Muhoja and Mkulu (2020) also conducted research in several public secondary schools available in Monduli district, Arusha region in Tanzania. Their research aimed to establish challenges facing heads of schools in performing procurement activities (para. 1). Findings revealed some of the limiting factors to procurement including, lack of procurement personnel, inadequate knowledge, skills and experience on procurement, insufficient funds, political interference, and favoritism and nepotism (Muhoja & Mkulu, 2020, para. 1). Examining closely to the challenges, many of them are directly connected to top–down style leadership existing in Tanzanian schools. For instance, in many secondary schools, the heads do not delegate powers to procurement and distribution of purchases functions.

One more research in Tanzania was carried out by Mazigo, though not in education background, it revealed a huge existence of corruption in the procurement process. Findings showed that corruption largely occurred in the process of tender specification, selection stage, the bidding process, and at delivery and costing stage (Mazigo, 2104, para. 1). The study by Mazigo shed much light on the procurement process carried out in secondary schools, because the process is the same, particularly in all public undertakings including public owned schools. It can be deduced that lack of the distributed leadership style is leading to so much of the inappropriate practices during the procurement and distribution process in Tanzanian secondary schools.

## Distributed Leadership and Teachers' Growth and Development

Teachers' growth and development is connected to professional growth of teachers. In different parts of the world teachers are developed professionally. Teachers' growth and development process is commonly known as staff development, in-service, skills training, and/or continuing education (Bredeson, 2000, p. 386). Teachers' growth and development is about training. It is the process of providing teachers with specific knowledge and skill in order to enable them to perform specific work or tasks. Soleiman and Khaliliyan (2012) emphasize, "Professional development usually takes place after finishing formal training for the purpose of keeping up-to-date with advancements in different fields... professional development is a never-ending process, it is a continuous process" (p. 363). Avalos (2011) defines teacher professional development as "a process through which teachers... learn how to learn, and transform their knowledge, competences, and skills into practice for benefit of their students' growth" (p. 10).

The common categories of teachers' professional growth and development in Tanzania include on-the-job training and off-the-job training. Under the on-the-job training, teachers learn various aspects of the job while at the same time actually performing these tasks. Some of the on-the-job training methods include: apprenticeship, job rotation, mentoring, or coaching. The off-the-job training method is where workers undergo training outside of their work environments; these include special courses or classes.

Several researches reveal the connection between teachers' professional growth and distributed leadership in schools available in Tanzania. The research carried out by Swai and Glanfield (2018, p. 183), aimed to look at the position of mathematics teacher leaders (MTLs) on the teacher-led professional learning (TLPL) method. The study suggested TLPL to be encouraged as a method to assist teachers teaching mathematics so as to become responsible for their professional learning. The method is suggested because it is empowering mathematics teachers to become teacher leaders for themselves instead of depending entirely on those in authority (the educational officers or school heads). Research findings revealed further that teachers were content with the facilitation led by their fellow teachers (Swai & Glanfield, 2018, p. 186). Empowering teachers themselves to lead is one of the features of informal leadership, and this is one aspect of distributed leadership. In fact informal leadership is a component of distributed leadership (see Spillane, 2006, p. 58). It was concluded that the TLPL might enable teachers to lead and support the professional learning of mathematics teachers within their schools. The research findings from the different study conducted by Nyenyembe et al. (2016, p. 188) revealed that teachers were more satisfied with their job when their school heads work closely with them through mentorship. Heads working together with teachers basically describes the component of distributed leadership.

Another research on professional development of teachers, integration, and use of information and communication technology (ICT) in their pedagogy was carried out by Swarts and Mwiyeria (2010, p. 25). Findings revealed inadequacy on use of ICT facilities including computers, mobile phones, availability of radios, modems, tablets, printers, photocopiers, lamination machines, and fax machines in secondary schools. Furthermore, many secondary school teachers were not competent on the use of some ICT's facilities including computers and smartphones. This tool could assist them to improve their teaching process (Swarts & Mwiyeria, 2010, p. 28). Unfortunately, some teachers could not get support from school heads or their fellow teachers. Other research still show heads could not support

ICT illiterate teachers in terms of training and coaching because they were illiterate too (Kenyatta, 2017, para. 1; Mfaume, 2019, p. 161; Mwila, 2018, p. 32; Ndibalema, 2015, para. 1). This simply means that neither schools heads nor the teachers assist each other on the use of ICT in the teaching and learning process. The researchers concluded through requesting the government to train both the teachers and those in administration so as to be competent on integration and use of ICT in the school's curriculum. It should be borne in our minds that failure to raise one another through mentoring and peer coaching is not linked to distributed leadership.

The research findings from Komba and Nkumbi (2008, p. 75), although a dated study, indicated that teachers' professional growth was adequately supported by school leadership, for instance, teachers were involved in preparation of school plans. In addition, teachers acted as leaders/facilitators in professional growth of themselves. Furthermore, findings indicated that district education officers, inspectors, and ward education coordinators supported teachers' professional development through permitting teachers to participate in seminars. The leaders also occasionally conducted seminars, also sensitizing teachers to take initiative on upgrading themselves. Findings from a study carried out by Komba and Nkumbi (2008) vividly showed the practice of distributed leadership from low leadership hierarchy (school head) to higher leadership hierarchy (the district leadership), where teachers were involved to a large extent in their professional development and growth (pp. 75–76).

Contrary, the recent research carried out by Losioki (2020, p. 96) indicated patchy leadership support from government and stakeholders in terms of mentorship, peer coaching, and action research as some factors hindering professional development of teachers in Mkuranga Tanzania. Research findings revealed further that nearly half (42.9%) of the teachers mentioned lack of support as one of the factors limiting their professional development (Losioki, 2020, p. 96). Lack of appropriate support, overreliance on traditional approach (teaching when the need arises), unclear policy, and fragmented approaches on professional development of teachers are common features mostly linked to top–down leadership style (see Avalos, 2011, p. 15). Komba and Mwakabenga (2019) also criticized the model of teachers' professional development commonly practiced in Tanzania. They asserted that the teachers' professional growth and development is haphazardly done. Most teachers' professional growth and development is done when there are new introduced changes in the curriculum instead of being on a continuous basis (Komba & Mwakabenga, 2019, pp. 2–3).

## Distributed Leadership and School Culture

Schipper et al. (2020) describe school culture as "ethos and social environment in schools, consisting of the administrative and organisational structures and how these interact in order to promote (or constrain) teacher professional learning" (p. 5). According to Atasoy (2020), "The concept of school culture explains the character of school as it reflects deep patterns of values, beliefs and traditions that have been composed over time" (p. 258). School culture consists of norms, values, beliefs, ceremonies, rituals, traditions, and myths understood by principals, teachers, students, and other stakeholders of the school community (Atasoy, 2020, p. 258, citing Stolp & Smith, 1994). Atasoy emphasises that, school leadership style shapes culture and culture affects leadership (p. 258). This could simply mean that, in the schools where distributed leadership is dominantly practiced, inevitably, school leaders in that particular school, the culture practiced will be to encourage sharing of responsibilities among school leadership and other members of staff.

Peterson and Deal (2002) support the role of formal and informal leaders as builders of positive school culture for effectual success of the schools.

> Strong, positive school cultures do not just happen. They are built over time by those who work in and attend the school and by the formal and informal leaders who encourage and reinforce values and traditions. (p. 17)

Research findings from a study carried out in South Africa by Glober et al. (2006, p. 470), acknowledge collaborative leadership (the element of distributed leadership) as a leadership style which creates a friendly environment for managing cultural diversity in schools. Ngcobo (2008, p. 7) also underscores the results as well in his study which was done in several township secondary schools available in South Africa. Research findings indicated that students in schools practicing communal style (the element of distributed leadership) performs well academically. Findings from the study conducted in Namibia by Smith and Amushigamo (2016) revealed the role of school leadership and culture on creating a strong positive outcome: "The data revealed an engaged school leadership that created a school that is characterised by respect, care, trust, edifying relationship, a sense of belonging, praise, acknowledgement and recognition and collaboration" (para. 1). Several studies conducted in Kenya still confirm the contribution of school culture and leadership on learners' academic performance (Jelagat, 2014, para. 1; Odongo, 2013, para. 1).

In Tanzania, several studies have been done focusing on distributed leadership and how collaborative, shared, or participative culture in schools is practiced by the schools' leadership. Moreover, the extent to which school culture embedded in distributed leadership effected students' achievement is as well researched. Mkwanda (2014, para. 1) investigated the contribution of school culture on students' academic performance in public secondary schools in Tunduru district in Tanzania. Findings revealed that school heads and teachers lacked much knowledge of the significance of school ceremonies, history, stories, vision and mission, school motto, values, and beliefs as to how they could contribute to learners' academic achievement. However, there were initiatives on implementing the positive school culture, particularly sports and games were done collaboratively (the piece of distributed leadership) between school leadership and staff members.

Muholi carried out research in Mbeya to examine how school culture mediates teachers' job satisfaction (Muholi, 2017, para. 1). One of the research findings indicated that unfriendly teachers' relationship with school leaders limited teachers' job satisfaction. The findings vividly indicated that school heads used many school rules and regulations which most likely made many teachers not satisfied with the job. As it has been explained in the previous paragraphs, excessive use of top–down leadership style by school heads limits teachers' job satisfaction and job performance.

Peter (2015) carried a study on the influence of school culture on teachers' commitment. The research was carried out in some community secondary schools available in Tanzania. Research findings about school leadership in connection to teachers' commitment indicated school leadership playing a positive impact as regards to teachers' commitment. Commitment of teachers was impacted by school leaders through "leadership support, participation in decision making, leaders' appreciation and recognition" (p. 84). It can simply be envisaged that through the school leadership sharing responsibilities (a component of distributed leadership) motivated and enhanced teachers' commitment as vividly shown by the research findings.

The doctorate research about culture and management of change was carried out by Van der Steen (2011) in Dodoma Tanzania. The research focused on "influence of staff attitudes and behaviors on the change management process" (p. 144). Van der Steen's research focused on two primary schools, but findings could shed much light to secondary schools. Findings revealed that "under hierarchical conditions and in accordance with local perceptions of relevance, successful management of change required a combination of... cooperation, communication, and close staff supervision" (p. 2). Van der Steen acknowledges that hierarchical leadership and shared leadership can work together toward affecting school management and pedagogical change. However, Van der Steen emphasises that change in management and/or staff attitudes and behaviors towards shared culture could lead to quality managerial and academic outcome.

## Synthesis of Evidence

Reviewed researches and other articles from Tanzania on the concept about distributed leadership and school instructional objectives have vividly indicated how distributed leadership is directly linked to achieving instructional objectives and good academic outcome (Aunga & Masare, 2017, p. 50; Felician, 2013, para. 1; Maige, 2016, p. 33). However, several studies showed how top–down leadership hindered fulfilment of school instructional objectives (Camara, 2014, para. 1; Chua & Mosha, 2015, p. 6; Komba, 2015, para. 1; Mgani, 2013, para. 1).

Regarding distributed leadership and school climate, a number of studies from Tanzania indicated various elements of climate which are directly connected to various features of distributed leadership. The features that revealed a connection between school climate and distributed leadership include: leadership gratefulness to teachers; teachers' empowerment; school leadership being transparent and communicative; and availability of school infrastructure (see Chachage et al., 2019, p. 41; Katera & Msafiri, 2020, pp. 3–4; Mkumbo, 2013, para. 1; Nkuba & Massomo, 2019, para. 1). But some research depicted inadequacy of school infrastructure (Lauwo & Mkulu, 2021, p. 80; Lyanga & Ming-kun, 2020, p. 44).

Another leadership function looked at by the researchers is procuring and distributing resources and how it is connected to distributed leadership. Several studies revealed that school committees (for primary schools) empowered school members in many areas including expenditure decisions, procurement of books and stationery (Masue & Askvik, 2016, p. 7). But in a different study done in secondary school context, findings revealed that the school board members' lacked key information which could help them to participate in making school decisions like planning (Maeda, 2015, p. 166; Muhoja & Mkulu, 2020, para. 1). In other research, dominance of hierarchical leadership and corruption limited the sharing of information about procuring and distributing of resources (Mazigo, 2014, para. 1).

Supporting teachers' growth and development and how it is linked to distributed leadership is another key function reviewed. Researchers from Tanzania revealed the following: In a study on learning mathematics, teachers were satisfied with the facilitation led by their fellow teachers (Swai & Glanfield, 2018, p. 183). Here, Swai and Glanfield depict the role of informal leadership in enabling teachers to acquire mathematics skills. However, in a different study on acquiring ICT competence, neither the school heads nor the teachers were aware of operating various ICT facilities; thus, they demanded training from higher education authority (Ndibalema, 2015, para. 1). Findings from the study done by Nyenyembe et al. (2016, p. 188) revealed that teachers were more satisfied with their job when their school heads worked closely with them through mentoring.

Nyenyembe and colleagues explained vividly on how in a distributed leadership style leaders and the lead raise one another. One more research showed that teachers' professional growth was adequately supported by school leadership, because teachers were involved in preparation of school plans (Komba & Nkumbi, 2008, p. 75). Nevertheless, another research and a recent one revealed unreliable leadership support from government and stakeholders in terms of mentorship, peer coaching, and action research (Losioki, 2020, p. 96). Lack of support from the leaders can be simply explained that the school leadership used hierarchical leadership style instead of distributed leadership.

Managing and developing school culture and the way it is connected to distributed leadership was also looked at by the researchers. Several researches revealed mixed findings in connection to distributed leadership. For instance, in the research done in Tunduru district in Tanzania, findings revealed that school heads as well as teachers lacked much knowledge about the significant elements of school culture. They did not understand that school ceremonies, history, stories, vision and mission, school motto, values, and beliefs as elements of school culture and these elements could contribute a lot to learners' academic achievement (Mkwanda, 2014, para. 1). Findings from a different research done in Mbeya indicated that unfriendly teacher relationships with school leaders restricted teachers' job satisfaction (Muholi, 2017, para.1). Van der Steen carried out a doctorate research about culture and management of change in Dodoma Tanzania. Findings indicated that successful management of change required a combination of dependable leadership, cooperation, communication, and close staff supervision. That is, successful management required the combination of top–down and distributed leadership which could contribute to effective ways for school management and pedagogical change (Van der Steen, 2011, p. 84). The last but not least evidence on the influence of collaborative and involvement school leadership culture towards enhancing the day-to-day performance of teachers is given in Peter's (2015) research. Findings revealed that "commitment of teachers was impacted by school leaders through leadership support, participation in decision making, leaders' appreciation and recognition" (p. 84). It can be simply presumed that Peter acknowledges the role of distributed leadership because it supports and enhances teachers' commitment towards fulfilling their day-to-day teaching responsibilities.

## CONCLUSIONS

This chapter aimed at exploring how school leadership functions in Tanzanian secondary schools are associated with distributed leadership. The sought school functions include completion of school instructional objectives; establishing a school climate; procuring and distributing resources; supporting teachers' growth and development; and managing and developing school culture. Among the reviewed studies, a good number of findings revealed the presence of components of distributed leadership. Nevertheless, various studies indicated dominance of hierarchical leadership model. Therefore it can be established that the school leadership functions practiced in Tanzanian secondary schools are imbedded both in distributed and hierarchical leadership styles. However, Tanzanian secondary schools might benefit very much in continuing moving from top–down leadership style and pay much attention to distributed leadership. This is because as long as distributed leadership involves formal leaders and informal leaders, the two categories of leadership could raise one another towards work. Moreover, as the research findings have shown from the reviewed literature, distributed leadership will motivate and enrich teachers' job satisfaction and results into demonstrable gains in students' quality learning.

## REFERENCES

Atasoy, R. (2020). The relationship between school principals' leadership styles, school culture and organisational change. *International journal of progressive education, 16*(5), 256–274.

Aunga, D. A. O., & Masare, O. (2017). Effect of leadership styles on teachers' performance in primary schools of Arusha district Tanzania. *International Journal of Educational Policy, Research and Review, 4*(4), 42–52.

Avalos, B. (2011). Teacher professional development in teaching and teacher education over ten years. *Teaching and Teacher Education, 27*(1), 10–20.

Babyegeya, E. (2002). *Educational planning and administration.* The Open University of Tanzania.

Boniface, R. M. (2019). Employee voice contexts and teacher retention in remote secondary schools in Tanzania. *African Journal of Teacher Education, 8,* 159–193.

Bredeson, P. V. (2000). The school principal's role in teacher professional development. *Journal of In-service Education, 26*(2), 385–401.

Camara, M. (2014). *The contribution of leadership styles on school achievement in secondary schools: A case study of Mpwapwa District, Tanzania* [Unpublished master's thesis]. University of Dodoma.

Cohen, J., McCabe, E. M., Michelli, N. M., & Pickeral, T. (2009). School climate: Research, policy, practice, and teacher education. *Teachers' College Record, 111*(1), 180–213.

Chachage, K., Walls, J., & Mwakalinga, Y. (2019). The role of caring in schools: A Tanzanian case study. *Journal of International and Comparative Education, 8*(1), 41–55. https://doi.org/10.14425/jice.2019.8.1.41

Chua, C., & Mosha, H. J. (2015). Managing school internal mechanisms for performance improvement in secondary education: Case of six secondary schools in Eastern Zone in Tanzania. *SAGE Open, 5*(4). https://doi.org/10.1177/2158244015610172

Delgado, M. L. (2014). Democratic leadership in middle schools of Chihuahua Mexico: Improving middle schools through democracy. *Journal of International Education and Leadership, 4*(1), 1–12.

Dernowska, U. (2017). Teacher and student perceptions of school climate: Some conclusions from school culture and climate research. *Journal of Modern Science, 1*(32), 63–82.

Dewey, J. (1998). The problem of logical subject-matter. In I. A. Hickman & T. M. Alexander (Eds.), *The essential Dewey, Vol. 2: Ethics, logic, psychology* (pp. 157–168). Indiana University Press. (Original work published 1938)

Dooley, K. E., Lindner, J. R., & Dooley, L. M. (2006). *Writing instructional objectives.* https://www.researchgate.net/publication/314537628_Writing_Instructional_Objectives

Felician, R. (2013). *Influence of teacher's participation in decision making on their job performance in public secondary school in Kilombero district* [Unpublished master's thesis]. Open University of Tanzania.

Glober, B. R, Moloi, K. C, Bisscoff, T. C., & Mestry, R. J. (2006). Creating school environment for the effective management of cultural diversity. *Educational Management Administration and Leadership, 34*(4), 449–472.

Gkoros, D. (2021). Distributed leadership in Greek public schools: Limits and conditions. *Journal of Education, Society and Behavioural Science, 34*(1), 93–102.

Harris, A. (2013). Distributed leadership: Friend or Foe? *Educational Management Administration and Leadership, 41*(5), 545–554.

Harris, A., & Spillane, J. P. (2008). Distributed leadership through looking glass. *Management in Education, 22*(1), 31–34.

Hassan, M. (2014). *The influence of secondary school heads' leadership attributes on students' academic performance in Mwanga district, Tanzania* [Unpublished master's dissertation]. University of Dar es Salaam.

Heikka, J., Waniganayake, M., & Hujala, E. (2013). Contextualizing distributed leadership within early childhood education: Current understanding, research evidence and future challenges. *Educational Management Administration and Leadership, 41*(1), 30–44.

Jelagat, B. (2014). *Influence of school culture on Kenya certificate of secondary education performance of public schools in Makadara District, Nairobi-Kenya* [Unpublished master's thesis]. Nairobi University.

Justus, F. (2013). *The contribution of heads of school leadership styles to teachers' job performance in selected secondary schools in Bagamoyo District, Tanzania* [Unpublished master's dissertation]. University of Dar es Salaam.

Kambambovu, M. E. (2018). *Assessment of leadership styles in relation to students' academic performance in secondary schools: A case of Tabora Municipality* [Unpublished master's thesis]. The Open University of Tanzania.

Katera, L., & Msafiri, D. (2020). *Learning environment and performance of primary education in Tanzania* (REPOA Brief. NO. PB 4/2020).

Kenyatta, F. (2017). *Teachers' perceptions on the use of information and communication technology as teaching and learning tool in public secondary schools in Tanzania: A case of Butiama district in Mara region* [Unpublished master's thesis]. University of Dodoma.

Kilicoglu, D. (2018). Understanding democratic and distributed leadership: How democratic leadership of schools principals related to distributed leadership in schools. *Educational Policy Analysis and Strategic Research, 13*(3), 6–23.

Komba, O. (2015). *The contribution of leadership styles on teachers' job performance in community secondary schools in Kilosa District in Tanzania* [Unpublished master's dissertation]. University of Dar es Salaam.

Komba, S. C., & Mwakabenga, R. J. (2019). *Teachers' professional development in Tanzania: Challenges and opportunities.* https://www.intechopen.com/chapters/70566

Komba, W. L., & Nkumbi, E. (2008). Teacher professional development in Tanzania: Perceptions and practices. *Journal of International Cooperation in Education, 11*(3), 67–83.

Lauwo, H., & Mkulu, D. G. (2021). Challenges facing community involvement in ensuring quality education in public secondary schools in Meru District, Arusha region Tanzania. *International Journal of English Literature and Social Sciences, 6*(1), 74–84.

Leithwood, K., Mascall, B., & Strauss, T. (2009). *Distributed leadership according to evidence.* Routledge.

Losioki, B. E. (2020). Professional development and empowerment among secondary school teachers in Mkuranga District, Tanzania. *Journal of Education and Practice, 11*(24), 92–98.

Lyanga, A. A., & Ming-kun, C. (2020). The impact of fee-free education policy to junior secondary schools in Tanzania. *Asian journal of education and social sciences, 13*(3), 2581–6268.

MacBeath, J., Oduro, G. K. T., & Water house, J. (2004). *Distributed leadership in action: A study of current practice in schools.* NCSL.

Maeda, C. M. (2021). Empowering locals through school governance: A case of secondary school boards in Tanzania. *East African Journal of Social and Applied Sciences, 3*(1), 188–199.

Maige, M. (2016). *The influence of participatory practice making upon secondary schools: Teachers' job satisfaction and commitment in Nyamagana District* [Unpublished master's thesis]. The Open University of Tanzania.

Manaseh, A. M. (2016). Instructional leadership: The role of heads of schools in managing the instructional programme. *International Journal of Educational Leadership and Management, 4*(1), 30–47.

Masue, O. S., & Askvik, S. (2014). Are school committees a source of empowerment? Insights from Tanzania. *International Journal of Public Administration, 40*(9), 780–791. https://doi.org/10.1080/01900692.2016.1201839

Mazigo, D. (2014). *Cause of corruption in construction public procurement in Tanzania: A case of Manyara region* [Unpublished master's dissertation]. Mzumbe University.

Mfaume, H. (2019). Awareness and use of a mobile phone as a potential pedagogical tool among secondary school teachers in Tanzania. *International Journal of Education and Development Using Information and Communication Technology, 15*(2), 154–170.

Mgani, V. D. (2013). *Leadership styles and school functioning: The case of Kilosa District secondary schools* [Unpublished master's thesis]. The Open University of Tanzania.

Mkumbo, K. (2013). *Does school environment affect students' achievement? An investigation into into the relationship between secondary school characteristics and academic performance in Tanzania.* https://learningportal.iiep.unesco.org/en/library/does-school-environment-affect-student-achievement-an-investigation-into-the-relationship

Mkwanda, L. A. (2014). *The contribution of school culture to students' academic performance: A study of public secondary schools in Tunduru district in Tanzania* [Unpublished master's thesis]. University of Dar es Salaam.

Muhoja, T., & Mkulu, D. G. (2020). Challenges facing heads of schools in performing procurement activities: A case of public secondary schools in Monduli District Arusha, Tanzania. *International Journal of Humanities and Education Development, 2*(6), 481–492. https://theshillonga.com/index.php/jhed/article/view/147

Muholi, B. J. (2017). *School-based culture mediating teachers job satisfaction and performance in secondary schools Mbeya region-Tanzania* [Unpublished master's thesis]. The Open University of Tanzania.

Mwila, P. (2018). Assessing the attitudes of secondary school teachers towards the integration of ICT in the teaching process in Kilimanjaro, Tanzania. *International Journal of Education and Development using Information and Communication Technology, 14*(3), 223–238.

Ndibalema, P. (2015). *Transforming teachers' professional competence in the use of ICT as a pedagogical tool: An experience of a community of practice learning group model in secondary schools in Tanzania* [Unpublished doctoral dissertation]. University of Dodoma.

Ngcobo, T. (2008, September 8–12). *Towards leadership for schools cultures associated with good academic performance in South African Township secondary schools: The power of organic emergence, diversity and service: Think globally act locally: A challenge to educational leaders* [Paper presentation]. The Commonwealth Council for Educational Administration and Management Conference, ICC Durban.

Nkuba, L. L., & Massomo, S. M. S. (2019). School climate and its influence on public secondary schools' performance in Mvomero District, Morogoro, Tanzania. *Asian Journal of Education and Social Studies, 4*(2), 1–11. https://journalajess.com/index.php/AJESS/article/view/30116

Nyenyembel, F. W., Maslowski, R., Nimrod, B. S., & Peter, L. (2016). Leadership styles and teachers' job satisfaction in Tanzanian public secondary schools. *Universal Journal of Education Research, 4*(5), 980–988.

Odongo, Z. O. (2013). *Influence of positive school culture on performance at Kenya Certificate of secondary education in public secondary schools in Rongo District, Kenya* [Unpublished master's thesis]. University of Nairobi. http://erepository.uonbi.ac.ke/handle/11295/56629

Peter, E. (2015). *A study of influence of school culture on teachers' professional commitment in community secondary schools in Tanzania: A case of Singida Municipality.* http://repository.udom.ac.tz/handle/20.500.12661/582

Peterson, K. D., & Deal, T. E. (2009). *The shaping school culture field book.* Jossey-Bass.

Pittaway, L., & Cope, J. (2007). Entrepreneurship education: A systematic review of evidence. *International Small Business Journal: Researching Entrepreneurship, 25*(5), 479–510.

Raphael, H. (2011). *Leadership styles and school effectiveness in Tanzania: A case study of public secondary schools in Iramba district* [Unpublished master's thesis]. University of Dar es Salaam.

Schipper, T. M., de Vries, S., Goei, S. L., & van Veen, K. (2020). Promoting a professional school culture through a lesson study? An examination of school culture, school conditions, and teacher self-efficacy. *Professional Development in Education, 46*(1), 112–129. https://doi.org/10.1080/19415257.2019.1634627

Sergiovanni, T. J. (1991). *The principalship: A reflective practice perspective.* Allyn & Bacon.

Sheppard, B., Hurley, N., & Dibbon, D. (2010, May 2). *Distributed leadership, teacher morale, and teacher enthusiasm: Unravelling the leadership pathway to school success* [Paper presentation]. American Educational Research Association, Denver, Colorado.

Smith, C., & Amushingamo, A. (2016). The perceived influence of school leadership on learner behaviour in a Namibian secondary school. *Educational Managemnet Administration and Leadership, 44*(4), 650–667. https://journals.sagepub.com/doi/abs/10.1177/1741143214559232

Soleiman, H., & Khaliliyan, M. (2012). Professional development between Iranian distance education PNU EFL university teachers and traditional non-PNU EFL university teachers. *Turkish Online Journal of Distance Education, 13*(3), 362–374.

Spillane, J. P. (2005). Distributed leadership. *The Educational Forum, 69*(2), 143–150.

Spillane, J. P. (2006). *Distributed leadership.* Jossey-Bass.

Spillane, J. P., Camburn, E. M., Pustejovsky, J., Pareja, A. S., & Lewis, G. (2009). Taking a distributed perspective in studying school leadership and management: The challenge of study operations. In A. Harris (Ed.), *Distributed leadership: Different perspectives* (pp. 47–80). Springer.

Spillane, J. P., Halverson, R., & Diamond, J. B. (2004). Towards a theory of leadership practice: A distributed perspective. *Journal of Curriculum Studies, 36*(1), 3–34.

Spillane, J. P., & Sherer, J. Z. (2004, April 12–16). *A distributed perspective on school leadership: Leadership practice as stretched over people and place* [Paper presentation]. American Education Association, San Diego, CA.

Swai, C. Z., & Glanfield, F. (2018). Teacher-led professional learning in Tanzania: Perspectives of mathematics teacher leaders. *Global Education Review, 5*(3), 183–195.

Swarts, P., & Mwiyeria, E. (2010). *Tanzania: ICT education situation analysis.* https://docplayer.net/30964883-Tanzania-ict-in-education-situational-analysis.html

Thapa, A., Cohen, J., D'Alessandro, A. H., & Guffey, S. (2013). *School climate research summary.* National School Climate Centre.

Thorpe, T., Holt, R., Pittaway, L., & Macpherson, A. (2006). Knowledge within small and medium sized firms: A systematic review of evidence. *International Journal of Management Review, 7*(4), 257–281.

Urio, P. J. (2012). *Effective leadership for quality improvement: Characteristics, practices and challenges in public secondary schools in Morogoro* [Unpublished doctoral dissertation]. University of Dar es Salaam.

Van der Steen, N. (2011). *School improvement in Tanzania: School culture and the management of change* [Unpublished doctoral dissertation]. Institute of Education, University of London.

CHAPTER 20

# PRIMARY RESOURCES AND PUBLIC PEDAGOGY

## A Case Study for Teacher Professional Development

**Minkie O. English**


### ABSTRACT

An exploratory and descriptive case study demonstrating how a piloted Art as Activism workshop requested by education leaders at a higher education institution and a museum, in New York City, was customized for teachers' professional development. Using an interdisciplinary conceptual framework rooted in learning within and from community, for knowledge expansion and technical skills acquisition, this workshop provided teachers with practical experiences to contextualize and re-contextualize historical and contemporary social issues and constructs best supported by public pedagogy critical theory. This teacher's professional development case study is a result of the workshops which utilized works of art, artists, and their artmaking practice as primary resources and field notes collected during the periods of study.


*On Leadership*, pages 377–387

## Background of the Study

Providing innovative ways to present pedagogy and address curriculum needs is the job of education leaders, as well as, addressing issues that challenge prevalent teaching practices, institutional constraints, and social patterns (Giroux, 2003). What is being taught in classrooms should be examined by and explained in, and by, the curriculum for critical thinking to be further developed. Such is the case with Artful Thinking, an arts-based program used by teachers and arts specialists across all grade levels to help teacher's use works of art in their curriculum to strengthen student thinking and learning through looking at and interpreting art, rather than making art (Tishman & Palmer, 2006).

Artful Thinking focuses on six thinking dispositions—questioning and investigating, observing and describing, reasoning, exploring viewpoints, comparing and connecting, and finding complexity—to help teachers create rich connections between works of art and topics they are teaching, while using the power of art as a force to develop students' thinking dispositions (Tishman & Palmer, 2006). While the Artful Thinking program's approach centered on looking at and interpreting art addresses the psychological and cognitive processes that allows a person to interpret or "see" art to have an aesthetic experience (Weir & Mandes, 2017), making art adds other intrinsic values to the learning process because process-focused art experiences also support physical learning, language and literacy, and social and emotional learning (Bongiorno, 2014). For younger children, Bongiorno (2014) characterized these process-focused art experiences as having no step-by-step instructions, no sample to follow and, no right or wrong way to explore and create, because it focuses on the experience and on exploration of techniques, tools, and materials so that the art is unique and original, the experience is relaxing or calming, the art is one's own, and the experience one's choice because the ideas are not readily available online.

Expanding on this approach, within the perspective of continuing education and learning, this research served as a case study to guide teachers through a process-focused art professional development experience. Through co-facilitated workshops with artists, their artmaking practice and artwork served as primary resources to create connections between works of art and topics they are teaching, while also guiding their creation of art to expand their learning. This case study specifically provides a public pedagogy perspective on how an Art as Activism workshop that was developed, piloted, and co-facilitated by an arts education researcher and working visual artists was used by a higher education institution (Medgar Evers College) and a cultural institution (Brooklyn Museum) to explore art and artmaking as primary resources, for professional development training for preservice and in-service teaching professionals. Utilizing an interdisciplinary conceptual framework, this study demonstrated how education leaders can support learning for teachers to understand and critically analyze primary resources, outside of their classrooms. Additionally, this study explored the collaboration between preservice and/or in-service teachers, higher education institutions, art institutions, and working artists in contributing to existing teacher professional development research and literature.

## Primary Resources and Public Pedagogy for Teachers' Professional Development in Arts Education

Public pedagogy is the science of learning through informal delivery and the analysis of cultural education, public space, popular culture, public intellectualism, and political struggle for citizenship in and beyond schools (IGI Global, n.d.). As leaders consistently provide support and resources to teachers they are scaffolding best practices within their schools, and their industry, to include voices and resources present in public discourse, but which might not be readily present or available to and for teachers to innovatively practice (Sandlin et al., 2010). Encouraging teaching and teachers' professional development that recognizes and include cultural references and resources ensures that leaders are empowering teachers to localize, globalize, indigenize, and enhance their curriculums based on public, institutional, and/or students' social and educational contexts, relevance, and responsiveness.

When leaders identify and support ways for teachers to engage with the local community through art, they are guiding the process and highlighting the resources that can be used and/or replicated by teachers. The U.S. Library of Congress (LoC) has an extensive digital collection of primary resource sets for teachers, for classroom instruction. LoC defines primary resources as "the raw materials of history—original documents and objects that were created at the time under study" (Library of Congress, n.d.). Therefore, raw materials like a person and their work of art which provides first-hand accounts, a viewpoint or original thinking, or new information of an event and/or experience are primary resources. Additionally, the artist process can serve as a primary resource because it is research of raw, or original materials, that others like teachers and students can base their research on and learn from. As a result, this study considered artists, their work of art (artwork), and art making practice as "raw materials of history" and therefore as primary resources alongside other primary resources utilized from digital databases like LoC. So, these Art as Activism workshops, and this research, adapted and operationalized LoC's definition to define artists, their work of art, and artmaking practice as primary resources, to increase the knowledge and skills of teaching professionals.

## Case Study Research Context

The Artist Talk Series, an exploratory project to work with emerging artists, was launched in 2016 to provide public engaging opportunities for the community-at-large and disadvantaged NYC public school students to engage in community spaces with artists and creative professionals. This series included workshops and artist talkbacks to allow people from any community to engage directly with individuals within the arts—art leaders, emerging visual and performance artists, and so on. After two sessions, feedback was provided that the workshops should be provided directly to teachers and educators as direct learning experiences with working artists. After several conversations with working artists, teachers, educators, and education leaders there was sufficient verbal confirmation that there was a lack of curated opportunities and workshops for teaching professionals to have the same learning experiences as their students, alongside their teaching peers. A pilot workshop was developed to focus on innovative ways to center art in classrooms, while serving to help teachers find the connections between curriculum and lesson planning conception and practice. The aim was to honor the teachers' experiences and connect what occurred in the everyday lives of students to their classroom. When education leaders can recognize that the forms of injustices that students face is also faced by teachers, and they are not separated from it, it is then that they can work to address what their leadership and public spaces can do together for teachers and their students.

Education leaders, Lawrence et al. (2019), found that primary sources can be used in content areas to increase disciplinary literacy instruction. By connecting local events in New York City to themes from the Library of Congress website and presenting these themes in workshops with (a) presenters from the Museum of the City of New York, the New-York Historical Society and (b) teacher educators from City University of New York and the Gotham Center for New York City History through walking tours, teachers were able to contextualize historical events and model historical inquiry using primary sources and museum artifacts. Using their study as supporting research, this chapter presents two co-facilitated workshops as cases of teacher's professional development which focused on creating connections between works of art, topics teachers are teaching, and the process of creating art to expand their creative and critical thinking dispositions.

## CONCEPTUAL FRAMEWORK

The conceptual framework that best aligned to support and understand the curricula for this public pedagogical concept for teacher's professional development was Salisbury University's Conceptual Framework (2013), which is an interdisciplinary professional learning community concept developed from discussion and analysis of coursework, classroom experiences, content, field experiences, and methods of evaluation, for teaching candidates and teaching professionals to feel supported in their current practice and towards their future growth (Salisbury University, 2013). The framework supports:

- *Informed and Reflective Practice:* Teachers as decision makers who through careful preparation and a thorough grounding in research and best practices, are supported by education leaders and local collaborative partners to question and reflect continuously in the pursuit of sound educational judgments.
- *Enhanced Student Learning:* Skilled and caring educators enhance learning and achievement when they recognize, appreciate, and build on the individual strengths and differences of every learner.
- *Scholarship:* Teachers ongoing scholarly inquiry, and leaders' integrity in their efforts to help teachers, as students, learn in local schools.
- *Collaboration:* Synergistic partnership that integrates the preparation of teachers' with advancing the knowledge base and supporting their professional development to improve student achievement in P–12 schools (Salisbury University, 2013, p. 6).

While these themes shape the core curriculum, it is the acquired knowledge and practiced skills that best influence educational professionals' preparedness and other outcomes (Salisbury University, 2013). According to this framework: (a) knowledge is addressed in content grounded in the arts and sciences; knowledge of learning, behavior, and development; knowledge of diversities; and in the review and analysis of data to help make informed and instructional decisions; and (b) in the skills acquired through practice and experience (Salisbury University, 2013). With this framework a case study plan was then developed. As such, this conceptual framework best supported the workshops and the critical theory employed by this research.

## Case Study Plan

As a data collection method for case studies, field notes are used in qualitative research to document contextual information (Phillippi & Lauderdale, 2018) that can be used for teaching and training (Mills et al., 2010). Field notes collected prior to, during, and after the workshops were used to guide the research question and examine the process and outcomes of the workshops, the public pedagogical approach, and the conceptual framework focused on engaging teachers and integrating art to expand and support their knowledge and skill needs. The research question that guided the workshops and this case study was: If the goal of teachers is to guide students to develop critical thinking and analytical skills through providing resources for learning, then how can artists, their artwork, and their artmaking practice augment critical and creative thinking for teachers in their own professional development?

## CASES

### Medgar Evers College Art as Activism Professional Development Workshop

In 2017 the Art as Activism professional development workshop was piloted at a higher education institution—Medgar Evers College in Brooklyn, New York—to a class of preservice teachers through a grant-funded opportunity with a higher education leader. It was piloted as a 2-hour writing workshop to support inquiry pedagogy that the professor (education leader) taught during the semester. The learning outcome for this workshop was for preservice teachers to understand how historical art activism movements can help critically guide teachers' analysis of various mediums of art and use that knowledge to plan and write lessons to support their curriculum. The arts education researcher provided preservice teachers with the contextual historical knowledge and framework of how social constructs were addressed by emerging artists during various art movements, as reactions to social issues. The visual artist provided the technical skills knowledge as a primary resource to support the historical knowledge provided by the arts education researcher. The visual artist discussed her art-making process—manipulating paper to create gowns which were then worn by models to capture images which contextualize, or re-contextualize, historical events and social constructs.

This workshop highlighted the realism art movement and the postmodernism art movement. However, it focused specifically on social realism and portraiture from painters, printmakers, and photographers as the visual art reference, and primary resources, to guide the practical experience for teachers' engagement with the artist while they created a lesson plan within a group setting. Utilizing visual references, as additional primary resources, from visual artists and public access resources like the LoC, the teachers were provided examples of how to compare art mediums within historical social contexts to frame the social causes that social realist (artists) throughout the various art movements focused on highlighting, through their art.

For the paintings art medium, two portraiture visual images were pulled from public access sources to present and compare how art was historically and presently (at the time of the workshop) utilized to present the contextual themes of identity, classism, racism, and overall social constructs. Works of art by two artists were presented and compared for critical analysis. At the time of this workshop one artist's artwork was on view at the Met Breuer for further viewing and engagement by the preservice teachers. For the photography art medium, one portraiture visual image was pulled from a public access source while the other portraiture belonged to the visual artist who was present. The same contextual themes were presented: identity, classism, racism, and overall social constructs. Works of art by another artist and the co-facilitating visual artist were presented and compared for critical analysis. The visual artist provided the preservice teachers with direct experiential knowledge on how she got started as an artist and her preferred choice of art making materials and art medium(s). She provided technical assistance and feedback to teachers who required more details as the lesson plans were being developed. For the illustrations/graphic design art medium, two portraiture visual images were pulled from public access sources to present and compare how these primary resources addressed the historical contextual themes of politics, classism, racism, activism/social justice, and overall social constructs. Works of art by two artists were presented and compared for critical analysis.

This cohort of preservice teachers were provided lesson plan expectations from their professor; targeted in the presentation to have a clear rationale for lesson planning, teaching, students' needs, and examples of how to present their information. They were divided into groups and provided 50 minutes to create their lesson plan presentation. Each group was also provided the following additional visual reference options: photographs from six emerging photographers and a civil rights and social justice graphic novel series. During their planning session within their groups, these preservice teachers were reminded by their education leader (professor) that because of students' diverse literacy needs they will need to differentiate the product, process, and content based on students' learning style, interest, and readiness. They were prompt to think about their own learning style, interest, and readiness while they worked individually within their groups. At the end of the 50 minutes, due to time constraints, each group was provided approximately 10 minutes to present an overview of their lesson plan to the rest of the class.

## Brooklyn Museum Art as Activism Professional Development Workshop

In 2019, the Art as Activism professional development workshop was piloted at a cultural institution—Brooklyn Museum in Brooklyn, New York—to teachers and artists/teaching artists, upon invitation by a museum education leader. This 2-hour workshop was customized and facilitated to support the work of the museum's teacher services programming. The learning outcome for this workshop was for teachers to question and re-contextualize images used as primary resources to analyze documents while engaging them in meaningful activities and conversations. Teachers were provided with a guide to help them understand: (a) how old/archival photographs may be used to critically analyze, contextualize, and re-contextualize past narratives within present-day experiences; (b) how past narratives influence how we understand and communicate present narratives and ideas; (c) how to view, understand, and provide students with equal access and opportunities to utilize overlooked, but available, primary resources; (d) how to engage in meaningful activities and conversations; and (e) how to utilize artwork and an artists' artmaking practice to understand how people and constructs within complex systems can work together for the same corrective outcome.

The arts education researcher provided the teachers with the contextual knowledge of how constructs influence narratives of visibility/invisibility, and when viewed through the visual artists' artwork and art making practice, the same can be understood and taught to students. The visual artist provided the technical skills knowledge through a discussion of his art making process—manipulating paper of captured images from his social activist experiences to contextualize/re-contextualize historical events. A senior museum instructor and teacher services coordinator provided a gallery walk through of a Brooklyn Museum exhibit. This helped teachers to further connect how the use of other works of art can serve to support and expand the knowledge and skills the teachers were acquiring and be used as contextual information for lesson planning and teaching about similar historical events for inquiry and social awareness.

This cohort of teachers had the option of using a list of curated photographs pulled from Brooklyn Museum's archives by the museum senior staff member, photos provided from the visual artists' archives, and/or photos from their own personal archives to imitate his artmaking practice to create their own piece of art as social activists. While the teachers were completing the art making activity they were asked to think about their reflective process (cognitive reflections) as they worked. The teachers were provided with questions to consider as reflective prompts to aid with their visual and cognitive analysis and, if needed, their descriptive write-up of the archival photos. The following questions included:

- Who are the subjects of this image?
- What might they be thinking or experiencing?
- Who, or what, is missing from this image that would contextualize it?
- What symbols are present in the image?
- What could be cut out or altered to be symbolically meaningful?

Using the photographs, the visual artists' art making process and tools, and the reflection prompts, the teachers manipulated, layered, wrote texts, and/or collaged the archival and contemporary photos. He guided them technically on how to cut out pieces (specific objects, architecture, people, etc.) from the archival photos and place them on the contemporary photo of their choice—allowing the archival photo to serve as composites, or fragments, within the contemporary photo. This allowed the teachers to be able to connectively utilize all the primary resources to contextualize/re-contextualize a narrative from their point of view.

## DISCUSSION

"Professional development is contingent on an inclusive process that establishes productive relationships for all who have a stake in the improvement of the educational enterprise" (Salisbury University, 2013, p. 24). The Art as Activism workshop was developed with this concept in mind and expanded to ensure it engaged its anticipated and unanticipated targeted audience equally. The original targeted audience were local New York City public school preservice and in-service teachers, however the second workshop also had participants from outside of New York City and at various career levels of teaching, teaching artists, and artists interested in teaching. With the support of both education leaders the workshops engaged artists, teachers/educators, a cultural institution, and/or a higher education institution.

The professional development workshops conducted at Medgar Evers College and Brooklyn Museum, in Brooklyn, NY, for preservice teachers, in-service teachers, and teaching artists provided them with access to publicly available archival resources, engagement with an emerging visual artist, knowledge of that artists' artmaking practice, and technical guidance from that artist. These workshops allowed these teachers to frame historical events/movements and contextualize social issues to understand how social constructs can be contextualized, or re-contextualized, within complex systems to critically analyze and understand how agency can be framed for teaching and lesson planning, to expose constructs and then correct narratives. Using various forms of resources defined and operationalized as primary resources, teachers scaffolded learning with supported rationale for lesson planning and teaching. Each teacher left the workshop with an understanding of how these various primary resources can be connected and used to frame a lesson plan as part of an overall curriculum, supported by an educational leader.

The simplified answer to the research question—If the goal of teachers is to guide students to develop critical thinking and analytical skills through providing resources for learning, then how can artists, their artwork, and their artmaking practice augment critical and creative thinking for teachers in their own professional development?—is yes. However, the support for teacher's professional development need not only come from educational institutions but can also come from cultural institutions which claim to challenge prevalent practices, constraints, and patterns in support of cultural awareness, learning and educating for change, and social responsibility and accountability. Continuous innovative approaches to professional development for teachers, in collaboration with these institutions, should always be working in concert for the benefit of education, students, schools, and the public.

Like the Artful Thinking program, these Art as Activism workshops allowed teachers and art content specialists from varied backgrounds and disciplines to learn new ways of using works of art in a curriculum and/or in their own practice to strengthen thinking and learning by looking at, interpreting, and making art. The participants of both workshops were provided resources and supported in questioning and investigating, observing and describing, reasoning, exploring viewpoints, comparing and connecting, and finding complexity to create rich connections between works of art and topics they are teaching or be provided perspectives of how they can use process-focused art experiences to develop their own thinking so they can better understand their student's thinking and further support their physical learning, language and literacy, and social and emotional learning.

## CONCLUSION

This exploratory and descriptive case study placed within the context of the Salisbury University conceptual framework, substantiated with the evidence collected and recounted by field notes from the Medgar Evers College and the Brooklyn Museum Art as Activism workshops, suggests that utilizing artists, their artwork, and their art making practices as primary resources to expand teachers knowledge and skills through professional development can serve as an option by innovative education leaders who are seeking diverse learning opportunities for teacher's professional development, their current practice, and future growth. As leaders support publicly available resources, they are working to help their teachers become informed and have a reflective practice, become more aware of their scholarship needs, actively seek out opportunities within their community and the community-at-large for further education, while collaborating with and working with primary resources for their enhanced learning and overall enhanced student learning. More specifically, the knowledge and technical skills that teachers acquired connected them with ways to use various types of resources to contextualize historical events for inquiry and provide social awareness to support their learning needs and professional outcomes.

This case study served as its own developing framework of how interdisciplinary leaders can work in any cultural and/or educational space, even of their own design, to collaboratively bridge gaps created by institutional priorities and plans, bias, constraints, and social formations or constructs. Interdisciplinary leadership provides that critical lens through which these constructs and social formations can be highlighted, critically analyzed, supported by innovative thinking and creations, and implemented with agency to try and reform those existing structures.

The implication from this case study reveals how this Art as Activism workshop, and various learning "raw materials," can be utilized as primary resources for teacher's professional development. Future research will focus on analyzing the collected quantitative data to support the implications and case study research outcomes with empirical evidence on how this interdisciplinary leadership approach for arts education professional development benefits teachers, artists, education institutions, cultural institutions, and the community-at-large.

## REFERENCES

Bongiorno, L. (2014). How process-focused art experiences support preschoolers. *Teaching Young Children, 7*(3). https://www.naeyc.org/resources/pubs/tyc/feb2014/process-art-experiences

Giroux, H. A. (2003). Public pedagogy and the politics of resistance: Notes on a critical theory of educational struggle. *Educational Philosophy and Theory, 35*(1), 5–16.

IGI Global. (n.d.). *What is public pedagogy?* https://www.igi-global.com/dictionary/public-pedagogy/62749

Lawrence, S. A., Langan, E., & Maurer, J. (2019). Using primary sources in content areas to increase disciplinary literacy instruction. *The Language and Literacy Spectrum, 29*(1), Article 1.

Library of Congress. (n.d). *Getting started with primary sources.* https://www.loc.gov/programs/teachers/getting-started-with-primary-sources/

Mills, A. J., Durepos, G., & Wiebe, E. (2010). *Encyclopedia of case study research* (Vols. 1-0). SAGE Publications.

Phillippi J., & Lauderdale J. (2018). A guide to field notes for qualitative research: Context and conversation. *Qualitative Health Research, 28*(3), 381–388. https://doi.org/10.1177/1049732317697102

Sandlin, J. A., Schultz, B. D., & Burdick, J. (Eds). (2010). *Handbook of public pedagogy: Education and learning beyond schooling.* Routledge.

Salisbury University. (2013). *Seidel school of education and professional studies professional education unit conceptual framework.* https://www.salisbury.edu/academic-offices/education/_files/conceptual-framework.pdf

Tishman, S. & Palmer, P. (November 2006). *Final report: Artful thinking. Project Zero.* http://pz.harvard.edu/sites/default/files/ArtfulThinkingFinalReport-1.pdf

Weir, C., & Mandes, E. (2017). *Interpreting visual art: A survey of cognitive research about pictures* (1st ed.). Routledge. https://doi.org/10.4324/9781351295444

# SECTION IV

## EXEMPLARS IN INTERDISCIPLINARY LEADERSHIP

CHAPTER 21

# THE MUTUAL ENGAGEMENT LEADERSHIP MODEL IMPLEMENTATION AND OUTCOMES AT CONWAY REGIONAL HEALTH SYSTEM

**Kateryna V. (Ligon) Pitchford**

## ABSTRACT

Interdisciplinary leadership sets a stage for horizontal organizational structure, which becomes an empowering mechanism for followers to take charge and equally participate in the organizational decision-making process and accountability for the outcomes (Bloomquist et al., 2018). Healthcare industry faces many challenges, which require innovative solutions in complex environments with multiple stakeholders' participation (Doublestein et al., 2015). Conway Regional Health System (CRHS) exemplifies application of the mutual engagement leadership model (Ligon, 2015, 2016), which promotes high organizational outcomes, high follower engagement in organization, culture of open communication, high collaboration and empowerment, and trust. CRHS celebrated its 100-year anniversary in 2021. CRHS offers

*On Leadership*, pages 391–419

complete healthcare services in six counties of northern central Arkansas. The purpose of this instrumental case study is to examine an implementation and outcomes of the mutual engagement leadership model in the setting of CRHS and under the CEO, Matt Troup's interdisciplinary leadership practices. Multiple source databases are analyzed using deductive thematic analysis.

Today's complex problems require interdisciplinary leadership approaches to their solutions, which includes collaboration within and between organizations, industries, and across communities. Interdisciplinary leadership is focused on interaction and collaboration between "context, culture, accountability, power, values, beliefs, ethics, and decision-making in which all members share responsibilities for processes and outcomes" (Bloomquist et al., 2018, p. 60). Interdisciplinary leadership is vital in today's healthcare since complex challenges require collaboration between all involved stakeholders and a "linear problem solving" strategy, that is a simple X, is not effective in the 21st century (Lees & Uri, 2018, p. 40; Thomas et al., 2019). Two main challenges noted for healthcare in the United States by 2050 are "physician shortages" and a focus on "patient-centered care" (Doublestein et al., 2015, p. 122). To meet future needs of the healthcare industry, present and future leaders must focus on "innovation and foresight" (Doublestein et al., 2015, p. 109). The United States Congressional Budget Office projects that U.S. healthcare costs will be "20 percent of the gross domestic product by 2050" (Doublestein et al., 2015, p. 122). The inflation of costs will require that healthcare institutions be innovative to survive.

In practice, an interdisciplinary leadership approach at the Conway Regional Health System (CRHS) established in 1921 in Arkansas, includes development of sustainable goals while addressing complex challenges through collaboration of all stakeholders from employees to community, in addition to partnering with external experts. Matt Troup, president and CEO of CRHS is focused on innovation, patient-centered care, and servant leadership (Campbell-Miller, 2020). Troup integrates the mutual engagement leadership model at the CRHS by creating a collaborative organizational environment, which is an integral part of interdisciplinary leadership. The mutual engagement leadership model is introduced in this instrumental case study of the CRHS (Stake, 2000). Internal and external data of the CRHS is analyzed using deductive thematic analysis to test implementation and outcomes of the mutual engagement leadership model (Ligon, 2015, 2016).

## PREFACE TO THE MUTUAL ENGAGEMENT LEADERSHIP MODEL

The mutual engagement leadership model (Ligon, 2015, 2016) is inspired by the toxic triangle model, developed by Padilla et al. (2007) and Kelley's

Followership Typologies (1992). In this paper, toxic and destructive leadership concepts will be used interchangeably. Destructive leadership is an expensive endeavor, with annual costs of $23 billion, affecting 13.6% of the United States workforce, according to Schyns and Schilling (2013). For the purposes of this case study, destructive leadership is defined as "the systematic and repeated behavior by a leader, supervisor, or manager that violates the legitimate interest of the organization by undermining and/or sabotaging the organization's goals, tasks, resources, and effectiveness and/or the motivation, well-being or job satisfaction of subordinates" (Einarsen et al., 2007, p. 208). The toxic triangle model conceptualizes destructive leadership, its roots, and contributing factors.

The toxic triangle model, developed by Padilla et al. (2007), attempts to review leadership from a complex and multidimensional perspective. It emphasizes direct influence of leaders, followers, and context to build a leadership model (see Figure 21.1).

Each element has their own triggers, which power the change of the component from constructive to destructive nature. When merged, the toxic nature of each element results in an eruption of destructive leadership. Triggers of destructive leaders are drawn mainly from the leader's personal traits. The susceptible followers are divided in two groups:

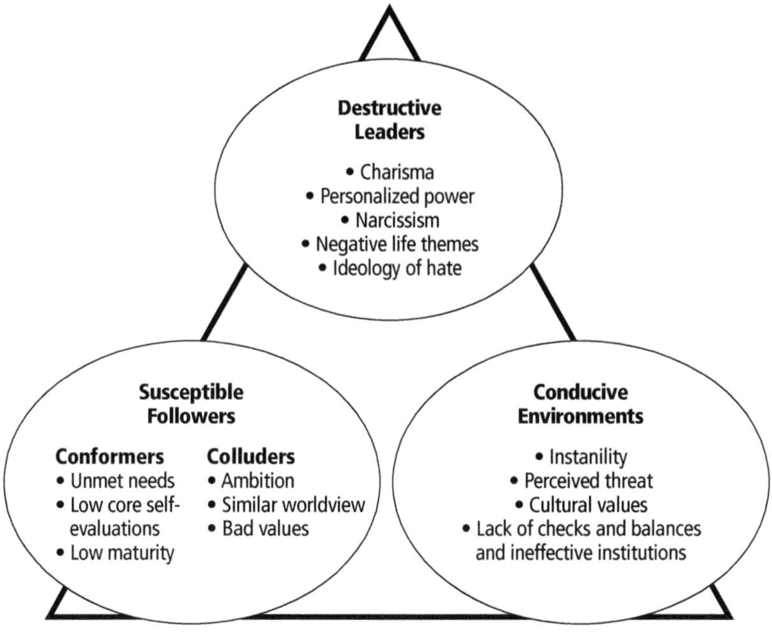


**Figure 21.1** The toxic triangle. *Source:* The toxic triangle: Elements in three domains related to destructive leadership. Adapted from Padilla et al. (2007, p. 180).

conformers, who obey out of dread, and colluders, who are a leader's active supporters. Both groups fulfill personal interests by following a destructive leader, whether for survival or power gains. The model would not be complete without environmental characteristics that create the conditions for destructive leadership to thrive, such as: low stability; upcoming risk and danger; "cultural values," promotion of individualism or collectivism in the country and organization; and weak or absent "checks and balances and institutionalization" (Padilla et al., 2007, p. 180). All such circumstances make for a ripe condition of takeover by emergent destructive leaders. When a toxic leader succeeds in the environment, the context of organization is changed to control the gained power.

Today, organizations draw from unique and diverse talents of personnel. Human and social capital progression has become a key in business success. Unfortunately, not every organizational environment is embracing personal development due to higher concerns for profits and production than for people. Some outcomes of toxic leadership, which decrease individual productivity and organizational performance, include: a closing of information exchange or communication (Tost et al., 2013); lack of job satisfaction (Bolman & Deal, 2008; Carlson et al., 2012; Tepper, 2000); conflict between work and family (Carlson et al., 2012; Davis & Scott, 2006; Tepper, 2000); and lack of empowerment by leaders (Lorinkova et al., 2013). There are many factors that have negative effects on organizational performance and destructive leadership relates to most of them.

By contrast, the mutual engagement leadership model looks at collaboration between a leader and followers under favorable context, while creating a collaborative organizational environment which holds an equilibrium of power and assures cooperation between the two. If the mutual engagement leadership model becomes unbalanced by forces generated by a leader or followers, the triangle rotates, and the leader or followers gain the most power in the organization. In the case of CRHS, the leader practices an interdisciplinary leadership approach by establishing a collaborative organizational environment or shared power context in the organization.

## The Mutual Engagement Leadership Model

Literature on leadership and followership can be reduced to five primary dynamics which take a different focus on leader/follower roles and interactions (Crossman & Crossman, 2011; Uhl-Bien et al., 2014). Three of the approaches (leader-centric, follower-centric, and relational) are focused on the leader's role in obtaining results. The other two approaches (role-based and constructionist followership) focus on the follower. The mutual engagement leadership model is grounded in the relational approach which comprises a leader, followers, and context and is focused on their interaction (Ligon, 2016).

The relational approach reflects organizational, political, economic, and environmental changes of the 21st century, which promote the context of collaboration between followers and leaders in horizontal organizational structures (Baker, 2007; Kellerman, 2007). The mutual engagement leadership model (Figure 21.2) is presented as the upside-down leadership triangle. This model, inspired by the toxic triangle model developed by Padilla et al. (2007) and Kelley's followership typologies (1992), attempts to review leadership from a complex and multidimensional perspective consisting of three main elements: leader, followers, and context. In the graphic representation of the model the leader and followers are mutually engaged while the collaborative organizational environment (context) holds equilibrium between equal players (Ligon, 2016). The context sets the stage for interactions between the leader and followers; development of organizational goals; and the search and implementation of internal and external solutions to complex problems.

It is important to note that triangular balance is delicate, if a leader or followers gain too much power, they can rotate the triangle. When a leader is on the bottom, they choose direction for the followers and create an organizational context. However, when *exemplary* followers gain voice, they can rotate the triangle by changing leader's roles and rebuilding an organizational context (Kelly, 1992). As a result of the rotation with context holding the balance, an organization establishes a strong foundation for mutual engagement between a leader and followers and holds each participant of the model accountable (Ligon, 2015, 2016).

A balanced model for mutual engagement leadership results in high organizational outcomes; high follower engagement in organization; a culture of open communication; high collaboration and empowerment; and trust. The CRHS is an example of the mutual engagement leadership

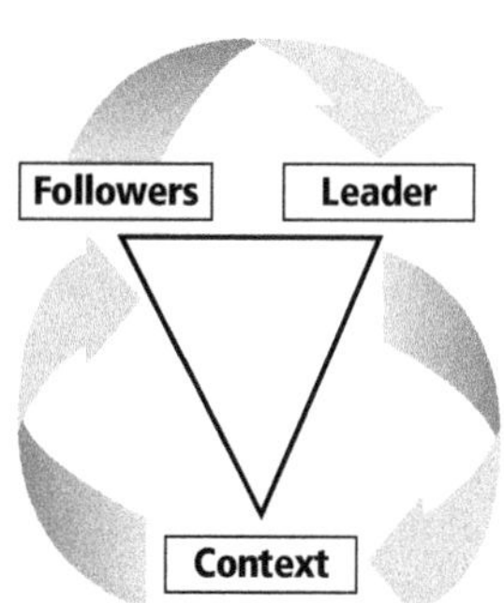


**Figure 21.2** The mutual engagement leadership model.

model in practice, which promotes collaborative organizational process (environment), defined as "the synergy between leadership and followership" (Ligon, 2016, p. 9).

## Research and Data Sources

### *Purpose of the Study*

The mutual engagement leadership model (Ligon, 2015, 2016) promotes establishment of the collaborative organizational environment, as an essential component of interdisciplinary leadership. The purpose of this instrumental case study is to examine the implementation and outcomes of the model in the setting of CRHS and under Matt Troup's leadership practices. To accomplish this goal, the overview of the leadership practices since Troup took over as a CEO in August of 2015 is summarized. The database includes internal surveys and reports, external partners surveys and reports, interviews and email communication with top leaders, public access reports, publications, CRHS website, public presentations, and audio materials from a podcast. CRHS external partners are Press Ganey Associates LLC, Modern Healthcare and Best Companies Group, Arkansas Business, and Quantros, Inc.

Support for the mutual engagement leadership model will promote effective interdisciplinary leadership practices in organizational settings.

### *Research Questions*

1. How is the mutual engagement leadership model implemented at Conway Regional Health System?
2. What interdisciplinary leadership practices at Conway Regional Health System contribute to establishment and preservation of the collaborative organizational context?
3. What organizational outcomes are recorded at Conway Regional Health System as a result of the mutual engagement leadership model application?

### *Research Design*

This instrumental case study is focused on implementation and outcomes of the mutual engagement leadership model at the CRHS (Mills et al., 2010). The quantitative data is provided to the investigator by the CRHS, which includes internal surveys and reports, in addition to external partners' surveys and reports. The qualitative data was collected and reviewed by the researcher and includes interviews and email communication with top leaders, public access reports, publications, CRHS website, public presentations, and audio materials from a podcast. The data analytical approach is conducted through correspondence and patterns as described by Stake (1995) and is focused on "the themes and relationships among the categories that are emerging from the data" as outcomes of the mutual engagement leadership model (Jones et al., 2014, p. 98). Specifically, deductive thematic analysis is used in the study (Braun, & Clarke, 2006; Creswell, 2014; Marks & Yardley, 2003). Thematic analysis creates a bridge between qualitative and quantitative analysis and is "useful for summarizing key features of a large data set" (Boyatzis, 1998; Nowell et al., 2017, p. 2). Codes and themes were generated deductively based on the conceptual framework of the mutual engagement leadership model (Nowell et al., 2017). CRHS was chosen for this study because the organization offers a multidimensional "opportunity to learn" (Stake, 2000, p. 446) about implementation and outcomes of the mutual engagement leadership model. Additionally, the CRHS instrumental case study can lead to the collective case study about the implementation of interdisciplinary leadership practices through the mutual engagement leadership model in other institutions (Stake, 2000).

***Internal and External Data***

CRHS established rigorous internal anonymous data collection practices, which help the top leadership team stay current on the internal issues, provide timely response to concerns, and develop better future foresight. External partners for data collection and reports include Press Ganey Associates LLC, Modern Healthcare and Best Companies Group, Arkansas Business, Quantros, Inc., and so on. These companies conduct independent data collection, analyses, comparison with other healthcare organizations and provide results, rank participants, and present awards and recognitions to healthcare facilities nationwide based on their performance.

The first external partner is Press Ganey Associates, LLC, which helps CRHS in the area of patient satisfaction since 2011 and in the area of employee engagement since 2015 (E. Shoffner, personal communication, March 2, 2021). Press Ganey, LLC is a well-recognized consulting company that collaborates with healthcare facilities nationwide and annually recognizes and awards leaders in the healthcare field. Dr. Irwin Press, PhD, and Dr. Rod Ganey, PhD partnered in 1984 to fulfill the mission of healthcare improvement in the nation through one of the first empirically supported instruments (Press Ganey Associates, LLC, 2021). Press Ganey's mission is "to reduce patient suffering by supporting the delivery of safe, high-quality, patient-centered care" (Press Ganey Associates LLC, 2022, para. 7). Currently, Press Ganey provides consulting services rooted in evidence-based scientific approaches to over 41,000 healthcare facilities nationwide. Press Ganey collects, investigates, and provides data to CRHS to evaluate several areas of employee engagement (organizational satisfaction, direct supervisor/manager, engagement indicator, and job satisfaction).

Another external partner is the Modern Healthcare and Best Companies Group along with *Arkansas Business,* which help rank CRHS compared to other healthcare facilities. Modern Healthcare and Best Companies Group and *Arkansas Business* use an identical questionnaire, which helps determine the best places to work for in healthcare nationwide and in businesses within the state of Arkansas respectfully. Modern Healthcare and Best Companies Group and *Arkansas Business* use the same survey which are randomly distributed among employees of the participating institutions. The survey evaluates eight categories (leadership and planning; corporate culture and communications; role satisfaction; work environment; relationship with supervisor; training, development, and resources; pay and benefits; and overall engagement) and helps determine the best places to work for from an employee perspective. In the CRHS case study only data collected and reported by Modern Healthcare and Best Companies Group is analyzed since an identical survey by *Arkansas Business* produced similar results. The primary difference between the two groups administering surveys was the number of employees who took both surveys; which showed an insignificant difference in the number of participants and yielded similar results (M.Troup, personal communication, February 24, 2021).

An additional partner is Quantros Inc., which for over 20 years has provided "software-based solutions to hospitals and hospital systems," according to their website (Quantros Inc., 2021, para.1). CRHS participates in the CareChex Awards system, "an innovative medical quality rating system module designed to assist providers in evaluating the quality of inpatient care that compares inpatient quality performance across all general, acute care, non-federal hospitals in the nation" (Healthcare Bluebook, 2022, para. 1). CareChex ranking system includes all hospitals, no self-reported data, in risk adjusted, considers patient mortality, readmission, complications, and patient safety (Healthcare Bluebook, 2022).

## Conway Regional Health System

According to their website, the CRHS provides "complete healthcare services to the growing communities of northern central Arkansas including Faulkner, Conway, Perry, Pope, Van Buren and Cleburne counties. Centered on a 150-bed, acute care medical center, the health system provides patients with a variety of services, such as: heart health, cancer care, women's health, surgery, rehabilitation" (CRHS, n.d.-d, para. 1). CRMC is a "community hospital  and not-for-profit health system" (CRHS, n.d.-b., p. 4). As of 2021, CRHS employs about 1,600 people, 1,100 of which work for CRMC (M. Troup, personal communication, February 24, 2021).

CRHS's mission is "to provide high-quality, compassionate healthcare services" (CRHS, n.d.-b, p. 1). CRHS' vision is "to be recognized as the regional leader in healthcare excellence" (CRHS, n.d.-b, p. 1). According to the 2019 Community Health Needs Assessments, ICARE values are the following:

- *Integrity:* We say what we mean, and we mean what we say.
- *Compassion:* We show concern and compassion for others.
- *Accountability:* We are answerable for our actions and decisions.
- *Respect:* We care about the well-being, dignity, and uniqueness of everyone.
- *Excellence:* We deliver our best every day and encourage innovation to continuously improve (p. 3).

CRMC and CRHS kept a strong performance recognition in the community. *Arkansas AY Magazine* recently recognized Troup as a 2020 Person of the Year and CRHS received recognition as 2020 Best Overall Company and AY's Best Hospital of 2020 and 2021. Additionally, CRHS has been consistently recognized as one of the Best Places to Work for 2017, 2018, 2020 by Modern Healthcare and Best Companies Group; Table 21.1 summarizes results for eight survey categories.

The CRHS work environment category has consistently shown high employee satisfaction. Other categories are still representing a strong performance; even though they lacked a consistent increase. Each category of this survey is reviewed in greater detail within the case study and in Appendixes A and B.

CRHS has shown consistently strong indicators of employee engagement since 2017. Press Ganey collects, investigates, compares, ranks, and

**TABLE 21.1 Best Places to Work for 2017, 2018, 2020 by Modern Healthcare and Best Companies Group**

| Year | Leadership and Planning | Corporate Culture and Communications | Role Satisfaction | Work Environment | Relationship With Supervisor | Training, Development and Resources | Pay and Benefits | Overall Engagement | Survey Average |
|---|---|---|---|---|---|---|---|---|---|
| 2020 | 84% | 83% | 89% | 91% | 86% | 80% | 78% | 90% | 85% |
| 2018 | 88% | 84% | 90% | 89% | 87% | 81% | 79% | 91% | 86% |
| 2017 | 84% | 82% | 87% | 84% | 84% | 75% | 78% | 87% | 82% |

*Note:* Number of participants in 2017: 191; 2018: 220; 2020: 228. Numbers shown represent the average percentage of respondents that answered *Agree Somewhat* or *Agree Strongly*.

provides data to CRHS to evaluate several areas of employee engagement such as satisfaction with the organization, direct supervisor/manager, job and engagement indicator. An important factor to recognize is that over 1,000 employees of CRHS were surveyed to collect this data (M.Troup, personal communication, February 24, 2021). Press Ganey data on employee engagement at CRHS, including national comparison, is presented below:

- 2020 PG rank 92nd percentile nationally
- 2019 PG rank 87th percentile nationally
- 2018 PG rank 80th percentile nationally
- 2017 PG rank 63rd percentile nationally
- 2016 PG rank 76th percentile nationally
- 2015 PG rank 32nd percentile nationally (R. Tyler, personal communication, March 22, 2021).

It is important to note that at CRHS not only employees and staff show high levels of engagement with the organization, but also physicians. As indicated previously, physician shortages are one of the complex upcoming problems in our country. Within healthcare, research indicates that engaged physicians contribute to organizational stability and patient-centered care, which ultimately helps build and sustain organizational value (Doublestein et al., 2015). "The most effective healthcare systems are those with the most-engaged physicians" (Gray et al., 2020, p. 954). CRHS has predominately high levels of physician activation, as physicians play an important role in the governance of their healthcare system (Gray et al., 2020; Patton, 2020). "Physician-led initiatives can have a profound impact on the efficiency, safety, and value of care delivery" (Gray et al., 2020, p. 955).

In December of 2020 CRHS named a surgeon with 30 years of medical experience and community engagement, Mike Stanton, MD, as a new chief of staff. Stanton's goals are to ensure establishments and maintenance of the cooperative environment and shared governance between CRHS 200 physicians, administration, and board of directors (Patton, 2020). High levels of physician engagement are a strong contributor to the "value-based healthcare system" (Gray et al., 2020, p. 957). At CRHS employees across various levels of organization show high levels of engagement, which can be attributed to an effective leadership style and strong organizational mission, vision, and core values, especially when engagement rankings have consistently increased since Troup's appointment (Kellerman, 2008). The next section examines internal and external leadership practices, which yield strong outcomes at CRHS.

## Leadership Practices at CRHS

CRHS administrative team incorporates interdisciplinary leadership styles to set a favorable environment for development and implementation of sustainable goals by seeking input from employees and community. There are several monthly and quarterly initiatives that take place to boost effective two-way communication and as a result, flatten the organization. Employees participate in quarterly town hall meetings, are encouraged to give direct feedback to the CEO, and have an opportunity to evaluate direct supervisors through skip level interviews conducted by Troup. Additionally, cross-departmental collaboration of 80 departments at CRHS is evaluated monthly through a success partner survey, which allows employees to rate departments they worked with in the last month (B. Gibbs, personal communication, February 26, 2021). After the data is collected and analyzed using internal and external experts, the CRHS administrative team evaluates survey results and investigates any issues that need action. Lastly, CRHS encourages input from the community to provide necessary services to the citizens, which has shown to be very valuable during the times of pandemic. Detailed review of employee engagement practices, community engagement initiatives, COVID-19 response and partnership expansion is presented next.

***Employee Engagement***

To engage employees in the decision-making process and mutual engagement, Troup created several internal initiatives:

- Mandatory town hall meetings followed by quarterly "pulse surveys" based on the scale developed by Dr. R. Wayne Boss (a professor in the Leeds School of Business at the University of Colorado). Troup and CRHS top leadership team review survey results and report on progress with any employees concerns during the next town hall meeting. During in person meetings, pre-COVID average participation yielded 650 employees; however, due to COVID-19 and the new virtual nature of meetings, participation rose to 1,100 employees, which showed a strong commitment from employees and administration to building powerful two-way communication practices.
- Initiated an "Ask the CEO" option at the end of "pulse surveys" to increase two-way dialogue.
- Established monthly success partner survey which measures cross-departmental effectiveness.

- Introduced the following employee benefits and initiatives: seventh paid holiday, Martin Luther King Day; One Team Rewards recognition program; relaxation lounge setup for employees with massage chairs; town hall gifts for employees each quarter; take home ready-made meals at a discount; new employee assistance program; initiated the formation of the diversity committee and clinical congress.
- Implemented quarterly skip level interviews conducted by the CEO to get direct feedback from employees about their supervisor's performance and leadership skills (B. Gibbs, personal communication, February 26, 2021).

CRHS leadership team is focused on building an accommodating and inclusive organizational environment through improving and securing employee satisfaction, engagement, collaboration, empowerment, two-way communication, and trust. Employees at CRHS exhibit a strong satisfaction with the leadership practices and planning initiatives; survey results are presented in Table 21.2.

The CRHS leadership and planning category has consistently shown a strong performance; however, it lacks a consistent increase. Additionally, CRHS partners with field experts to engage staff in the decision-making process. Troup recognizes that start-up thinking is the key to overcoming many obstacles the organization faces. His strive for sustainable goals development and practical solutions to complex problems, prompted Troup to incorporate outside talent and expertise. Startup Junkie Consulting (Innovation Junkie) of Fayetteville, Arkansas provided CRHS with consulting. In 2019 the first daylong workshop included 100 leaders from CRHS, who worked with 13 teams pitching various innovative ideas. Some of the ideas

**TABLE 21.2 Leadership and Planning Category: Best Places to Work for by Modern Healthcare and Best Companies Group**

| # | Category Question | 2017 | 2018 | 2020 |
|---|---|---|---|---|
| 1 | I understand the long-term strategy of this organization. | 88 | 93 | 89 |
| 2 | I have confidence in the leadership of this organization. | 88 | 91 | 88 |
| 3 | The leaders of this organization care about their employees' well-being. | 84 | 89 | 85 |
| 4 | Senior leaders live the core values of the organization. | 86 | 90 | 86 |
| 5 | There is adequate planning of departmental objectives. | 79 | 85 | 81 |
| 6 | There is adequate follow-through of departmental objectives. | 77 | 82 | 80 |
| 7 | The leaders of this organization are open to input from employees. | 83 | 86 | 82 |
| | **Average** | **84** | **88** | **84** |

*Note:* Number of participants in 2017: 191; 2018: 220; 2020: 228. Numbers shown represent the percentage of respondents that answered *Agree Somewhat* or *Agree Strongly*.

that were implemented included "letting emergency room patients check in online before arriving at the ER, having food service workers rather than nurses deliver meals, and selling premade meals for less than $15 to hospital workers" (Campbell-Miller, 2020, p. 11). Troup recognizes that healthcare industry disruptions require innovative outlook in order to stay relevant and satisfy patients' needs. At CRHS new ideas are pitched, implemented, and followed up on within 3–6 months in order to check if they are meeting desired outcomes, need revision, or termination (Campbell-Miller, 2020).

***Community Engagement***

In addition to internal engagement, CRHS strives to increase external engagement between community and CRHS by offering new and well-established benefits to the community. According to the Community Health Needs Assessment 2019, established benefits are the following:

- Physician recruitment, which strives to bring needed physicians to address community needs.
- AED (automated external defibrillators) donations to organizations across CRHS's service area.
- Safety town program in collaboration with the Junior Auxiliary of Conway to share safety tips with kindergartners.
- "Kids Run Arkansas" event to increase physical activity among children in Faulkner County.
- Diabetes self-management education program.
- AR SAVES in collaboration with the UAMS Center for Distance Health to provide timely neurological care to the patients with stroke symptoms.

CRHS used qualitative and quantitative data to develop the Community Health Needs Assessment 2019, which indicated that the community seeks assistance in the following areas: obesity; nutrition and exercise; access to care; chronic disease management and diabetes; smoking and vaping. CRHS developed a 3-year action plan to address these areas in Faulkner County. Additionally, CRHS started a series of podcasts where any member of the community can meet CRHS employees (from CEO to a nurse) to ask questions and address concerns.

***COVID-19 Response and Partnership Expansion***

In the community, Conway Regional partnered with three institutions of higher education: Central Baptist College, University of Central Arkansas, and Hendrix College, and the Conway Public School District, to form the COVID-19 Conway Education Consortia. The purpose of the consortia was to provide testing, tracing, and guidance on health and safety. Conway is known as the city of colleges and the COVID-19 Conway Education Consortia was a significant way for CRHS to respond to the community needs during the pandemic.

In public presentations to local noon Rotary club in 2020 and on the CRHS podcast *One Team, One Promise,* three college presidents expressed their gratitude to Matt Troup and CRHS for their ongoing collaboration during the pandemic. Troup himself stated during his participation in Rotary events that CRHS has never done such an inclusive partnership with institutions of higher education (Troup, 2020; Troup & Bradley, 2021). After the pandemic year the COVID-19 Conway Education Consortia was labeled a success. The CRHS leadership team met weekly with leaders of three higher education institutions and the superintendent of the local school system to keep up with COVID-19 community updates. Since the start of the pandemic in March 2020, CRHS has provided COVID-19 testing, contact tracing, and additional services for students and employees of the COVID-19 Conway Education Consortia (Troup & Bradley, 2021).

## The Mutual Engagement Leadership Model Outcomes at CRHS

Since Troup became a president and CEO, he has built a strong collaborative organizational environment, which equalizes and promotes shared power practices between leaders and followers at CRHS. This environment is instrumental for the implementation of interdisciplinary leadership. Troup has exhibited strong interdisciplinary leadership competencies in his tenure at CRHS (Negandhi et al., 2015). He effectively leads vision, mission, and strategic planning development, while being a successful change agent. Troup exposes CRHS to internal and external influences, which keep the organization innovative. He truly built a strong team through integrating ICARE values every day in his leadership and CRHS. Troup's leadership focus has been recognized on multiple levels and resulted in robust organizational outcomes. CRHS employees consistently show high follower engagement, satisfaction with leadership, and long-term planning initiatives. In the past 6 years, CRHS has built an innovative culture which embraces an open information exchange, employee's collaboration, empowerment, and trust. Organizational trust, strong ethical and moral practices at CRHS are built through professional clinical shared governance (PCSG) of CRMC which was established in 2015. CRHS goal is to provide in the local community "high-quality, compassionate healthcare services" (CRHS, 2021a, p. 1). The purpose of PCSG is "to provide a mechanism to establish, uphold, and communicate its values and standards within CRHS" (CRHS, 2021a, p. 2). PCSG operates through four levels of governance councils: department councils; patient care governing congress; patient care leadership council; and CRHS executive councils (CRHS, 2021a). Modern Healthcare and Best Companies Group and Press Ganey surveys report high levels of employee trust and satisfaction with ethical and moral practices at CRHS.

Strong leadership outcomes and outstanding employee performance have been recognized on many levels. Below is the list of significant expansions, recent awards, and recognitions that CRHS and its employees obtained:

- Service expansion: Neurospine surgery, sleep medicine, and plastic surgery.
- Location expansion: A new 42,530 square-foot medical office building and a new family practice clinic in Greenbrier; taking over management of Dardanelle Regional Medical Center, formerly known as River Valley Medical Center; Conway Regional Surgical Associates expansion into Russellville and Clinton.
- Certified in 2021 by Great Place to Work, "the global authority on workplace culture, employee experience, and the leadership behaviors proven to deliver market-leading revenue, employee retention and increased innovation" (CRHS, 2021b, para. 3).
- Magnet designation from the American Nurses Credentialing Center in 2019 as a "reflection of nursing professionalism, teamwork, and superiority in patient care" (CRHS, 2020, para. 2). "Only 8% of hospitals nationwide achieve Magnet Recognition status" (CRHS, 2020, para. 5).
- Received 52 CareChex awards by Quantros in 2018, including:
  - #1 Hospital in the Central Arkansas Market for Medical Excellence in Overall Hospital Care
  - #1 Hospital in the State for Patient Safety in Orthopedic Care
  - #1 Hospital in the State for Medical Excellence in Women's Health
- Two Press Ganey awards for physician engagement in 2019: The Guardian of Excellence and the Pinnacle of Excellence awards. The annual Guardian of Excellence award indicates that during January–December 2018, CRHS physician engagement scores were in the top 5% for each reporting period for the award year with "a minimum of 30 completed surveys per year and received a 40% or higher response rate during the specified timeframe" (Press Ganey Associates LLC, 2019, p. 2).
  - The annual Pinnacle of Excellence award presented annually to the "top performing organizations on the basis of extraordinary achievement" (Press Ganey Associates LLC, 2019, p. 4). The Pinnacle of Excellence award indicates that between January 2017 and January 2019 CRHS physicians completed a minimum of 10

surveys and "received a 40% or higher response rate in their two most recent survey periods" (Press Ganey Associates LLC, 2019, p. 5). Most importantly, CRHS physicians' engagement received the highest overall score in their market category of 100–499 physicians (Press Ganey Associates LLC, 2019). CRHS currently have over 125 active staff physicians (CRHS, n.d.-c).

- Best Place to Work recognition in 2017, 2018, 2020 by Modern Healthcare and Best Companies Group.
- AY's Best Overall Company of 2021 (AY Magazine, 2021).
- AY's Best Hospital of 2020 and 2021 (CRHS, n.d.-a).

In the realm of high rewards and recognitions, it is important to reflect on patient satisfaction with CRHS. Press Ganey patient satisfaction surveys are distributed via mail to the released patients with the paid stamp envelope to return the responses or electronically (email and text). Data collected during 2011–2020 measured patient satisfaction with outpatient units; inpatient units; ambulatory surgery; and emergency department. The percentile rankings are based on the mean score ranking within the Press Ganey database, which includes other participating hospitals in the nation (E. Shoffner, personal communication, March 2, 2021). CRMC patient satisfaction percentile compared to other national hospitals is presented in Table 21.3.

This data shows inconsistency of patient satisfaction with CRHS units' performance. Possible explanation of such low and inconsistent patience satisfaction can be explained by the nationwide study conducted by Fenton et al. (2012) between 2000 and 2007 in the United States. The study collected data from adult respondents ($N = 51{,}946$) and showed that high patient satisfaction was associated with "lower emergency department utilization, higher inpatient utilization, greater total healthcare expenditures, and higher expenditures on prescription drugs" (Fenton et al., 2012, p. 407). Additionally, "patients with the highest degree of satisfaction also had significantly greater mortality risk" (Fenton et al., 2012. p. 409). The study suggests that healthcare providers should provide patient centered care based on proven results rather than strive for patient satisfaction (Fenton et al., 2012).

**TABLE 21.3 CRMC Press Ganey Patient Satisfaction Percentile Ranking (2011–2020) Compared to the Press Ganey Database**

| Service | 2011 | 2012 | 2013 | 2014 | 2015 | 2016 | 2017 | 2018 | 2019 | 2020 |
|---|---|---|---|---|---|---|---|---|---|---|
| Outpatient Units | 22nd | 29th | 39th | 45th | 43rd | 38th | 41st | 32nd | 51st | 47th |
| Inpatient Units | 52nd | 62nd | 67th | 70th | 62nd | 70th | 79th | 80th | 79th | 65th |
| Ambulatory Surgery | 15th | 15th | 18th | 26th | 32nd | 29th | 37th | 39th | 50th | 42nd |
| Emergency Department | 12th | 7th | 22nd | 15th | 17th | 23rd | 70th | 43rd | 56th | 38th |

Next section presents a detailed overview of survey results, which report employee engagement, culture of open communication, collaboration, and empowerment. An Appendix A includes survey results about CRHS employees' Ooverall Engagement and Pay and Benefits by Best Places to Work for by Modern Healthcare and Best Companies Group, in addition to CRHS Engagement Indicator in comparison with AHA-7 Average, which includes Arkansas, Louisiana, Oklahoma, and Texas, and the National Healthcare Average by Press Ganey. CRHS Overall Engagement indicator has consistently shown high employee satisfaction and consistent increase in the employee eagerness of going to work; satisfaction with the environment where they can perform their best, and soliciting care provided by CRHS to friends. The CRHS Pay and Benefits category has consistently shown employee satisfaction and consistent increase in the employee perception of fair pay and satisfaction with healthcare and organizational benefits. CRHS Employee Survey 2020 rating Engagement Indicator in comparison with AHA-7 Average and the National Healthcare Average by Press Ganey, reports higher engagement compared to other healthcare institutions in the United States.

To reflect on employee engagement, voluntary turnover rates will be reviewed in Table 21.4. The voluntary turnover rates during 2011–2015 showed an increasing trend; 2016–2019 showed a decreasing trend under the new leadership of Troup. Year 2020 or COVID-19 year showed an increase in voluntary turnover rate, which can be attributed to the pandemic rather than leadership practices.

Despite precautions that virtual leadership practices may result in decreasing engagement of followers in an organization, CRHS has seen an increase in employee engagement (Kligler, 2017) during the COVID-19

**TABLE 21.4 Voluntary Turnover Rates at CRHS (2011–2020)**

| Year | Turnover Rate |
|---|---|
| 2020 | 13.4% |
| 2019 | 9.9% |
| 2018 | 12.0% |
| 2017 | 15.0% |
| 2016 | 16.4% |
| 2015 | 18.0% |
| 2014 | 17.4% |
| 2013 | 16.9% |
| 2012 | 13.5% |
| 2011 | 12.3% |

pandemic. Pre-COVID-19 quarterly town hall meetings were held in person but had to be changed to a virtual format. After quarterly town hall meetings, employees were asked to complete an electronic quarterly "pulse survey." During pre-COVID times the number of respondents ranged between 600–700, during COVID-19 times it increased to about 1,100 participants (M. Troup, personal communication, February 24, 2021). This increase in employee participation coincides with the survey results presented in Table 21.5, which report employees' high satisfaction with organizational culture and open communication.

Additionally, CRHS employees exhibit consistent high levels of satisfaction with organizational effort towards employee's collaboration and individual empowerment. Employees are highly satisfied with their work roles; realistic deadlines and work autonomy; recognition they receive from supervisor and organization; safe and comfortable work environment; work–life balance; relationship with a supervisor; distribution of organizational

**TABLE 21.5 Corporate Culture and Communications: Best Places to Work for by Modern Healthcare and Best Companies Group**

| # | Category Question | 2017 | 2018 | 2020 |
|---|---|---|---|---|
| 1 | This organization's corporate communications are frequent enough. | 92 | 93 | 91 |
| 2 | This organization's corporate communications are detailed enough. | 92 | 94 | 90 |
| 3 | I have a good understanding of how this organization is doing financially. | 79 | 86 | 75 |
| 4 | I can trust what this organization tells me. | 86 | 83 | 83 |
| 5 | This organization treats me like a person, not a number. | 83 | 87 | 80 |
| 6 | This organization gives me enough recognition for work that is well done. | 67 | 74 | 72 |
| 7 | Staffing levels are adequate to provide quality products/services. | 59 | 62 | 75 |
| 8 | Quality is a top priority with this organization. | 88 | 89 | 88 |
| 9 | Safety is a top priority with this organization. | 90 | 90 | 88 |
| 10 | I believe there is a spirit of cooperation within this organization. | 89 | 88 | 86 |
| 11 | My employer enables a culture of diversity. | 88 | 88 | 89 |
| 12 | I like the people I work with at this organization. | 94 | 95 | 94 |
| 13 | At this organization, employees have fun at work. | 84 | 87 | 87 |
| 14 | I feel I can express my honest opinions without fear of negative consequences. | 70 | 76 | 76 |
| 15 | Changes that may affect me are communicated to me prior to implementation. | 63 | 74 | 76 |
| | **Average** | **82** | **84** | **83** |

*Note:* Number of participants in 2017: 191; 2018: 220; 2020: 228. Numbers shown represent the percentage of respondents that answered *Agree Somewhat* or *Agree Strongly*.

resources; and opportunities for individual training and development. For more details refer to an Appendix B, which includes seven tables highlighting survey results ranging from employee role satisfaction to CRHS rating by employees in comparison with AHA-7 Average and the National Healthcare Average by Press Ganey.

## CONCLUSION

CRHS is an excellent example of the mutual engagement leadership model at work. Troup's interdisciplinary leadership practices have built a strong collaborative organizational environment, which created "synergy between leadership and followership" at CRHS (Ligon, 2016, p. 9). Successful interdisciplinary leadership practices established successful lateral and vertical communication, cross-departmental alliance, and dynamic feedback on all organizational levels at CRHS. His inclusive and serving approach towards employees and community have set a stage for followers' empowerment on multiple organizational levels, which proliferated human and social capital to boost organizational performance and at the same time improve healthcare quality in the local community and Arkansas. Also, innovative practices at CRHS add value to patients, the community, and all stakeholders involved.

Through implementation and outcomes of the mutual engagement leadership model, CRHS is set to meet future demands of U.S. healthcare. Troup's 6-year leadership journey at CRHS provides solid guiding principles to the enactment of the model and CRHS's impressive list of awards, recognitions, and high-top rankings among other healthcare organizations prove the success of the mutual engagement leadership model, which validates effective interdisciplinary leadership practices in organizational settings.

## APPENDIX A

**TABLE 21.A1 Overall Engagement: Best Places to Work for by Modern Healthcare and Best Companies Group**

| # | Category Question | 2017 | 2018 | 2020 |
|---|---|---|---|---|
| 1 | Overall, I am very satisfied with my employer. | 91 | 94 | 91 |
| 2 | **Most days, I look forward to going to work.** | **82** | **85** | **86** |
| 3 | My job provides me with a sense of meaning and purpose. | 89 | 93 | 92 |
| 4 | I am proud to work for this organization. | 90 | 92 | 90 |
| 5 | **I feel this organization has created an environment where I can do my best work.** | **79** | **89** | **89** |
| 6 | I am willing to give extra effort to help this organization succeed. | 92 | 95 | 94 |
| 7 | I plan to continue my career with this organization for at least two more years. | 84 | 90 | 89 |
| 8 | **I would recommend this organization's products/services to a friend.** | **91** | **89** | **92** |
| 9 | I would recommend working here to a friend. | 85 | 92 | 89 |
| | **Average** | **87** | **91** | **90** |

*Note:* # of participants in 2017: 191; 2018: 220; 2020: 228. Numbers shown represent the percentage of respondents that answered *Agree Somewhat* or *Agree Strongly*.

**TABLE 21.A2 Pay and Benefits: Best Places to Work for by Modern Healthcare and Best Companies Group**

| # | Category Question | 2017 | 2018 | 2020 |
|---|---|---|---|---|
| 1 | **My pay is fair for the work I perform.** | **55** | **60** | **65** |
| 2 | **Overall, I'm satisfied with this organization's benefits package.** | **76** | **80** | **82** |
| 3 | I'm satisfied with the amount of vacation (or Paid Time Off). | 80 | 83 | 73 |
| 4 | I'm satisfied with the sick leave policy. | 71 | 64 | 71 |
| 5 | I'm satisfied with the amount of healthcare paid for. | 78 | 78 | 77 |
| 6 | **I'm satisfied with the dental benefits.** | **83** | **86** | **87** |
| 7 | **I'm satisfied with the vision care benefits.** | **84** | **85** | **87** |
| 8 | I'm satisfied with the retirement plan benefits. | 87 | 85 | 82 |
| 9 | **I'm satisfied with the life insurance benefits.** | **83** | **83** | **84** |
| 10 | I'm satisfied with the disability benefits. | 83 | 81 | 81 |
| 11 | I'm satisfied with the tuition reimbursement benefits. | 75 | 81 | 75 |
| | **Average** | **78** | **79** | **78** |

*Note:* # of participants in 2017: 191; 2018: 220; 2020: 228. Numbers shown represent the percentage of respondents that answered *Agree Somewhat* or *Agree Strongly*.

**TABLE 21.A3 CRHS Employee Survey Rating Engagement Indicator in Comparison With AHA-7 Average and the National Healthcare Average by Press Ganey**

| 2020 Item Order | 2020 # of Responses | 2020 Item Text | 2020 Score | 2020 vs. National AHA-7 Average | 2020 vs. National Healthcare Average |
|---|---|---|---|---|---|
| 1 | 1,179 | I am proud to tell people I work for CRHS. | 4.49 | **+.12** | **+.23** |
| 2 | 1,165 | I would stay with CRHS if offered a similar position elsewhere. | 4.16 | **+.15** | **+.28** |
| 3 | 1,176 | I would recommend CRHS to family and friends who need care. | 4.45 | **+.16** | **+.23** |
| 4 | 1,158 | I would like to be working at CRHS three years from now. | 4.32 | **+.09** | **+.20** |
| 5 | 1,175 | I would recommend CRHS as a good place to work. | 4.42 | **+.21** | **+.33** |
| 6 | 1,177 | Overall, I am a satisfied employee. | 4.31 | **+.20** | **+.31** |

*Note:* **Bold** font indicates a statistically significant point difference.
Threshold for 2020: ±.06 compared to the National AHA-7 Average (American Hospital Association Region 7: Arkansas, Louisiana, Oklahoma, and Texas) and the National Healthcare Average.

## APPENDIX B

**TABLE 21.B1 Role Satisfaction: Best Places to Work for by Modern Healthcare and Best Companies Group**

| # | Category Question | 2017 | 2018 | 2020 |
|---|---|---|---|---|
| 1 | **I like the type of work that I do.** | **94** | **96** | **96** |
| 2 | I am given enough authority to make decisions I need to make. | 88 | 88 | 87 |
| 3 | I believe my job is secure. | 81 | 91 | 87 |
| 4 | **Deadlines at this organization are realistic.** | **88** | **89** | **91** |
| 5 | I feel I am valued in this organization. | 78 | 83 | 81 |
| 6 | **I feel part of a team working toward a shared goal.** | **83** | **88** | **88** |
| 7 | **I am able to maintain a reasonable balance between work and my personal life.** | **84** | **84** | **89** |
| 8 | My job makes good use of my skills and abilities. | 90 | 91 | 88 |
| 9 | I have a clear understanding of my job role. | 94 | 95 | 93 |
| 10 | **I understand the importance of my role to the success of the organization.** | **93** | **93** | **93** |
| 11 | Most days, I feel I have made progress at work. | 87 | 93 | 91 |
| | **Average** | **87** | **90** | **89** |

*Note:* # of participants in 2017: 191; 2018: 220; 2020: 228. Numbers shown represent the percentage of respondents that answered *Agree Somewhat* or *Agree Strongly*.

**TABLE 21.B2 Work Environment: Best Places to Work for by Modern Healthcare and Best Companies Group**

| # | Category Question | 2017 | 2018 | 2020 |
|---|---|---|---|---|
| 1 | My physical working conditions are good. | 84 | 95 | 93 |
| 2 | **My general work area is adequately heated/cooled.** | **85** | **89** | **89** |
| 3 | **There is adequate noise control to allow me to focus on my work.** | **81** | **86** | **89** |
| 4 | **My workspace has adequate privacy for me to do my job.** | **81** | **83** | **90** |
| 5 | **I feel physically safe in my work environment.** | **90** | **91** | **93** |
| | **Average** | **84** | **89** | **91** |

*Note:* # of participants in 2017: 191; 2018: 220; 2020: 228. Numbers shown represent the percentage of respondents that answered *Agree Somewhat* or *Agree Strongly*.

**TABLE 21.B3 CRHS Employee Survey Rating Employee in Comparison With AHA-7 Average and the National Healthcare Average by Press Ganey**

| 2020 Item Order | 2020 # of Responses | 2020 Item Text | 2020 Score | 2020 vs. National AHA-7 Average | 2020 vs. National Healthcare Average |
|---|---|---|---|---|---|
| 1 | 1,173 | My work unit works well together. | 4.40 | **+.17** | **+.22** |
| 2 | 1,178 | I like the work I do. | 4.54 | .00 | **+.08** |
| 3 | 1,171 | The environment at CRHS makes employees in my work unit want to go above and beyond what's expected of them. | 3.96 | **+.23** | **+.38** |
| 4 | 1,174 | My job makes good use of my skills and abilities. | 4.28 | +.05 | **+.16** |
| 5 | 1,154 | I have sufficient time to provide the best care/service for our clients/patients. | 3.99 | **+.10** | **+.28** |
| 6 | 1,178 | I can enjoy my personal time without focusing on work matters. | 4.02 | +.01 | **+.13** |
| 7 | 1,179 | I am able to disconnect from work communications during my free time (emails/phone etc.). | 3.94 | –.04 | +.05 |
| 8 | 1,177 | I rarely lose sleep over work issues. | 3.99 | **+.06** | **+.19** |
| 9 | 1,177 | I am able to free my mind from work when I am away from it. | 3.93 | –.02 | **+.12** |
| 10 | 1,163 | I see every patient/client as an individual person with specific needs. | 4.61 | .00 | +.04 |
| 11 | 1,147 | I care for all patients/clients equally even when it is difficult. | 4.59 | –.03 | +.02 |
| 12 | 1,177 | My work is meaningful. | 4.59 | +.02 | **+.11** |
| 13 | 1,178 | The work I do makes a real difference. | 4.52 | –.01 | **+.07** |
| 14 | 1,157 | My coworkers value individuals with different backgrounds. | 4.29 | **–.09** | **+.06** |

*Note:* Bold font indicates a statistically significant point difference.
Threshold for 2020: +/–.06 compared to the National AHA-7 Average (American Hospital Association Region 7: Arkansas, Louisiana, Oklahoma, and Texas) and the National Healthcare Average.

**TABLE 21.B4 Relationship With Supervisor: Best Places to Work for by Modern Healthcare and Best Companies Group**

| # | Category Question | 2017 | 2018 | 2020 |
|---|---|---|---|---|
| 1 | My supervisor treats me fairly. | 86 | 89 | 88 |
| 2 | My supervisor treats me with respect. | 86 | 91 | 89 |
| 3 | My supervisor handles my work-related issues satisfactorily. | 83 | 88 | 85 |
| 4 | My supervisor handles my personal issues satisfactorily. | 88 | 92 | 88 |
| 5 | **My supervisor acknowledges when I do my work well.** | **83** | **83** | **85** |
| 6 | My supervisor tells me when my work needs improvement. | 89 | 88 | 87 |
| 7 | My supervisor is open to hearing my opinion or feedback. | 81 | 87 | 85 |
| 8 | My supervisor helps me develop to my fullest potential. | 79 | 84 | 81 |
| 9 | I feel I can trust what my supervisor tells me. | 79 | 83 | 85 |
| | **Average** | **84** | **87** | **86** |

*Note:* # of participants in 2017: 191; 2018: 220; 2020: 228. Numbers shown represent the percentage of respondents that answered *Agree Somewhat* or *Agree Strongly*

**TABLE 21.B5 CRHS Employee Survey Rating Manager in Comparison With AHA-7 Average and the National Healthcare Average by Press Ganey**

| 2020 Item Order | 2020 # of Responses | 2020 Item Text | 2020 Score | 2020 vs. National AHA-7 Average | 2020 vs. National Healthcare Average |
|---|---|---|---|---|---|
| 1 | 1,176 | The person I report to treats me with respect. | 4.47 | +.05 | **+.08** |
| 2 | 1,176 | The person I report to cares about my job satisfaction. | 4.32 | **+.12** | **+.17** |
| 3 | 1,175 | I am satisfied with the recognition I receive for doing a good job. | 4.01 | **+.14** | **+.25** |
| 4 | 1,169 | I am involved in decisions that affect my work. | 3.91 | **+.10** | **+.20** |
| 5 | 1,173 | When appropriate, I can act on my own without asking for approval. | 4.13 | +.05 | **+.09** |
| 6 | 1,178 | The person I report to encourages teamwork. | 4.38 | **+.09** | **+.14** |
| 7 | 1,179 | I respect the abilities of the person to whom I report. | 4.39 | +.05 | **+.10** |
| 8 | 1,176 | The person I report to is a good communicator. | 4.07 | –.03 | +.04 |
| 9 | 1,165 | The person I report to treats all employees equally regardless of their background. | 4.41 | N/A | **+.15** |

*Note:* Bold font indicates a statistically significant point difference.
Threshold for 2020: ±.06 compared to the National AHA-7 Average (American Hospital Association Region 7: Arkansas, Louisiana, Oklahoma, and Texas) and the National Healthcare Average.

**TABLE 21.B6 Training, Development and Resources: Best Places to Work for by Modern Healthcare and Best Companies Group**

| # | Category Question | 2017 | 2018 | 2020 |
|---|---|---|---|---|
| 1 | **This organization provided as much initial training as I needed.** | **82** | **84** | **88** |
| 2 | This organization provides as much ongoing training as I need. | 82 | 87 | 85 |
| 3 | **This organization provides the technology, equipment, and resources I need to do my job well.** | **78** | **85** | **88** |
| 4 | The computer or other hardware I use to do my job is dependable. | 73 | 82 | 81 |
| 5 | The software and program applications I use to do my job are adequate. | 75 | 83 | 79 |
| 6 | Technology issues are resolved in a timely manner. | 83 | 84 | 79 |
| 7 | Technology issues affecting my work are communicated to me in a timely manner. | 83 | 87 | 84 |
| 8 | I understand what is expected for career advancement. | 82 | 83 | 82 |
| 9 | I am encouraged to explore growth or advancement opportunities within the organization. | 73 | 80 | 73 |
| 10 | There is room for me to advance at this organization. | 61 | 69 | 70 |
| 11 | **I trust that if I do good work, I will be considered for a promotion.** | **52** | **65** | **68** |
| | **Average** | **75** | **81** | **80** |

*Note:* # of participants in 2017: 191; 2018: 220; 2020: 228. Numbers shown represent the percentage of respondents that answered *Agree Somewhat* or *Agree Strongly*.

**TABLE 21.B7 CRHS Employee Survey Rating Organization in Comparison With AHA-7 Average and the National Healthcare Average by Press Ganey**

| 2020 Item Order | 2020 # of Responses | 2020 Item Text | 2020 Score | 2020 vs. National AHA-7 Average | 2020 vs. National Healthcare Average |
|---|---|---|---|---|---|
| 1 | 1,143 | Different work units work well together at CRHS. | 4.02 | **+.14** | **+.26** |
| 2 | 1,171 | CRHS conducts business in an ethical manner. | 4.35 | **+.16** | **+.24** |
| 3 | 1,118 | I am satisfied with my benefits. | 4.01 | **+.17** | **+.31** |
| 4 | 1,176 | CRHS provides high-quality care and service. | 4.46 | **+.15** | **+.23** |
| 5 | 1,176 | CRHS supports me in balancing my work life and personal life. | 4.08 | +.05 | **+.20** |
| 6 | 1,166 | CRHS makes every effort to deliver safe, error-free care to patients. | 4.43 | **+.10** | **+.19** |
| 7 | 1,165 | My pay is fair compared to other healthcare employers in this area. | 3.84 | **+.36** | **+.48** |
| 8 | 1,174 | My work unit is adequately staffed. | 3.45 | +.03 | **+.18** |
| 9 | 1,175 | I get the training I need to do a good job. | 4.10 | .00 | **+.11** |
| 10 | 1,172 | Patient safety is a priority at CRHS. | 4.50 | +.03 | **+.16** |
| 11 | 1,176 | CRHS treats employees with respect. | 4.28 | **+.19** | **+.33** |
| 12 | 1,158 | CRHS provides career development opportunities. | 4.06 | **+.16** | **+.28** |
| 13 | 1,157 | I get the tools and resources I need to provide the best care/service for our clients/patients. | 4.11 | **+.08** | **+.20** |
| 14 | 1,169 | CRHS values employees from different backgrounds. | 4.37 | –.02 | **+.10** |
| 15 | 1,164 | CRHS demonstrates a commitment to workforce diversity. | 4.32 | **–.13** | **+.09** |
| 16 | 1,148 | All employees have an equal opportunity for promotion regardless of their background. | 4.20 | –.01 | **+.16** |

*Note:* Bold font indicates a statistically significant point difference.
Threshold for 2020: ±.06 compared to the National AHA-7 Average (American Hospital Association Region 7: Arkansas, Louisiana, Oklahoma, and Texas) and the National Healthcare Average.

## REFERENCES

AY Magazine. (2021). *AY's best of 2020 winners.* https://www.aymag.com/ays-best-of-2020-winners/

Baker, S. (2007). Followership: The theoretical foundations of a contemporary construct. *Journal of Leadership and Organizational Studies, 14*(1), 50–60. https://doi.org/10.1177/0002831207304343

Bloomquist, C. D., Georges, L., Ford, D. J., & Breen, J. M. (2018). Interdisciplinary leadership practices in graduate leadership education programs. *Journal of Leadership Studies, 12*(2), 60–63. https://doi.org.ucark.idm.oclc.org/10.1002/jls.21579

Braun, V., & Clarke, V. (2006). Using thematic analysis in psychology. *Qualitative Research in Psychology, 3*(2), 77–101. https://doi.org/10.1191/ 1478088706qp063oa

Boyatzis, R. (1998). *Transforming qualitative information: Thematic analysis and code development.* SAGE Publications.

Bolman, L. G., & Deal, T. E. (2008). *Reframing organizations: Artistry, choice and leadership* (4th ed.). Jossey Bass.

Campbell-Miller, S. (2020). Established Arkansas companies seek startup mindset. *Arkansas Business, 37*(6), 1, 10–11.

Carlson, D., Ferguson, M., Hunter, E., & Whitten, D. (2012). Abusive supervision and work-family conflict: The path through emotional labor and burnout. *Leadership Quarterly, 23*(5), 849–859. https://doi.org/10.1016/j.leaqua.2012.05.003

Conway Regional Health System. (n.d.-a). *Awards & recognition.* https://www.conwayregional.org/about/quality-care/awards-recognition

Conway Regional Health System. (n.d.-b). *Community health needs assessment 2019.* https://www.conwayregional.org/docs/default-source/crhs/reports/finalforweb-chna2019-121619.pdf?sfvrsn=1189f449_5

Conway Regional Health System (n.d.-c). *Physicians.* https://www.conwayregional.org/about/physicians

Conway Regional Health System (n.d.-d). *About Conway Regional Health System.* https://www.conwayregional.org/about

Conway Regional Health System. (2020, September 15). *Conway regional medical center receives magnet designation.* https://www.conwayregional.org/about/news/conway-regional/2021/01/04/conway-regional-medical-center-receives-magnet-designation

Conway Regional Health System. (2021a). *Bylaws of professional clinical shared governance.*

Conway Regional Health System. (2021b, April 2). *Conway regional health system earns 2021 great place to work certification.* https://conwayintranet.mhpteamsi.com/about/news/conway-regional/2021/04/01/conway-regional-health-systems-earns-2021-great-place-to-work-certification

Crossman, B., & Crossman, J. (2011). Conceptualizing followership—A review of the literature. *Leadership, 7*(4), 481–497. https://doi.org/10.1177/1742715011416891

Creswell, J. W. (2014). *Research design: Qualitative, quantitative, and mixed methods approaches* (4th ed.). SAGE Publications

Davis, G. R., & Scott, R. (2006). *Organizations and organizing: Rational, natural and open systems perspectives.* Routledge.

Doublestein, B., Lee, W, & Pfohl, R. (2015). Healthcare 2050: Anticipatory leadership, physician shortages, and patient-centered care. In M. Sowcik, A. Andenoro, M. Mcnutt, & S. Murphy (Eds.), *Leadership 2050: Critical challenges, key contexts and emerging trends* (pp. 109–126). Emerald Publishing.

Einarsen, S., Aasland, M. S., & Skogstad, A. (2007). Destructive leadership behaviour: A definition and conceptual model. *The Leadership Quarterly, 18*(3), 207–216. https://doi.org/10.1016/j.leaqua.2007.03.002

Fenton, J. J., Jerant, A. F., Bertakis, K. D., & Franks, P. (2012). The cost of satisfaction: A national study of patient satisfaction, healthcare utilization, expenditures, and mortality. *Archives of Internal Medicine, 172*(5), 405–411. https://doi.org/10.1001/archinternmed.2011.1662

Gray, C., Parvataneni, H., & Bozic, K. (2020). Value-based healthcare. *Clinical Orthopaedics and Related Research, 478*(5), 954–957. https://doi.org/10.1097/CORR.0000000000001234

Healthcare Bluebook. (2022). *Hospital quality awards: An objective comparison.*https://www.quantros.com/hospital-quality-awards-objective-comparison/

Jones, S. R., Torres, V., & Arminio, J. (2014). *Negotiating the complexities of qualitative research in higher education: Fundamental elements and issues* (2nd ed.). Routledge.

Kellerman, B. (2007). What every leader needs to know about followers. *Harvard Business Review, 85*(12), 84–91.

Kellerman, B. (2008). *Followership: How followers are creating change and changing leaders.* Harvard Business Press.

Kelley, R. (1992). *The power of followership.* Doubleday.

Kligler, B. (2017, April 18). Leading a virtual team. *Explore, 13*(4), 277–278.

Lees, D. W., & Uri, T. (2018). Using a systemic design paradigm to develop sustainability leadership and build organizational interdisciplinary sustainability platforms. *Creighton Journal of Interdisciplinary Leadership, 4*(1), 35–49.

Ligon, K. V. (2015, October 14–17). *The destructive leader's impact on organizational culture* [Poster session]. 17th Annual Global Conference of International Leadership Association, Barcelona, Spain.

Ligon, K. V. (2016). *Measuring followership: An empirical investigation of the Kelley followership questionnaire-revised* (Order No. 10245303). https://www.proquest.com/openview/03469bfcff5fbcf2c7afe6ad25b1c7da/1?pq-origsite=gscholar&cbl=18750

Lorinkova, N. M., Pearsall, M. J., & Sims, H. P., Jr. (2013). Examining the differential longitudinal performance of directive versus empowering leadership in teams. *Academy of Management Journal, 56*(2), 573–596. http://dx.doi.org/10.5465/amj.2011.0132

Marks, D., & Yardley, L. (2003). *Research methods for clinical and health psychology* (1st ed.). SAGE Publications.

Mills, A. J., Durepos, G., & Wiebe, E. (2010). *Encyclopedia of case study research* (Vols. 1-0). SAGE Publications. https://doi.org/10.4135/9781412957397

Nowell, L. S., Norris, J. M., White, D. E., & Moules, N. J. (2017). Thematic analysis: Striving to meet the trustworthiness Criteria. *International Journal of Qualitative Methods, 16*(1), 1–17. https://doi.org/10.1177/1609406917733847

Negandhi, P., Negandhi, H., Tiwari, R., Sharma, K., Zodpey, S. P., Quazi, Z., Gaidhane, A., Jayalakshmi N, Gijare, M., & Yeravdekar, R. (2015). Building interdisciplinary leadership skills among health practitioners in the twenty-first century: An innovative training model. *Frontiers in Public Health, 3,* Article 221. https://doi.org/10.3389/fpubh.2015.00221

Padilla, A., Hogan, R., & Kaiser, R. B. (2007). The toxic triangle: Destructive leaders, susceptible followers, and conducive environments. *Leadership Quarterly, 18*(3), 176–194. https://doi.org/10.1016/j.leaqua.2007.03.001

Patton J. (2020). Surgeon picks up the torch. *501 Life Magazine, 12*(8), 27

Press Ganey Associates LLC. (2019). *2019 Press Ganey Award criteria.* https://www.pressganey.com/docs/default-source/awards/2019-press-ganey-award-criteria.pdf

Press Ganey Associates LLC. (2021). *History & mission.* https://www.pressganey.com/about/history-mission

Press Ganey Associates LLC. (2022a). *About Press Ganey.* https://www.pressganey.com/about-us/news/forsta

Press Ganey Associates LLC. (2022b). *Press Ganey Award criteria.* https://www.pressganey.com/sites/default/files/2022-05/2022%20Press%20Ganey%20Awards%20Program%20Criteria%20FINAL.pdf

Quantros, Inc. (n.d.). *Hospital quality awards: An objective comparison.* https://www.quantros.com/hospital-quality-awards-objective-comparison/

Quantros, Inc. (2021). *About.* https://www.quantros.com/about/

Schyns, B., & Schilling, J. (2013). How bad are the effects of bad leaders? A meta-analysis of destructive leadership and its outcomes. *The Leadership Quarterly, 24*(1), 138–158. https://doi.org/10.1016/j.leaqua.2012.09.001

Stake, R. E. (1995). *The art of case study research.* SAGE Publications.

Stake, R. E. (2000). Case studies. In N. K. Denzin & Y. S. Lincoln (Eds.), *Handbook of qualitative research* (2nd ed.; pp. 435–454). SAGE Publications.

Tepper, B. J. (2000). Consequences of abusive supervision. *Academy of Management Journal, 43*(2), 178–190.

Thomas, E. V., Wells, R., Baumann, S. D., Graybill, E., Roach, A., Truscott, S. D., Crenshaw, M., & Crimmins, D. (2019). Comparing traditional versus retrospective pre-/post-assessment in an interdisciplinary leadership training program. *Maternal & Child Health Journal, 23*(2), 191–200.

Troup, M. (2020, Oct. 20). *Event leading through Zoom: Effective team management.* Jeff Farris Leadership Academy Rotary District 6170..

Troup, M., & Bradley, P. (Hosts). (2021, March 17). *COVID education consortia* [Audio podcast episode]. In One Team One Promise. https://www.conwayregional.org/about/podcasts?fbclid=IwAR1_UTcm_EPChJIfzdVJViVpLAmNLbg-FIwkrmjMAT4CZn3ytEMNlh8h_DI

Tost, L. P., Gino, F., & Larrick, R. P. (2013). When power makes others speechless: The negative impact of leader power on team performance. *Academy of Management Journal, 56*(5), 1465–1486. https://doi.org/10.5465/amj.2011.0180

Uhl-Bien, M., Riggio, R. E., Lowe, K. B., & Carsten, M. K. (2014). Followership theory: A review and research agenda. *The Leadership Quarterly, 25*(1), 83–104. https://doi.org/10.1016/j.leaqua.2013.11.007

CHAPTER 22

# BECOMING AN INTEGRATED LEADER

**Alyncia M. Bowen**

## ABSTRACT

As leadership is a position of influence and impact on others, it is paramount for all individuals aligned with the title of "leader" to learn their personal leadership style, drive, and compass. Likewise, it is important for all leaders to determine when to shift and or realign their strategic goals. Having served in a leadership role for the better half of 25 years it has become acutely apparent that one approach is not appropriate for every industry, organization, or the individuals that are being led. Experienced leaders are aware of their leadership style and are thereby able to pivot when deemed necessary. This chapter is an autoethnographic approach of this author's journey of becoming an integrated leader during disruption, both internally and externally, by capitalizing on the experience gleaned while leading in two nonprofit organizations, one a service organization and the other an institution of higher education. As an integrated leader it is necessary to (a) synthesize key learning from prior experiences, (b) identify and leverage transferable skills, (c) develop a mode of continuous personal and professional development, and (d) transfer knowledge that is meaningful for those that follow.

*On Leadership*, pages 421–437

During the past 50 years, research in leadership has resulted in more than 1,000 studies in an attempt to determine the definitive styles, characteristics, or personality traits of great leaders (George et al., 2007). The popularity of the topic of leadership has remained a constant for research for several centuries, even as early as the mid 1800s. Today effective leaders seek to remain relevant and knowledgeable. Defining leadership is a pervasive challenge that is flavored with experience, history, and developed competencies. For this writing the following two positions on leadership will serve as the foundation. Northouse (2013) shared, "Some define leadership in terms of the power relationship that exists between leaders and followers. From this viewpoint, leaders have power that they wield to effect change in others" (p. 5). "Leadership is an evolving concept that invokes the interactive influence that occurs when, in a given context, some people accept someone as their leader to achieve common goals" (Alberto, 2012, p. 4). Today's leader has to be able to identify the strengths in others and teach them how to leverage both their strengths and weaknesses to their advantage. As a leader it has been a delight and a challenge to balance the needs of the organization with the needs of my team.

Having served in two nonprofit private organizations, this author was presented with turbulence and disruption both internally and externally. Healthcare is dynamic and ever changing. Serving in leadership during multiple recessions, major healthcare reforms at both the local and federal level, and during the September 11, 2001 attack provided a unique opportunity to pivot and develop personally and professionally. After serving in healthcare for over 23 years, an opportunity to work in higher education became available. The shift reaffirmed that leadership skills and competencies are transferable and that the act of leading itself is not contingent upon the industry in which one works.

During an informal conversation with a profound visionary senior leader, this author was asked, "What is your gray?" While simple in nature this question forced the author to really delve into the parameters that have formulated my leadership style, journey, position, and influence. Clearly the diverse industries served as pivotal points along my leadership journey. But what is the role of the gray? The question is best illustrated in Figure 22.1. The overlap in the segments below represents the gray. The answer had to cross the boundaries of healthcare, business, and education. The gray as it were, is my present place of leading. As such, leaders with multi-industry experiences should evaluate how the gray influences their current leadership style and or practice.

Ihama (2017) shared that "to be integrated means every aspect of something is linked and well-coordinated" (para. 1). The gray is the interwoven intricacies of a leaders' values, morals, and competencies. As such these attributes are ingrained in one's leadership practice and style.

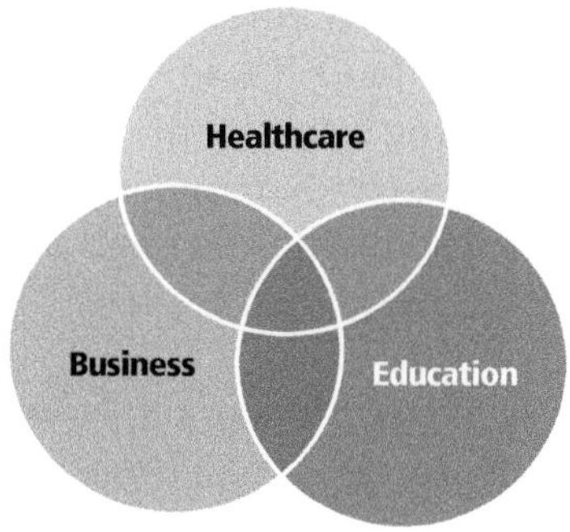


**Figure 22.1** The gray.

This intrinsic nature contributes to the interdisciplinary nature of being an integrated leader.

## HISTORICAL PERSPECTIVE

The proverbial question, "Are leaders born or made?" is often at the core of the exploration of the topic of leadership. To begin providing a perspective of leadership it was important to research the origin, the etymology of leadership. Grace (2003) posits:

> The root word of leadership—lead—has a history of change in both form and meaning, from its origin (around 800 A.C.E.) to its evolution into the concept of leader (around 1300 A.C.E.), and finally to leadership in the mid-19th century... The root word of leadership is *lead* from the Anglo-Saxon Old English word *loedan,* the casual form of *lithan*—to travel... The use of the word *leader* in the English language in the English language (beginning around 1300 A.C.E.) demonstrated awareness of a new role in society. (p. 3)

In addition, Kelly (2014) posits that "when one studies the etymology of the word lead, leader and leadership and its ancient relative *Ducere,* one can begin to appreciate why there is so much complexity and variance in our modern understanding of what leaders do and what leadership is" (para. 2).

Leadership principles are values translated into action. Having a solid base of values and testing them under fire enables one to develop the principles used in leading. For example, a value such as "concern for others" might be translated into a leadership principle such as "create a work environment where people are respected for their contributions, provided job security, and allowed to fulfill their potential" (George et al., 2007, p. 4). Theoretical frameworks of leadership theories and its application to the workplace has been extensively researched for more than 3 decades. Conger and Benjamin (1999) defined leadership as centered on ideas, vision, and direction, emphasizing inspiring people with goals, as opposed to day-to-day execution. When asked where individuals learn their leadership skills, employees often suggest that it is through their past experiences on the job or through associating with their leaders.

> *Kurt Lewin stated, "There's nothing so practical as a good theory."*
>
> —Greenwood & Levin, 1998, p. 9

## The Great Man Theory

The existence of the great man theory has roots as early as the mid 1800s. Early as the 19th century the question of whether or not leaders were born or made invoked discussions. Additional questions regarding what set great leaders apart from their peers and how they defied the odds were also topics of discussion and debate. Thomas Carlyle put forth the idea that "the world's history is nothing more than a collection of biographies belonging to great men" (Villanova, 2019, para. 3). Accordingly, there are two assumptions that are made that are foundational to the great man theory:

- Great leaders are born possessing certain traits that enable them to rise and lead.
- Great leaders can arise when the need for them is great. (Villanova, 2019, para. 3).

The belief of how great leaders emerge is still being debated in the 21st century and yet there are truths to both assumptions and others yet to be shared. For example, during the COVID-19 pandemic the test of leadership provided a platform for great leaders to shine, emerging leaders to thrive, and unknown leaders to enter into a new arena of "presence." In times of great turmoil and uncertainty the strength and capabilities of a leader emerges. When there are no historical examples that neatly fit the current ailment, great leaders emerge due to their ability to remain open to innovative ideas and adapt to change.

In many instances, Carlyle would refer to great leaders as heroes. Today there are individuals who are true heroes. They are unsung, unknown to the general population but nonetheless heroes to the constituents in which they influence.

## Transactional and Transformational Leadership

James MacGregor Burns has been accredited with expanding the transactional and transformational theories of leadership. "Transactional leadership seeks to maintain organizational stability through regular social exchanges leading to goal achievement for leaders and their followers" (Arenas et al., 2017, p. 20). In this approach the self interests of both the leader and the follower are satisfied. Transactional leaders promote, comply, and provide both rewards and punishments. In the transactional model, according to Malik et al. (2014), change initiatives are a team effort.

Conversely, transformational leaders garner the employees trust in the work relationship. Flynn and Sylva (2019) posits that transformational leaders look beyond their own interests for the good of the organization. This leadership style is concerned with the followers' attitudes, behaviors, and performance outcomes (Northouse, 2013). It is further noted that transformational leaders encourage a positive, motivated, inspirational, and creative culture (Moriano et al., 2014). This premise could also suppose that transformational leaders are also authentic and transparent. According to Wren (2018) this leader type cultivates growth, commitment, and motivation thereby increasing commitment and productivity.

## DISRUPTION

Being afforded the privilege of being trained in both the Six Sigma and Lean Six Sigma management model in 2001 provided a stage for managing change within the healthcare organization that this author served. "Six Sigma is a management model that originated in the 1980s by an employee of Motorola. While the original intent of the model was designed as a means of ensuring the organization's existence, it has since evolved into a modality for communicating organizational changes and outcomes" (Bowen, 2020, p. 32). In recollection the management model was strongly resisted by many of the employees. This was largely due to many of them being involved in initiatives that were presented and were either dismissed or they failed. A common term for a change initiative that did not survive time was "flavor of the month." As one of the 44 individuals selected to be trained in the Six Sigma/ Lean Six Sigma management model, uncertainty of how the organization would be positively impacted loomed. To demonstrate their commitment, the leadership of the organization, at that time, provided each one of the practitioners with a contract that permitted them to return to their previous role after a 2-year commitment as a practitioner. This type of commitment was new and made the 2-year dedication less daunting. The formal training entailed 6 months in a classroom setting, passing four exams and completing two approved projects. One with "hard" savings that could be tied to the bottom line and the second on "soft" savings. The soft savings were aligned with improving employee morale and or satisfaction. Parallel to the transformational process of Six Sigma/Lean Six Sigma, the organization determined to re-awaken the spirit values in the workplace. In short, the organization embarked upon a culture shift that promoted the servant leader approach. This approach will be explored later in this writing.

The first year the Six Sigma/Lean practitioners spent a great deal of time explaining the management model to project stakeholders and using their tools in their newly developed toolkit. The first year projected internal savings were met with ease. And, the culture of the organization began to embrace the change model, Six Sigma, and the practitioners. Trust was cultivated and soon the Six Sigma practitioners were introduced to more challenging problems. Each year the organization experienced quantifiable savings beyond the projected goals. By the end of the second year, many of the practitioners remained in their role, others were hired into vacant or newly formed leadership roles. Soon the thought of the flavor of the month was no longer a language found in the organization. This new-found trust in the "process" also promoted the culture shift that was taking place.

An opportunity arose to become an operational director of a division that was not meeting their financial projections. Also, morale in the division was at an all-time low. The immediate thought for this writer was, what tools could be carried forward to this present situation. Interestingly it was not until this writer crossed the thresholds of this new opportunity that it became apparent that the terms—courageous and authentic surfaced as viable tools.

## Servant Leadership

The servant leadership way of leading was introduced to this writer during a period of culture transformation within a healthcare organization. The question to be addressed was, "How do we re-awaken the spirit values in the workplace?" Interestingly the catholic-based healthcare organization found itself at a pivotal time that required assessment of who they were and why they were present in their community. Key to sustainability was determining how to maintain the principles and values upon which it was founded.

During organized retreats and leadership gatherings, teachings and trainings took place on understanding one's personal values and how they aligned with the organization's values. An outcome of the training was that the leader was empowered to support the evaluation of personal and divisional values within the business units in which they served. Boyum (n.d.) states:

> The term servant is defined as, "one who is under obligation to work for the benefit of a superior and to obey his or her commands." . . . The original term servant leader often is accredited to Christianity and the teachings of Jesus. In the Biblical text, Jesus gives instruction on the qualities of a leader, the role of the leader and the issue of power or (authority) of a leader . . . Thus, a servant leader is a person who has an innate desire to lead by serving, serves to align with own beliefs, and strives to meet the highest priorities of others. (p. 8)

Greenleaf (1977), the seminal leader of the phrase servant leadership posits that

> the servant-leader is servant first . . . It begins with the natural feeling that one wants to serve, to serve first. Then conscious choice brings one to aspire to lead. That person is sharply different from one who is leader first, perhaps because of the need to assuage an unusual power drive or to acquire material possessions. For such it will be a later choice to serve—after leadership is established. The leader-first and the servant-first are two extreme types. Between them there are shadings and blends that are part of the infinite variety of human nature . . . The difference manifests itself in the care taken by the servant-first to make sure that other people's highest priority needs are being served. (p. 13)

Aligning the work of Burns with servant leadership suggests that servant leadership is an example of transformational leadership. Transformational leaders tend to appeal to the moral values of those that they lead. Likewise, the primary tenants of a servant leader are to improve those that they lead. This is a form of transformation. Boyum (n.d.) suggests that the servant leadership literature claims that such a leader is grounded in values, manages values, and manages vision as a means of improving performance.

## Authentic Leadership

The practice of leading is dynamic. The concept has evolved from transformational leadership to authentic leadership (Walumbwa & Wernsing, 2013). Transformational, transactional, and authentic leadership approaches foster trust. Berberoglu (2015) argued that organizational commitment played a significant role in employees' behaviors. Luthans and Avollio (2003) suggest that authentic leadership is a form of positive leadership. Walumbwa et al. (2008) states:

> It is a pattern of leader behavior that draws upon and promotes both psychological capabilities and positive ethical climate to foster greater self-awareness, an internalized moral perspective, balanced information processing and

relational transparency on the part of leaders working with followers, fostering positive development. (p. 93)

No one can be authentic by trying to imitate someone else. You can learn from others' experiences, but there is no way you can be successful when you are trying to be like them. People trust you when you are genuine and authentic, not a replica of someone else (George et al., 2007). As a Six Sigma/Lean practitioner working with many leaders in varying roles was an expectation. This afforded opportunities to observe different approaches to leading.

Early in the process all practitioners were aligned directly with the Six Sigma deployment leader. Later the reporting structure aligned with an organizational vice president or c-suite leader. It was when aligned with a VP named Todd (pseudonym) that it became very obvious that developing relationships was one of my deficits. The straight to the point approach that was comfortable did not foster trust and engagement. Todd took the time to "push" my boundaries whenever possible. It was this writer/leader's response to the prodding that made the difference. Developing a new comfort of listening provided an awareness that could only be fathomed. Learning to hear to learn versus respond was one of the great competencies developed.

Eigel and Kuhnert (2005) observed that "authentic leadership is related to many different characteristics such as self-awareness, self-esteem, trustworthiness, integrity, respect for others, high emotional intelligence, transformational leadership, and other noble characteristics" (p. 358). It is the foundation that provokes the belief that leadership is a journey that implores a commitment to continuously developing oneself. The journey to authentic leadership begins with understanding one's individual life story and using the context of one's experiences to define the grey; to find the place where inspiration thrives.

## Internal Disruption

Authentic leaders thrive in the realm of transparency, genuineness, and honesty. They demonstrate a passion for their purpose, practice their values consistently, and lead with their hearts as well as their heads. They establish long-term, meaningful relationships, and have the self-discipline to get results. They know who they are.

When trust is broken it is difficult to bridge the divide. A lesson learned by a former leader was to listen to hear and learn. When listening to develop an allegiance to a preconceived plan of action, it is easy to not hear. In an instance when an organizational restructure took place, the leader-based changes on what they heard. Clearly, the leader was listening but it was difficult deciphering between what was being said as, "Please change things" or "I am just venting." Unfortunately, what they heard was not what was being said and the result was mistrust and confusion. The "CHANGE" was not well received and the response was disheartening. As a leader in this environment it became apparent that healing was necessary. Not physical, but emotional. There were hurt persons and listening to their pain was heart wrenching, but necessary. In this instance, as an authentic leader it was necessary to allow time and consistency to become the bridge towards a better working environment.

## Open-Door Policy

Years ago, as a new leader it was ingrained in me to keep an open door. Make certain those that follow "feel that you are approachable." Allow them the freedom of coming in to sit and dialogue. This was important to learn as a new leader and soon became a norm. The door stayed open and people who reported to me and those who did not report to me would frequent my office. The only barrier to access were those that were there before the person seeking access. For many years the physical and emotional door was open for any and everyone. Before entering into higher education, it became very apparent that the open-door policy worked too well. For instance, as soon as it appeared as if the office was open, people entered to talk, to receive guidance, and/or advice. While it was enjoyable meeting the needs, it also meant longer days, nights, and oftentimes weekends. As a leader most of my days are spent in meetings, when there is office time, it is important to follow through on projects, and other tasks that need to be completed.

The open-door policy was another lesson that was in my leader's toolbox. This policy is great when physically in a shared space. When the pandemic (COVID-19) hit, many organizations left their physical buildings. The transformation for many occurred within 24 hours. Ironically, for this writer/leader, 60 days after joining a new division in the organization, the senior leadership team informed everyone to take what they needed to work remotely. I was new to this team who had just experienced a difficult internal disruption, and now we were no longer in the same building. Day 1, in the midst of many unknowns, communication took place. The leader liaison became an invaluable role. Serving as both the conduit between leadership and my team and my team and leadership. This became my new normal. A parallel thought was, how do we bring individuals together in the middle of a pandemic? One in which we are commissioned to remain socially distant. Here is where rephrasing occurred—socially, is not the same as remaining physically distant? During the pandemic the thought was we are physically distant but we would need to become or remain socially present.

In healthcare, a variable for shift change is that the nurse meets with their replacement nurse prior to ending their shift. In some instances, depending on the care provided, multi-disciplinary team members meet in a huddle to discuss the plans of care, the acuity of the patient, and so on. The huddle concept is not new and it is often used in team-oriented sports. Four days into the work from home environment the team met, via Zoom, to just "talk." The rules of the huddle—no work conversations, cameras can be on or off and what is discussed in the huddle, stays in the huddle. Most preferred to have their cameras on. George et al. (2007) shared that

> leadership principles are values translated into action . . . For example, a value such as "concern for others" might be translated into a leadership principle such as "create a work environment where people are respected for their contributions, provided job security, and allowed to fulfill their potential. (p. 4)

Almost 2 years into the pandemic and the team still "huddles." The time ranges from 45–60 minutes. Communication of what is going on in one's life, births, deaths, gains, losses, gardens, and grandchildren are some of the discussions that take place. As a new leader to this team, the huddle provided direct contact to the team. It provided an opportunity to listen; to see; to connect. The huddle was not the only means for communicating but proved vital. In the pandemic it became this leaders' purpose to speak one on one with everyone at varying points in time. It was during an HR observed performance review that a colleague shared, "I don't know when it happened but it did happen. I now enjoy coming to work. I enjoy working with my leader. I can talk about anything and that makes me glad" (N.A., March 2021). The huddle was another tool transferred from a prior experience, another tool in the toolbox.

Discovering one's authentic leadership requires a commitment to developing oneself. Time must be allocated to crafting one's potential. In a pandemic, external development opportunities evaporate. Conferences and trainings were drying up and the team was disappointed in their inability to attend their sessions. During one of the huddles some of the team members shared about a book they were reading. That sharing sparked the idea of creating a book club. Immediately, excitement filled the meeting space and the book club was born. During the first 6 months of the pandemic the team read three books and discussed what they read. In some instances, the authors were contacted to share further insight into their publication. That action brought additional delight.

As a leader it is important to remain innovative. The book club was an innovative means of promoting professional development. Due to canceled conferences, there was flexibility in the budget for the purchase of the books for the book club. Every team member received their books via mail at no expense. Lesson learned, as a leader do not be afraid to color outside of the lines. Don't be afraid to try something new.

It can be overwhelming to mend a broken team. The first 90 days we began the work of creating the culture we desired. When we were together in the office setting, we met to discuss what that culture looked like. Keywords—autonomy, trust, respect, authenticity, and courage emerged. Initially, as a new leader to this team it was important to just listen and hear what was being said and what was not being said. It was important to respect where they were. Yes, it was painful and intense. One day, one of the team members asked me to give input. What was said was purposeful and intentional. Soon the conversations flowed and as the new leader, I was no longer an outsider.

Within 30 days of joining the team, individual performance evaluations were due. This was difficult because there was a period of internal disruption and realignment. The evaluation process went as well as could be expected and now it was time to establish new goals for the next 6 months. The number one goal was related to cultivating and maintaining the culture we desired. How do you measure a culture shift? Very carefully. As a team we discussed our progression and recognized that it takes time to make a true shift in culture.

Somewhere between the 60th day and the 365th day the team that was internally broken has mended and is thriving. The culture of autonomy, respect, trust, authenticity, and courage is where we thrive, and how do we know it exists? Our peers, the organization as a whole has noticed and that inspires continued work toward the future.

The life stories of authentic leaders cover the full spectrum of experiences—including the positive impact of prior leaders, teachers, mentors, and so forth—there are also negative experiences that shape one's leadership style. The loss of a job, loss of a close friend or relative, feelings of exclusion and rejection from individuals who once supported you. This author often refers to such events as "life." The resiliency of authentic leaders is not predicated only on how they lead others but it also entails how they balance life—professional and personal. Most leaders have a multifaceted support system that includes spouses or significant others, families, mentors, close friends, and colleagues. They also build their networks over time, as the experiences, shared histories, and openness with people close to them foster the trust and confidence they need in times of difficulty, transition, and uncertainty. Oftentimes leaders give more support than they receive.

George et al. (2007) shared:

> When the 75 members of Stanford Graduate School of Business's Advisory Council were asked to recommend the most important capability for leaders to develop, their answer was nearly unanimous: self-awareness. Yet many leaders, especially those early in their careers, are trying so hard to establish themselves in the world that they leave little time for self-exploration. They

> strive to achieve success in tangible ways that are recognized in the external world—money, fame, power, status, or a rising stock price. Often their drive enables them to be professionally successful for a while, but they are unable to sustain that success. As they age, they may find something is missing in their lives and realize they are holding back from being the person they want to be. Knowing their authentic selves require the courage and honesty to open up and examine their experiences. As they do so, leaders become more humane and willing to be vulnerable. (pp. 3–4)

## Self-Care

To my surprise the pandemic also provided some instrumental learnings, new lessons. Initially there was no divide between work and home. The remote work environment fed the desire to stay connected to this author's team. Sleep was a concept and it became increasingly apparent that work had invaded every part of this leader's life. It was during a session with my executive coach when the topic of self-care arose. "What lesson am I demonstrating to my team in regards to self-care?" That question landed like a knockout punch. Being available is important. Remember the open-door policy? In the virtual world there is no physical door to open or close. The virtual door is always open. It never shuts. The computer rarely was shut down and when not physically planted in front of it, access was available through the iPad or cell phone. Connection was constant. While practicing developing personal boundaries it became very apparent that this was an area that had no boundaries. As a leader, it is important to lead by example. A lesson learned during the pandemic was that self-care is not an area that should be compromised. As I became my own priority, the team took note. It was another topic for discussion during our huddles. The ability to reset is important when leading others. Taking a break is not a bad thing, it is a necessity.

For this author self-care included establishing boundaries and reframing the open-door concept. For example, there were new start times and end times, no weekend work unless it was absolutely necessary. It also meant carving out time to revisit the gym and getting massages on a regular basis. The self-awareness shared in the section of the authentic leader section, includes being aware of one's limitations and formulating boundaries. This allows the leader to have a confident, steady presence, even during stressful times.

## Green Space

A few years ago, the concept of green space was introduced as a means for providing grass, trees, and other aesthetics to urban areas. The intended consequence was to introduce areas by which individuals felt invited to relax or participate in recreational activities. In the early 1990s city planners in the city that I dwell in determined to build a multi-level mall near the center of downtown. It was a novel idea. The mall was to assist in luring shoppers away from the suburban malls to the beautiful downtown structure. This author was present on the day of the ribbon cutting, and, when the stores were not able to sustain sales and ultimately closed.

In the center of a growing city in the Midwest was a now lifeless structure. All around this blighted vision, growth, development, and building was taking place. The looming structure was a constant reminder that times were changing and the center of the city shopping structure was no longer desired. In recent years, mid-2000s it became increasingly apparent that the Midwest city needed additional downtown housing. The city was growing rapidly, attracting new employers, sports teams, and enthusiasts. In fact, in the middle of the global pandemic headlines read "56 Urban Development Projects Under Construction in 2020" (Warren, 2020, p. 1). The concept of downtown housing exploded and down went the blighted downtown mall. In its place, housing, areas to play, and grass. As housing began to develop in the space of the mall, it was determined that there was an opportunity to re-shape the landscape. Soon more green grass grew where there was once pavement. The space now holds small outside concerts and events. The infusion of physical green space was provided to transform an otherwise concrete presence to one that promotes serenity and connectivity. Likewise, creating greenspace in one's schedule is an intentional step that promotes times for creativity.

Software upgrades can sometimes be a nuisance. One day, while waiting for a virtual meeting and replying to email messages, green times began to appear on the work calendar. Historically it was a badge of honor to share the "busyness" of the work calendar with others. Meetings started as early as 7:00 a.m. and ended as late as 9:00 p.m. with no breathing space. The day that these "green" meetings called focus time started appearing on my calendar was intriguing. Unbeknownst to me my admin had begun placing "green space" on my calendar. During a one on one she explained that she was placing holders on the calendar because she was "tired of my calendar, my busy days." The constant maneuvering the unyielding maze of time slots was difficult and promised much unnecessary anxiety. So daily the green space opened, and it was during that time it became feasible to "work" on projects and assignments. The green space provided a break from the pace of the day to "think... create... innovate." Today, the green space is a desired norm. Leaders need time to create and innovate. This was another lesson learned during COVID-19 and another tool for this writer's toolbox.

*Everyone wanted to be like Jack (Welch), he explains. Leadership has many voices. You need to be who you are, not try to emulate somebody else*

—George et al., 2007, para. 2

## INTEGRATED LEADERSHIP

James MacGregor Burns, one of the pioneers of leadership studies, began the integrative theory of leadership in hopes of legitimizing the field of leadership. Integrated leadership is an amalgamation of several styles of leadership. The tenants of integrated leadership embrace creating a vision that inspires, motivates, and engages those that follow. The approach also suggests that the integrated leader embodies the attributes of a coach; one who provides meaningful guidance, not solutions. A fundamental truth of an integrated leader is their orientation to the organization's mission and culture. This individual aligns with transformational leadership in that they lead with the outcome of positive changes in those that follow. As a results-oriented leader, it is important to understand and value the diverse situations that may arise in the quest for the most optimal outcome. "Leadership requires a more nuanced view of the world because it involves people: what motivates them, what their interests are, and how engaged they become" (McNulty, as cited by Maxwell, 2019, p. 2). The view of the integrated leader expands beyond one dimension by expanding to a multi-faceted, prism-like view of people, processes, and the work to be performed. One of the tenants of integrated leadership is that "things" are linked and well-coordinated; that it is intradisciplinary and transdisciplinary.

Observably leading a team into a harmonized culture requires the competencies aligned with being an integrated leader. Figure 22.2 illustrates the foundational elements of being an integrated leader. This leader is

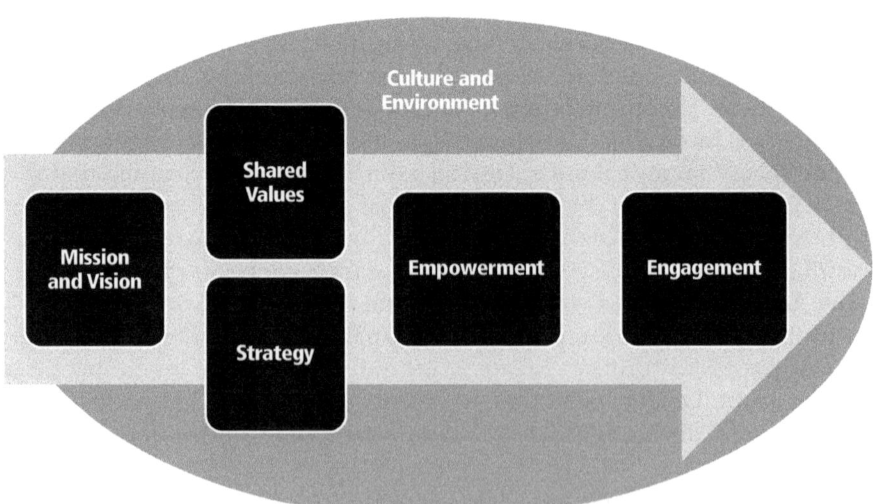


**Figure 22.2** Integrated leadership model.

mission and vision oriented and maintains a sense of awareness. In all practicality the ability to align goals, and objectives with the organization's goal provides the employee with a reminder that what they do matters. Therefore, creating an environment of shared values is fundamental in creating the desired culture. In the instance of the team that this leader serves, some of the shared values are autonomy, authenticity, courage, and transparency. When the members embrace the same values then cultural transformation takes place and in the end the individuals are empowered and engaged.

George et al. (2007) postulates that the journey to leadership begins with understanding the story of your life. That life story provides the context for your experiences, and through it, one can find the inspiration to make an impact in the world. The world being those that you serve on a daily basis. This journey to becoming an integrated leader is ever evolving. Having served as a transactional, transformational, and authentic leader provided the underpinnings for emerging and developing as an integrated leader. Using prior experiences as the palate for leading has been insightful for both the team and the author.

Integrative leadership is an emerging leadership approach that fosters collective action across many types of boundaries in order to achieve the common good. It brings together interdisciplinary leadership concepts and practice rooted in five major sectors of society—business, government, nonprofits, media, and community. It focuses on leadership development at all levels, from individual to around the world (Crosby, 2008). To be an effective integrated leader it is important to maintain coordination and to harmoniously link one's thoughts, words, and actions. Consistent actions, makes one predictable enough for others to follow.

There are many leadership styles. As such, the interdisciplinary leadership approach incorporates the complex relationships of culture, power, beliefs, accountability, and decision-making. The intersection of these variables contributes to being an effective leader. One of the formidable challenges afforded a leader is the ability to collaborate in a meaningful interdisciplinary manner. The ability to work in an interdisciplinary manner means that "work crosses the boundaries of disciplines, borrowing tools, concepts, and methodologies, combining them in new relationships" (Blackmore & Kandiko, 2010, p. 5). When a leader fosters an interdisciplinary approach, he or she is able to "focus on real world problems and offer solutions that make a difference" (Blackmore & Kandiko, 2010, p. 6). The ability to view problems from the varying lenses provided in an interdisciplinary approach creates an environment that deciphers and yields outcomes that are more robust.

Having effective leaders influenced my leadership style. Recently, Todd, my former vice president, was elevated to a new role with a new organization. When I extended my congratulations, Todd's response riveted me. He said, "I could not have done this without you." This statement reinforced once again that leaders cannot lead without followers and each follower teaches a lesson that can be used to develop one's leadership capacity.

## REFERENCES

Alberto, S. (2016). What is leadership? *Journal of Business Studies Quarterly, 8*(1), 1–5.

Arenas, F. J., Tucker, J., & Connelly, D. A. (2017). Transforming future air force leaders of tomorrow: A path to authentic transformational leadership. *Air & Space Power Journal, 31*(3), 18–33.

Boyum, G. (n.d.). *The historical and philosophical influences on Greenleaf's concept of Servant Leadership: Setting the stage for theory building.* https://files.eric.ed.gov/fulltext/ED501687.pdf

Berberoglu, A. (2015). Organizational commitment and perceived organizational performance among healthcare professionals: Empirical evidence from a private hospital in Northern Cyprus. *Journal of Economics and Behavioral Studies, 7*(1), 64–71. https://doi.org/10.22610/jebs.v7i1(J).563

Blackmore, P., & Kandiko, C. (2010). Chapter 3 Interdisciplinary leadership and learning. In M. Davies, M. Devlin, M. Tight (Eds.), *Interdisciplinary higher education: Perspectives and practicalities* (pp. 55–74). Emerald Group Publishing Limited.

Bowen, A. (2020). Developing a knowledge worker (Six Sigma) community of practice: A case study. *Journal for Advancing Business Education,* 2(1), 28–45.

Conger, J. A., & Benjamin, B. (1999). *Building leaders: How successful companies develop the next generation.* Jossey-Bass.

Crosby, B. (2008). *Theoretical foundations of integrative leadership.* http://integralleadershipreview.com/5000-feature-article-theoretical-foundations-of-integrative-leadership/

Eigel, K. M., & Kuhnert, K. W. (2005). Authentic development: Leadership development level and executive effectiveness. In W. L. Gardner, B. J. Avolio, & F. O. Walumbwa (Eds.), *Authentic leadership theory and practice: Origins, effects and development monographs in leadership and management* (Vol. 3; pp. 357–385). Emerald Publishing Group.

Flynn, M. B., & Silva, E. O. (2019). Criticizing and legitimizing patent monopolies. In M. Ellis (Ed.), *Critical global semiotics: Understanding sustainable transformational citizenship* (pp. 160–172). Routledge.

George, B., Sims, P., McLean, A. N., & Mayer, D. (2007). *Discovering your authentic leadership.* Harvard Business Review. https://hbr.org/2007/02/discovering-your-authentic-leadership

Grace, M. (2003). *Origins of leadership: The etymology of leadership.* http://www.ila-net.org/Publications/Proceedings/2003/mgrace.pdf

Greenleaf, R. K. (1977). *Servant leadership: A journey into the nature of legitimate power and greatness.* Paulist Press.

Greenwood, D. J., & Levin, M. (1998). *Introduction to action research: Social research for social change.* SAGE Publications.

Ihama, A. (2017). *Integrated leadership: The impact of morals, values and ethics.* About Leaders. https://aboutleaders.com/integrated-leadership/#gs.dfj687

Kelly, R. (2014). *The root of leadership: They etymological root of leadership, lead and leader.* https://www.leadershipissues.org/the-root-of-leadership/

Luthans, F., & Avolio, B. J. (2003). Authentic leadership: A positive developmental approach. In K. S. Cameron, J. E. Dutton, & R. E. Quinn (Eds.), *Positive organizational scholarship* (pp. 241–261). Barrett-Koehler.

Malik, W. U., Javed, M., & Hassan, S. T. (2017). Influence of transformational leadership components on job satisfaction and organizational commitment. *Pakistan Journal of Commerce and Social Sciences, 11*(1), 147–166. https://www.econstor.eu/handle/10419/188286

Maxwell, J. C. (2019). *Leader Shift: The 11 essential changes every leader must embrace.* Harper Collins Publishing.

Moriano, J. A., Molero, F., Topa, G., & Mangin, J. P. L. (2014). The influence of transformational leadership and organizational identification on intrapreneurship. *International Entrepreneurship and Management Journal, 10*(1), 103–119. https://doi.org/10.1007/s11365-011-0196-x

Northouse, P. G. (2013). *Leadership theory and practice* (6th ed.). SAGE Publications.

Villanova University. (2019, May 6). *The great man theory of leadership explained.* https://www.villanovau.com/resources/leadership/great-man-theory/#:~:text=That%20is%20the%20foundation%20upon,biographies%20belonging%20to%20great%20men

Walumbwa, F., Avolio, B., Gardner, W., Wernsing, T., & Peterson, S. (2008). Authentic leadership: Development and validation of a theory-based measure. *Journal of Management, 34*(1), 89–126. https://digitalcommons.unl.edu/managementfacpub/24

Warren, B. ( 2020, December 4). 56 urban development projects under construction in 2020. *Columbus Underground.* https://columbusunderground.com/56-urban-development-projects-under-construction-in-2020-bw1/

Wren, C. (2018). *Employee perceptions of leadership styles that influence workplace performance* [Unpublished doctoral dissertation]. Walden University. https://scholarworks.waldenu.edu/dissertation

CHAPTER 23

# CROSSOVER LEADERSHIP

## An Autoethnography on Interdisciplinary Leadership and Transformation

**John Nestor**

### ABSTRACT

Given the complexity of 21st century challenges facing the private and public sectors, transformative leadership is critical for success. Leadership research, theory, and practice are studied, but there is a further need for an examination of firsthand experiences of interdisciplinary leaders. This autoethnography examines the author's multi-industry leadership practices that have transformed underperforming organizations into best practices in manufacturing, law enforcement, K–12, and higher education. Key leadership principles, themes, and lessons learned shared within this unique study are grounded in 30 years of successful crossover leadership in both the public and private sectors that can support the development of today's leaders.

*On Leadership*, pages 439–456

## My Father, My Mentor. My Leadership Evolution.

My father, a former school superintendent, was a naval aviation mechanic during WWII He maintained fighter aircrafts and had close relationships with aviators dependent upon him for reliable aircraft. He was impressed with their swagger; he believed it to be a necessary attribute for mission success. The first leadership lesson my father learned from fighter pilots and he conveyed to me was, "No dare, no flair, no success." He talked me into joining a U.S. Naval J.R.O.T.C. unit during the Vietnam War. Crossover interdisciplinary leadership training had begun for me.

The aircraft carrier became a "postage stamp" in the Atlantic moments after the helicopter takeoff from the U.S.S. Iwo Jima for a simulated assault with the Marines. Upon landing, I disembarked from the helicopter as trained and was quickly tagged a "casualty." I was taken on a helicopter back to receive medical care. As a young man, I was oblivious to the risks of landing on a moving carrier. I also did not know how close we came to danger when our carrier almost collided broadside with our supply ship. Risk taking was inherent with advancing the mission—no dare, no flair, no success. After my immersion day with U.S. Navy Seals and fast boat attacks, wind and water in my face were exhilarating, as it should be metaphorically in your organization, when success is shared and celebrated. For example, later in life as a business leader, words cannot capture the look on our employees' faces on the factory floor the day I had the high school band march in, or a time we shut down to dip ice cream for employees. The message was clear; change was happening, and it's going to be good. Weeks prior, employees had the opportunity to view a large banner I installed, visible anywhere in the factory; it simply read "CHANGE." It triggered questions and employee engagement because inquiring minds wanted to know. Disengaged minds do not care, whereas engaged minds align their purpose to the mission, but only when leaders align mission to employees' purpose.

I was not born a crossover interdisciplinary leader. I learned. I am a product of theory, crossover experiences, and caring mentors. Examples of this development include time with my late father on the tennis courts and in living room discussions prepared me, along with leadership and policy graduate studies. On the tennis court, he outsmarted me and tested my endurance and skill. In the living room, he engaged with me between those amazing smoke rings he produced from his pipe. I was intrigued by his real-life leadership challenges he shared while he was a high school principal and superintendent. Each story started with a problem, a review of the facts, and the interests of each side. He asked me how I would solve it and then shared his resolution. My shallow responses proved to my mentor I was not ready to lead, but I was ready to learn.

Themes emerged from our problem-solving discussions, followed by the takeaways. His primary theme stuck with me: engage and value team members. At times, even he was struck by the importance of employee engagement, such as the time he walked down a long West Virginia school hallway to surprise a janitor with an appreciation certificate and red rose. The janitor thought he was in trouble until my father's explanation. The janitor then broke down to tears. No school superintendent had ever taken the time to visit just him. This lesson became a foundational cornerstone of my leadership.

Given the complexities of 21st century challenges facing the private and public sectors, transformative leadership is critical for success. Leadership research, theory, and practice are critical, but there is also a need for an examination of firsthand experiences of interdisciplinary crossover leaders. In high school, my counselor asked what I wanted to be when I grew up. I replied, "An educator, business executive, police officer, or military officer." I could not choose just one, so I did all of them. That wasn't a plan. During my crossover careers I realized there were overarching leadership practices which crossed over public and private sector leadership positions. The following are crossover lessons learned from an evolution in interdisciplinary leadership, as reflected in firsthand experiences.

1. *Landscape complexities and challenges.* What are some of today's leadership complexities and challenges in the day-to-day operations?
2. *Traits of crossover leaders.* What are the traits of these unusual leaders? (Crossover leaders are diamonds in the rough, often overlooked for leadership opportunities). "Researchers have found that even expert researchers operating in their domain of expertise are vulnerable to inattentional blindness" (Drew et al., 2013); if human resource specialists aren't looking for crossover leaders, they won't be found.
3. *Leadership practices.* What were the personal crossover leadership practices I utilized to create best practices in a failing industry, a failing school, and a failing higher education law enforcement department?
4. *Overarching organizational drivers.* What are the overarching organizational drivers which supported each organizational transformation?

## Landscape Complexities and Challenges-Survival Tips

As a chief of police of a large U.S. urban college, my superior and media liaison bombarded me with questions during critical incidents. In times of rapid change and complexity, digital information is immediately accessible.

Accuracy is the first casualty. Today's leaders require a proactive and reactive mindset, reliant on contingency planning. Leaders cannot ponder and squander during a critical incident. Reaction in real time is the new normal. It separates the frozen from the chosen. Listen, learn, act, and reassess.

Engage fearlessly with every working hour, with self-discipline and confidence. A leader's response to critical events outside their control are also positive opportunities to shape the organization's future with strategic responses. Today's effective leaders recognize disruptions as opportunities to engage, advance the mission, redirect, and affirm. Engagement with employees for the first time in the trenches during a critical event is too late. It also implies the organization cares more about the critical event than the team.

Disengaged employees create chasms which impacts employee retention, productivity, work quality, and constituent support, whereas engaged employees "are involved in, enthusiastic about, and committed to their work and workplace" (Gallup, n.d., para. 1). Dauble (2019) reported that 52% of small businesses claimed it was hard to find qualified hires and 63% of those surveyed in larger businesses emphasized the same difficulty. Intentional leaders routinely engage their teams in meaningful work, discussions, and timely resolution of concerns. This increases the likelihood of employee retention and attraction.

Law enforcement and education have their own chasm to bridge with constituents. 58% of the public indicated policing needs to change (Crabtree, 2020). In 2019 elections, 51% of new K–12 tax levies were voted down in Ohio (Nestor & Nestor-Lane, 2020). There are significant opportunities for dynamic leaders to advance strategic planning through community or constituent engagement. In my own experience, a campus police public forum was a turning point in community relations. Asking parents, teachers, or industrial customers for critiques led to a transformed school and significant market gains respectively, as "engagement leads to better outcomes and deeper support to accomplish goals that otherwise may be impossible" (Nestor & Nestor-Lane, 2020, p. 26).

The ability to improvise, adapt, overcome, and engage defines both Marines and crossover leaders. Smart crossover leaders create smart teams to move big rocks; they astutely and quickly identify knowledgeable, passionate, and coachable core team members to accomplish agreed upon missions.

## TRAITS OF CROSSOVER INTERDISCIPLINARY LEADERS

Crossover interdisciplinary leaders are instrumental when a fresh set of eyes and innovative thinking are needed for transformation. They ask different questions than insiders to uncover strengths, weaknesses, opportunities, and threats. They identify, analyze, and mitigate risks which contribute to disengagement, dysfunction, loss of productivity, innovation, and quality deficiencies.

### Crossover Leaders Are Quietly Guided by Three Questions

1. What inhibits this organization?
2. What can enhance this organization?
3. What can I do to help or hinder?

Sometimes being helpful means to stand down and get out of the way. An effective classroom teacher realizes the person who does the work does the learning. The same lesson crosses over to an organization. Learning requires doing, like assigned and meaningful opportunities for team members to advance the mission and own the outcomes.

As an example, my first instructive leadership failure was in my role as a young volunteer CEO of a countywide EMS system. I introduced a specialized rescue concept and failed to involve others in the work; thus, the concept was confined to my own limited experience. I failed to look behind to see if anyone was following or needed coaching. The specialized rescue unit disbanded as quickly as it was formed. Even good ideas fail without followers. This lesson informed my future endeavors and helped formulate critical questions that can quietly guide leaders and help to learn through failure.

### Crossover Leaders Provide Psychological Safety for Their Direct Reports on Day 1

The leader's introductory message conveys the door is always open, and constructive opinions will never endanger jobs. Subordinate military personnel ask, "Permission to speak freely." The leader in the public and private sectors grants this freedom on Day 1, and all days thereafter. Fear muzzles: empowerment unleashes. Not once did I turn down an employee at any level who needed time to talk. It made for some long days, but it was worth it.

### Crossover Leaders Have a Knack for Affecting Hard Change

The leader realizes the fear of transformative change can sidetrack the best of team members. The leader has periodic check-ins to engage with the team. Assurance is given that change is incremental and flexible. Strategic direction is adjusted for the common good. Crossover leaders understand that conflict parallels progress. The leader tolerates and balances an acceptable level of organizational conflict in the transition to a new equilibrium, a step toward transformation. Insecure leaders squash conflict and noise, inadvertently squashing their best innovators and any hope for the future. I admired an assistant when he entered my office and said, “You are expecting too much, too fast. Not all of us can work at your rate.” I needed to hear that before morale and mission suffered. Effective leaders also benefit from an open-door policy while affecting challenging change.

### Uncertainty Is Unsettling for the Leader, and Employees

Crossover leadership provides the “night vision” for an organization to find clarity by cutting through the clutter, fog, and noise. Crossover leaders make the deep dives into the bowels of the organization to understand and mitigate sources of uncertainty or chaos. The leader reassures and equips the team to envision the end game.

### Crossover Leaders Are "Mavericks." They Draw Their Strength From a Proven Record of Transformation in Diverse Arenas

Mavericks are true hearted and courageous, to name a few traits. They challenge the status quo and believe in their own vision (Khair, 2016). They seek the right moment and opportunity to connect to constituents to dramatize key beliefs or to jumpstart the mission. For example, as a student teacher I entered the cafeteria on day one with my food tray. All eyes were on me. Instead of walking to the teachers’ lunch table, I changed direction and sat with a table of students, creating a moment of silence and puzzled looks from teachers and students alike. The earth had seemingly stopped spinning on its axis, and it was my fault. I ate a tater tot and the cafeteria roared back to life. Lesson learned—the priority of leadership is connecting with the led. Never waste a teaching moment.

“Mavericks” are driven to engage, not because of an outgoing personality. Many may be introverts outside of their work, like me. They’re cause-driven, with a deep and burning despise for mediocrity and the status quo. A fire in their core ignites when they see the ordinary and envision the extraordinary. It may be puzzling that others cannot see the same vision. Mavericks cannot unsee the envisaged state or simply “turn it off.” To transform, leaders start with their vision, and reverse engineer a successful pathway forward to the desired outcome. They are confident because achievement has already been realized in their mind. However, transformative, crossover leaders tend to get ahead of their skis, excited by a future that only they can see, until their vision is shared.

Not everyone will arrive at the train station at the same time. That is ok. The leader is not deterred. The leader's eye is on the prize. The leader is patient and adds color and form to the canvas to assist the team in seeing the vision, and the benefits of a transformation. When success comes, this leader is not surprised. Success had already been envisioned and celebrated in the mind of the leader before the process started. This is an intrinsic motivator, and their path to a legacy.

### Crossover Leaders Are Intrinsically Motivated by Personal Fulfillment

My late father and mentor tagged me as a "divine discontent." The maverick in me will turn myself into a pretzel just to improve a process or an organizational climate.

Tested in the public and private arenas, I was able to transform three failing organizations by translating these crossover interdisciplinary leadership traits into the following leadership practices.

## LEADERSHIP PRACTICES: BUSINESS AND INDUSTRY

### The Practice of Improvising

Promoted to executive vice president of Riten Industries, Inc. (a business specializing in machine tool manufacturing), I was responsible for operations, U.S. markets, and tasked to open international markets. The owner made it clear my first week the company could fail if our order backlog did not increase. We had a formidable mission: to increase our market share in a shrinking market and economic downturn, and at the beginning of the skilled labor shortage. On paper, failure looked inevitable. Engage, improvise, adapt, and overcome. We improvised in every manner and strategically doubled the company's sales. I learned a great deal at the feet of the savvy owner, and he trusted and adopted my emphasis on process improvement and team engagement. I had confidence our strategic improvements would translate to customer confidence.

One strategy was to connect employees to the vision of the company. Employees had lacked a sense of purpose. They had no connection to the customers' end use of the machine tools. To drive home the importance of their skill and purpose, I showed them pictures of where Riten's machine tools were used to produce components for the space shuttle, aircraft, turbines, and vehicles of all makes. I shared end user success stories when our products improved the quality of our customers' products. We also engaged our team when our products failed expectations and sat down to document and improve our manufacturing processes. Our team's success became connected to our customers' success.

## The Practice of Leaving a Legacy

Riten became quality driven, cost effective, and established its competitive edge in the emerging global market of the 1980s. We implemented data-driven decision-making, advanced machinery and cellular manufacturing, continuous improvement and "just in time" inventories. We rebranded this small manufacturer into a giant with contemporary marketing, trade show displays, bold packaging, and product demonstration videos. We improvised at every level to become quality driven, starting first with our valued employees. I then served on a U.S. manufacturers global marketing committee to assist similar companies in selling abroad. Years later, I was invited back for a 50th anniversary founding party. The company had grown even more. An employee unknown to me was introduced and stated, "You are a legend around here." I was humbled and it reinforced that employees want to make a difference. Riten's new motto, "Solutions, not excuses," aligned with the philosophy and culture I was fortunate to help install. My team changed the culture, saved the company, and doubled jobs. The owner reminded me they had implemented everything in the business plan I had left behind. Mission accomplished.

## The Practice of Creating Opportunities

I had targeted two of the nation's largest distributors to carry Riten's machine tool line. I could never get face time with one owner from New York City by standing in long lines at trade shows, so I approached him in the hotel lobby and made my pitch. Impressed with my doggedness, he became a customer that day. Another customer target, the largest industrial distributor in the South, sent me a trial order. Within an hour of our product being installed on their customer's CNC lathe, it failed. The same day we made a heroic recovery. We packaged a replacement tool and I personally drove it 40 miles to the Columbus, Ohio airport and booked a flight for the tool. The customer received the replacement the same day, no charge. Riten's owner asked me, "Did you really just do all of that at our expense?"

I replied, "Yes. Deduct it from my paycheck because I know it will come back to us." A week later we received a letter from their president, awarding all future business to Riten. His letter said, "In all my years in business, we have never experienced that level of customer service." Leaders add value by creating opportunity when it appears there is none.

### Lessons Learned in Business and Industry

- Leaders steer the course, check radar, mitigate threats, and engage in every opportunity, good and bad. A strategic plan without a passionate, engaging leader is a sleek jet with no engines: forever grounded.
- Leaders know some business is not worth having. I terminated a long-term distributor and subsequent business for his pattern of abuse of our customer service team.
- Leaders grow the business as they can afford it. If the pace exceeds the capacity for exceptional customer service and quality, the interests of the corporation, employees, and customers have been jeopardized.
- Leaders realize cute slogans alone do not get it done.
- Leaders seize opportunities to come to the sides of their team members during hard times.

A move from Riten's hometown to a company we acquired in Iowa resulted in my pivot and return to K–12 education, where I focused on completing my policy and leadership graduate degrees. I once asked Riten's owner why he hired a former teacher turned consultant. He said, "Educators relate, motivate, and innovate. The rest can be learned." I valued that he saw something in me I did not: an interdisciplinary skill set. In my subsequent leadership positions, the business management skills learned at Riten became my foundation and path to crossover leadership.

## LEADERSHIP PRACTICES IN EDUCATION

### The Practice of Owning It. The Strategy for School Turnaround

To initiate my return to K–12 education, as the executive vice president of Riten, I had greeted a local school superintendent at our Rotary meeting. I asked if would believe me if I said I wanted to re-enter teaching. He said, "No I would not!" He later hired me as a traveling teacher between two rural buildings, assigned to failing, misbehaving classes. No surprise, the previous teachers had quit mid-year. I took a massive pay cut and was featured in the *Ohio School Boards Association Journal* for making the switch from industry and returning to education (Nestor, 1994).

On day one with students, I passed around a rock from my visit to Alcatraz prison. I told students the rock was symbolic of ultimate failure and said, "The Marines have landed. My mission is to help you succeed and 'avoid the rock.'" They did. I remain in contact with many to this day. I was promoted to the building principal soon after being selected as the county's "Outstanding Teacher of the Year." In the summer before becoming principal, I sat with individual teachers and asked them about building strengths, weaknesses, opportunities, and threats. A school board member told me, "You have inherited a cesspool." The former principal resigned. I had a track record for turnarounds and enjoyed the challenge. In 3 years, I targeted metrics that mattered, and the building experienced an incredible transformation. We increased attendance, significantly decreased discipline problems, increased honor roll participation, and eradicated school bullying.

I had been the principal for only a few weeks when a young student came up to me and said, "I'm not afraid to come to school anymore." My strategy was simple. Own and engage every building problem. In front of the entire student body and staff on day one, I had said, "If someone bullies you, they're bullying me. Come to my office any day, any time, immediately after you've been bullied, and I will take care of it." It only took a few examples for word to spread, and the bullying stopped. I owned it. Staff and students now owned a safe, friendly environment. My staff and I were invited to the state capitol and presented a school improvement award from the governor, a first for a rural Ohio school. The local Common Pleas court judge and parent described the transformed school as the "best public 'private' school." Prior to the transformation, he had plans to remove his daughter from the school, but I had assured him a turnaround was coming.

## The Practice of Engagement

Promoted to the district office, I spearheaded a presentation I had named "Land Rich, Dirt Poor," to the Ohio House Finance and Appropriations Committee on behalf of large rural districts, at the invitation of then Chairperson John Carey. Our district could not wait for state funding to replace buildings 100 years old. Passion, confidence, and data at my side, I lobbied for a change on the timing when rural school facilities were funded. The process for special need districts was eventually absorbed into Ohio Rev. Code 3318.36, the Expedited Local School Building Assistance Program. The change accelerated rural and urban construction which benefited students, staff, and contributed to community development and business retention. Own it. Engage it.

## Lessons Learned in Education

- Astute leaders do not wait to learn organizational deficiencies. Ask employees and expedite a strategic plan built on consensus to address the needs. Resolve less complicated issues first to demonstrate sincerity, success, and to build momentum for continued systemic improvement.
- Effective leaders recognize the importance of timing and disengagement. Most decisions do not have to be made the same day. Sometimes it is best to let it percolate a day or two for additional insight.
- Leaders know metrics matter. Numbers mattered in industry, and I introduced performance metrics and continuous improvement for the first time in our school district before it was mandated by the state.
- Effective leaders engage in interest-based negotiations on matters of importance. While a graduate assistant to the Ohio State executive dean, a legal conflict with a convention hotel had attorneys at an impasse. I was familiar with the hotel from my business days and asked if I could try to resolve it. The dean laughed, "Sure, you can't do any worse." I addressed the interests of both parties, resolved the matter, and avoided significant costs for both sides. I had previously negotiated a corporate acquisition at Riten; this learned, interest-based interdisciplinary skill transferred nicely.
- Crossover leaders recognize staff and students do not want to fail, but organizations are not always structured for their success either. Leaders quickly identify factors that inhibit performance and lower job satisfaction, then put in place measures to enhance learning, satisfaction, and the work atmosphere.
- Leaders must engage families at the building and district level as if they were equity partners in a corporation who share in the accountability and outcomes of their schools.
- Leaders develop replacements before departure. They pay attention to overlooked talent in the underrepresented. Provide your mentees a set of facts and ask what they would do if they were in your position. Future leaders will emerge.
- Leaders recognize talent acquisition is mindful of interdisciplinary experience and skills which may be used to direct and transform any organization.
- Educational leaders can benefit from business management immersion experiences.

- Business leaders can reject raw materials at the dock which do not meet a quality standard. K–12 education leaders cannot reject their students at entry.
- Crossover leaders humbly accept they do not know everything. I entered my doctoral program as an overconfident former industry executive vice president. The last question asked at my dissertation defense was, "What was your biggest take away from Ohio State?" I replied, "How little I know, and how much more there is to learn." "Good answer," said the dean.

During a K–12 district administrative morning meeting was when the World Trade Center was attacked. Our meeting stopped. My mind flashed to how my parents were impacted by Pearl Harbor. My father had served in the U.S. Navy. My mother was a top-secret code decipherer. Motivated by their examples, I transitioned my reserve police officer and Ohio Military Reserves experience into a full-time career. I was recruited to develop emergency management protocols at a major urban college. (I had just implemented such protocols in the local school district.) I was eventually promoted to the director of public safety and chief of police of the college. Once again, I was assigned to a failing organization. It was poorly managed and poorly supported, with no strategic direction. Navy jargon? It was a ship adrift anchored to nothing.

## MY LEADERSHIP PRACTICES: LAW ENFORCEMENT

### The Practice of Surviving a Crucible

Factors that hindered transformation of this failing campus police department into a national best practice were daunting. They included poor hiring practices, little support from inside or outside, and resistance from within the department and college administration. A crucible for a Marine is a weeklong final test with limited food and sleep. It is meant to validate their physical and mental toughness and moral training. This organization transformation validated my physical and mental stamina, and my moral training.

### The Practice of Achieving Stability in Chaos

It can take 3 years to stabilize and transform an organization. I sensed I only had months to stabilize it and provide strategic solutions and direction. A career counselor told me I had an uncanny ability to see what others didn't, to see through the fog and create order from chaos. He called it my night vision. The department and administration had not comprehended how close the unit was to implosion.

## The Practice of Planning Is Multi-Faceted and Interconnected

My immediate action plan became a three-prong approach. A labor-management committee was created to create a safe space for employee dialogue. Second, a department strategic planning process for the eventual transformation was initiated. Third, always the hardest, job performance accountability. Navy jargon: "The ship is more than the crew"; a few officers were jeopardizing the department and the college by poor judgment and performance. They were eventually replaced with stringent hiring practices and competitive pay.

## The Practice of Smart Community Policing

The mission of enforcement was transformed to balance service, diversity, and relationship building, the three-prong approach. Our smart use of data to deter and reduce crime significantly reduced thefts. As I learned in education and business, numbers mattered. Critical to success and my survival was trusting in my process. More importantly, department personnel had to trust in the process. I reminded them transformation would lead to fulfilling, rewarding careers. The ultimate measure of success would be when outsiders came to see a best practice in action. We built it and they came. It was the first college department with a data-driven strategic plan. It was named as the college's only best practice in the college's Higher Learning Commission accreditation and evaluation (nonpublic) report. The report even suggested other college departments should follow our example. The campus became known as one of the safest U.S. urban campuses (Spaces4Learning, 2016).

## The Practice of Deeply Caring

A department with deep hurts requires deep caring. The transformation was accomplished, but not without mental and professional scars for several. Four personnel, core to the organizational transformation, were lost to natural causes during my tenure. I often think of them: Lees, Gatliff, Karas, and Murphy. Prior to Murphy's passing, I asked him how he wanted to be remembered. Murphy replied, "Just tell them I did my job." Heart and mission, aligned. Mission accomplished.

## LESSONS LEARNED IN LAW ENFORCEMENT

- *Leaders listen.* At the core of any organization are personnel driven to make a difference. They aspire to add purpose and value to the mission. Find them. Listen. Integrate their ambitions. The gift of leadership is providing the team a purpose to report to work.
- *Leaders do not quit when inconvenient.* When I was offered back my former position, I declined. Cut and run is not an option after a commitment is made.
- *Leaders recognize when it is time to stand down and assess if the mission is still current.* Adjustments are made as needed before the organization goes off rail.
- *Leaders ensure employees' talents, passion, and experience align to their roles.* When personnel are not properly assigned, it becomes the organization's responsibility for a reassignment, if practical. Termination of dedicated employees erodes trust.
- *Leaders understand the needs and interests of their unions, in advance of bargaining.* The last collective bargaining process during my tenure negotiated a union contract in the shortest time in the college's history according to the president, less than 2 weeks.
- *Leaders are accessible and flexible.* The night shift complained department meetings were held during their daytime slumber. The next department meeting was at 3:00 a.m., and yes, I attended.
- *Leaders realize an organization with no vision has no purpose.* Even engaged employees will wander and worry about an unplanned future. The disengaged create their own vision of division and disgruntlement. A shared vision creates a unified and forward moving department.
- *Leaders know their positional power is granted to them in trust, not by job title.* The leader relies on established trust to balance corrective actions while maintaining organizational stability. A confident leader wears their authority lightly.
- *Leaders know setbacks are teaching moments.* Leaders accept responsibility and accountability. Better yet, leaders position departments to prevent setbacks with adequate planning, direction, resources, training, and coaching.

Overarching, interdisciplinary organizational drivers are like the roof trusses which support ceilings. On a day-to-day basis, the trusses go unnoticed unless one would split, fall, and bring the house down. Overarching organizational drivers, like trusses, bolster and maintain sound, organizational structure.

## OVERARCHING ORGANIZATIONAL DRIVERS

### Organization Driver: A Foot in the Moment. A Foot in the Future. Contingency Minded

Running radar on the U.S.S. Iwo Jima taught the value of recognizing bogeys (suspicious radar contacts) before engagement. A similar aim of leadership is less surprises. This requires knowledge of the organization's past so as not to repeat mistakes. Also required is having a foot in the moment, and a foot in the future. Situational awareness in real time, all the time, is every team member's charge; your radar is on for unanticipated surprises, risks, or opportunities to advance the mission. The organization has contingency plans. An organization cannot control every event, but it can control its responses. Responses shape the future.

### Organization Driver: Data Driven. Knowledge Rich

I remember it like it was yesterday when the Riten president entered my office and asked, "How are we doing?" I replied, "We're doing fine." He smiled and pointed at my sales representatives' map. "Oh, they're doing just fine too," I said. He made it a teaching moment. "John, it's about the numbers. How are we doing?" Got it. I responded with shipment totals and if we were plus or minus for the year on our specific goals.

In off campus higher education course programming, I tracked course enrollment and identified "bread and butter" courses. I correlated future schedules to student and workforce demands. The knowledge gained from data directed the decisions and increased enrollments to the level that was able to further successfully advocate for a new regional campus be constructed.

Prior to continuous improvement in K–12, schools were ironically data rich but knowledge poor, meaning data was collected, but not studied for planning and improvement. As a building principal of a failing school, I met with students, parents, and staff to identify improvement opportunities. I tracked metrics on attendance, discipline, and honor roll participation, to name a few, and employed building level strategies to impact success. Metric data was updated on my principal's office public bulletin board. It displayed significant improvement trends. When parents or teachers would question progress, I'd point to the data.

Taking the helm of an aircraft carrier at night forced me to trust the navigational data. No ship is on course 100% of the time, as it is buffeted by wind and currents. Similarly, no organization is on track all the time, so it is important to adjust the course as needed. Grounding a ship is frowned upon. Data and the knowledge gained are change agents for targeted success and transformation.

## Organization Driver: Success Driven, Values Oriented

When I was a first-year teacher and a volunteer CEO of a fledgling county-wide emergency medical system (EMS), the board of directors told me in my first meeting the system would likely fail that year. I replied, "Not on my watch." A few laughed because I had nothing to base that on other than confidence, passion, and belief in the mission. Over 40 years later, the same EMS system transported my parents. An early challenge evolved from the volunteer EMS crew: experiencing lapses in their judgment which had been ignored by past leadership. Their behaviors were causing damage to our values and the organizational brand. I confronted the crew and placed them on notice. The organization eventually flourished thereafter with renewed values, additional volunteers, and thousands of dollars in donations. Leaders diminish fear of failure with risk analysis, strategic planning, and mitigation. Bostock and Riley (2018), translating Pliny the Elder, state, "How many things are looked upon as quite impossible until they have been actually effected?" The road from good to great requires organizational values, and a leader who envisions success where others only see impossibility.

## Organization Driver: No Echo Chambers

A Riten sales representative and former Marine taught me "management does not like bad news." An ineffective leader insulates their office with subservient direct reports accustomed to reporting good news only. Direct reports conceal problems, making matters worse. A leader's job description should include: "Will intentionally seek the organization's hidden strengths, weaknesses, opportunities, and threats in open forums, surveys, and one-on-one engagement with frontline employees." An effective leader trusts, verifies, and demands the bad news too.

An engaging leader avoids an "echo chamber," defined by *Oxford Learner's Dictionaries* (n.d.) as "an environment in which a person encounters only beliefs or opinions that coincide with their own, so that existing views are reinforced, and alternative ideas are not considered." My first echo chamber was during a higher education directors' meeting when we were asked for ideas to increase student enrollment. More experienced directors stared into the distance and said nothing. I suggested an alternate and obvious idea: Ask the students. The administrator incredulously replied we would not ask the students; we would ask each other, and the directors nodded in compliance. My instinct was confirmed. My colleagues had shut down several meetings ago. This administrator had failed to nurture a culture of acceptance for innovation.

### Organization Driver: A Culture of Form, Focus, and Care

Effective crossover leaders create work environments which provide form, focus, and care. Less effective leaders may offer one or two, but highly effective leaders create work cultures which offer all three. An ideal work culture is organized to strategically enhance performance and hinder anything that gets in the way. A caring culture provides an intentional family-like atmosphere which seeks and addresses employee concerns in a timely manner. The end result is a culture that retains and attracts employees.

## CLOSING

As a crossover, transformative leader, the challenging obstacles to leadership are the resistance to change, a fear of what change could bring, and a deep satisfaction of organizational mediocrity in the upper ranks. No one is challenging leaders to take deep dives into their organizations to identify and mitigate deficiencies in their organizations. This lack of engagement communicates indifference to the ranks and the team will reciprocate with the same attitude. The interdisciplinary crossover leader is uniquely equipped for the challenge. Newton's laws of motion (Encyclopedia Britannica, n.d.) in part states that a body at rest remains at rest unless acted on by an external force. Analogously, an organization waiting for a crossover leader to act. Robert F. Kennedy (1966) said midway through his University of Cape Town speech:

> Each time a person stands up for an ideal or acts to improve the lot of others or strikes out against injustice, he sends forth a tiny ripple of hope, and crossing each other from a million different centers of energy and daring, those ripples build a current, which can sweep down the mightiest walls of oppression and resistance.

Start making ripples. Become the legend you were meant to be.

## REFERENCES

Bostock, J., & Riley, H. T. (Eds.). (2018). *The natural history of Pliny* (Pliny the Elder, Author). Taylor and Francis. (Original work published ca. A.D. 77)

Encyclopedia Britannica. (n.d.). Newton's laws of motion. In *Encyclopedia Britannica Online.* Retrieved February 3, 2020 from https://www.britannica.com/science/Newtons-laws-of-motion

Crabtree, S. (2020, July 22). *Most Americans say policing needs major change.* Gallup. https://news.gallup.com/poll/315962/americans-say-policing-needs-major-changes.aspx

Drew, T., Võ, M. L. H., & Wolfe, J. M. (2013). The invisible gorilla strikes again: Sustained inattentional blindness in expert observers. *Psychological Science, 24*(9), 1848–1853.

Dauble, J. (2019, May 8). *CNBC and survey monkey release latest small business survey results.* CNBC. https://www.cnbc.com/2019/05/08/cnbc-and-surveymonkey-release-latest-small-business-survey-results.html

Gallup. (n.d.). *Gallup Daily: U.S. employee engagement.* https://news.gallup.com/poll/180404/gallup-daily-employee-engagement.aspx#:~:text=Gallup%20defines%20engaged%20employees%20as,predict%20important%20organizational%20performance%20outcomes

Kennedy, R. F. (1966, June 6). *Day of affirmation address* [Transcript]. https://www.jfklibrary.org/learn/about-jfk/the-kennedy-family/robert-f-kennedy/robert-f-kennedy-speeches/day-of-affirmation-address-university-of-capetown-capetown-south-africa-june-6-1966

Khair, H. (2016). The 10 qualities of a Maverick Leader. *Mavericks Unlimited.* https://www.mavericksunlimited.com/about-us

Nestor, J. C. (1994). How can we do less? *Ohio School Boards Association Journal, 38*(7), 30–32.

Nestor, J. C., & Nestor-Lane, S. (2020). Community engagement: Messy, yet necessary. *Ohio School Boards Association Journal, 64*(2), 26–29.

Oxford Learner's Dictionaries. (n.d.). Echo chamber. In *Oxford Learner's Dictionaries.com.* Retrieved September 25, 2022 from https://www.oxfordlearnersdictionaries.com/us/definition/english/echo-chamber

Spaces4Learning. (2016, September). *College planning & management.* https://spaces4learning.com/Issues/2016/09/CPM-September-2016.aspx

# ABOUT THE EDITORS

**Denver J. Fowler** currently serves as the associate dean of graduate and undergraduate studies at California State University, Bakersfield. He has over a decade of experience in the higher education setting as an adjunct/assistant/associate professor (tenured), graduate program coordinator, doctoral program chair, department chair, interim dean, and associate dean. Prior to matriculating into higher education, Dr. Fowler served as a coach, teacher (tenured), athletic director, technology coordinator, and school administrator in the PreK–12 educational setting. His research is focused on leadership, namely as it applies to the superintendency and principalship. He is the author of numerous books, chapters, journal articles, and articles in practitioner magazines focused on educational leadership. Visit Dr. Fowler's Amazon Author page at: https://www.amazon.com/Dr.-Denver-J.-Fowler/e/B087WZT12G%3Fref=dbs_a_mng_rwt_scns_share

**Meghan B. Raehll** currently serves as the assistant dean of the Center for Teaching Excellence at Franklin University in Columbus, Ohio. As an award-winning educator, trainer, and leader, Dr. Raehll has taught in higher education for over 15 years and is a growth-focused educational leader with expertise spanning global programs, instructional quality, data analytics, accreditation processes, cross-functional team leadership, instructional coaching, and faculty development. In

*On Leadership*, pages 457–458

addition to working in higher education, Dr. Raehll also serves as an elected official presiding as trustee in Berlin Township, Delaware County, Ohio.

Dr. Raehll completed her Doctorate in Philosophy (PhD) from the State University of New York at Buffalo, Educational Specialist degree (EdS) from the University of Kentucky, Master of Arts in philosophy (MA) from Duquesne University, Master of Divinity (MDiv) from Ashland Theology Seminary, Master of Arts in religion (MA) from Trinity International University.

# ABOUT THE CONTRIBUTORS

**Akshay Sateesh** was born in India, raised in Malaysia, and now lives in San Diego, California with his wife and two children. He combined his experiences from the life sciences industry and applied improvisation, to create a leadership development firm, Ziksana Consulting, that activates the world of work through play to help companies scale their culture and strategy. Ziksana has had extensive experience supporting fortune 100 and scaling companies around the globe. Akshay loves to dive, play pickleball, surf, and transform into a professional mime for his children's school events.

**Stan Amaladas** is an associate professor at Baker College, Centre for Graduate Studies, Flint, MI. Stan's scholarly interests include, ecosystemic thinking, leadership studies, peace leadership, and higher education program and curriculum design with a specific focus on Leadership Studies. His writings are partially informed by his 15-year tenure with the Canadian Federal Public Service. He has published two books, *Intentional Leadership: Getting to the Heart of the Matter, Leadership Studies: A Desire for Shared Agreement* (Routledge, 2017), co-edited a volume on *Peace Leadership: A Quest for Connectedness* (Routledge, 2017), and published numerous articles on Leadership. One particular leadership experience that cautions his reflections and writing on leadership is grounded in the adage that the power to lead is the power to mislead and

*On Leadership*, pages 459–470

destroy. Relationally, Stan is a proud Gran'Pa of two beautiful grandsons. Married for 41 years, he continues to enjoy being with his soul-partner and wife, Miriam.

**Seneka Arrington**, PhD, LPC-S, LMFT-S, NCC, is a licensed professional counselor, licensed marriage and family therapist, and national certified counselor. With twelve years of specialized experience in mental health, family, career, and group counseling Dr. Gainer currently serves as an assistant professor at Jacksonville University. For the past decade, she has occupied multiple leadership roles, including president of the National Employment Counseling Association and governing council representative for the American Counseling Association. Dr. Gainer is the CEO of The Gainer Group, Counseling and Consulting. She prioritizes leadership and advocacy and strives to bridge the gap between research and practice, emphasizing the importance of connection, collaboration, and translating research findings into clinically meaningful information. https://drseneka-gainer.clientsecure.me/ www.linkedin.com/in/senekaa

**Gilbert Arinaitwe** is a research associate in the Faculty of Education, University of Tasmania, Australia. He was a schoolteacher at Kigezi high school for 2 years prior to working as a lecturer for over 15 years at several Ugandan universities including Makerere University, Kyambogo University, Uganda Christian University, and Uganda Management and Technology University. Arinaitwe was head of Department of Education at Bishop Barham University College for four years and concurrently served as an assistant academic registrar for 2 years. Arinaitwe received his Bachelor of Arts in education from Uganda Christian University (Uganda), Master of Philosophy in education from NLA University College (Norway), and PhD in education from the University of Tasmania (Australia). His current research interests are in rural education, teacher retention, teacher engagement, and teacher work lives.

**Alyncia Bowen** serves as the dean of the Ross College of Business, executive director of the Franklin University Leadership Center, and co-executive director of the Global Center for Healthcare Education and has taught both domestically and internationally. She earned her doctorate in organization and management from Capella University, MSA in healthcare administration from Central Michigan University, and Bachelor of Arts in sociology from Capital University. Dr. Bowen has over 23 years healthcare leadership experience. She is a certified Lean/Six Sigma black belt and has trained yellow, white, green, and black belts. Her publications in the areas of intellectual communities of practice, knowledge workers, intersectionality of Black female education leaders and integrated leadership. Dr. Bowen serves on the board of trustees for three Columbus, Ohio nonprofit organizations.

**Ben Brooks** is an assistant professor of interdisciplinary studies teaching in the leadership studies program at Kennesaw State University. He previously worked as associate faculty and senior class advisor at NYU's Gallatin School of Individualized Study, as a teaching assistant professor in multidisciplinary studies and leadership studies at West Virginia University, and was a Fulbright Scholar in Hungary. Dr. Brooks' scholarly interests include metacognition, ethical instruction, critical pedagogy, and higher education program and curriculum design with specific areas of focus in interdisciplinary studies and leadership studies. His work has appeared in the *Journal of Leadership Studies, New Directions for Student Leadership*, and *Issues in Interdisciplinary Studies*.

**Kyle Butler** is a professor in the School of Education at Union University and a former secondary science teacher. At Union, he teaches graduate students pursuing initial teacher licensure and doctoral candidates in the Doctor of Education (EdD) program. His scholarly interests include teacher education, teacher leadership, the teaching and learning of science, problem-based learning, professional learning communities, technology integration, and teacher-directed action research.

**AJ Crabill** was raised in and out of foster care from birth until high school. AJ bounced around enough to have attended 11 schools prior to graduation. He attended urban, suburban, and rural schools; private, public, and parochial schools; lived with White families and families of color; lived in racist communities and inclusive communities; experienced loving homes and homelessness. Guided by the idea that student outcomes don't change until adult behaviors change and drawing on his intimate familiarity with the triumphs and terrors of America's safety nets for children, AJ has devoted much of his adult life to advocating for the well-being of our nation's most vulnerable youth. AJ currently serves as conservator (receiver) at DeSoto, Texas Independent School District; education faculty at the Leadership Institute of Nevada; collaborator with the Effective School Boards Initiative; and director of governance at the Council for the Great City Schools. AJ has served as board member for the Missouri School Boards Association; board member for the International Policy Governance Association; policy committee member for the National School Boards Association; advisory board member for SXSW Edu; board chair for Kansas City, Missouri Public Schools; and deputy commissioner of education for the Texas Education Agency.

**Minkie O. English**, MPA, is an independent researcher, data and evaluations specialist, and project manager with a special interest in inquiry-based and project-based learning. She holds a master's in public administration and her research focuses on engaging communities through education and the arts. She has over 15 years' experience in healthcare and hospital administration services and New York City government. For the last 4 years, she has been working and consulting with various service models. For more information visit, www.MinkieEnglishConsulting.com and https://printbyprintgroup.com/

**Tracey France.** Prior to her leadership effectiveness role at the University of Worcester, Tracey has 15 years of leadership and consultancy experience working across the education and skills sector for a local authority and as an inspector of schools. She has led the implementation of strategic policy, interacting with regional and national organizations across public, voluntary and private sectors. In her current role she designs and delivers bespoke leadership programs for the education and healthcare sectors, providing a range of leadership coaching and facilitation of systems leadership with a focus on building capacity between organizations and securing impactful collaborative systems and networks. Tracey is passionate about the transformation of senior people and her expertise lies in the development of honest, powerful, and enabling relationships. She specializes in one to one coaching, team facilitation of senior executives and leadership development.

**Elizabeth Goryunova** is assistant professor of leadership and organizational studies at the University of Southern Maine. She is a scholar and practitioner of global leadership. Prior-to-academia, Elizabeth served as the president and CEO of World Trade Center Utah, as a member and treasurer of the Utah District Export Council, appointed by the U.S. secretary of commerce, and as the U.S. private sector liaison officer to the World Bank Group and IDB, connecting researchers, entrepreneurs, and business leaders with projects financed globally by the International Financial Institutions. Her current scholarly research interests and publications are on leadership in a global context (cross-cultural effectiveness, D&I, complexity theory), and leadership education (both: capacity to lead in a digitally transformed environment, and digital technology-enhanced instruction). She also consults on business strategy, operations, and procurement policies/procedures of the international financial institutions.

**Kathy L. Guthrie** is associate professor in the higher education program, director of the Leadership Learning Research Center, and coordinator of the undergraduate certificate in leadership studies at Florida State University. Kathy's research focuses on leadership learning, socially just leadership education, and professional development for student affairs professionals in leadership education. Kathy has developed and taught both undergraduate and graduate courses in leadership and higher education. Kathy has authored/co-authored over 50 refereed journal articles and book chapters, and co-edited 4 issues in the New Directions series. She co-authored *Operationalizing Culturally Relevant Leadership Learning* (Information Age Publishing, 2021), *Engaging in the Leadership Process: Identity, Capacity, and Efficacy of College Students* (Information Age Publishing, 2021), and *The Role of Leadership Educators: Transforming Leadership* (Information Age Publishing, 2018), and co-edited *Shifting the Mindset* (Information Age Publishing, 2021) and *Changing the Narrative: Socially Just Leadership Education* (Information Age Publishing, 2018). Guthrie has served on several editorial boards and is currently the associate editor of the *New Directions for Student Leadership* series.

**Ashlee Hover** is assistant professor in the Womack Educational Leadership Department at Middle Tennessee State University and a former elementary school teacher. At MTSU, Dr. Hover teaches pre-service and in-service K–12 teachers and school administrators. She serves as the program coordinator for the curriculum and instruction online master's degree at MTSU. Her research includes studies of child development, teacher education, performance-based assessments, and digital learning in the classroom.

**Pei Hu** is a doctoral candidate in the higher education program at Florida State University. Her research interests focus on leadership education and international student education. Currently, she serves as a graduate assistant for the Leadership Learning Research Center, responsible for conducting leadership research projects and teaching in the undergraduate certificate in leadership studies. Pei received her bachelor's degree in Chinese literature and linguistics from

Jianghan University in China and obtained her master's degree in higher education at Florida State University.

**Aishwarya Joshi** currently serves as an assistant professor at the University of Vermont. She is a state-licensed mental health counselor in Ohio, and an NBCC board certified counselor in the United States, with nine years of experience providing mental health services both nationally and internationally. In addition she currently serves as a diversity, equity and inclusion (DEI) director for Huruma Rescue Mission, Inc in Embu, Kenya; regional ambassador for Urban Leaders Fellowship and the Chi Sigma Iota, International Leadership Fellow. Aishwarya has previously served as an Urban Leaders fellow, addressing public policy issues pertaining to racial disparities for the immigrant population in Denver, Colorado. She also has published articles that discuss oppression, social inequities experienced by various minority sub-groups in the United States. Profile: linkedin.com/in/aishwarya-joshi-lpc-ncc-b5129896

**Anne Katz** is a clinical associate professor of early childhood education in the Department of Curriculum and Instruction in the College of Education at the University of Houston. Dr. Katz served as a collaborator on a National Institute of Health (NIH) grant, contributing close reading workshops to prepare undergraduates to pursue biomedical science careers. She has previously provided professional development in content-area literacy for educators through three federal Teacher Quality grants. Dr. Katz recently served as a member of the Notable Books for a Global Society (NBGS) Awards Committee of the International Literacy Association, and is currently chairing a Research and Practitioner Award for innovative uses of NBGS books.

**Revocatus C Kuluchumila** holds a Master of Educational Leadership and Management from Newcastle University (United Kingdom) under the sponsorship of Ford Foundation. He is currently working as an executive secretary of the Tanzania Educational Leadership and Research Organization (TELRO). TELRO is a registered NGO working in Tanzania Mainland. TELRO aims to raise and update school leadership skills and competences. Earlier, he worked at Shinyanga Commercial Institute teaching economics for approximately 10 years. He then moved to Archbishop Mihayo University College of Tabora in the Department of Educational Foundations, where he taught school leadership and research courses for more than 7 years.

His research interest is in school leadership and has published articles and books in school leadership.

**Joe Lasley** teaches organizational and leadership studies as assistant professor at the University of Southern Maine. He earned his PhD in leadership studies at the University of San Diego, where he researched group dynamics and leadership in role-playing games. His experience includes over a decade facilitating organizational leadership development while working in student affairs/higher education including residential life, student leadership programs, personnel selection, training, and military, and veteran programs. His interests and research involve group dynamics, experiential learning, creativity, and leadership development. Specifically, how adults play and can leverage the power of gaming for leadership, learning, and development. His consulting practice can be found at Gamenamic.org. Dr. Joe has participated in and worked for many experiential and transformational group dynamics leadership experiences in the past decade including group relations events & training. Joe is a co-creator with Group Relations International, and a member of the Adaptive Leadership Network (ALN).

**Karl-Sue Marriott,** full professor, serves as the director of the Forensic Science Program in the School of Justice Studies at Roger Williams University (RWU). She has served as PI and CoPI on several NIH, NASA, DoD, and NSF funded biomedical research projects. Dr. Marriott received her PhD in chemistry from the University of the West Indies, Jamaica (Mona Campus), and completed postdoctoral research in cannabinoid chemistry at Clemson University with Professor John W. Huffman. She joined the faculty at Savannah State University (SSU) 2006–2021, where she established the Bachelor of Science degree program in forensic science. Recognized as a program of distinction in the USG under her leadership, the forensic science program at SSU actively engages in immersive integrative student-centered research. In Fall 2016, Dr. Marriott completed establishment of the first, one-of-a-kind 3D virtual reality (VR) crime scene facility for training undergraduates. She is also the founding director for the Visual, Immersive, and Tangible Applications in Learning (VITAL) STEM imaging exploration center established at SSU in 2020. Dr. Marriott is a self-taught freehand painter-artist and was a 2018 TEDxSavannah speaker.

**David T. Marshall** is an assistant professor in the College of Education at Auburn University. His research has focused on how K–12 education can be reformed to better serve all students. Specifically, his work has focused

on school choice and charter schools, the impact the COVID-19 pandemic has had on K–12 education, and innovative approaches for preparing teachers. His recent book, *COVID-19 and the Classroom: How Schools Navigated the Great Disruption* (Lexington Books, 2022), shares social science research on how schools handled the pandemic and documents what this period of time was like for K–12 education. Dr. Marshall earned a PhD from Virginia Commonwealth University in educational research and evaluation. He formerly taught middle and high school social studies in both traditional public schools as well as in public charter schools in Philadelphia, Pennsylvania. In the Summer of 2020, Dr. Marshall is currently chair of the Alabama Public Charter School Commission.

**Richard D. "Rick" Megahan** is a 30-year Army Infantry veteran, recipient of two awards of the Combat Infantryman's Badge. Since 2018, he has been a senior instructor in the Norwich University College of Graduate & Continuing Studies (CGCS), Strategic Studies and Defense Analysis (SSDA) program. He has served as deputy commandant of cadets at New Mexico Military Institute and assistant commandant of cadets at Norwich University. He is the founder/owner of RealLeaderNow LLC, a service disabled veteran owned small business providing client-based adaptive leadership and mission command curricula and programs. COL Megahan is a graduate of the U.S. Army War College, and holds a master's degree in military arts and sciences from the U.S. Army Command and General Staff College. COL Megahan lives in Goodyear, Arizona with his wife and best friend of 44 years, Mary.

**Brianne (Brie) Morettini** is an associate professor in the Department of Interdisciplinary and Inclusive Education in the College of Education at Rowan University. She teaches doctoral courses on research literature and analysis, and undergraduate courses on working with families and communities, inclusive education, and elementary education. She draws on a sociocultural theoretical framework to research beginning teacher identity development, beginning teachers' perspectives on teaching, and the use of self-study methodologies to uncover and acknowledge epistemological frames. She considers the intersections of theory and practice in her teaching and research. She has published her work in book chapters and peer-reviewed journals. She also presents her work at national and international research conferences.

**John C. Nestor** is a cross-over leader with prior roles in K–12 teaching and administration, Columbus State Community College directorships, and vice president of Riten Industries, Inc. He received his doctorate in policy and leadership while serving as the executive dean's administrative assistant at The Ohio State University. He is founder and senior consultant at Nestor Management Consulting, LLC. Special thanks to editing by Sarah Nestor-Lane, educator, and consultant for the company. Dr. Nestor can be reached at DrJohn@nestormanagementconsulting.com

**Natalie Neugebauer** is a doctoral student in educational psychology at Auburn University. Previously, Natalie received her BS in psychology from Georgia State University and worked as a research assistant for Emory University. Currently, Natalie is a graduate assistant in Auburn's Ralph Brown Draughon Library. Her research interests encompass school choice decision-making for parents of children with special needs, including charter schools, and the inclusion of children on the spectrum.

**Elizabeth Ostler** is the manager of graduate enrichment programs at the Gabelli School of Business where she oversees the Gabelli Thoughtful Leadership Certification program. She is also the founder and storyteller-in-chief of Life's Echoes. She offers workshops and opportunities for people to stand in their truth and tell their stories. Liz is a theater-maker specializing in directing and puppetry. She's the creator of communal theater, an approach to creating theater rooted in the belief that theater should be a communion between the audience and the theater event. Liz is editor-in-chief and writer at the LDS Women's Project. She holds an MFA in theater directing from Brooklyn College and a BA in liberal arts from Sarah Lawrence College. Liz is a doctoral candidate at Fordham University in the contemporary learning and interdisciplinary studies program. Her research focus is on cultural master narratives and belonging.

**Kateryna V. Pitchford** has been an associate professor of business at Central Baptist College in Conway, Arkansas since 2015. Fluent in three languages—English, Russian, and Ukrainian—Dr. Pitchford graduated with a Bachelor of Business Administration and Labor Economics degree from Dnipropetrovsk National University, Ukraine; received a master's degree in business administration from

Harding University; obtained a graduate certificate in sociology from the Appalachian State University; and graduated with a PhD in leadership studies from the University of Central Arkansas in 2016. Dr. Pitchford is an active member of her community, currently serving in the Noon Conway Rotary Club and is chair of the Jeff Farris Leadership Academy (2020–2022). A native of Dnipropetrovsk, Ukraine, Dr. Pitchford lives in Conway with her husband, Jeff, and daughters Elizabeth, Sophia, and Macie.

**Paul Sheehan** is the education systems lead for the school effectiveness team at The University of Worcester, United Kingdom. Paul holds a master's in executive coaching and mentoring. The focus of his work is team facilitation, one to one coaching, and leadership development both in schools and other public sector organizations. His expertise lies in the development of powerful, trusting, and enabling relationships. The transformational possibilities generated by these relationships, allied to challenging the orthodoxies for individuals, teams, and organizations are central drivers in his impactful work.

**Carla Solvason** is senior lecturer in the Department for Children and Families at the University of Worcester. Prior to this role she was an elementary school teacher, a schools' advisor for a charity supporting children with communication needs and a researcher. Carla takes a lead on research in her department, overseeing all student research and supporting colleagues in their own research development and publication; she is also the pathway lead for the master's in early childhood. Carla champions qualitative approaches to research and is particularly interested in ethical, respectful, and collaborative approaches, an area which she has published widely within. Carla's own longitudinal research project, carried out with a group of senior educational leaders, was the impetus for the joint chapter in this book.

**Maria Stephenson** is a senior lecturer in education in the School of Education, University of Worcester, United Kingdom. She is pathway lead for the MA in education (leadership & management) and has conducted qualitative research in the field of ethical leadership and ethical decision-making. She champions methods such as elite and specialized interviewing and is particularly interested in understanding how leaders develop through collaborative engagement within groups of their peers. Other recent work includes exploring the notion of inclusive leadership, and its underpinning principles such as equality, fairness, dignity, respect, and democracy.

**Valerie A. Storey**, PhD, has over 45 years of experience in K–12 and higher education in both the United States and the United Kingdom. As an associate professor emerita and program lead for educational leadership doctoral and master programs, she has facilitated the leadership development of administrators and doctoral students, presented at state, national, and international conferences, and published on various aspects of leadership for academic equity. Prior to matriculating into higher education, Dr. Storey served as a teacher, school administrator (academic & pastoral) in the secondary education setting. Her research interests include coaching of aspiring educational leaders, women in leadership, succession planning, equity, inclusion, and school diversification. She has written and published over 50 peer reviewed research papers/books and professional articles. Visit Dr. Storey's Amazon Author page at https://www.amazon.com/author/valerie_a_storey

**Marlee J. Tavlin** is a PhD candidate in contemporary learning and interdisciplinary research at Fordham University with a focus on out of school time (OST) STEM and equity. She earned her MA in anthropology and education from Columbia University with a focus on urban education. She is a member of several national honor societies including Phi Kappa Phi where she earned the 2020 Love of Learning Award. Her research focus and personal passion are to research, develop, and ultimately implement more STEM based OST programs that are accessible to a diverse range of students and their families. She has a decade of experience as an OST STEM educator at major institutions of learning such as the American Museum of Natural History and as a researcher and evaluator who has worked on large scale projects that focus on improving STEM education for NYC students such as the evaluation of CS4ALL. Her current and past projects have only strengthened this passion to diversify OST STEM learning and make it more accessible to underrepresented populations. Marlee was born and raised in New York City and resides there with her family, beloved dog Chili and turtle.

**Joshua Tipton** is a middle school administrator and former assistant professor of education and Doctor of Education program director. Dr. Tipton continues to serve as an instructor at Middle Tennessee State University and Lincoln Memorial University, where he teaches and directs graduate students pursuing initial teacher licensure and doctoral candidates in the instructional leadership concentration. Dr. Tipton's service as an educator includes teaching middle and high school social studies, middle and high school administration, and district supervision. His scholarly interests and expertise include Indigenous studies, teacher education, educational policy, instructional leadership and administration, and social justice education.

**Lisa Vernon-Dotson** is dean of the Dwight Shar College of Education at Ashland University. She formerly served as professor and chair in the Department of Interdisciplinary and Inclusive Education at Rowan University. Lisa is a former classroom teacher and teacher leader. Her research focuses on teacher leadership, distributed leadership models, and special education teacher education.

**John Williamson** is professor emeritus in the faculty of education, University of Tasmania, Australia. He was a school teacher in Australia and England prior to an academic career lasting over 30 years. During this time, he has held senior educational and leadership positions in several Australian universities, including chair of the academic senate, and dean of education at the University of Tasmania. John is a graduate in arts, education, and public policy and attended three Australian universities, the University of New South Wales, the University of Sydney, and Curtin University, and his PhD is from the University of Leicester, United Kingdom. He is a fellow of the Australian Teacher Education Association and a fellow of the Royal Society of Arts, United Kingdom. He has conducted research for several Australian state departments of education, for Commonwealth of Australia funding agencies, and for the OCED. His research has investigated classroom pedagogy, the initial preparation of teachers, and teacher work lives. John has been a board member of a state authority responsible for teacher registration and he is currently a member of national authorities responsible for teacher education and professional standards, and the provision of teacher workforce data.

**Kathryn Woods** is an associate professor in the Department of Leadership and Organizational Administration at Austin Peay State University in Clarksville, TN. She teaches courses in leadership development, organizational innovation, gender and leadership, and small group leadership. Her research interests include organizational behavior, leadership development, leadership education, and diversity in leadership.

www.ingramcontent.com/pod-product-compliance
Ingram Content Group UK Ltd.
Pitfield, Milton Keynes, MK11 3LW, UK
UKHW020130290926
15471UKWH00003B/396

9 798887 300924